Variable Plants and Herbivores
in Natural and Managed Systems

Variable Plants and Herbivores in Natural and Managed Systems

Edited by

ROBERT F. DENNO

Department of Entomology
University of Maryland
College Park, Maryland

MARK S. McCLURE

Department of Entomology
The Connecticut Agricultural Experiment Station
New Haven, Connecticut

1983

ACADEMIC PRESS

A Subsidiary of Harcourt Brace Jovanovich, Publishers
New York   London
Paris   San Diego   San Francisco   São Paulo   Sydney   Tokyo   Toronto

ACADEMIC PRESS, INC.
111 Fifth Avenue, New York, New York 10003

United Kingdom Edition published by
ACADEMIC PRESS, INC. (LONDON) LTD.
24/28 Oval Road, London NW1 7DX

Library of Congress Cataloging in Publication Data

Main entry under title:

Variable plants and herbivores in natural and managed
   systems.

   Includes index.
   1. Insects--Host plants.   2. Insect-plant relationships.   3. Insect control.   4. Botany--Variation.
5. Insects--Variation.   I. Denno, Robert F.
II. McClure, Mark S.
QL496.V37 1983   581.5'264   82-22666
ISBN 0-12-209160-4

PRINTED IN THE UNITED STATES OF AMERICA

83 84 85 86   9 8 7 6 5 4 3 2 1

Contents

Part II. Sources of Interplant Variation and Consequences for Herbivores   221

7. Ecology of Host-Selection Behavior in Phytophagous Insects

MARK D. RAUSHER

8. Influence of Vegetation Texture on Herbivore Populations: Resource Concentration and Herbivore Movement

PETER KAREIVA

9. Tracking Variable Host Plants in Space and Time

ROBERT F. DENNO

10. Effects of Host-Plant Variability on the Fitness of Sedentary Herbivorous Insects

RODGER MITCHELL

15. Phytochemical Variation, Colonization, and Insect Communities: The Case of Bracken Fern (*Pteridium aquilinum*)

CLIVE G. JONES

16. Hypotheses on Organization and Evolution in Herbivorous Insect Communities

PETER W. PRICE

Part V. Host Variability and Herbivore Pest Management   597

17. Genetics of Plant–Herbivore Systems: Interactions between Applied and Basic Study

FRED GOULD

18. Manipulation of Host Suitability for Herbivore Pest Management

J. DANIEL HARE

Contributors

Numbers in parentheses indicate the pages on which the authors' contributions begin.

D. N. ALSTAD (413), Department of Ecology and Behavioral Biology, University of Minnesota, Minneapolis, Minnesota 55455

ROBERT F. DENNO (1, 91, 291, 463), Department of Entomology, University of Maryland, College Park, Maryland 20742

G. F. EDMUNDS, JR. (413), Department of Biology, University of Utah, Salt Lake City, Utah 84112

DOUGLAS J. FUTUYMA (427), Department of Ecology and Evolution, State University of New York at Stony Brook, Stony Brook, New York 11794

FRED GOULD (599), Department of Entomology, North Carolina State University, Raleigh, North Carolina 27650

J. DANIEL HARE (655), Department of Entomology, The Connecticut Agricultural Experiment Station, New Haven, Connecticut 06504

CLIVE G. JONES (513), New York Botanical Garden Cary Arboretum, Millbrook, New York 12545

PETER KAREIVA (259), Division of Biology, Brown University, Providence, Rhode Island 02912

VERA ABER KRISCHIK (463), Department of Entomology, University of Maryland, College Park, Maryland 20742

MARK S. McCLURE (1, 125), Department of Entomology, The Connecticut Agricultural Experiment Station, New Haven, Connecticut 06504

RODGER MITCHELL (343), Department of Zoology, The Ohio State University, Columbus, Ohio 43210

CHARLES MITTER (427), Department of Entomology, University of Maryland, College Park, Maryland 20742

PETER W. PRICE (559), Department of Biological Sciences, Northern Arizona University, Flagstaff, Arizona 86011

MICHAEL J. RAUPP (91), Department of Entomology, University of Maryland, College Park, Maryland 20742

MARK D. RAUSHER (223), Department of Zoology, Duke University, Durham, North Carolina 27706

DAVID F. RHOADES (155), Department of Zoology, University of Washington, Seattle, Washington 98195

C. A. RYAN (43), Institute of Biological Chemistry and Biochemistry/ Biophysics Program, Washington State University, Pullman, Washington 99164

JACK C. SCHULTZ (61), Department of Biological Sciences, Dartmouth College, Hanover, New Hampshire 03755

J. MARK SCRIBER (373), Department of Entomology, University of Wisconsin, Madison, Wisconsin 53706

THOMAS G. WHITHAM (15), Department of Biological Sciences, Northern Arizona University, Flagstaff, Arizona 86011, and Biology Department, Museum of Northern Arizona, Flagstaff, Arizona 86001

Preface

The causes of spatial and temporal variation in host plants and the effects of variable resources on herbivores are currently receiving the attention of ecologists, evolutionary biologists, and agricultural, forest, and urban entomologists. How the world stays green despite the presence of herbivorous insects with their great potential for reproductive increase and how plants with relatively long generation times and low recombination rates have been able to stay in the evolutionary "arms race" with their insect parasites are questions that continue to interest biologists. Host-plant heterogeneity viewed at several levels may be a key to disclosing how and why seemingly disadvantaged plants are so successful despite their herbivores. Understanding the dynamics of plant–herbivore relationships and applying this knowledge in agriculture and silviculture are the themes of this volume.

This book is unlike predecessors that dealt with coevolution of plants and herbivores. We have emphasized the individual, population, species, and community responses of herbivores to plant variation rather than the detailed nature of that variation (for example, secondary plant chemistry). These are theoretical questions that now excite basic scientists and also offer material to applied biologists that may prove instrumental in establishing new crop and pest-management programs. Although insects are the major subjects of chapters in this volume, other important groups of economic plant parasites are discussed as well, including fungi, bacteria, and viruses.

The book is not a series of reviews per se, but rather a continuum of integrated but not overlapping chapters which often incorporate the original research findings of the authors with appropriate reference and review material. The first four parts discuss variability as a mechanism of defense used by plants against their parasites and the effects of variability on herbivores at several different levels of complexity. In Part I, sources of within-plant variation are considered, as are its effects on the distribution and abundance of herbivores. Part II examines interplant variation and the coevolutionary problems it poses for herbivores and the ecological and evolutionary responses of these animals. Part III discusses the role of host variability in the evolution of feeding specialization, genetic differentiation, and race formation. The importance of host variation to the organization of herbivore communities is presented in Part IV. Part V considers the ways in which host-plant variability can be manipulated for the management of herbivore pest populations.

No volume could hope to elucidate all the issues that are posed by this rapidly expanding field. We think, however, that this treatise reveals many complexities of plant–herbivore relationships and greatly advances our understanding of them.

Robert F. Denno
Mark S. McClure

Variability: A Key to Understanding Plant–Herbivore Interactions

ROBERT F. DENNO

MARK S. McCLURE

Superficially, plants appear to be at a disadvantage when compared to their herbivores in both ecological and evolutionary time. The reproductive potential of many herbivores is incredibly high, which seemingly poses a major threat to their host plants. Furthermore, how plants with relatively long generation times and low recombination rates (compared to their herbivores) stay in the evolutionary arms race is not immediately clear (Whitham, 1981; Chapter 1; Whitham and Slobodchikoff, 1981; Edmunds and Alstad, 1981; Alstad and Edmunds, Chapter 12; Gill and Halverson, in press). Herbivores should break the defenses of long-lived plants faster than plants can erect new ones (Whitham, 1981).

However, Hairston *et al.* (1960) noted that plants are abundant and remain largely intact despite their herbivores. Thus there is an apparent paradox. Hairston *et al.* (1960) suggested that the best clues to what regulates herbivore populations are to be found in the analysis of the exceptional cases in which terrestrial herbivores have become numerous enough to deplete the vegetation. They point out that outbreaks of herbivores often involve introduced species that have arrived without their entourage of natural enemies. Indeed, when predators are excluded by caging in the field, populations of herbivores can increase dramatically (Morris, 1972; Solomon *et al.*, 1976; Eickwort, 1977; Holmes *et al.*, 1979; Kroll and Fleet, 1979; Tallamy and Denno, 1981; Gradwohl and Greenberg, 1982). If predators and/or parasites are selectively killed by the application of pesticides, resurgence of phytophagous insects and mites can occur (Huffaker and Spitzer, 1951; Huffaker and Kennett, 1956; Huffaker *et al.*, 1962; Flaherty and Huffaker, 1970; van den Bosch *et al.*, 1971; Wood, 1971; DeBach, 1974; McClure, 1977a). Also, field releases of parasites or predators have been shown to suppress populations of

1

herbivorous pests (Tothill *et al.*, 1930; Muir, 1931; DeBach and Hagen, 1964; DeBach *et al.*, 1971; DeBach, 1974). Last, populations of herbivorous insects can increase in the field due to a delay in the numerical response of predators (Vince *et al.*, 1981; Denno *et al.*, in preparation). Information like this, accumulating since the turn of the twentieth century, led to the conclusion by Hairston *et al.* (1960) that herbivores are more often than not predator-limited and are seldom food-limited.

During the decade that followed, Hairston, Smith, and Slobodkin received considerable criticism for their conclusion that herbivores are seldom food-limited. Murdoch (1966) and Ehrlich and Birch (1967) examined the logic, consistency, and methodology of the paper by Hairston *et al.* (1960) and suggested that their conclusions or hypotheses were not acceptable. It is in these critical reviews that we find the seeds of host-plant variability and its importance in regulating herbivore populations. For instance, Murdoch (1966) recognized that all green plant material may not be edible to herbivores in a given area and, consequently, that it is invalid to conclude that predation or some other controlling factor is occurring merely by observing that plants are abundant and remain largely intact despite their herbivores. Slobodkin *et al.* (1967) responded to the criticisms leveled at their original paper, but to a large degree they maintained their initial contention that populations of herbivores are usually not limited by their food supply. The controversy emerging from this series of papers focused the attention of ecologists on the host plant as having a potential influence on herbivore distribution and abundance.

Development of theory concerning the importance of parasites and predators in herbivore population dynamics has been paralleled by applied work that suggests an important effect of host-plant variation on herbivorous pests. Varieties of wheat, grapes, and apples resistant to insect attack were recognized in the late nineteenth century (Lindley, 1831; Ortman and Peters, 1980), and our knowledge of the resistance of plants to herbivores has grown ever since (Snelling, 1941; Painter, 1951, 1958; Beck, 1965; Maxwell *et al.*, 1972; Gallun *et al.*, 1975; Maxwell and Jennings, 1980). Unfortunately, the knowledge gained by horticulturalists, plant breeders, plant physiologists, plant pathologists, and entomologists of intraspecific plant variation and its effect on herbivores has seldom been integrated with the ecological theory surrounding herbivore population regulation. Only beginning in the 1960s has there been strong emphasis in the theoretical literature on the host plant as something more than the inert, homogeneous substrate on which the dynamic interactions among predators, prey, and competitors are staged and where the effects of physical factors are felt.

The insecticidal properties of plants have been known for several centuries. Water extracts of tobacco (Solanaceae) were used to kill sucking insects in 1690, rotenone (Leguminosae) was used to kill leaf-feeding caterpillars in 1848, and pyrethrum (Compositae) has been used as an insecticide since 1800 (Ware, 1982). Furthermore, the pure alkaloid nicotine was isolated in 1828, the active chemical ingredient of rotenone was isolated in 1892, and the ester, alcohol, and acid fractions of pyrethrum were identified between 1909 and 1924 (Matsumura, 1975). Despite this long-standing knowledge of the toxic properties of plants by agriculturists and natural-product chemists, the role that secondary plant chemicals likely play in plant–herbivore coevolution has been realized only recently. Fraenkel (1959, 1969) and Ehrlich and Raven (1964) were among the ecologists who recognized early the importance of allelochemicals as *defenses* against herbivores. Since then the literature documenting the diversity, distribution, concentration, structure, metabolism, and antiherbivore properties of allelochemicals present in plants has grown tremendously (e.g., Harborne, 1972, 1978; Wallace and Mansell, 1976; Rosenthal and Janzen, 1979, and references cited therein).

With knowledge of the evolution of novel enzymes that could detoxify the secondary chemicals associated with particular plants, Ehrlich and Raven (1964) argued for the possibility that new avenues of plant exploitation and subsequent speciation could be open to herbivores. Their emphasis and that of others (e.g., Dethier, 1954) concerned host selection and exploitation at the level of the plant species, but they did not include details of how plant chemistry might affect the population dynamics of herbivores. It was not until the late 1960s that articles frequently implicated plant nutrition and allelochemistry in herbivore population dynamics, and at this time the data base was strongly skewed toward plant nutrition (e.g., Feeny, 1968, 1970; Dixon, 1970; Way and Cammell, 1970; Osborne, 1973; Southwood, 1973; White, 1974, 1976; Mattson and Addy, 1975; McNeill and Southwood, 1978; Rhoades, Chapter 6).

Recall the suggestion of Hairston *et al.* (1960) that the clues to herbivore population regulation lie in situations in which outbreaks occur. There is an extensive literature indicating that insect population growth is inversely related to host-plant vigor (Mattson and Addy, 1975). For instance, nutrient and moisture stress results in physiological changes in trees that render them susceptible to insect attack (Berryman, 1972; Mattson and Addy, 1975; Mattson, 1980). Native trees grown in stressed ornamental plantings incur higher densities of herbivores than those occurring naturally in wood lots, even though parasites are similarly abundant in both habitats (Pinto, 1980). Also, fertilization can alter host plants in ways that make them more or less susceptible to herbivore attack (Rodriguez, 1951, 1972; Mattson and Addy, 1975; Jones, 1976; Slansky and Feeny, 1977; McNeill and Southwood, 1978; Mattson, 1980; McClure, 1980; Tingey and Singh, 1980; Scriber, 1982; Denno *et al.*, in prep.). Regular pruning of trees and shrubs results in new foliage and alters physiology such that herbivore populations increase (Owen, 1971; Hall, 1977). Also, insect feeding may induce physiological changes in hosts that render foliage less suitable for subsequent generations of phytophagous insects (Haukioja and Niemelä, 1977; Ryan, 1978; Chapter 2; Niemelä et al., 1979; Haukioja, 1980; Raupp and Denno, Chapter 4; Rhoades, Chapter 6). In addition to the array of environmental factors that effect the susceptibility of the host to herbivore attack, there is also a genetic component to intraspecific variation in plant morphology, allelochemistry, and nutrition (Cooper-Driver et al., 1977; Hunt and von Rudloff, 1977; Lincoln and Murray, 1978; Chew and Rodman, 1979; Maxwell and Jennings, 1980; Whitham, 1981; Chapter 1; Whitham and Slobodchikoff, 1981; Krischik and Denno, Chapter 14). These data not only suggest that host plants are as important as predators and parasites in dictating the distribution and abundance of herbivores, but they also document the existence of variation in the resistance of plants and plant parts to herbivore attack. Indeed, plants are not homogeneous substrates where ecological interactions occur; they are heterogeneous participants themselves. We are just beginning to realize the central position host-plant variability (e.g., variation in morphology and chemistry) plays in the regulation of herbivore populations.

Until very recently the scale of host-plant variation receiving the most attention has been at the intraspecific level, where differences in structure, chemistry, density, or dispersion among individual plants in a population or among plant populations result in differential loads of herbivores (Kuhn and Low, 1955; Kogan, 1972; Dolinger et al., 1973; Levin, 1973; Root, 1973, 1975; Webster et al., 1973; Hedin et al., 1974; White, 1974, 1976; Hoxie et al., 1975; Johnson, 1975; Mattson and Addy, 1975; Ralph, 1977; Seaman et al., 1977; Smith, 1977; Edmunds and Alstad, 1978, 1981; McClure, 1979; Denno et al., 1980, 1981; Kareiva, Chapter 8; Krischik and Denno, Chapter 14; to name just a few).

Intraplant variation in morphology, nutrition, and defensive chemistry may well be as important an obstacle for herbivores to overcome as interplant variation in these features (see Whitham, Chapter 1; Schultz, Chapter 3). Dixon (1970) showed that both young and senescent sycamore (Acer pseudoplatanus) leaves are rich in amino nitrogen, which leads to the development of large, fecund aphids and large populations of these herbivores. During the summer, mature leaves contain less amino nitrogen, aphids are food limited, and their populations crash. Pine sawflies feed only on old foliage of jack pine and avoid juvenile needles early in the growing season (Ikeda et al., 1977). The basis of this feeding pattern is a resin acid that occurs only in the juvenile foliage. As the season progresses and the young needles mature, the concentration of the chemical decreases and the foliage becomes acceptable to the larvae. The precise timing of larval acceptance of juvenile foliage indicates a highly specific relationship between sawflies and their host tree, based on the chemical composition of the foliage (Ikeda *et al.*, 1977).

Herbivores themselves can alter the physiology of the plant part on which they feed, further increasing intraplant variation in leaf quality. Way and Cammell (1970), in an elegant set of experiments, showed that aggregates of aphids can act as "sinks," diverting nutrients from distant parts of the plant and flourishing on mature leaves that otherwise would be unsuitable to a single aphid. McClure (1977b, 1979, 1980) argued that scale insects significantly reduce the concentration of nitrogen in hemlock foliage, making certain branches on an individual tree unsuitable for future consumption. Also, herbivores and pathogens may induce changes in defensive chemistry that render that foliage less suitable for future feeding (Loebenstein and Ross, 1963; Green and Ryan, 1972; Kuc, 1976; Haukioja and Niemelä, 1977, 1979; Niemalä *et at.*, 1979; Cruickshank, 1980; West, 1981; Ryan, Chapter 2; Raupp and Denno, Chapter 4; Rhoades, Chapter 6). Superior competitors can restrict the distribution of inferior ones to a less suitable position on a tree, where nutrients are less available (McClure, Chapter 5). Thus, as a result of developmental and environmental factors and pest-induced plant defenses and changes in nutrition, individual plants can become a highly heterogeneous habitat for herbivores (Whitham, 1981). Furthermore, Whitham (1981; Chapter 1) and Whitham and Slobodchikoff (1981) have suggested that individual plants are mosaics of genetic variability, which has profound effects on herbivores. Somatic mutations arising in plants can be inherited by naturally occurring mechanisms of sexual and asexual reproduction. Coupled with long life span, large clone size, and the complete regeneration of buds each year, the occurrence of somatic mutations may permit a plant or clone to develop as a genetically diverse individual (Whitham and Slobodchikoff, 1981). If somatic mutations carry with them features of resistance, then an individual tree may represent a mosaic of genotypes that effectively prevents herbivores from evolving specific metabolic pathways to overcome plant defense (Whitham and Slobodchikoff, 1981; Whitham, Chapter 1).

We want to emphasize that various scales of variation in plant quality exist, all of which are important to herbivores. Herbivores must distinguish suitable from unsuitable species of host plants. Within a plant species there is considerable variation in chemistry and morphology among individuals in a population, and as just discussed a single plant or clone is an extremely heterogeneous array of choices with which herbivores must contend. To make a wrong decision can have drastic consequences on the fitness of a plant parasite. Superimposed over this spatial scale of variation is a temporal one that adds a dynamic component to an already complex set of alternatives. The ultimate result is that favorable resources are ephemeral (resource state changes rapidly) and scattered among a finely divided array of less-suitable and unacceptable resources (Jones, Chapter 15; Price, Chapter 16). Thus host-plant variation poses major tracking problems for herbivores and significantly affects their population regulation (Southwood, 1973; Mattson and Addy, 1975; Rhoades, Chapter 6; Denno, Chapter 9). Moreover, because host heterogeneity results in clumped populations, herbivores can be more apparent and vulnerable to their predators and parasites (Whitham, 1981). Also, plant heterogeneity probably contributes significantly to the shaping of herbivore communities. Such variability undoubtedly acts as a filter, imposing major constraints on when and where herbivores may colonize a plant (Jones, Chapter 15). Price (Chapter 16) argues that under the condition of finely divided and changing resource states many resources remain uncolonized in ecological time, and herbivore communities are likely to result from colonization of resources by species in the absence of competition as an organizing force.

We are not suggesting that parasites, predators, pathogens (e.g., Hairston et al., 1960), or physical factors (e.g., Denno et al., 1981) do not contribute significantly to the population dynamics of herbivores. However, we do feel that host-plant heterogeneity contributes significantly to the environmental "squeeze play" imposed on herbivores and affects their distribution and abundance. Indeed, the seeming advantage enjoyed by herbivores, with their relative short generation times and high recombination rates compared to plants, may be countered in part by the inherent variation of their hosts and the predicament this poses for them (Whitham and Slobodchikoff, 1981; Whitham, 1981; Chapter 1; Edmunds and Alstad, 1981; Alstad and Edmunds, Chapter 12; Gill and Halverson, in press).

Because of the profound, potentially negative effects of plant variability on herbivore abundance, it is not surprising that the reduction of interplant variability by agriculturists and silviculturists elevates some herbivores to pest status (Feeny, 1976; Edmunds and Alstad, 1981; Hare, Chapter 18). However, agriculturists may be able to turn the tables on herbivores by manipulating or exploiting host-plant variability to reduce pest density. Aside from trying to control or manipulate plant heterogeneity, simply understanding how herbivores are affected by plant variability may promote the development of more efficient, finely tuned pest-management programs. Specific information on the genetics of resistance and plant–pest interactions (Alstad and Edmunds, Chapter 12; Mitter and Futuyma, Chapter 13; Gould, Chapter 17), the searching and host-selecting behavior of herbivores (Rausher, Chapter 7), the spatial and temporal deployment patterns of resistant crop varieties (Kareiva, Chapter 8; Hare, Chapter 18), the seasonal variation in sensitivity of plants to defoliation (Krischik and Denno, Chapter 14), and the degree of synchrony between plant and insect developmental processes (Hare, Chapter 18) will provide needed insight for sophisticated pest management. Furthermore, how other agricultural practices (e.g., fertilization) change host suitability and promote pest outbreaks and how host-plant resistance and biological control can be used compatibly to depress pest populations warrant careful consideration. As we gain knowledge of the impact of plant variability on herbivores, we must ask how this new information can be employed to better manage our agricultural and silvicultural pests. To that end we feel this book focuses on important issues.

ACKNOWLEDGMENTS

We sincerely appreciate the reviews of Dan Hare, Charles Mitter, and Michael Raupp of earlier drafts of this chapter.

REFERENCES

Beck, S. D. (1965). Resistance of plants to insects. *Annu. Rev. Entomol.* **10,** 207–232.

Berryman, A. A. (1972). Resistance of conifers to invasion by bark beetle fungus associations. *BioScience* **22,** 598–602.

Chew, F. S., and Rodman, J. E. (1979). Plant resources and chemical defense. In "Herbivores: Their Interaction with Secondary Plant Metabolites" (G. A. Rosenthal and D. H. Janzen, eds.), pp. 271–307. Academic Press, New York.

Cooper-Driver, G. A., Finch, S., Swain, T., and Bernays, E. A. (1977). Seasonal variation in secondary plant compounds in relation to the palatability of *Pteridium aquilinum. Biochem. Syst. Ecol.* **5,** 177–183.

Cruickshank, I. A. M. (1980). Defenses triggered by the invader: Chemical defenses. In "Plant Disease: An Advanced Treatise" (J. G. Horsfall and E. B. Cowling, eds.), Vol. 5, pp. 247–267. Academic Press, New York.

DeBach, P. (1974). "Biological Control by Natural Enemies." Cambridge Univ. Press, London/New York.

DeBach, P. and Hagen, K. S. (1964). Manipulation of entomophagous species. In "Biological Control of Insect Pests and Weeds" (P. DeBach, ed.), pp. 429–458. Van Nostrand-Reinhold, Princeton, New Jersey.

DeBach, P., Rosen, D., and Kennett, C. E. (1971). Biological control of coccids by introducted natural enemies. In "Biological Control" (C. B. Huffaker, ed.), pp. 165–194. Plenum, New York.

Denno, R. F., Raupp, M. J., Tallamy, D. W., and Reichelderfer, C. F. (1980). Migration in heterogeneous environments: differences in habitat selection between the wing forms of the dimorphic planthopper, *Prokelisia marginata* (Homoptera: Delphacidae). *Ecology* **61**, 859–867.

Denno, R. F., Raupp, M. J., and Tallamy, D. W. (1981). Organization of a guild of sap-feeding insects: equilibrium vs. nonequilibrium coexistence. *In* "Insect Life History Patterns: Habitat and Geographic Variation" (R. F. Denno and H. Dingle, eds.), pp. 151–181., Springer-Verlag, Berlin and New York.

Denno, R. F., Krischik, V. A., and Hanks, L. M. Population dynamics of a salt marsh-inhabiting planthopper on host plants of variable nutritional quality: an experimental study. In preparation.

Dethier, V. G. (1954). Evolution of feeding preferences in phytophagous insects. *Evolution* **8**, 33–54.

Dixon, A. F. G. (1970). Quality and availability of food for a sycamore aphid population. *Symp. Brit. Ecol. Soc.*, **10**, 271–286.

Dolinger, P. M., Ehrlich, P. R., Fitch, W. L., and Breedlove, D. E. (1973). Alkaloid and predation patterns in Colorado lupine populations. *Oecologia* **13**, 191–204.

Edmunds, G. F., and Alstad, D. N. (1978). Coevolution in insect herbivores and conifers. *Science* **199**, 941–945.

Edmunds, G. F., and Alstad, D. N. (1981). Responses of black pineleaf scales to host plant variability. *In* "Insect Life History Patterns: Habitat and Geographic Variation" (R. F. Denno and H. Dingle, eds.), pp. 29–38. Springer-Verlag, Berlin and New York.

Ehrlich, P. R., and Birch, L. C. (1967). The balance of nature and population control. *Am. Nat.* **101**, 97–107.

Ehrlich, P. R., and Raven, P. H. (1964) Butterflies and plants: a study in coevolution. *Evolution* **18**, 586–608.

Eickwort, K. R. (1977). Population dynamics of a relatively rare species of milkweed beetle (*Labidomera*). *Ecology* **58**, 527–538.

Feeny, P. P. (1968). Effect of oak leaf tannins on larval growth of the winter moth *Operophtera brumata*. *J. Insect Physiol.* **14**, 805–817.

Feeny, P. P. (1970). Seasonal changes in oak leaf tannins and nutrients as a cause of spring feeding by winter moth caterpillars. *Ecology* **51**, 565–581.

Feeny, P. P. (1976). Plant apparency and chemical defense. *Recent Adv. Phytochem.* **10**, 1–40.

Flaherty, D. L., and Huffaker, C. B. (1970). Biological control of Pacific mites and Willamette mites in San Joaquin Valley vineyards. I. Role of *Metaseiulus occidentalis*. *Hilgardia* **40**, 267–308.

Fraenkel, G. (1959). The raison d'etre of secondary plant substances. *Science* **129**, 1466–1470.

Fraenkel, G. (1969). Evaluation of our thoughts on secondary plant substances. *Entomol. Exp. Appl.* **12**, 473–486.

Gallun, R. L., Starks, K. J., and Guthrie, W. D. (1975). Plant resistance to insects attacking cereals. *Annu. Rev. Entomol.* **20**, 337–357.

Gill, D. E., and Halverson, T. G. Fitness variation among branches within trees. *In* "Evolutionary Ecology" (B. Shorrocks, ed.). Blackwell, London. In press.

Gradwohl, J., and Greenberg, R. (1982). The effect of a single species of avian predator on the arthropods of aerial leaf litter. *Ecology* **63**, 581–583.

Green, T. R., and Ryan, C. A. (1972). Wound-induced proteinase inhibitor in plant leaves: a possible defense mechanism against insects. *Science* **175**, 776–777.

Hairston, N. G., Smith, F. E., and Slobodkin, L. B. (1960). Community structure population control, and competition. *Am. Nat.* **94**, 421–425.

Hall, R. W. (1977). The population biology of *Aphis nerii* B. d. F. on oleander. Ph.D. Dissertation, University of California, Davis.

Harborne, J. B., ed. (1972). "Phytochemical Ecology." Academic Press, New York/London.

Harborne, J. B., ed. (1978). "Biochemical Aspects of Plant and Animal Coevolution." Academic Press, New York and London.

Haukioja, E. (1980). On the role of plant defenses in the fluctuation of herbivore populations. *Oikos* **35**, 202–213.

Haukioja, E., and Niemelä, P. (1977). Retarded growth of a geometrid larva after mechanical damage to leaves of its host tree. *Ann. Zool. Fenn.* **14**, 48–52.

Haukioja, E., and Niemelä, P. (1979). Birch leaves as a resource for herbivores: seasonal occurrence of increased resistance in foliage after mechanical damage of adjacent leaves. *Oecologia* **39**, 151–159.

Hedin, P. A., Maxwell, F. G., and Jenkins, J. N. (1974). Insect plant attractants, feeding stimulants, repellents, deterrents, and other related factors affecting insect behavior. *Proc. Summer Inst. Biol. Control Plant Insects Dis., 1972* pp. 494–527.

Holmes, R. T., Shultz, J. C., and Nothnagle, P. (1979). Bird predation on forest insects: an exclosure experiment. *Science* **206**, 462–463.

Hoxie, R. P., Wellso, S. G., and Webster, J. A. (1975). Cereal leaf beetle response to wheat trichome length and density. *Environ. Entomol.* **4**, 365–370.

Huffaker, C. B., and Kennett, C. E. (1956). Experimental studies on predation: predator and cyclamen mite populations on strawberries in California. *Hilgardia* **26**, 191–222.

Huffaker, C. B., and Spitzer, C. H. (1951). Data on the natural control of the cyclamen mite on strawberries. *J. Econ. Entomol.* **44**, 519–522.

Huffaker, C. B., Kennett, C. E., and Finney, G. L. (1962). Biological control of the olive scale *Parlatoria oleae* (Colvee) in California by imported *Aphytis maculicornis* (Masi) (Hymenoptera: Aphelinidae). *Hilgardia* **32**, 541–636.

Hunt, R. S., and von Rudloff, E. (1977). Leaf-oil-terpene variation in western white pine populations of the Pacific Northwest. *For. Serv.* **23**, 507–516.

Ikeda, T., Matsumura, F., and Benjamin, D. M. (1977). Chemical basis for feeding adaptation of pine sawflies, *Neodiprion rugifrons* and *Neodiprion swainei*. *Science* **197**, 497–498.

Johnson, H. B. (1975). Plant pubescence: an ecological perspective. *Bot. Rev.* **41**, 233–258.

Jones, F. G. W. (1976). Pests, resistance and fertilizers. *Proc. Int. Potash Inst., 12th*, pp. 233–258.

Kogan M. (1972). Intake and utilization of natural diets by Mexican bean beetle, *Epilachna varivestis:* A multivariate analysis. *In* "Insect and Mite Nutrition: Significance and Implication in Ecology Management" (J. G. Rodriguez, ed.), pp. 107–126. North-Holland Pub., Amsterdam.

Kroll, J. C., and Fleet, R. R. (1979). Impact of woodpecker predation on overwintering within-tree populations of the southern pine beetle *(Dendroctonus frontalis)*. *In* "The Role of Insectivorous Birds in Forest Ecosystems" (J. G. Dickson, R. N. Conner, R. R. Fleet, J. G. Kroll, and J. A. Jackson, eds.), pp. 269–281. Academic Press, New York.

Kuc, J. A. (1976). Phytoalexins. *In* "Encyclopedia of Plant Physiology," Vol. 4 (R. Heitefuss and P. H. Williams, eds.), pp. 632–652. Springer-Verlag, Berlin and New York.

Kuhn, R., and Low, I. (1955). Resistance factors against *Leptinotarsa decemlineata* (Say) isolated from the leaves of wild *Solanum* species. *In* "Origins of Resistance to Toxic Agents" (M. G. Sevag, R. D. Reid, and O. E. Reynolds, eds.), pp. 122–132. Academic Press, New York.

Levin, D. A. (1973). The role of trichomes in plant defense. *Q. Rev. Biol.* **48**, 3–15.

Lincoln, D. E., and Murray, M. J. (1978). Monogenic basis for reduction of (+) – pulegone to (−) – menthone in *Mentha* oil biogenesis. *Phytochemistry,* **17**, 1727–1730.

Lindley, G. (1831). "A Guide to the Orchard and Kitchen Garden." Landon, Longmans, Ress, Orme, Brown, & Green Publishers, London.

Loebenstein, G., and Ross, A. (1963). An extractable agent induced in uninfested tissues by localized virus infections that interferes with infection by tobacco mosaic virus. *Virology* **20**, 507–517.

McClure, M. S. (1977a). Resurgence of the scale, *Fiorinia externa* (Homoptera: Diaspididae), on hemlock following insecticide application. *Environ. Entomol.* **6**, 480–484.

McClure, M. D. (1977b). Population dynamics of the red pine scale, *Matsucoccus resinosae* (Homoptera: Margarodidae): the influence of resinosis. *Environ. Entomol.* **6**, 789–795.

McClure, M. S. (1979). Self-regulation in populations of the elongate hemlock scale, *Fiorinia externa* (Homoptera: Diaspididae). *Oecologia* **39**, 25–36.

McClure, M. S. (1980). Foliar nitrogen: a basis for host suitability for elongate hemlock scale, *Fiorinia externa* (Homoptera: Diaspididae). *Ecology* **61**, 72–79.

McNeill, S. and Southwood, T. R. E. (1978). The role of nitrogen in the development of insect/plant relationships. *In* "Biochemical Aspects of Plant and Animal Coevolution" (J. B. Harborne, ed.), pp. 77–98. Academic Press, New York and London.

Matsumura, F. (1975). "Toxicology of Insecticides." Plenum, New York.

Mattson, W. J. (1980). Herbivory in relation to plant nitrogen content. *Annu. Rev. Ecol. Syst.* **11**, 119–161.

Mattson, W. J., and Addy, N. D. (1975). Phytophagous insects as regulators of forest primary production. *Science* **190**, 515–522.

Maxwell, F. G ., and Jennings, P. R. (1980). "Breeding Plants Resistant to Insects." Wiley, New York.

Maxwell, F. G., Jerkins, J. N., and Parrot, W. L. (1972). Resistance of plants to insects. *Adv. Agron.* **24**, 187–265.

Morris, R. F. (1972). Predation by wasps, birds, and mammals on *Hyphantria cunea*. *Can. Entomol.* **104**, 1581–1591.

Muir, F. (1931). The insects and other invertebrates of Hawaiian sugar cane fields. *Publ. Exp. Stn., Hawaii. Sugar Plant. Assoc.*

Murdoch, W. W. (1966). "Community structure, Population Control, and Competition"— a critique. *Am. Nat.* **100**, 219–226.

Niemelä, P., Aro, E. M., and Haukioja, E. (1979). Birch leaves as a resource for herbivores: damage-induced increase in leaf phenols with trypsin inhibiting effects. *Rep. Kevo Subarct. Res. Stn.* **15**, 37–40.

Ortman, E. E., and Peters, D. C. (1980). Introduction. *In* "Breeding Plants Resistant to Insects" (F. G. Maxwell and P. R. Jennings, eds.), pp 3–13. Wiley, New York.

Osborne, D. J. (1973). Mutual regulation of growth and development in plants and insects. *Symp. R. Entomol. Soc. London* **6**, 33–42.

Owen, D. F. (1971). Species diversity in butterflies in a tropical garden. *Bio. Conserv.* **3**, 191–198.

Painter, R. H. (1951). "Insect Resistance in Crop Plants." Macmillan, New York.

Painter, R. H. (1958). Resistance of plants to insects. *Annu. Rev. Entomol.* **3**, 267–290.

Pinto, L. J. (1980). Resource utilization patterns of a complex of hymentopterous parasitoids associated with obscure scale *(Melanaspis obscura)* on pin oak *(Quercus palustris).* M.S. Thesis, Entomol. Dept., University of Maryland, College Park.

Ralph, C. P. (1977). Effect of host plant density on populations of a specialized, seed-sucking bug, *Oncopeltus fasciatus. Ecology* **58**, 799–809.

Rodriguez, J. G. (1951). Mineral nutrition of the two-spotted spider mite, *Tetranychus bimaculatus* Harvey. *Ann. Entomol. Soc. Am.* **44**, 511–526.

Rodriguez, J. G. (1972). "Insect and Mite Nutrition." Elsevier/North Holland, Amsterdam.

Root, R. B. (1973). Organization of a plant–arthropod association in simple and diverse habitats: the fauna of collards *(Brassica oleracea). Ecol. Monogr.* **43**, 95–124.

Root, R. B. (1975). Some consequences of ecosystem texture. *In* "Ecosystem Analysis and Prediction" (S. A. Levin, ed.), pp. 83–97. Soc. Ind. Appl. Math., Philadelphia.

Rosenthal, G. A., and Janzen, D. H., eds. (1979). "Herbivores: Their Interaction with Secondary Plant Metabolites." Academic Press, New York.

Ryan, C. A. (1978). Proteinase inhibitors in plant leaves: a biochemical model for pest-induced natural plant protection. *Trends Biochem. Sci.* **5**, 148–150.

Scriber, J. M. (1982). Nitrogen nutrition of plants and insect invasion. *In* "Nitrogen in Crop Protection" (R. D. Hauck, ed.). Am. Soc. Agron., Madison, Wisconsin.

Seaman, F., Likefahr, M. J., and Mabry, T. J. (1977). The chemical basis of the natural resistance of *Gossypium hirsutum* L. to *Heliothis. Proc.—Beltwide Cotton Prod. Res. Conf.* pp. 102–103.

Slansky, F., and Feeny, P. P. (1977). Stabilization of the rate of nitrogen accumulation by larvae of the cabbage butterfly on wild and cultivated food plants. *Ecol. Monogr.* **47**, 209–228.

Slobodkin, L. B., Smith, F. E., and Hairston, N. G. (1967). Regulation in terrestrial ecosystems, and the implied balance of nature. *Am. Nat.* **101**, 109–124.

Smith, R. H. (1977). Monoterpenes of ponderosa pine xylem resin in western United States. *USDA For. Serv. Tech. Bull.* **1532**, 1–48.

Snelling, R. O. (1941). Resistance of plants to insect attack. *Bot. Rev.* **7**, 543–586.

Solomon, M. E., Glen, D. M., Kendall, D. A., and Milsom, N. F. (1976). Predation of overwintering larvae of codling moth *(Cydia pomonella* L.) by birds. *J. Appl. Ecol.* **13**, 341–352.

Southwood, T. R. E. (1973). The insect/plant relationship—an evolutionary perspective. *Symp. R. Entomol. Soc. London* **6**, 3–30.

Tallamy, D. W., and Denno, R. F. (1981). Alternative life history patterns in risky environments: An example from lacebugs. *In* "Insect Life History Patterns: Habitat and Geographic Variation" (R. F. Denno and H. Dingle, eds.). pp. 129–147. Springer-Verlag, Berlin and New York.

Tingey, W. M., and Singh, S. R. (1980). Environmental factors influencing the magnitude and expression of resistance. *In* "Breeding Plants Resistant to Insects" (F. G. Maxwell and P. R. Jennings, eds.), pp. 89–113. Wiley, New York.

Tothill, J. D., Taylor, T. H. C., and Paine, R. W. (1930). "The Coconut Moth in Fiji: A History of its Control by Means of Parasites." Publ. Imp. Bur. Entomol, London.

van den Bosch, R., Leigh, T. F., Falcon, L. H., Stern, V. M., Gonzalez, D., and Hagen, K. S. (1971). The developing program of integrated control of cotton pests in California. *In* "Biological Control" (C. B. Huffaker, ed.), pp. 377–394. Plenum, New York.

Vince, S. W., Valiela, I., and Teal, J. M. (1981). An experimental study of the structure of herbivorous insect communities in a salt marsh. *Ecology* **62**, 1662–1678.

Wallace, J. W., and Mansell, R. L. (1976). "Recent Advances in Phytochemistry: Biochemical Interaction between Plants and Insects." Plenum, New York.

Ware, G. W. (1982). "Fundamentals of Pesticides." Thomson Publications, Fresno, California.

Way, M. J., and Cammell, M. (1970). Aggregation behavior in relation to food utilization by aphids. *Symp. Br. Ecol. Soc.* **10**, 229–247.

Webster, J. A., Gage, S. H., and Smith, D. H. (1973). Suppression of the cereal leaf beetle with resistant wheat. *Environ. Entomol.* **2,** 1089–1091.

West, C. A. (1981). Fungal elicitors of the phytoalexin response in higher plants. *Naturwissenschaften* **68,** 447–457.

White, T. C. R. (1974). A hypothesis to explain outbreaks of looper caterpillars, with special reference to populations of *Selidosema sauvis* in a plantation of *Pinus radiata* in New Zealand. *Oecologia* **16,** 279–301.

White, T. C. R. (1976). Weather, food and plagues of locusts. *Oecologia* **22,** 119–134.

Whitham, T. G. (1981). Individual trees as heterogeneous environments: adaptation to herbivory or epigenetic noise? *In* "Insect Life History Patterns: Habitat and Geographic Variation" (R. F. Denno and H. Dingle, eds.), pp. 9–27. Springer-Verlag, Berlin and New York.

Whitham, T. G., and Slobodchikoff, C. N. (1981). Evolution by individuals, plant–herbivore interactions, and mosaics of genetic variability: the adaptive significance of somatic mutations in plants. *Oecologia* **49,** 287–292.

Wood, B. J. (1971). The importance of ecological studies to pest control in Malaysian plantations. *In* "Crop Protection in Malaysia" (R. L. Wastie and B. J. Wood, eds.), pp. 187–196. Incorp. Soc. Planters, Kuala Lumpur.

Robert F. Denno
Department of Entomology
University of Maryland
College Park, Maryland

Mark S. McClure
Department of Entomology
The Connecticut Agricultural Experiment Station
New Haven, Connecticut

PART I

Sources of Intraplant Variation and Consequences for Herbivores

Interactions between plants and their herbivores have often been viewed as if they were confrontations between populations, with little regard for the uniqueness and complexity of the individual combatants. Individual plants were often envisioned as a uniform resource for herbivores, each plant part (foliage, stem, cones, roots, etc.) homogenous within each plant and with phenology, nutrition, and defensive chemistry similar to that of its neighbors. We have now come to appreciate that individual plants are highly heterogeneous hosts in space and time, which makes it extremely difficult for herbivores to be adapted to all aspects of their variable host at the same time. Thus intraplant variation serves as a primary means by which relatively long-lived hosts defend themselves against their rapidly evolving parasites. The chapters that follow in this part discuss the numerous factors that contribute to variation within the individual host plant, the importance of resource variability as a plant defense mechanism, and the ecological and evolutionary consequences of intraplant variation for herbivores.

In Chapter 1, Whitham develops the logic of intraplant variation as a plant defense and discusses the impact of variation within individual trees of narrowleaf cottonwood on *Pemphigus* gall aphids. Whitham explains how intraplant variation may be an evolved trait that allows a plant not only to manipulate the behavior of its herbivores and their predators but also direct the evolution of its herbivores along less destructive pathways. The mosaic pattern of host variation in cottonwood "squeezes" the aphid between two opposing selective pressures, both of which negatively affect its survival and reproduction.

The way in which herbivores contribute to variation in their host plants by inducing chemical defense is addressed by Ryan in Chapter 2. From original work on induced proteinase-inhibitor synthesis in tomato and from other work on induced phytoalexin production in beans, Ryan provides evidence that plant cell-wall fragments released at the wound site are involved in the mechanism of induced chemical protection against insects, fungi, bacteria, and viruses. Ryan suggests that many induced plant defensive responses may involve similar communication systems. In Chapter 3, Schultz explains how individual forest trees are highly heterogeneous resources and habitats for herbivores and discusses the impact of intraplant variation on the life history and behavior of defoliating insects. Schultz presents a model using forest-tree-dwelling caterpillars that predicts the ways in which herbivores compromise their habitat selection and feeding behavior to maximize fitness on their heterogeneous hosts.

The role of within-plant heterogeneity in determining the spatial and temporal distributions of herbivores is the main focus of Chapter 4. Raupp and Denno illustrate how intraplant variation in leaf age, host nutrition, and defensive chemistry affect temporal and spatial distributions of foliar-feeding insects. Using evidence gathered from their willow leaf–beetle system, they elucidate how interactions with herbivores, predators, and abiotic factors can modify the distribution of herbivores, predicted from spatial patterns of plant nutrients and allelochemicals. The interaction of multiple factors results in niche separation between adult and juvenile stages that share a common resource. McClure (Chapter 5) considers the ways in which competition between herbivores further adds to the complexity of individual trees as habitats and how competition may alter predictions of insect distribution and abundance, based solely on measures of host-plant nutrition and defensive chemistry. Using the system of exotic scale insects on eastern hemlock, McClure illustrates how competing herbivores may reduce the fitness of others by spatially excluding them from optimal resources on the host plant and by altering the nutritional quality of the host plant in time, making it less suitable for subsequent generations. Rhoades (Chapter 6) concludes Part I by discusssing how the nutritional and defensive chemistry of host plants can be altered in response to physical stress and herbivore attack and how these phytochemical changes in the host can influence the population dynamics of herbivores and the incidence of their outbreaks. Rhoades generates a nonmathematical model of broad applicability to herbivore-outbreak phenomena to predict herbivore distribution and abundance from measures of plant nutrition and defensive chemistry.

CHAPTER 1

Host Manipulation of Parasites: Within-Plant Variation as a Defense against Rapidly Evolving Pests

THOMAS G. WHITHAM

I. INTRODUCTION

The disparity between parasites and their host plants in generation times and recombination potential leads to a fundamental problem in the coevolutionary interactions of these two groups: Why don't pathogens, parasites, and herbivores break the defenses of their host plants? This is especially perplexing when it is considered that the supposedly single genotype of an individual host plant may be perpetuated by cloning for thousands of years and yet during that time be exposed to ever-changing pests.

As a possible answer to these anomalies I will expand upon the hypothesis that an individual plant is a mosaic of resistance to parasite attack and that pests cannot or are not likely to be adapted to all parts of the mosaic at once (Whitham, 1981). Quantitative and/or qualitative variation in the defenses of an individual host plant or clone may represent a key defense that permits the plant to simultaneously manipulate both its parasites and their predators and to direct the evolution of its pests to minimize their destructive impact. Variation as a defense may place plant pests in an evolutionary "squeeze play" that even rapidly

VARIABLE PLANTS AND HERBIVORES
IN NATURAL AND MANAGED SYSTEMS

evolving pests cannot easily surmount. To the extent that these hypotheses are correct, our current concepts of plants and their coevolutionary interactions must be modified to incorporate a more dynamic view of plants than was previously suspected.

After developing the logic of variation as a plant defense, I will empirically examine the impact of variation within individual trees of narrowleaf cottonwood *(Populus angustifolia)* on the parasite *Pemphigus betae.*

II. VARIATION AS A PLANT DEFENSE

Because plant resistance acts as a selective filter in which pathogens, parasites, and herbivores unable to attack the plant are selected against, the survivors may interbreed to produce a new biotype or race that can successfully attack the formerly resistant host plant. In several documented cases, single genes for resistance in the host population have been overcome within 1–3 yr of their widespread use (Knott, 1972). For example, from 1941 to 1957 four different cultivars of oats resistant to crown rust were released sequentially in the United States. After an initially successful resistant period, each cultivar succumbed to the rapidly evolving rust; up to 30% of the oat crop was lost before a new cultivar was released (Frey *et al.*, 1973). The rapidity with which the defenses of cultivars can be broken is a severe problem because it typically takes 10–15 yr to produce a new resistant variety, and tree varieties require even more time (Painter, 1966).

Examples of evolution of the ability to successfully attack formerly resistant plants or overcome pesticides by parasites and other plant pests are common. For example, with economically important insects the evolution of races capable of attacking formerly resistant varieties are most commonly observed with aphids (Gallun *et al.*, 1975). This is probably due to their parthenogenetic reproduction and relatively short generation time, which permit new races to become abundant in one or two growing seasons. There are also now at least eight races of Hessian flies that can attack wheat plants that have different genes for resistance (Gallun *et al.*, 1975). Other examples include the evolution of many "superfly" races, when DDT was used extensively (DeBach, 1974). Similarly, it appears that the natural use of tannins by many oaks to precipitate proteins and negatively affect digestion and growth of larval lepidopterans (Feeny, 1970) has been overcome by other lepidopterans that have evolved specialized gut characteristics. Berenbaum (1980) noted that a high gut pH could prevent tannins from binding to proteins and suggested that this adaptation may have permitted the lepidopterans that employ this counter-adaptation to radiate onto plants with tannin defenses.

Because these examples suggest that no single "ultimate weapon" exists or can exist for long in the face of rapidly evolving parasites, it is pertinent to examine the role of variation as a plant defense. Variation in the host population has long been recognized to be important in preventing rapidly evolving pathogens from becoming virulent (Rosen, 1949; Van der Plank, 1963; Browning and Frey, 1969; Knott, 1972; Frey et al., 1973, 1979; Browning, 1974; Gallun et al., 1975; Browning et al., 1977, 1979; Cowling, 1978; Day, 1978; Schmidt, 1978; Leonard and Czochor, 1980; Robinson, 1980; Segal et al., 1980).

Variation in the host population makes adaptations by pathogens more difficult. Different kinds of host resistance act to reduce the selective coefficients placed upon the pathogen population because no single change or mutation by a pathogen will confer great fitness. For example, with a highly variable host population a mutant pathogen may be able to utilize or infect a specific host genotype, but the problems of successful detection and subsequent spread to like host genotypes are exceedingly difficult. To reduce the susceptibility of our economically important crops (e.g., wheat), agronomists have sought to increase variation in the host population by mixing varieties in time and space. This includes varietal rotation, in which genes for resistance are rotated on an annual basis to reduce their exposure and keep the evolving pathogen population continually off balance. It also includes the use of mutilines, in which strains differing only in their resistance characteristics are planted as mixtures in the same field, and the use of multigene cultivars, which simultaneously employ several genes for resistance in the same plant. The goal of such man-designed strategies is to mimic the diversity of natural ecosystems by keeping the level of variation sufficiently high that no single pathogen can break the defenses of all strains and spread in epidemic proportions (Browning, 1974; Segal et al., 1980).

Even more importantly, it is argued that such variation can be used to stabilize the pathogen population and even select for simple races that lack the ability to reach epidemic proportions (Van der Plank, 1963; Browning and Frey, 1969; Knott, 1972; Frey et al., 1973, 1979; Leonard and Czochor, 1980). With the widespread use of single cultivars of oats, the whole of the North American continent became one vast epidemiological unit for crown rust (*Puccinia coronata* Cda var. *avenae* Frazier and Ledingham). Such genetic uniformity resulted in the boom-or-bust cycles of pathogen infection, which have already been mentioned (Frey et al., 1973). Because the rust overwinters in southern Texas and migrates north into Canada along the "*Puccinia* path," a joint Canadian–American effort has been initiated to break up the epidemiological unity of this large region. The *Puccinia* path was divided into three latitudinal belts, into which ten different genes for resistance were deployed. The northern, central, and southern regions were assigned three, three, and four of these genes, respectively, and each group was composed so that no known crown rust race could parasitize a resistance gene in more than one region. Thus the rust survivors of one belt would not be adapted to another belt, and with gene rotation and/or new gene introductions the crown rust cycle covering thousands of miles should be broken. It is thought that the useful "life span" of resistant genes can be greatly increased with these methods and that such variation has long-term usefulness.

Although it is relatively easy to appreciate how variation in annual monocultures may foil the advances of rapidly evolving pathogens, that variation is important in annual agronomic crops begs the question, How do long-lived trees or any clonal species that purportedly have a single genotype exposed for hundreds or even thousands of years cope with their pathogens, parasites, and herbivores (which have short generation times and the potential to evolve rapidly)?

The importance of this question is enhanced by the following four observations.

1. Following the work of Flor (1971), which demonstrated a gene-for-gene interaction between pathogens and their hosts, the research of Edmunds and Alstad (1978) indicated that some insects may become genetically adapted to an individual host tree. If an individual host tree represents a sufficiently large resource to favor the evolution of such specific adaptations, then an individual tree may be considered as a monoculture.

2. Even small monocultures can become susceptible to evolving pathogens over a short period of time. For example, under greenhouse conditions Leijerstam (1972) found that, when a resistant wheat variety was exposed to the avirulent pathogen *Erysiphe gramminis* f. sp. *tritici,* after only 438 days mutations in the pathogen population resulted in three different virulent races that successfully attacked the previously resistant wheat variety.

3. Because parasites and other plant pests have short generation times, their potential to evolve races virulent to an individual host plant increases with the life span of the host. In comparisons of longevity of broadleaf and conifer trees common to North American, Barbour *et al.* (1980) estimated the average longevity of broadleaf species to be approximately 200 yr and the average longevity of conifers to be about

1000 yr. Thus, even though a plant may not represent a monoculture in space like agronomic crops, it may represent a monoculture in time due to long life span.

4. Perhaps far more important than the life span of the individual is the life span of the genotype. Because many plants reproduce vegetatively, the life span of the genotype (genet) may be much in excess of the life span of the vegetatively produced individual (ramet). For example, with creosote bush (Larrea tridentata), even though the vegetatively produced ramet may live for only 200 yr, the genet can be as old as 11,700 yr (Vasek, 1980). Equal in importance to longevity is the size of the genet. The larger it is, the more it approaches a traditional monoculture, thereby increasing the probability of detection and successful colonization. Kemperman and Barnes (1976) described clones of aspen (Populus tremuloides) that covered 81 ha (200 acres) or more. One smaller clone covered 43.3 ha and was composed of 47,000 ramets that had an average diameter breast high of 28 cm and averaged 18.3 m in height. Although the average age of each ramet was 105 yr, because clone size is very likely a function of age it is speculated that such clones date back to the Pleistocene and may be even older in areas where no glaciation occurred. The following examples show that even herbaceous plants, which are not generally thought of as being long-lived, can form clones that are old and of large size. Individual clones of bracken fern (Pteridium aquilinum) may be 1400 yr old and cover an area of 138,400 m^2 (Oinonen, 1967a,b). Similarly, clones of goldenrod (Solidago missouriensis) may be 1000 yr old and composed of as many as 10,000 stalks or ramets (W. J. Platt, personal communication).

When taken in combination, these four observations suggest that individual long-lived native plants or clones may be exposed to attack by rapidly evolving pathogens, parasites, and herbivores. A potential solution to the dilemma of long-lived plants that face rapidly evolving enemies is that plants are mosaics of variability. If true, individual plants or clones have long employed the strategy of variation that man has only recently discovered as a protection for his economically important crops.

A current nonplant example of how variation in itself can be an important strategy is represented by the parasitic protozoan Trypanosoma, which is transmitted by the tsetse fly to both man and domestic animals, with potentially devastating effects. Even though the mammalian immune system is highly effective in developing appropriate antibodies to complex with foreign substances, "the trypanosome survives in the bloodstream of the mammalian host by periodically altering its antigenic profile so that the developing immune response of the host is abortive" (Turner, 1980, p. 13). Thus by employing variation the parasite manages to stay ahead of a host defense that is also capable of changing but that is hindered by the lag time between the appearance of an altered antigen and the production of appropriate antibodies. It is also known that clones of trypanosomes grown from a single organism can develop many variant forms; these are expected to number in the hundreds. Such variability suggests that each trypanosome contains all the genetic information necessary to produce the variant forms (Turner, 1980). It would appear that trypanosome virulence is not conferred by a single overwhelming toxin or offensive weapon but by *variability within the individual*, for which effective countermeasures are difficult to develop.

In comparison with the trypanosome, in which variability is highly adaptive and clonally derived from a single organism, similar variability has been demonstrated with clonal populations of potatoes (Shepard *et al.*, 1980). Clonal populations regenerated from single leaf-cell protoplasts of the potato cultivar Russet Burbank exhibited high variation in disease-resistance characters, tuber shape, yield, maturity date, photoperiod requirements for flowering, and plant morphology. Although the genetic mechanisms have yet to be determined, it would appear that substantial genetic variation exists within individual plants (at least in expression). It also appears that the observed variation is stable, and the enhanced resistance to early blight and late blight suggests that such cloning techniques may be important to varietal improvement. Contrary to traditional logic, the cloning techniques with potatoes seem to produce more useful variability than has resulted from the past 50 yr of conventional breeding programs.

These examples demonstrate the feasibility of extensive and adaptive variation arising within a single individual or clone. A priori there are no reasons why the branches of a single tree or the various parts of the same clone could not employ such variation as a strategy against their parasites. There are at least three genetic mechanisms whereby individual plants could develop as mosaics of variability such that different leaves of the same shoot, different branches of the same tree, and/or different trunks of the same clone could differ qualitatively and/or quantitatively in their defenses. These include (1) somatic mutations and chimeras, in which individual plants develop as genetic mosaics, (2) induced factors such as pest-induced plant defenses, in which parasite attack triggers a defensive response that may vary depending upon the intensity of attack, and (3) developmental patterns of plant growth in which genes are turned on or off, depending upon age or some other patterns of plant growth. The first of these mechanisms has been reviewed by Whitham and Slobodchikoff (1981), and the latter two have been briefly discussed by Whitham (1981; see also Ryan, Chapter 2; Schultz, Chapter 3; Raupp and Denno, Chapter 4; McClure, Chapter 5; Rhoades, Chapter 6).

The following sections of this chapter will examine the variation that can be observed in individual trees of *Populus angustifolia* and the impact of this variation on its primary parasite, a gall aphid, *Pemphigus betae*. Although the mechanism(s) of host variation are as yet unknown, the unexpected level of variation in the resistance of different parts of the same plant may well be adaptive and represent a host strategy to manipulate the behavior of its parasites to minimize their negative impact.

III. HOST SELECTION BY *PEMPHIGUS* GALL APHIDS

The successful colonization of any tree involves two individuals representing different generations. To clarify this important point a brief review of the complex life cycle of *Pemphigus* aphids is required. At bud break in early spring, colonizing stem mothers emerge from eggs that overwinter in the deep fissures of cottonwood trees, and they migrate to the developing leaves where they induce galls. Although many stem mothers die during the gall-forming period, which lasts approximately 3–5 days, even these leave an identifiable scar that can later be recognized (Whitham, 1978). From previous experiments it is known that a colonizing stem mother can produce either a successful gall or a scar, but not both. This feature permits accurate censusing of not only the survivors that successfully form galls and produce offspring, but also those that died attempting colonization. On some host trees as many as 100% of all colonizers die during this critical colonizing period.

Although wingless, stem mothers are highly mobile and discriminate between leaves, shoots, and branches within an individual host tree. Within a few days of settling, successful stem mothers are enclosed within a hollow gall, and, depending upon the aphid and host species, by midsummer they parthenogenetically produce up to several hundred progeny. With gall maturation in midsummer, the mature, winged progeny of the stem mother migrate to a secondary host (usually a herbaceous plant), where they go underground and feed on the roots (Harper, 1958, 1963). On the secondary host a generation of wingless females are produced, and these in turn give birth to the fall winged migrants that return to the cottonwood trees. Back on the primary host a sexual generation is produced, and after mating each female lays a single overwintering egg to complete the life cycle. From this complex life cycle two

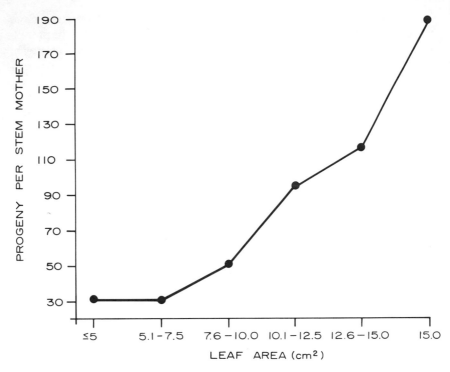

Fig. 1. Individual leaves of the same host plant vary greatly in their suitability to aphids. The effects of mature leaf size on the reproductive success of stem mothers is shown. Stem mothers occupying the largest leaves produced 189 ± 11.7 progeny, whereas those occupying the smallest leaves produced only 32 ± 7.3 progeny. Only leaves with single predator-free galls were used. Adapted from Whitham (1978).

individuals representing different generations are involved in successful host selection: the fall migrants determine which host tree will be colonized and the stem mother determines which branch, shoot, and leaf will be colonized. The failure of either generation to make precise settling decisions results in reduced fitness.

The preferred gall site is the base of a leaf that attains large size at maturity. These leaves result in the highest survival rates, number of progeny, mature dry body weights, and other measures of relative fitness (Whitham, 1978). For example, Fig. 1 shows the increase in the number of progeny per colonizing stem mother as a function of the mature leaf-size occupied. To control for the negative effects of density (when more than one stem mother colonizes the same leaf), only leaves with one gall were included in this analysis. Stem mothers colonizing the largest available leaves (>15 cm²) produced six times more progeny than stem mothers occupying the smallest leaves (≤5 cm²). Because of differential fitness the selection pressure for colonizing stem mothers to discriminate between leaves is very high, and they do so with considerable accuracy (Whitham, 1980). Also note that previous experiments (Whitham, 1978) confirm that stem mothers do *not* inject substances into the leaf to induce large size.

Host preference is negatively correlated with the concentration of phenolics (Zucker, 1982, also unpublished data), which have been strongly implicated in the defensive chemistry of many plants (Levin, 1971). Zucker (1982) showed that the chemical environment of these aphids, both between and within individual trees, is not at all uniform. Within a single leaf the concentration of total leaf phenols on or near the midrib where the gall is formed increases from the base of the leaf to the leaf tip (Fig. 2). Colonizing stem mothers nearly always attempt to form their galls at the base of the leaf, where the concentration of phenolics is lowest. When aphid densities are high, several galls may be formed on the same leaf. When this occurs, stem mothers that formed galls more distally on the leaf blade, where phenol concentrations were significantly higher, suffered higher mortality, fewer progeny, and a general reduction in other measures of relative fitness (Whitham, 1978, 1980). Similarly, small leaves, which aphids avoid, have a higher concentration of phenolics than the preferred large leaves. In paired comparisons of leaves of extreme size on individual shoots, the smallest leaves averaged more total phenols per milligram of dry leaf tissue than the largest leaves by a factor of 1.7 (Zucker, 1982).

In agreement with these findings of variation within an individual leaf and among leaves of the same shoot, similar differences exist among trees in which aphids prefer low concentrations of total phenols (Zucker, 1982). In examining two adjacent trees that exhibited a six-fold difference in aphid density, the concentration of phenolics in leaves of the preferred tree was approximately one-third that of the avoided tree. These findings demonstrate that although other factors such as nutrients or available nitrogen may be important, aphid preference has known biochemical correlates that are consistent at all levels of host selection.

IV. BETWEEN-PLANT VARIATION IN RESISTANCE

Colonizing aphids may exhibit a 150-fold difference in preference for individual trees growing near one another in the same grove. Such selective settling behavior reflects an underlying pattern of host resistance that is correlated with aphid survival and reproduction. Consequently, the selection of an individual tree by the fall migrants is a crucial phase in the life cycle, affecting fitness.

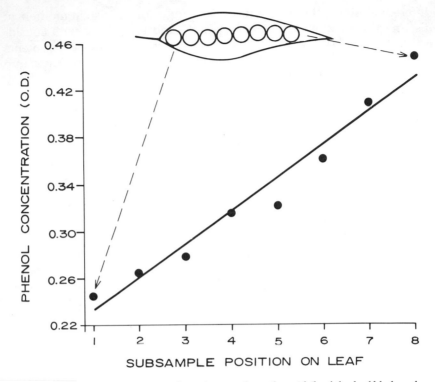

Fig. 2. Subsamples of leaf tissue collected on or along the midrib of the leaf blade, where galls are formed, reveal that the concentration of phenolics (O.D., optical density), is lowest at the base of the leaf, where stem mothers prefer to form galls ($r = 0.980$, $P < 0.01$, $n = 8$). The data presented here are from a single representative leaf. Leaves were collected at the time of aphid settling. Adapted from Zucker (1982).

Several *Pemphigus* species show similar preferences for individual host trees. Because colonizing aphids selectively settle where their fitness is highest (Whitham, 1978, 1980), there is a strong ecological basis for equating colonizer preference and the density of colonizers. Throughout this chapter density is defined as the number of colonizers per leaf, which includes both those stem mothers that survived to reproduce and those that died during gall formation, leaving a scar as evidence of their attempt. Table I shows aphid preferences, measured as gall density and survival rates for *Pemphigus populitransversus* and *P. populicaulis* on eastern cottonwood (*Populus deltoides*). These data were collected from a grove near Columbus, Ohio. All trees were of similar size, approximately 7 m in height, and all grew within 40 m of one another. Approximately 2000 leaves were sampled randomly from all sides and heights of each

TABLE I
Between-Tree Variation in Suitability for Aphids[a]

	Pemphigus populitransversus		Pemphigus populicaulis	
Mean leaf size (cm²) (± 1 SE, n)	Galls/2000 leaves (no. leaves examined[b])	Survival (%) (no. galls examined)	Galls/2000 leaves (no. leaves examined[b])	Survival (%) (no. galls examined)
13.6 (±1.18, 202)	15.0 (1732)	24.4 (41)	0	— (0)
14.8 (±1.26, 273)	0 (1780)	— (0)	0	— (0)
19.7 (±1.18, 296)	1.0 (1995)	— (1)	0	— (0)
25.6 (±1.16, 222)	16.5 (1092)	23.1 (13)	0	— (0)
28.7 (±1.51, 217)	5.6 (5003)	31.9 (47)	6.0	26.7 (15)
37.1 (±1.75, 251)	27.6 (1523)	77.1 (35)	6.6	— (5)
39.2 (±1.50, 238)	17.2 (1510)	45.5 (44)	6.6	55.6 (9)
39.3 (±1.03, 484)	29.1 (4057)	66.1 (59)	6.4	69.2 (13)
39.9 (±1.00, 491)	72.6 (2508)	68.1 (91)	1.6	— (2)
65.6 (±1.63, 219)	59.4 (1043)	72.0 (182)	42.2	82.9 (35)

[a]Shown are the densities and survival rates of two *Pemphigus* gall aphid species on different host trees of eastern cottonwood (*Populus deltoides*). Both aphid species preferentially colonize large-leaved trees, where survival rates are greatest.
[b]The same leaves were used for both *Pemphigus populicaulis* and *P. populitransversus*.

of 10 trees. Trees were selected on the basis of their representing a continuum of leaf sizes, which presumably reflected differences in the concentrations of secondary compounds and/or nutritional differences.

Both aphid species clearly preferred the large-leaved trees. The most abundant aphid species, *Pemphigus populitransversus*, showed a strong preference for the largest-leaved trees (Spearman rank correlation, $r_s = 0.879$, $P < 0.001$). Similarly, *P. populicaulis* was relatively common only on the largest-leaved tree ($r_s = 0.812$, $P < 0.005$).

Aphid selectivity (or the avoidance of individual trees) has probably evolved in response to differential survival. Survival was measured as the percentage of colonizing stem mothers that survived to reproduce. *Pemphigus populitransversus* survival increased from only 24% on the smallest-leaved tree to 72% on the largest-leaved tree ($r_s = 0.738$, $n = 8$, $P < 0.025$). Similarly, for *P. populicaulis* survival increased from 27% on the smallest-leaved tree to 83% on the preferred largest-leaved tree ($r_s = 1.00$, $n = 4$, $P < 0.05$). For both aphid species the discriminatory host-selection behavior was adaptive because aphid survival on the largest-leaved tree was greater than on the smallest-leaved tree by a factor of approximately 3.

Even stronger patterns of aphid host preference and survivorship have been observed at study sites in Utah with *Pemphigus betae* on *Populus angustifolia*. In an examination of 33 mature trees it was found that on large-leaved trees, where survival was as high as 76%, aphid preference or gall density was as high as 729 galls per 1000 leaves. On small-leaved trees, where survival could be as low as 0%, densities were as low as 5 galls per 1000 leaves (Whitham, 1981, also unpublished data). Clearly, the differences between trees can be great, and aphids that failed to respond to these differences suffered higher mortality.

Censuses of *Pemphigus betae* on *Populus angustifolia* during consecutive years show that, even though the aphid population may fluctuate from one year to the next, aphid preference for individual trees remains relatively constant (T. G. Whitham, unpublished data). This is particularly interesting, considering that the complex life cycle of these aphids, involving migration between a primary and secondary host, requires the subsequent recolonization of preferred trees each year. Whether or not these aphids have become genetically adapted to an individual host tree is unknown. That such specific adaptation may occur is enhanced by the trees' vegetative reproduction, which increases their exposure to rapidly evolving pests. Even though individual cottonwoods are not known to be long-lived, the genetic age of the clone, which may be composed of up to 55 mature trees (T. G. Whitham, unpublished data), is probably far in excess of the life span of any individual tree. Furthermore, preliminary morphological comparisons of clones of resistant and susceptible trees grown under laboratory conditions indicate that the differences in resistance between trees or clones are genetically determined.

V. WITHIN-PLANT VARIATION IN RESISTANCE

The variation in resistance to aphid attack within a single host tree can be as great as the variation in resistance between extreme trees in the population. Figure 3 shows how an estimated 53,000 galls (containing approximately 2,100,000 aphids) of *Pemphigus betae* were distributed on 20 branches of a single 20-m tree. All branches equal to or more than 5 cm in diameter were censused by randomly sampling approximately 400 leaves per branch (2778 galls on 7424 leaves were examined). Leaves were individually measured for size, and each gall was examined to determine if the gall had been successfully formed and contained a viable stem mother and her progeny or if the stem mother had died during the brief gall-forming period at bud break. The number of leaves for each branch was estimated from comparisons with representative branches, on which the total number of leaves had been determined by counting. Because the number of progeny per stem mother is strongly correlated with her mature dry body weight (Whitham, 1978), total aphid

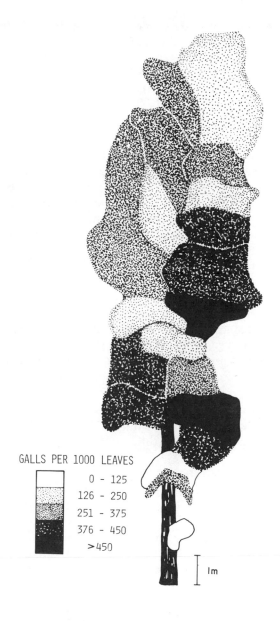

GALLS PER 1000 LEAVES

0 - 125
126 - 250
251 - 375
376 - 450
>450

1 m

Fig. 3. This schematic of a 20.1-m *Populus angustifolia* tree shows how an estimated 53,000 galls, containing approximately 2,100,000 aphids, are distributed over 20 branches. The mosaic pattern of aphid settling is nonrandom and reflects an underlying mosaic pattern of host resistance (see text for explanation). The size of each branch reflects total leaf area. Drawing by Pam Lunge.

numbers were estimated by determining the mean dry body weight of 60 stem mothers collected at random over the entire tree. Using the regression equation $y = 425.22x - 10.82$, the average stem mother (weighing 0.210 mg) produced 78 progeny. Although 49% of all colonizing stem mothers died during the gall-forming process, using this estimate of reproductive success the remaining 26,900 galls should have contained approximately 2,100,000 aphids or about 1.5 aphids per square centimeter of leaf area.

The observed pattern of aphid settling shows that adjacent branches as well as branches at various heights can have very different parasite loads. Gall densities per branch ranged from 19 to 794 galls per 1000 leaves, with a mean gall density for the entire tree of 324 galls per 1000 leaves. This represents a 42-fold difference in the extremes of aphid preference for one branch over another. One-way analysis of variance (ANOVA) shows that this distribution could not have resulted from the random settling of colonizing stem mothers ($P < 0.001$). The observed level of variation between branches of the same tree is of the same order of magnitude that exists between extreme trees in the population.

The mosaic pattern of aphid settling, in which colonizing stem mothers avoid those small-leaved branches where mortality is highest, reflects an underlying pattern of host resistance. Figure 4 shows the survival rates of colonizing stem mothers on individual branches of the tree shown in Fig. 3. Survival is given as the percentage of colonizing stem mothers that survive to form galls and reproduce. Survival on individual branches ranges from 26 to 58%, which is significantly correlated with the mean leaf size of the host branch ($r = 0.71$, $P < 0.01$). These data demonstrate the existence of real differences between branches that affect aphid fitness.

Colonizing aphids, even though very small (about 0.6 mm in length), are highly mobile and somehow discriminate between branches. Figure 5, based on data from Fig. 3, shows that colonizing stem mothers avoided the small-leaved branches, where mortality during gall formation was highest, and selectively settled on the large-leaved branches ($r = 0.68$, $P < 0.01$). For example, gall densities ranged from only 19 galls per 1000 leaves on a branch where only 33% of the colonizers survived to a high of 794 galls per 1000 leaves on a branch where 58% of the colonizers survived. The differential in survival rates is a direct measure of the advantage gained by discriminating between branches.

These patterns have been replicated in even greater detail on another, nearby 18.0-m tree that supported an estimated 81,000 galls containing approximately 4,500,000 aphids (T. G. Whitham, unpublished data). As in the previous example, the observed pattern of aphid settling showed

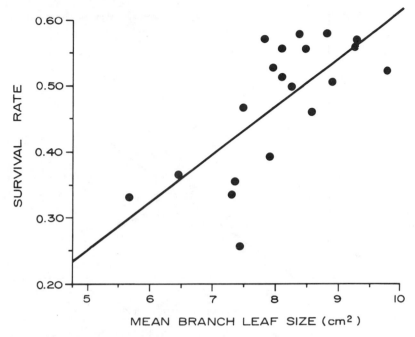

Fig. 4. Aphid survival during the colonizing period is highest on large-leaved branches. Survival of colonizing stem mothers per branch is plotted as a function of the mean leaf size of the host branch occupied ($r = 0.71$, $P < 0.01$, $n = 20$). All 20 branches are from the same tree, shown in Fig. 3.

that adjacent branches as well as branches at various heights could have very different parasite loads. Gall densities ranged from 30 to 950 galls per 1000 leaves, with an average density of 480 galls per 1000 leaves. Survival rates were more extreme than in the first example ranging from 0 to 72%, and those branches where survival was lowest were avoided. Furthermore, it was found that the differences between branches also significantly affected the mature dry body weight of the stem mother and the number of her progeny. Thus, regardless of the mechanisms that produce variation within an individual host plant, colonizing stem mothers clearly respond to the mosaic of suitabilities, and this response greatly increases individual success.

In agreement with the findings that the variation in resistance *between* trees remains relatively constant in consecutive years, the mosaic pattern of host resistance *within* a single tree also remains relatively constant from one year to the next. T. G. Whitham (unpublished data) found that the branches within a single tree that were preferred in 1980 were also

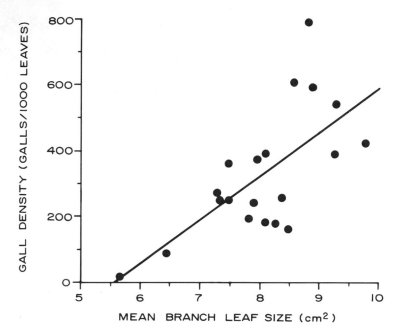

Fig. 5. Colonizing stem mothers selectively settle on large-leaved branches, where survival is highest. Branch preference or the density of galls per 1000 leaves is plotted as a function of the mean leaf size of the host branch occupied ($r = 0.68$, $P < 0.01$, $n = 20$). Data are from the tree shown in Fig. 3.

preferred in 1981, demonstrating that branch differences remain constant (at least over a 2-yr period) and that the branches where mortality is highest are continually avoided. Such selectivity is remarkable because the complex life cycle of these aphids, involving migration between two different hosts, requires that individual trees and branches must be recolonized each year.

VI. IMPACT OF WITHIN-PLANT VARIATION ON PARASITES

The next questions to address are, How can variation be adaptive to the host plant, and What are its impacts on the parasite population? Whitham (1981) predicted that host variation would have at least three major impacts on the parasite population. First, variation would make the host less apparent to its parasites by increasing the probability that inappropriate settling and feeding decisions would be made, thereby reducing parasite fitness and impact on the host. Second, variation would increase the level of competitive interactions for superior host resources, resulting

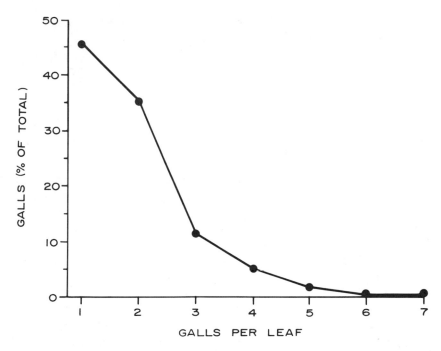

Fig. 6. Over the entire tree 54.2% of all galls were clumped on the same leaves, with two to seven galls occupying a single leaf. This distribution was produced from the cumulative data from all branches of the tree shown in Fig. 3, in which branches were weighted according to the number of leaves they supported.

in greater parasite mortality. Third, the clumping of parasites at specific sites would make them more apparent and vulnerable to their predators than if they were able to disperse more evenly over the host plant. In the remainder of this section I will develop the argument that by concentrating its parasites at specific sites the host plant can significantly reduce parasite numbers.

The net effect of host variation is not only to concentrate colonizing aphids on specific branches but also to concentrate them on specific leaves. Figures 3–5 show that the mosaic pattern of branch suitability causes colonizing aphids to clump. As the density of colonizing aphids on individual branches increases, the percentage of the aphid population that doubles-up on the same leaves (two or more colonizing stem mothers or galls per leaf) also increases. For example, on the tree shown in Fig. 3, as the density of galls rose from 19 to 794 galls per 1000 leaves on different branches, the percentage doubling-up on the same leaves increased from 0 to 81%. Figure 6 shows how aphids doubled-up on the same leaves over the entire tree. These estimates are based on samples

Table II
Increased Competitor Density Negatively Affects Aphid Fitness[a, b]

Galls/leaf	Progeny/stem mother	Leaf size (cm²)
1	90 ± 7.3 (143)	13.7 ± .31 (143)
2	59 ± 4.8 (224)	14.0 ± .30 (143)

[a]Numbers adjacent to means indicate ± 1 SE; numbers in parentheses indicate sample sizes.
[b]To measure the effect of competitor density on the number of progeny per stem mother, only predator-free galls on leaves of nearly identical size were examined.

from all branches (includes the examination of 2778 galls) and are adjusted for branch size. Thus over the entire tree 54.2% of all colonizing stem mothers doubled-up with 2–7 stem mothers occupying the same leaf.

Although leaves that mature to large size can support more stem mothers and their progeny (Whitham, 1978, 1980), stem mothers that colonize the same large leaf are at a disadvantage. To examine the effects of doubling-up on the reproductive success of stem mothers, only predator-free galls on leaves of the same size were used to determine relative fitness. In comparisons of reproductive success, the average stem mother, occupying leaves singly, produced 90 progeny, whereas stem mothers that shared a leaf with another stem mother produced an average of only 59 progeny (Table II). Consequently, stem mothers occupying leaves singly gained a 53% increase in the number of progeny produced (ANOVA, $P < 0.001$).

The observed levels of doubling-up (Fig. 6) and the observed yield of progeny by stem mothers occupying leaves singly (Table II) can be used to measure the effect of host variation on the aphid population. If all leaves of the host plant had been equal, so that colonizing stem mothers could have dispersed over the host with only one gall per leaf, the aphid population would have been 32% higher. Thus aphid responses to host variation results in colonization of the same leaves where competitive interactions between aphids reduces the parasite population and, presumably, their impact on the host plant.

In addition to the negative effects of competition discussed previously, there is evidence indicating that on some host trees the presence of a gall induces a defensive response in which galled leaves are selectively abscised. Such premature leaf fall results in the death of all aphids in the gall (unpublished data) and is similar to observations made by Faeth et al. (1981) on leaf miners. When a tarpaulin was placed on the ground beneath a tree, it was found that some leaves fell from the tree in May and early June, nearly a month before the aphids matured and several

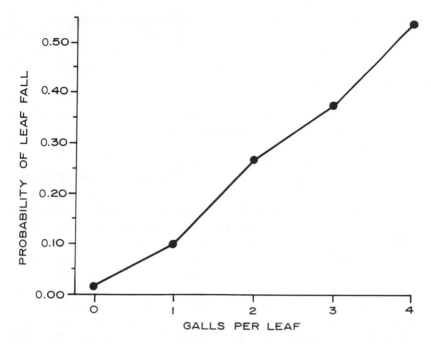

Fig. 7. As the number of galls per leaf increases, so does the probability of premature leaf abscision and aphid death. The probability of premature leaf fall is plotted as a function of the number of galls formed on the leaf.

months before the leaves would normally abscise. Upon closer examination it was found that nearly all of the leaves on the ground contained galls, whereas the density of galls on the tree was much lower, indicating that galled leaves were selectively dropped by the host tree. From the distribution of galled and gall-free leaves both on the tree and on the ground it was possible to calculate the probability of a galled leaf's being abscised or dropped by the host tree. Figure 7 shows that galled leaves have a much higher probability of premature leaf fall than gall-free leaves. For example, leaves without any galls had less than 2% chance of being abscised, whereas galled leaves (leaves with one or more galls) had 21% chance of being abscised. By summing over all gall-density categories (one to four or more galls per leaf), we calculated that the observed leaf fall resulted in 28% of all galls dropping from the tree before the aphids in these galls matured.

High levels of variation within a single host plant may be viewed as an efficient mechanism for concentrating parasites at specific sites, so that fewer leaves need be abscised to achieve the same loss of parasites.

Figure 7 shows that, as the number of galls per leaf increased from one to four or more galls per leaf, the probability of premature leaf fall increased linearly from 10 to 54%. It would appear that only at low gall densities (per leaf) can aphids perhaps prevent premature leaf fall. Regardless of the mechanisms, however, by clumping its parasites at specific sites the host plant can increase the probability of premature leaf fall and literally shed even more aphids than would have been possible had the aphids been distributed evenly over all leaves and branches.

Clumping also increases the probability of detection by predators. The level of predation on branches with high gall densities can be nearly twice as great as on adjacent branches with low gall densities (45% versus 25%, respectively; Whitham, 1981, also unpublished data). Such selective foraging by predators is predicted by optimal foraging theory (Charnov, 1976; Krebs, 1978). As preferred food items become more abundant or as travel time between prey items decreases, the profitability of increased specialization on a specific prey type increases. From the predator's viewpoint, the concentration of aphids makes selective foraging on branches with high gall densities and specialization on aphids more profitable (see also Tullock, 1971; Schultz, Chapter 4). From this perspective it would appear that the potential exists for the host plant to manipulate the settling behavior of its parasites to reduce their numbers through competition and premature leaf fall and, simultaneously, manipulate the behavior of the predators of aphids as well.

VII. DISCUSSION

This chapter has assumed that aphids represent a significant drain on the host plant. This is the most common failing of plant–parasite interaction studies, and it is crucial for future experiments to precisely quantify parasite impact on host fitness. Unless such experiments demonstrate impact, however, there remains the real possibility that parasites and other pests have no impact on their hosts and may even be beneficial, as suggested by Owen and Wiegert (1976) and Owen (1980). To quantify parasite impact on the host in this system, we are currently cloning resistant and susceptible trees (and branches) for field tests. Obviously, these must be long-term experiments, and this necessity probably accounts for the present general lack of evidence in natural systems. Only with such experiments can one critically examine what may turn out to be a small yearly impact. A very small impact, however, compounded over the remaining life span of a long-lived plant or clone, could be enormous at the end of 100 or 1000 yr and could result in large reproductive differentials among the genotypes in the host population. For this reason, experiments undertaken to study parasite impact on the host plant should be robust and precise enough to discriminate between relatively small differences.

Even with these possible failings in mind, this study has demonstrated an unexpected high level of variation in the resistance to parasite attack within an individual host plant that rivals the range of variation observed between extreme trees in the population. Gall densities ranged from 5 to 729 galls per 1000 leaves among trees at the same study site, and among branches of the same tree gall densities ranged from 19 to 794 galls per 1000 leaves. It is difficult to regard such within-plant variation as noise in the system, particularly when the mosaic pattern of variation is reflected in differential survival rates, number of progeny, and strong aphid preference for specific branches that persists from year to year. Aphid selectivity is not surprising, however, because previous studies of these aphids have demonstrated their precision in local habitat-selection behavior (within a branch) and a capability of achieving 84% of their potential reproductive success in discriminating between leaves of different quality and competitor densities (Whitham, 1980, also unpublished data). Although such discriminatory behavior appears impressive, the best they can do may be highly restricted by the host plant and represent an example of Van Valen's Red Queen's hypothesis (1973, p. 25), in which "it takes all the running you can do to stay in the same place."

Because of host variation, the specialized aphid parasites of *Populus* are caught between two opposing selection pressures, both of which negatively affect their survival and reproduction. Host variability gives an advantage to aphids that discriminate between branches, but this results in clumping, and the negative effects of clumping (competition, premature leaf fall, and predation) favor hyperdispersion or random settling. Selection may favor plants that increase the degree that these two opposing selective pressures interact. This may be thought of as a squeeze play that is brought about by opposing selection pressures, in which the aphids are caught in the middle (see Price et al., 1980, for examples of three interacting trophic levels). That the variation in resistance within a single tree can be as great as the variation in resistance between trees in the population may in an evolutionary sense represent a quantitative measure of the host plant's effort to play off the opposing selection pressures.

In response to the negative effects of clumping, territorial behavior may have evolved as an aphid counteradaptation. Because host leaves are highly variable in quality and because the most favorable large leaves are relatively rare, most colonizing stem mothers are forced to double-up on the same leaves (Whitham, 1978, 1980). The negative effects of clumping, however, give a great advantage to aphids that avoid clumping, and they may have been important in the evolution of territorial behavior. Whitham (1979) showed that large, dominant stem mothers successfully defend superior gall sites and that this limits density. Such behavioral adaptations are only partially effective and appear to break down at very high densities. As many as 24 colonizing stem mothers have been observed trying to colonize the same leaf, but no more than 4 can survive on a single leaf. If these aphids had not evolved territorial behavior to limit density, presumably the negative effects of clumping on the aphid population would have been even more severe.

The opposing selection pressures operating on aphids are diverse and independent of one another. For example, if aphids were able to eliminate any one of the negative effects of clumping (competition, premature leaf fall, or predation) the remaining two could still represent a significant selection pressure. In comparison with single responses by the host, such diversity makes it more difficult for counteradaptations to evolve because no single aphid trait will confer great fitness. Thus variation within the host plant and the diversity of responses to parasite attack should at the very least delay counteradaptations by their parasites.

Although colonizing aphids are presently capable of successfully attacking only a small portion of the host mosaic (those relatively rare large leaves in which the concentration of phenolics or other plant defenses are lowest), aphids could evolve the ability to utilize small leaves. Why haven't they? Assuming there is a cost involved with detoxification or increased virulence (Van der Plank, 1963), in the absence of a toxin or genes for resistance in the host the mutant parasite race with specialized detoxification mechanisms should be selected against. Leonard (1977), in summarizing results on a few plant pathogens, demonstrated that the selective coefficients against unnecessary genes for virulence ranged from 0.12 to 0.42. This is a very important point because in the absence of host resistance a simple pathogen lacking virulence will be evolutionarily favored. Leonard (1969), Nelson (1978), Leonard and Czochor (1980), and others have used this logic as a cornerstone for examining the evolution of equilibria in plant–pathogen populations.

Using the concept of trade-offs between host resistance and parasite fitness, quantitative and/or qualitative variation in the host plant may select for simple parasite races that lack the ability to reach epidemic proportions and seriously damage the host plant. For example, aphids could have evolved the ability to utilize small leaves, which are more heavily defended or of poorer nutritive value, but as long as large leaves are superior to small leaves selection will favor those aphids that are most efficient on the superior, large leaves. It would appear that the presence of a few large leaves could favor aphid races that are not adapted to attack the majority of the host plant. Thus the mosaic pattern of variation in the host plant could be an evolved trait that allows the plant to not only manipulate the behavior of its parasites and their predators but also direct the evolution of their parasites along less destructive pathways. Such coevolved interactions are most likely to be observed in gall-forming insects because of the long-term association of these parasites and their host plants and the highly interactive nature of the gall-forming process (Mani, 1964).

Within-plant variation as a potential mechanism permitting hosts to direct the evolution of their parasites may be particularly important when considering that (1) parasites may become genetically adapted to an individual host tree, (2) even small monocultures can become susceptible to evolving pathogens over a short period of time, and (3) the ability of rapidly evolving parasites to break the defenses of their hosts increases with the life span of the plant or clone, the size of the clone, and its genetic uniformity. Viewed in this perspective, within-plant variation arising by any of the mechanisms described in Section I may represent the only long-term host defense against rapidly evolving pests.

VIII. SUMMARY

Research on agronomic crops makes it clear that variation in the host population, both in time and space, is an important plant defense against rapidly evolving parasites and other plant pests (see Hare, Chapter 18). Here I extend the adaptive role of variation in a population to consider the adaptive role of variation within an individual tree or clone. The potential importance of variation within an individual plant is emphasized by two major points.

1. Through race formation, pests may become adapted to an individual host plant, and such adaptations may occur over a relatively short period of time.

2. Long life span and/or large clone size increases the exposure of the host genotype to plant pests with short generation times and the potential to evolve rapidly.

Because of these and other factors, long-lived plants in natural eco-systems may be exposed to attack by rapidly evolving parasites, pathogens, and herbivores.

To examine this hypothesis, individual trees of *Populus angustifolia* have been examined for within- and between-host variation in resistance to the attack of their primary insect parasite, *Pemphigus* gall aphids. The following points have been demonstrated.

1. Colonizing aphids discriminate between individual leaves and branches of the host tree.
2. The settling pattern of colonizing aphids reflect an underlying mosaic of host resistance that affects aphid fitness.
3. Variation within a single host plant sharply reduces parasite numbers through the negative effects of clumping, premature leaf fall, and increased predation.
4. The variation in resistance to aphid attack among different branches of the same tree is of the same order of magnitude as the variation in resistance between extreme trees in the population.

These data suggest that variation within the individual host plant may act to stabilize the pest population at levels far lower than would have been achieved with a uniform host substrate. Within-plant variation may represent a plant strategy that allows the host plant to manipulate its parasites and their predators to directly reduce pest numbers and simultaneously direct the evolution of parasites along less harmful pathways. Although much more research needs to be conducted on impact of parasites on host plants and the mechanisms involved in host variation, these data suggest that within-plant variation may be a highly adaptive and evolved plant trait rather than noise in an otherwise orderly system.

ACKNOWLEDGMENTS

I gratefully acknowledge the use of facilities provided by Joe Begay and Rhet White from the Utah Power and Light Company and Eugene G. Bozniak and Dawn M. Gatherum from the Botany Department of Weber State College. Judge Thornley K. Swan graciously allowed us to camp on his property. This work would not have been possible without the support of NSF Grants DEB7905848 and DEB8005602. Helpful comments and suggestions were provided by William J. Platt, Peter W. Price, O. J. Reichman, C. N. Slobodchikoff, and Alan Williams. K. T. Leonard, Rodger Mitchell, Marr D. Simons, and William V. Zucker provided critical reviews of the manuscript. Extensive sampling of trees and analyses would not have been completed without the help of Tom Buckley, Phil Gaddis, Rocky Harrison, Alan Williams, and Debra L. Wright.

REFERENCES

Barbour, M. G., Burk, J. H., and Pitts, W. D. "Terrestrial Plant Ecology." Benjamin/ Cummings, Menlo Park, California.

Berenbaum, M. (1980). Adaptive significance of midgut pH in larval Lepidoptera. *Am. Nat.* **115**, 138–146.

Browning, J. A. (1974). Relevance of knowledge about natural ecosystems to development of pest management programs for agro-ecosystems. *Proc. Am. Phytopathol. Soc.* **1**, 191–199.

Browning, J. A., and Frey, K. J. (1969). Multiline cultivars as a means of disease control. *Annu. Rev. Phytopathol.* **7**, 355–382.

Browning, J. A., Simons, M. D., and Torrres, E. (1977). Managing host genes: epidemiologic and genetic concepts. *In* "Plant Disease: An Advanced Treatise" (J. G. Horsfall and E. B. Cowling, eds.), Vol. 1, pp. 191–212. Academic Press, New York.

Browning, J. A., Frey, K. J., McDaniel, M. E., Simons, M. D., and Wahl, I. (1979). The bio-logic of using multilines to buffer pathogen populations and prevent disease loss. *Indian J. Genet. Plant Breed.* **39**, 3–9.

Charnov, E. L. (1976). Optimal foraging: attack strategy of a mantid. *Am. Nat.* **110**, 141–151.

Cowling, E. B. (1978). Agricultural and forest practices that favor epidemics. *In* "Plant Disease: An Advanced Treatise" (J. G. Horsfall and E. B. Cowling, eds.), Vol. 2, pp. 361–381. Academic Press, New York.

Day, P. R. (1978). The genetic basis of epidemics. *In* "Plant Disease: An Advanced Treatise" (J. G. Horsfall and E. B. Cowling, eds.), Vol. 2, pp. 263–285. Academic Press, New York.

DeBach, P. (1974). "Biological Control by Natural Enemies." Cambridge Univ. Press, London/New York.

Edmunds, G. F., Jr., and Alstad, D. N. (1978). Coevolution in insect herbivores and conifers. *Science* **199**, 941–945.

Faeth, S. H., Connor, E. F., and Simberloff, D. (1981). Early leaf abscission: a neglected source of mortality for folivores. *Am. Nat.* **117**, 409–415.

Feeny, P. P. (1970). Seasonal changes in oak leaf tannins and nutrients as a cause of spring feeding by winter moth caterpillars. *Ecology* **51**, 565–581.

Flor, H. H. (1971). Current status of the gene-for-gene concept. *Annu. Rev. Phytopathol.* **9**, 275–296.

Frey, K. J., Browning, J. A., and Simons, M. D. (1973). Management of host resistance genes to control diseases. *Z. Pflanzenkr. Pflanzenschutz* **80**, 160–180.

Frey, K. J., Browning, J. A., and Simons, M. D. (1979). Management systems for host genes to control disease loss. *Indian J. Genet. Plant Breed.* **39**, 10–21.

Gallun, R. L., Starks, K. J., and Guthrie, W. D. (1975). Plant resistance to insects attacking cereals. *Annu. Rev. Entomol.* **20**, 337–357.

Harper, A. M. (1958). Notes on behavior of *Pemphigus betae* Doane (Homoptera: Aphididae) infected with *Entomophora aphidis* Hoffm. *Can. Entomol.* **90**, 439–440.

Harper, A. M. (1963). Sugar-beet root aphid, *Pemphigus betae* Doane (Homoptera: Aphididae) in southern Alberta. *Can. Entomol.* **95**, 863–873.

Kemperman, J. A., and Barnes, B. V. (1976). Clone size in American aspens. *Can. J. Bot.* **54**, 2603–2607.

Knott, D. R. (1972). Using race specific resistance to manage the evolution of plant pathogens. *J. Environ. Qual.* **1**, 227–231.

Krebs, J. R. (1978). Optimal foraging: decision rules for predators. *In* "Behavioral Ecology: An Evolutionary Approach" (J. R. Krebs and N. B. Davies, eds.), pp. 23–63. Blackwell, Oxford.

Leijerstam, B. (1972). Studies in powdery mildew on wheat in Sweden. III. Variability of virulence in *Erysiphe graminis* f. sp. *tritici* due to gene recombination and mutation. *Natl. Swed. Inst. Plant Prot., Contrib.* **15**, 231–248.

Leonard, K. J. (1969). Genetic equilibria in host–pathogen systems. *Phytopathology* **59**, 1858–1863.

Leonard, K. J. (1977). Selection pressures and plant pathogens. *Ann. N.Y. Acad. Sci.* **287**, 207–222.

Leonard, K. J., and Czochor, R. J. (1980). Theory of genetic interactions among populations of plants and their pathogens. *Annu. Rev. Phytopathol.* **18**, 237–258.

Levin, D. A. (1971). Plant phenolics: an ecological perspective. *Am. Nat.* **105**, 157–181.

Mani, M. S. (1964). "Ecology of Plant Galls." Junk, The Hague.

Nelson, R. R. (1978). Genetics of horizontal resistance to plant disease. *Annu. Rev. Phytopathol.* **16**, 359–378.

Oinonen, E. (1967a). The correlation between the size of Finnish bracken (*Pteridium aquilinum* (L.) Kuhn) clones and certain periods of site history. *Acta For. Fenn.* **83**, 1–51.

Oinonen, E. (1967b). Sporal regeneration of bracken in Finland in the light of the dimensions and age of its clones. *Acta For. Fenn.* **83**, 3–96.

Owen, D. F. (1980). How plants may benefit from the animals that eat them. *Oikos* **35**, 230–235.

Owen, D. F., and Wiegert, R. G. (1976). Do consumers maximize plant fitness? *Oikos* **27**, 488–492.

Painter, R. H. (1966). Lessons to be learned from the past experience in breeding plants for insect resistance. *In* "Breeding Pest Resistant Trees," pp. 349–366. Pergamon, Oxford.

Price, P. W., Bouton, C. E., Gross, P., McPheron, B. A., Thompson, J. H., and Weis, A. E. (1980). Interactions among three trophic levels: influence of plants on interactions between insect herbivores and natural enemies. *Annu. Rev. Ecol. Syst.* **11**, 41–65.

Robinson, R. A. (1980). New concepts in breeding for disease resistance. *Annu. Rev. Phytopathol.* **18**, 189–210.

Rosen, H. R. (1949). Oat percentage and procedure for combining resistance to crown rust, including race 45, and *Helminthosporium* blight. *Phytopathology* **39**, 20.

Schmidt, R. A. (1978). Diseases in forest ecosystems: the importance of functional diversity. *In* "Plant Disease: An Advanced Treatise" (J. G. Horsfall and E. B. Cowling, eds.), Vol. 2, pp. 287–315. Academic Press, New York.

Segal, A., Manisterski, J., Fischbeck, G., and Wahl, I. (1980). How plant populations defend themselves in natural ecosystems. *In* "Plant Disease: An Advanced Treatise" (J. G. Horsfall and E. B. Cowling, eds.), Vol. 5, pp. 75–102. Academic Press, New York.

Shepard, J. F., Bidney, D., and Shahin, E. (1980). Potato protoplasts in crop improvement. *Science* **208**, 17–24.

Tullock, G. (1971). The coal tit as a careful shopper. *Am. Nat.* **105**, 77–80.

Turner, M. (1980). How trypanosomes change coats. *Nature, (London)* **284**, 13–14.

Van der Plank, J. E. (1963). "Plant Diseases: Epidemics and Control." Academic Press, New York.

Van Valen, L. (1973). A new evolutionary law. *Evol. Theory* **1**, 1–30.

Vasek, F. C. (1980). Creosote bush: long-lived clones in the Mojave Desert. *Am. J. Bot.* **67,** 246–255.

Whitham, T. G. (1978). Habitat selection by *Pemphigus* aphids in response to resource limitation and competition. *Ecology* **59,** 1164–1176.

Whitham, T. G. (1979). Territorial behavior of *Pemphigus* gall aphids. *Nature (London)* **279,** 324–325.

Whitham, T. G. (1980). The theory of habitat selection: examined and extended using *Pemphigus* aphids. *Am. Nat.* **115,** 449–466.

Whitham, T. G. (1981). Individual trees as heterogeneous environments: Adaptation to herbivory or epigenetic noise? *In* "Insect and Life History Patterns: Habitat and Geographic Variations" (R. F. Denno and H. Dingle, eds.), pp. 9–27. Springer-Verlag, Berlin/New York.

Whitham, T. G., and Slobodchikoff, C. N. (1981). Evolution by individuals, plant–herbivore interactions, and mosaics of genetic variability: the adaptive significance of somatic mutations in plants. *Oecologia* **49,** 287–292.

Zucker, W. V. (1982). How aphids choose leaves: the role of phenolics in host selection by a galling aphid. *Ecology* **63,** 972–981.

Thomas G. Whitham
Department of Biological Sciences
Northern Arizona University
Flagstaff, Arizona
and
Biology Department
Museum of Northern Arizona
Flagstaff, Arizona

CHAPTER 2

Insect-Induced Chemical Signals Regulating Natural Plant Protection Responses

C. A. RYAN

I. INTRODUCTION

Plants have evolved a variety of strategies to defend themselves against higher animals, insects, microbes, and viruses, including the ability to respond to attacks by producing toxic chemicals. A number of responses to pest attacks are mediated by signals that are released from the attack sites and transported to uninfected or unwounded cells, where they trigger, within a few hours, biochemical processes that produce chemicals that have primary roles in plant defense. In some instances, chemicals are produced at or near the wound site, apparently to arrest the attacking pests during the initial attack (Green and Ryan, 1972; Kuć, 1976; Keen and Bruegger, 1977; Grisbach and Ebel, 1978; Kojima et al., 1979; Mahadevan, 1979; Cruickshank, 1980; Stoessl, 1980; Uritani, 1978; West, 1981). In other cases, there are responses that take place in unwounded tissues, even several centimeters away from the wound site, that are apparently directed against a persistent attack or against future attacks by the same or other pests (Loebenstein and Ross, 1963; Thielges, 1968; Green and Ryan, 1972; Giebel, 1974; Haukioja and Niemelä, 1977; Rhoades, 1979; Niemelä et al., 1979; Sequeira, 1979; McIntyre, 1980; Goodman, 1980; Hamilton, 1980; Sela, 1981). Some examples of these types of responses are presented in Table I. While not comprehensive, these examples include responses that are initiated by insect attacks, nematode infestations, fungal and bacterial invasion, and viral infections.

VARIABLE PLANTS AND HERBIVORES
IN NATURAL AND MANAGED SYSTEMS

Table I

Pest-Induced Protective Systems Involving Short-Duration Responses

Pest	Damage	Plant	Plant response	References[a]
Insects				
Colorado potato beetle	Grazing or mechanical wounding	*Solanum tuberosum, Lycopersicon esculentum*	Proteinase inhibitor accumulation in unwounded leaves	1,2
Chewing insects	Mechanical wounding	*Betula pubescens*	Total phenolics increase in unwounded leaves	3,4
Chewing insects	Mechanical wounding	*Solanum bicolor*	HCN release at wound site	5,6
Neamatodes				
Several genera	Infection	Several genera	Subsequent infective nematodes died or development was delayed	7,8
Fungi				
Many genera	Infection	Many genera	Phytoalexin increase	9–16
Bacteria				
Pseudomonas solanacearum	Infection	*Nicotiana tabacum*	Immunity to subsequent infection	17,18
Virus				
TMV	Infection polycarboxylates or polyanions	*Nicotiana tabacum*	Induced resistance to subsequent infection	19–21

[a] References: 1, Ryan (1970); Green and Ryan (1972); 3, Haukioja and Niemalä (1977); 4, Niemalä *et al.* (1979); 5, Dement and Mooney (1974); 6, Kojima *et al.* (1979); 7, Giebel (1974); 8, McIntyre (1980); 9, Kuć (1976); 10, Keen and Bruegger (1977); 11, Grisbach and Ebel (1978); 12, Mahadevan (1979); 13, Cruickshank (1980); 14, Stoessl (1980); 15, Uritani (1978); 16, West (1981); 17, Sequeira (1979); 18, Goodman (1980); 19, Loebenstein and Ross (1963); 20, Hamilton (1980); 21, Sela (1981).

Until recently, little was known of the chemical nature of the signals that are apparently involved in inter- and intratissue communication during pest attacks. Studies of two systems, insect-induced proteinase-inhibitor accumulation in tomato plants (Ryan, 1978; Bishop *et al.*, 1981; Ryan *et al.*, 1982) and phytoalexin production in soybeans (Hahn *et al.*, 1981), castor beans (Lee and West, 1981a,b; Bruce and West, 1982), and peas (Walker-Simmons *et al.*, 1983), have provided new insights into the mechanisms of chemical communication in plants that occur during such attacks. The evidence strongly supports a role for plant cell-wall fragments, released at the wound site, as informational macromolecules that communicate to receptor cells in nearby or distal tissues that the plant is under attack. These data imply an even more intriguing possibility that both systems may have evolved from an ancient ancestral communication system, and they raise the possibility that some of the other plant-protection responses, such as those shown in Table I, may also employ fundamentally similar communication systems for monitoring pest attacks.

The initial recognition that plant cell-wall fragments are informational macromolecules resulted from the combined evidence that was developing in three separate research programs, those on (1) insect or wound-induced proteinase-inhibitor syntheses in tomato leaves (Bishop *et al.*, 1981; Ryan *et al.*, 1982), (2) fungal-induced phytoalexin synthesis in soybeans (Hahn *et al.*, 1981), and (3) phytoalexin synthesis in castor beans (Lee and West, 1981a,b; Bruce and West, 1982). Information from all three laboratories has been crucial in recognizing the relationships between the signals emanating from pest attacks and the release of large, biologically active cell-wall polysaccharides and, later, in recognizing that the signals may also involve much smaller oligosaccharide fragments.

A brief background into these systems will be presented, together with a review of the data that have led to the conclusion that cell-wall fragments are indeed informational macromolecules that initiate biochemical processes involved in plant protection.

II. PROTEINASE INHIBITORS AND NATURAL PLANT PROTECTION

A. Background

Proteinase inhibitors are polypeptides and proteins that combine tightly with proteolytic enzymes ($K_i = 10^{-7}-10^{-12}$ M) to inhibit their catalytic activity. Natural inhibitors of the four mechanistic classes of proteinase have been reported in plants (Ryan, 1973), but the majority of inhibitors from plants are specific for the serine class of proteinases that are commonly found as the major food-protein-digesting enzymes of microorganisms and animals, including insects. Comprehensive reviews of proteinase inhibitors have been written (Laskowski and Sealock, 1977; Laskowski and Kato, 1980), and their properties will not be discussed in detail here.

Proteinase inhibitors are widely distributed in the plant kingdom, particularly in seeds and tubers, where they often represent several percent of total protein (Liener and Kakode, 1969; Ryan, 1973; Richardson, 1977). Proteinase-inhibitor proteins may be the most common antinutritional factors in plants, but, when cooked, their toxic properties are usually lost, and they can become excellent food proteins (Huang et al., 1981). The properties of certain plant proteins (e.g., proteinase inhibitors and lectins) that allow them to be transformed from potentially toxic forms in seeds and tubers to nutritionally acceptable proteins by cooking may have provided major advantage to primitive man in competing for food (Leopold and Ardrey, 1972).

Interest in proteinase inhibitors as protective agents against insects originated with the research of Mikel and Standish (1947), who found that certain pests do not develop normally when they consume soybean products. Lipke et al. (1954) employed a feeding-assay system with larvae of Tribolium confusum to test the toxicity of soybean products and proteinase inhibitors toward these organisms. Raw soybean meal significantly retarded growth and pupation, but the purified trypsin inhibitor did not seem to be the cause. However, an inhibitor of invertebrate proteolytic-enzyme activity was present that was apparently different from the soybean trypsin inhibitor.

Birk and Applebaum (1960) followed these initial studies by comparing the effects of various proteinase inhibitors in soybean meal on both the development of Tribolium castanenum larvae and the proteolytic-enzyme activity in their midgut homogenates. They confirmed the presence of two fractions that inhibited both the growth of the larvae and the proteolytic activity of the midgut proteinases. Two fractions were isolated that possessed inhibitory activity against both trypsin and Tribolium proteolytic enzymes. However, one fraction was isolated (Birk et al., 1963) that inhibited midgut proteolytic activity of both T. confusum and T. castaneum but that was entirely free of inhibition toward mammalian trypsin and chymotrypsin. An inhibitor of a Tribolium proteinase was also found in wheat (Applebaum and Konijn, 1966).

The proteolytic activities of the larvae of Tenebrio molitor appear to be more like the mammalian enzymes than the Tribolium enzymes (Applebaum *et al.*, 1964). Thus, although some of the insect midgut proteolytic enzymes are similar to those of higher animals, some are quite different. This work made it apparent that the specificities of the inhibitors can be quite different among seed varieties and must be considered in determining their effectiveness as pest deterrents (Applebaum, 1964). Two examples of the differential effects of purified proteinase inhibitors on insects have been reported. Janzen *et al.* (1977) demonstrated that the development of *Callosobruchus maculatus* larvae (bean eaters) was not seriously affected by the addition of pure soybean trypsin inhibitor in their diets at 1 or 5% levels. However, a mixture of partially purified potato inhibitors in the diet at the 5% level was lethal. Similarly, the addition of 2–5% soybean inhibitor to diets of corn borer larvae (which thrive on corn; Steffins *et al.*, 1978) inhibited growth and delayed pupation, whereas addition of proteinase inhibitors from corn (*Zea mays*) to the diets had no effect. These may be examples of evolutionary adaptations that have somehow circumvented the activity of some inhibitors, but not others.

Potato tuber proteinase inhibitors have also been shown to inhibit growth of a variety of bacterial strains (Mosolov *et al.*, 1976; Senser *et al.*, 1974; Ryan *et al.*, 1983), presumably through inhibitory specificities. With regard to specificity toward proteolytic enzymes, it is worth noting that potato tubers contain the only known plant tissues that possess inhibitors against all five of the major animal pancreatic enzymes (Ryan, 1980) as well as enterokinase (Lau *et al.*, 1980), which activates the animal intestinal protease trypsin, which, in turn activates zymogens of elastase, chymotrypsin, and the carboxypeptidases. Thus raw potatoes can effectively shut down the entire array of the intestinal proteinases of animals.

The concentration of specific inhibitors in plant tissues may be important with respect to resistance, as suggested by research with *Callosobruchus*. Gatehouse *et al.* (1979) provided an important new insight into this aspect of effectiveness when they found that a single variety of cowpea (*Vigna unguiculata*) out of 5000 tested in a breeding program in Nigeria possessed resistance toward *C. maculatus*. The resistant variety contained about twice the level of trypsin inhibitors compared to any other variety. An inhibitor was isolated (by affinity chromatography) that possessed inhibitory activity against both trypsin and chymotrypsin. The toxic effects of this inhibitor were confirmed in feeding studies with *C. maculatus* larvae. When the inhibitor was fed at 0.8% of the diet, the insects all died. At 0.1%, however, over 80% of the larvae survived and pupated. These levels reflected levels of the inhibitor in the resistant variety (>0.5%) and in susceptible varieties (<0.5%). Thus in this case there appears to be a threshold of inhibitor content in the seeds that may be important to resistance.

The relationship between the concentration of proteinase inhibitors in seeds and pest resistance received further support in a study of smut resistance in wheat (Yamaleev *et al.*, 1980). Russian workers demonstrated that a strong positive correlation exists between trypsin-inhibitor content of spring and durum wheat and resistance or susceptibility to hard smut. Of 180 selections, trypsin-inhibitor levels were significantly higher in the seeds in selections with the best resistances. It is not yet known if this inhibitor is the *Tribolium* inhibitor previously found in wheat (Applebaum and Konijn, 1966).

Both specificity and concentration therefore may be major factors in determining the effectiveness of proteinase inhibitors as plant defenses. For an inhibitor to be effectively toxic, it must specifically inhibit either an important digestive enzyme(s) or the conversion of the precursors of inactive zymogens to their active enzymes. Given the presence of specific proteinase inhibitors, their concentration in the consumed food becomes a major factor in the toxicity. It is quite possible that, through the years, man's selection of plant varieties to increase yields and improve other horticultural characteristics of specific crops may have reduced the levels of certain proteinase inhibitors and eliminated their effectiveness in plant protection.

B. Insect-Induced Proteinase Inhibitors in Tomato Leaves

Our research concerned with the wound-induced accumulation of proteinase inhibitors in tomato (*Lycopersicon esculentum*) leaves began in the early 1960s, beginning with our isolation (Ryan and Balls, 1962; Balls and Ryan, 1963) and characterization (Balls and Ryan, 1963; Ryan, 1966; Melville and Ryan, 1972) of a chymotrypsin-inhibitor protein from Russet Burbank potato (*Solanum tuberasum*) tubers. The inhibitor was eventually called inhibitor I (Ryan, 1966) when a second inhibitor, called inhibitor II, was identified (Ryan, 1966), isolated, and characterized (Bryant *et al.*, 1976) from Russet Burbank potatoes. Inhibitors I and II are potent inhibitors of the serine endopeptidases trypsin and chymotrypsin.

Inhibitor I has a molecular weight of 41,000 and is composed of subunits with molecular weights of about 8100 (Richardson *et al.*, 1976; Plunkett *et al.*, 1982). It is, therefore, a pentamer in its native state (Plunkett *et al.*, 1982). Each subunit possesses an active site that is specific for chymotrypsin, and the apparent K_i for the inhibition of chymotrypsin is about 10^{-9} M (Plunkett *et al.*, 1982). Inhibitor II has a molecular weight of about 23,000 (Melville and Ryan, 1972; Plunkett *et al.*, 1982), is composed of two subunits, and strongly inhibits both trypsin and chymotrypsin, with K_i values of about 10^{-8} and 10^{-7} M, respectively (Plunkett *et al.*, 1982). Both inhibitors I and II strongly inhibit elastase (Plunkett *et al.*, 1982), but the kinetics of the inhibition have not been studied in detail.

The amino acid sequence of potato inhibitor I has been determined (Richardson, 1974; Richardson and Cossins, 1974, 1975) as has part of the sequence of potato inhibitor II (Iwasaki *et al.*, 1977). The amino acid sequences of tomato-leaf inhibitors I and II are in progress (Ryan *et al.*, 1983). No sequence homology has been detected between inhibitors I and II, nor have immunological relationships been found. The inhibitors have been assigned to two unrelated classes that have presumably evolved independently within the Solanaceae (Laskowski and Kato, 1980). Inhibitors have been identified in barley (Svendsen *et al.*, 1980) and a leech species (Seemuller *et al.*, 1980) that display extensive amino acid sequence homologies with potato inhibitor I. This is the first unambiguous homology found between an animal and a plant proteinase inhibitor (Svendsen *et al.*, 1983).

Inhibitors I and II are found in both potato and tomato leaves (Green and Ryan, 1972). The presence of inhibitors in potato tubers appears to be regulated by physiological signals that are under developmental control, whereas the concentrations of the leaf inhibitors from both potato and tomato leaves are regulated by signal(s) released by stimuli from the environment (Ryan *et al.*, 1968; Ryan, 1980).

While studying the levels of inhibitors in leaves under different environmental conditions, we found that leaves of tomato and potato plants responded to Colorado potato beetle attack by accumulating proteinase inhibitor I (Green and Ryan, 1972, 1973). We found that the response was due to the chewing injury to the plant and that any type of severe wounding caused the levels of the inhibitor to increase significantly, even in undamaged leaves. After wounding, both proteinase inhibitors I and II as well as carboxypeptidase inhibitor (Graham and Ryan, 1981) and an inhibitor of enterokinase (Lau *et al.*, 1980) are known to accumulate in tomato and potato leaf cells over a period of several hours, reaching several hundred micrograms of inhibitor per gram of leaf tissue (>1% of soluble protein of the leaf). Inhibitor I accumulates at about twice the rate of inhibitor II (Gustafson and Ryan, 1976).

Inhibitors I and II accumulate as protein globules or membraneless bodies in the central vacuole, or lysosomal compartment, of the cells

(Shumway *et al.*, 1970, 1976). It has been demonstrated that virtually all of the accumulated inhibitors I and II in tomato leaf cells are found within vacuoles isolated from leaves of wounded tomato plants (Walker-Simmons and Ryan, 1977). The two inhibitors are synthesized as pre-proteins that are about 3 kilodaltons larger than the native inhibitors in *in vitro* translation systems (Nelson and Ryan, 1980). The preproteins may be involved in the transport of these proteins into the vacuolar compartment, as has been reported for many other compartmented proteins in cells of a number of plant and animal tissues (Sabatini *et al.*, 1982). The compartmentation of the newly accumulated inhibitors in the central vacuole (lysosome) provides a location where they can survive for long periods of time.

C. The Proteinase-Inhibitor Inducing Factor (PIIF)

The magnitude of the chemical signals, or wound hormone (called PIIF; Green and Ryan, 1972) that is released at or near the wound site depends upon both the location and the severity of the wound. Transport of the factor to unwounded leaves occurs within 2–3 hr after wounding (Makus *et al.*, 1980). The transport apparently takes place in the phloem and is directed primarily upward to younger leaves (Makus *et al.*, 1980).

PIIF has been isolated by various techniques from tomato leaves, yielding a single broad peak from Sephadex G75, and the activity is consistently associated with oligo- and polysaccharide fractions that exhibit a molecular weight of about 5000 to 10,000. Properties of highly purified PIIF preparations, such as loss of activity upon either prolonged acid hydrolysis or periodate oxidation, and their monosaccharide compositions suggested to us that PIIF was a pectic-like substance (Ryan, 1978; Ryan *et al.*, 1982). PIIF, as isolated from tomato leaves, was subsequently identified as a highly methylated polysaccharide containing galacturonic acid, rhamnose, galactose, arabinose, and fucose (Ryan *et al.*, 1982). These studies revealed that PIIF is somewhat similar in composition to rhamnogalacturonan I, which is a well-defined fraction of the sycamore (*Acer pseudoplatanus*) cell wall, which may be released from the cell walls by an *endo-α-1,4*-polygalacturonase (Sharp *et al.*, 1980; McNeil *et al.*, 1980) isolated from the fungus *Colletotricum lindemuthianum*. This further implied that tomato PIIF is also a fragment of the plant cell wall (Ryan *et al.*, 1982). More importantly, the sycamore cell-wall-derived rhamnogalacturonan I was found to be as active as tomato PIIF in inducing proteinase-inhibitor accumulation in young tomato plants (Ryan *et al.*, 1982).

Not all pectic polysaccharides exhibit PIIF activity; no activity was detected in samples of larch or sycamore arabinogalactan, in rhamno-galacturonan II (Ryan *et al.*, 1982), or in one sample of citrus pectin (Sunkist), although pectin from two other manufacturers (MCP and Pen Gel), exhibited moderate PIIF activities. Mono-, di-, and tri-α-1,4-linked galacturonic acids exhibited little capacity to induce proteinase inhibitors in excised tomato plants (Ryan *et al.*, 1982).

Further studies (Bishop *et al.*, 1981) revealed that oligosaccharides possessing proteinase-inhibitor inducing activity could be prepared from demethylated tomato PIIF by digesting it with a highly purified *endo*-α-1,4-polygalacturonase from the fungus *Rhizopus stolonifer* (Lee and West, 1981b). Similar oligosaccharides could be isolated from purified tomato cell walls by degradation with a mixture of tomato pectinesterase and tomato endopolygalacturonase. However, in all cases the oligosaccharides were less active than the larger PIIF polysaccharides (Hahn *et al.*, 1981).

A hypothesis was presented that included a hormonal role for pectic oligosaccharide fragments that are released from the site of injury as a result of pest attack (Bishop *et al.*, 1981). These oligosaccharides would be produced by degradation of the plant cell wall, either by hydrolytic enzymes that are compartmented in the plant and mixed with the cell wall during wounding or that are introduced into the plant by invading pests (Bishop *et al.*, 1981). The oligosaccharides that are produced, or products induced by their presence, would then be transported rapidly to unwounded cells to react with specific receptors on, or in, target cells, to induce either directly or indirectly the synthesis and accumulation of proteinase-inhibitor proteins. The conversion of tomato PIIF into small oligosaccharides by fungal endopolygalacturonase required pectinesterase, implying that the latter enzyme may play a role in the process of PIIF release *in vivo* and that demethylation of cell walls or their products may be additional levels of control of the formation or release of active PIIF (Ryan *et al.*, 1982a).

Two important observations in our studies with tomato leaves have extraordinary relationships with the fungal-induced phytoalexin accumulation in castor beans and soybeans. Data from studies of both of these latter systems clearly implicate pectic-like oligosaccharides as elicitor molecules of glycinol synthesis in soybeans (Hahn *et al.*, 1981) and casbene synthesis in castor beans (Lee and West, 1981a,b; Bruce and West, 1982). Both of these elicitor systems are further discussed in the following sections, and the possible relationships between the regulation of elicitation of these fungal systems and the regulation of insect-wound-induced proteinase-inhibitor induction are addressed.

D. Fungal-Induced Phytoalexin Synthesis

It is clear that the interaction of plants with fungi and bacteria is very complex and that the barriers of the plant to infection can be both physical and chemical. A major emphasis in studying host–pathogen interactions has been to understand the antifungal phytoalexins and phytoalexin-like compounds that are induced in tissues near the sites of attack of pathogenic organisms as a defense mechanism. Several reviews have appeared that thoroughly discuss the phytoalexin response and the types of phytoalexin molecules that are synthesized (Kuć, 1976; Keen and Bruegger, 1977; Grisbach and Ebel, 1978: Mahadevan, 1979; Cruickshank, 1980; Stoessel, 1980; Uritani, 1978; West, 1981). The diversity of the phytoalexins is considerable and includes chemicals of several classes, including isoflavonoids, sesquiterpenes, diterpenes, polyacetylenes, dihydrophenanthrenes, and stilbenes (West, 1981). The most thoroughly studied of the phytoalexins are from the most important agricultural crops of the Leguminosae and Solanaceae.

When certain pathogens attack plants, substances are released (or are produced) called *elicitors* that induce (elicit) synthesis of specific phytoalexins in cells near the pathogen-attack site, apparently to help arrest fungal invasion of these cells. The natural elicitors have been termed *biotic* elicitors (Hargreaves and Bailey, 1978), in contrast to an array of nonbiological or abiotic elicitors that have been reported, and they have been the object of much research in recent years. Three types of biotic elicitors are now recognized as being biopolymers (West, 1981): (1) fungal cell-wall polysaccharides, (2) glycoproteins, and (3) *endogenous* elicitors, which appear to be fragments of the plant cell wall.

The first type of elicitors, the fungal cell-wall polysaccharide elicitors (West, 1981), are either highly branched glucans, having mainly β-1,3 or β-1,4 linear chains, branched with β-1,6 linkages, or β-1,4-glucosamine polymers (called chitosans; Hadwiger and Beckman, 1980), which are found in cell walls of certain pathogenic fungi. All of these polysaccharides can be either mechanically, physically, or enzymatically released from fungal cell walls during infection. The mechanisms of how these polysaccharides trigger phytoalexin production is unknown.

Glycoprotein preparations from fungi have been reported to evoke elicitor activities in various plants. One is a polypeptide of molecular weight 8000 isolated from *Monolinic fructicola* mycelial extracts (West, 1981). The others appear to be larger proteins or glycoproteins. Until recently, little was known of how the polypeptides or proteins elicited phytoalexin synthesis.

Lee and West (1981a,b) have demonstrated that the *Rhizopus stolonifer* endopolygalacturonase, a glycoprotein, acts as an elicitor of the phytoalexin casbene in castor bean seedlings. The catalytic activity of the enzyme is now known (Bruce and West, 1982) to be necessary for its function as an elicitor. Incubation of the enzyme with pectin, polygalacturonic acid, or castor bean cell homogenates that exhibit moderate elicitor activities considerably increases their elicitor activities. This evidence strongly supports a role for pectic fragments produced by the fungal endogalacturonase (Bruce and West, 1982) as intermediates in the process of elicitation of casbene activity.

Ryan *et al.* (1982) and Bishop *et al.* (1981) had previously reported that oligosaccharides released from tomato pectic polysaccharides by the action of the *Rhizopus* endogalacturonase (Ryan, 1978; Bishop *et al.*, 1981) provided by C.A. West are active inducers of proteinase inhibitors in detached tomato leaves. These oligosaccharides, produced from a 5- to 10-kilodaltons active PIIF fraction by the *Rhizopus* endogalacturonase, are also active in eliciting casbene synthesis in castor beans (Bruce and West, 1982).

The third class of elicitors, the endogenous elicitors, were recognized by Hargreaves and Bailey (1978), who reported the presence of constitutive, or endogenous, elicitors in bean hypocotyl tissues. The endogenous elicitors were not characterized, but they are small molecules the properties of which are not unlike those of small pectic polysaccharides or oligosaccharides of the type produced by $endo$-α-1,4-polygalacturonase on plant cell walls.

The endogenous elicitor of the soybean phytoalexin glycinol has been identified as a soluble polysaccharide fraction arising from soybean cell walls (Hahn *et al.*, 1981). The elicitor-active material is rich in galacturonic acid and contains small amounts of rhamnose, suggesting that the elicitor is a fragment of a pectic polysaccharide. This fraction has also been shown to be an active elicitor of casbene is castor bean cotyledons (Bruce and West, 1982). Endogenous-elicitor-active oligosaccharides have also been obtained from cell walls of suspension-cultured tobacco, wheat, and sycamore. Several pectin-like polysaccharides, including pectin, polyuronide, and rhamnogalacturonan I, contain small to moderate eliciting activity, but when fragmented by hydrolysis with 2 N trifluoroacetic acid for 4 hr, elicitor activities increases severalfold. Rhamnogalacturonan ronan I had previously been shown to have a strong proteinase-inhibitor inducing activity in tomato leaves. Furthermore, a pectin lyase from a bacterial pathogen that elicited phytoalexin synthesis in soybeans has been found (P. Albersheim *et al.*, unpublished data). The implications of all of these reports are that the cell-wall-degrading enzymes from pathogenic fungi and bacteria may be releasing pectic fragments that signal the plant to respond to the attacks.

Hadwiger and Beckman (1980) have reported that chitosans, components of fungal and insect cell walls, are highly active in inducing the synthesis of the phytoalexin pisatin in pea cotyledons. In collaboration with Hadwiger, we have now found that small chitosan fragments are the most potent PIIF-like substances we have yet to assay (over 50-fold more potent than tomato-leaf PIIF; Walker-Simmons et al., 1983). Conversely, several of our tomato PIIF preparations (pectic polysaccharides and oligosaccharides), exhibit phytoalexin-inducing activity in the pisatin assay—in the same range of concentrations in which they induce proteinase inhibitors in tomato leaves.

The cumulative results of these experiments demonstrate that structural elements in both plant and fungal cell walls possess a spectrum of gene-activating activity. This implies that in cells of a wide variety of plant genera receptors are present that have a similar biochemical basis for regulating the genes of both proteinase inhibitors and phytoalexins. The diversity of the responses is even broader when the biochemical pathways of the phytoalexins are considered (Stoessl, 1980). Casbene, a diterpene, requires an entirely different pathway for synthesis than those of either glycenol or pisatin. Thus the oligosaccharides activate a variety of genes in different tissues, presumably by way of a common receptor mechanism. Furthermore, polysaccharide or oligosaccharide informational macromolecules may not be limited to just the regulation of genes of proteinase inhibitors and phytoalexins; they may regulate genes involved in other defense responses. Many examples are now known of pest-induced resistances to insects, fungi, bacteria, and viruses (see Table I). Chemical messages are apparently released and transported in these systems to trigger those responses. It is possible that cell-wall fragments may be information macromolecules that are fundamental components in the initial steps in many such processes. Our present model for such relationships is shown in Table II.

Although some regulatory role for oligo- and polysaccharides is strongly supported by the evidence, the structural bases for these messages and their reception are still not clear. They could involve carbohydrate structural features and perhaps lectins or lectin-like receptors, or they could involve other structural components that are associated with cell-wall fragments such as lipids.

A report by Bostock et al. (1981) demonstrated that elicitor activity could be extracted from the pathogenic fungus *Phytophthora infestans* with a mixture of chloroform and methanol. The most active elicitors of

Table II
Pest-Induced Plant Resistances

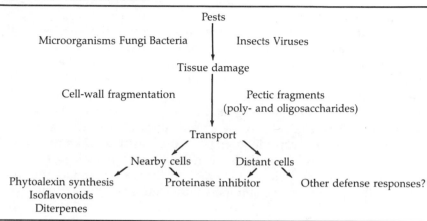

phytoalexins in the extracts were eicosapentaenoic acid and arachidonic acids, which are precursors in animals of prostaglandins (Murphy *et al.*, 1979). Cell-wall preparations of the fungal cell wall also yielded the two components. This report raises important questions about the possible role of lipids in phytoalexin induction and the possible relationship of the cell walls as carriers of lipids or as inducers of lipid-releasing systems. However, neither of the lipid compounds are found in plant tissues and, therefore, may not be related to the endogenous elicitors of the plants.

III. SUMMARY

Overall, the information concerning pectic degradation and its relationship to insect attack and fungal and bacterial pathogenesis suggests a general role of carbohydrates as signals to monitor both types of pest attacks. However, we still recognize that the structures of the plant and fungal polysaccharides are complex, and the basis for their possible regulatory roles is not fully understood. Full understanding of the biologically active structures of PIIF, of the elicitors, and of molecules involved in other chemical communication systems in plants indeed provide some of the most interesting, challenging, and potentially useful research areas to study plant–pest interactions.

This emerging area of research has already provided novel insights into chemical communication in plants in response to pest attacks, and it suggests many new avenues of research for studying the biochemical basis of plant responses to herbivore attacks. The insect damage itself can mix cellular components in an abnormal way to release signals that are transported to healthy cells. These signals may trigger biochemical processes that can quantitatively and qualitatively change the plant tissue and significantly affect the continued feeding by the attacking insects. Thus plant variability in the ability to release signals and to receive and amplify these signals and the specificity of the defense responses all become aspects of consideration. Our present state of knowledge is indeed limited, but the limitations are the challenges, in biology, ecology, molecular biology, and biochemistry, to further explore and better understand the variability of plant–pest interactions.

REFERENCES

Applebaum S. (1964). Physiological aspects of host specificity in the Bruchidae. I. General considerations of developmental compatibility. *J. Insect Physiol.* **10**, 783–788.

Applebaum S., and Konijn, A. (1966). The presence of a *Tribolium*-protease inhibitor in wheat. *J. Insect Physiol.* **12**, 665–669.

Applebaum S., Birk, Y., Harpaz, I., and Bondi, A. (1964). Comparative studies on proteolytic enzymes of *Tenebrio molitor* L. *Comp. Biochem. Physiol.* **11**, 85–103.

Balls, A. K., and Ryan, C. A. (1963). Concerning a crystalline chymotryptic inhibitor from potatoes, and its binding capacity for the enzyme. *J. Biol. Chem.* **238**, 2976–2982.

Birk, Y., and Applebaum, S. W. (1960). Effect of soybean trypsin inhibitors on the development and midgut proteolytic activity of *Tribolium castaneum* larvae. *Enzymologia* **22**, 318–326.

Birk, Y., Gertler, A., and Khalef, S. (1963). Separation of a *Tribolium*-protease inhibitor from soybeans on a calcium phosphate column. *Biochim. Biophys. Acta* **67**, 326–328.

Bishop, P. D., Makus, D. J., Pearce, G., and Ryan, C. A. (1981). Proteinase inhibitor-inducing factor activity in tomato leaves resides in oligosaccharides enzymically released from cell walls. *Proc. Natl. Acad. Sci. U.S.A.* **78**, 3536–3540.

Bostock, R. M., Kuć, J. A., and Laine, R. A. (1981). Eicosapentaenoic and arachidonic acids from *Phytophthora infestans* elicit fungitoxic sesquiterpenes in the potato. *Science* **212**, 67–69.

Bruce, R. J., and West, C. A. (1982). Elicitation of casbene synthetase activity in castor bean: the role of pectic fragments of the plant cell wall in elicitation by a fungal endopolygalacturonase. *Plant Physiol.* **69**, 1181–1188.

Bryant, J., Green, T. R., Gurusaddaiah, T., and Ryan, C. A. (1976). Proteinase inhibitor II from potatoes: Isolation and characterization of its protomer components. *Biochemistry* **15**, 3418–3824.

Cruickshank, I. A. M. (1980). Defenses triggered by the invader: Chemical defenses. *In* "Plant Disease: An Advanced Treatise" (J. G. Horsfall and E. B. Cowling, eds.), Vol. 5, pp. 247–267. Academic Press, New York.

Dement, W. A., and Mooney, H. A. (1974). Seasonal variation in the production of tannins and cyanogenic glucosides in the chaparral shrub, *Heteromeles arbutifolia*. *Oecologia* **15**, 65–76.

Gatehouse, A., Gatehouse, J., Dobie, P., Kilminster, A., and Boulter, D. (1979). Biochemical basis of insect resistance in *Vigna unguiculata*. *J. Sci. Food Agric.* **30**, 948-958.

Giebel, J. (1974). Biochemical mechanisms of plant resistance to nematodes. *J. Nematol.* **6**, 175–184.

Goodman, R. N. (1980). Defenses triggered by previous invaders: Bacteria. *In* "Plant Disease: An Advanced Treatise" (J. G. Horsfall and E. B. Cowling, eds.), Vol. 5, 305-317. Academic Press, New York.

Graham, J. S., and Ryan, C.A. (1981). Accumulation of a metallo-carboxypeptidase inhibitor in leaves of wounded potato plants. *Biochem. Biophys. Res. Commun.* **101**, 1164–1169.

Green, T. R., and Ryan, C. A. (1972). Wound-induced proteinase inhibitor in plant leaves: a possible defense mechanism against insects. *Science* **175**, 776–777.

Green, T. R., and Ryan, C. A. (1973). Wound-induced proteinase inhibitor in tomato leaves. *Plant Physiol.* **51**, 19–21.

Grisebach, H., and Ebel, J. (1978). Phytoalexins, chemical defense substances of higher plants? *Angew. Chem., Int. Ed. Engl.* **17**, 635–647.

Gustafson, G. and Ryan, C. A. (1976) Specificity of protein turnover in tomato leaves. *J. Biol. Chem.* **251**, 7004–7010.

Hadwiger, L. A., and Beckman, J. M. (1980). Chitosan as a component of pea–*Fusarium solani* interactions. *Plant Physiol.* **66**, 205–211.

Hahn, M. G., Darvill, A. G., and Albersheim, P. (1981). Host–pathogen interactions. XIX. The endogenous elicitor, a fragment of a plant cell wall polysaccharide that elicits phytoalexin accumulation in soybeans. *Plant Physiol.* **68**, 1161–1169.

Hamilton, R. I. (1980). Defenses triggered by previous invaders: viruses. *In* "Plant Disease. An Advanced Treatise" (J. G. Horsfall and E. B. Cowling, eds.), Vol. 5, pp. 333-343. Academic Press, New York.

Hargreaves, J. A., and Bailey, J. A. (1978). Phytoalexin production by hypocotyls of *Phaseolus vulgaris* in response to constitutive metabolites released by damaged bean cells. *Physiol. Plant Pathol.* **13**, 89–100.

Haukioja, E., and Niemelä, P. (1977). Retarded growth of a geometrid larva after mechanical damage to leaves of its host tree. *Ann. Zool. Fenn.* **14**, 48–52.

Huang, D. Y., Swanson, B. G., and Ryan, C. A. (1981). Stability of proteinase inhibitors in potato tubers during cooking. *J. Food Sci.* **46**, 287–290.

Iwasaki, T., Wada, J., Kiyohara, T., and Yoshikawa, M. (1977). Amino acid sequence of an active fragment of potato proteinase inhibitor IIb. *J. Biochem. (Tokyo)* **82**, 991–1004.

Janzen, D. H., Juster, H. B., and Bell, E. A. (1977). Toxicity of secondary compounds to the seed-eating larvae of the bruchid beetle *Callosobruchus maculatas*. *Phytochemistry* **16**, 223–227.

Keen, N. T., and Bruegger, B. (1977). Phytoalexins and chemicals that elicit their production in plants. *ACS Symp. Ser.* **62**, 1-26.

Kojima, M., Poulton, J. E., Thayer, S. S., and Conn, E. E. (1979). Tissue distribution of dhurrin and of enzymes involved in its metabolism in leaves of *Sorghum bicolor*. *Plant Physiol.* **63**, 1022–1028.

Kuć, J. A. (1976). Phytoalexins. *Plant Physiol. New Ser.* **4**, 632-652.

Laskowski, M., Jr., and Kato, I. (1980). Protein inhibitors of proteinases. *Annu. Rev. Biochem.* **49**, 593–626.

Laskowski, M., Jr., and Sealock, R. W. (1977). Protein proteinase inhibitors, molecular aspects. *In* "The Enzymes" (P. D. Boyer, ed.), 3rd ed., Vol. 3, pp. 375-473. Academic Press, New York.

Lau, A., Ako, H., and Werner-Washburne, M. (1980). Survey of plants for enterokinase inhibitors. *Biochem. Biophys. Res. Commun.* **92**, 1243–1249.

Lee, S.-C., and West, C. A. (1981a). Polygalacturonase from *Rhizopus stolonifer*, an elicitor of casbene synthetase activity in castor bean. *Plant Physiol.* **67**, 633–639.

Lee, S.-C., and West, C. A. (1981b). properties of *Rhizopus stolonifer*, an elicitor of casbene synthetase activity in castor bean (*Ricinus communis* L.) seedlings. *Plant Physiol.* **67**, 640–654.

Liener, I., and Kakade, M. L. (1969). Protease inhibitors. *In* "Toxic Constituents of Plant Foodstuffs" (I. E. Liener, ed.), pp. 8–66. Academic Press, New York.

Leopold, A. C., and Ardrey, R. (1972). Toxic substances in plants and the food habits of early man. *Science* **176**, 512–513.

Lipke, H., Fraenkel, G. S., and Liener, I. E. (1954). Effect of soybean inhibitors on growth of *Tribolium confusum*. *J. Agric. Food Chem.* **2**, 410–414.

Loebenstein, G., and Ross, A. (1963). An extractable agent induced in uninfected tissues by localized virus infections, that interferes with infection by tobacco mosaic virus. *Virology* **20**, 507–517.

McIntyre, J. L. (1980). Defenses triggered by previous invaders: nematodes and insects. *In* "Plant Disease: An Advanced Treatise" (J. G. Horsfall and E. B. Cowling, eds.), Vol. 5, pp. 333–343. Academic Press, New York.

McNeil M., Darvill, A. G., and Albersheim, P. (1980). Structure of plant cell walls. X. Rhamnogalacturonan I, a structurally complex pectic polysaccharide in the walls of suspension-cultured sycamore cells. *Plant Physiol.* **66**, 1128–1134.

Mahadevan, A. J. (1979). Biochemical aspects of plant-disease resistance. *J. Sci. Ind. Res.* **38**, 156–171.

Makus, D., Zuroske, G., and Ryan, C. A. (1980). The direction and rate of transport of the proteinase inhibitor inducing factor out of wounded tomato leaves. *Plant Physiol.* **65**, Suppl., 150.

Melville, J. C., and Ryan, C. A. (1972). Chymotrypsin inhibitor from potatoes. *J. Biol. Chem.* **247**, 3445–3453.

Mikel, C. E., and Standish, J. (1947). Susceptibility of processed soy flour and soy grits in storage to attack by *Tribolium castaneum* (Herbst). *Minn., Agric. Exp. Stn., Tech. Bull.* **178**, 1–20.

Mosolov, V. V., Loginova, M. D., Fedurkina, N. V., and Benken, I. I. (1976). The biological significance of proteinase inhibitors in plants. *Plant Sci. Lett.* **7**, 77–80.

Murphy, R., Hammarström, S., and Samuelsson, B. (1979). Leukotriene C: a slow-reacting substance from murine mastocytoma cells. *Proc. Natl. Acad. Sci. U.S.A.* **76**, 4275–4279.

Nelson, C. E., and Ryan, C. A. (1980). *In vitro* synthesis of pre-proteins of vacuolar compartmented proteinase inhibitors that accumulate in leaves of wounded tomato plants. *Proc. Natl. Acad. Sci. U.S.A.* **77**, 1975–1979.

Niemelä, P., Aro, E. M., and Haukioja, E. (1979). Birch leaves as a resource for herbivores; damage-induced increase in leaf phenols with trypsin-inhibiting effects. *Rep. Kevo. Subarct. Res. Stn.* **15**, 37–40.

Plunkett, G., Senear, D. F., Zuroske, G., and Ryan, C. A. (1982). Proteinase inhibitors I and II from leaves of wounded tomato plants: purification and properties. *Arch. Biochem. Biophys.* **213**, 463–472.

Rhoades, D. F. (1979). Evolution of plant chemical defense against herbivores. *In* "Herbivores: Their Interaction with Secondary Plant Metabolites" (G. A. Rosenthal and D. A. Janzen, eds.), pp. 3–54. Academic Press, New York.

Richardson, M. (1974). Chymotryptic inhibitor I from potatoes: the amino acid sequence of sub-unit A. *Biochem. J.* **137**, 101–112.

Richardson, M. (1977). The proteinase inhibitors of plants and micro-organisms. *Phytochemistry* **16**, 159–169.

Richardson, M., and Cossins, L. (1974). Chymotryptic inhibitor I from potatoes: the amino acid sequences of subunit-B, subunit-C and subunit-D. *FEBS Lett.* **45**, 11–13.

Richardson, M., and Cossins, L. (1975). Chymotryptic inhibitor I from potatoes: the amino acid sequences of subunits B, C, and D, corrigendum. *FEBS Lett.* **52**, 161.

Richardson, M., Barker, R. D. J., and McMillan, R. T. (1976). Re-examination of the molecular weight of chymotryptic inhibitor I from potatoes. *Biochem. Soc. Trans.* **4**, 1077–1078.

Ryan, C. A. (1966). Chymotrypsin inhibitor I from potatoes: reactivity with mammalian, plant, bacterial, and fungal proteinases. *Biochemistry* **5**, 1592–1596.

Ryan, C. A. (1973). Proteolytic enzymes and their inhibitors in plants. *Annu. Rev. Plant Physiol.* **24**, 173–196.

Ryan, C. A. (1978). Proteinase inhibitors in plant leaves: a biochemical model for pest-induced natural plant protection. *Trends Biochem. Sci.* **5**, 148–150.

Ryan, C. A. (1980). Wound-regulated synthesis and vacuolar compartmentation of proteinase inhibitors in plant leaves. *Curr. Top Cell. Regul.* **17**, 1-23.

Ryan, C. A., and Balls, A. K. (1962). An inhibitor of chymotrypsin for *Solanum tuberosum* and its behavior toward trypsin. *Proc. Natl. Acad. Sci. U.S.A.* **48**, 1839–1844.

Ryan, C. A., Huisman, O. C., and Van Denburgh, R. W. (1968). Transitory aspects of a single protein in tissues of *Solanum tuberosum* and its coincidence with the establishment of new growth. *Plant Physiol.* **43**, 589–596.

Ryan, C. A., Bishop, P., Pearce, G., Darvill, A., McNeil, M., and Albersheim, P. (1982). A sycamore cell wall polysaccharide and a chemically related tomato leaf polysaccharide possess similar proteinase inhibitor-inducing activities. *Plant Physiol.* **68**, 616–618.

Ryan, C. A., Walsh, K., and Titani, K. (1983). In preparation.

Sabatini, D., Kreibich, G., Morimoto, T., and Adesnik, M. (1982). Mechanisms for the incorporation of proteins in membranes and organelles. *J. Cell Biol.* **92**, 1–22.

Seemuller, U., Eulitz, M., Fritz, H., and Strobel, A. (1980). Structure of the elastase-cathepsin G inhibitor of the leech *Hirudo medicinalis. Hoppe-Seyler's Z. Physiol. Chem.* **361**, 1841–1846.

Sela, I. (1981). Plant-virus interactions related to resistance and localization of viral infections. *Adv. Virus Res.* **26**, 210–237.

Senser, F., Belitz, H. D., Kaiser, K. P., and Santarius, K. (1974). Suggestion of a protective function of proteinase-inhibitors in potatoes: inhibition of proteolytic activity of microorganisms isolated from spoiled potato tubers. *Z. Lebensm.-Unters. -Forsch.* **155**, 100–101.

Sequeira, L. (1979). The acquisition of systemic resistance by prior inoculation. *In* "Recognition and Specificity in Plant Host Parasite Interactions" (J. M. Daly and I. Uritani, eds.), pp. 231-252. Univ. Park Press, Baltimore, Maryland.

Sharp, J. R., Darvill, A. G., McNeil, M., and Albersheim, P. (1980). Rhamnogalacturan II, a complex pectic polysaccharide in the walls of growing plant cells. *Plant. Physiol.* **65**, Suppl. 23.

Shumway, K., Rancour, J. M., and Ryan, C. A. (1970). Vacuolar protein bodies in tomato leaf cells and their relationship to storage of chymotrypsin inhibitor I protein. *Planta* **93**, 1–14.

Shumway, K., Yang, V. V., and Ryan, C. A. (1976). Evidence for the presence of proteinase inhibitor I in vacuolar bodies of plant cells. *Planta* **129**, 161–165.

Steffins, R., Fox, F. R., and Kassell, B. (1978). Effect of trypsin inhibitors on growth and metamorphosis of corn borer larvae, *Ostrinia nubilalis* (Huebner). *J. Agric. Food Chem.* **26**, 170–174.

Stoessl, A. (1980). Phytoalexins—a biogenetic perspective. *Phytopathol. Z.* **99**, 251–272.

Svendsen, I., Martin, B., and Jonassen, I. B. (1980). Characteristics of hiproly barley. III. Amino acid sequences of two lysine-rich proteins. *Carlsberg Res. Commun.* **45**, 79-85.

Svendsen, I., Boisen, S., and Hejgaard, J. (1982). Amino acid sequence of serine protease inhibitor CI-2, potato inhibitor I and leech eglin. *Carlsberg Res. Commun.* **47**, 45–53.

Thielges, B. A. (1968). Altered polyphenol metabolism in the foliage of *Pinus sylvestris* associated with European pine sawfly attack. *Can. J. Bot.* **46**, 724–725.

Uritani, I. (1978). The biochemistry of host response to infection. *Prog. Phytochem.* **5**, 29-64.

Walker-Simmons, M., and Ryan, C. A. (1977). Immunological identification of proteinase inhibitors I and II in isolated tomato leaf vacuoles. *Plant Physiol.* **60**, 61–63.

Walker-Simmons, M., Hadwiger, L., and Ryan, C. A. (1983). *Biochem. Biophys. Res. Comm.* **110**, 194–199.

West, C. A. (1981). Fungal elicitors of the phytoalexin response in higher plants. *Naturwissenschaften* **68**, 447–457.

Yamaleev, A. M., Mukhsinov, V. K., Isaev, R. F., Yamaleeva, A. A., and Krivchenko, V. I. (1980). Activity of protease inhibitors and resistance of wheat to the causal agent of hard smut. *S-kh. Biol.* **15**, 143–144.

C. A. Ryan

Institute of Bilogical Chemistry and Biochemistry/Biophysics Program
Washington State University
Pullman, Washington

CHAPTER 3

Habitat Selection and Foraging Tactics of Caterpillars in Heterogeneous Trees

JACK C. SCHULTZ

I. INTRODUCTION

A. Host Heterogeneity and Insect Foraging Behavior

The "arms race" between insects and their hosts is usually viewed as an interaction between uniform populations (Dixon, 1970; Dawkins and Krebs, 1979). Single plant traits, for example, water, are thought to act uniformly on all insects in a population at all times. We are now beginning to appreciate that individual host plants and plant populations are not uniform for many traits; they are highly heterogeneous in space and time (Whitham, 1981). This has important consequences for herbivorous insects.

VARIABLE PLANTS AND HERBIVORES
IN NATURAL AND MANAGED SYSTEMS

First, if host-plant tissues or host plants vary in quality, insects have the option of avoiding unsuitable or less suitable food. We should expect to find specific preferences for individual plants, for different tissues within a single plant, and even careful foraging among tissue units (e.g., individual leaves) within a single plant. The option to avoid plant traits that reduce feeding effectiveness and thus act as selective agents on insects may be an alternative to the evolution of insect digestive adaptations.

Second, host-plant heterogeneity acts to place herbivorous insects in many compromise situations. For example, plant tissues possess multiple traits that can affect insect feeding (e.g., Hegnauer, 1962; Gibbs, 1974; Rhoades and Cates, 1976; Rhoades, 1979). If these traits covary negatively among tissue units, an individual insect may find itself faced with antagonistic feeding or digestive demands. If enemies cue on specific tissues or locations, act in a density-dependent fashion, or are more likely to contact herbivores searching for food, risk from natural enemies will be high when food is variable (Jones, 1979; Lawton and McNeill, 1979; Moran, 1980), and there will be a strong compromise between obtaining good-quality food and escaping predation.

Third, because the contact rate between individual insects in a population and poor-quality (or "well-defended") tissues is reduced when tissues are variable, the strength of directional selection on insects may be reduced (Maiorana, 1979). This should increase the useful lifetimes of defensive tree traits (Whitham, 1981). Overall, less tree tissue may be consumed and primary consumption may be stabilized at low levels through evolutionary time.

B. Studies of Foraging Behavior on Heterogeneous Hosts

Unfortunately, the foraging behavior of folivorous insects such as caterpillars on single hosts (and even among hosts) has received little attention (see Hassell and Southwood, 1978; Matthews and Matthews, 1978). Habitat selection, feeding-site preference, and tissue preferences are better studied for piercing–sucking insects than they are for folivorous insects. Phloem-feeding insects appear to recognize differences among tissues in nutrient quality and focus feeding on high-nutrient tissues or tissue units (Dixon, 1970; Prestidge, 1982). Gall-making aphids identify superior-quality tree leaves and compete for these tissue units (Whitham, 1978). Psyllids (White, 1970; Journet, 1980) apparently identify superior-quality leaves and branches on their host trees.

Studies of actual foraging behavior of caterpillars are scarce for at least three reasons. First, attention to caterpillar biology tends to be focused on a very few outbreak-pest species during outbreak events, and emphasis is given to population phenomena, not individual behavioral traits. These species may be biologically unique, and their behavior may not reflect the more typical behavior of insects at endemic population levels (Nothnagle, et al., 1982). Second, host trees are generally assumed to be uniform environments. As such, there is no particular reason to find food selection interesting. Third, there is a problem of the priorities in foraging goals for caterpillars. What might be most important for a caterpillar to do during foraging—accumulate energy, meet minimal nutrient requirements, or avoid toxins?

Generalizations about the importance of heterogeneity include little information or even speculation about the mechanics of insect interactions with variable plants, that is, What is the direct impact on insects? Moreover, only a few studies have dealt with variation *within* plants, the level at which foraging behavior is influenced. This chapter concentrates on the potential impact of within-plant variability on the behavior of individual insects, together with the evolutionary consequences of this impact.

In Section II I will describe some of the ways in which a forest tree may vary as a food source and feeding site for insects, focusing on spatial patterns in leaf variability from a caterpillar's viewpoint. The influence of leaf-quality variation on caterpillar foraging will then be described, and the broader implications of these observation will be discussed, including consequences for insect community structure, insect species diversity, potential inter- and intraspecific competition among insects, and stabilization of the evolutionary interation between long-lived plants and their folivorous insects.

II. PATTERNS OF FEEDING-SITE VARIATION IN TREE CANOPIES

A. Variation and Spatial Arrays of Leaf Quality

A long list of leaf traits, including toughness, nitrogen and micronutrient content, and concentration of a host of secondary compounds, have been shown to vary intrinsically within and among forest-tree canopies (Schultz et al., 1982). For example, adjacent leaves on single sugar maple branches may differ by a factor of 2 or more on any given date for several traits, including tanning coefficient, a measure of digestibility (Fig. 1). Leaves of different values appear randomly arrayed on branch segments; the position of a leaf of a given value is unpredictable on individual branches.

Yellow birch leaves exhibit trait-dispersion patterns that may be more predictable in space (Fig. 1). As is often the case, younger leaves possess unique chemical and physical characteristics (McKey, 1979; Whitham, 1981). Because yellow birch produces new leaves about every 10 days during the growing season, at particular growth points (Sharik and Barnes, 1976), the position of leaves with "young" traits can be predicted fairly well. Young leaves have consistently higher total phenol and water content as well as lower toughness (Schultz et al., 1982). Age-related variation localizes leaves of a particular quality in relatively small patches at or near the sites of active plant growth (e.g., tips of branches). An emerging generalization may be made that the distribution of leaves with particular traits will differ greatly between determinate-growth tree species and continuously flushing species (see Kozlowski and Clausen, 1966).

Several of the causes of within-canopy heterogeneity reviewed by Whitham (1981; Chapter 1) would result in larger canopy sections that differ in quality. For example, one whole side of a tree may differ in quality as insect food when compared with the rest of the canopy (White, 1970; Schoonhoven, 1977).

Mechanical damage (Haukioja and Niemela, 1978), the presence of bacteria that process secondary compounds (Lovett and Duffield, 1981), and previous attack by a variety of organisms (McIntyre, 1980; Matta, 1980) would also create food-quality mosaics within a tree canopy. Patch size and distribution should vary with the "inducing" factor.

Leaf shape and size can be important determinants of food quality (Heinrich, 1971), and they vary enough in some tree species to make leaves unavailable as food (J. C. Schultz, unpublished). Parasitoids may use leaf-shape cues to locate insect hosts (Vinson, 1975; Vinson and Iwantsch, 1980).

Leaf size can strongly influence feeding success and population dynamics of several kinds of insects (Whitham, 1981). Leaf size and biomass could be important to caterpillars for several reasons, including visibility and protection from predators and the impact that local food abundance can have on movement patterns (see later discussion). Areas and weights of adjacent leaves in individual sprays of sugar maple, beech, and yellow birch can differ by a factor of 2 (Schultz et al., 1983). Significant differences in leaf size and weight also exist between the top and lower portions of the canopies of these trees. So there is both large-scale and small-small

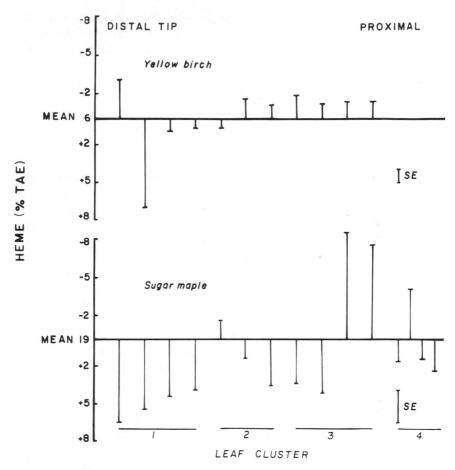

Fig. 1. Value, in terms of digestibility, of individual leaves on individual sprays of yellow birch *(Betula lutea)* and sugar maple *(Acer saccharum)*. Horizontal axes are mean values (as percentage tannic acid equivalents; Schultz *et al.*, 1981) all leaves on the branch. Each vertical bar represents one leaf, expressed in units of deviation from the branch mean. Upward-deviating bars indicate more digestible, higher quality leaves; downward deviations represent less digestible leaves. In both cases, branch terminus is at left; for yellow birch this means that the two left-most leaves are less than 10 days old. Sugar maple leaves are all even-aged and grow in clusters, as indicated. One standard error of the branch mean shown lower right. HEME, Hemoglobin assay (see Schultz *et al.*, 1981).

heterogeneity in the amount of biomass available per unit area (and hence per bite) in these canopies.

Leaf-surface features, such as trichomes and glandular hairs, can be important feeding deterrents for insects (Levin, 1973). Trichome development and type change vary greatly as oak leaves develop, and coverage and type can differ greatly among individual trees of the same species (Hardin, 1979). Physical leaf-quality traits may have various spatial distributions. Age-determined features may be widely scattered in small patches. Individual variation of undetermined cause may occur in much larger patches (see Hardin, 1979).

B. Extrinsic Influences on Feeding-Site Quality

Factors external to the physiological or developmental organization of the tree can influence site quality, either by altering the physiological state of the tissue or by acting directly upon insects (Whitham, 1981). For example, sugar maple leaves growing in direct sunlight exhibit reduced water content, increased toughness, and various chemical changes, including altered secondary compound composition (Table I). Even on the same branch, total phenol content (as percentage tannic acid equivalents or %TAE; Schultz *et al.*, 1981) and hydrolyzable tannins (as %TAE, using iodate test; Bate-Smith, 1977) are greater in "sun" leaves, whereas tanning coefficients (as %TAE in hemoglobin precipitation; Schultz *et al.*, 1981) and condensed tannins (%TAE in proanthocyanidin method; Bate-Smith, 1975) do not differ. See Schultz *et al.* (1981) for sampling sites and details.

The suitability of feeding sites and the availability of tissues may be determined directly by physical factors as well as by altering leaf traits per se. A tree leaf that remains in a sun fleck for very long may become too warm or dry for comfort, forcing a feeding insect to reject or abandon it. Southwood (1973) pointed out that plant surfaces are difficult for insects to grip and regarded "slipperiness" as a major evolutionary hurdle for phytophagous insects. The stability of leaves or other tissues in the wind may represent an important quality criterion for some herbivorous species. Wind motion could also cause bumping with adjacent tissues, damaging potential food and dislodging insects. This problem ought to be particularly severe at the very top of tree canopies, and it will produce relatively local variation (see Wilson, 1980).

C. Natural Enemies Influence Site Quality

A feeding site and hence the tissues at that site may differ in suitability because of differences in predation or parasitism risks (Heinrich, 1979; Schultz, 1982). Tree architecture may influence accessibility to prey for

Table I
Values of Six Leaf-Quality Factors for Individual "Sun- and Shade-Grown" Sugar Maple (*Acer saccharum* Marshall) Leaves

Factor[a]	Sun	Shade	Significance[b] (P)	Leaves per treatment
%TAE[c]	24.07 ± 6.06[d]	16.40 ± 1.64	0.001	48
HEME (%TAE)	51.31 ± 11.65	43.77 ± 17.31	>0.05	48
TI − %TAE	63.20 ± 39.70	22.3 ± 9.66	0.004	48
PA − %TAE	1.66 ± 0.41	1.01 ± 0.48	>0.05	48
Toughness (g/cm²)	204.4 ± 33.1	165.7 ± 27.3	0.000	48
Water (%)	54.3 ± 1.0	59.7 ± 3.0	0.0003	36

[a]See Schultz *et al.* (1982) and text for methods.
[b]Statistical methods, analysis of variance (ANOVA) and Kruskal–Wallis rank test, on arcsine-transformed data where necessary.
[c]HEME, Hemoglobin assay; PA, proanthocyanidin test; %TAE, percentage tannic acid equivalents; TI, iodate test.
[d]Means ± standard deviations.

vertebrate or invertebrate predators (Greenberg and Gradwohl, 1980). Birds and parasitoids may use specific cues in searching for insects in trees (Alcock, 1973; Vinson and Iwantsch, 1980), including structures modified by prey (e.g., rolled leaves), damage resulting from herbivory (Heinrich, 1979, also personal communication), and chemicals deposited by feeding caterpillars (Vinson, 1975). Time spent feeding creates a high-risk area if predators search in an area-restricted fashion around such cues (Croze, 1970). Invertebrate predators must deal with their own predators and may find their search constrained by safety (Charnov, 1976); their hunting activity should be focused on certain plant tissues or regions. The scale of heterogeneity generated by these effects will be relatively small, and the activities of predators and parasites will further fragment suitable patches, defined by intrinsic leaf qualities. As host (caterpillar) densities increase, larger and larger areas will become unsuitable, so the scale of heterogeneity may change with host densities and as the season progresses.

Pathogens are commonly encountered on leaf surfaces by foraging caterpillars (Doane, 1976; Tanada, 1976). Little is known about the spatial array and variance in density of these organisms at endemic insect population levels, but older leaves on a tree may have accumulated more pathogenic cells through time (Schultz, 1982). Gypsy moth larvae find food coated with the pathogenic bacterium *Bacillus thuringiensis* unsuitable on the basis of taste (Yendol *et al.*, 1975). Feeding by other insects in suitable patches may focus pathogens there, effectively breaking otherwise good feeding sites into smaller sites, or destroying them completely. The scale of disease patches in a canopy should be a function of insect-host densities and the longevity of pathogens on leaf surfaces.

III. THE IMPACT OF VARIABILITY ON DEFOLIATING INSECTS

A. Compromises Forced upon Caterpillars

The variable factors described in Section II should place caterpillars in difficult, compromised situations. Multiple leaf-quality traits, varying together or separately, may impose digestive or other costs on individuals consuming them (Dolinger et al., 1973; Feeny, 1975). Selective feeding may reduce such costs, but it cannot eliminate them. Synergistic interactions among leaf traits may alter their effectiveness (Eisner and Halpern, 1971; Schoonhoven, 1976), and other leaf traits may antagonize each other (e.g., Oates et al., 1980).

Physical factors and nutritional needs may interact in an antagonistic fashion, although field studies are few (Tingey and Singh, 1980; Scriber and Slansky, 1981). Although some caterpillars have very narrow thermal optima (Sherman and Watt, 1973), the impact of temperature on digestive processes is at present obscure (Heinrich, 1981; Scriber and Slansky, 1981). Because the caterpillar's temperature may influence disease susceptibility (Heinrich, 1981) and because being in the sun may increase susceptibility to parasites (Vinson, 1975), the costs and benefits of being in the sun may conflict.

Price et al. (1980) and Schultz (1982) have reviewed some ways in which variable food quality within and between plants can influence susceptibility to predators, parasites, and disease and force compromises in food choice for folivores. Feeding in specific sites can cue enemies or focus their activities on high prey densities (Croze, 1970; Vinson and Iwantsch, 1980). Food quality may influence resistance to enemies directly (Roeske et al., 1976; Tanada, 1976; Koike et al., 1979; Price et al., 1989; Vinson and Iwantsch, 1980); this effect should vary as food eaten varies in quality. Contact with and exposure to predators and parasites may be increased if searching for suitable leaves increases movement (Schultz, 1982).

Compromises probably exist between food-getting and other risks as well. Many caterpillars appear to fall out of trees; movement in search of food should exacerbate this. Metabolic costs of movement could be substantial, so there ought to be a direct trade-off between looking for superior food and losses in growth and reproduction. Chewing activity doubles the resting metabolism of caterpillars (Aidley, 1976), and, judging from studies of other insects (Herreid *et al.*, 1981, on cockroaches), costs of walking must be considerably higher.

B. The Caterpillar as a Model System

Although many forest Lepidoptera include widely divergent tree taxa in their diets (Holloway and Hebert, 1979), food discrimination must be based upon distinctive leaf traits. We should expect some insects to evolve the capacity to deal with some of these traits, but not all of them, and to recognize and seek out superior tissues.

Caterpillars have several characteristics that make them good systems for studying food selection. The major function of a lipidopteran (or sawfly) larva is to accumulate as much material as possible, as quickly as possible, without being caught by predators or being parasitized or diseased (Heinrich, 1979). There are no significant competing functions; caterpillars do not mate, defend territories, or feed young. They translate as much food as possible directly into adult fitness (clutch sizes). There is usually a good correlation between final body weight and adult fecundity (Scriber and Slansky, 1981). Hence, there are a few well-defined factors of importance to caterpillars: feeding success (determined by food quality and defined by growth and final pupal weight), metabolic costs (which may be subtracted from feeding success directly as growth decrement and which should be increased by movement), and avoidance of risks (predation, parasitism, disease, and physical risk; expressed as survivorship to the next feeding opportunity).

Tree-dwelling caterpillars are generally linear foragers that walk to food. They search for food directly along tree branches, so that path lengths and patch sizes are predetermined and leaves of various qualities are encountered in direct proportion to their abundances. We may assess the spatial array of potential foods of various quality levels, although many of the traits that determine quality are "invisible" chemical or physical characteristics; bioassays are often necessary to uncover leaf differences.

Although lepidopteran larvae can discriminate among complex chemical mixtures (Dethier, 1979), they have limited sensory capacities; olfaction is limited to very short distances, and food selection requires contact with the tissue (Dethier, 1970). Hence, behavioral "choices" may be observed readily through careful observation.

C. Threshold Discrimination between Leaves

Given leaf-quality variability and these limitations on caterpillar behavior, how are decision rules likely to be organized as a caterpiller searches for food? If leaves encountered have some frequency distribution of values, the best a caterpillar could do by eating every leaf encountered would be to obtain the mean value of that distribution over some sampling (feeding) period. However, if the caterpiller can inspect and reject low-quality leaves while selecting others, there are several ways in which a better-than-average food value can be obtained.

A number of reasonable assumptions about caterpillars must be made before we can erect reasonable hypotheses about caterpillar leaf choice. Caterpillar time and/or mobility constraints are such that only one leaf can be inspected and judged at a time. Caterpillar memory is likely to be poor because of the simplicity of the central nervous system. It is assumed at the start that a caterpillar can only eat one leaf (or a portion of a leaf) before seeking another, that there is no competition for leaves, that leaves vary in value (with mean and variance contributing to growth and fecundity), that leaves do not manipulate choices by changing in value faster than the decision (tasting) process, and that leaves of different values are encountered randomly.

Under these conditions, eating the first leaf encountered will gain, through foraging time, food with a value equal to the mean of the distribution of the tree. If every leaf could be eaten, then the expected yield in food (and presumed contribution to growth and fitness) would increase linearly with distance traveled or time spent searching (Fig. 2). But empirical observation (J. C. Schultz, personal observations, and see later discussion) indicates that careful choices are made by caterpillars as they forage. Leaves are not taken sequentially, except by a few colonial defoliators (e.g., tent caterpillars, *Malacosoma* spp.; webworms, *Hyphantria cunea;* various sawflies). Even if some leaves are rejected and others selected, choice may still be random, in which case the overall food-value yield will equal the mean for the leaf population.

Assuming that search is organized to maximize the food value yield over foraging time, what other tactics are possible? According to models of mate choice suggested by Janetos (1980), individuals may establish a threshold leaf value, choosing only leaves "better" than some value. Such a fixed-threshold search tactic provides a greater-than-average return over *n* leaves (mates), but this can yet be improved.

The threshold value may be altered (lowered) if no leaves of this quality are found within some minimal time or after some number

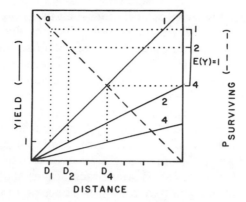

Fig. 2. Food-value yield and probability of survival of a caterpillar foraging some distance along a branch, when every leaf encountered is eaten. Yield accumulates linearly with distance, but more slowly if food is one-half as valuable (2) or one-fourth as valuable (4). For an expected yield of 1 unit, decreasing food value decreases the probability of continuing (increases risk) proportionately. Similar results would be obtained if one-half or one-fourth of the leaves were eaten as encountered (i.e., if every second or fourth leaf were eaten). No selectivity is expressed by the insect.

searched. Hunger would be an appropriate cue, and it could reset the threshold criterion. This tactic will always produce a better yield than the fixed threshold, but, as the number of leaves searched increases, the two tactics converge in expected yield (Janetos, 1980), because as more leaves are searched, the chance of encountering one of threshold value increases. Hence, for a given variance in leaf quality, very widely spaced leaves of threshold or better quality make each tactic equally profitable. The spatial array of leaves varying in quality could influence yield as strongly as leaf-quality variance. If a caterpillar can safely and at low cost search long distances, it may hold to a fixed threshold and be "choosy"; but if search distances are restricted, it may best become less choosy, varying its threshold. If risks become high enough during search, selection will favor caterpillars with more catholic tastes.

For mate choice, Janetos (1980) examined one other tactic, *optimal one-step choice*. For caterpillars, this would mean eating an encountered leaf only if its yield is better than that expected from leaves encountered during the time it takes to consume the present leaf. This type of choice involves additional conditions. First, it is most important in situations that are strongly time- or distance-constrained. If the chance and cost of experiencing a negative energy balance (expending more in search than can be returned) are large or if other risks (e.g., predators) are very strong, then such constraints may apply. Second, this tactic demands some estimate by the caterpillar of the spatial distribution or at least variance of leaf quality. The ability to use this type of search tactic will be strongly influenced by the availability of reliable information about the location of suitable leaves.

In trees with highly organized arrays of leaves of various qualities, for example, those in which leaf quality is age-related, insects may employ the optimal one-step method, using spatial or substrate cues to locate preferred leaves. Conifer-feeding sawflies, which prefer young needles, use such cues to bypass unsuitable leaves and focus search on younger, terminal needles (Ghent, 1958). It seems doubtful that most insects would have the capacity to use this tactic in more-random leaf arrays (e.g., sugar maple, as described previously), although semisocial foraging may provide additional cues (Fitzgerald, 1980).

For all of these tactics, a function describing the expected yield to growth and fitness of a leaf chosen from n leaves potentially encountered is a monotonically increasing, asymptotic curve (Fig. 3; see Janetos, 1980: appendix, for mathematical justification). I conclude that some threshold basis is most likely to be employed by caterpillars because of constraints on memory and available information and because time constraints are strong (see later discussion). This conclusion is consistent with two other independent theoretical treatments (Levins and MacArthur, 1969; Oster and Heinrich, 1976).

But do caterpillars behave as though these guesses about their tactics are reasonable? Do they really make choices, and what can we infer about the basis of choice from their behavior? Unfortunately, the available information on foraging behavior of caterpillars is miniscule. However, what there is in the literature and the preliminary results of our studies currently underway at the Hubbard Brook Experimental Forest in New Hampshire may provide some clues.

Caterpillars do indeed select individual leaves within a canopy for feeding, and chosen leaves are not often adjacent. Even during outbreaks, scattered damage appears first and eventually becomes widespread enough to anastamoze (Bryant and Raske, 1975).

Gypsy moths seem to prefer certain branches on poplar trees (Schoonhoven, 1977), and spruce budworms carefully inspect and select foraging sites (McGugan, 1954; Heron, 1965). Bryant and Raske (1975) showed that the spatial variance in damage by the birch casebearer (*Coleophora fuscendinella* Zeller) is distributed so that at least eight leaves are required to form a sampling unit for feeding activity. Several leaf-feeding insects

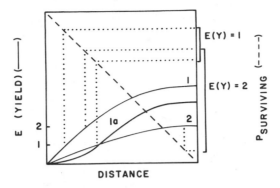

Fig. 3. Expected food-value yield and probability of survival of a caterpillar foraging along a branch as a function of selection of leaves of some minimum value from a frequency distribution of leaf values. Yield curve 2 represents the case in which approximately one-half of the leaves meet threshold criteria (when compared with case 1). As the proportion of suitable leaves encountered declines, risk increases, but more dramatically than in the linear cases (Fig. 2). Case 1a represents the effects of damage induction; leaves near the last feeding site are of reduced value because of feeding activity nearby. Hence, expected yield accumulates slowly as foraging begins.

have strong preferences for portions of three canopies (Raske and Bryant, 1977; Nielson, 1978). Larsson and Tenow (1979) attributed low digestion efficiencies and slow growth in the sawfly *Neodiprion sertifer* Georffr. to failure to choose the most nutritious needles on the host tree. Herrebout et all. (1963) showed that several caterpillar species feeding on scots pine orient to needles in stereotyped ways.

Insect preferences based on leaf age are often strong in conifer-feeding species (Knerer and Atwood, 1973; Beckwith, 1975; Togashi and Takahashi, 1977; Larsson and Tenow, 1979; J. C. Schultz, unpublished). Cates and Rhoades (1977) cited a number of other examples for nonconifers. In most cases, strong differences between tissues of different ages in terms of secondary compounds or nutrient levels have been identified.

Much finer age-based discriminations may be made. Caterpillars of the sphingid *Paonius excaecatus* Smith and Abbot, hatching from a single clutch of eggs taken from a female and reared under constant conditions (25° C.; 6:18 hr dark:light) on yellow birch leaves from two age classes, failed to grow and experience high mortality on the younger leaves (Fig. 4). The reason for these results, however, was not consumption of poor or toxic material by those fed young leaves; instead it was refusal to eat

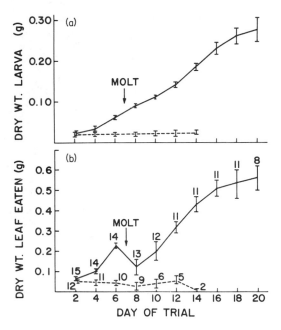

Fig. 4. Dry-weight accumulation (a) and consumption (b) by larvae of *Paonius excaecatus* (Sphingidae) on young (– – –) and old (——) yellow birch *(Betula lutea)* leaves (see text for methods). Larvae refused to eat young leaves.

young leaves (Fig. 4). The young leaves appear to have antifeedant properties, and this caterpillar discriminates between leaves from a single branch, which differ in age by about a month (Sharik and Barnes, 1976). We know that these leaf age classes differ in total phenol content (Schultz *et al.*, 1982) and in phenolic composition (Baldwin and Schultz, 1983), but we do not know what cues are used by this caterpillar species. They are clearly intrinsic to the leaves; no positional or other information was available to larvae in these experiments.

Detailed behavorial observations of several caterpillar species indicate that choices are made during foraging. For example, on 20 July 1981, six fifth-instar individuals of the notodontid *Heterocampa guttivitta* Walker were observed continuously for 5 hr while they fed, rested, and foraged on sugar maple (a preferred host) in nature. During this time, these caterpillars moved a total of 970 cm, passing at least 776 leaves; they tasted (mandibulated leaf edges) 98 leaves, accepting 30 (31%) of them for sustained feeding. Clearly *H. guttivitta* is a relatively choosy feeder. The basis of choice could not be observed, although individuals returning to leaves already rejected once were consistent in rejecting such leaves a second (and third) time. Individuals sampling a leaf rejected by a conspecific were also observed to reject the same leaf.

Similar observations of gypsy moths, geometrids (*Euchlaena serrata* Drury), sphingids (*Paonius myops* Smith and Abbot), and noctuids (*Colocasia propinquilinia* Grote) gave similar results; considerable time and effort were expended in searching over long distances while tasting, rejecting, and accepting certain leaves. The basis of choice sometimes appears to be position (*P. myops*), spatial array (*C. propinquilinia*), or is undetermined and probably chemical (e.g., *Heterocampa guttivitta*; J. C. Schultz, unpublished).

D. A Qualitative Cost–Risk–Benefit Analysis of Foraging Tactics

Assuming that the eventual fitness of the caterpillar as reflected by its size at pupation and fecundity as an adult is a direct, positive function of food assimilation, then it is reasonable to presume that the better the quality of the food that a caterpillar can ingest, the greater its fitness will be. If trees are truly variable, then not all leaves contribute equally to fitness accumulation, and, as I have argued earlier, we can expect caterpillars to employ a variable- or fixed-threshold discrimination rule, choosing some leaves on which to feed and rejecting others.

The null hypothesis or situation in which caterpillars accept any leaf (or select randomly) is also interesting. A caterpillar behaving this way would suffer growth and fitness reduction compared with one making "superior" choices, but it would avoid some risks and costs associated with movement and search. This is probably a viable strategy for some caterpillars (Haukioja and Niemelä, 1978; Larsson and Tenow, 1979), but, for now, let us concentrate on the problems of finding superior leaves.

If leaves are uniformly low in quality, or if some are unavailable or low in quality but the animal eats them all, then yield increases linearly but slowly with distance or time (Fig. 2). As the search distance or time increases, risk accumulates, and the probability of surviving to continue the search decreases (Fig. 2). For a given yield, an insect foraging among low- or variable-quality leaves will experience a lower probability of continuing (higher risk) than one foraging among uniformly high-quality leaves (Fig. 2). Hence, even when leaves are taken as encountered, if they are of low or variable quality the risk per food assimilated is higher.

If one leaf is chosen from some variable, finite set encountered, then the cumulative expected yield rises curvilinearly and asymptotically with distance or time (Fig. 3). The same general relationship between food value and risk obtains; as leaves become more variable, the risk per yield increases. However, the impact of decreasing average food value is much greater than in the uniform, linear first case. Hence, if variability is important enough to force choices, for example, if some leaves have significant antifeedant properties, then risks suffered while searching for a given food yield are increased well beyond the influence of average food value alone.

Metabolic costs of movement should interact with food variability in similar ways. When food is highly variable, distance traveled to obtain a given yield will increase, and along with it metabolic costs of movement increase. Hence, the return in yield per unit distance or time will be decreased if distances are long between acceptable leaves. These costs may be balanced or offset by selecting leaves of sufficiently high quality, but at some search distance there will never be a leaf superior enough to warrant the expense (and concomitant risk) of traveling farther. Hence, there should be direct compromises among (1) the acceptability threshold (the maximum growth or fitness "cost" an individual bears in consuming a given leaf), (2) the metabolic expenditure necessary to reach a leaf of given value, and (3) the risk experienced in searching long enough. These three factors will determine the average distance traveled and the threshold of leaf suitability employed by a caterpillar species.

The variance in leaf quality and its spatial array strongly influence these three factors. If patches of suitable leaves are small and widely scattered, much travel time and effort will be necessary to fill the gut only a few times. The relationship between patch size and quality on the one hand and gut volume on the other may be very important. If gut volume is large and passage slow, then a caterpillar may fill the gut several times on a single leaf and travel a considerable distance before the gut empties. If the gut volume is low or passage fast, exploiting widely separated feeding sites may be more costly.

Even if a large number of adjacent leaves is suitable in terms of food quality, the focused action of predators and parasites or the unfocused action of shifting physical factors should dissect such a patch into many smaller portions. For this reason even apparently large, uniform patches of older, even-aged leaves on some tree limbs may not be the grand expanses of suitable food they seem. As we have seen, even-aged leaves may differ drastically over short distances. My impression from observing caterpillars is that most suitable patches comprise one to four leaves.

The goals of this kind of analysis of compromise ought to include the ability to make predictions about important caterpillar and tree traits. For example, if we know the risk levels involved in movement and the levels of leaf-quality variation important to a caterpillar species, can we predict its movement frequency and distance? Can we calculate the number of leaves actually available to a given species and project population dynamics from a knowledge of feeding and growth efficiencies and resource abundance? More likely, can we predict what a caterpillar must look like to live in a tree having a certain variance and spatial array of leaf qualities while minimizing risk? Under what conditions is feeding only at night preferable to feeding around the clock? Trees differing in leaf-quality variance and/or spatial array will favor feeding by insects with different acceptability thresholds, movement rules, and adaptations to reduce risk. Analyses of these compromises may help us understand how host-plant insect faunas are organized and how their diversities are determined. A more quantitative approach would be desirable, but for now we know so little about the impact of leaf variability on growth and about caterpillar behavior that this is not possible.

E. Adaptive Syndromes of Caterpillars

The problem of being an arboreal caterpillar, then, consists of trade-offs among costs of search, risks while searching, and "costs" of handling poor-quality leaves (expressed as reduction in growth contribution per unit time due to toxicity, digestion inhibition, or investment in digestive or detoxification adaptations). Balancing these factors should result in a finite set of adaptive syndromes or "ways of being a caterpillar." Some species may minimize movement; others may express characteristics that reduce the risks of movement while selecting more or less freely among widely scattered variable leaves. Some may reduce travel and risk by developing digestive or detoxification traits that minimize feeding costs. As pointed out in Section I, no species appears to have become a perfect food-cost minimizer through exclusively physiological means; in general, empirical evidence suggests that if food-cost minimization occurs, it involves at least some feeding selectivity. However, various adaptations can increase the proportion of variable leaves regarded as suitable and falling above the acceptability threshold.

The balance among feeding costs, risks, and movement costs can be illustrated as an inelastic compromise or trade-off surface (Fig. 5). For lack of more-reasonable assumptions, relationships among feeding cost (growth–fitness decrement due to handling poor food), movement costs (metabolic expenditures), and predation risk (probability of surviving to assimilate more food) are depicted as linear. The area of the surface describes the overall reduction in fitness of the organism due to the

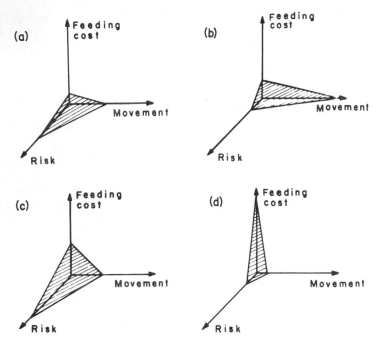

Fig. 5. Trade-off planes of selected caterpillar syndromes. Costs of feeding (e.g., metabolic costs of digestion, reduced growth, etc.), movement (metabolic costs of reduced growth), and risks (e.g., probability of capture of reduced growth due to time spent hiding) increase in direction of arrows (see text for details). (a) Selective feeding (days). (b) Selective feeding (nights; aposematic). (c) Day feeding (cryptic). (d) Food mimic.

three factors. Although risk and other costs are not necessarily of the same units, in some cases risk may be translated into a growth cost. For example, for insects that evade risks by remaining motionless and not feeding for some periods, reduced growth is an inevitable consequence, so risk and other costs may be expressed in similar cost units. The evolutionary "problem" is how the three corners will be arranged in response to differential variability, predation, etc. Natural selection should favor a reduction along any cost axis, but this will result in an increase along the other two. The adaptive syndromes (or apparent evolutionary "solutions") of different caterpillar species are represented by different orientations of the trade-off plane.

Several potential caterpillar syndromes are depicted in Fig. 5. Selective feeding by day may yield low feeding costs, but movement costs will be moderate to high, and the risk of being detected by predators quite high (Fig. 5a). By feeding selectively at night, risks and feeding costs can be reduced greatly, but movement costs may be high (to locate the very best leaves; Fig. 5b). However, feeding at night limits the amount of time available for assimilation and growth (to only 6 hr per day during June in northern forests). To maintain the growth rate it might have feeding around the clock, a night-feeder's risk would have to be reduced significantly and leaf choice would have to produce a much improved yield over that obtainable under high risks during the day. Aposematic insects, because they are protected from predation, have a low risk value and can move as much as necessary to select the best leaves. However, they do not escape movement costs, and there may be additional costs (added to movement or feeding costs) of sequestration.

Some caterpillars are cryptic but still feed during the day, usually in brief bouts (Herrebout et al., 1963; see later discussion). Extensive movement should be precluded because of risk, so costs may be fairly high and careful feeding and careful leaf choice may be impossible (Fig. 5c). Risk will be fairly significant, because some small-scale movement is necessitated by feeding. If leaves are chosen for feeding only at night and feeding proceeds around the clock, then more than one leaf cannot be consumed during daylight hours, so growth may be slow. If leaves are selected from time to time, even during the day, then movement costs and risks climb.

Other caterpillar species may mimic their own food (Fig 5d). Examples from eastern North America include Heterocampa spp., Schizura spp. (Notodontidae), Cepphis armataria Herrich-Schäffer and Nematocampa filamentaria Guenee (Geometridae), among others. These species resemble not only the substrates on which they feed, but also the damage they do. Effectiveness depends on motionlessness and substrate specificity. Such an individual does not resemble other tissues and is especially conspicuous when moving on nonfood substrates. Hence, movement is strongly constrained and risk is kept low by remaining in place and feeding seldom and/or in very brief bouts. Because so much time is spent on a single leaf, feeding costs may be very high. In the extreme, caterpillars of this type may spend an entire lifetime on one leaf or, as in leaf miners, within one leaf. Such a species has no choice of leaf once settled, so first choice by the larvae or choices made by the ovipositing female are very important.

As insects grow larger, it is reasonable to assume that their profitability to predators (e.g., birds) and thus their risk will increase. The cost of movement should also change with size (Scriber and Slansky, 1981). To balance the trade-off plane, feeding costs and/or movement costs will have to be reduced. Induction of detoxification systems may occur more readily in late-instar caterpillars (Gould and Hodgson, 1980), and later instars are typically more tolerant of poor food quality (Chan *et al.*, 1978; M. Montgomery, personal communication), perhaps balancing increasing risks. If movement costs and feeding costs cannot be changed, then we should expect substantial changes in the predator-avoidance traits of insects as they grow larger. This is often the case (Young, 1972; Schultz, 1981).

F. Real Adaptive Syndromes

Herrebout *et al.* (1963) described the feeding behavior and appearances of seven species of lepidopteran larvae living on Scots pine (*Pinus sylvestris* L.). All were cryptic, and did some significant proportion of their feeding during the day, although several species fed primarily at night. Species active during the day fed in very short bouts but completed growth in much less time than those that fed primarily or exclusively at night (Herrebout *et al.*, 1963). One of the day-feeding caterpillar species, *Hyloicus pinastri* L. (Sphingidae), was shown to be taken more often by birds than the others, and all of the day-feeding species were more readily apparent to birds. Although the investigators speculated that the day-active species were less cryptic in appearance, they did not measure the degree to which this was due to daytime feeding activity.

Restricting the feeding period does indeed slow growth. Larvae of the cutworm *Agrotis orthogonia* Morr. (Noctuidae) were maintained on suitable diets, but half of them were only permitted to feed for 2 hr per day (McGinnis and Kasting, 1959). No data on diurnal feeding patterns were presented, but this restriction (from 24 hr possible feeding time per day to 2 hr) extended the larval life 36% and reduced final weight. One consequence of extending larval life should be extension of the period of susceptibility to predators and parasites.

Three closely related geometrid species (*Pero honestaria* Walter, tribe Azelinini; *Anagoga occiduaria* Walker; and *Cepphis armataria* tribe Anagonini) can all be found feeding on the understory shrub striped maple (*Acer pensylvanicum* L.) and on mountain maple (*Acer spicatum* Lam.) at the same time during July. During July 1978, 40 individuals of each geometrid species were confined in the laboratory on sprays of striped maple, and their activity was observed at 2-hr intervals around the clock. Leaf area consumed between each observation was measured using a graphpaper grid, and 2-hr "rations" were calculated as the proportion of total 24-hr feeding performed during each 2-hr block. In addition, the average 2-hr meal size was calculated and corrected for caterpillar dry

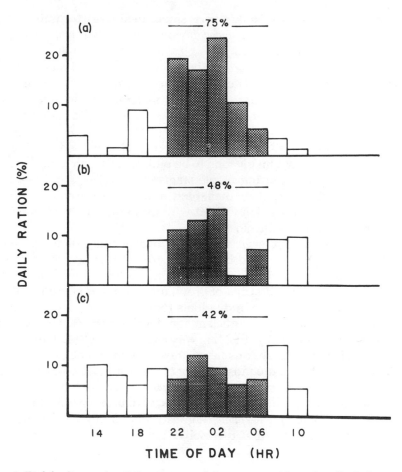

Fig. 6. Diel feeding and activity patterns of three geometrid species. Shaded areas are hours of darkness. Meal sizes are corrected for dry weight of larvae. Meal size (mm²/g): (a) 3.8 [CV, coefficient of variation of meal size (amount eaten per 2-hr period)] = 92%; night moves = 39%. (b) 4.2; CV = 45%; night moves = 39%. (c) 1.1; CV = 33%.

weight, and the number of changes in positions (moves) was counted for the first two species every 2 hr.

Pero ate about 3.8 mm² per gram dry weight every 2 hr, doing about 75% of its daily feeding after dark (Fig. 6a). Most of its movements also occurred after dark. *Anagoga* had a similar meal size but fed during any 2-hr interval around the clock (Fig. 6b); its feeding appeared almost rhythmic. The feeding distribution of *Cepphis* was almost uniform around the clock (Fig. 6c), and it took a very small meal size (1.1 mm^2/g dry wt). So *Pero* is a night feeder, *Anagoga* day or night, and *Cepphis* is equally likely to feed around the clock.

Pero larvae vary in color but tend to be brown or gray, and their surface traits (striations, rugosities) match older maple stems very well (Fig. 7a). It is on older stems, far from the leaves, that these individuals hide during the day, moving fairly long distances to select leaves at night, when 75% of their feeding occurs.

Anagoga larvae are also polymorphic for color; the individuals found on striped and mountain maple tend to be pinkish and match the surface texture of young, leaf-bearing maple stems closely (Fig. 7b). They are cryptic when within reach of their food and can move very slightly ("leaning" toward the leaves) to feed without becoming very conspicuous; they feed around the clock.

As noted previously, *Cepphis* mimics its own feeding damage. Individuals are rough in form and brown (Fig. 7c) and hang upside down from the veins of the leaf on which they are feeding. From a distance they resemble the tattered strips of browning tissue left behind as they skeletonize a leaf. Two to six individuals forage together on a leaf, and only one or two leaves are sufficient for development (J. C. Schultz, personal observation). Individuals are very small, yet they feed in minute bouts, possibly to minimize conspicuousness. I predict that we shall find that the traveler, *Pero,* is the most choosy of the three, selecting superior leaves to balance travel costs, whereas *Cepphis* may have no choice of leaves. Hence, one prediction would rank variability in development time from *Pero* (lowest) to *Cepphis* (highest), depending on the quality of the leaf on which they find themselves.

G. Complications Arising from Temporal Variability

It would appear that some of the difficulties encountered by caterpillars could be reduced if they were to feed only at night to minimize risks, carefully selecting leaves when risks are low and growing slowly.

This is not possible because, at least in temperate forests, the environment in which they live changes during the developmental period. Food quality overall may decline sharply as the season progresses (Feeny, 1970; Schultz *et al.*, 1982), so feeding costs may increase beyond the control of the insect. Physical factors change continuously during

Fig. 7. Natural daytime postures and resting sites of *Pero honestaria* (a), *Anagoga occiduaria* (b), and *Cepphis armataria* (c) on striped maple *(Acer pensylvanicum).*

the growth season; for example, cold night conditions may abate later in the summer. As a result, adaptive syndromes involving night feeding may be possible in midsummer, but not in the spring. Parasites may have important "phenological windows" (Cheng, 1970; Lawton and McNeill, 1979), so temporal shifts in parasitism risk may constrain the seasonal occurrence of caterpillars with particular traits. Bird predation increases dramatically as nestlings are produced in temperate forests (Holmes *et al.*, 1979); adaptive traits that provide protection under low predation pressure may not be suitable later, when that pressure increases sharply.

These sorts of changes should contribute to the validity of the assumption with which we started, that it is to a caterpillar's advantage to complete development as quickly as possible, reaching as large a size as possible during this period. There may be a direct correlation between the minimum size necessary for pupation and the degree of change and predictability in a caterpillar's feeding environment.

Short-term, induced changes in leaf quality can also have important effects on caterpillar adaptive syndromes. Local induction (along a branch) of reduced leaf quality should depress the expected yield curve by making the first few leaves encountered in the search unsuitable (Fig. 3). This will increase the travel distance and time necessary to obtain a given food yield, and hence increase risks. Feeding by conspecifics (Haukioja and Niemelä, 1978) or even by unrelated organisms (McIntyre, 1980; Matta, 1980) reduces the relative food abundance for others through time and increases risk all around. The shape and patch size of the canopy mosaic will change as the growth season progresses.

IV. CONCLUSIONS

A. Impacts on Forest Insect Communities

There are several broad consequences of variability in the forest tree environment. Sharply varying habitat characteristics (e.g., food quality or predation pressure) may influence insect community structure. When no caterpillar species can express sufficient adaptive latitude to successfully exploit all parts of the canopy habitat at all times, more than one species may exploit a host (Schroeder and Malmer, 1980). For example, it seems highly likely that the nutritional and chemical properties of black cherry (*Prunus serotina* Ehrh.) vary throughout the growth season, yet Schroeder and Malmer (1980) found that each seasonal cohort assimilates material and grows with equal efficiency. They concluded that the herbivore community on black cherry consists of an aggregation of species, each of which can tolerate one range of environmental factors but which must enter and exit the system through the appropriate phenological window to avoid conditions with which it is unprepared to deal. Singular cases like this are well known (e.g., Feeny, 1970), and the entire Hubbard Brook caterpillar community (for the three major tree species) seem to turn over in a similar fashion (Schultz et al., 1978, and unpublished).

It seems possible that tree habitat heterogeneity could influence contemporaneous caterpillar species coexistence and community species richness as well. There appears to be a huge number of variable tree traits that insect species might exploit differentially. It is clear that all caterpillar species are not the same when we look closely and that all trees (or even leaves) are not the same. Patterns in the diversity of appearance ("aspect diversity"; Rand, 1967) among caterpillars in a forest may be more readily predicted by analyzing the need to minimize risks under various food-locating constraints.

The idea that food limitation and hence competition are not possible among canopy-feeding insects because they rarely consume much food (see, e.g., Lawton and Strong, 1981) fails to account for differential resource availability and suitability. The ability to feed only on a subset of leaves or in a narrow set of circumstances may greatly restrict food availability and insect abundance (Lawton and McNeill, 1979). Feeding by one insect may effectively remove a much larger portion of a tree canopy from the pool of resources available to others because of spreading induction effects, increased concentration of disease organisms, or increased concentration in that area by predators or parasites. Depending on insect densities overall, considerable portions of tree canopies may become unavailable as food for some herbivores because of accumulated induction of leaf defenses (see Ryan, Chapter 2; Rhoades, Chapter 6) and spread of pathogens by other insects.

B. Impact of Variability on Consumption Levels

Host-plant variability can increase the effectiveness of natural enemies of defoliators. This direct impact on insect populations should help restrict primary consumption. Perhaps more importantly, being variable may slow the evolution of the "perfect pest" (Beck and Schoonhoven, 1980). If most or all leaves in tree canopies were suitable, defoliation levels would be very high. Alternatively, if practically none were available, evolution would proceed so that defoliation eventually would become very great. However, if there is a cost associated with adapting to the plant tissue, defoliation should really be less by some amount reflecting this cost. There is no evidence to suggest that the cost of adapting to tree traits is so high that insect populations are influenced enough to keep defoliation at its average level, below 7% per year (Mattson and Addy, 1975; Scriber, 1979). So, the "best" situation for trees (adaptive or not on the part of the trees) is some intermediate level of defense. I suggest that packaging leaf quality in certain ways (high spatial and temporal variability) increases the effectiveness of natural enemies, reducing further defoliation at intermediate levels of leaf quality.

Under these circumstances, avoidance of particularly bad tissues in an option for insects, and the contact rate with (and selective pressure from) "bad" tissues is reduced. One result should be stability of the relationships between insects and long-lived trees. This stability is achieved via complex interactions among herbivores, parasites, predators, and diseases, and it is enhanced by spatial and temporal plant variability. Clearly, "Why does the world remain green?" has a complex answer, and each answer thus far proposed is partly correct. All of these parts must be assembled, however, to truly understand how this system works.

ACKNOWLEDGMENTS

D. Dussourd, J. R. Howe V, and M. J. Richards helped gather behavioral data. I. T. Baldwin performed chemical analysis, and M. J. Richards drew the figures. The manuscript benefited from criticisms by I. T. Baldwin, R. T. Holmes, P. J. Kareiva, P. J. Nothnagle, and T. S. Whitham. Research supported by NSF grants DEB 76-82905 and 80-22174 to JCS and R. T. Holmes.

REFERENCES

Aidley, D. J. (1976). Increase in respiratory rate during feeding in larvae of the armyworm, *Spodoptera exempta. Physiol. Entomol.* **1**, 73–75.
Alcock, J. (1973). Cues used in searching for food by red-winged blackbirds *(Agelaius phoeniceus). Behaviour* **46**, 174–188.
Baldwin, I. T., and Schultz, J. C. (1983). In preparation.
Bate-Smith, E. C. (1975). Phytochemistry of proanthocyanidins. *Phytochemistry* **14**, 1107–1113.
Bate-Smith, E. C. (1977). Astringent tannins of *Acer* species. *Phytochemistry* **16**, 1421–1426.
Beck, S. D., and Schoonhoven, L. M. (1980). Insect behavior and plant resistance. *In* "Breeding Plants Resistant to Insects" (F. G. Maxwell and P. R. Jennings, eds.), pp. 115–136. Wiley-Interscience, New York.
Beckwith, R. C. (1975). Influence of host foliage on the Douglas-fir tussock moth. *Environ. Entomol.* **5**, 73–77.
Bryant, D. G., and Raske, A. G. (1975). Defoliation of white birch by the birch casebearer, *Coleophora fuscedinella* (Lepidoptera: Coleophorideae). *Can. Entomol.* **107**, 217–223.

Cates, R. G., and Rhoades, D. F. (1977). Prosopis leaves as a resource for insects. *In* "Mesquite: Its Biology in Two Desert Scrub Ecosystems" (B. B. Simpson, ed.), pp. 61–83. Dowden, Hutchinson, & Ross, Stroudsburg, Pennsylvania.

Chan, B. G., Waiss, A. C., Jr., and Lukefahr, M. (1978). Condensed tannin, an antibiotic chemical from *Gossypium hirsutum*. *J. Insect Physiol.* **24,** 113–118.

Charnov, E. L. (1976). Optimal foraging: the attack strategy of a mantid. *Am. Nat.* **110,** 41–151.

Cheng, L. (1970). Timing of attack by *Lypha dobia* Fall (Diptera: Tachinidae) on winter moth, *Operophtera brumata* (Lepidoptera: Geometridae) as a factor affecting parasite success. *J. Anim. Ecol.* **39,** 313–320.

Croze, H. (1970). Searching image in carrion crows. *Z. Tierphyschol.* **5,** 1–86.

Dawkins, R., and Krebs, J. R. (1979). Arms races between and within species. *Proc. R. Soc. London, Ser. B* **205,** 489–511.

Dethier, V. G. (1970). Chemical interactions between plants and insects. *In* "Chemical Ecology" (E. Sondheimer and J. B. Simeone, ed.), pp. 83–102.

Dethier, V. G. (1979). The importance of stimulus patterns for host-plant recognition and acceptance. *Symp. Biol. Hung.* **16,** 67–70.

Dixon, A. F. G. (1970). Quality and availability of food for a sycamore aphid population. *In* "Animal Populations in Relation to Their Food Resources" (A. Watson, ed.), pp. 271–287. Blackwell, Oxford.

Doane, C. D. (1976). Ecology of pathogens of the gypsy moth. *In* "Perspectives in Forest Entomology" (J. F. Anderson and H. K. Kaya, eds.), pp. 285–293. Academic Press, New York.

Dolinger, P. M., Ehrlich, P. R., Fitch, W. L., and Breedlove, D. E. (1973). Alkaloid and predation patterns in Colorado lupine populations. *Oecologia* **13,** 191–204.

Eisner, T., and Halpern, B. P. (1971). Taste distortion and plant palatability. *Science* **172,** 1362.

Feeny, P. P. (1970). Seasonal changes in oak leaf tannins and nutrients as a cause of spring feeding by winter moth caterpillars. *Ecology* **51,** 565–581.

Feeny, P. P. (1975). Biochemical coevolution between plants and their insect herbivores. *In* "Coevolution of Animals and Plants" (L. E. Gilbert and P. R. Raven, eds.), p. 246. Univ. of Texas Press, Austin.

Fitzgerald, T. D. (1980). An analysis of daily foraging patterns of laboratory colonies of the eastern tent caterpillar, *Malacosoma americanum* (Lepidoptera: Lasiocampidae), recorded photoelectrically. *Can. Entomol.* **112,** 731–738.

Ghent, A. W. (1958). Studies of the feeding orientation of the jack pine sawfly, *Neodiprion pratti banksianae* Roh. *Can. J. Zool.* **36,** 175–183.

Gibbs, R. D. (1974). "Chemotaxonomy of Flowering Plants," Vols. 1–4. McGill-Queen's Univ. Press, Montreal.

Gould, F., and Hodgson, E. (1980). Mixed function oxidase and glutathione transferase activity in last instar *Heliothis virescens* larvae. *Pestic. Biochem. Physiol.* **13,** 34–40.

Greenberg, R., and Gradwohl, J. (1980). Leaf surface specializations of birds and arthropods in a Panamanian forest. *Oecologia* **46,** 115–124.

Hardin, J. W. (1979). Patterns of variation in foliar trichomes of eastern North American *Quercus*. *Am. J. Bot.* **66,** 576–585.

Hassell, M. P., and Southwood, T. R. E. (1978). Foraging strategies of insects. *Annu. Rev. Ecol. Syst.* **9,** 75–78.

Haukioja, E., and Niemelä, P. (1978) Birch leaves as a resource for herbivores: seasonal occurrence of increased resistance in foliage after mechanical damage of adjacent leaves. *Oecologia* **39,** 151–159.

Hegnauer, R. (1962). "Chemotaxonomie der Pflanzen," Vols. 1–6. Birkhaeuser, Stuttgart.

Heinrich, B. (1971). The effect of leaf geometry on the feeding behavior of caterpillars of *Manduca sexta* (Sphingidae). *Anim. Behav.* **19**, 119–124.

Heinrich, B. (1979). Foraging strategies of caterpillars: leaf damage and possible predator avoidance strategies. *Oecologia* **42**, 325–337.

Heinrich, B. (1981). Ecological and evolutionary perspectives. *In* "Insect Thermoregulation" (B. Heinrich, ed.), pp. 235–302. Wiley-Interscience, New York.

Heron, R. J. (1965). The role of chemotactic stimuli in the feeding behavior of spruce budworm larvae on white spruce. *Can. J. Zool.* **43**, 247–269.

Herrebout, W. M., Kuyten, P. J., and DeRuiter, L. (1963). Observations on colour patterns and behavior of caterpillars feeding on Scots pine. *Arch. Neerl. Zool.* **15**, 315–357.

Herreid, D. F., II, Prawel, D. A., and Full, R. J. (1981). Energetics of running cockroaches. *Science* **212**, 331–333.

Holloway, J. D., and Hebert, P. D. N. (1979). Ecological and taxonomic trends in macro-lepidopteran host plant selection. *Bio. J. Linn. Soc.* **11**, 229–251.

Holmes, R. T., Schultz, J. C., and Nothnagle, P. J. (1979). Bird predation on forest insects: an exclosure experiment. *Science* **206**, 462–463.

Janetos, A. C. (1980). Strategies of female mate choice: a theoretical analysis. *Behav. Ecol. Sociobiol.* **7**, 107–112.

Jones, R. (1979). Predator-prey relationships with particular reference to vertebrates. *Biol. Rev. Cambridge Philos. Soc.* **54**, 73–97.

Journet, A. R. P. (1980). Intraspecific variation in food plant favourability to phytophagous insects: Psyllids on *Eucalyptus blakelyi* M. *Ecol. Entomol.* **5**, 249–261.

Knerer, G., and Atwood, C. E. (1973). Diprionid sawflies: polymorphism and speciation. *Science* **179**, 1090–1099.

Koike, S., Iizuka, T., and Mizutani, J. (1979). Determination of caffeic acid in the digestive juices of silkworm larvae and its antibacterial activity against the pathogenic *Streptococcus faecalis* AD-4. *Agric. Biol. Chem.* **43**, 1727–1731.

Kozlowski, T. T., and Clausen, J. J. (1966). Shoot growth characteristics of heterophyllous woody plants. *Can. J. Bot.* **44**, 827–843.

Larsson, S., and Tenow, O. (1979). Utilization of dry matter and bioelements in larvae of *Neodiprion sertifer* Geoffr. (Hym., Diprionidae) feeding on Scots pine *(Pinus sylvestris* L.). *Oecologia* **43**, 157–172.

Lawton, J. H., and Strong, D. R., Jr. (1981). Community patterns and competition in folivorous insects. *Am. Nat.* **118**, 317–338.

Lawton, J. H., and McNeill, S. (1979). Between the devil and the deep blue sea: on the problem of being a herbivore. *Symp. Br. Ecol. Soc.* **20**, 223–244.

Levin, D. A. (1973). The role of trichomes in plant defense. *Q. Rev. Biol.* **48**, 3–15.

Levins, R., and MacArthur, R. (1969). An hypothesis to explain the incidense of monophagy. *Ecology* **50**, 910–911.

Lovett, J. V., and Duffield, A. M. (1981). Allelochemicals of *Camelina sativa. J. Appl. Ecol.* **18**, 283–290.

McGinnis, A. J., and Kasting, R. (1959). Nutrition of pale western cutworm, *Agrotis orthogonia* Morr. (Lepidoptera: Noctuidae) I. *Can. J. Zool.* **37**, 259–266.

McGugan, B. M. (1954). Needle-mining habits and larval instars of the spruce budworm. *Can. Entomol.* **86**, 439–454.

McIntyre, J. L. (1980). Defenses triggered by previous invaders: nematodes and insects. *Plant Dis.* **5**, 333–343.

McKey, D. (1979). The distribution of secondary compounds within plants. *In* ""Herbivores: their Interaction with Secondary Plant Metabolites" (G. A. Rosenthal and D. H. Janzen, eds.), pp. 56–133. Academic Press, New York.

Maiorana, V. C. (1979). Nontoxic toxins: the energetics of coevolution. *Biol. J. Linn. Soc.* **11,** 387–396.

Matta, A. (1980). Defenses triggered by previous diverse invaders. *Plant Dis.* **5,** 345–361.

Matthews, R. W., and Matthews, J. R. (1978). "Insect Behaviour." Wiley-Interscience, New York.

Mattson, W. J., and Addy, N. D. (1975). Phytophagous insects as regulation of forest primary productivity. *Science* **190,** 515–522.

Moran, V. C. (1980). Interactions between phytophagous insects and their *Opuntia* hosts. *Ecol. Entomol.* **5,** 153–164.

Nielson, B. O. (1978). Food resource partitioning in the beech leaf-feeding guild. *Ecol. Entomol.* **3,** 193–201.

Nothnagle, P. J., Schultz, J. C., and Lorimer, N. (1982). In preparation.

Oates, J. F., Waterman, P. A., and Choo, G. M. (1980). Food selection by the south Indian leaf-monkey, *Presbytis johnii,* in relation to leaf chemistry. *Oecologia* **45,** 45–56.

Oster, G., and Heinrich, B. (1976). Why do bumblebees major? A mathematical model. *Ecol. Monogr.* **46,** 129–133.

Prestidge, R. A. (1982). Instar variation, adult consumption, oviposition and nitrogen utilization efficiencies of leaf hoppers feeding on different quality food (Auchenorrhyncha: Homoptera). *Ecol. Entomol.* **7,** 91–101.

Price, P. W., Bouton, C. E ., Gross, P., McPheron, B. A., Thompson, J. N., and Weis, A. E. (1980). interactions among three trophic levels: influence of plants on interactions between insect herbivores and natural enemies. *Annu. Rev. Ecol. Syst.* **11,** 41–65.

Rand, A. S. (1967). Predator prey interactions and the evolution of aspect diversity. *Atas Simp. Sobre Biota Amazonica* **5,** 73–83.

Raske, A. G., and Bryant, D. G. (1977). Distribution, survival, and intra-tree movement of late-instar birch casebearer larvae on white birch (Lepidoptera: Coleophoridae). *Can. Entomol.* **109,** 1297–1306.

Rhoades, D. F. (1979). Evolution of plant chemical defense against herbivores. *In* "Herbivores: Their Interaction with Secondary Plant Metabolites" (G. A. Rosenthal and D. H. Janzen, eds.), pp. 4–54. Academic Press, New York.

Rhoades, D. F., and Cates, R. G. (1976). Toward a general theory of plant antiherbivore chemistry. *Recent Adv. Phytochem.* **10,** 168–213.

Roeske, C. N., Seiber, J. N., Brower, L. P., and Moffitt, C. M. (1976). Milkweed cardenolides and their comparative processing by monarch butterflies *(Danaus plexippus L.). Recent Adv. Phytochem.* **10,** 93–166.

Schoonhoven, L. M. (1976). On the variability of chemosensory information. *Symp. Biol. Hung.* **16,** 261–266.

Schoonhoven, L. M. (1977). Feeding behaviour in phytophagous insects: on the complexity of the stimulus situation. *Colloq./Int. C.N.R.S.* **265,** 291–298.

Schroeder, L. A., and Malmer, M. (1980). Dry matter, energy, and nitrogen conversion of Lepidoptera and Hymenoptera larvae fed leaves of black cherry. *Oecologia* **45,** 63–71.

Schultz, J. C. (1981). Adaptive changes in antipredator behavior of a grasshopper during development. *Evolution* **35,** 175–179.

Schultz, J. C. (1983). Impact of variable plant defensive chemistry on susceptibility of insects to natural enemies. *In* Plant Resistance to Insects" (P. Hedin, ed.), pp. 37–55. Am. Chem. Soc., Washington, D.C.

Schultz, J. C., Nothnagle, P. J., and Holmes, R. T. (1978). Dietary preferences and patterns of occurrence of Lepidoptera larvae in a northern hardwoods forest. *J. N. Y. Entomol. Soc.* **46,** 320.

Schultz, J. C., Baldwin, I. T., and Nothnagle, P. J. (1981). Hemoglobin as a binding substrate in the quantitative analysis of plant tannins. *J. Agric. Food. Chem.* **29,** 823–826.

Schultz, J. C., Nothnagle, P. J., and Baldwin, I. T. (1982). Individual and seasonal variation in leaf quality of two northern hardwood tree species. *Am. J. Bot.* (in press).

Schultz, J. C., Holmes, R. T., and Nothnagle, P. J. (1983). In preparation.

Scriber, J. M. (1979). The effects of sequentially sitching food plants upon biomass and nitrogen utilization by polyphgous and stenophagous *Papilio* larvae. *Entomol. Exp. Appl.* **25,** 203–215.

Scriber, J. M., and Slansky, F., Jr. (1981). The nutritional ecology of immature insects. *Annu. Rev. Entomol.* **26,** 183–211.

Sharik, T. L., and Barnes, B. V. (1976). Phenology of shoot growth among diverse populations of yellow birch *(Betula allegheniensis)* and sweet birch *(B. lenta). Can. J. Bot.* **54,** 2122–2129.

Sherman, D. W., and Watt, W. B. (1973). The thermal ecology of some *Colias* butterfly larvae. *J. Comp. Physiol.* **83,** 25–40.

Southwood, T. R. E. (1973). The insect/plant relationship—an evolutionary perspective. *Symp. R. Entomol. Soc. London* **6,** 3–30.

Tanada, Y. (1976). Ecology of insect viruses. *In* "Perspectives in Forest Entomology" (J. F. Anderson and H. K. Kaya, eds.), pp. 265–283. Academic Press, New York.

Tingey, W. M., and Singh, S. R. (1980). Environmental factors influencing the magnitude and expression of resistance. *In* "Breeding Plants Resistant to Insects" (F. G. Maxwell and P. R. Jennings, eds.), pp. 87–113. Wiley-Interscience, New York.

Togashi, K., and Takahashi, F. (1977). Preferential feeding of the last instar larvae of *Dendrolimus spectabilis* Butler (Lepidoptera: Lasiocampidae) on the old needles of *Pinus thunbergii* Parl. in the field. *Jpn. J. Ecol.* **27,** 159–162.

Vinson, S. B. (1975). Biochemical coevolution between parasitoids and their hosts. *In* "Evolutionary Strategies of Parasitic Insects and Mites" (P. W. Price, ed.), pp. 14–48. Plenum, New York.

Vinson, S. B., and Iwantsch, G. F. (1980). Host suitability for insect parasitoids. *Annu. Rev. Entomol.* **25,** 397–419.

White, T. C. R. (1970). Some aspects of the life history, host selection, dispersal, and oviposition of adult *Cardiaspina densitexta* (Homoptera: Psyllidae). *Aust. J. Zool.* **18,** 105–117.

Whitham, T. G. (1978). Habitat selection by pemphigus aphids in response to resource limitation and competition. *Ecology* **59,** 1164–1176.

Whitham, T. G. (1981). Individual trees as heterogeneous environments: adaptation to herbivory or epigenetic noise? *In* "Insect Life History Patterns; Habitat and Geographic Variation" (R. F. Denno and H. Dingle, eds.), pp. 9–27. Springer-Verlag, Berlin/New York.

Wilson, J. (1980). Macroscopic features of wind damage to *Acer pseudoplatanus* L. and its relationship with season, leaf age, and windspeed. *Ann. Bot. (London)* [N.S.] **46,** 303–311.

Yendol, W. G., Hemlen, R. A., and Rosario, S. B. (1975). Feeding behavior of gypsy moth larvae on *Bacillus thuringiensis*-treated foliage. *J. Econ. Entomol.* **68,** 25–27.

Young, A. M. (1972). Adaptive strategies of feeding and predator-avoidance in larvae of neotropical butterfly, *Morphopeleides linipide, J. N. Y. Entomol. Soc.* **80,** 66–69.

Jack C. Schultz
Department of Biological Sciences
Dartmouth College
Hanover, New Hampshire

CHAPTER 4

Leaf Age as a Predictor of Herbivore Distribution and Abundance

MICHAEL J. RAUPP
ROBERT F. DENNO

I. INTRODUCTION

Herbivorous insects are confronted with variation originating at several levels that likely confounds their ability to utilize plant resources to the fullest degree. The spatial arrangement of a host plant and its nonhost associates in a community can have a major impact on a herbivore's ability to colonize and remain on its food (Root, 1973; Tahvanainen and Root, 1972; Cromartie, 1975; Ralph, 1977; Bach, 1980a,b; Kareiva, Chapter 8). Even after having successfully located a patch of potential hosts, a herbivore is likely to find substantial variation among individuals of the same species within the patch (Hanover, 1975; Edmunds and Alstad, 1978, 1981; Denno *et al.*, 1981). To complicate matters further, individual plants are mosiacs of resources that vary temporally and spatially in their suitability as food for herbivores (Whitham, 1981).

Whitham (1981) identified four mechanisms as the sources of within-plant variation in resource quality. First, epigenetic factors such as nutrient or water deficiency affect plant tissues differentially (Kozlowski, 1971; Zimmermann and Brown, 1971). Second, the feeding activities of herbivores may reduce the quality of damaged leaves and their neighbors for subsequent feeding (Haukioja and Niemelä, 1976, 1977, 1979), creating patches of less suitable foliage interspersed with foliage of higher quality (Whitham, 1981). A third source of within-plant variation arises from mutation of somatic tissues (Whitham and Slobodchikoff, 1981; Whitham, 1981). The fourth source, which we shall consider in much more detail, is the variation that results from ontogenetic changes in plants (Whitham, 1981).

The effect aging has on the suitability of plant leaves as a food resource for herbivores has been treated extensively in several reviews (Feeny, 1976; Rhoades and Cates, 1976; McNeill and Southwood, 1978; McKey, 1979; Rhoades, 1979; Mattson, 1980; Scriber and Slansky, 1981; Krischik and Denno, Chapter 14). In general, the concentrations of important nutrients such as nitrogen in leaves decrease with age (McNeill and Southwood, 1978; Mattson, 1980; Scriber and Slansky, 1981), and some classes of defensive compounds increase, whereas other decrease (Feeny, 1976; Rhoades and Cates, 1976; Rhoades, 1979; McKey, 1979). Around these patterns have arisen predictions concerning where and when herbivores will be found on their host plants (Rhoades and Cates, 1976; Cates, 1980).

One objective of this chapter is to examine how well changes in the suitability of leaves predict temporal and spatial patterns of herbivores on their host plants. We first outline how the quality of plant leaves as food for herbivores varies with time and how this variation affects herbivore fitness, as measured, for example, by survivorship, growth, development, and reproduction. With this evidence, we discuss the impact that age-dependent changes in foliage quality have on within-plant distributions of herbivores. Next, using the imported willow leaf beetle (*Plagiodera versicolora* Laich.), we demonstrate that spatial distributions of some herbivores do not coincide with distributions expected by nutritional considerations alone. Interactions with other herbivores, predators, and abiotic factors impose different constraints on herbivores at various times during development. The result of this variation may be divergence among stages in the sites they occupy on their host plants and a failure of herbivore distributions to conform with predicted patterns.

II. TEMPORAL VARIATION IN LEAF QUALITY

A. Diurnal Changes in Leaf Quality

Temporal changes in the content of nutrients, water, and secondary chemicals in leaves result in corresponding changes in the quality of food for herbivores. Durzan (1968b) found diurnal fluctuations in the nitrogen content of white spruce *(Picea glauca)* leaves, buds, and roots. Near the onset of dormancy the total soluable nitrogen of leaves was greatest at sunrise and again in the late afternoon. The moisture content of plant leaves also may vary on an hourly basis during the course of a day. Haukioja *et al.* (1978) demonstrated that the leaves of mountain birch *(Betula pubescens* ssp. *tortuosa)* have a higher moisture content during the morning than in the evening. Durzan (1968c) reported a similar finding for leaves of *Picea glauca.* These fluctuations in nutrient and water content of leaves are likely related to diurnal variation in photosynthetic rates, which in turn are affected by air temperature, relative humidity, light intensity, and soil moisture (Durzan, 1968b,c).

The content of allelochemicals such as alkaloids and terpenes also fluctuates diurnally in the leaves of plants (Robinson, 1974; Seigler and Price, 1976). For example, Fairbairn and Wassel (1964) found that the leaves of the poppy *Papaver somniferum* contain more morphine in the morning than in the afternoon, yet foliar levels of codeine and thebaine exhibit the opposite trend. Robinson (1974) has cited other examples of diurnal variation in the alkaloid content of plants. There is evidence that diurnal variation in the nutrient, moisture, and allelochemical content of leaves affects the suitability of leaves as food for herbivores. Grison (1952) demonstrated that the fecundity of *Leptinotarsa decemlineata* is greater when fed potato leaves excised in the morning compared to leaves picked in the afternoon. Furthermore, Haukioja *et al.* (1978) found that leaves of *Betula pubescens* ssp. *tortuosa* vary diurnally in their suitability as food for the spring-feeding geometrid *Oporinia autumnata.* Larvae of *O. autumnata* develop faster when fed morning- rather than evening-picked leaves. When the experiment was repeated later in the season with a sawfly, *Dineura virididorsata,* no clear differences were found between morning or evening leaves. Haukioja *et al.* (1978) suggested that diurnal fluctuations in the moisture content of birch leaves may play a role in reducing the quality of evening leaves in June and July. However, later in the season diurnal changes in leaf moisture were not as dramatic, and the growth and development of *D. virididorsata* larvae were not influenced by this factor.

B. Seasonal Changes in Leaf Quality

The nutrient, water, and allelochemical profiles of plant leaves also vary on time scales greater than 24 hr. The content of some nutrients (e.g., total nitrogen) generally decline with leaf age (Feeny, 1970; McNeill and Southwood, 1978; Mattson, 1980; Denno et al., 1981; Scriber and Slansky, 1981; Kraft and Denno, 1982). However, certain types of nitrogenous compounds (e.g., soluble nitrogen in the form of amino acids) may have several maxima over the course of the season as materials are transported to expanding leaves or developing buds and away from senescent tissues. These processes may account for high levels of soluble nitrogen in the leaves of plants in the fall as well as in the spring (Durzan, 1968a; Dixon, 1970; Parry, 1974; Beevers, 1976; Carter and Cole, 1977; McNeill and Southwood, 1978).

Often correlated with the changes in nitrogen content of plant leaves are changes in their moisture content. Seasonal declines in the moisture content of plant leaves are believed by many to reduce the suitability of leaves as food for defoliators (Feeny, 1970; Mattson, 1980; Scriber and Slansky, 1981; Kraft and Denno, 1982). Qualitative and quantitative differences in defensive compounds found in young versus old leaves were identified by two research groups investigating plant and herbivore interactions. Feeny (1975, 1976), Rhoades and Cates (1976), and Rhoades (1979) separated plants and their tissues into two general categories based on their relative probabilities of being discovered by herbivores. Apparent plants and tissues are those likely to be discovered by herbivores, owing to their abundance and/or persistence. The other end of the spectrum is represented by unapparent plants and tissues, those that escape herbivores because they are rare and/or ephemeral. These authors suggested that apparent plants or tissues (e.g., mature leaves) are protected by allelochemicals that are present in quantitive amounts and that reduce the digestibility of foliage. Scriber and Slansky (1981) included in this category compounds such as silica, resins, tannins, oils, waxes, lignin, and fibers and suggested that concentrations of these compounds generally increase as leaves age. Unapparent tissues appear to be protected by allelochemicals that are active in low concentrations and deter feeding by generalist herbivores (Feeny, 1975, 1976; Rhoades and Cates, 1976; Rhoades, 1979; Scriber and Slansky, 1981, and references therein). Although these patterns appear to be true for a great variety of plants (Feeny, 1975; Futuyma, 1976; Rhoades and Cates, 1976; McKey, 1979; Rhoades, 1979), there are exceptions. For example, Rhoades and Cates (1976) reported that the young leaves of the desert shrubs *Larrea tridentata* and *L. cuneifolia* contain greater concentrations of resins that act in a quantitative way to reduce leaf digestibility. However, the young leaves of *Larrea* actually are a more apparent resource than mature leaves because they are maintained during drought (when mature leaves are shed) and are produced during periods of growth following rain. Given these phenological details it is clear that young leaves are defended like other apparent tissues by containing higher levels of digestibility-reducing compounds.

How does the suitability of leaves as food for defoliators change as leaves age? Most investigations of this question have included feeding herbivores leaves of different ages and measuring changes in one or more traits related to the survivorship, growth, or reproduction of cohorts. We have compiled the results of some of the studies in Table I. Variation in leaf age has been evaluated in two ways. Some researchers collected leaves for bioassays early in the growing season (young leaves) and later in the season (old leaves; e.g., Feeny, 1970; Hough and Pimentel, 1978; Mitter *et al.*, 1979; Kraft and Denno, 1982). For plants that produce leaves in a single synchronous flush (e.g., oaks and maples) this technique is justified. However, other herbaceous plants and some woody ones produce leaves for prolonged periods of time (Phillips, 1976; Kitayama *et al.*, 1979; Raupp, 1982), and comparisons between young and old leaves can be made on leaves excised on the same date.

The first parameter summarized in Table I is the survivorship of immature stages. Almost without exception larvae survive better when reared on young leaves. The three extraordinary cases involve the noctuids *Chaetaglaea sericae* and *Metaxaglaea viatica* and the diprionid sawfly *Neodiprion swainei*. The greater mortality of noctuids results because larvae are unable to locate small new leaves in large sleeve cages (Schweitzer, 1979), and the greater mortality of sawfly larvae fed young leaves results from higher concentrations of a deterrent chemical in young leaves of jack pine *(Pinus banksiana;* Ikeda *et al.*, 1977a,b).

The second parameter outlined in Table I is the developmental period of immature stages. The data clearly indicate that the developmental periods for herbivores are generally shorter when they eat young leaves. The exceptions to this pattern are larvae of *Neodiprion swainei* fed young jack pine needles. Higher levels of resin acids in young needles may slow the development of larvae (Ikeda *et al.*, 1977a,b). The advantages of rapid growth and development appear numerous. Feeny (1976) and Price *et al.* (1980) suggested that prolonged development may result in greater juvenile mortality because vulnerable stages are exposed to predators for longer periods of time. For example, we found first-instar larvae

TABLE I

Effects of Leaf Age on the Fitness of Juvenile and Adult Herbivores

		Juvenile traits			Adult traits		
Herbivore	Host	Survivorship[a]	Developmental period[b]	Size[a]	Survivorship[a]	Fecundity[a]	Reference
Lepidoptera							
Tortricidae							
Choristoneura fumiferana	Abies balsamea					X	Greenbank (1956)
Geometridae							
Alsophila pometaria	Acer rubrum		X	X			Mitter et al. (1979)
Ennomos subsignarius	Carya glabra	X	X			X	Drooz (1970)
Ennomos subsignarius	Quercus rubra	X	X			X	Drooz (1970)
Operophtera brumata	Quercus robur			X			Feeny (1970)
Lymantriidae							
Lymantria dispar	Quercus alba	X	X	X		X	Hough and Pimentel (1978)
Lymantria dispar	Quercus rubra	X	X				Hough and Pimentel (1978)
Lymantria dispar	Fagus grandifolia	X	X				Hough and Pimentel (1978)
Lymantria dispar	Acer saccharum	X	X				Hough and Pimentel (1978)
Lymantria dispar	Tsuga canadensis	X					Hough and Pimentel (1978)
Orgyia pseudotsugata	Abies concolor			X			Cates (1980)

Insect	Host plant				Reference
Arctiidae					
Hyphantria cunea	*Malus pumila*	X	X	X	Morris (1967)
Hyphantria cunea	*Morus rubra*		—	0	Cates (1980)
Noctuidae					
Spodoptera eridania	*Lotus corniculatus*		X		Scriber (1978)
Xylena curvimacula	*Prunus serotina*	X	0		Schweitzer (1979)
Lithophane hemina	*Betula lenta*	0	X		Schweitzer (1979)
Lithophane hemina	*Quercus coccinea*	X	X		Schweitzer (1979)
Lithophane grotei	*Acer rubrum*	X	X		Schweitzer (1979)
Lithophane grotei	*Prunus serotina*	X	X		Schweitzer (1979)
Lithophane innominata	*Salix* sp.	X	X		Schweitzer (1979)
Pyreferra citrombra	*Hamamelis virginiana*	X	X		Schweitzer (1979)
Eupsilia sidus	*Quercus palustris*	X			Schweitzer (1979)
Eupsilia sp.	*Quercus coccinea*	X			Schweitzer (1979)
Eupsilia morrisoni	*Quercus velutina*	X	X		Schweitzer (1979)

(Continued)

TABLE I (*Continued*)

Herbivore	Host	Juvenile traits			Adult traits		Reference
		Survivorship[a]	Developmental period[b]	Size[a]	Survivorship[a]	Fecundity[a]	
Eupsilia devia	Aster cordifolia	0		X			Schweitzer (1979)
Metaxaglaea semitaria	Vaccinium corymbosum	X					Schweitzer (1979)
Metaxaglaea semitaria	Vaccinium atrococcum	X					Schweitzer (1979)
Metaxaglaea viatica	Quercus palustris	X					Schweitzer (1979)
Metaxaglaea viatica	Pyrus ×purpurea	−X0		X			Schweitzer (1979)
Metaxaglaea viatica	Pyrus sp.	X					Schweitzer (1979)
Chaetaglaea tremula	Vaccinium vacillans	X					Schweitzer (1979)
Chaetaglaea sericea	Vaccinium corymbosum			0			Schweitzer (1979)
Chaetaglaea sericea	Quercus coccinea	−		X			Schweitzer (1979)
Eucirroedia pampina	Acer rubrum	X		−			Schweitzer (1979)
Eucirroedia pampina	Quercus palustris	X					Schweitzer (1979)
Jodia rufago	Quercus palustris	X					Schweitzer (1979)

98

					Reference
Coleptera					
Coccinellidae					
Epilachna varivestis	Glycine max	-X			Kitayama et al. (1979)
Chrysomelidae					
Haltica lythri	Epilobium hirsutum	X			Phillips (1976)
Leptinotarsa decemlineata	Solanum tuberosum	X			Grison (1952)
Leptinotarsa decemlineata	Solanum dulcamara	X			de Wilde et al. (1969)
Leptinotarsa decemlineata	Solanum tuberosum		X	0	Cibula et al. (1967)
Leptinotarsa decemlineata	Lycopersicon esculentum		X	X	Cibula et al. (1967)
Labidomera clivicollis	Asclepias sp.		0	0	Eickwort (1977)
Plagiodera versicolora	Salix spp.	X	X	X	Raupp (1982)
Trirhabda bacharidis	Baccharis halimifolia		X	X	Kraft and Denno (1982)
Pyrrhalta luteola	Ulmus sp.		X	X	Wene (1968)
Hymenoptera					
Diprionidae					
Neodiprion swainei	Pinus banksiana	0	-	-	All and Benjamin (1975)

[a] X, Greater survivorship, size, or fecundity for herbivores fed young rather than old leaves; 0, no difference between treatments; –, greater survivorship, size, or fecundity for herbivores fed old rather than young leaves.

[b] X, Shorter period of development for herbivores fed young rather than young leaves; 0, no difference between treatments; –, longer period of development for herbivores fed young rather than old leaves.

of the leaf beetle *Plagiodera versicolora* to be much more vulnerable to attack by coccinellid larvae than were third instars. First-instar coccinellid larvae had little trouble subduing first-instar *P. versicolora*, but they were generally unable to capture the larger third instars. Blau (1981) suggested that when the rates of larval mortality exceed those of the pupal or adult stages selection will act to constrict the larval period. Cole (1954), Lewontin (1965), and MacArthur and Wilson (1967) reached a similar conclusion for species colonizing fluctuating environments, where resources may be superabundant for periods of time. This may be especially important for multivoltine species inhabiting seasonal environments. A reduction in the age to first reproduction is also predicted in stable environments when juvenile mortality varies (Murphy, 1968; Stearns, 1976; Tallamy and Denno, 1981) and in fluctuating environments when adult mortality varies (Schaffer, 1974; Stearns, 1976; Tallamy and Denno, 1981).

The third parameter summarized in Table I is the size of immature stages, expressed as either larval or pupal weight or length. With three exceptions larvae raised on young leaves either grew to a larger size or showed no size difference compared to larvae raised on older leaves (Table I). The first exception, *Hyphantria cunea*, attained greater size when reared on old leaves of *Morus rubra*, probably for the same reason that survivorship was greater on old leaves; old leaves contain less noxious latex than young leaves (Cates, 1980). The second case involved larvae of the geometrid *Eucirroedia pampina* raised on old leaves of red maple *(Acer rubrum)*. Schweitzer (1979) suggested that *E. pampina* attained greater weight because the tree used for rearing produced a second flush of new leaves late in the season, when mature leaves were usually present. The larvae of *Neodiprion swainei* fed young pine needles were smaller than those fed mature needles, presumably for the same reasons that survivorship and growth were poorer on young needles (All and Benjamin, 1975; Ikeda *et al.*, 1977a,b). The contributions of large body size to the fitness of a herbivore may be numerous. Several studies have demonstrated good correlations between body size and fecundity in Lepidoptera (Campbell, 1962; Drooz, 1965; Hough and Pimentel, 1978). Furthermore, Blau (1981) noted that oviposition rate and total fecundity may also be related to adult body size.

In addition to the direct correlation between body size and fecundity, larger individuals may have greater fitness for other reasons. Large body size may enhance an individual's ability to escape or repel predators (Schoener and Janzen, 1968; Calow, 1977). For example, third-instar *Plagiodera versicolora* larvae are much less susceptible than first instars to small coccinellid predators (Raupp, 1982).

Table II
Fitness Traits of *Plagiodera versicolora* Adults Fed Young or
Old Willow Leaves for 20 days

	Fitness trait		
Treatment	Average age to first reproduction[a]	Average clutch size[b]	Average number of clutches[a]
Young	8.4	12.2	8.9
Old	16.6	9.6	1.8

[a]Treatments differed significantly; $P < 0.001$ (Mann–Whitney test).
[b]Treatments differed significantly; $P < 0.05$ (Mann–Whitney test).

Other advantages to large body size include the ability to better withstand environmental rigors such as drought and food stress (Wasserman and Mitter, 1978; Blau, 1981) and increased ability to defend resources from competitors (Blau, 1981). Furthermore, large body size may enhance colonizing ability (Dingle *et al.*, 1980; Blau, 1981) and allow more effective thermoregulation in some environments (Blau, 1981).

Few studies have examined the effect of leaf age on the survivorship of adult insects. In some insects, such as the gypsy moth *(Lymantria dispar)*, the adult stage may be short-lived and reproduction confined to a single bout. Others, such as *Plagiodera versicolora*, may be reproductively active for several months, and the effects of eating mature foliage can have a major impact on survivorship and fecundity. For example, we fed *P. versicolora* adults young and old willow leaves and found the intrinsic rate of increase for the cohort on young leaves to be greater than that of adults fed old ones by a factor of 10, as a result of greater survivorship and fecundity. The evidence presented in Table I indicates that, for herbivores with extended reproduction, young plant leaves are a better resource than old ones.

In all studies involving Lepidoptera, larvae reared on young leaves have had greater fecundity as adults. The beetles surveyed also show a strong trend for greater fecundity on young versus old leaves. In the case of *Plagiodera versicolora* this resulted because adults reproduced earlier and laid larger clutches more frequently (see Table II). Young leaves were not the best resource for adults of the Mexican bean beetle *(Epilachna varivestis)*, because Kitayama *et al.* (1979) found that adults laid more eggs when fed mature versus young or senescent soybean leaves. The greater fecundity resulted primarily from an increased egg-mass production rate rather than an increase in the number of eggs contained in each mass.

III. TEMPORAL AND SPATIAL PATTERNS OF HERBIVORY

Based on the evidence presented thus far it seems reasonable that herbivores would respond in predictable ways to temporal changes in the
quality of their host plants as food. For example, Haukioja *et al.* (1978)
suggested that daily fluctuations in the suitability of leaves could impose
a temporal pattern on herbivore feeding activity. Although Haukioja *et
al.* (1978) failed to observe such a pattern in *Oporinia autumnata*, diurnal
patterns of feeding activity are well documented in other species of
Lepidoptera (Young, 1972; Heinrich, 1979). For example, Young (1972)
found that larvae of the butterfly *Morpho peleides limpida* feed primarily
in the morning and evening and attributed this pattern to the effects of
predation and perhaps temperature. However, diurnal fluctuations in
leaf quality could also contribute to this pattern. The idea that diurnal
variation in leaf quality imposes constraints on herbivore feeding deserves more attention.

Because of the changes in nutrients, moisture, allelochemicals, and
structural defenses in leaves as they age and the impact of leaf age on
herbivore fitness, we would expect some tissues to be preferred over
others and the distribution of herbivores in time and space to reflect this
preference. Rhoades and Cates (1976) predicted that the feeding behavior
of herbivores would vary in a predictable way based on their degree of
specialization. Given equal tissue abundance, they suggested that specialists, those herbivores largely adapted to qualitative defenses present
in their host plant, should feed preferentially on young host leaves that
contain higher levels of nutrients and water and lower levels of digestibility-reducing compounds. In contrast, generalists lacking the physiology to contend with the toxic allelochemicals that are present in young
leaves may prefer the older leaves of their host plant (Rhoades and
Cates, 1976; Cates, 1980).

This hypothesis was first rigorously tested by Rhoades and Cates
(1976), who examined tissue preference of insects feeding on desert
shrubs. They found that when feeding distributions were adjusted for
the relative abundance of young and old leaves several species of Lepidoptera and Coleoptera conformed to the prediction. A more recent
and extensive study has provided further support for this hypothesis
(Cates, 1980).

Just as herbivores discriminate between leaves in space, they may also
discriminate between tissues in time. McNeill and Southwood (1978)
described several cases in which the temporal abundance of sucking

insects is closely linked to seasonal changes in the nutritional profile of their host. Rockwood (1974) defoliated calabash trees *(Crescentia alata)* at a time when only mature leaves were usually present and found that adults of the flea beetle *Oedionychus* colonized and exploited the new leaves of defoliated trees but not the leaves of unaltered trees.

In some cases the consequences of asynchrony with host phenology are so severe that selection has acted to closely link the life cycle of herbivores with key phenological events of their hosts. Both Feeny (1970) and Mitter *et al.* (1979) found that the success of winter moth and cankerworm larvae depends largely upon how closely egg hatch coincides with the production of new leaves. Hatching too early may result in larvae not finding food, whereas hatching too late may force larvae to contend with older, less suitable leaves (Feeny, 1976). Consequently, Feeny (1970) and Mitter *et al.* (1979) suggested that strong selection has resulted in the synchrony of egg hatch with bud break.

Considering plants that produce leaves in a single well-synchronized flush, Rhoades and Cate's (1976) hypothesis suggests that the assemblage of herbivores feeding on plants may vary temporally, with specialists dominating the fauna near the time of leaf production and generalists becoming more common as leaves age. Although a rigorous test of this hypothesis remains to be performed, Cates (1980) has noted that some polyphagous feeders exploit the young leaves of their hosts (Feeny, 1970; Mitter *et al.*, 1979). Cates (1980) has suggested that this may result because the young leaves of some plants (e.g., oaks) lack toxic defenses.

Having outlined how the nutritional status of plants can vary in time and how this may affect spatial and temporal patterns of herbivores, we shall now discuss how factors indirectly related or unrelated to plant nutrition but directly related to leaf age can affect the spatial distribution of insects on their host. This type of tissue specialization is analogous to the "ecological monophagy" referred to by Gilbert (1979) to describe the narrowing of a herbivore's host range, which results when one or more ecological factors override or act in concert with nutritional ones. Examples of this type of specialization are well known for many species of Lepidoptera and may depend on factors such as the predictability and relative abundance of host plants in a habitat (Singer, 1971; Gilbert and Singer, 1975; Wiklund, 1974b, 1975; Gilbert, 1979). Other factors affecting the suitability of plants and their parts for herbivores include the foraging behavior of predators, interactions with other herbivores, and the abiotic environment (McClure, 1974; Hassel and Southwood, 1978; Price *et al.*, 1980; Denno *et al.*, 1981).

IV. A Case Study of Within-Plant Variation and Its Effect on Herbivore Distribution

The herbivore–plant system we report on involves the imported willow leaf beetle (*Plagiodera versicolora*) and one of its host plants, the weeping willow (*Salix babylonica*). This system demonstrates that spatial distributions of herbivores on the host may not be solely or even primarily determined by nutritional and defensive constraints. Furthermore, we propose that the determinants of within-plant distributions of herbivores vary with the developmental stage utilizing the plant. Factors determining adult distributions are not necessarily the same ones affecting the distribution of larvae, pupae, or eggs.

A. Biology of the Imported Willow Leaf Beetle

Plagiodera versicolora is a specialist that feeds on plants of the genera *Salix* and *Populus* (Salicaceae; Herrick, 1935; Johnson and Lyon, 1976; Wilcox, 1979). The life history of this beetle is similar to many other species in the Chrysomelinae. Adults overwinter beneath loose bark and litter near willow trees. In Maryland, adults colonize willows in April within one month of bud break. Eggs are laid in clusters on willow leaves, where both larvae and adults feed and larvae often pupate. This species is multivoltive over much of its geographic range (Johnson and Lyon, 1976; Raupp, 1982).

B. Growth of Weeping Willow

Like other species of *Salix*, *S. babylonica* produces leaves on many shoots for much of the growing season. New leaves may be produced every 2–3 days and be retained on a shoot for more than 2 months (M. J. Raupp, unpublished data). Rapid rates of leaf production coupled with long retention times and a prolonged period of dominance by apical meristems result in shoots that bear numerous leaves arranged in a linear sequence, with the youngest leaves at the apex and the oldest ones at the base. This pattern of growth provides a spatial gradient of different-aged leaves, where spatial distributions of herbivores can be observed and compared.

C. Distribution of Life Stages of the Imported Willow Leaf Beetle

The spatial distribution of insects on plants reflects feeding and/or oviposition decisions made at one or several times during development. Mitchell (1981) has pointed out that in highly mobile insects such as Orthoptera host choice can be exercised at each feeding bout. For less mobile insects such as the larvae of holometabolous insects and hemimetabolous insects like aphids and scale insects, the choice of food is often determined by females during oviposition or brood production (Mitchell, 1981).

By observing the spatial distribution of *Plagiodera versicolora* we determined whether adults and larvae of this specialized insect prefer the young leaves of their host, as predicted by Rhoades and Cates (1976) and Cates (1980). Next, as a corollary to this hypothesis we tested whether young leaves serve as perferred oviposition sites for *P. versicolora*. This idea was explicitly stated by Rockwood (1974) and is supported by several authors, who have suggested that butterflies preferentially oviposit on plants where larval growth and development is favored (Wiklund, 1974a; Chew, 1975, 1977; Feeny, 1975; Gilbert and Singer, 1975; Rausher, 1978).

On several dates during the 1979, 1980, and 1981 growing seasons the positions of beetle eggs, larvae, pupae, and adults were observed on several willow trees. On each date several hundred branchlets were examined around entire trees and at various heights (1–10 m) in the canopies. The locations of individuals in each developmental stage (egg, larva, pupa, adult) were observed and expressed in terms of leaf age. Leaf age was defined as the position of a leaf relative to the apical meristem of the shoot. The first expanded leaf at the apex of a branchlet was designated leaf 1 and each leaf proximal from the apex received a consecutively greater number.

Observations made over 3 yr were grouped into three time periods (April, June, and August). Within each time period, the position of eggs, first- and third-instar larvae, pupae, and adults were compared with an analysis of variance. Means for each stage were separated with a Student–Newman–Keuls multiple-comparison test. The results of this survey (Fig. 1) reveal an interesting general pattern. On all dates adults occurred on younger leaves, but the eggs, larvae, and pupae occurred on older leaves. These results indicate that adults utilized different-aged leaves for feeding than they did for oviposition. Eggs occurred consistently near the middle of the branchlets rather than near apexes where adults fed.

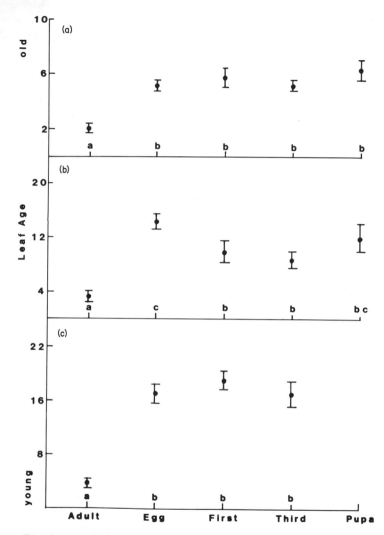

Fig. 1. Distribution of adults, eggs, first- and third-instar larvae, and pupae of *Plagiodera versicolora* among different-aged willow leaves during three time periods. Means (± 1 SE) are given. Average number of leaves present on actively growing branchlets: (a) April, 9.1; (b) June, 18.4; (c) August, 30.7. During each time period, distributions of all stages were compared with an analysis of variance and found to differ significantly (F tests, P < 0.01). A Student–Newman–Keuls test separated means that differ significantly (P < 0.05). On each date means sharing a common letter did not differ significantly.

To determine why adult beetles preferred young host leaves the following experiment was performed. In June 1980, 28 pairs of adults (consisting of one male and one female) were obtained from a laboratory colony and assigned to one of two treatments within 24 hr of eclosion. Half were fed young leaves (leaves from positions 1–5 on active branchlets), and the remainder received old leaves (leaves 10–15). The results of this experiment (Table II) indicate that young willow leaves are a better resource for adults of *Plagiodera versicolora*. Females fed young leaves laid eggs significantly sooner than those fed old ones. Furthermore, the clutch size and number of clutches per 20 days were greater when females ate young leaves. Reproductive data and spatial distributions of adults conform well with other studies of leaf age on beetle fecundity (Phillips, 1976) and the pattern predicted by Rhoades and Cates (1976) and Cates (1980). However, eggs were not deposited and larvae did not feed on young leaves, as had been expected.

To help resolve this contradiction we first attempted to evaluate the quality of different-aged leaves as food for the juvenile stages of *Plagiodera versicolora*. Leaf quality was evaluated twice during the growing season. During June 1979 a cohort of 200 first-instar larvae less than 24 hr old was divided into two groups. Half were raised on young leaves (leaves 1–5), and the remainder received older leaves (leaves 8–13). The experiment was repeated in August 1980. At this time leaves were categorized as young (leaves 1–5), medium (leaves 15–20), or old (leaves 30–35). Cohorts of 70 larvae were used in each treatment.

Larvae raised on different-aged leaves responded in a manner similar to that of the adults (Fig. 2). During both June and August leaf age affected developmental period (days to adult) and adult weight attained by larvae. Larvae reared on older leaves took longer to develop and produce smaller adults. In June, mortality did not differ between larvae raised on young and old leaves. However, in August, significant differences in mortality occurred, with larvae reared on old leaves showing the greatest mortality.

Results of our bioassays with larvae agree with those discussed previously. However, from these findings we would have expected eggs and larvae to occur on young host leaves instead of those in intermediate age, especially in light of the fact that young willow leaves, thoughout the growing season, are generally higher in nitrogen and water content and less tough than old leaves (Raupp, 1982). To resolve this apparent anomaly, we investigated the possibility that factors other than nutritional ones vary among leaves of different age and that this variation contributes to the observed distribution of *Plagiodera versicolora* on its host.

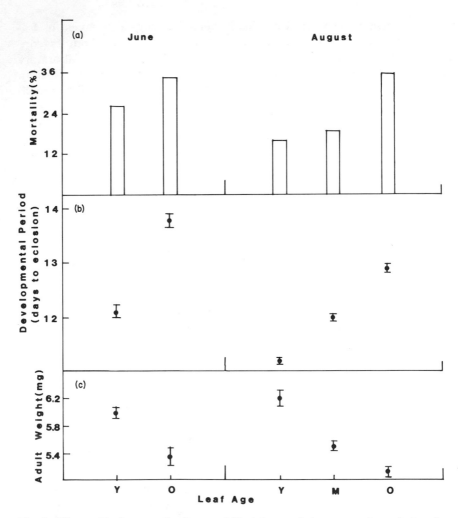

Fig. 2. Effects of leaf age on the fitness of *Plagiodera versicolora* at two times during the season. (a) Comparison of the mortality of larvae fed young (Y) and old (O) willow leaves in June, and young, medium (M), and old leaves in August. In June, mortality did not differ for larvae fed young and old leaves (X^2, $P < 0.30$). However, in August, mortality differed among treatments (X^2, $P < 0.001$). (b) Comparison of the developmental period of larvae fed different aged leaves. Means (± 1 SE) are given. At both times of the year larvae fed young leaves required less time to develop than those fed old leaves (June, t test, $P < 0.001$; August, F test, $P < 0.001$). (c) Comparison of the weight of adults produced by larvae fed different-aged leaves. At both times of the year larvae fed young leaves produced larger adults than larvae fed old ones (June, t test, $P < 0.005$; August, F test, $P < 0.001$).

D. Modifying Effects of Plant Growth

The distribution of sessile stages such as eggs or small larvae of insects is the result of two processes. First, the location of egg masses reflects decisions made by females during oviposition. The location of masses may then be modified by growth characteristics of the host plant. Raupp (1982) found that willows produce young leaves for much of the growing season. For each young leaf added at the apex of a growing branchlet the relative position of each sessile stage will increase by 1. Therefore, decisions made by ovipositing females are potentially obscured by plant growth characteristics.

To help elucidate the degree to which plant growth modifies the distribution of immobile stages of *Plagiodera versicolora*, we first measured the ovipositional behavior of 20 females under laboratory conditions. Daily observations were made on the positions of all egg masses and their frequency among age classes of leaves. This distribution was compared with the one of egg masses observed in the field. A χ^2 analysis failed to detect differences between the two distributions ($\chi^2_9 = 11.329$, $P < 0.30$). Therefore, we conclude that the location of *P. versicolora* eggs was little affected by the growth characteristics of the plant and likely reflects ovipositional decisions made by females.

This may not be the case for all herbivores utilizing willow. If eggs require a long time to develop, hatchlings may find themselves on leaves substantially older than those on which females oviposited. For example, during the last week of April 1981, a female poplar tent maker [*Ichthyura inclusa* (Lepidoptera: Notodontidae)] deposited 78 and 50 eggs on the third and fourth leaves of a willow branchlet bearing 7 leaves. By the time eggs hatched, 1 month later, the branchlet bore 8 more leaves, and larvae hatched and fed on the eleventh and twelfth leaf of 15.

In summary, it appears that plant growth characteristics can modify spatial distributions of insects on their hosts. This will be especially true when disparities between plant growth rates and the development of sessile stages are great as was the case with eggs of *Ichthyura inclusa*. When development is relatively rapid (as it is for the eggs of *Plagiodera versicolora*), ovipositional choices of females determine more closely the food resource encountered by first-instar larvae.

E. Herbivory, Abscission, and Leaf Suitability

Leaves disappear from plants in bits and pieces, as a result of attack by herbivores and pathogens, and as entire units, by the process of abscission brought on by these agents or by aging. When herbivory, abscission, or both processes vary among leaves in predictable ways, the suitability of leaves for herbivore oviposition and development will also vary. For example, Raupp and Denno (1980) reported that several species of willow defoliators occurred on and fed on young willow leaves. The herbivores included Lepidoptera belonging to the families Noctuidae, Notodontidae, and Tortricidae, Coleoptera in the Chrysomelidae and Scarabeidae, and a tenthredinid sawfly. Furthermore, older age classes of leaves were abscissed more frequently than young ones. The developmental stage most susceptible to interference from defoliators or displacement due to abscission is the egg, because of its immobility. We proposed that if leaf disappearance exerts a selective force on oviposition behavior, then the distribution of eggs should be negatively related to the likelihood that a leaf will lose area through defoliation or disappear due to abscission.

In May 1980 we observed leaf-area loss in a cohort of leaves found on 34 branchlets. We ranked leaf age classes by the likelihood that they would lose substantial amounts of tissue due to defoliators or abscission. Age classes losing the greatest area received the highest rank. During the same time interval we recorded the location of egg masses on a large sample of branchlets ($n > 100$) and ranked leaf age classes according to the frequency with which they bore eggs. We then correlated the disappearance rank for each age class of leaves with the egg-occurrence rank and found a significant negative relationship (Fig. 3). This relationship indicated that females deposited eggs on the leaves least likely to lose leaf area through the combined activities of other defoliators and leaf abscission.

Two apparently anomalous points (leaves 1 and 4) were found in this relationship (Fig. 3). Leaves at position 1 bore far fewer egg masses than might be expected from the overall relationship. When the fate of leaf 1 is considered, the reason for the lack of eggs seems clear. Leaf 1 soon enters age classes 2, 3, and 4, which are likely to be fed upon by defoliators. Females ovipositing on leaf 1 would force their progeny to contend with the other herbivores that feed on these slightly older leaves.

The opposite extreme was observed in leaf 4, where many more eggs than expected were found. Again, analysis of the fate of leaf 4 provides a probable explanation. Leaf 4, because it has passed through the age classes most susceptible to defoliation, is likely to be a safe site for eggs to develop with little risk of disruption by herbivores or disappearance due to abscission.

In summary, this study provides evidence that the suitability of leaves for some herbivore stages may be affected by factors indirectly related

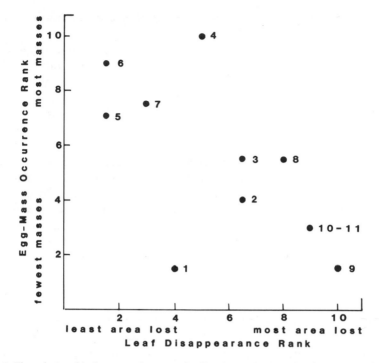

Fig. 3. The relationship between the area of willow leaves lost by abscission and defoliation and the occurrence of *Plagiodera versicolora* egg masses. Leaves with the least area lost received the lowest rank, and those leaves losing the most area received the highest rank. Leaves bearing the most egg masses received the highest rank, and those with the fewest eggs were ranked lowest. Numbers accompanying points indicate leaf-position classes. A Spearman rank correlation indicated a significant negative relationship between the leaf area lost and the number of egg masses deposited ($r_s = 0.664$, $P < 0.025$).

to their ability to support the growth and development of larvae. In this case differential herbivory and abscission appear to make both young and old leaves less suitable oviposition sites for *Plagiodera versicolora*.

Other studies have demonstrated that interactions with conspecifics or individuals of different species operating at the same trophic level can alter spatial distributions of insects on their hosts. Williams and Gilbert (1981) demonstrated that ovipositing *Heliconius* butterflies avoided leaves already having butterfly eggs, thereby reducing the probability for larval cannibalism. McClure (1974; Chapter 5) studied interactions between two species of scale insects and found that *Fiorina externa* displaced *Tsugaspidiotus tsugae* from the most nutritious feeding sites. Furthermore, Whitham (1979, 1980) reported that competition among female gall aphids determined their distribution within and among leaves on a single poplar tree.

Price (1975) suggested that one outcome of holometabolism is a reduction of competitive interactions between juvenile and adult stages. In many holometabolous orders (e.g., herbivorous Lepidoptera, Hymenoptera, and some Coleoptera) adult resources are vastly different than those of immature stages. However, in other herbivorous beetles (e.g., some epilachnine coccinellids and many chrysomelids) adults and juveniles may share the same resource in time and space. Although females of *Plagiodera versicolora* may be unable to dictate the feeding sites of other herbivores on willow, they can determine to a large extent where their own larvae feed. Although we lack specific data documenting competition between the adults and larvae of *P. versicolora*, it is clear that females select older leaves for oviposition, thereby reducing the herbivore load on young leaves. This pattern is consistent with Price's (1975) contention that niche divergence may reduce competition in holometabolous insects.

F. Predator Search and Leaf Suitability

To this point we have considered the impact that host plants and other herbivores can have on within-plant distributions of defoliators. Now we shall discuss the possibility that the activities of predators vary in space and can also affect the suitablility of leaves for some stages of *Plagiodera versicolora*. Weseloh (1974) and Price *et al.* (1980) have suggested that the rate at which herbivore are attacked may depend upon the plant part they occupy. Attack rates may be lower when herbivores occupy plant parts that are less freqently searched, inaccessible, or refractory to the searching movements of enemies (Price *et al.*, 1980).

Hassell (1978), after examining several studies of parasitoid and predator searching behavior, concluded that over at least part of the range of host densities enemies spend more time searching where prey are abundant. In patches where prey are abundant, predators increase their searching activity and simultaneously increase their residence time in the patch (Hassel, 1978). For example, Banks (1957) found that larvae of the coccinellid beetle *Adalia bipunctata* greatly increase their turning movements upon encountering aphids, thereby facilitating further encounters with prey.

As reported previously, the larvae of many willow-feeding Lepidoptera and Hymenoptera prefer to feed on the young leaves. Furthermore, during 1981 we surveyed the location of 65 individual aphids and found that most occupied the third leaf from the tip on branchlets (branchlets averaged 16 leaves). These findings agree with those of Horsfield (1977) and Denno *et al.* (1980), who demonstrated preferences in sucking insects for the terminal, young leaves of their host plants. At the same time that aphids were present, the eggs and larvae of *Plagiodera versicolora* and coccinellid and chrysopid predators were common. If these predators search young terminal leaves more frequently or longer, then young leaves should be less suitable for *P. versicolora* eggs and larvae. Hence, selection should favor females that oviposit on slightly older leaves.

The location of *Plagiodera versicolora* eggs and larvae on old leaves agrees with the egg and larval distribution of other herbivores. Young (1972) and Young and Moffett (1979) found females of *Morpho peleides limpida* and *Mechanitis isthmia* ovipositing and larvae feeding on older leaves of *Machaerium* and *Solanum*, respectively. Furthermore, Young (1972) suggested that in *Morpho peleides limpida* the choice of larval resting cites and timing of feeding bouts may be adjusted to patterns of predator activity.

The notion that the searching behavior of predators and parasitoids can modify spatial distributions of insects has been proposed by several authors (Zwölfer, 1975; Lawton, 1978; Price *et al.*, 1980). Both Zwölfer (1975) and Price *et al.* (1980) have suggested that herbivorous insects may compete for predator-free sites, where activities such as feeding, pupation, and oviposition occur with less risk. The outcome of this interaction may be niche separation. Although we have not tested this idea explicitly, the observed distributions of *Plagiodera versicolora* eggs and larvae relative to those of adults and other willow herbivores supports this contention.

Factors other than prey density may affect the searching behavior of predators and, concomitantly, make some leaves less suitable for prey than others. As they feed, herbivores leave telltale evidence of their presence. For example, Heinrich (1979) suggested that vertebrate predators used visual cues, in this case feeding damage, to help them locate their insect prey on plant leaves. In addition to visual cues like leaf damage, herbivores often leave chemical cues that are used by enemies to locate prey. These cues include chemicals left at that time of oviposition, chemicals secreted from mandibular and labial glands during feeding, plant substances released as a result of feeding damage, and chemicals present in the feces of prey (Arthur, 1981; Greany and Hagen, 1981; Vinson, 1981; Weseloh, 1981).

Of particular interest in understanding the distribution of *Plagiodera versicolora* eggs is the observation that adult beetles defecate on young leaves as they feed. This effect is so pronounced that adult *P. versiocolora*

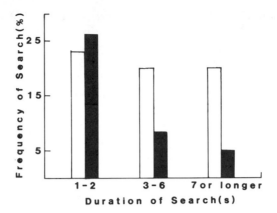

Fig. 4. The searching behavior of *Hippodamia convergens* adults on willow leaves with and without *Plagiodera versicolora* feces. Searches were divided into three categories, those lasting 1–2, 3–6, and 7 or more sec. The number of searches in each category differed significantly between leaves with (□) and without (■) feces (X^2, $P < 0.01$). Generally, leaves with feces were searched for longer periods of time.

feeding sites can be identified from those of other herbivores by the presence of feces alone. In 1981 we examined the searching behavior of adults of the generalist coccinellid *Hippodamia convergens* on willow leaves with and without adult feces. We found that leaves with beetle feces were searched more frequently and for longer periods of time than leaves of equal size lacking fecal deposits (Fig. 4). Because young leaves are more likely to bear adult feces and, consequently, may be more thoroughly searched by predators, they may be less suitable sites for oviposition. Hence, females may avoid areas where predator search is concentrated and lay eggs on older leaves.

G. Abiotic Factors and Leaf Suitability

In addition to the factors previously discussed, features of the physical environment vary within plants and may make some leaves less suitable than others for herbivores. Dixon (1970) found that, during the summer, temperatures in the upper canopy of sycamore trees (*Platanus*) approach the lethal level for the sycamore aphid (*Drepanosiphum platanoides*) and that during these weeks aphids colonize leaves in the lower canopy of the tree. Similar distributions have been found in other sucking insects on sycamore (McClure and Price, 1975).

Another factor that affects the suitability of leaves for herbivores is their spatial position relative to one another. Dixon and McKay (1970) demonstrated that the suitability of sycamore leaves for aphids was reduced when leaves were closely juxtaposed. During periods of wind, these leaves collided and disrupted the feeding activities of aphids. As a result, leaves with undersurfaces in close proximity to others were less likely to be colonized by aphids.

Because of the growth characteristics of willow shoots we suspected that some willow leaves are less suitable for juveniles of *Plagiodera versicolora* because they are more likely to be involved in collisions with adjacent foliage. By adding leaves for prolonged periods of time, willow shoots can elongate more than 1 m in a single growing season. Winds, even light breezes, cause these long branchlets to sway and collide with adjacent foliage. Young leaves at the apex of flexible branchlets appear much more likely to be involved in collisions and consequently seem a less suitable site for juvenile stages to occupy.

We tested this hypothesis with eggs and larvae of *Plagiodera versicolora*. These stages were chosen because displacement from the host poses the greatest relocation problems for these small, relatively sessile stages. In a series of experiments we determined whether survivorship of juveniles varied between young (terminal) and old (basal) leaves. Eggs or first-instar larvae were placed on leaves near the tip and the base of a willow branchlet, and the disappearance of juveniles from both positions were compared. Our results strongly support the contention that under both mild and severe weather conditions eggs are more likely to be dislodged from young than from old leaves (Fig. 5). Similar results were found for first-instar larvae exposed to an artificial breeze of 9 km/hr. After 5 min, 58% of the larvae were dislodged from young leaves, but only 29% were dislodged from old ones (χ^2, $P < 0.01$). As in the studies of Dixon (1970) and Dixon and McKay (1970), we have shown that the relative position a leaf occupies in space can affect its suitability for herbivores and contribute to their spatial distribution on the host.

V. CONCLUDING REMARKS

The nutrition and allelochemistry of leaves varies diurnally and seasonally (Fairbairn and Wassell, 1964; Durzan, 1968a,b,c; Burbott and Loomis, 1969; Adams, 1970; Feeny, 1970; Dement and Mooney, 1974; Parry, 1974; Robinson, 1974; Lawton, 1976; Seigler and Price, 1976; McNeill and Southwood, 1978; Mattson, 1980; Scriber and Slansky, 1981; Kraft and Denno, 1982; Raupp, 1982). Eating leaves at different times of the day or on different days during a leaf's development can have a major impact on one or more attributes of a herbivore's fitness (Grison, 1952; Greenbank, 1956; Cibula *et al.*, 1967; Morris, 1967; Wene, 1968; De Wilde, 1969;

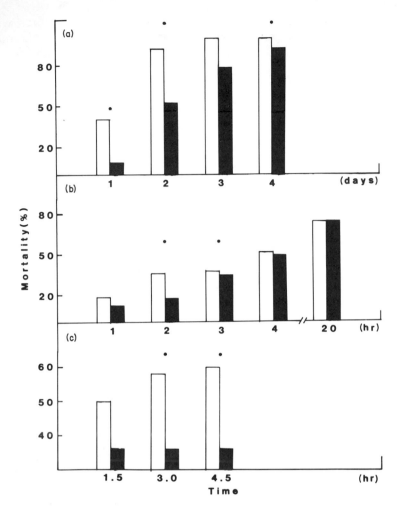

Fig. 5. Mortality of *Plagiodera versicolora* eggs placed on young (□) and old (■) willow leaves during mild and severe (thunderstorm) weather conditions in May (a, mild), June (b, mild), and July (c, severe). During each time interval, mortality of eggs on young and old leaves was compared with a X^2 test. Intervals in which mortality differed significantly ($P < 0.05$) are marked (·). Eggs placed on young leaves generally incurred greater mortality than eggs on old leaves.

Drooz, 1970; Feeny, 1970; All and Benjamin, 1975; Phillips, 1976; Haukioja *et al.*, 1978; Hough and Pimentel, 1978; Kitayama *et al.*, 1979; Mitter *et al.*, 1979; Schweitzer, 1979; Cates, 1980; Kraft and Denno, 1982; Raupp, 1982). Therefore, it is not surprising that herbivores show preferences for certain tissues in time (Feeny, 1970; McNeill, 1973; Parry, 1974; Rockwood, 1974; McNeill and Southwood, 1978; Mitter *et al.*, 1979; Kraft and Denno, 1982) and in space (White, 1970; McNeill, 1973; All and Benjamin, 1975; Woodwell *et al.*, 1975; Phillips, 1976; Rhoades and Cates, 1976; Ives, 1978; McNeill and Southwood, 1978; Cates, 1980; Denno *et al.*, 1981).

Does a general pattern exist that allows us to predict when or where herbivores will be found feeding on their host plants? For sucking insects, temporal and spatial abundances are often correlated with age-related changes in the content of soluble nutrients such as nitrogen (Dixon, 1970; McNeill, 1973; Parry, 1974; McNeill and Southwood, 1978). This may result in a preference for nutrient-rich tissues such as young leaves and seed heads (McNeill and Southwood, 1978; Denno *et al.*, 1980) and abundance peaks in spring, when new tissues are developing, and in fall, when both tissue development and nutrient recovery increase soluble nutrients (McNeill and Southwood, 1978). Exceptions to this generality include the psyllid *Cardiaspina densidextra*, which prefers the mature leaves of *Eucalyptus* trees over the young or senescent leaves because mature leaves may possess higher concentrations of soluble nutrients (White, 1970).

The fitness measures of many defoliators summarized in this chapter implicate young leaves as a superior food resource. Based on this evidence we would predict, as Rockwood (1974) did, that defoliators should select young leaves as feeding sites. However, Rhoades and Cates (1976) suggested that the allelochemicals present in young leaves would mitigate against generalists attempting to feed there and cause a divergence in tissue preference between specialists and generalists. Their empirical studies of defoliators support this contention (Rhoades and Cates, 1976; Cates, 1980); however, notable exceptions exist (Cates, 1980). Some polyphagous herbivores such as the moths studied by Feeny (1970) and Mitter *et al.* (1979) exploit the young leaves of their hosts. The oligophagous sawflies studied by All and Benjamin (1975) prefer older leaves of pines because of the presence of deterrent chemicals in young leaves. Females of the oligophagous cabbage butterfly *(Pieris rapae,)* select older leaves of *Brassica* as oviposition sites (Ives, 1978). Also, the oligophagous butterfly *Mechanitis isthmia* selects the older leaves of *Solanum* for oviposition, and larvae feed on those leaves (Young and Moffett, 1979).

Just as the presence of allelochemicals can modify the basic nutritional suitability of leaves and affect hervibore distributions, ecological factors can alter leaf suitability as well. Hassell and Southwood (1978), Gilbert (1979), and Price *et al.* (1980) have suggested that the distribution of some insects on their host plants results from a compromise among nutritional constraints and other factors that are indirectly or unrelated to nutrition. Although young leaves support better growth, development, reproduction, and survivorship of *Plagiodera versicolora* larvae and adults, young leaves are an unfavorable site for some immature stages for a variety of reasons. Young leaves are more likely to disappear through feeding by adults of *P. versicolora* and a variety of other willow defoliators. Also, young leaves near active meristems may be preferentially colonized by other herbivores, thereby concentrating predators. Adult beetles leave traces of their presence on young leaves, and this too may concentrate predator search. Furthermore, the young leaves of willows shed eggs and small larvae more than old leaves as they sway and collide with adjacent foliage. For these reasons female beetles select somewhat older foliage for oviposition sites and force their offspring to contend with a less nutritious resource, but one on which overall survivorship is greater. The outcome of these interactions is niche divergence among the developmental stages of *P. versicolora* and a failure of spatial distribution to conform with the pattern predicted by the nutritional characteristics of leaves alone.

In conclusion, we suggest that the distribution of herbivores on their host plants reflects a compromise among various factors that vary in time and space. The nutrient content of plant leaves appears to vary in predictable ways, and for many herbivores spatial and temporal distributions will closely reflect patterns of host nutrients (Feeny, 1970, 1976; Rockwood, 1974; Phillips, 1976; Rhoades and Cates, 1976; Mitter *et al.*, 1979; Cates, 1980; Denno *et al.*, 1980; Kraft and Denno, 1982). For other herbivores, distributions of allelochemicals may be the primary determinants of feeding sites (All and Benjamin, 1975; Ikeda *et al.*, 1977a,b). From our studies and others it is clear that interactions with members of the same trophic level, trophic levels above, and the abiotic environment may supercede or modify host effects in establishing hervibore distributions (Dixon and McKay, 1970; McClure, 1974; Zwölfer, 1975; Hassell and Southwood, 1978; Gilbert, 1979; Heinrich, 1979; Young and Moffet, 1979; Price *et al.*, 1980; Denno *et al.*, 1981). To establish a pattern in light of the richness and complexity of these interactions remains a challenge for those who attempt to understand the distribution and abundance of herbivores on plants.

ACKNOWLEDGMENTS

John Davidson, David Inouye, William Mellors, and Douglass Miller criticized earlier drafts of this chapter, and Mark McClure provided helpful comments on the final version. Joan Russo, Helen Lindsey, and Shirley Donkis typed various portions of the manuscript. To these people we extend our thanks.

Scientific Article no. A-3227, Contribution no. 6298 of the Maryland Agricultural Experiment Station, Department of Entomology.

REFERENCES

Adams, R. P. (1970). Seasonal variation of terpenoid constituents in natural populations *Juniperus pinchottii* Sudw. *Phytochemistry* **9**, 397–402.

All, J. N., and Benjamin, D. M., (1975). Influence of needle maturity on larval feeding preference and survival of *Neodiprion swainei* and *N. rugifrons* on jack pine, *Pinus banksiana*. *Ann. Entomol. Soc. Am.* **68**, 579–584.

Arthur, A. P. (1981). Host acceptance by parasitoids. *In* "Semiochemicals: Their Role in Pest Control" (D. A. Nordlund, R. L. Jones, and W. J. Lewis, eds.), pp. 97–120. Wiley, New York.

Bach, C. E. (1980a). Effects of plant density and diversity on the population dynamics of a specialist herbivore, the striped cucumber beetle, *Acalymma vittata* (Fab.). *Ecology* **61**, 1515–1530.

Bach, C. E. (1980b). Effects of plant diversity and time of colonization on an herbivore–plant interaction. *Oecologia* **44**, 319–326.

Banks, C. J. (1957). The behavior of individual coccinellid larvae on plants. *Anim. Behav.* **5**, 12–24.

Beevers, L. (1976). "Nitrogen Metabolism in Plants." Am. Elsevier, New York.

Blau, W. S. (1981). Latitudinal variation in the life histories of insects occupying disturbed habitats: A case study. *In* "Insect Life History Patterns: Habitat and Geographic Variation" (R. F. Denno and H. Dingle, eds.), pp. 75–95. Springer-Verlag, Berlin/New York.

Burbott, A. J., and Loomis, W. D. (1969). Evidence for metabolic turnover of monoterpenes in peppermint. *Plant Physiol.* **44**, 173–179.

Calow, P. (1977). Ecology, evolution, and energetics: A study in metabolic adaptation. *Adv. Ecol. Res.* **10**, 1–62.

Campbell, J. M. (1962). Influence of larval environment on adult size and fecundity in the moth, *Panaxia dominula* L. *Nature (London)* **192**, 282.

Carter, C. I., and Cole, J. (1977). Flight regulation in the green spruce aphid *(Elatobium abietinum)*. *Ann. Appl. Biol.* **86**, 137–151.

Cages, R. G. (1980). Feeding patterns of monophagous, oliogophagous, and polyphagous insect herbivores: The effect of resource abundance and plant chemistry. *Oecologia* **46**, 22–31.

Chew, F. S. (1975). Coevolution of pierid butterflies and their cruciferous foodplants. I. The relative quality of available resources. *Oecologia* **20**, 117–128.

Chew, F. S. (1977). Coevolution of pierid butterflies and their crucifer foodplants. II. The distribution of eggs on potential foodplants. *Evolution* **31**, 568–579.

Cibula, A. B., Davidson, R. H., Fisk, F. W., and LaPidus, J. B. (1967). Relationship of free amino acids of some solanaceous plants to growth and development of *Leptinotarsa decemlineata* (Coleoptera: Chysomelidae). *Ann. Entomol. Soc.* **60**, 626–631.

Cole, L. C. (1954). The population consequences of life history phenomena. *Q. Rev. Biol.* **29**, 103–137.

Cromartie, W. J., Jr. (1975). The effect of stand size and vegetational background on the colonization of cruciferous plants by herbivorous insects. *J. Appl. Ecol.* **12**, 517–533.

Dement, W. A., and Mooney, H. A. (1974). Seasonal variation in the production of tannins and cyanogenic glucosides in the chaparral shrub, *Heteromeles arbutifolia*. *Oecologia* **15**, 65–76.

Denno, R. F., Raupp, M. J., Tallamy, D. W., and Reichelderfer, C. F. (1980). Migration in heterogeneous environments: Differences in habitat selection between the wingforms of the dimorphic planthopper, *Prokelisia marginata* (Homoptera: Delphacidae). *Ecology* **61**, 859–867.

Denno, R. F., Raupp, M. J., and Tallamy, D. W. (1981). Organization of a guild of sap-feeding insects: Equilibrium vs. nonequilibrium coexistence. In "Insect Life History Patterns: Habitat and Geographic Variation." (R. F. Denno and H. Dingle, eds.), pp. 151–181. Springer-Verlag, Berlin/New York.

De Wilde, J., Bongers, W., and Schooneveld, H. (1969). Effects of host plant age on phytophagons insects. Entomol. Exp. Appl. 12, 714–720.

Dingle, H., Blakley, N. R., and Miller, E. R. (1980). Variation in body size and flight performance in mildweed bugs (Oncopeltus). Evolution 34, 356–370.

Dixon, A. F. G. (1970). Quality and availability of food for a sycamore aphid population. Symp. Br. Ecol. Soc. 10, 271–286.

Dixon, A. F. G., and McKay, S. (1970). Aggregation in the sycamore aphid, Drepanosiphum platanoides (Schr.) (Hemiptera: Amphididae) and its relevance to the regulation of population growth. J. Anim. Ecol. 39, 439–454.

Drooz, A. T. (1965). Some relationships between host, egg potential, and pupal weight of the elm spanworm, Ennomos subsignarius (Lepidoptera: Geometridae). Ann. Entomol. Soc. Am. 58, 243–245.

Drooz, A. T. (1970). Rearing the elm spanworm on oak or hickory. J. Econ. Entomol. 63, 1581–1585.

Durzan, D. J. (1968a). Nitrogen metabolism of Picea glauca. I. Seasonal changes of free amino acids in buds, shoot apices, and leaves, and the metabolism of uniformly labelled C^{14}-L-arginine by buds during the onset of dormancy. Can. J. Bot. 46, 909–919.

Durzan, D. J. (1968b). Nitrogen metabolism of Picea glauca. II. Diurnal changes of free amino, amides, and guanidine compounds in roots, buds, and leaves during the onset of dormancy of white spruce seedlings. Can. J. Bot. 46, 921–928.

Durzan, D. J. (1968c). Nitrogen metabolism of Picea glauca. II. Diurnal changes of amino acids, amides, protein, and chlorophyll in leaves of expanding buds. Can. J. Bot. 46, 929-937.

Edmunds, G. F., and Alstad, D. N. (1978). Coevolution in insect herbivores and conifers. Science 199, 941–945.

Edmunds, G. F., and Alstad, D. N. (1981). Responses of black pineleaf scales to host plant variability. In "Insect Life History Patterns: Habitat and Geographic Variation" (R. F. Denno and H. Dingle, eds). pp. 29–38. Springer-Verlag, Berlin/New York.

Fairbairn, J. W., and Wassel, G. M. (1964). The alkaloids of Papaver somniferum L.: Evidence for rapid turnover of the major alkaloids. Phytochemistry 3, 253–258.

Feeny, P. (1970). Seasonal changes in oak leaf tannins and nutrients as a cause of spring feeding by winter moth caterpillars. Ecology 51, 565–581.

Feeny, P. (1975). Biochemical coevolution between plants and their insect herbivores. In "Coevolution of Animals and Plants" (L. E. Gilbert and P. R. Raven, eds.), pp. 3–19. Univ. of Texas Press, Austin.

Feeny, P. (1976). Plant apparency and chemical defense. Recent Adv. Phytochem. 10, 1–40.

Futuyma, D. J. (1976). Food plant specialization and environmental predictability in Lep-idoptera. Am. Nat. 110, 285–292.

Gilbert, L. E. (1979). Development of theory in analysis of insect–plant interactions. In "Analysis of Ecological Systems" (D. J. Horn, R. Mitchell, and G. R. Stairs, eds.), pp. 117–154. Ohio State Univ. Press, Columbus.

Gilbert, L. E., and Singer, M. C. (1975). Butterfly ecology. Annu. Rev. Ecol. Syst. 6, 365–397.

Greany, P. D., and Hagen, K. S. (1981). Prey selection. In "Semiochemicals: Their Role in Pest Control" (D. A. Nordlund, R. L. Jones, and W. J. Lewis, eds.), pp. 121–136. Wiley, New York.

Greenbank, D. O. (1956). The role of climate and dispersal in the initiation of outbreaks of the spruce budworm in New Brunswick. J. Zool. 34, 453–476.

Grison, P. A. (1952). Relation entre l'état physiologique de la plantehote, *Solanum tuberosm*, et la fécondité du dorophyre, *Leptinotarsa decemlineata* Say. *Trans. Int. Congr. Entomol., 9th, 1951* Vol. 1, pp. 331–337.

Hanover, J. W. (1975). Physiology of tree resistance to insects. *Annu. Rev. Entomol.* **20**, 75–95.

Hassell, M. P. (1978). "The Dynamics of Arthropod Predator–Prey Systems." Princeton Univ. Press, Princeton, New Jersey.

Hassell, M. P., and Southwood, T. R. E. (1978). Foraging strategies of insects. *Annu. Rev. Ecol. Syst.* **9**, 75–98.

Haukioja, E., and Niemelä, P. (1976). Does birch defend itself actively against herbivores? *Rep. Kevo Subarct. Res. Stn.* **13**, 44–47.

Haukioja, E., and Niemelä, P. (1977). Retarded growth of a geometrid larva after mechanical damage to leaves of its host tree. *Ann. Zool. Fenn.* **14**, 48–52.

Haukioja, E., Niemelä, P. (1979). Birch leaves as a resource for herbivores: Seasonal occurrence of increased resistance in foliage after mechanical damage of adjacent leaves. *Oecologia* **39**, 151–159.

Haukioja, E., Niemelä, and Iso-Iivari, L. (1978). Birch leaves as a resource for herbivores. II. Diurnal variation in the usability of leaves for *Oporinia autumnata* and *Dineura virididorsata*. *Rep. Kevo. Subarct. Res. Stn.* **14**, 21–24.

Heinrich, B. (1979). Foraging strategies of caterpillars, leaf damage and possible predator avoidance strategies. *Oecologia* **42**, 325–337.

Herrick, G. W. (1935). "Insect Enemies of Shade Trees." Cornell Univ. Press (Comstock), Ithaca, New York.

Horsfield, D. (1977). Relationships between feeding of *Philaenus spumarius* (L.) and the amino acid concentration in the xylem sap. *Ecol. Entomol.* **2**, 259–266.

Hough, J. A., and Pimentel, D. (1978). Influence of host foliage on development, survival, and fecundity of the gypsy moth. *Environ. Entomol.* **7**, 97–102.

Ikeda, T., Matsumura, F., and Benjamin, D. M. (1977a). Mechanisms of feeding discriminating between matured and juvenile foliage by two species of pine sawflies. *J. Chem. Ecol.* **3**, 677–694.

Ikeda, T., Matsumura, F., and Benjamin, D. M. (1977b). Chemical basis for feeding adaptation of pine sawflies, *Neodiprion rugifrons* and *Neodiprion swainei*. *Science* **197**, 497–499.

Ives, P. M. (1978). How discriminating are cabbage butterflies? *Aust. J. Ecol.* **3**, 261–276.

Johnson, W. T., and Lyon, H. H. (1976). "Insects that Feed on Trees and Shrubs." Cornell Univ. Press, Ithaca, New York.

Kitayama, K., Stinner, R. E., and Rabb, R. L. (1979). Effects of temperature, humidity and soybean maturity on longevity and fecundity of the adult Mexican bean beetle, *Epilachna varivestis*. *Environ. Entomol.* **8**, 458–464.

Kozlowski, T. T. (1971). "Growth and Development of Trees," Vol. 1. Academic Press, New York.

Kraft, S. J., and Denno, R. F. (1982). Feeding responses of adapted and non-adapted insects to the defensive properties of *Baccharis halimifolia* L. (Compositae). *Oecologia* **52**, 156–163.

Lawton, J. H. (1976). The structure of the arthropod community on bracken. *Bot. J. Linn. Soc.* **723**, 187–216.

Lawton, J. H. (1978). Host plant influences on insect diversity: the effects of space and time. *In* Diversity of Insect Faunas" (L.A. Mound and N. Waloff, eds.), pp. 105–125. Blackwell, Oxford.

Lewontin, R. C. (1965). Selection for colonizing ability. *In* "The Genetics of Colonizing Species" pp. 77–91. (H. G. Baker and G. L. Stebbins, eds.), Academic Press, New York.

MacArthur, R. H., and Wilson, E. O. (1967). "The Theory of Island Biogeography." Princeton Univ. Press, Princeton, New Jersey.

McClure, M. S. (1974). Biology of *Erythroneura lawsoni* (Homoptera: Cicadellidae) and coexistence in the sycamore leaf-feeding guild. *Environ. Entomol.* **3**, 59–68.

McClure, M. S., and Price, P. W. (1975). Competition and coexistence among sympatric *Erythroneura* leafhoppers (Homoptera: Cicadellidae) on American sycamore. *Ecology* **56**, 1388–1397.

McKey, D. (1979). The distribution of secondary compounds within plants. *In* "Herbivores: Their Interaction with Secondary Plant Metabolites" (G. A. Rosenthal and D. H. Janzen, eds.). pp. 56–134. Academic Press, New York.

McNeill, S. (1973). The dynamics of a population of *Leptoterna dolabrata* in relation to its food resources. *J. Anim. Ecol.* **42**, 495–507.

McNeill, S., and Southwood, T. R. E. (1978). Role of nitrogen in the development of insect–plant relationships. *In* "Biochemical Aspects of Plant and Animal Coevolution" (J. B. Harborne, ed.), pp. 77–98. Academic Press, New York.

Mattson, W. J., Jr. (1980). Herbivory in relation to plant nitrogen content. *Annu. Rev. Ecol. Syst.* **11**, 119–161.

Mitchell, R. (1981). Insect behavior, resource exploitation, and fitness. *Annu. Rev. Entomol.* **26**, 373–396.

Mitter, C., Futuyma, D. J., Schneider, J. C., and Hare, J. D. (1979). Genetic variation and host plant relationships in a parthenogenetic moth. *Evolution* **33**, 777–790.

Morris, R. F. (1967). Influence of parental food quality on the survival of *Hyphantria cunea*. *Can. Entomol.* **99**, 24–33.

Murphy, G. I. (1968). Pattern in life history and the environment. *Am. Nat.* **102**, 391–403.

Parry, W. H. (1974). The effects of nitrogen levels in Sitka spruce needles on *Elatobium abietinum* in north-eastern Scotland. *Oecologia* **15**, 305–320.

Phillips, W. M. (1976). Effects of leaf age on feeding 'preference' and egg laying in the chrysomelid beetle, *Haltica lythri*. *Physiol. Entolmol.* **1**, 223–226.

Price, P. W. (1975). "Insect Ecology." Wiley, New York.

Price, P. W., Burton, C. E., Gross, P., McPheron, B. A., Thompson, J. N., and Weis, A. E. (1980). Interactions among three tropic levels: Influence of plants on interactions between insect herbivores and natural enemies. *Annu. Rev. Ecol. Syst.* **11**, 41–65.

Ralph, C. P. (1977). Effect of host plant density on populations of a specialized, seed-sucking bug, *Oncopeltus fasciatus*. *Ecology* **58**, 799–809.

Raupp, M. J. (1982). Spatial distribution and seasonal abundance of the imported willow leaf beetle, *Plagiodera versicolora* Laich: The effect of plant nutrition and defence, physical factors, and activities of competitors and predators. Ph.D. Dissertation, University of Maryland, College Park (unpublished).

Raupp, M. J., and Denno, R. F. (1980). Interactions among willow herbivores as a determinant of feeding and oviposition of the imported willow leaf beetle, *Plagiodera versicolora* Laich. (Coleoptera: Chrysomelidae). *J. N.Y. Entomol. Soc.* **88**, 67.

Rausher, M. D. (1978). Search image for leaf shape in a butterfly. *Science* **200**, 1071–1073.

Rhoades, D. F. (1979). Evolution of plant chemical defense against herbivores. *In* "Herbivores: Their Interaction with Secondary Plant Metabolites" (G. A. Rosenthal and D. H. Janzen, eds.) pp. 4–54.

Rhoades, D. F., and Cates, R. (1976). Toward a general theory of plant antiherbivore chemistry. *Recent Adv. Phytochem.* **10**, 168–213.

Robinson, T. (1974). Metabolism and function of alkaloids in plants. *Science* **184**, 430–435.

Rockwood, L. L. (1974). Seasonal changes in the susceptibility of *Crescentia alata* leaves to the flea beetle *Oedionychus* sp. *Ecology* **55**, 142–148.

Root, R. B. (1973). Organization of a plant–arthropod association in simple and diverse habitats. The fauna of collards *(Brassica oleracea)*. *Ecol. Monogr.* **43**, 95–124.

Schaffer, W. M. (1974). Selection for optimal life histories: The effects of age structure. *Ecology* **55**, 291–303.

Schoener, T. W., and Janzen, D. H. (1968). Notes on environmental determinants of tropical versus temperate insect size patterns. *Am. Nat.* **102**, 207–224.

Schweitzer, D. F. (1979). Effects of foliage age on body weight and survival of larvae of the tribe Lithophanini (Lepidoptera: Noctuidae). *Oikos* **32**, 403–408.

Scriber, J. M. (1978). Cyanogenic glycosides in *Lotus corniculatus*. *Oecologia* **34**, 143–155.

Scriber, J. M., and Slansky, F. (1981). The nutritional ecology of immature insects. *Annu. Rev. Entomol.* **26**, 183–211.

Seigler, D., and Price, P. (1976). Secondary compounds in plants: Primary function. *Am. Nat.* **110**, 101–105.

Singer, M. C. (1971). Evolution of food-plant preferences in the butterfly *Euphydryas editha*. *Evolution* **25**, 383–389.

Stearnes, S. C. (1976). Life history tactics: a review of ideas. *Q. Rev. Biol.* **51**, 3–47.

Tahvanainen, J. O., and Root, R. B. (1972). The influence of vegetational diversity on the population ecology of a specialized herbivore, *Phyllotreta cruciferae* (Coleoptera: Chrsyomelidae). *Oecologia* **10**, 321–346.

Tallamy, D. W., and Denno, R. F. (1981). Alternative life history patterns in risky environments: An example from lacebugs. *In* "Insect Life History Patterns: Habitat and Geographic Variation" (R. F. Denno and H. Dingle, eds.), pp. 129–147. Springer-Verlag, Berlin/New York.

Vinson, S. B. (1981). Habitat location. *In* "Semiochemicals: Their Role in Pest Control" (D. A. Nordlund, R. L. Jones, and W. J. Lewis, eds.), pp. 51–77. Wiley, New York.

Wasserman, S.S., and Mitter, C. (1978). The relationship of body size to breadth of diet in some Lepidoptera. *Ecol. Entomol.* **3**, 155–160.

Wene, G. P. (1968). Biology of the elm leaf beetle in southern Arizona. *J. Econ. Entomol.* **61**, 1178–1180.

Weseloh, R. M. (1974). Host related microhabitat preferences of the gypsy moth larval parasitoid, *Parasetigena agilis*. *Environ. Entomol.* **3**, 363–364.

Weseloh, R. M. (1981). Host location by parasitoids. *In* "Semiochemicals: Their Role in Pest Control" (D. A. Nordlund, R. L. Jones, and W. J. Lewis, eds.), pp. 79–95. Wiley, New York.

White, T. C. R. (1970). Some aspects of the life history, host selection, dispersal, and oviposition of adult *Cardiaspina densidextra*. *Aust. J. Zool.* **18**, 105–117.

Whitham, T. G. (1979). Territorial behavior of *Pemphigus* gall aphids. *Nature (London)* **279**, 324–325.

Whitham, T. G. (1980). The theory of habitat selection: Examined and extended using *Pemphigus* aphids. *Am. Nat.* **115**, 449–466.

Whitham, T. G. (1981). Individual trees as heterogeneous environments: Adaptation to herbivory or epigenetic noise? *In* "Insect Life History Patterns: Habitat and Geographic Variation" (R. F. Denno and H. Dingle, eds.), pp. 9–27. Springer-Verlag, Berlin/New York.

Whitham, T. G., and Slobodchikoff, C. N. (1981). Evolution by individuals, plant–herbivore interactions, and mosaics of genetic variability: The adaptive significance of somatic mutations in plants. *Oecologia* **49**, 287–292.

Wiklund, C. (1974a). The concept of oligophagy and the natural habitats and host plants of *Papilio machaon* L. in Fennoscandia. *Entomol. Scand.* **5**, 151–160.

Wiklund, C. (1974b). Oviposition preferences in *Papilio machaon* in relation to the host plants of larvae. *Entomol. Exp. Appl.* **17**, 189–198.

Wiklund, C. (1975). The evolutionary relationship between adult oviposition preference and larval host range in *Papilio machaon* L. *Oecologia* **18**, 185–197.

Wilcox, J. A. (1979). "Leaf Beetle Host Plants in Northeastern North America," World Nat. Hist. Publ. Plexus Publishing, Marlton, New Jersey.

Williams, K. S., and Gilbert, L. E. (1981). Insects as selective agents on host plant morphology: egg mimicry reduces egg laying by butterflies. *Science* **212**, 467–469.

Woodwell, G. M., Whittaker, R. H., and Houghton, R. A. (1975). Nutrient concentration in plants in the Brookhaven oak–pine forests. *Ecology* **56**, 318–322.

Young, A. M. (1972). Adaptive strategies of feeding and predator avoidance in the larvae of the butterfly *Morpho peleides limpida* (Lepidoptera: Morphoidae). *J. N.Y. Entomol. Soc.* **80**, 60–82.

Young, A. M., and Moffett, M. W. (1979). Behavioral regulatory mechanisms in populations of the butterfly *Mechanitis isthmia* in Costa Rica: adaptations to host plants in secondary and agricultural habitats. *Dtsch. Entomol. Z.* **26**, 21–38.

Zimmermann, M. H., and Brown, C. L. (1971). "Trees: Structure and Function." Springer-Verlag, Berlin/New York.

Zwölfer, H. (1975). Speciation and niche diversification in phytophagous insects. *Verh. Dtsch. Zool. Ges.* **67**, 394–401.

Michael J. Raupp

Robert F. Denno
Department of Entomology
University of Maryland
College Park, Maryland

CHAPTER **5**

Competition between Herbivores and Increased Resource Heterogeneity

MARK S. McCLURE

I. INTRODUCTION

A. Competition in Herbivorous Insects

The view that competition plays a key role in structuring animal communities is central to current thinking in ecology (Cody and Diamond, 1975; Hutchinson, 1978). Where species occur in time and space and how species utilize resources are often explained by interspecific competition. However, Lawton and Strong (1981) have contended that interspecific competition is too rare or impuissant to regularly structure insect communities on plants. They have suggested that autecological factors such as a harsh and changing climate, host-plant phenology,

125

chemical and physical changes in host tissue, and patchiness of food-plant resources are of greater importance to herbivorous insects than competition (also see Jones, Chapter 15). Lawton and Hassell (1981) reviewed the relatively few examples of interspecific competition among insects and concluded that in most cases competition was asymmetrical, that is, one species had a marked effect on the other but that there was no detectable reciprocal effect. They argued that the infrequency of reciprocal competition in nature undermines the importance of interspecific competition in the organization of insect communities.

Lawton and Strong (1981) listed several authors who have argued that population densities of herbivorous insects are usually too low to produce interspecific competition and others who have amended this notion (e.g., that during insect outbreaks densities could be sufficiently high to produce transitory competition). However, Lawton and Strong (1981) wrote that they do not believe that rare population eruptions are the cause of community structure in insects (also see Price, Chapter 16).

Although the frequency and importance of competition among herbivorous insects are currently being challenged, there is little doubt that, when densities are high, herbivorous insects can experience competition and that competition further increases the heterogeneity of resources within individual plants. This chapter will describe the ways in which competition contributes to the spatial and temporal variation in the quality of a host plant for resident herbivorous insects and how this may alter predictions of insect distribution and abundance based solely on measures of host nutrition and defensive chemistry.

B. Outbreak Populations of Herbivorous Insects

Competition is apt to have its most obvious impact on the fitness of herbivorous insects during population outbreaks. Changes in host-plant phytochemistry and in the regulatory influence of natural enemies have been cited as the most common causes for insect outbreaks. Numerous factors, including weather, host age, host phenology, and herbivory can contribute to insect outbreaks by causing phytochemical changes in the host plant (see Rhoades, Chapter 6). Based upon his own work with psyllids and looper caterpillars and on numerous examples from the literature, White (1969, 1974, 1976) hypothesized that outbreaks of phytophagous insects occur when food plants become a richer source of nitrogen, when they are stressed by random fluctuations of the weather. Numerous studies by Dixon (1970, 1975, 1979) have demonstrated the importance of herbivore density and seasonal variation in food quality to the reproductive behavior of the sycamore aphid, *Drepanosiphum platanoides*. Similarly, outbreaks of the green spruce aphid, *Elatobium abietinum* (Kloft and Ehrhardt, 1959; Parry, 1974, 1976), and the spruce budworm, *Choristoneura fumiferana* (Kimmins, 1971), have been attributed to changes in the nutritional quality of the food related to herbivore-induced stress and host-plant phenology.

Population outbreaks and competition in herbivorous insects can also be stimulated by the removal of the regulatory influence of natural enemies. There are numerous cases in which populations of herbivorous insects increased sharply where habitats have been rendered unsuitable for natural enemies by insecticide application of drift (Ripper, 1956; Edmunds, 1973; McClure, 1977a) or by contamination with dust materials (Bartlett, 1951; Edmunds, 1973). But the most common and best examples of high population densities and competition in herbivorous insects in the absence of natural enemies involve introduced species. Often introduced into a new locale without their cohort of natural enemies from the homeland, exotic herbivorous insects often increase in number rapidly, to a level at which competition is the most influential regulatory factor on their populations. Indeed, one of the classic examples of interspecific competition and competitive exclusion involved introduced species (DeBach and Sundby, 1963). As we shall see, communities of introduced herbivorous insects offer great potential for insight into competition and its contribution to the variability of resources within the host plant in time and space.

II. INTRODUCED SPECIES: A UNIQUE ENCOUNTER BETWEEN PLANT AND HERBIVORE

A. Population Dynamics of Introduced Herbivorous Insects

Herbivorous insects and their host plants can be viewed as coevolving, interdependent, biochemical systems. The degree of balance between these two systems is often a function of the length of their association in evolutionary time. When herbivorous insects and their host plants have coevolved, as in the case of endemic species, the relationship between herbivore and host plant is often very intimate. Consequently, endemic herbivores are apt to respond to subtle physical and biochemical changes in their host plants (see Jones, Chapter 15). This relationship between host-plant quality and herbivore fitness is so interdependent that Mattson and Addy (1975) have proposed that insects can serve as regulators of primary production in forest systems. Numerous examples of the intimate coevolutionary relationships that endemic herbivorous insects and their host plants share are presented elsewhere in this book (see Mitchell, Chapter 10; Krischik and Denno, Chapter 14).

Where herbivorous insects and their host plants have had little or no coevolutionary history, as in the case of introduced species, an intimate relationship between herbivore and host plant is seldom apparent. Instead, herbivorous insects introduced into a habitat with a hospitable climate and a suitable host plant often find conditions favorable for rapid population growth. With abundant food and little environmental resistance from host-plant defenses or natural enemies, their numbers often increase rapidly to a level at which resource limitations regulate population growth through competition. Accordingly, the fitness of introduced herbivorous insects is often a function of their compatability with the phenology of the new host and their ability to cope with the deleterious effects of their own population densities on the food supply.

Some of the most intensive studies of competition and of the population dynamics of introduced herbivorous insects have involved scale insects (Homoptera: Coccoidea). Scale insects are well represented among the hundreds of exotic insect species that have established themselves as serious pests throughout the world. DeBach and Rosen (1976) listed 47 exotic scale pests belonging to the single family Diaspididae, the armored scales. Numerous exotic scales have become such serious pests that population-dynamics studies and biological-control projects have been initiated at considerable expense (see DeBach, 1974; DeBach *et al.*, 1971; Caltagirone, 1981).

Of the numerous coccoids introduced onto the island of Bermuda during this century (Bennett and Hughes, 1959), the two armored scales that attack *Juniperus bermudiana* are among the most destructive and best studied. Populations of *Lepidosaphes newsteadi* (Sulc.) and *Carulaspis minima* (Targ.) grew rapidly during the first few years after their introduction, killing many trees. Initially *L. newsteadi* was the more abundant scale, but soon *C. minima* displaced *L. newsteadi* as the major killer of Bermuda cedar. Thompson (1954) suggested that the sudden decline in *L. newsteadi* abundance was due to its inability to compete with *C. minima*.

Studies of the population dynamics of the exotic red-pine scale, *Matsucoccus resinosae* Bean & Godwin, a serious pest of *Pinus resinosa* Ait. in the northeastern United States, also illustrate the importance of herbivore interactions to scale fitness. The rapid buildup of scale populations and the subsequent deterioration of red pine as a host were shown to have a profound influence upon scale biology, behavior, and population dynamics, leading to reduced scale fitness (McClure, 1977c). The nutri-

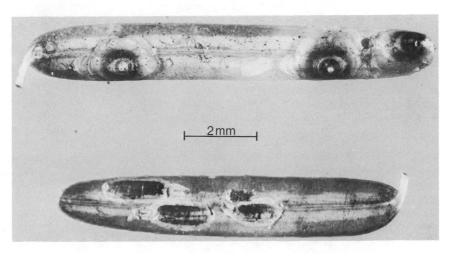

Fig. 1. Third-instar females (adults) of *Tsugaspidiotus tsugae* (top) and *Fiorinia externa* (bottom) on the undersides of needles of *Tsuga canadensis*.

tional quality of red pine for feeding scales was improved initially by herbivory but then was reduced with the progressive and irreversible injury to the host.

Newbery (1980a,b,c) and Hill and Newbery (1980) examined long-term changes in populations of *Icerya seychellarum* (Westw.), a margarodid scale introduced on Aldabra atoll in the Indian Ocean. They found that leaf phenology greatly influenced scale development and that the scale significantly reduced the growth and survival of its host plant, *Euphorbia pyrifolia* Lam. A decline in the level of the infestation in spite of the abundance of plant material for attack was attributed to qualitative changes in the scale population or its host plants.

B. The Exotic Armored Scales of Eastern Hemlock

One of the best examples showing the importance of host plant phenology and herbivore density to the population dynamics of introduced insects involves two armored scales on hemlock. Because much of this chapter will focus on this hemlock–scale system to exemplify how competition between herbivores can contribute to the spatial and temporal heterogeneity of resources within plants, a brief historical and biological sketch of these exotic scales is appropriate. The elongate hemlock scale, *Fiorinia externa* Ferris (Fig. 1), and a circular hemlock scale, *Tsugaspidiotus tsugae* (Marlatt) (Fig. 1; both Homoptera: Diaspididae), infest and often kill eastern hemlock, *Tsuga canadensis* (L.) Carrière, in the northeastern United States. *Fiorinia externa* was first discovered in 1908 in Queens, New York (Sasscer, 1912; Ferris, 1936); *T. tsugae* was first discovered in 1910 on exotic hemlocks shipped to New Jersey from Japan (Marlatt, 1911; Weiss, 1914). Both scales have been collected from *Tsuga sieboldii* Carrière (Siebold hemlock) in Japan, the probable homeland of these insects (Takahashi and Takagi, 1957; Takagi, 1963).

Readily dispersed by the wind (McClure, 1977b), these scales have expanded their distributions well into the natural range of *Tsuga canadensis*. They now share many native and exotic evergreen hosts, including at least 57 species from several genera (McClure and Fergione, 1977). On the principal host, eastern hemlock, crawlers (the mobile first-instar nymphs) of both scales usually colonize the lower surface of the youngest needles in the lower part of the crown and feed on the fluid contents of the mesophyll cells. Overlap of the feeding sites of these two scales is almost complete (McClure, 1980b).

The life histories of *Fiorinia externa* and *Tsugaspidiotus tsugae* on hemlock in Connecticut differ considerably (McClure, 1978). *Fiorinia externa* is primarily univoltine, completing one generation in summer. Only a small portion of the eggs produced by this summer generation hatch to initiate an unsuccessful second generation in autumn. *Tsugaspidiotus tsugae* is bivoltine, completing one generation in summer and one in autumn. The effects of voltinism on the dynamics of hemlock scale populations have been examined (McClure, 1981).

Before examining the evidence that these scales do compete and that competition does contribute to the complexity of individual trees as habitats, let us review the literature on the nutritional requirements of herbivorous insects and establish the nutritional basis for fitness in these exotic hemlock scales.

III. NUTRITIONAL REQUIREMENTS OF HERBIVOROUS INSECTS

A. Herbivory in Relation to Plant Nitrogen Content

White (1978) proposed that the single most important factor limiting the abundance of many, if not all, animals is a relative shortage of nitrogenous food for the very young. Because of its central role in all metabolic processes as well as in cellular structure and genetic coding, nitrogen is a critical element in the growth of all organisms (Mattson, 1980). McNeill and Southwood (1978) and Mattson (1980) have reviewed and examined the evidence that nitrogen is scarce and perhaps limiting for many herbivores and that, in response to this selection pressure, herbivores have evolved behavioral, morphological, physiological, and other adaptations to fully utilize the nitrogen available in their host plants.

There is an expanding amount of evidence indicating that nitrogen is critical to the survival and development of many organisms (see Mattson, 1980). Yet the quantitative nutritional requirements of dietary nitrogen and the utility of various forms of host nitrogen are still poorly known for herbivorous insects (Friend, 1958; Scriber and Slansky, 1981). Generally, piercing and sucking insects are favored by an increase in the soluble nitrogen component of their food. Auclair (1963) and Dixon (1970) have provided evidence that free amino acids and amides are major sources of dietary nitrogen for aphids and scales and that these can be incorporated and utilized directly. Because nearly 90% of the nitrogen in plants is present in the form of free amino acids and proteins (Long, 1961), determination of nitrogen content of foliage (e.g., by Kjeldahl analysis) probably provides a good estimate of the maximum amount of nitrogen available for insect growth (Feeny, 1970) and, therefore, represents a sound approach to studying herbivore nutrition. However, because not all forms of nitrogen are suitable for insect utilization (see Mattson, 1980), we must remain somewhat uncertain of conclusions derived solely from analyses of total nitrogen content.

B. Factors Affecting Nitrogen Availability in Plants

The suitability of a host plant as food is governed by a complex interaction of factors (see Scriber and Slansky, 1981). For example, moisture stress on the host plant can significantly alter food quality for herbivorous insects through its impact on nitrogen uptake and metabolism (Mattson and Addy, 1975). A shortage of water has been considered the single most important factor giving rise to conditions suitable for insect outbreaks (Stark, 1965; White, 1974, 1976, 1978). Besides the phytochemical changes that result from fluctuations in the amount of moisture available to plants, the water content of the food itself also influences the ability of phytophagous insects to assimilate the necessary food for their survival, growth, and development. For example, Scriber (1977, 1978, 1979) and Reese and Beck (1978) have shown the importance of food water content to the efficiency of nitrogen utilization for various species of Lepidoptera.

Plant allelochemicals also affect the availability of nitrogen for herbivorous insects. This subject has been dealt with extensively in the literature (see Rhoades and Cates, 1976; Rosenthal and Janzen, 1980), and it is addressed elsewhere in this book (see Ryan, Chapter 2; Jones, Chapter 15). In brief, whether or not a herbivore will feed on a given plant and how much and how fast it will consume food often depends upon the repellence–attractance characteristics of allelochemicals (see Chapman, 1974). Allelochemicals also influence the availability of nitrogen to herbivores by forming nonutilizable chemical complexes with proteins (see Cates and Rhoades 1977; Swain, 1977) and through effects on the herbivore's nutritional physiology (see Beck and Reese, 1976; Reese, 1978).

IV. FOLIAR NITROGEN: A BASIS FOR FITNESS IN ELONGATE HEMLOCK SCALE

A. Scale Fitness on Hemlock Fertilized with Nitrogen

Factors that determine the suitability of a host plant for its resident herbivorous insects have seldom been studied directly in forest systems. Most studies have been correlative, examining the responses of a herbivore population to changes in the nutritional quality of the host induced by numerous factors ranging from plant age and phenology to soil moisture and fertility to pollution (Mattson and Addy, 1975). There have been few attempts with forest tree species to manipulate experimentally the amount of organic nitrogen available to resident insect populations and, subsequently, to monitor their fitness. One experiment conducted in a Connecticut forest on *Fiorinia externa* indicated that the fitness of scale populations on eastern hemlock is influenced by the nutrient composition, texture, and moisture content of the soil (McClure, 1977b). Scale nymphs incurred less mortality and developed at a faster rate on the more vigorous hemlocks and those that had been fertilized. The varying degrees of scale fitness among seven experimental conditions were attributed to differences in the nutritional quality of the host.

An experiment to determine the importance of nitrogen to the fitness of *Fiorinia externa* on eastern hemlock was conducted during 1976–1978 at Lockwood Farm, Connecticut Agricultural Experiment Station, Mt. Carmel, Connecticut (McClure, 1980a). A group of 12-yr-old trees was fertilized in spring with 50 g of ammonium nitrate (NH_4NO_3), 17.5 g nitrogen per tree, and then artificially infested with crawlers of *F. externa*. Using a modified Kjeldahl technique (Glowa, 1974) for analyzing total nitrogen, I found that fertilization prior to flush significantly increased the amount of nitrogen in the subsequent young needles, which im-

Table I
Effect of Fertilization on the Nitrogen Concentration of Young Hemlock Needles and Subsequent Effects on the Survival, Development Rate [a] and Fecundity of Fiorinia externa [b]

Treatment	Nitrogen in needles	Survival of nymphs (%)	Females with eggs (%)	Eggs per female (number)
Fertilized	5.64 ± 0.39	81.5 ± 4.6	42.2 ± 5.2	13.3 ± 2.1
Unfertilized	4.28 ± 0.37	68.5 ± 7.9	13.5 ± 3.8	9.3 ± 1.9

[a] Measured as percentage of females with eggs.
[b] Numbers are means (± 1 SD). All parameters differed significantly between fertilized and unfertilized trees (all $P < 0.005$ by ANOVA).
[c] Data from McClure (1980a). Copyright 1980, the Ecological Society of America.

proved the survival, development rate (measured as the percentage of females with eggs on a particular sampling date such that the greater the percentage, the faster the development rate), and fecundity of those scales that colonized this young, nitrogen-rich foliage (Table I). The increased amount of nitrogen made available to nymphs by fertilization was probably responsible for improved scale fitness.

B. Relative Suitability of Plant Species as Hosts

The relationship between foliar nitrogen concentration and the suitability of 14 species from five genera of native and exotic conifers for *Fiorinia externa* was examined during 1977 and 1979 at the Bartlett Arboretum in Stamford, Connecticut, and at the Montgomery Pinetum in Greenwich, Connecticut (McClure, 1980a). Included were five species of *Abies, Cedrus atlantica* Manetti, three of *Picea, Pseudotsuga menziesii* (Mirbel) Franco and four of *Tsuga*. The amount of nitrogen in the young foliage of each tree during the time of peak colonization by *F. externa* was determined by Kjeldahl analysis and related to the density, survival, development rate, and fecundity of the scale population residing on that foliage. On those plant species whose needles contained higher amounts of nitrogen, scale populations incurred up to 41% less mortality, developed up to 47% faster, produced twice the number of eggs per female, and attained a density greater by a factor of 10 than did populations on tree species with lower foliar nitrogen concentrations during the peak colonization time of nymphs (Fig. 2).

The availability of nitrogen to feeding nymphs is an important factor determining the fitness of *Fiorinia externa* on hemlock and on its numerous other coniferous hosts. Survival, development rate, and fecundity were all influenced by differences in the concentration of foliar

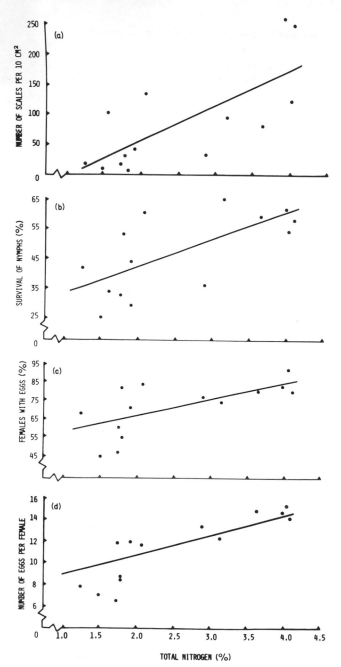

Fig. 2. Relationships between the total nitrogen concentration of the young foliage of 14 host species during peak colonization by nymphs of *Fiorinia externa* and the density of these colonists that survived to maturity (a, $r = 0.74$**), their survival (b, $r = 0.70$**), their development rate (measured as percentage of females with eggs; c, $r = 0.64$**), and their fecundity (d, $r = 0.74$**). *, $P < 0.05$; **, $P = <0.01$ by linear regression analysis. Data from McClure (1980a). Copyright 1980, the Ecological Society of America.

nitrogen associated with fertilization, interplant variation, and host phenology. Although numerous other factors, including foliar water concentration, rate of consumption, efficiency of nitrogen utilization, and intraspecific competition probably also influenced the ability of nymphs to obtain and assimilate essential nutrients, there is little doubt that nitrogen is important to the fitness of populations of hemlock scales.

Having established the nutritional basis for scale fitness, we shall now examine factors that influence the quality and availability of food for hemlock scales and the effects of herbivore competition on spatial and temporal variation of resources within the tree.

V. QUALITY AND AVAILABILITY OF FOOD FOR EXOTIC HEMLOCK SCALES

A. Phenological Compatability with the New Host Plant

1. Seasonal Trends in Foliar Nitrogen and Water Content

Concentrations of foliar nitrogen and water in trees are usually highest at leaf flush, and then they decline throughout the season (see Mattson, 1980), which imposes a strong selective pressure on herbivores to synchronize their onset of feeding with leaf flush. Yet, as in the case of eastern hemlock, time of flush can vary considerably over relatively short distances. Among 10 sites that I sampled in Fairfield County, Connecticut, separated by a maximum of only 30 km, the percentage of buds that had opened by early May varied between 4 and 100% (Fig. 3). Time of flush was related to the start of the growing season at each site, which was determined from meterological data compiled by Brumbach (1965). Although time of flush in the 10 hemlock forests varied by several days, there was a constant trend at each site for decreasing foliar nitrogen and water concentrations from May through July (Fig. 4). Foliar nitrogen dropped from 2.7 to 1.5% and foliar water from 90 to 60% during the 10-week period.

2. Colonization Times of Hemlock Scales

The phenologies of *Fiorinia externa* and *Tsugaspidiotus tsugae* on hemlock differed among the 10 sites. Mean colonization time by *F. externa* crawlers occurred in mid-June, about 1 month prior to that of *T. tsugae*. At every location *F. externa* colonized the young foliage at least 2 weeks prior to *T. tsugae*, when concentrations of foliar nitrogen and water were higher (Table II). Even though differences in foliar nitrogen and water concentrations between the colonization times of *F. externa* and *T. tsugae* were relatively small, differences in the nutritional quality of hemlock of this magnitude have been related to significant trends in survival and

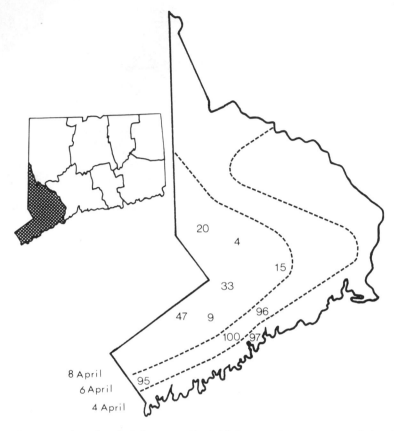

Fig. 3. Location of ten hemlock forests in Fairfield County, Connecticut, coinhabited by *Fiorinia externa* and *Tsugaspidiotus tsugae*. Numbers give the mean percentage of the hemlock buds in 1978 (based upon 200 buds on each of ten trees per site) that had opened by 8 May. Dashed lines define three zones wherein the start of the growing season in April differs by 2 days between adjacent zones, as determined from meterological data compiled by Brumbach (1965).

fecundity of hemlock scales (McClure, 1980a). Therefore, by virtue of its earlier colonization time, *F. externa* had a nutritional advantage over *T. tsugae.*

B. Scale-Induced Changes in the Food Supply

Scale colonization sites and herbivory itself also affect the quality and availability of food for hemlock scale nymphs, thereby further increasing the heterogeneity of resources in time and space. Experiments conducted

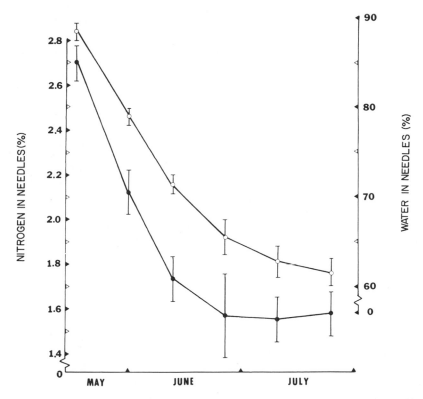

Fig. 4. Mean (± 1 SD) percentage nitrogen (●) and water (○) in the young hemlock needles in ten hemlock forests in southwestern Connecticut, coinhabited by *Fiorinia externa* and *Tsugaspidiotus tsugae*. Data from McClure (1980b). Copyright 1980, the Ecological Society of America.

in the greenhouse demonstrated that young hemlock needles contained significantly higher concentrations of nitrogen than 1-yr-old needles and that trees infested with *Fiorinia externa* had significantly less foliar nitrogen after only 7 weeks of feeding than either uninfested trees or those infested with *Tsugaspidiotus tsugae* (Table III; see McClure, 1980a,b). Experiments conducted in a field plot of 14-yr-old hemlocks at Lockwood Farm confirmed that feeding by *F. externa* nymphs reduced the nutritional quality of the food available later during the season (McClure, 1980a). Foliar nitrogen concentrations were significantly lower on infested trees than on uninfested trees after 7 weeks (Table III).

Studies of natural populations of *Fiorinia externa* in a hemlock forest in Ridgefield, Connecticut, revealed that herbivory had an important effect on the amount of food available not only during the current season but also during the following year (McClure, 1979a,b, 1980a). On 10

Table II

Nitrogen and Water Concentrations in Young Needles of Mature Hemlocks during
Colonization by *Fiorinia externa* and *Tsugaspidiotus tsugae*

Site	Colonization by Fiorinia externa		Colonization by Tsugaspidiotus tsugae		
	Nitrogen (%)	Water (%)	Nitrogen (%)	Water (%)	Weeks following F. externa
Greenwich	2.03	75.3	1.73	64.9	2
Norwalk	1.91	75.0	1.55	62.9	2
Darien	1.90	75.3	1.64	64.5	2
Westport	1.82	75.1	1.67	66.9	2
Stamford	1.77	69.3	1.69	61.9	2
Wilton	1.64	68.8	1.57	62.8	2
New Canaan	1.62	69.2	1.52	61.7	2
Ridgefield	1.61	67.0	1.46	61.3	4
Easton	1.58	67.4	1.49	61.9	4
Redding	1.46	64.6	1.32	60.1	6

[a]10 sites in Fairfield County, Connecticut. Numbers are means.

hemlocks supporting densities ranging (in 1977) from 30.0 to 232.5 scales per 100 needles, there were significant differences in the biomass (quantity) and total nitrogen concentration (quality) of the young needles the following year (1978). The average dry weight of 20 young needle clusters ranged from 0.25 to 0.51 g, and total nitrogen from 1.46 to 2.77% dry weight. Both of these parameters were significantly negatively correlated with scale density on the 10 hemlocks during the previous year (Fig. 5). These data support conclusions drawn from the greenhouse and field-plot experiments that herbivory does reduce the nutritive value of the host plant and that it further adds to the complexity of individual trees as habitats.

The fitness of 1978 scale populations at Ridgefield varied significantly in response to differences in the nutritive value of the 10 hemlocks that had supported various scale densities during 1977. Scales of the 1978 generation that colonized high-nitrogen needles of trees lightly infested during 1977 suffered less mortality and produced a greater number of eggs than those that colonized low-nitrogen needles of trees lightly infested during 1977 (McClure, 1980a). Significant positive correlations were obtained between nitrogen concentration of 1978 foliage and scale survival and fecundity (Fig. 6). Because scale densities on each of the 10 hemlocks fluctuated greatly for 3 yr (see McClure, 1979a), it is unlikely that the differential fitness of the 1978 generation on these trees was due

Table III
Effects of Needle Age and Feeding by Hemlock Scales on the Foliar Nitrogen Concentration of Hemlock Trees[a]

Experiment	Infestation	Scales per 100 needles	Total nitrogen (%)	
			Young needles	1-yr-old needles
Greenhouse	None	—	4.11 ± 0.57	3.03 ± 0.23[b]
(4-yr-old trees)	Fiorinia externa	124.4 ± 24.3	3.36 ± 0.25[b]	2.92 ± 0.29[b]
	Tsugaspidiotus tsugae	135.6 ± 30.4	4.02 ± 0.72[b]	3.28 ± 0.47[b]
Field plot	None	—	5.02 ± 0.17	
(14-yr-old trees)	Fiorinia externa	132.6 ± 29.7	4.28 ± 0.37[c]	

[a] Data from McClure (1980a,b). Copyright 1980, the Ecological Society of America.
[b] $P < 0.01$ (ANOVA).
[c] $P < 0.0005$ (ANOVA).

to inherent intraspecific variation in nutrient quality or defensive chemistry, as has been proposed by Edmunds and Alstad (1978) for populations of black-pine leaf scale on ponderosa pine (also see Alstad and Edmunds, Chapter 12). These data support those from experiments at Lockwood Farm that indicated that fitness of hemlock scales is related to the amount of foliar nitrogen available, which is itself affected by the previous level of herbivory on the host plant.

C. Competition between Hemlock Scales

1. Density-Dependent Fitness

The evidence presented thus far indicates that the nutritional quality of hemlock, measured as foliar nitrogen and water concentrations, is important to the survival, development rate, and fecundity of hemlock scales and that the quality and availability of food in time and space are functions of host phenology and scale density. Studies of Fiorinia externa (McClure, 1979a,b, 1980a) concluded that scale fitness is reduced by intraspecific competition, which depletes the amount of nitrogen and water available to nymphs. Another study (McClure and Fergione, 1977) hypothesized that interspecific competition was responsible for the negative correlation between densities of F. externa and Tsugaspidiotus tsugae in 11 coinhabited hemlock forests in southwestern Connecticut.

The effects of scale density on the relative fitness of Fiorinia externa and Tsugaspidiotus tsugae on eastern hemlock has been examined in a

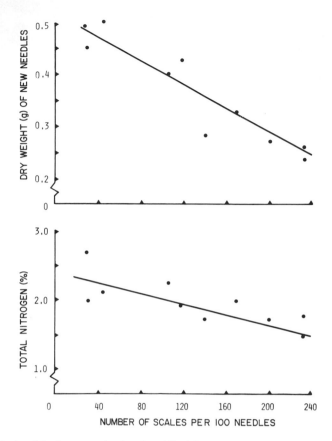

Fig. 5. Relationships between the density of *Fiorinia externa* on ten mature hemlocks during 1977 and the mean biomass ($r = -0.94$**) and nitrogen concentration ($r = -0.76$**) of the young needles of those trees during 1978. Probabilities are as in Fig. 2. Data from McClure (1980a). Copyright 1980, the Ecological Society of America.

Darien, Connecticut, forest (McClure, 1980b). For 3 yr the density, survivorship, and fecundity of both scales were monitored on six trees where each species occurred alone and on six trees where both species coexisted. The six trees in each group were chosen to represent a range of total scale density from lightly infested to heavily infested so that density effects on scale fitness could be evaluated. In pure and in mixed-species infestations percentage of survival and fecundity of *F. externa* was significantly negatively correlated with its own density, indicating that its fitness was adversely affected by density (Table IV). *Tsugaspidiotus tsugae* had no apparent adverse affect on the fitness of *F. externa* in mixed infestations, as neither survival nor fecundity of *F. externa* were related

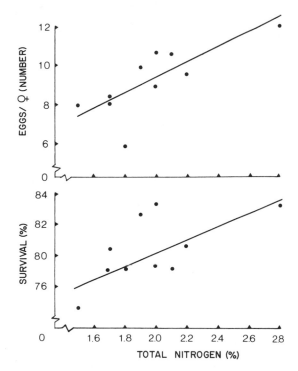

Fig. 6. Relationships between the total nitrogen concentration (dry weight) of the young needles of ten mature hemlocks and the mean fecundity ($r = 0.70^*$) and survivorship ($r = 0.70^*$) of *Fiorinia externa* residing on those trees. Probabilities are as in Fig. 2. Data from McClure (1980a). Copyright 1980, the Ecological Society of America.

to either *T. tsugae* density or total scale density. Survival and fecundity of *T. tsugae* were not significantly correlated with its own density in either pure or mixed infestations, but they were significantly negatively correlated with density of *F. externa* on coinhabited trees. This suggested that *T. tsugae* fitness was more adversely affected by *F. externa* density than by its own density.

Experiments conducted in the greenhouse (McClure, 1980b) established that *Fiorinia externa* and *Tsugaspidiotus tsugae* compete at population densities typical of those that occur in hemlock forests in southwestern Connecticut, identified factors responsible for the apparent competitive advantage of *F. externa* leading to its greater fitness in mixed infestations, and demonstrated how competition can contribute to resource heterogeneity. Groups of 4-yr-old hemlocks obtained from a common nursery stock were infested either with *F. externa* only, with *T. tsugae* only, or with both species such that total scale densities on all

Table IV

Relationships between Density, Survival, and Fecundity of Hemlock Scales on Six Mature Hemlocks[a]

Infestation	Density (scales per 100 needles)	Density used in analysis	Survival of nymphs Range (%)	Survival of nymphs P[b]	Eggs per female Range (number)	Eggs per female P[b]
Pure						
Fiorinia externa	37.5–182.0	Own	93.0–54.5	<0.001	16.6–8.4	<0.05
Tsugaspidiotus tsugae	16.5–138.0	Own	90.5–41.4	NS[c]	52.8–22.7	NS
Mixed						
Fiorinia externa	22.0–238.0	Own	93.0–59.7	<0.01	15.8–7.8	<0.01
		T. tsugae		NS		NS
	38.0–288.0	Both		NS		NS
Tsugaspidiotus tsugae	8.5–159.5	Own	81.5–33.5	NS	45.9–20.0	NS
		F. externa		<0.01		<0.01
	38.0–288.0	Both		NS		NS

[a]Numbers are means. Data from McClure (1980b). Copyright 1980, the Ecological Society of America.
[b]Calculated by linear regression.
[c]Not significant.

groups of trees would be similar. Hemlocks were infested either at the time of each species' peak colonization in the field (2 weeks apart) or simultaneously (by delaying the colonization time of *F. externa* for 2 weeks), the latter an unlikely occurrence under natural conditions. In pure infestations a significantly greater number of crawlers of both species colonized the nitrogen-rich young needles rather than the 1-yr-old needles containing relatively low nitrogen [$Ps < 0.01$ by analysis of variance (ANOVA); Table V]. In the mixed infestations where the two species colonized simultaneously, both scales again colonized the preferred young needles significantly more often ($Ps < 0.01$). However, in mixed infestations where *F. externa* colonized 14 days before *T. tsugae*, simulating natural conditions, most *T. tsugae* colonized the less preferred older needles ($Ps < 0.01$). This indicates that the previous establishment of *F. externa* nymphs forced *T. tsugae* to colonize the less nutritious older needles. The significance of this shift by *T. tsugae* to less nutritious older needles on trees colonized earlier by *F. externa* was apparent in comparing mortality incurred by nymphs on young and 1-yr-old growth (Table V). For all infestation groups mortality was significantly greater among nymphs feeding on low-nitrogen, 1-yr-old needles than on nitrogen-rich young growth ($Ps < 0.05$). Therefore, under natural conditions where hemlock scales coexisted, the later colonization time of *T. tsugae* and the behavioral shift to older, less nutritious foliage reduced its fitness relative to that of *F. externa*.

The effects of scale density on the relative competitive abilities of *Fiorinia externa* and *Tsugaspidiotus tsugae* were apparent from the degrees of mortality incurred by each species in pure versus mixed infestations (Table V). Percentage of mortality among *F. externa* colonists on young and 1-yr-old needles was 35 and 27% lower in mixed infestations than in pure infestations, whereas mortality among *T. tsugae* colonists was 76 and 42% higher in mixed infestations than in pure infestations. Because total scale densities on all infestation groups were similar (Table V), these data indicate that *F. externa* had a greater adverse affect on *T. tsugae* fitness than did *T. tsugae* have on itself. Therefore, in mixed infestations *F. externa* was the superior competitor. This is a good example of how one competing herbivore reduces the fitness of another by spatially excluding it from optimal resources and how competition can contribute to the heterogeneity of resources within plants.

2. Competitive Exclusion

The differential fitness of *Fiorinia externa* and *Tsugaspidiotus tsugae* on eastern hemlock has been clearly related to differences in the quality and availability of food for nymphs in time and space. *Fiorinia externa*, by virtue of its earlier colonization time and superior competitive ability,

Table V

Effects of Cohabitation and Time of Colonization on the Selection of Colonization Sites by Hemlock Scales and on Their Subsequent Survivorship.[a]

Infestation	Time of colonization	Scales per 200 needles	Colonization (%)		Mortality	
			Young needles	1-yr-old needles	Young needles	1-yr-old needles
Pure						
Fiorinia externa	8 June	136.4 ± 29.6	90.5 ± 15.6	9.5 ± 7.0	16.2 ± 2.2	18.3 ± 1.2
Fiorinia externa	22 June	114.3 ± 24.3	89.9 ± 17.2	10.1 ± 6.3	25.2 ± 2.3	29.7 ± 4.6
Tsugaspidiotus tsugae	22 June	179.6 ± 35.6	74.2 ± 13.0	25.8 ± 6.8	23.8 ± 3.3	30.6 ± 3.8
Mixed						
Fiorinia externa	8 June	77.5 ± 21.3	74.5 ± 19.7	25.5 ± 8.7	10.6 ± 3.0	13.3 ± 4.3
Tsugaspidiotus tsugae	22 June	101.4 ± 17.3	42.0 ± 7.0	58.0 ± 9.1	37.2 ± 4.1	46.4 ± 3.4
Fiorinia externa	22 June	68.3 ± 19.7	81.2 ± 19.1	18.8 ± 8.7	18.8 ± 3.3	25.5 ± 6.8
Tsugaspidiotus tsugae	22 June	83.7 ± 19.6	69.3 ± 13.9	30.7 ± 10.7	28.6 ± 2.3	35.3 ± 3.6

[a]Number are means (± 1 SD). See Section V,C for probabilities (calculated by ANOVA). Data from McClure (1980b). Copyright 1980, the Ecological Society of America.

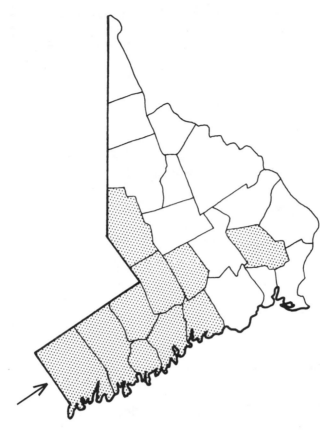

Fig. 7. The distribution of *Fiorinia externa* and *Tsugaspidiotus tsugae* among the 23 towns of Fairfield County, Connecticut. The stippled towns are those in which *F. externa* was present at more of the sampled sites than *T. tsugae*; unshaded towns are those in which *T. tsugae* was more widely distributed. A total of 232 sites was sampled (minimum of 5 sites per town). The arrow indicates the direction of the prevailing winds, the likely path of scale invasion from New York City. Data from McClure (1980b). Copyright 1980, the Ecological Society of America.

has a distinct nutritional advantage over *T. tsugae*. Because of this nutritional advantage, one might expect that *T. tsugae* populations are relatively unsuccessful where they coexist with *F. externa*. There is substantial evidence that *F. externa* does outcompete and eventually excludes *T. tsugae* from mixed-species infestations.

The first evidence derives from a comparison of the distributions of *Fiorinia externa* and *Tsugaspidiotus tsugae* in Fairfield County, Connecticut, (McClure and Ferigone, 1977; Fig. 7). *Fiorinia externa* was widely distributed among sites in the towns closest to New York City, where the scale had been introduced, and sparse in towns farther from this infestation center. Although we would expect a similar distribution for *T. tsugae*, which invaded Connecticut from New York before *F. externa*, such is not the case. Instead, *T. tsugae* was sparse in towns where *F. externa* was widespread and abundant where *F. externa* incidence was low. This peculiar distribution of *T. tsugae* in Fairfield County could have been the result of continuing competitive exclusion of *T. tsugae* from areas where *F. externa* had subsequently invaded and established extensive infestations.

Additional evidence of the ability of *Fiorinia externa* to exclude *Tsugaspidiotus tsugae* competitively derives from trends in relative abundance of hemlock scales during a 5-yr period on four trees at each of 10 sites in Fairfield County, Connecticut, where the two scales had coexisted in 1976 (Table VI). At 9 of the sites *T. tsugae* had been excluded after 3 yr, and at the other site its relative abundance had declined sharply after 5 yr.

Experiments conducted in the greenhouse from 1978 to 1981 also demonstrated the ability of *Fiorinia externa* to exclude *Tsugaspidiotus tsugae* from coinhabited trees. In pure infestations mean densities of both species remained relatively constant during the 5-yr period (Table VII). On coinhabited trees mean densities of *F. externa* nearly doubled while numbers of *T. tsugae* were reduced more than 90%. On some trees *T. tsugae* had been completely eliminated.

VI. SUMMARY AND CONCLUSIONS

There is some question as to the importance of interspecific competition in the organization and evolution of insect–herbivore communities (see Price, Chapter 16). However, there is little doubt that when herbivore densities are high, such as in outbreak populations of indigenous species or in populations of exotic species soon after introduction, competition can occur and can contribute to the heterogeneity of resources in individual host plants. Unlike endemic communities in which fitness of herbivores is often governed by an intimate coevolutionary relationship with the host plant, the fitness of introduced herbivorous insects is more often a function of their compatability with the phenology of the new host plant and their ability to cope with density-related changes in the quality and availability of food. Competition and its impact on the population dynamics of herbivorous insects and on the spatial and temporal heterogeneity of resources can be appraised best in such relatively young and simple communities, where resources are abundant

Table VI

Density and Relative Abundance of *Tsugaspidiotus tsugae* Cohabited with *Fiorinia externa*[a]

Site	*Tsugaspidiotus tsugae* (per 100 young needles)	Total scales occupied by *Tsugaspidiotus tsugae*				
		1976	1977	1978	1979	1980
Westport	80.5 ± 7.1	93.3	98.0	97.0	85.3	46.4
Norwalk	29.3 ± 4.6	80.1	2.6	[b]	[b]	[b]
Stamford	28.5 ± 6.3	75.0	37.8	16.1	[b]	[b]
Darien	28.8 ± 7.8	74.6	1.4	[b]	[b]	[b]
Redding	3.0 ± 1.3	60.0	13.6	[b]	[b]	[b]
Ridgefield	2.5 ± 1.1	55.6	33.3	[b]	[b]	[b]
Easton	2.3 ± 1.1	43.4	2.1	[b]	[b]	[b]
Wilton	1.3 ± 0.9	4.9	0.3	[b]	[b]	[b]
New Canaan	4.0 ± 0.3	3.5	3.2	[b]	[b]	[b]
Greenwich	1.5 ± 0.6	1.4	1.2	[b]	[b]	[b]

[a] Over a 5-yr period (1976–1980) at 10 sites in Fairfield County, Connecticut. Numbers are means (± 1 SD).
[b] *Tsugaspidiotus tsugae* excluded.

Table VII
Effects of Cohabitation on Density of Hemlock Scales on Hemlock Trees[a]

	Density			
	1978[b]		1981	
Infestation	Young needles	Total needles	Young needles	Total needles
Pure				
Fiorinia externa	124.4 ± 24.3	136.3 ± 23.4	114.2 ± 11.9	146.2 ± 16.2
Tsugaspidiotus tsugae	135.6 ± 30.4	275.5 ± 36.3	133.4 ± 10.8	258.2 ± 22.5
Mixed				
Fiorinia externa	63.2 ± 13.1	87.6 ± 12.3	117.2 ± 6.6	152.8 ± 10.6
Tsugaspidiotus tsugae	44.2 ± 9.2	177.2 ± 17.6	4.2 ± 3.9	7.6 ± 4.9

[a]Numbers are means (± 1 SD) of scales on 100 needles each on young, 1-yr-old greenhouse trees.
[b]Data from McClure (1980b). Copyright 1980, the Ecological Society of America.

initially and factors regulating population growth are few compared to endemic communities.

The community of armored scales on eastern hemlock illustrates the unique and precarious relationships that exotic herbivorous insects share with each other and with their new host plant and the ways in which competing herbivores can increase the heterogeneity of resources within individual plants. The differential fitness of *Fiorinia externa* and *Tsugaspidiotus tsugae* on eastern hemlock has been related to differences in the quality and availability of food for nymphs in time and space. The greater fitness of *F. externa* is due to a nutritional advantage, which resulted from its earlier colonization time and its superior competitive ability. *Fiorinia externa* is able to reduce the fitness of *T. tsugae* by spatially excluding this competitor from optimal resources and by reducing the nutritional quality of the habitat for subsequent generations. Evidence that colonization time and competitive superiority provide *F. externa* with a nutritional advantage over *T. tsugae* is as follows.

1. The availability of nitrogen to feeding nymphs is an important factor determining scale fitness on eastern hemlock and on numerous other coniferous hosts. Survival, development rate, and fecundity are all influenced by changes in concentrations of foliar nitrogen associated with fertilization, herbivory, and host phenology. Because the concen-

tration of nitrogen declines during the season as the foliage matures, the earlier colonization time of *F. externa* provides nymphs with a nutritional advantage over *T. tsugae*. The significantly greater survival of *F. externa* that colonize greenhouse hemlocks during its natural colonization time (8 June) compared to those that settled 2 weeks later (*Ps* < 0.01 by ANOVA: see Table V) attests to the nutritional advantage of early colonization.

2. Concentrations of nitrogen are significantly higher in young hemlock needles than in the 1-yr-old foliage. Previous colonization of the preferred young needles by *F. externa* forces *T. tsugae* crawlers to settle on the older foliage, where they subsequently incur greater mortality. Clearly, under natural conditions where hemlock scales coexist, the later colonization time of *T. tsugae* and the behavioral shift to older, low-nitrogen foliage will further reduce its fitness.

3. Feeding by *F. externa* nymphs significantly reduces the amount of nitrogen in the young hemlock foliage available to *T. tsugae* nymphs that colonize 2–6 weeks later. Consequently, *T. tsugae* nymphs in mixed-species infestations have even less food available for their survival, growth, and development. Indeed, the greater mortality to *T. tsugae* on greenhouse hemlocks that have been colonized previously by *F. externa* (compared to trees colonized by both scales simultaneously) indicates that *F. externa* reduces the quality and availability of food for *T. tsugae*.

4. High scale density has deleterious effects on the survival and fecundity of *F. externa* and *T. tsugae* (as observed for 3 yr in a Darien, Connecticut, forest). These data and those from greenhouse experiments demonstrate that hemlock scales do experience intraspecific and interspecific competition at densities commonly encountered in forests and that *F. externa* has a greater adverse effect on *T. tsugae* fitness than on its own. Intraspecific competition is more important in regulating *F. externa* populations, whereas interspecific competition has a greater regulatory impact on *T. tsugae* populations. *Fiorinia externa* is the superior competitor and excludes *T. tsugae* from coinhabited trees in the greenhouse and in hemlock forests throughout southwestern Connecticut.

These studies on the exotic scale insects of eastern hemlock illustrate how intraspecific and interspecific competition between herbivores further adds to the complexity of individual trees as habitats. Competing herbivores may reduce the fitness of others by spatially excluding them from optimal resources on the host plant and by altering the nutritional quality of their habitat temporally, making it less suitable for subsequent generations. Accordingly, competition between herbivores and its contribution to spatial and temporal variation in the quality of a host plant may significantly alter prediction of insect distribution and abundance based solely on measures of host-plant nutrition and defensive chemistry.

REFERENCES

Auclair, J. L. (1963). Aphid feeding and nutrition. *Annu. Rev. Entomol.* **8**, 439–490.

Bartlett, B. R. (1951). The action of certain "inert" dust materials on parasitic Hymenoptera. *J. Econ. Entomol.* **44**, 891–896.

Beck, S. D., and Reese, J. C. (1976). Insect–plant interactions: nutrition and metabolism. *Recent Adv. Phytochem.* **19**, 41–92.

Bennett, F. D., and Hughes, I. W. (1959). Biological control of insect pests in Bermuda. *Bull. Entomol. Res.* **50**, 423–436.

Brumbach, J. J. (1965). The climate of Connecticut. *Conn. Geol. Nat. Hist. Surv. Bull.* **99**, 1–215.

Caltagirone, L. E. (1981). Landmark examples in classical biological control. *Annu. Rev. Entomol.* **26**, 213–232.

Cates, R. G., and Rhoades, D. F. (1977). Patterns in the production of antiherbivore defenses in plant communities. *Biochem. Syst. Ecol.* **5**, 185–193.

Chapman, R. F. (1974). The chemical inhibition of feeding by phytophagous insects: a review. *Bull. Entomol. Res.* **64**, 339–363.

Cody, M. L., and Diamond, J. M. (1975). "Ecology and Evolution of Communities." Belknap Press, Cambridge, Massachusetts.

DeBach, P. (1974). "Biological Control by Natural Enemies." Cambridge Univ. Press, London and New York.

DeBach, P., and Rosen, D. (1976). Armoured scale insects. *In* "Studies in Biological Control" (V. L. Delucchi, ed.), pp. 139–178. Cambridge Univ. Press, London/New York.

DeBach, P., and Sundby, R. A. (1963). Competitive displacement between ecological homologues. *Hilgardia* **34**, 105–166.

DeBach, P., Rosen, D., and Kennet, C. E. (1971). Biological control of coccids by introduced natural enemies. *In* "Biological Control" (C. B. Huffaker, ed.), pp. 165–194. Plenum, New York.

Dixon, A. F. G. (1970). Quality and availability of food for a sycamore aphid population. *In* "Animal Populations in Relation to their Food Resources" (A. Watson, ed.), pp. 271–278. Blackwell, Oxford.

Dixon, A. F. G. (1975). Seasonal changes in the fat content, form, state of gonads and length of adult life in the sycamore aphid, *Drepanosiphum platanoides* (Schr.). *Trans. R. Entomol. Soc. London* **127**, 87–100.

Dixon, A. F. G. (1979). Sycamore aphid numbers: the role of weather, host and aphid. *In* "Population Dynamics" (R. M. Anderson, B. D. Turner, and L. R. Taylor, eds.), pp. 105–121. Oxford Univ. Press, London and New York.

Edmunds, G. F., Jr. (1973). Ecology of black pine leaf scale (Homoptera: Diaspididae). *Environ. Entomol.* **2**, 765–777.

Edmunds, G. F., Jr., and Alstad, D. N. (1978). Coevolution in insect herbivores and conifers. *Science* **199**, 941–945.

Feeny, P. (1970). Seasonal changes in oak leaf tannins and nutrients as a cause of spring feeding by winter moth caterpillars. *Ecology* **51**, 565–581.

Ferris, G. F. (1936). Contributions to our knowledge of the Coccoidea (Homoptera). *Microentomology* **1**, 1–16.

Friend, W. G. (1958). Nutritional requirements of phytophagous insects. *Annu. Rev. Entomol.* **3**, 57–74.

Glowa, W. (1974). Zirconium dioxide, a new catalyst, in the Kjeldahl method for total nitrogen determination. *J. Assoc. Off. Anal. Chem.* **57**, 1228–1230.

Hill, M. G., and Newbery, D. McC. (1980). The distribution and abundance of the coccid *Icerya seychellarum* Westw. on Aldabra atoll. *Ecol. Entomol.* **5**, 115–122.

Hutchinson, G. E. (1978). "An Introduction to Population Ecology." Yale Univ. Press, New Haven, Connecticut.

Kimmins, J. P. (1971). Variation in the foliar amino acid composition of flowering and non-flowering balsam fir [*Abies balsamea* (L.) Mill.] and white spruce [*Picea glauca* (Moench) Voss] in relation to outbreaks of the spruce budworm [*Choristoneura fumiferana* (Clem)]. *Can. J. Zool.* **49**, 1005–1011.

Kloft, W., and Ehrhardt, P. (1959). Zur Sitkalauskalamität in Nordwestdeutschland. *Waldhygiene* **2**, 47–49.

Lawton, J. H., and Hassell, M. P. (1981). Asymmetrical competition in insects. *Nature (London)* **289**, 793–795.

Lawton, J. H, and Strong, D. R., Jr. (1981). Community patterns and competition in folivorous insects. *Am. Nat.* **118**, 317–338.

Long, C. (1961). "Biochemist's Handbook." Van Nostrand-Reinhold, Princeton, New Jersey.

McClure, M. S. (1977a). Resurgence of the scale, *Fiorinia externa* (Homoptera: Diaspididae), on hemlock following insecticide application. *Environ. Entomol.* **6**, 480–484.

McClure, M. S. (1977b). Dispersal of the scale *Fiorinia externa* (Homoptera: Diaspididae) and effects of edaphic factors on its establishment on hemlock. *Environ. Entomol.* **6**, 539-544.

McClure, M. S. (1977c). Population dynamics of the red pine scale, *Matsucoccus resinosae* (Homoptera: Margarodidae): the influence of resinosis. *Environ. Entomol.* **6**, 789–795.

McClure, M. S. (1978). Seasonal development of *Fiorinia externa, Tsugaspidiotus tsugae* (Homoptera: Diaspididae), and their parasite *Aspidiotiphagus citrinus* (Hymenoptera: Aphelinidae): importance of parasite–host synchronism to the population dynamics of two scale pests of hemlock. *Environ. Entomol.* **7**, 863–870.

McClure, M. S. (1979a). Self-regulation in populations of the elongate hemlock scale, *Fiorinia externa* (Homoptera: Diaspididae). *Oecologia* **39**, 25–36.

McClure, M. S. (1979b). Self-regulation in hemlock scale populations: role of food quantity and quality. *Misc. Publ. Entomol. Soc. Am.* **11**(3), 33–40.

McClure, M. S. (1980a). Foliar nitrogen: a basis for host suitability for elongate hemlock scale, *Fiorinia externa* (Homoptera: Diaspididae). *Ecology* **61**, 72–79.

McClure, M. S. (1980b). Competition between exotic species: scale insects on hemlock. *Ecology* **61**, 1391–1401.

McClure, M. S. (1981). Effects of voltinism, interspecific competition and parasitism on the population dynamics of the hemlock scales, *Fiorinia externa* and *Tsugaspidiotus tsugae* (Homoptera: Diaspididae). *Ecol. Entomol.* **6**, 47–54.

McClure, M. S., and Fergione, M. B. (1977). *Fiorinia externa* and *Tsugaspidiotus tsugae* (Homoptera: Diaspididae): distribution, abundance, and new hosts of two destructive scale insects of eastern hemlock in Connecticut. *Environ. Entomol.* **6**, 807–811.

McNeill, S. and Southwood, T. R. E. (1978). The role of nitrogen in the development of insect/plant relationships. *In* "Biochemical Aspects of Plant and Animal Coevolution" (J. B. Harborne, ed.), pp. 77–98. Academic Press, New York and London.

Marlatt, C. L. (1911). A newly-imported scale-pest on Japanese hemlock (Rhynch.). *Entomol. News* **22**, 385–387.

Mattson, W. J., Jr. (1980). Herbivory in relation to plant nitrogen content. *Annu. Rev. Ecol. Syst.* **11**, 119–161.

Mattson, W. J. and Addy, N. D., (1975). Phytophagous insects as regulators of forest primary production. *Science* **190**, 515–522.

Newbery, D. McC. (1980a). Infestation of the coccid, *Icerya seychellarum* (Westw.), on the mangrove *Avicennia marina* (Forsk.) Vierh. on Aldabra atoll, with special reference to tree age. *Oecologia* **45**, 325–330.

Newbery, D. McC. (1980b). Interactions between the coccid, *Icerya seychellarum* (Westw.), and its host tree species on Aldabra atoll. I. *Euphorbia pyrifolia* Lam. *Oecologia* **46**, 171–179.

Newbery, D. McC. (1980c). Interactions between the coccid, *Icerya seychellarum* (Westw.) and its host tree species on Aldabra atoll. II. *Scaevola taccada* (Gaertn.) Roxb. *Oecologia*, **46**, 180–185.

Parry, W. H. (1974). The effect of nitrogen levels in Sitka spruce needles on *Elatobium abietinum* (Walker) populations in northeastern Scotland. *Oecologia* **15**, 305–320.

Parry, W. H. (1976). The effect of needle age on the acceptability of Sitka spruce needles to the aphid, *Elatobium abietinum* (Walker). *Oecologia* **23**, 297–313.

Reese, J. C. (1978). Chronic effects of plant allelochemicals on insect nutritional physiology. *ACS Symp. Ser.* **62**, 129–152.

Reese, J. C., and Beck, S. D. (1978). Interrelationships of nutritional indices and dietary moisture in the black cutworm, *Agrotis ipsilon*, digestive efficiency. *J. Insect Physiol.* **24**, 473–479.

Rhoades, D. F., and Cates, R. G. (1976). Toward a general theory of plant antiherbivore chemistry. *Recent Adv. Phytochem.* **10**, 168–213.

Ripper, W. E. (1956). Effect of pesticides on balance of arthropod populations. *Annu. Rev. Entomol.* **1**, 403–438.

Rosenthal, G. A., and Janzen, D. H., eds. (1979). "Herbivores: Their Interaction with Secondary Plant Metabolites." Academic Press, New York.

Sasscer, E. R. (1912). The genus *Fiorinia* in the United States. *U. S. Dep. Agric., Bur. Entomol. Tech. Ser.* **16**, 75–82.

Scriber, J. M. (1977). Limiting effects of low leaf-water content on the nitrogen utilization, energy budget, and larval growth of *Hyalophora cecropia* (Lepidoptera: Saturniidae). *Oecologia* **28**, 269–287.

Scriber, J. M. (1978). The effects of larval feeding specialization and plant growth form on the consumption and utilization of plant biomass and nitrogen: an ecological consideration. *Entomol. Exp. Appl.* **24**, 694–710.

Scriber, J. M. (1979). Post-ingestive utilization of plant biomass and nitrogen by Lepidoptera: legume feeding by the southern armyworm. *J.N.Y. Entomol. Soc.* **87**, 141–153.

Scriber, J. M., and Slansky, F., Jr. (1981). The nutritional ecology of immature insects. *Annu. Rev. Entomol.* **26**, 183–211.

Stark, R. W. (1965). Recent trends in forest entomology. *Annu. Rev. Entomol.* **10**, 303–324.

Swain, T. (1977). Secondary compounds as protection agents. *Annu. Rev. Plant Physiol.* **28**, 479–501.

Takagi, S. (1963). *Fiorinia externa* on *Tsuga sieboldii* in Japan. *Insecta Matsum.* **26**, 115–117.

Takahashi, R., and Takagi, S. (1957). A new genus of Diaspididae from Japan (Coccoidea, Homoptera). *Konchu* **25**, 102–105.

Thompson, W. R. (1954). Biological control work on cedar scales in Bermuda. *Rep. Commonw. Entomol. Conf., 6th, 1954*, pp. 89–95.

Weiss, H. B. (1914). Notes on three imported insects occurring in New Jersey. *J. Econ. Entomol.* **7**, 250–251.

White, T. C. R. (1969). An index to measure weather-induced stress of trees associated with outbreaks of psyllids in Australia. *Ecology* **50,** 905–909.

White, T. C. R. (1974). A hypothesis to explain outbreaks of looper caterpillars, with special reference to populations of *Selidosema sauvis* in a plantation of *Pinus radiata* in New Zealand. *Oecologia* **16,** 279–301.

White, T. C. R. (1976). Weather, food and plagues of locust. *Oecologia* **22,** 119–134.

White, T. C. R. (1978). The importance of a relative shortage of food in animal ecology. *Oecologia* **33,** 71–86.

Mark S. McClure
Department of Entomology
The Connecticut Agricultural Experiment Station
New Haven, Connecticut

CHAPTER 6

Herbivore Population Dynamics and Plant Chemistry

DAVID F. RHOADES

I. INTRODUCTION

Two main schools of thought have arisen to explain large temporal fluctuations in abundance of animals. One school (Andrewartha and Birch, 1954; Milne, 1957) proposed that physical factors, particularly variation in weather, that were themselves independent of animal numbers (density-independent factors) are the main determinants of animal abundance. The other school (Nicholson, 1954; Wellington, 1957, 1960; Chitty, 1960; Klomp, 1964) proposed that biotic factors, such as competition for food and levels of predation, parasitism, and disease, the effects of which were presumed to vary with population density (density-dependent factors), largely determine changes in animal abundance. Because ample evidence exists that both climatically and biotically induced changes in mortality and natality exert important influences on animal populations, a spirited debate ensued (*Cold Spring Harbor Symposia on Quantitative Biology* **22**, 1957). Also disputed were the meanings of the concept of population "regulation," whether animal populations were indeed regulated and by what mechanisms, and whether factors could be meaningfully categorized into density-independent and density-dependent groups. Much of the controversy centered on the population dynamics of small herbivorous animals, particularly phytophagous insects and microtine rodents. This debate subsided but was not resolved, and it now appears that neither density-dependent factors nor density-independent factors as they were originally conceived, nor even a combination, can satisfactorily explain temporal fluctuation in the abundance of animals, even though there are ways of including both kinds of factors in a more general theory (Horn, 1968; Enright, 1976).

I suggest that an important reason for the continuing inability of population models to satisfactorily explain or predict large fluctuations in numbers is their general failure to include changes in the quality as well as quantity of food resources. To develop satisfactory population models for herbivorous animals it is probable that food-plant nutritional and defensive characteristics must be taken into acount. Inclusion of these factors can provide a direct causal link between "density-dependent" and "density-independent" influences on herbivore population dynamics.

In this chapter I examine the changes in nutritional quality of plants (to herbivores) induced by physical and biotic stress of plants, defensive responses of plants to herbivore attack, and direct and indirect effects of changes in food quality on fitness, population growth, and other properties of herbivores. Offensive adaptations of herbivores that enable them to discriminate between suitable and unsuitable food and that enable them to actively increase the nutritional quality of plants or circumvent induced defensive responses of plants are also discussed. I propose a theory of herbivore population outbreaks in which stability in plant–herbivore relationships is viewed as resulting from a balance of offensive and defensive power among plants, herbivores, and members of higher trophic levels. In this model, population instabilities result from the perturbing influences of plant physical stress, climatic change leading to change in the geographic range of herbivores, and migration of herbivores between different portions of their range. This theory incorporates that of White (1969, 1974, 1976), which attributes herbivore outbreaks largely to physical stress-induced changes in proximate nutritional quality of plants, and those of Haukioja and Hakala (1975) and Benz (1974, 1977), which attribute population cycles largely to active defensive responses by plants.

II. EFFECTS OF STRESSFUL ENVIRONMENTS ON THE PROXIMATE NUTRITIONAL QUALITY OF PLANTS

It is generally accepted that atypical weather conditions, especially drought, excessive precipitation, and unusually hot or cold temperatures, are causally associated with increase in abundance of phytophagous insects (Wellington et al., 1950; Uvarov, 1957; Rudnew, 1963). In some cases the effect of weather has been attributed to a direct action on the insects (Klomp, 1968; Wellington et al., 1975), but in others the insects have been shown to be well adapted to climatic extremes (Morris et al., 1958), and in general the mechanism by which weather influences insect fitness remains obscure (Gunn, 1960; Dempster, 1963). This correlation between unusual weather and insect outbreaks has been examined by White (1969, 1974, 1976; see also Rudnew, 1963), who argued that the correlation is often largely due to effects upon the plants rather than upon the insects. White (1969, 1974, 1976) suggested that plant stress, particularly that induced by drought, can lead to enhanced proximate nutritional quality of plants, which in turn results in lowered mortality and increased fecundity of phytophagous insects (see also Kimmins, 1971). For example, in the case of grasses and forbs, drought stress can lead to a 53% increase in total available carbohydrates and an 88% increase in total foliage nitrogen content (Abd El Rahman et al., 1971; Abd El Rahman, 1973). Soluble metabolites of potential nutritional importance to animals such as proline, sugars, glycerol, malate, and shikimate increase in concentration in plant tissues in response to drought, freezing, salinity, or root flooding stresses (Levitt, 1972; Harborne, 1977; Mali and Mentha, 1977). The reasons for these changes in concentrations of primary metabolites are poorly understood. Increased tissue solute concentrations in plants under conditions of water deficit or freezing could contribute directly to plant resistance to tissue damage from desiccation or ice-crystal formation by lowering the vapor pressure or freezing point and increasing the osmotic pressure of the tissues. In some cases it is possible that the observed high concentrations of total nitrogen and low-molecular-weight primary metabolites in plants grown under stressful conditions are due, in whole or part, to low tissue concentrations of other unmeasured substances such as cellulose, lignin, or defensive compounds.

Other stressful influences on plants that are associated with insect outbreaks include nutrient-poor soils, competition, pollution, overmaturity, disease, and damage during cultural operations (Table I). Interestingly, removal of the stressful condition is often associated with higher mortality of the insects and collapse of the outbreak (White, 1974, 1976).

Stark (1965) has reviewed the effects of forest fertilization on fitness of pest insects. For species of pine, beech, and oak, fertilization usually markedly increases tree resistance to defoliating insects, resulting in increased larval mortality, reduction in adult female weight, and decreased population levels (see also Haukioja and Niemelä, 1976). In some cases fertilization has led to an increase in insect damage, but Stark (1965) has suggested that such results often may be due to overfertilization. Similarly, severely nutrient-stressed plants are often more susceptible to disease than those grown under optimal nutritional conditions, yet plants receiving a large excess of nutrients may be predisposed to disease (Huber, 1980).

It thus appears that plants often exist in a suboptimal physiological condition due to physical stress, which renders them more susceptible to herbivores and disease. This increased susceptibility may be due to an enhanced proximate nutritional quality of stressed plants as proposed by White (1969, 1974, 1976) or, more probably, to an imbalance between proximate nutritional quality and intrinsic plant defenses. The latter contention is supported by the fact that although forest fertilization usually leads to an increase in plant resistance to insects, increased resistance is also, in some cases, associated with increased proximate nutritional quality of the foliage (Buttner, 1961; Smirnoff and Bernier, 1973).

III. THEORY OF PLANT DEFENSE

Few workers question that plants display physical and chemical defensive adaptations. Abundant evidence has accumulated to implicate plant secondary metabolites as defensive compounds in plant–plant, plant–pathogen, and plant–herbivore interactions (Harborne, 1978; Rosenthal and Janzen, 1979), and there is little doubt that all plants possess chemical defensive systems against consumers. However, our understanding of how and why various classes of secondary metabolites are

Table I

Factors that Predispose Plants to Outbreaks of Phytophagous Insects

Insect	Reference[a]	Predisposing factor
Swain jack pine sawfly	1	Poor, sandy soils
Lodgepole needle miner	1	Nutrient-poor, low-water-capacity soils
Pine defoliators	1	Soils deficient in nitrogen.
Red-headed pine sawfly	1	Soils with poorly developed or disturbed profile or trees competing with other vegetation
Defoliators	1	Ridge tops where soil moisture depletions and other stresses are most severe or nutrient-poor soils
Stem coccid	1	Air pollution
Phytophagous insects	1	Pollution
Hemlock looper	1	Poor growing conditions for several years
Southern pine beetle	1,2	Damage during harvest; poor drainage, low soil fertility; slow growth and dense stocking conditions; rapidly changing climatic conditions, moisture surplus, or deficit; or monoculture
Fir engraver beetle	1	Trees weakened by competition, drought, or disease
Gypsy moth	3	Poor, shallow soils, xeric sites; drought-stricken trees; extremes in meterologic conditions; or ice damage to trees
Spruce budworm	4	Several warm, dry summers; tree over-maturity
Bark beetles and other phytophagous insects	5	Trees weakened by forest fires, lightning, disease, or drought
Elm bark beetle	6	"Weakened" elm trees
Engelmann spruce beetle	7	Windthrow or mature and overmature trees
Pest insects	8	Monocultured, even-aged trees, or monocultured crops
Bark beetles	9	Freshly cut, lightning-struck, or girdled trees
Douglas-fir tussock moth	10	Dry sites
Aphids	11	Drought
European pine sawfly	12	Drought and low soil nutrients

[a]References: 1, Mattson and Addy (1975); 2, Kalkstein (1976); 3, Bess et al. (1947), Leonard (1974) Campbell and Sloan (1977); 4, Morris et al. (1958); 5, Evans (1971); 6, Peacock et al. (1971); 7, Wygant (1958); 8, Varley et al. (1975), Root (1973); 9, Hanover (1975); 10, Lessard (1974); 11, Owen (1976); 12, Larsson and Tenow (1982).

distributed between and within plants, how these substances act and interact in the target organisms, their relative cost to plant metabolism, and the mechanisms that consumers have evolved to detoxify or tolerate defensive substances is still rudimentary.

It seems axiomatic that the evolution of defensive adaptations in plants should proceed as a function of both historical and ecological factors. On one hand, selection pressure in ecological time provides the driving force for change in the complement of defensive adaptations in plants. On the other hand, selection at any given time can act only to modify an existing set of adaptations, which should reflect past selection pressure on ancestral types. The dual importance of historical and ecological factors in determining secondary chemistry is illustrated by the very existence of plant secondary chemical systematics as a subject. Ultimately, theories of plant defense will include full consideration of both historical and ecological effects. Such a synthesis was attempted, to some degree, by Dethier (1954) and Erhlich and Raven (1965), but, given the enormity of the task and the number of unknowns, more-recent work has tended to concentrate on either historical or ecological considerations.

Swain (1978) suggested that the distribution of secondary metabolites among taxa of plants can be understood in historical terms. He found that tannins, lignin, and other phenolics are characteristic of ancient plant groups such as gymnosperms and ferns, whereas alkaloids, toxic nonprotein amino acids, cyanogens, and glucosinolates are found mainly in the more advanced angiosperms. Swain concluded that the former group of substances evolved early in plant evolution and has been retained in primitive living taxa, whereas the latter group is of relatively recent origin.

Janzen (1973a,b), McKey (1974), Feeny (1975, 1976), Futuyma (1976), Rhoades and Cates (1976), and Rhoades (1979) have emphasized the importance of risk, cost, and value, operating in ecological time, in the maintenance and evolution of patterns in the defensive attributes of plants. In short, they proposed that the amount and type of defense evolved in plants and their various tissues is related to the risk plants face from consumers, the value of their individual tissues, and the costs of defense. For conceptual purposes plant defensive metabolites have been divided into two basic types, *qualitative* and *quantitative* defensive compounds (Feeny, 1975) or, alternatively, *toxins* and *digestibility-reducing substances*, respectively (Rhoades and Cates, 1976). Qualitative defensive compounds such as alkaloids, glucosinolates, cardenolides, cyanogenic substances, and nonprotein amino acids, many of which interfere with internal metabolism of herbivores, are characteristically present at low concentration ($< 2\%$ dry weight) in plant tissues and possess properties facilitating their synthesis, storage, and transport within plants. Though cheap for the plant to synthesize, transport, and store, qualitative defensive substances are thought to have a limited protective ability against coevolved herbivores that have developed detoxification or tolerance mechanisms. Quantitative defenses such as tannins, resins, silica, lignin, and refractory carbohydrates, many of which act to reduce the digestibility of plant tissues to herbivores, are characteristically present in large quantities (~5–20% dry weight for tannins) and are thought to be more costly to the energy budget of plants than qualitative defenses. Though costly, quantitative defenses provide more protection to plants than qualitative defenses because they act in a dosage-dependent fashion, even against highly coevolved herbivores. The defense type employed by a plant species or individual plant tissue is mainly determined by the *apparency* (Feeny, 1976) or *predictability* and *availability* (Rhoades and Cates, 1976) of the plant or plant tissue as a food resource to herbivores and other enemies. Unpredictable (unapparent) resources such as herbaceous, early-successional, and rare plants, or young, rapidly flushed leaves of woody plants escape from enemies in space and time and, consequently, the plants use cheap qualitative defenses. On the other hand, predictable (apparent) resources such as woody perennial, climax, and common plants, particularly the persistent tissues of these plants such as mature leaves, bark, and wood, are easy for herbivores to locate and, consequently, the plants use costly quantitative defenses. Thus, in ecological time, fitness loss of apparent and unapparent plants due to herbivores and other consumers should be similar, because each type of plant has evolved defenses appropriate to its risk.

Approximately 80% of woody perennial dicot species contain tannins, as opposed to about 15% of herbaceous dicot species, indicating the importance of quantitative defense for the former group (Bate-Smith and Metcalf, 1957; Rhoades and Cates, 1976). Many plants use both qualitative and quantitative defenses, and in these cases qualitative defenses are usually concentrated in more ephemeral tissues, whereas quantitative defenses are usually concentrated in the more persistent tissues (Feeny, 1976; Rhoades and Cates, 1976).

Within plants the value of individual tissues can vary. Growing shoots and young leaves are more valuable to plants than mature leaves (McKey, 1974, 1979). Therefore, for plants of indeterminate growth form, which do not produce their leaves in a sudden flush, we can expect higher commitment to defense in young leaves than in mature ones.

The historical and ecological interpretations for the gross pattern of distribution of secondary substances among trees and herbs are reconciled by the fact that many herbaceous plants are members of taxa thought to have evolved more recently than characteristically woody taxa (Cronquist, 1968). Examination of the distribution of secondary metabolites within plant families that contain both woody, apparent members and herbaceous, unapparent members (e.g., Compositae and Leguminosae) may help evaluate the relative importance of historical and ecological factors.

Some of the ideas, assumptions, and proposed general correlations in the ecological scheme have been challenged (DiFeo, 1977; Bernays, 1978, 1981; Jung *et al.*, 1979; Swain, 1979; Bernays *et al.*, 1981; Fox, 1981). It is beyond the scope of this chapter to examine the questions raised. Let it suffice to say that there appears to be no new synthesis that better explains the observed patterns. It should be emphasized that the scheme is tentative and may require modification, but I believe that the central importance of risk, cost, and value will be retained, superimposed on historical effects.

It has become clear that plants not only contain constitutive defensive chemical systems, but also that the levels of defensive substances in plants can change in response to physical stress (Section IV) and attack by herbivores (Section V). In addition, the importance of variation in amount and type of constitutive chemical defense among individual plants of the same species and among different parts of the same plant has been clarified. Within- and between-plant variation in constitutive defensive chemistry has been extensively discussed elsewhere in this book (see particularly Whitham, Chapter 2; Schultz, Chapter 3; Alstad and Edmunds, Chapter 12; and also Rhoades, 1979). I shall therefore not discuss such variation further except to emphasize that any factor reducing defensive chemical variation within plant communities, between plants within a species, or between different parts of the same plant is likely to have a negative effect on plant defensive capabilities and to promote attack by consumers. Investigation of the responsive nature of plant defenses, variation in constitutive defenses within and between plants, and the costs of various defensive systems to plant metabolism, in my view, are the most exciting and potentially rewarding areas of current research in plant defense.

IV. EFFECT OF PHYSICAL STRESS ON PLANT DEFENSES

If we assume that plants possess finite energy and nutrient resources that can be allocated to various plant functions, to accommodate various contingencies that plants face, we can conclude that energy or nutrients allocated to a particular need will decrease the amounts available to meet other requirements. Similarly, any circumstance that reduces the size of the energy and nutrient budget will reduce the amount available for allocation (Mooney, 1972; Mooney and Chu, 1974; Rhoades, 1979; McLaughlin and Shriner, 1980). Growth, reproduction, defense, and the accomodation of physical stresses are probably all important energy- and nutrient-requiring activities of plants. We can therefore expect that physical stress of plants, by reducing the size of the energy and nutrient budget or by requiring its expenditure to accomodate the stress, may result in a lower commitment to defense by the plant in some cases.

Lowered plant defensive capability resulting from physical stress has been best documented in the case of coniferous trees under attack by bark beetles (Vité, 1961; Smith, 1961; Hanover, 1975). Attacked trees respond by flooding beetle galleries with oleoresin, which "pitches out" and drowns or toxifies the beetles. In trees experiencing a water deficit, the resin-exudation pressure is reduced, resulting in increased beetle survival and, sometimes, death of the tree.

In general though, the effects of physical stress on the content of secondary chemicals in plants are complex. There is no question that a variety of physical stresses, including drought, high or low temperature extremes, shade, etiolation, nutrient stress, and pollution, can have dramatic effects on the concentrations of secondary chemicals in plants. Concentrations of some substances decrease, but, on the other hand, concentrations of many others increase in response to physical stress (Rhoades, 1979). In addition, there are a number of conflicting reports concerning the effects of stress on levels of secondary metabolites in plants (see James, 1950; Mothes, 1960). For instance, Nowaki *et al.* (1976) studied the effect of nitrogen fertilization on content of glycoalkaloids in potato leaves in two consecutive years. In the first year of the study the weather was warm and sunny. During this season unfertilized potatoes produced leaves containing high levels of glycoalkaloids, whereas leaves of fertilized potatoes contained low levels. In contrast, during the second season, which was cool and cloudy, the opposite result was obtained.

To explain the confusing effects of stress on levels of secondary compounds in plants, Rhoades (1979) proposed that plants generally possess two or more defensive chemical systems of differing cost. Under physical stress, plants compensate by decreasing their commitment to costly defenses but also, sometimes, by increasing their commitment to less costly but less effective defenses. Applied to the results of Nowaki *et al.* (1976), this suggests that, under poor growing conditions (cool and cloudy), potatoes use glycoalkaloids as a leaf defense and that levels of these substances are increased with increasing nitrogen availability. Under good growing conditions (warm and sunny), potatoes also utilize mainly glycoalkaloids, if available nitrogen levels are low, but when fertilized they switch to an unidentified, more costly and effective system. Proteinase inhibitors (Ryan, 1979; Chapter 2) are possible candidates for this unidentified system.

To date, there have been few studies of the effects of stress on two or more defensive chemical systems operating in the same plant simultaneously. Concentrations of cyanogenic substances are high and concentrations of tannin low in shaded bracken fern, and vice versa for unshaded plants (Cooper-Driver et al., 1977). This single example supports the reallocation hypothesis.

Other factors that need to be taken into account when considering the effect of stress on the defensive posture of plants are the degree of adaptation of the plant to physical stress and whether the stress is transient or sustained. Conditions that might be considered stressful to plants in general can be expected to have little effect on highly adapted plants. For example, water-deficit stress would be expected to have minimal effect on the defensive posture of desert plants. Transient stresses may have effects that differ markedly from sustained ones. It has been argued (see previous discussion) that stresses that reduce the size of the plant's energy and nutrient budget or that cause diversion of energy and nutrients to accomodate the stress will reduce the resources available for allocation to other contingencies such as defense. However, there is no absolute requirement that allocation to defense be reduced under these conditions, only that the sum total of resources to be allocated be reduced. Indeed, under some sustained stressful conditions we might expect greater commitment to defense in spite of the decreased resource base. An example may be the effect of sustained low soil nutrient availability. Janzen (1974) has argued that the value of tissues in plants growing on nutrient-poor soils is higher than that of plants growing on nutrient-rich soils due to replacement costs. From this Janzen predicted that plants grown on impoverished soils would be found to contain greater concentrations of defensive secondary compounds than plants growing on rich soils. McKey et al. (1978) have provided evidence that this is true (see also Coulson et al., 1960a,b; Davies et al., 1964a,b). Under conditions of sustained stress, in which it is adaptive for the plant to increase its resource allocation to defense in spite of a lower resource base, we can expect a severely curtailed allocation to other activities such as growth and reproduction.

If a stress is short-lived, the risk of attack by consumers during the period of stress is low because little time is available for consumers to locate the plant and/or build up a high population. Because of this element of escape from consumers, lowered defensive capability of plants may occur more commonly in response to stresses that over the evolutionary history of the plant have usually proven to be short-lived than in response to stresses that have usually proven to be long-lived.

In summary, the effects of physical stress on concentrations of secondary metabolites in plants are complicated and poorly understood. Partial explanation of the effects may be obtained by assuming that stressed plants reallocate resources among defensive systems of differing cost and effectiveness, but many questions remain. We greatly need detailed studies of the effects of a variety of transient and sustained stresses on each of the several different secondary-metabolite systems that most plants appear to contain. It is clear, however, that physical stress can have important effects on levels of secondary metabolites in plants. Therefore, it is likely that the predisposition of herbivore outbreaks to occur on physically stressed plants is due to an imbalance between proximate nutritional quality and defensive capability rather than to changes in proximate nutritional quality alone.

V. DEFENSIVE RESPONSES OF PLANTS TO HERBIVORE ATTACK

There is mounting evidence that plant defensive systems can be altered not only by physical stress, but also by biotic stress from herbivores and other consumers. At the simplest level, breakdown of precursors such as glucosinolates and cyanogens to release toxic substances or the release of tannins from vacuoles during tissue damage are plant defensive responses. Attack of plants by herbivores or pathogens or simulated herbivore damage can also initiate much more complex sequences of events in plants to reduce present and future damage.

According to Benz (1977), Standfuss may have been the first to suggest that attack by herbivores can lead to decreased food quality of plant tissues to subsequent herbivores. Standfuss found that rearing Lepidoptera for several successive years on the same individual trees gave unsatisfactory results due, apparently, to increasing malnutrition of the larvae. He interpreted these results as indicating the existence of active self-protection mechanisms in plants (Standfuss, 1896, in Benz, 1977).

Green and Ryan (1972), in a seminal paper, reported that mechanical or Colorado potato beetle damage to tomato or potato leaves leads to a systemic increase in concentration of proteinase inhibitors in the plants. Oligosaccharides, liberated from the damaged tissues during wounding, travel in the vasular system to initiate accumulation of proteinase inhibitors throughout the plant in a matter of hours (Green and Ryan,

1973; Ryan, 1979, Chapter 2). They suggested that this may reduce subsequent herbivore attack. However, deterrent or antibiotic effects of the induced response against herbivores have not been demonstrated.

Davies and Schuster (1981) found that mechanical wounding of pea and soybean stems, tobacco leaves, and corn roots can lead to rapid, massive, and enduring formation of polyribosomes, indicating enhanced protein-synthesizing capacity in tissues adjacent to and distant from the site of injury. The signal is apparently generated in less than 15 min and is transmitted through the plant at a rate in excess of 30 mm/min. Although the wound-induced plant products and their functions are unknown, the results illustrate the speed with which systemic changes can occur in response to plant injury.

Benz (1974, 1977) has shown that defoliation of larch (Larix decidua) by the larch budmoth (Zeiraphera diniana) in subalpine forests of Switzerland leads to a delayed flush of smaller needles the following year. These needles have an abnormally high fiber content and a reduced nitrogen content, and they may sometimes be covered with a layer of oleoresin. They are less palatable and assimilable for the budmoth larvae, leading to high mortality of the larvae and low fecundity of surviving adults. Benz indicated that the induced resistance disappears within 4–5 yr. Benz suggested that induced responses in plants subjected to insect attack may be common, representing a major cause of the collapse of phytophagous insect populations.

Haukioja and co-workers at Kevo in northern Finland mechanically damaged leaves of birch (Betula pubescens) and observed an increase in total phenolic content and phenolic trypson inhibitor content of neighboring undamaged leaves 2 days later (Haukioja and Niemelä, 1976, 1977; Niemelä et al., 1979). Larvae of the autumnal moth (Oporinia autumnata) fed these leaves exhibited retarded pupation and lower pupal weights than larvae fed control leaves. The rapid induced response appears to be greatest in the spring and early summer, because it was detected in bioassays using several species of Lepidoptera and Hymenoptera in spring, early summer, and midsummer, but not in late summer using two other species of Hymenoptera (Haukioja and Niemelä, 1979). The rapid response was more intense for strains of birch from southern Finland, where population fluctuations of O. autumnata are minimal, than for strains from northern Finland, where population fluctuations are more pronounced (Haukioja, 1980). Retarded pupation and low pupal weights of O. autumnata were also observed for larvae fed leaves of birch that were artificially defoliated the previous year, as compared to those fed leaves from control trees (Haukioja and Niemelä, 1977). This long-term response was greater for northern birch strains than for southern ones (Haukioja, 1980). These latitudinal differences in short- and long-term response of birch to artificial damage were also reflected on a local scale along an altitudinal gradient extending from a higher elevation where *O. autumnata* outbreaks occur to a lower elevation where they do not (Haukioja, 1980). It thus appears that in *O. autumnata* outbreak regions the birches exhibit a weak, immediate defensive response but a strong one the following year, whereas the opposite occurs at altitudes and geographical regions where *O. autumnata* populations are more stable. Much of the research by the Kevo group was designed to test a theory of herbivore cycles and periodic outbreaks based on herbivore-induced changes in plant nutritional quality formulated by Haukioja and Hakala (1975).

Similarly, Werner (1979) has shown survival of the spear-marked black moth *(Rheumaptera hastata)* fed leaves from paper birch *(Betuta papyrifera)* defoliated in previous years decreased compared to those fed leaves from undefoliated controls. The intensity of the effect increased with degree of previous defoliation (1–3 yr defoliation), but no effect of current defoliation was found. The chemical changes responsible for the decreased nutritional quality of the leaves of defoliated trees are unknown.

Wallner and Walton (1979) found that larvae of the gypsy moth *(Lymantria dispar)* reared in the field on artificially defoliated gray birch *(Betula populifolia)* and black oak *(Quercus velutina)* had longer development times and lower pupal weights compared to control insects. The effects occurred during the first year of defoliation and were magnified during the second year. As in the case of *B. papyrifera*, the factors responsible for the decreased nutritional quality of the leaves of defoliated trees are unknown.

Smith (1982) has found that repeated grazing by three or more generations of *Urania fulgens* (Lepidoptera: Uraniidae) larvae on an individual *Omphalea* (Euphorbiaceae) vine results in a response, presumably chemical, that greatly lowers the chances of survival and prolongs the development time of *U. fulgens* that subsequently attempt to eat it. Smith suggested that this host-plant response may, at least in part, be responsible for the large-scale migration of *Urania* moths observed in Central America and lowland tropical South America, and it may also be the factor producing the 4- and 8-yr cycles in abundance of the insects.

Bryant (1981, 1982), following Klein (1977), has shown that adventitious shoots and young stems of paper birch, balsam poplar *(Populus balsamifera)*, quaking aspen *(P. tremuloides)*, and other plant species are much less palatable and nutritious to snowshoe hares than small-diameter mature stems. This is due, in part, to the greater concentrations of terpene phenolic resins in young growth. Severe winter browsing during hare population maxima causes the production of large numbers of these unpalatable juvenile shoots. Bryant (1982) suggested that depletion of the supply of small-diameter mature stems during an outbreak forces the hares to feed on adventitious shoots (produced in response to the browsing pressure) and low-preference browse species, resulting in a hare population crash. The juvenile stems mature within 2 or 3 yr, leading to a large increase in amount of high-quality winter browse. The hare population then rebounds and overshoots the supply of high-quality stems, leading to another crash. According to Bryant (1982), the time delay between production of juvenile stems and their maturation is of the correct magnitude to explain the recurring 10-yr population fluctuations of snowshoe hares as due to a stable limit cycle (May, 1972). Although the production of resistant juvenile growth in response to attack of mature stems can be considered to be a plant defensive response, it is, at least as envisioned by Bryant (1982), a passive one. Whether adventitious shoots produced in response to hare browsing are more resistant to hares than juvenile stems or adventitious shoots in general or whether changes occur in existing stems in response to browsing is unknown.

Rhoades (1983) found that tent caterpillar larvae *(Malacosoma californicum pluviale)* fed detached leaves of red alder *(Alnus rubra)* trees undergoing attack by tent caterpillars in the spring grew more slowly, died at a faster rate, and produced fewer egg masses than insects fed leaves from control trees. This change in foliage quality was induced within a period of 27 days from the initiation of attack by relatively light grazing levels (11% estimated leaf-area loss) and was associated with an increased proanthocyanidin content of the foliage. The response was systemic because it occurred in leaves on branches protected from attack. Similarly, fall webworm larvae *(Hyphantria cunea)* fed detached leaves from Sitka willow trees *(Salix sitchensis)* undergoing attack in late summer by fall webworms or raised in the field on these trees grew more slowly than corresponding control larvae (Rhoades, 1983). The response was systemic and occurred within a time period of 15–35 days from the initiation of attack. Because the response was observed in leaves that had already attained full size before the trees were attacked, these results show that plant responses to insect attack are not confined to early phases of leaf development. The chemical basis of the change in leaf quality of Sitka willow is unknown.

The black grass bug *(Labops hesperius)* can be a serious agricultural pest, causing reduced palatability and nutritive value of infested grasses to cattle (Todd and Kamm, 1974; Kamm and Fuxa, 1977; Higgins *et al.*,

1977). Reduced palatability of infested wheatgrass (*Agropyron interme-dium*) is associated with an increased fiber content of the grass and occurs in spite of an increased crude-protein content. These changes take place in less than 8 weeks from the initiation of *L. hesperious* attack.

Other examples suggesting that herbivore or mechanical damage to plants can lead to increased content of putative defensive substances or decreased growth rate and increased mortality or deterrence of herbi-vores have been reviewed by Rhoades (1979; see also Carroll and Hoff-man, 1980, discussed later). These plant responses are common and probably universal. They do not appear to be restricted to any particular taxonomic group of plants or to plants of any particular growth form. Usually, the responses are systemic, as would be expected for effec-tiveness against mobile consumers. Short-term responses (minutes, days) occurring during the period of attack can be expected to influence the fitness of attacking herbivores, whereas long-term responses (years) may affect fitness of subsequent herbivores or generations of herbivores. If defenses are costly to plant metabolism, relaxation of defense following attack is to be expected. Relaxation times varying between days and years have been observed.

Until recently, most experimental work and theory concerning the effects of plant defensive systems on plant–herbivore interactions fo-cused on preformed or constitutive defenses. In plant pathology, how-ever, the dual importance of constitutive and inducible plant defenses has long been recognized (Müller and Börger, 1941; Müller, 1956; Horsfall and Cowling, 1980). Inoculation with fungi (Suzuki, 1980), bacteria (Goodman, 1980), or viruses (Hamilton, 1980) can increase the resistance of plants to further challenges by the same or different pathogens. Attack by nematodes may also induce resistance to further attack, but the evi-dence is sparse (McIntyre, 1980). In the case of fungi, the mechanisms of induced resistance are fairly well understood. Local induced resistance involves the accumulation of low-molecular-weight phytoalexins and polymeric lignins and tannins in the region of infection (Harborne and Ingham, 1978; Beckman, 1980; Cruickshank, 1980). Systemic resistance induced by fungi may involve the accumulation of low-molecular-weight compounds and protein or glycoprotein enzyme inhibitors and agglu-tinins, mediated by a long-distance communication system in the plant (Kuć and Caruso, 1977; Suzuki, 1980). Mechanisms of resistance induced by viruses and bacteria are poorly understood, but local resistance may involve the accumulation of lignins and tannins (Beckman, 1980). A phosphoglycoprotein that has been likened to the interferons has been isolated from tobacco following inoculation with tobacco mosaic virus

(Hamilton, 1980). Accumulation of lectin-like agglutinizing substances has been observed following inoculation of plants with bacteria (Goodman, 1980).

The importance of induced plant defenses in disease dynamics, by controlling the spread of disease within and between plants, is beyond reasonable doubt. Similarly, plant defensive responses should have profound effects on herbivore population dynamics. It is probable that the intensity and rates of induction and relaxation of defensive responses, characteristic for each plant species or plant–herbivore interaction, are important variables that, together with other influences such as plant physical stress and effects of parasitism, predation, and disease on herbivores, determine herbivore population patterns.

The relative contributions of changes in proximate nutrients versus changes in defensive chemicals, and *de novo* synthesis versus transport to changes in nutritional quality of plants induced by herbivore attack are unknown. Rhoades (1979) suggested that short-term responses may involve mainly qualitative defensive substances that are cheap for plants to synthesize and transport to tissues under attack from elsewhere in the plant, whereas long-term responses may involve mainly quantitative defenses such as tannins, lignin, and resins. However, induced increases in leaf content of tannin-like substances have been observed within days (Niemelä *et al.*, 1979) and weeks (Rhoades, 1983) of damage to birch and alder, respectively, indicating that changes in content of tannin-like substances are not restricted to long-term reactions. Induced responses can be expected to have less effect on highly coevolved specialist herbivores than on generalists. This may be especially true for responses involving qualitative defenses.

Plant defensive responses should affect both the attacking species and other species attacking the plant. For two species that feed on the same tissue, induction by the first species should often have a negative effect on the second species. The resulting mutual interference should resemble that produced in classical competitive interactions, but in this case proceeding in the absence of a limiting resource. On the other hand, for species utilizing different tissues, the effect of the inducing species on other species is likely to be positive if the plant reallocates defensive materials to the attacked tissue at the expense of other tissues. This may result in mutual facilitation between consumers. Insect or artificial defoliation of trees often increases their susceptibility to secondary attack by boring insects and pathogens (Schoeneweiss, 1967; Wargo, 1972; Dunbar and Stevens, 1975, 1976; Schultz and Allen, 1977). For example, black oak is often heavily attacked by bark beetles and fungi following defoliation by insects (Staley, 1965; Nichols, 1968), and this is associated with a decreased content of phenolics in the bark following defoliation (Parker, 1977).

Escape in space and time (Janzen, 1970, 1971; Root, 1973) from herbivores is probably an important component of defense for young leaves of temperate trees, which characteristically flush out their leaves in a sudden burst. Asynchrony between bud burst and egg hatch can be an important source of larval insect mortality (Feeny, 1970; Haukioja, 1980). Larval mortality is increased if egg hatch is too early or too late. In the former case no food is available, and in the latter case leaves have matured sufficiently such that they are no longer an optimal food due, in the case of pedunculate oak *(Quercus rober)*, to increasing levels of tannins and lowered levels of nitrogen (Feeny, 1970). It is thus reasonable that trees subject to heavy attack of young leaves by herbivores would gain advantage by unpredictable leaf flush. This seems to be so for pedunculate oak, in which timing of bud burst varies yearly and by as much as 2 weeks among individual trees in a given year (Feeny, 1970). Delayed spring leaf flush by larch (*Larix decidua*; Benz, 1977) and birch (*Betula pubescens*; Haukioja and Niemelä, 1977) and variable flushing of birch (Haukioja, 1980) following defoliation the previous year are additional examples. Early shedding of leaves attacked by mining insects may represent another phenological defensive response to insect attack (Faeth *et al.*, 1981).

VI. OFFENSIVE ADAPTATIONS OF HERBIVORES FOR DISCRIMINATION BETWEEN SUITABLE AND UNSUITABLE FOOD AND FOR SYNCHRONIZING REPRODUCTION WITH THE AVAILABILITY OF SUITABLE FOOD

In coevolved systems such as plant–herbivore relationships, adaptations evolved in one member are subject to evolved counteradaptation in other members. Indeed, the balance between defensive adaptations evolved in lower members of trophic systems and offensive adaptations evolved in higher members to counter these defenses is probably responsible for the persistence and long-term stability of producer–consumer interactions (Section XI). The evolution of defensive metabolites in plants has led to concurrent evolution in herbivores of the ability to detect these substances, avoid plant tissues that contain concentrations sufficient to overload evolved accommodation mechanisms, and preferentially attack plants that are in a vulnerable condition due to stress. It has also led to the use by adapted herbivores of plant defensive substances as cuing stimuli to aid in the recognition of suitable food. In this way, herbivores have, in part, "turned the tables" on plants.

An enormous literature has accumulated concerning the proximate aspects of food selection by herbivorous animals (see Dethier *et al.*, 1960; Wood *et al.*, 1970; Arnold and Hill, 1972; Schoonhoven, 1973; Hedin *et al.*, 1974; Harborne, 1977; Kogan, 1977; Staedler, 1977; Bernays and Chapman, 1978; Chapman and Blaney, 1979; Dethier, 1980). Herbivores discriminate between suitable and unsuitable food via sensitive smell and taste receptors and, to a lesser degree, visually. In general, food selection is determined by positive responses to sugars, salts, amino acids, and other primary nutrients, coupled with positive and negative responses to secondary plant metabolites. Plant secondary metabolites deterrent to nonadapted herbivores often elicit positive feeding responses in adapted herbivores. Examples include glucosinolates in crucifers (Schoonhoven, 1967; Van Emden, 1972), polysulfides and mercaptans in onions (Matsumoto, 1970), chlorogenic acid in potatoes (Hsiao and Fraenkel, 1968), saponins in alfalfa (Hsiao, 1969), phaseolunatin, a bean cyanogenic glycoside (Naya and Fraenkel, 1963), gossypol in cotton (Maxwell *et al.*, 1963; Hedin *et al.*, 1974), sparteine, an alkaloid of scotch broom (Smith, 1966), cucurbitacins, the bitter principles of cucumbers and other squashes (Chamblis and Jones, 1966), hypericin in St. John's wort (Rees, 1969), and monoterpenes and other compounds (Norris and Kogan, 1980).

The strong stimulatory influence of plant secondary chemicals on feeding or oviposition of some pest insects has led, in the past, to attempts to control the pests by selective breeding for plants with low concentrations of secondary constituents, with unfortunate results. For example, cucumbers selected for low leaf cucurbitacin content to control cucumber-specific beetles are decimated by a general pest, the two-spotted mite (Da Costa and Jones, 1971a,b). Glandless strains of cotton low in gossypol, developed to control the boll weevil, which is attracted to gossypol, are much more susceptible to attack by blister beetles and many other species of general pest insects (Maxwell *et al.*, 1965; Norris and Kogan, 1980). Strains of alfalfa selected for low saponin content, to control the alfalfa weevil and prevent bloat in cattle, are more heavily attacked by the pea aphid (Hanson *et al.*, 1973). Similarly, lupine cultivars selected for low alkaloid content, to improve palatability and nutritional value to cattle, are heavily attacked by thrips (Gustafsson and Gadd, 1965). It seems that all plant breeding programs designed to control specific pests or improve forage quality to domestic animals, by reducing the concentrations of secondary metabolites in plants (see Matches *et al.*, 1973), incur a high risk of increased general pest problems.

Herbivores can detect and preferentially attack stressed food plants or tissues. The grasshopper *Melanopus differentalis* discriminates between wilted and turgid sunflower leaves, eating more of the former when offered a choice (Lewis, 1979). Aphids are very sensitive to the physiological condition of their host plants and remain on plants that are particularly suitable, due to stress or other factors, but they leave those that are less suitable (McLean and Kinsey, 1968; Van Emden, 1972). Many species of bark beetles select host trees on the basis of volatile compounds released from the tree, due to deterioration of its physiological condition from physical stress or previous attack by insects or pathogens (Wood, 1982).

Herbivores can time their reproductive cycles by detecting cuing substances in their food plants, thereby insuring that reproduction coincides with the availability of suitable food. Desert locusts *(Schistocerca gregaria)* spend long periods feeding upon mature and senescent vegetation, during which time they do not become sexually mature (Osborne, 1973). After rains, when the locusts have access to young foliage, they become sexually mature. Concentrations of gibberellins (plant growth hormones) are high in young foliage and low in senescent foliage. If gibberellin A_3 (GA_3) is supplied to female locusts feeding on senescent vegetation, they become sexually mature as soon as those feeding on young foliage (Ellis *et al.*, 1965; Osborne, 1973). A remarkably paralled effect of GA_3 on reproduction in the mouse *Mus musculus* has been observed (Olsen, 1981). Administration of GA_3 in amounts similar to those that they would ingest from young vegetation, doubled the proportion of females entering estrus and producing litters. In contrast, Visscher (1980) has reported negative effects of the plant growth hormones GA_3 and abscisic acid on grasshopper fecundity, and Chrominski *et al.* (1982) have reported both negative and positive effects of the plant growth hormone ethylene on grasshoppers. However, in both studies (Visscher, 1980; Chrominski *et al.*, 1982) it is unclear whether the exogenous hormones acted directly upon the insects or induced changes in the food plants that secondarily affected the insects.

Colorado potato beetles readily oviposit on young potato leaves, but, in the presence of only aged potato leaves, oviposition is inhibited (de Wilde *et al.*, 1969). Food-plant age can also affect differentiation of offspring of the pea aphid (Mittler and Sutherland, 1969; Sutherland, 1969). Aphids raised on seedlings produce mainly apterous (wingless) progeny, whereas those raised on mature leaves of the same species of plant produce mainly alate (winged) progeny.

There is evidence that both initiation and termination of reproduction by the vole *Microtus montanus* is under the influence of cuing substances

in food plants. A compound (6-MBOA) produced when young grami-
noid foliage is damaged induces a high incidence of testicular hypertrophy in males and a high incidence of pregnancy in females, when
administered in artificial diets to nonbreeding winter populations of the
voles (Berger *et al.*, 1981; Sanders *et al.*, 1981). On the other hand, cinnamic acids, present in high concentrations in senescent foliage, cause
decreased uterine weight, inhibition of follicular development, and cessation of breeding activity when it is fed to *M. montanus* (Berger *et al.*,
1977). Interestingly, DIMBOA, the precursor of 6-MBOA, is a resistance
factor to the European corn borer in young maize plants (Klun *et al.*,
1967). This illustrates, once again, how the same chemical system can
have either positive or negative effects on herbivores, depending on
their degree of adaptation.

VII. OFFENSIVE ADAPTATIONS OF HERBIVORES THAT STRESS, INCREASE THE NUTRITIONAL QUALITY OF, OR CIRCUMVENT INDUCED DEFENSIVE RESPONSES OF PLANTS

If physical stress can render plants more suitable for herbivore growth
and development, we can expect some herbivores to have evolved adaptations that severely stress their food plants. Species of *Ips* and *Dendroctonus* bark beetles commonly mass-attack individual host trees by
using aggregation pheromones (Hanover, 1975; Vité and Franke, 1976;
Coster and Johnson, 1979; Prokopy, 1981). Resin-exudation pressure is
so reduced by the large number of attacking beetles that the tree suc-
cumbs. Girdling of terminal twigs by boring beetles (*Oncideres, Agrilus;*
Johnson *et al.*, 1976; Mares *et al.*, 1977), sawflies *(Hartigia)*, and Lepidoptera *(Periploca;* Johnson *et al.*, 1976), followed by oviposition or feeding on the dying terminal are relatively common. The grasshopper
Melanopus differentialis preferentially feeds on sunflower leaves wilted
from stem girdling by the beetle *Mecas inornata* (Lewis, 1979), and other
insects also invade beetle-girdled stems (Mares *et al.*, 1977). Some insects
damage the leaf petiole prior to feeding on the leaf (Carroll and Hoffman,
1980). Larvae of the alder sawfly *(Eriocampa ovata)* cut all main veins of
a leaf of red alder *(Alnus rubra)* prior to feeding on the distal region
(D. F. Rhoades, unpublished observation). Girdling and petiole and vein
damage probably prevent the mobilization of defensive chemicals into
the feeding region, or cause the accumulation of nutrients in it, or both.
Stream damming by beavers may, in addition to other functions, serve

to stress the surrounding vegetation by root flooding and increase its nutritional quality. The extensive girdling of willows and other trees by beavers may have a similar function.

In other cases herbivores kill or severely stress parts of plants and then feed on tissues remote from the site of damage. *Phloeosinus* bark beetle adults cut deep grooves in terminal twigs of host cypress trees, resulting in characteristic "flagging" of the trees by dead terminals. The adult beetles then oviposit in the trunk and larger stems (Johnson *et al.*, 1976). Severe damage to broadleaf trees can result from ovipositional flagging by periodical cicadas (Johnson *et al.*, 1976). Female cicadas oviposit in slits cut into twigs and small branches, many of which subsequently die (Lloyd and White, 1976). Upon hatching, the larvae fall to the ground and feed upon the roots of the tree by sucking from xylem vessels (White and Strehl, 1978). Flagging and stem girdling by root weevils (*Scythropus*, *Nemocestes*; Johnson *et al.*, 1976) are further examples of damage to food-plant tissues remote from the main feeding sites. These behaviors have possibly evolved to stress the host plant, leading to generally lowered plant defensive capability and increased nutritional quality, or to cause diversion of defensive metabolites from the food tissues to those previously attacked. For example, cicada flagging, by decreasing the plant aerial biomass, may cause the tree to adjust its root–shoot ratio by senescing parts of its root system (see Head, 1974) so that the composition of the root xylem sap becomes favorable for establishment of the young cicada nymphs.

Carroll and Hoffman (1980) have reported that mechanically damaged leaves of the squash *Cucurbita moschata* mobilize substances, possibly cucurbitacins, to the damaged region within 40 min. This response inhibits feeding by the beetle *Epilachna tredecimnota* but stimulates feeding by the beetle *Acalymma vittata*, which is known to exhibit a positive feeding response to cucurbitacins (Da Costa and Jones, 1971b). When feeding on squash leaves, *E. tredecimnota* cuts a circular trench around a piece of leaf tissue, so that only a few veins and pieces of lower epidermis hold the encircled leaf section in place. The beetle then feeds on the excised area. Carroll and Hoffman have proposed that this trenching behavior is an adaptation of the insect to defeat the plant response. Stimulation of feeding by *A. vittata* suggests that this specialized insect is largely immune to the effects of the mobilized substances, may utilize them in host location, and/or may even directly benefit from their presence in the food (see Berenbaum, 1981; Bernays and Woodhead, 1982; McFarlane and Distler, 1982). These results illustrate the complexity of offense and defense to be expected in coevolved interactions. In the face of attack by highly adapted herbivores, plant defenses or defensive responses may have little effect or even a negative effect on plant fitness.

In general, we can expect a continuum of effect of plant defensive responses on herbivores, varying in their degree of adaptation. Generalist herbivores, or hervibores that do not usually eat the plant in question or plants containing a similar defensive system, should be more negatively affected by plant defensive response than coevolved specialists with highly developed ability to metabolize and excrete defensive substances in their food plants (Millburn, 1978; Scheline, 1978; Brattsten, 1979), tolerate the substances in other ways (Rosenthal et al., 1977, Vaughan and Jungreis, 1977; Berenbaum, 1978; 1980), or utilize them (Rothschild, 1973; Rosenthal et al., 1977; Bernays and Woodhead, 1982). It is thus no surprise that the Colorado potato beetle (Leptinotarsa decemlineata), a specialist of Solanaceae, is not affected by wound-induced accumulation of proteinase inhibitors in potato (T. Jeker, C. Mueller, and U. Volkart, in Benz, 1977).

In many cases, plant pathogens successfully invade susceptible hosts, not so much because they can detoxify or tolerate the defensive response of their host plant, but rather because they are not recognized as foreign by the plant, and defensive responses are not induced (Sequeira, 1980). Recognition phenomena, akin to the acceptance of self and rejection of nonself in animals, are extremely important in determining the outcome of interactions between plants and potential pathogens (Sequeira, 1980). Recognition may similarly be important in plant–herbivore interactions. If herbivores possess adaptations to suppress the recognition of attack in plants, herbivore damage to plants should be a less effective inducer of defensive responses than an equivalent amount of mechanical damage, in some cases. In other cases herbivores may be more effective, depending upon the degree of adaptation and acquired immunity of plant and herbivore or, in other words, which participant is "in the driver's seat" in the particular interaction.

To date, there do not appear to have been any systematic studies comparing the intensity of plant defensive responses induced by mechanical versus herbivore damage. However, there is now considerable evidence indicating that regrowth rates of plants following grazing by grasshoppers and ungulates or mechanical clipping plus application of animal saliva or saliva components can differ significantly from regrowth rates following clipping alone (Reardon et al., 1972, 1974; Dyer and Bokhari, 1976; Dyer, 1980; Capinera and Roltsch, 1980; Detling and Dyer, 1981; Detling et al., 1981). In some cases regrowth was reduced compared to clipped controls, in others it was stimulated, and in still others no difference was observed. These various effects on regrowth rates are probably manifestations of underlying offensive–defensive interactions between the plants and herbivores in which enhanced plant growth rates, compared to clipped controls, are associated with an induced increase in food quality that is caused by herbivore salivary secretions, whereas decreased growth rates are associated with an induced decrease in food quality that is controlled by the plant. Preferential feeding by the grasshopper *Melanopus differentialis* on sunflower leaves previously damaged by insects or infected with fungi (Lewis, 1979) is also suggestive of interactions between plant and consumers, resulting in increased food quality of the attacked tissues.

Salivary secretions of most major groups of plant-sucking invertebrates, namely heteropterous bugs, aphids, psyllids, mites, and nematodes, are strongly suspected or have been shown to contain plant-growth-controlling substances, including indoleacetic acid (Miles, 1968a; Osborne, 1973; Markkula *et al.*, 1976; Hori, 1976; Hori and Endo, 1977, and references therein; Dropkin, 1979; Norris, 1979). Hemipterous saliva often contains polyphenoloxidase enzymes, which appear to oxidatively neutralize plant defensive phenolic compounds and/or be involved in the production of auxin-like compounds *in situ* (Miles, 1968a,b, 1978). The midgut fluid and regurgitate of a grasshopper also contains polyphenoloxidase, though it is not known if it is also present in the saliva (Rhoades, 1977). Some lepidopteran leaf miners retard senescence of leaves in which they are feeding. Mined areas of leaves and the caterpillars contain high levels of cytokinins (Osborne, 1973). Aphids often exhibit higher reproductive rates when clumped than when dispersed on plants (Way and Cammel, 1970). This has been interpreted as due to passive source–sink effects in the flow of phloem nutrients. A more likely explanation is that it reflects an active offensive–defensive interaction between aphids and the plant, in which aphids are better able to gain the upper hand when clumped.

Lepidoptera that feed colonially as larvae are generally more successful when raised *en masse* than when raised singly or in small groups on their food plant. The converse is true for solitary species (Wellington, 1957; Iwao, 1968; Shiga, 1976; Peters and Barbosa, 1977). Haukioja and coworkers have shown that on poor birch-leaf diets (leaves in which defensive responses have been induced by mechanical damage) crowded autumnal moth larvae have a shorter larval period and form heavier pupae than solitary larvae (Haukioja, 1980). As with aphids, these results may reflect an underlying battle between plant and insects in which numerical amplification of an offensive stimulus produced by the larvae can suppress or reverse defensive responses in the plant. On good birch-leaf diets (previously uninduced), solitary autumnal moth larvae do better than crowded ones (Haukioja, 1980; see also Iwao, 1968; Gruys, 1970). This may indicate that, if a defensive response has not already been stimulated, it is less likely to be induced by one larva than by many. To carry the speculation a stage further, it is possible that colonial and solitary herbivores have evolved alternate strategies for dealing with plant defensive responses. Offensive stimuli produced by colonial herbivores can, in concert, overcome and reverse defensive responses attempted by the plant. In contrast, solitary species use a strategy of stealth, possibly employing salivary "anesthetics" to prevent the plant from recognizing that it is under attack. Accordingly, epideictic pheromones (Prokopy, 1981), which are produced by phytophagous and other insects to influence their spacing patterns, may have a previously unrecognized adaptive function. The effects of crowding on fitness of colonial and solitary herbivores and on food-plant chemistry should be a fertile area for future study, not only with respect to plant defensive responses but also with respect to herbivore offensive adaptations.

Control of plant metabolism by substances introduced by the consumer into the plant is exemplified by gall-forming arthropods that cause diversion of the vascular system of the plant and profound developmental and structural changes in surrounding tissues (Miles, 1968a,b; Dieleman, 1969; Carter, 1973; Osborne, 1973; Norris, 1979) and that may even usurp the defensive system of the plant for their own protection (Janzen, 1977). However, it is unlikely that the balance of offense and defense always lies in the direction of the gall-maker. Depending on the degree of adaptation of host and gall-maker, we can expect the balance to shift in favor of one or the other.

Some insects, particularly boring beetles, are totally dependent on ectosymbiotic relationships with viruses, mycoplasms, bacteria, fungi, protozoa, or nematodes to achieve successful attack (Norris, 1979; Wood, 1982). The symbionts, which are carried in special pouches on the insect such as mycangia, infect and propagate in the plant, increase the nutritional quality of infected tissues to the insect, and, in some cases, themselves become the main food source.

Thus plants are far from being static food resources for herbivores and other consumers, as they have been commonly viewed in the past. Plant nutritional quality can vary as a function of both physical and biotic stress. There is evidence that plants defensively respond to attack by herbivores and that herbivores possess adaptations to exploit and induce favorable changes in the nutritional quality of their food plants. In my view, we have barely scratched the surface of an intricate system of offensive stimuli and defensive responses and acquired immunity, which are modulated by the physical environment.

VIII. DIRECT AND INDIRECT EFFECTS OF FOOD-PLANT NUTRITIONAL QUALITY AND DEFENSIVE POSTURE ON FITNESS OF HERBIVORES

Growth rate, survival, and fecundity of invertebrate and vertebrate herbivores are dependent upon concentrations of proximate nutrients, especially proteins, in their food (Watson 1970; Mattson, 1981; Scriber and Slansky, 1981) and also upon concentrations of defensive substances (Wallace and Mansell, 1976; Harborne, 1978; Rosenthal and Janzen, 1979). It is also probable that susceptibility of herbivores to pathogens, parasites, and predators is often related to the quality of herbivore diets (Price et al., 1980).

A variety of stressful conditions, including crowding, excessively high or low temperatures, application of toxic chemicals, and suboptimal diets, have been shown to render herbivores more susceptible to pathogens (Steinhaus, 1958; Tanada, 1976). The encapsulation reaction is an important defense of insects against invading endoparasites (Salt, 1963; Askew, 1971; Nappi, 1975). Eggs or larvae of the parasites are recognized as foreign by host hemocytes, which then surround and encapsulate them. Successful encapsulation, often accompanied by melanization, results in death of the parasite. Normal health and longevity are often shown by adult hosts containing encapsulated parasites (Muldrew, 1953). The effectiveness of the encapsulation reaction is greatly dependent on the physiological condition of the host and can be decreased by stressful influences, including poor nutrition and the application of toxic chemicals to the host (Muldrew, 1953; Salt, 1956, 1964; van den Bosch, 1964). Cheng (1970) found that when winter moth larvae were feeding on oak, a preferred food plant, the larvae grew more rapidly and were able to encapsulate a higher proportion of tachinid parasites than when feeding on other plants. Salt (1956, 1964) found that starved larvae of the wax moth were unable to successfully encapsulate an ichneumonid parasite, whereas unstarved larvae could do so. Van den Bosch (1964) observed a similar effect of starvation on encapsulation in beetle hosts. In "unhealthy" larvae of the larch sawfly, only 37% of parasite eggs were encapsulated versus 80–100% in "healthy" larvae (Muldrew, 1953).

Similarly, resistance to predation can depend on the physiological condition and nutritional status of herbivores. Bouton et al. (1980) studied relative predation by pentatomids on larvae of the Mexican bean beetle feeding on two soybean strains that varied in their nutritional quality to the beetles. They found that the predators more effectively reduced the population of beetles when the beetle larvae were feeding on the "resistant" soybean strain, on which the larvae grew more slowly. Okamoto (1966) found that suitability of an aphid as food to a coccinellid predator varied greatly with the plant on which the aphids were raised. Unhealthy (or parasitized) larvae of the fall webworm are more easily subdued by a pentatomid predator than healthy larvae (Morris, 1963e). Morris suggested that the pentatomids act in a selective fashion, attacking weakened larvae in the same way that carnivorous mammals selectively eliminate weakened prey. Late-instar fall webworms and eastern tent caterpillars repel pentatomid predators by throwing them from the web and entangling them in it, whereas young larvae fall easy prey (Sullivan and Green, 1950).

Apparently, influences that weaken or cause herbivores to grow more slowly often render them more susceptible to their enemies. Therefore, fitness of herbivores should depend upon the nutritional quality of their food plants acting not only through direct effects upon their mortality and fecundity but also through indirect effects upon their susceptibility to parasitism, predation, and disease. Favorable changes in the nutritional quality of plants induced by physical stress on plants or by offensive adaptations of herbivores should increase herbivore fitness via both direct and indirect pathways. Similarly, decreased nutritional quality of food plants, caused by relaxation of physical stress on plants or defensive response of plants, should have the opposite direct and indirect effects on herbivore fitness.

These ideas may be particularly applicable in cases in which altered food quality is due to changes in proximate nutrients and digestibility-reducing substances. Food-plant toxins that act on internal metabolism of animals can sometimes have a greater negative effect on parasitoids and predators than on the host (Campbell and Duffy, 1979; Price et al., 1980). In cases of food-plant quality altered due to changes in content of toxins, the relative effects on fitness of host, parasites, and predators should depend on the relative degree of adaptation of each participant to the toxins.

IX. CHANGES IN HERBIVORE PROPERTIES DURING POPULATION FLUCTUATIONS

A feature of many outbreaks of forest insects is that larval mortality is low and adult fecundity high for several years during the increase phase, whereas the opposite is true during the retrogression (White, 1969, 1974, 1976, van den Bos and Rabbinge, 1976; Mason et al., 1977; Campbell, 1981). Usually, this is attributed to changes in food quantity due to foliage depletion (Mason, 1981), but it could often be due to changes in foliage quality. In many cases population collapse occurs before most of the foliage has been consumed (Morris, 1963d; White, 1969, 1974, 1976), or population decline continues, following foliage regrowth, in a way that cannot be accounted for by parasitism and disease (Wellington, 1960; van den Bos and Rabbinge, 1976). Incidence of parasitism and disease is often low during population increase but high in the decline (Miller, 1963b; Kaya, 1976; Baltensweiler et al., 1977). Usually, this is attributed to low rates of increase of parasites and pathogens, but it could also be due to increased susceptibility of the hosts during the collapse phase due to low food-plant nutritional quality.

Striking changes in larval *quality* observed during population increases and decreases are consistent with changing nutrition. Western tent caterpillar *(Malacosoma californicum pluviale)* colonies contain both active and relatively inactive individuals (Wellington, 1957, 1960, 1965). As infestations of tent caterpillars on red alder and other deciduous trees peak and decline, the proportion of sluggish adults and larvae increases, larvae do not move as far from their tents when feeding, tent size decreases, and larval mortality rates increase. Colonies containing a high proportion of inactive larvae are more susceptible to disease than active colonies (Wellington et al., 1975). Wellington (1964) has suggested that these changes are due to selective emigration of the more active adults, giving rise to a progressive decrease in population vitality and, finally, local extinction. Wellington (1960) further suggested that these qualitative changes may be a primary cause of periodic tent caterpillar outbreaks and may represent a self-regulatory mechanism for the insects. It is difficult to imagine a selective mechanism leading to population auto-regulation as proposed by Wellington and others (see following discussion), but the effects can be interpreted as resulting from decreased food quality caused by plant reaction. I found (unpublished observation) that western tent caterpillars grew much faster on red alder during 1977, a peak population year (Fig. 1), than 1978, the year of population collapse, or 1979. From the time of egg hatch, at the beginning of April, until mid-May the caterpillars grew faster in 1977 than in 1979 by a factor of approximately 5. The eggs hatched on similar dates, when the foliage was in a similar phenological stage, in 1977 and 1979. The mean of daily minimum and maximum temperatures, averaged from the time of egg hatch to mid-May, was 0.6°C higher in 1977 than in 1979, whereas rainfall totaled 39.1 and 37.6 mm, respectively, over the same periods (measured at Seattle–Tacoma Airport, 8 km from the study site). These minor differences in environmental conditions are unlikely to have caused such large differences in growth rates between 1977 and 1979. The results are consistent with, but do not prove, decreased food quality during the population collapse. However, Myers (1981) could find no evidence for

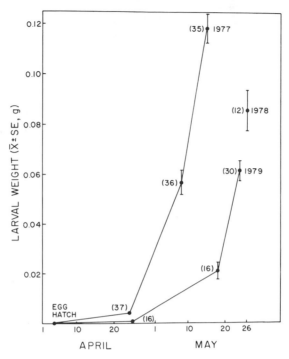

Fig. 1. Growth of *Malacosoma californicum pluviale* larvae on *Alnus rubra* trees at Kent, King County, Washington, in 1977–1979. Larval size was determined photographically and converted to weight by the use of a standard curve, except for sampling dates 26 May 1978 and 18 May 1979, when the larvae were weighed. Each colony was on a different tree. For each colony an average larval weight was determined; then a mean weight for all colonies was calculated over the number of colonies measured (numbers in parentheses).

change in food quality of wild rose *(Rosa nutkana)* during a population decline of western tent caterpillars.

Baltensweiler and co-workers (1977) have shown that a dark form of larch budmoth proliferates for four to five generations during the increase phase of budmoth outbreaks on European larch, whereas the proportion of a light-colored ecotype, which grows more slowly but is less subject to food stress, increases during the collapse phase over four to five generations. During the increase phase, parasitism is low and the parasitoid complex is dominated by ichneumonids, whereas during the collapse phase, parasitism is high and the complex is dominated by eulophids. Low incidence of eulophid parasitism during the host-density increase is due partly to ineffective paralysis of the host and to altered behavior of the host; in other words, budmoth larvae are more resistant to eulophids during increase than during collapse. The probable importance of defensive reaction by larch in contributing to budmoth population fluctuations has been discussed by Benz (1977) and Baltensweiler and co-workers (1977).

Leonard (1970, 1971) has examined qualitative changes in gypsy moth populations taking place during the course of outbreaks. As density increases, there comes a point at which smaller larvae are produced. Leonard has suggested that these smaller larvae remain in an active state that enhances their chances for dispersal by wind and has hypothesized that this is a self-regulating mechanism for gypsy moth populations. However, Capinera and Barbosa (1976) found that smaller larvae have a decreased tendency to disperse relative to the larger larvae, in direct contradiction to Leonard's hypothesis. Again, the observations are consistent with changes in food quality.

Changes in herbivore properties during population cycles are often so dramatic that several workers have suggested that they are due to genetic changes in the herbivores. Such genetic changes have been proposed for spruce budworm (Campbell, 1962), larch budmoth (Baltensweiler, 1971), and voles (Chitty, 1967). It has even been suggested that genetic changes in herbivores are actually driving population fluctuations (Campbell, 1962; Chitty, 1967; Krebs et al., 1973; Myers and Krebs, 1974; Lorimer, 1979), though the mechanisms producing such rapid (~3–10 generations) directional selection have not been convincingly explained. Van den Bos and Rabbinge (1976) have questioned Baltensweiler's genetic interpretation of phase transition in larch budmoth, suggesting that polymorphism may be due to nongenetic plasticity, and, similarly, Christian and co-workers (1965) have proposed a nongenetic interpretation of phenotypic changes in voles. For many years solitaria, gregaria, and other phases of locusts were thought to be distinct species, but it is now known that these phases are expressed within a common genotype (Uvarov, 1921; Kennedy, 1956; Nolte, 1974). In addition, for several species of phytophagous insects and grouse, qualitative changes in larvae or chicks during population fluctuations are associated with variation in yolk content or size of eggs due to maternal nutrition (Wellington, 1965; Morris, 1967; Leonard, 1970; Moss et al., 1974), strongly implying a nongenetic basis. If selection pressure from parasitism, predation, food quality, and other influences varies throughout population fluctuations, some genetic changes in the herbivores seem inevitable (see Haukioja, 1980). However, it is doubtful that genetic changes can be sufficient to account for the observed phenotypic changes or to actually drive population fluctuations.

Chitty (1957), Nicholson (1957), Wellington (1960), Christian and co-workers (1965), and Leonard (1970) have proposed that decreased fecundity, migratory behavior, and other characteristics of herbivores in high and declining populations are population autoregulatory adaptations, though the mechanism whereby the animals have evolved the ability to autoregulate their population numbers remains a mystery. In my view, phenotypic changes are probably largely nongenetic in origin. They are probably induced by changing food quality, resulting from physical stress of plants (White, 1976) and defensive–offensive interaction between plants and herbivores as previously described. In some cases (e.g., locusts, larch budmoth) this has resulted in the differentiation of distinct phases, each expressing a set of morphological and physiological characteristics suitable for the food condition and population density in which they normally occur (see Section XI,D). In less developed cases (e.g., gypsy moth, voles, tent caterpillars) distinct phases are not recognizable, although behavioral and morphological differences are evident.

X. POSSIBLE PHEROMONAL INTERACTIONS AMONG PLANTS AND HERBIVORES

There is evidence, albeit preliminary and tentative, that some plants are sensitive and can respond defensively to signals emanating from nearby plants experiencing attack by insects. Rhoades (1983) has found that attack by tent caterpillars (*Malacosoma californicum pluviale*) of Sitka willow trees can induce altered leaf quality not only in attacked trees but also in nearby unattacked Sitka willows. Figure 2 represents a bioassay of the quality of leaves from three groups of willow trees: a test group of 10 willows, a nearby control group of 10 willows intermingled with the test trees (average distance between each control tree and the nearest test tree = 3.3 m), and a far control group of 20 willows 1.6 km from the test site. Short-term growth (21 hr) of groups of tent caterpillars fed leaves detached from each tree was measured periodically throughout the experiment (Fig. 2, top). The growth results are expressed as the average growth rates (percentage) for larvae fed leaves from each group of willows relative to those fed leaves from the far control groups. On the indicated date (Fig. 2.), tent caterpillar colonies were attached to the test trees (LOAD), and the numbers of caterpillars present on the trees were censused periodically thereafter (Fig. 2, bottom). Migration of larvae from the test trees and onto control trees was prevented by the use

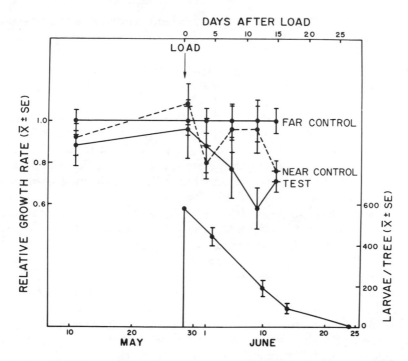

Fig. 2. Growth (% increase in fresh weight per unit time) of *Malacosoma californicum pluviale* larvae fed detached leaves in the laboratory from test and near control *Salix sitchensis* trees, relative to growth of larvae fed leaves from a far control group. On the indicated date, *M. californicum pluviale* colonies were placed on the test trees (LOAD) and numbers of caterpillars remaining on the trees were censused periodically thereafter (see text).

of tanglefoot bands. Prior to load there were no significant differences in growth of laboratory insects fed leaves from each of the three groups of trees, nor were differences found in the first three assays after load. However, on 9 June, 11.5 days after load, larvae fed leaves from the test trees grew significantly more slowly than those fed leaves from the near or far controls (Fig. 1; $P < 0.05$, Newman–Keuls multiple-range test). In the subsequent assay on 12 June, 14.5 days after load, larvae fed leaves from both test and nearby control trees grew more slowly than those fed leaves from the far controls ($P < 0.01$). Leaf-area loss due to insects was estimated at 15.8 ± 1.0% (SE) for the test trees, 1.1 ± 0.1% for the near controls, and 1.6 ± 0.2% for the far controls, at the end of the experiment. Excavation of willows at the test site revealed no evidence of subterranean root connections between trees. Rhoades (1983) has suggested that these results may be due to detection by the near control trees of pheromonal substances emitted by the attacked trees or the caterpillars.

In a similar experiment using Sitka willows and fall webworm *(Hyphantria cunea)*, Rhoades (1983) obtained no evidence for unusual effects during the first year of attack; altered leaf quality (lowered growth rates of assay webworms) occurred in the attacked trees but not in a nearby control group of trees approximately 60 m from the test trees. None of these had been attacked by fall webworm during the previous 3 yr (and probably not during their lifetime) because they were 5 yr old and no outbreaks of fall webworm had occurred in the area during that period. The experiment was repeated the following year, and this time leaf quality was altered in both attacked trees and in the nearby control groups, as compared to far control trees (Rhoades, unpublished).

It thus appears that with "naive" willows no unusual effects are observed, but that in the year following "immunization" of the site by webworms both attacked and nearby unattacked trees can respond. With respect to the experiments with tent caterpillars, all trees had been attacked by tent caterpillars 3–4 yr previously, during a natural outbreak. Since that time we have been conducting experiments on willows within a few tens of meters of the test and nearby control trees with tent caterpillars brought in from elsewhere each spring.

Haukioja (1980) has briefly reported that the presence of feces of the autumnal moth in the soil below previously defoliated birch trees elicits a stronger defensive response in the trees. E. Haukioja (personal communication) thinks that this effect is probably due to substances in the feces that are taken up by the roots of the trees. It could also be due to volatile substances in the feces produced by the insects or derived from the birch diet. Benz (1977) has cryptically noted that the decreased quality of larch foliage associated with collapse of larch budmoth outbreaks "may be triggered in trees which become not visibly damaged [p. 157]."

Meager as the evidence is at the present time, I propose the following.

1. There is a level of interaction between plants and herbivores, previously unsuspected, involving pheromonal signals generated by plants in response to herbivore attack and detectable by unattacked plants.

2. Herbivores also emit signals, the function of which is to confuse, suppress, mimic, or otherwise interfere with the signals generated by plants.

3. Communication with other plants is a major function of volatile terpenes and other substances ubiquitously emitted at low levels by plants into the atmosphere.

XI. THEORY OF HERBIVORE OUTBREAKS

In the broad, philosophical sense, most trophic interactions can be regarded as mutualistic in that disruption of any single trophic level would lead to collapse or drastic change of all other levels (for discussion and application of the *mutualistic approach* to plant–herbivore interactions see Mattson and Addy, 1975; Jermy, 1976; Owen and Wieger, 1976; Stenseth, 1978; Owen, 1980; and Owen and Wiegert, 1981). However, this *mutualism* probably evolved under, and is maintained by, selection resulting from conflicting interests of the various participants, because convincing mechanisms whereby two or more independently reproducing groups of organisms can altruistically evolve adaptations for the common good have not been demonstrated. Even cases of trophic interactions generally regarded as mutualistic, such as pollination and fruit dispersal, can probably be best understood in terms of conflicting interest between plant and vector (McKey, 1975; Rhoades and Bergdahl, 1981; Wheelright and Orians, 1982). Evolutionary mechanisms aside, it is probably more useful to view trophic relationships as being maintained by a balance of opposing forces rather than by some nebulous teleological force of common interest, because this immediately focuses attention on what the nature of these opposing forces might be, and it leads to testable predictions.

From this viewpoint, I suggest that stability in interactions among plants, herbivores, and consumers at higher trophic levels is most usefully regarded as resulting from a balance of offensive and defensive power among the participants. Conversely, that instability results from perturbations of the stabilizing, opposing forces. We have seen previously what the nature of some of these opposing forces may be. Plants have evolved defensive systems, and herbivores have evolved the ability to neutralize these systems. Plants can decrease their nutritional quality when attacked, and there is emerging evidence that herbivores, in turn, manipulate the nutritional quality of their food plants. Herbivores are adapted to defend themselves against enemies at the next higher trophic level, and members of this level possess offensive adaptations (Vinson and Iwantsch, 1980a,b; Edson *et al.*, 1981; Shaw, 1981; Beckage, 1982; Schmidt, 1982), and so on to higher levels. The interactions between these opposing sets of adaptations have resulted in long-term stability, because trophic systems persist. So it is easy to see how short-term perturbations that increase or decrease the efficacy of defensive or offensive adaptations of any of the members of the trophic structure are liable to lead to a shift in population numbers, and how short-term perturbations that are applied and then released are liable to lead to population fluctuations.

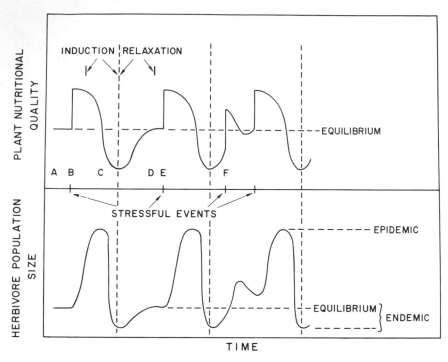

Fig. 3. Model of herbivore population fluctuations based on changes in food-plant nutritional quality, caused by physical stress of the plants and attack-induced defensive responses of the plants (see text).

A. Perturbation A: Physical Stress of Food Plants

Because physical stress of plants appears to be a particularly important perturbation, we can construct the following scheme. At the long-term equilibrium herbivore population level, population growth is checked by plant defense systems that decrease herbivore fecundity, increase mortality, and importantly, increase herbivore susceptibility to natural enemies by negatively affecting herbivore defensive systems against these enemies (Fig 3, A). Stressful influences acting on plants, particularly weather extremes, cause an imbalance between their proximate nutrient content and defensive capabilities, resulting in increased nutritional quality to herbivores (Fig. 3, B). High-quality food leads to decreased mortality, increased fecundity, and resistance to enemies in the herbivores. Herbivore populations increase rapidly, especially under conditions of low plant-species and defensive diversity, outstripping those of natural enemies. Given that physical stress is sufficiently relaxed during the period of herbivore buildup, the plants respond to the high levels of herbivory by increasing their commitment to defense, such that their nutritional quality is decreased below the equilibrium level (Fig. 3, C). This causes collapse of the herbivore population to below the equilibrium level, directly by nutritional effects and by decreasing the resistance of the herbivores to natural enemies, which build up rapidly during the collapse phase. The plants then relax their defenses. In the absence of further perturbations, equilibrium plant nutritional quality and herbivore populations are reestablished (Fig. 3, D).

In this model, there is no reason to expect overcompensatory oscillations in herbivore population numbers to take place during reestablishment of equilibrium (for models that depend on overcompensatory oscillations, see Wangersky and Cunningham, 1958; May et al., 1974; Berryman, 1978a,b). If herbivore population return times are short compared to plant defensive relaxation times, the herbivore population should closely track plant nutritional quality back to the equilibrium level. If herbivore population return times are long compared to defensive relaxation times, plant nutritional quality may well overshoot the equilibrium level, but as herbivore populations slowly approach the equilibrium level, plant nutritional quality will do so as well.

If, following reestablishment of equilibrium, additional plant stress occurs, this will cause another fluctuation in the herbivore population (Fig. 3, E). However, if a stressful event closely follows a previous one, before the plants have relaxed their defenses from the previous attack, a significant new population increase may not occur (Fig. 3, F). We can therefore see that randomly occurring stressful events can give rise to population cycles of more or less constant periodicity. Depending on the defensive induction and relaxation times in individual cases and the frequency of stressful events, the model can accommodate fluctuations with constant periodicity and aperiodic ones, both of which are common.

Time delays in negative-feedback processes have featured prominently in several mathematical models of animal population fluctuations (Wangersky and Cunningham, 1958; May, 1973; May et al., 1974; Berryman, 1978a,b), but the nature of the biological processes giving rise to the time lags remains obscure (Berryman, 1978a). Possibly, induction and relaxation times of changes in plant nutritional quality can fulfull the requirements for time delays in these models or similar ones (see Bryant, 1982). In any case, the qualitative model presented here should be readily amenable to mathematical treatment.

If physical stress to the plants is prolonged during the period of herbivore buildup, herbivore populations may rise to such high levels and constitute such a drain on the energy reserves of the already weakened plants that the ability of the plants to react defensively may be seriously impaired. This could result in continuous high population levels for extended periods and, in extreme cases, to total destruction of the resource, followed by herbivore population collapse due to lack of food. Similarly, if growing conditions for plants are benign and defensive relaxation times long, the herbivore populations will likely remain below the equilibrium level for extended periods. Relaxation times may be particularly long in the case of induced quantitative defenses in persistent tissues, such as long-lived leaves of evergreen plants, because remetabolism or translocation of quantitative defensive substances may be energetically costly.

This analysis suggests that the epidemic state is a disequilibrium condition and that at low levels of abundance herbivore populations may approach long-term equilibrium only for brief periods, when physical conditions are stable (Fig. 3). This differs from the interpretation of Morris (1963c) and McLeod (1979), who have suggested that equilibrium conditions exist at both high and low levels of herbivore abundance, with extrinsic factors causing shifts between these two alternative equilibrium points. The main difference between the present treatment and "classical" models is that it stresses changes in quality of both food and herbivores taking place during population fluctuations, whereas classical models have considered only quantitative changes.

All of the main features in this model have been cited singly or in various combinations to explain outbreaks of cyclic oscillations in herbivore numbers (White, 1969, 1974, 1976; Benz, 1974, 1977; Haukioja and Hakala, 1975; Haukioja, 1980; Bryant, 1982; Smith, 1982). It may be applicable to cases of herbivore population fluctuation that appear to be triggered by environmental extremes, such as spruce budworm (discussed in Section XI,E), locusts (White, 1976), sucking insects (White, 1969, 1974), and bark beetles (Vité, 1961). At least two mathematical models have been developed that take herbivore-induced changes in food quality into account. Both are models of the 8- to 10-yr population cycles of larch budmoth in the upper Engadin Valley of Switzerland and stem from the work of Benz (1974, 1977). The model of van den Bos and Rabbinge (1976) includes changes in nutritional quality of larch foliage induced by budworm defoliation in addition to the classical factors: egg predation, parasitism, temperature acting directly on the insects, incoincidence between egg hatch and leaf flush, and amount of food. The model of Fischlin and Baltensweiler (1979) is discussed in Section XI,C.

If physical stress of plants is important in initiating herbivore outbreaks, we can expect outbreaks to be more common or more severe at sites particularly stressful for the plants (Table I) or in marginal habitats, such as at the edges of geographical or altitudinal ranges of plants, given that the ranges of plants and herbivores overlap. On a global scale, insect population densities do tend to be more variable from year to year in areas of low, unpredictable rainfall that in areas of high, predictable rainfall (Wolda, 1978).

B. Perturbation B: Physical Stress of Herbivores—Climatic Change

A second perturbation likely to give rise to fluctuation is physical stress that acts directly on herbivores or their enemies, as emphasized in classical density-independent models, and there is little doubt that climatic extremes can inflict significant direct mortality (Wellington *et al.*, 1975). However, there is also a mechanism whereby subtle changes in the physical environment acting on herbivores could give rise to population instability at the edges of their ranges. In cases in which the food plants have a wider geographic or altitudinal range than the herbivores, the range of the herbivores is probably determined partly by their tolerance to the physical environment, particularly temperature. Plant populations occurring beyond the long-term avarage range of the herbivores should have evolved weaker defensive systems against the herbivores than plant populations growing within this range.

Thus, in the short term, when physical conditions are benign for a number of years we can expect the herbivores to invade areas beyond their long-term average range and rapidly increase in numbers on the relatively unprotected plants. This, in turn, could lead to genetic differentiation in the types of defense mechanisms possessed by plant populations occurring within and outside the long-term range. Within the range there would be selection for high constitutive defences and strong short-term responses that affect the attacking herbivores, because the herbivores are usually present in the environment. Outside, but near to, the long-term average herbivore range there would be selection for low constitutive defenses, weak short-term responses, but strong long-term responses, because initial attack will likely be followed by heavier attack in subsequent years. Further outside the average range the plants should evolve weak constitutive, short-term, and long-term inducible defenses. These arguments are weakened by the fact that they consider only a single herbivore species, whereas in reality many herbivores with partly overlapping and contiguous ranges usually feed on a given plant species. However, the existence of recognition phenomena, producing specificity of plant response to attack by particular herbivore species and offensive adaptations of herbivores, would strengthen the arguments.

If genetic differentiation of plant populations takes place, herbivore populations should be relatively stable at the center of their range due to strong plant constitutive defences and rapid plant responses. At the edges of their ranges, herbivore populations should be more unstable due to rapid population increase on plants with weak constitutive defenses and weak short-term responses, followed by population collapse caused by long-term plant response. In the northern hemisphere, during periods of climatic cooling, herbivore population instabilities should develop along the southern margins of herbivore ranges, whereas during periods of climatic warming instabilities should occur along the northern margins and near the upper altitudinal limits of herbivore ranges. Complementary population instabilities should occur in the southern hemisphere.

Since the early 1800s there has been a general climatic warming trend throughout the world, particularly during winter in the northern hemisphere at high and temperate latitudes (Lamb, 1969; Brinkmann, 1976). For instance, average winter temperatures in central England have risen about 1.5°C over this period (Lamb, 1969). Massive outbreaks of the autumnal moth are confined to the northern regions of Fennoscandia and are more intense at high elevations, whereas in southern Fennoscandia the populations fluctuate little (Haukioja, 1980). In northern Finland, vole populations fluctuate over a wider range of population densities than in southern Finland, where the vole populations have a more endemic nature (Teivainen, 1981). Vole cycles also have higher amplitudes in northern Norway than in the south (Kalela, 1962; Christiansen, 1975), and reports of extensive vole damage to trees began to appear in the late 1800s (Christiansen, 1975). Intense population cycles of the larch budmoth occur mainly in high valleys above 1300 m, whereas at low elevations fluctuations are of the latent type (van den Bos and Rabbinge, 1976). The forest tent caterpillar (*Malacosoma disstria*) occurs throughout the United States from Florida to California, the state of Washington to Maine, often reaching outbreak proportions with a period of about 11 yr (Hodson, 1941). General and local outbreaks have been much more frequent in the northern states. There were 36.9 outbreak years per 10^5 km^2 reported in the northeastern United States (Maine, New Hampshire, Vermont, Massachusetts, New York, Connecticut) versus 6.3 in the east (Pennsylvania, New Jersey, Virginia) and 4.1 in the southeast (South Carolina, Mississippi, Louisiana) during the period 1886–1940. The corresponding figures for the west coast are Washington (11.0), Oregon (4.0), and California (0.5; all calculated from Hodson,

1941). Recorded outbreaks in the central states are sparse but concentrated along the northern border of the United States, particularly in northern Minnesota (Hodson, 1941; Duncan and Hodson, 1958).

All of these observations are consistent with effects of recent climatic warming and previous genetic differentiation in chemical defenses of food-plant populations, as described previously. That these geographical and altitudinal variations in population stability are not due to latitude or climatic severity per se is substantiated by the fact that, in general, tropical insects appear to fluctuate in abundance to about the same degree as temperate ones (Janzen, 1974; Wolda, 1978). The intensities of short- and long-term defensive chemical responses of southern and northern Finnish strains of birch also fit the expected pattern (Haukioja, 1980). Given time, selection of northern plant populations and invasion by southern plant genotypes should increase the stability of northern and high-altitude populations of herbivores. Since about 1940, a slight cooling trend has developed in the northern hemisphere (Brinkmann, 1976). If it continues it should contribute to this stabilization process. Insofar as the global warming trend may have contributed to increased water stress of southern plant populations, we may expect herbivore population instability to have developed at the southern margins of the ranges of plants as well as at the northern margins of the ranges of herbivores.

C. Perturbation C: Migration of Herbivores between Different Portions of Their Range

A third perturbation of the trophic system likely to lead to fluctuation in herbivore populations and food-plant nutritional quality is migration of herbivores between different portions of their range. A strategy of attack by herbivores can be imagined in which they invade a portion of their range occupied by plants that, because they have not experienced recent attack, are of high nutritional quality or are susceptible to herbivore offensive stimuli. From the initial immigrants, populations build rapidly and events proceed as outlined in Fig. 3, B–D, but, instead of collapsing to a low endemic population followed by reestablishment of equilibrium (Fig. 3, D), the herbivores emigrate during the collapse phase to initiate another cycle elsewhere. Thus in this scheme population fluctuations are driven by intrinsic properties of the trophic system. Large-scale emigration of adults is a common feature of high-density herbivore populations. This is true of spruce budworm (Morris *et al.*, 1958; Rainey,

1979; Greenbank *et al.*, 1980), locusts (Dempster, 1963; Rainey, 1979), African armyworm (Rainey, 1979; Khasimuddin, 1981a), tent caterpillars (Brown, 1965; Shepherd, 1979), bark beetles (Berryman, 1979; Carle, 1979), and microtine rodents (Thompson, 1955; Krebs *et al.*, 1973). Population fluctuations of these herbivores and many others may involve a contribution from the migration mechanism.

Smith (1982) has invoked this type of model to explain population fluctuation and migration of *Urania* moths. Baltensweiler and Fischlin (1979) have proposed a qualitative model to account for the 8- to 10-yr population cycles of larch budmoth by a similar mechanism. Migration of adults from latent populations at low altitudes to the high-altitude outbreak zone initiates an outbreak, which then collapses under the influence of decreased larch nutritional quality induced by defoliation. As pointed out in Section XI,B, population cycles of the larch budmoth at high altitudes may also involve a contribution from climatic warming. Fischlin and Baltensweiler (1979) have also created a mathematical model that is similar to the qualitative model but based on indigenous populations of budmoth.

D. Other Influences on Herbivore Population Stability

The population model described in Fig. 3 depends upon the intervention of factors such as weather extremes extrinsic to the trophic system to periodically synchronize properties of the participants (e.g., plant nutritional quality). In models of this kind, it is easy to understand how population fluctuations could occur and how periodicity (or lack of it, depending on frequency of stressful events and defensive induction and relaxation times) can be maintained. However, in models based solely on intrinsic properties of the trophic system such as migration (Section XI,C; see also Fischlin and Baltensweiler, 1979), one wonders why natural individual variation in values for the driving variables (e.g., tendency to migrate, rate and degree of change in plant nutritional quality) does not lead to damping of the oscillations and, finally, to a stable equilibrium. Lloyd and Dybas (1966) have shown how cyclic emergence of periodic cicadas would rapidly dampen under the influence of quite small temporal variations in periodicity among individuals, unless severe penalities accrue to nonsynchronized emergers. Synchronous population fluctuations over wide geographical areas, for example, those of larch budmoth (Baltensweiler and Fischlin, 1979), tent caterpillars (Hodson, 1941), Douglas-fir tussock moth (Williams *et al.*, 1979), and voles (Teivaninen, 1981), are particularly difficult to account for using models based solely on intrinsic properties of the trophic system. Wide geographic synchrony suggests the intervention of extrinsic factors, such as weather, operating over the entire range, but often none are apparent. I suggest two effects that are likely to contribute to the maintenance of population oscillation in intrinsically driven systems and to widespread synchrony of population fluctuations.

1. Communication between food plants exists, such that the level of defense in an individual plant is keyed more to levels of attack experienced by the plant population as a whole than that experienced by itself.

2. Herbivores commonly possess offensive adaptations that are effective on naive plants, which have not experienced recent attack, but they are less effective on recently attacked plants. The efficacies of these offensive adaptations are increased by many herbivores acting in concert, so that asynchronous individuals are penalized.

If offensive adaptations of herbivores are common, facilitation between herbivore species that simultaneously utilize the same tissue of a given plant species should occur in some cases. In other cases, mutual interference via induced plant defensive responses should occur (Section V). This may explain why attempts to explain patterns of co-occurrence of phytophagous insects and other herbivores through competition theory (see Lawton and Strong, 1981), have met with little success. Classical competition theory, based in changes in amount of resources, is inappropriate in analyses of interactions between herbivores if these interactions are mediated largely through induced decreases and increases in quality of resources rather than decreases in amount.

Although all herbivore populations fluctuate to some degree, population levels of some species are much more variable and rise to much higher levels than others. Herbivore generation times and intrinsic rates of population increase are obviously involved to some degree. Invertebrate and small vertebrate herbivores often have shorter generation times and higher reproductive rates than large vertebrate herbivores. Doubtless this contributes to the higher variability of population numbers in the former groups, by allowing their populations to rapidly respond to favorable changes in food quality. However, there are great differences in population stabilities even among invertebrate and small vertebrate species. I suggest that this variation may be due to fundamental differences in attack strategies.

For example, insect species with low and relatively constant populations may use a strategy based on stealth. Eggs are widely dispersed to minimize the degree of herbivory on any particular plant and the probability that defensive responses will be induced. Salivary components that suppress plant recognition of damage would aid this process. This strategy would lead to relatively low and stable populations because, if herbivore populations rose above a critical level, plant defensive responses would likely be induced. In contrast, herbivores with unstable populations may use an opportunistic strategy in which they preferentially attack plants weakened by physical stress (perturbation A). Or, alternatively, opportunists may use the tactic of surprise by actively migrating into naive populations of food plants (perturbation C), which are particularly nutritious and susceptible to offensive stimuli. High food quality and numerical amplification of offensive stimuli lead to a rapid and large increase in population. The plants then become immunized and the herbivores emigrate. As part of the opportunistic strategy, eggs would often be deposited in masses (e.g., spruce budworm, Douglas-fir tussock moth, gypsy moth, tent caterpillars), because many larvae acting in concert can more effectively subdue the plant. The answer to the question, "Why do some species [of butterflies] cluster their eggs rather than deposit them singly?" posed by Stamp (1980, p. 367) may thus be that the former group are opportunists, whereas the latter are stealthy. It follows that egg-clustering species of herbivores should have more variable populations than those that deposit eggs singly.

Phase changes in herbivores may be due to a transition from one strategy to the other (see Section IX). For instance, the *solitaria* phase of locusts may use stealth. Physical stress of food plants, by increasing food nutritional quality, induces transition to the opportunistic *gregaria* phase. Having built up a large population, the locusts then migrate en masse to areas of unstressed but naive plants, which they can subdue with offensive stimuli by reason of their large numbers. Transition of the solitary green and nonblack forms of the African armyworm to the gregarious, migratory black form (Khasimuddin, 1981a,b; Odiyo, 1981) may involve a similar mechanism.

In summary, the theory of herbivore population fluctuations described here views these processes as akin to the development of disease in populations of animals or plants (see Berryman, 1978b), invoking effects of host stress, postattack host responses, acquired host immunity, genetic variation in immunity, and offensive adaptations in consumers. I have speculated that plant–herbivore interactions may be mediated by phenomena in which plants can differentiate between mechanical and herbivore damage; that herbivores possess adaptations to suppress recognition by plants of their activities and cause increases in the nutritional quality of plants, and even that pheromonal interactions among plants and between plants and herbivores may be involved. The evidence for pheromonal interactions is sparse, but I envision a *battle at the pheromonal level* mediated through signals generated by attacked plants, defensive responses of nearby unattacked plants in response to these signals, and countersignals produced by herbivores to disrupt the system of communication between plants. If so, interactions at the level of gustation, plant tissue chemistry, and catabolic detoxification may, in many cases, assume a secondary role. If not, the basic scheme remains intact.

Effects of the three main perturbations, (1) food-plant stress, (2) herbivore range changes caused by climatic change, and (3) herbivore migration may be combined to explain population fluctuations of many herbivore species. For example, spruce budworm, locust, and bark beetle epidemics might be accounted for mainly by perturbations (1) and (3), Douglas-fir tussock moth mainly by (1), autumnal moth, larch budmoth and voles by (2) and (3), *Urania* moths mainly by (3), and so on.

These ideas can be readily tested.

1. Does physical stress of plants increase their nutritional quality to herbivores, and, if so, what are the chemical changes taking place? In plants that contain both costly quantitative and cheap qualitative defenses, of which there are many, is there evidence that the plants decrease their commitment to the costly system while increasing their commitment to the cheaper defenses during physical stress?

2. Can current or previous herbivore attack lead to decreased nutritional quality of plants? If so, how much damage, how long a time period, does it take for these changes to be induced, and how long is required for relaxation?

3. Is the nutritional quality of food plants higher during herbivore population increase than during collapse and the endemic state?

4. Are herbivores more resistant to predators, parasites, and pathogens during the increase phase than during collapse and the endemic state?

5. Can herbivores induce increased nutritional quality in naive plants but not in plants that have experienced recent attack?

6. Can herbivore attack lead to changes of nutritional quality, not only in attacked plants but also in nearby unattacked plants?

E. Application to Outbreaks of the Spruce Budworm

Morris and collaborators (1958; Morris, 1963a) carried out extensive studies of factors important in predisposing and initiating attacks of spruce budworm on balsam fir (*Abies balsamea*) in eastern Canada. At that time, little was known of plant defense, nothing of defensive reaction by plants, and the main thrust of the research concerned classical density-dependent and density-independent effects of weather, para-sitism, disease, predation, and competition for food on budworm num-bers. From hindsight we can see that many of the effects can be explained in terms of changes in plant defense and nutritional quality in response to physical stress and herbivore attack.

Dense, even-aged, continuous stands of mature and overmature bal-sam fir over large areas are the major factors predisposing outbreaks of spruce budworm. Given these predisposing factors, an outbreak can be triggered by three or four consecutive hot, dry summers.

> The mechanism through which it [weather] operates is not fully understood, but apparently the effects of climate are relatively indirect. The budworm is well adjusted to extremes in Canadian climate and direct mortality attributable to meteorological extremes is only rarely observed [Morris et al., 1958, p. 143].

It seems likely that drought stress, acting upon the trees to lower their resistance to budworm, is the triggering factor.

Two major outbreaks of budworm have occurred in an even-aged stand of balsam fir studied by Morris and co-workers (1958; Morris, 1963a) with peaks of budworm abundance in 1915 and 1952. Both out-breaks lasted approximately 10 yr and were preceded by several con-secutive years of summer drought. However, a particularly severe period of summer drought extending from the early to the late 1920s did not result in an outbreak. This may have been due to selective kill of the most susceptible trees in the 1915 outbreak, but tree mortality was light in this outbreak. By the late 1920s, the expected time of initiation of the "missing outbreak," the trees were some 15–20 yr older, and thus, pre-sumably, more susceptible than trees during the 1915 outbreak. A pos-sible reason why no outbreak occurred in the late 1920s is unrelaxed defensive capability of the trees resulting from the 1915 outbreak, and, if so, this suggests a defensive relaxation time of at least 5 yr, possibly more than 10 yr.

The 1952 outbreak was studied in detail (Morris, 1963a). Survival of larvae (S_L) from the third instar until pupation was the most important factor determining overall generation survival (Morris, 1963b). Surpris-ingly, S_L was found to be positively correlated with larval density, in contrast to the expected density-dependent decrease in larval survival (Watt, 1963). It was postulated that this was due either to inherited low vigor at low densities or to predators (e.g., birds) that caused significant mortality to larvae at low densities but that were numerically unable to respond to high prey densities (Watt, 1963). Little evidence was pro-duced in support of either hypothesis. The effect could be due to high larval mortality in the endemic condition caused by poor food. Climatic stress to the trees then resulted in improved food quality, leading to high populations of larvae with low mortality rates.

Mortality due to starvation and predation was low throughout the outbreak (Morris, 1963d, f). Parasitism caused heavy mortality only during the final stages of collapse and during the endemic state (Miller, 1963b). In addition, in severe outbreaks of the spruce budworm, "parasites have certain limitations to their behavior which are not yet understood . . . where the number of hosts attacked per adult parasite is . . . considerably reduced" (Morris et al., 1958, p. 145; see also Miller, 1963b) compared to moderate outbreaks. These observations are consistent with increased budworm resistance to parasites during the increase phase of the outbreak, particularly at the most favorable sites, compared to that in the final stages of collapse and the endemic state.

A negative relationship was found between fecundity of budworm and a cumulative index of defoliation obtained by summing defoliation indices over several previous years, but no relationship was found between fecundity and current foliage availability (Miller, 1963a). This indicates that lowered fecundity was not due to starvation but to some property of the foliage associated with repeated damage.

Emigration of adult budworms from heavily infested regions has been noted repeatedly (Morris et al., 1958; Clark, 1979; Rainey, 1979; Sanders, 1979) and studied in detail by Greenbank et al. (1980). In New Brunswick 79% of the migrating moths were females carrying 40–50% of their reproductive output (Greenbank et al., 1980). These moths can be carried up to several hundred kilometers before realighting. If they land in stands of trees with heavy current defoliation they continue migrating, whereas most moths arriving in lightly defoliated stands remain there (Greenbank et al., 1980).

Balsam fir and other hosts of spruce budworm contain many secondary chemicals that are potentially important in defending the trees against attack by spruce budworm and other herbivores. The foliage and other parts of firs, and conifers in general, contain large quantities of terpenes, lignin, tannins, and other phenolics (Hegnauer, 1962; Mirov, 1967; Hanover, 1975; Manville et al., 1977). Puritch and Nijholt (1974) found that attack by the balsam wooly aphid (Adelges piceae) on firs (Abies grandis and A. amabilis) is associated with the deposition of juvabione-related compounds in the annual ring of wood produced during infestation. Similarly, Thielges (1968) observed a systemic increase in polyphenol content of foliage of Pinus sylvestris attacked by the European pine sawfly (Neodiprion sertifer). Clearly, spruce budworm food plants or their congeners (Browne, 1968) are able to defensively respond to attack by insects.

Thus many features of spruce budworm outbreaks are explained by the previously outlined theory, and I hope that this analysis will prove useful in current attempts to understand and model spruce budworm outbreaks (Holling *et al.*, 1977, 1979; Clark, 1979). The frequent occurrence of severe and sustained epidemics of spruce budworm in eastern Quebec, New Brunswick, and Maine (Clark, 1979; Sanders, 1979), near the northeastern margins of the range of spruce budworm, suggests that climatic warming may also play an important role in the population dynamics of this insect (see Section XI,B).

F. Application to Microtine Outbreaks

Eruptive or cyclic behavior of populations of small herbivorous vertebrates, particularly microtine rodents (Chitty, 1960; Pitelka, 1964; Krebs *et al.*, 1973), hares and rabbits (Wagner and Stoddart, 1972; Keith, 1974; Bryant, 1982), and grouse (Moss *et al.*, 1974), have long been of interest to ecologists, agriculturalists, and game biologists. A host of explanatory hypotheses have been advanced, involving interactions with predators, food shortage, periodic fires, disturbances caused by man, and weather (Keith, 1974; Moss *et al.*, 1974).

Populations of microtine rodents (voles and lemmings) cycle with a period of 3 or 4 yr over a wide range of latitudes and habitats (Keith, 1974), but cycles are particularly pronounced at high latitudes (Kalela, 1962; Christiansen, 1975; Teivainen, 1981). A striking parallel between insect and microtine cycles is that in both cases population peaks and declines are associated with major qualitative changes in the herbivores. Reproductive rate and survival are highest during the increase phase of microtine cycles. The decrease phase is associated with delayed sexual maturity and lowered reproductive rate, reduced growth rates, lowered survival of all age classes, increased susceptibility to disease and predators, and splenic and adrenal hypertrophy (Findlay and Middleton, 1934; Elton *et al.*, 1935; Thompson, 1955; Dawson, 1956; Christian, 1971; Pearson, 1971; Keith, 1974). Dispersal of individuals is high throughout the peak years (Thompson, 1955; Krebs *et al.*, 1973). Food shortage is not thought to be a major factor causing decline in most cases (Krebs and DeLong, 1965; Chitty *et al.*, 1968).

Chitty (1960, 1967) has argued that traditional hypotheses involving predation, disease, and food depletions are inadequate to account for microtine cycles. Instead, Chitty suggested that selection favors different genotypes at various stages of the cycle, accounting for qualitative differences in the animals, and that genetic changes are fast enough to drive the cycles, rather than merely correlated with them. In a test of this hypothesis, Krebs *et al.* (1973) found that microtines dispersing from outbreak epicenters differed behaviorally and genetically from those that remained, though no cause and effect relationships were established. On the other hand, Christian and co-workers (1965) proposed that the qualitative changes are nongenetic, resulting from hormonal imbalance due to stressful interactions among individuals at high population density. Both Chitty and Christian have interpreted qualitative changes in the mammals as population autoregulatory mechanisms, but, as with insects, qualitative changes are probably better interpreted as resulting from altered food quality.

Decrease in availability of preferred foods at high population density, originally proposed by Lack (1954), was also suggested as a cause of microtine population decline by Batzli and Pitelka (1971). Freeland (1974), reanalyzing the data of Batzli and Pitelka (1971), suggested that microtines reduce the availability of nontoxic food plants during population buildup and are forced to eat a higher proportion of toxic plants at peak densities. A second reanalysis by Batzli and Pitelka (1975) and additional data provided by Schlesinger (1976) do not support Freeland's hypothesis, though, as pointed out by Batzli and Pitelka (1975), there are difficulties in deciding what is toxic to microtines.

Surprisingly, none of these workers has suggested that plants may respond directly to grazing pressures by changing their suitability as food. Therefore, few data are available concerning possible defensive reaction by microtine food plants. However, alfalfa, listed by Freeland (1974) as the second most preferred food plant of *Microtus pennsylvanicus*, produces coumestrol when attacked by aphids. This estrogenic compound cause's lowered fertility in sheep (Hanson *et al.*, 1965; Loper *et al.*, 1967; Loper, 1968).

Qualitative changes in food plants have been invoked by Pitelka (1964) and Schultz (1964) to explain cycles in arctic microtines (lemmings). They hypothesize that, in years following an outbreak, nutrient availability to the plants is reduced due to slow breakdown of fecal matter and animal remains, leading to reduced growth and lowered nutritional quality of the plants and, in turn, to lower populations of lemmings. Evidence for the *nutrient-recovery hypothesis* has been slow to materialize, but, in any event, the hypothesis still regards the plant as a passive partner in the interaction. Increased content of phenolic compounds in foliage of *Carex aquatilis*, a dominant sedge and a food plant of lemmings (Thompson, 1955; Pitelka, 1957; Batzli and Jung, 1980), in the season following mechanical grazing (Table II) is the first evidence that plants may not be passive participants in this system.

Table II

Phenolics of Previously Clipped and Unclipped *Carex aquatilis* from Atkasook, Alaska[a]

Clipped		Unclipped		
X̄	SD	X̄	SD	Component
41.17	0.04	41.61	0.44	Water (%)
36.50	0.97[b]	28.64	0.46	Folin–Denis (FD) total phenolics (725 nm, dry weight)[c]
18.76	0.97[b]	13.46	1.02	FD phenolics absorbed by casein[d]
14.08	0.51[b]	10.77	0.19	FD phenolics not absorbed by casein[d]
0.18	0.03[b]	0.12	0.01	Proanthocyanidins (550 nm, dry weight)[c]
0.58	0.14	0.41	0.07	Flavonols (vanillin reaction, 500 nm, dry weight)[c]

[a]S. Archer and D. F. Rhoades (unpublished). Two 0.5-m^2 plots of *C. aquatilis* were clipped to a short stubble on 26 June 1976 and reclipped five times at 10-day intervals thereafter. On 20 July 1977, three samples were obtained from the previously clipped plots by clipping the plants to approximately 2–3 cm above their bases. Each sample was a composite obtained from both plots. Unclipped samples were obtained from a control area between the plots (no previous clipping). The samples were immediately submerged in 85% methanol (in water) and later homogenized and filtered before analysis. Subsamples of fresh leaves were oven-dried at Atkasook to determine water content.
[b]Averages significantly different ($P < 0.05$, two-tailed t test).
[c]Methods of Swain and Hillis (1959).
[d]Method available upon request.

Though some workers have emphasized the importance of inclement weather in causing population declines in microtines (Fuller, 1969; Fuller *et al.*, 1969), most workers have not ascribed a critical importance to physical factors (Pitelka, 1957; Batzli and Pitelka, 1971; Krebs *et al.*, 1973). Rather, they have viewed them as influences that modulate rather than cause eruptions and declines. This suggests that microtine cycles may be largely intrinsically driven by a combination of migration and plant reaction. The possibility that the particularly high-amplitude population cycles observed at high latitudes are due to climatic warming is discussed in Section XI,B.

XII. CONCLUSION

Despite a prolonged and intense interest in herbivore-outbreak phenomena, due to their agricultural, silvicultural, and theoretical importance, relatively little progress has been made in understanding their causes. Though many theories have been proposed, not a single example exists of an outbreak that has been explained or mathematically modeled to give satisfactory predictions of future population trends. The general failure of herbivorous insect population models in this respect is well known (Baltensweiler, 1968; Fye, 1974; Stehr, 1974; Waters and Stark, 1980). Although it can be argued that fault lies in the mathematics rather than in the data base, the probable reason for continued failure is the general assumption of passive participation by the plants.

Recent discoveries that the nutritional quality of plants is affected by physical stress and that plants can defensively react to attack by herbivores, together with the realization that these changes can significantly affect herbivore population dynamics, promises to open a new phase in analysis of eruptive plant–herbivore interactions, following the pioneering work of T. R. Green and C. A. Ryan, T. C. R. White, G. A. Benz and E. Haukioja and T. Hakala. Inclusion of plant nutritional and defensive properties, and changes thereof, in the analysis can reunify the classical and previously unresolved dichotomy between "density-independent" and "density-dependent" effects on herbivore populations, by showing how variations in the physical environment can have an indirect effect on parasites, pathogens and predators of herbivores. "Competition" between herbivores may be mediated not so much by changes in the amount of food available as by changes in food quality caused by herbivory.

I have attempted to describe nonmathematical models of broad applicability to herbivore-outbreak phenomena. Doubtlessly, parts of these models will prove overemphasized or applicable only in particular cases, but I am hopeful that the coherent overall picture will prove useful. When the major factors described here have been measured and included in quantitative models, we can expect that the predictive power of these models will be significantly improved. Similarly, we can expect improvement in the biological control of pest insects (Batra, 1982). These programs have been unsuccessful in most cases (Beirne, 1974; DeBach, 1974), probably because the philosophy and practice of biological control has changed little over several decades (Way, 1977).

Other suggestions in this chapter are of a much more speculative nature. If plants commonly possess inducible defensive responses, it is reasonable to suppose that herbivores have evolved adaptations to suppress or even reverse these responses. At present, the evidence for such adaptations is sparse and mostly inferential, but I believe they will prove to be just as common as inducible defensive responses in plants are proving to be. The suggestions that plants use pheromones to communicate with each other and that herbivores also emit air-borne chemicals to interfere with this process may be assessed as wildly speculative. But, given our lack of progress in understanding and controlling herbivore population fluctuations, in spite of enormous past and present effort and expenditure on such pests as spruce budworm, Douglas-fir tussock moth, larch budmoth, gypsy moth, nun moth, tent caterpillars, bark beetles, locusts, voles, rabbits, and many others, it seems almost certain that major effects are not being taken into account.

XIII. SUMMARY

Research into the mechanism and causes of fluctuations in population numbers of herbivorous animals has been hampered by the general assumption that plants play a passive role in the interaction. We now know that plants actively defend themselves, that these defenses are sensitive to physical stress to the plants, and that they can be increased by plants in response to herbivore attack. These discoveries should lead to rapid progress in the theory and practice of pest management.

ACKNOWLEDGMENTS

I thank G. H. Orians, N. E. Beckage, A. B. Adams, G. A. Benz, J. P. Bryant, G. E. Edmunds, D. J. Futuyma, D. Harvell, E. Haukioja, C. S. Holling, C. Jones, J. Landal, N. Lorimer, J. Myers, S. Rudolph, C. C. Smith, J. Smith, G. VanVliet, T. C. R. White, and T. Whitham for commenting on various versions of the manuscript and N. E. Beckage and G. VanVliet for providing information. L. Erckmann, S. Cook, A. B. Adams, J. C. Bergdahl, and C. Baron took part in the experimental work. This work was supported by National Science Foundation grants DEB 7703258 and DEB 8005528.

REFERENCES

Abd El Rahman, A. A. (1973). Effect of moisture stress on plants. *Phyton* **15,** 67–86.
Abd El Rahman, A. A., Shalaby, A. F., and Monayeri, M. O. (1971). Effect of moisture stress on metabolic products and ions accumulation. *Plant Soil* **34**(1), 65–90.
Andrewartha, H. G., and Birch, L. C. (1954). "The Distribution and Abundance of Animals." Univ. of Chicago Press, Chicago.
Arnold, G. W., and Hill, J. L. (1972). Chemical factors affecting selection of food plants by ruminants. *In* "Phytochemical Ecology" (J. B. Harborne, ed.), pp. 71–101. Academic Press, New York.
Askew, R. R. (1971). "Parasitic Insects." Heinemann, London.
Baltensweiler, W. (1968). The cyclic population dynamics of the grey larch tortrix, *Zeraphera griseana* Hübner (= *Semasia diniana* Guenée) (Lepidoptera: Tortricidae). *In* "Insect Abundance" (T. R. E. Southwood, ed.), pp. 88–97. Blackwell, Oxford.
Baltensweiler, W. (1971). The relevance of change in the composition of the larch bud moth populations for the dynamics of its numbers. *In* "Dynamics of Populations" (P. J. den Boer and G. R. Gradwell, eds.), pp. 208–219. Pudoc, Wageningen, The Netherlands.

Baltensweiler, W., and Fischlin, A. (1979). The role of migration for the population dynamics of the larch bud moth, *Zeiraphera diniana* Gn. (Lep. Tortricidae). *Mitt. Schweiz. Entomol. Ges.* **52**, 259–271.

Baltensweiler W., Benz, G., Bovey, P., and Delucchi, V. (1977). Dynamics of larch bud moth populations. *Annu. Rev. Entomol.* **22**, 79–100.

Bate-Smith, E. C., and Metcalf, C. R. (1957). Leuco-anthocyanins. 3. The nature and systematic distribution of tannins in dicotyledonous plants. *J. Linn. Soc. London, Bot.* **55**, 669–705.

Batra, S. W. T. (1982). Biological control in agroecosystems. *Science* **215**, 134–139.

Batzli, G. O., and Jung, H. G. (1980). Nutritional ecology of microtine rodents: resource utilization near Atkasook, Alaska. *Arct. Alp. Res.* **12**, 483–499.

Batzli, G. O., and Pitelka, F. A. (1971). Condition and diet of cycling populations of the California vole, *Microtus californicus*. *J. Mammal.* **52**, 141–163.

Batzli, G. O., and Pitelka, F. A. (1975). Vole cycles: test of another hypothesis. *Am. Nat.* **109**, 482–487.

Beckage, N. E. (1982). Incomplete host developmental arrest induced by parasitism of *Manduca sexta* larvae by *Apanteles smerinthi*. *Ann. Entomol. Soc.* **75**, 24–27.

Beckman, C. H. (1980). Defenses triggered by the invader: physical defenses. In "Plant Disease" (J. G. Horsfall and E. B. Cowling, eds.), Vol. 5, pp. 225–245. Academic Press, New York.

Beirne, P. B. (1974). Status of biological control procedures that involve parasites and predators. *Proc. Summer Inst. Biol. Control Plant Insects Dis.*, *1972* pp. 69–76.

Benz, G. (1974). Negative Rückkoppelung durch Raum- und Nahrungskonkurrenz sowie Zyklische Veränderung der Nahrungsgrundlage als Regelprinzip in der Populationsdynamik des Gruen Lärchenwicklers, *Zeiraphera diniana* (Guenée) (Lep. Tortricidae). *Z. Angew. Entomol.* **76**, 196–228.

Benz, G. (1977). Insect-induced resistance as a means of self defense in plants. *Eucarpia/IOBC Work. Group Breed. Resistance Insects Mites, Bull, SROP, 1977/1978* pp. 155–159.

Berenbaum, M. (1978). Toxicity of a furanocoumarin to armyworms: a case of biosynthetic escape from insect herbivores. *Science* **201**, 532–534.

Berenbaum, M. (1980). Adaptive significance of midgut pH in larval Lepidoptera. *Am. Nat.* **115**, 138–146.

Berenbaum, M. (1981). Effects of linear furanocoumarins on an adapted specialist insect (*Papilio polyxenes*). *Ecol. Entomol.* **6**, 345–351.

Berger, P. J., Sanders, E. H., Gardner, P. D., and Negus, N. C. (1977). Phenolic plant compounds functioning as reproductive inhibitors in *Microtus montanus*. *Science* **195**, 575–577.

Berger, P. J., Negus, N. C., Sanders, E. H., and Gardner, P. D . (1981). Chemical triggering of reproduction in *Microtus montanus*. *Science* **214**, 69–70.

Bernays, E. A. (1978). Tannins: an alternative viewpoint. *Entomol. Exp. Appl.* **24**, 244–253.

Bernays, E. A. (1981). Plant tannins and insect herbivores: an appraisal. *Ecol. Entomol.* **6**, 353–360.

Bernays, E. A., and Chapman, R. F. (1978). Plant chemistry and acridoid feeding behavior. In "Biochemical Aspects of Plant and Animal Coevolution" (J. B. Harborne, ed.), pp. 99–141. Academic Press, New York.

Bernays, E. A., and Woodhead, S. (1982). Plant phenols utilized as nutrients by a phytophagous insect. *Science* **216**, 201–202.

Bernays, E. A., Chamberlain, D. J., and Leather, E. M. (1981). Tolerance of acridids to ingested condensed tannin. *J. Chem. Ecol.* **7**, 247–256.

Berryman, A. A. (1978a). Population cycles of the Douglas-fir tussock moth (Lepidoptera: Lymantridae): the time-delay hypothesis. *Can. Entomol.* **110**, 513–518.

Berryman, A. A. (1978b). Towards a theory of insect epidemiology. *Res. Popul. Ecol.* **19**, 181–196.

Berryman, A. A. (1979). Dynamics of bark beetle populations: analysis of dispersal and redistribution. *Mitt. Schwiez. Entomol. Ges.* **52**, 227–234.

Bess, H. A., Spurr, S. H., and Littlefield, E. W. (1947). Forest site conditions and the gypsy moth. *Harv. For. Bull.* **22**, 1–56.

Bouton, C. E., Price, P. W., and Kogan, M. (1980). Chemical defense in plants and its relevance to the third trophic level. Cited in Price *et al.* (1980).

Brattsten, L. B. (1979). Biochemical defense mechanisms in herbivores against plant allelochemicals. *In* ""Herbivores: Their Interaction with Secondary Plant Metabolites" (G. A. Rosenthal and D. H. Janzen, eds.), pp. 200–270. Academic Press, New York.

Brinkmann, W. A. R. (1976). Surface temperature trend for the northern hemisphere—updated. *Quat. Res. (N.Y.)* **6**, 355–358.

Brown, C. E. (1965). Mass transport of forest tent caterpillar moths *Malacosoma disstria* Hubner by a cold front. *Can. Entomol.* **97**, 1073–1075.

Browne, F. G. (1968). "Pests and Diseases of Forest Plantation Trees." Oxford Univ. Press (Clarendon), London and New York.

Bryant, J. P. (1981). Phytochemical deterrence of snowshoe hare browsing by adventitious shoots of four Alaskan trees. *Science* **213**, 889–890.

Bryant, J. P. (1982). The regulation of snowshoe hare feeding behaviour during winter by plant antiherbivore chemistry. *Proc. Int. Lagomorph. Conf., 1st, 1979* (in press).

Buttner, H. (1961). The effect of fertilizer applied to host plants on mortality and development of forest pests. *Schriftenr. Landesforstverwaltung Baden-Württemberg, Freiburg im Breisgau* **11**, 1–69.

Campbell, B. C., and Duffy, J. J. (1979). Tomatine and parasitic wasps: potential incompatability of plant-antibiosis with biological control. *Science* **205**, 700–702.

Campbell, I. M. (1962). Reproductive capacity in the genus *Chorinstoneura* Led. (Lepidoptera: Tortricidae). I. Quantitative inheritance and genes as controllers of rates. *Can. J. Genet. Cytol.* **4**, 272–288.

Campbell, R. W. (1981). Evidence for high fecundity among certain North American gypsy moth populations. *Environ. Entomol.* **10**, 663–667.

Campbell, R. W., and Sloan, R. J. (1977). Release of gypsy moth populations from innocuous levels. *Environ. Entomol.* **6**, 323–330.

Capinera, J. L., and Barbosa, P. (1976). Dispersal of first-instar gypsy moth larvae in relation to population quality. *Oecologia* **26**, 53–60.

Capinera, J. L., and Roltsch, W. J. (1980). Response of wheat seedlings to actual and simulated migratory grasshopper defoliation. *J. Econ. Entomol.* **73**, 258–261.

Carle, P. (1979). La dispersion des coléoptères forestiers nusibles. *Mitt. Schweiz. Entomol. Ges.* **52**, 133–156.

Carroll, C. R., and Hoffman, C. A. (1980). Chemical feeding deterrent mobilized in response to insect herbivory and counteradaptation by *Epilachna tredecimnota*. *Science* **209**, 414–416.

Carter, W. (1973). "Insects in Relation to Plant Disease." Wiley, New York.

Chambliss, O. L., and Jones, C. M. (1966). Cucurbitacins: specific insect attractants in Cucurbitaceae. *Science* **153**, 1392–1393.

Chapman, R. F., and Blaney, W. M. (1979). How animals perceive secondary compounds. *In* "Herbivores: Their Interaction with Secondary Plant Metabolites" (G. A. Rosenthal and D. H. Janzen, eds.), pp. 161–198. Academic Press, New York.

Cheng, L. (1970). Timing of attack by *Lypha dubia* Fall. (Diptera: Tachinidae) on the winter moth *Operophtera brumata* (L.) (Lepidoptera: Geometridae) as a factor affecting parasite success. *J. Anim. Ecol.* **39**, 313–320.

Chitty, D. (1957). Self regulation of numbers through changes in viability. *Cold Spring Harbor Symp. Quan. Biol.* **22**, 277–285.

Chitty, D. (1960). Population processes in the vole and their relevance to general theory. *Can. J. Zool.* **38**, 99–113.

Chitty, D. (1967). The natural selection of self-regulatory behaviour in animal populations. *Proc. Ecol. Soc. Aust.* **2**, 51–78.

Chitty, D., Pimentel, D., and Krebs, C. J. (1968). Food supply of overwintered voles. *J. Anim. Ecol.* **37**, 113–120.

Christian, J. J. (1971). Fighting, maturity and population density in Microtus pennsylvanicus. *J. Mammal.* **52**, 556–567.

Christian, J. J., Lloyd, J. A., and Davis, D. E. (1965). The role of endocrines in the self-regulation of mammalian populations. *Recent Prog. Horm. Res.* **21**, 501–578.

Christiansen, E. (1975). Field rodent damage in Norway. *Ecol. Bull.* **19**, 37–43.

Chrominski, A., Neumann Visscher, S., and Jurenka, R. (1982). Exposure to ethylene changes numphal growth rate and female longevity in the grasshopper Melanopus sanguinipes. *Naturwissenschaften* **69**(1), 45–46.

Clark, W. C. (1979). Spatial structure relationships in a forest insect system: simulation models and analysis. *Mitt. Schweiz. Entomol. Ges.* **52**, 235–257.

Cooper-Driver, G. A., Finch, S., Swain, T., and Bernays, E. (1977). Seasonal variation in secondary plant compounds in relation to the palatability of Pteridium aquilinum. *Biochem. Syst. Ecol.* **5**, 211–218.

Coster, J. E., and Johnson, P. C. (1979). Dispersion patterns of Dendroctonus frontalis and its predator Thanasimus dubius: influence of behavioral chemicals. *Mitt. Schweiz. Entomol. Ges.* **52**, 309–322.

Coulson, C. B., Davies, R. I., and Lewis, D. A. (1960a). Polyphenols in plant, humus, and soil. I. Polyphenols of leaves, litter and superficial humus from mull and mor sites. *J. Soil Sci.* **11**, 20–29.

Coulson, C. B., Davies, R. I., and Lewis, D. A. (1960b). Polyphenols in plant, humus and soil. II. Reduction and transport by polyphenols of iron in model soil columns. *J. Soil Sci.* **11**, 30–44.

Cronquist, A. (1968). "The Evolution and Classification of Flowering Plants." Houghton, Boston, Massachusetts.

Cruickshank, I. A. M. (1980). Defenses triggered by the invader: chemical defenses. *In* "Plant Disease" (J. G. Horsfall and E. B. Cowling, eds.), Vol. 5, pp. 247–267. Academic Press, New York.

Da Costa, C. P., and Jones, C. M. (1971a). Cucumber beetle resistance and mite susceptibility controlled by the bitter gene in Cucumis sativus L. *Science* **172**, 1145–1146.

Da Costa, C. P., and Jones, C. M. (1971b). Resistance in cucumber, Cucumis sativus L. to three species of cucumber beetles. *HortScience* **6**, 340–342.

Davies, E., and Schuster, A. (1981). Intercellular communication in plants: Evidence for a rapidly generated, bidirectionally transmitted wound signal. *Proc. Natl. Acad. Sci. U.S.A.* **78**(4), 2422–2426.

Davies, R. I., Coulson, C. B., and Lewis, D. A. (1964a). Polyphenols in plant, humus and soil. III. Stabilization of gelatin by polyphenol tanning. *J. Soil Sci.* **15**. 299–309.

Davies, R. I., Coulson, C. B., and Lewis, D. A. (1964b). Polyphenols in plant, humus and soil. IV. Factors leading to increase in biosynthesis of polyphenol in leaves and their relationship to mull and mor formation. *J. Soil Sci.* **15**, 310–318.

Dawson, J. (1956). Splenic hypertrophy in voles. *Nature (London)* **178**, 1183–1184.

DeBach, P. (1974). "Biological Control by Natural Enemies." Cambridge Univ. Press, London/New York.

Dempster, J. P. (1963). The population dynamics of grasshoppers and locusts. *Biol. Rev. Cambridge Philos. Soc.* **38**, 490–529.

Dethier, V. G. (1954). Evolution of feeding preferences in phytophagous insects. *Evolution* **8**, 33–54.

Dethier, V. G. (1980). Evolution of receptor sensitivity to secondary plant substances with special reference to deterrents. *Am. Nat.* **115**, 45–66.

Dethier, V. G., Brown, B., and Smith, C. (1960). The designation of chemicals in terms of the responses they illicit from insects. *J. Econ. Entomol.* **53**(1), 134–136.

Detling, J. K., and Dyer, M. I. (1981). Evidence for potential plant growth regulators in grasshoppers. *Ecology* **62**, 485–488.

Detling, J. K., Ross, C. W., Walmsley, M. H., Hilbert, D. W., Bonilla, C. A., and Dyer, M. I. (1981). Examination of North American bison saliva for potential plant growth regulators. *J. Chem. Ecol.* **7**, 239–246.

de Wilde, J., Bonger, W., Schooneveld, H. (1969). Effects of host plant age on phytophagous insects. *Entomol. Exp. Appl.* **12**, 714–720.

Dieleman, F. L. (1969). Effects of gall midge infestation on plant growth and growth regulating substances. *Entomol. Exp. Appl.* **12**, 745–749.

DiFeo, D. R., Jr. (1977). Qualitative and quantitative natural products chemistry of a desert plant community, Andalgalá Valley, Argentina: a chemical-ecological study. Ph.D. Dissertation, University of Texas, Austin.

Dropkin, V. H. (1979). How nematodes induce disease. *In* "Plant Disease" (J. G. Horsfall and E. B. Cowling, eds.), Vol. 4, pp. 219–238. Academic Press, New York.

Dunbar, D. M., and Stevens, G. R. (1975). Association of two-lined chestnut borer and shoestring fungus with mortality of defoliated oak in Connecticut. *For. Sci.* **21**, 169–174.

Dunbar, D. M., and Stevens, G. R. (1976). The bionomics of the twolined chestnut borer. *In* "Perspectives in Forest Entomology" (J. F. Anderson and H. K. Kaya, eds.), pp. 73–83. Academic Press, New York.

Duncan, D. P., and Hodson, A. C. (1958). Influence of the forest tent caterpillar upon the aspen forests of Minnesota. *For. Sci.* **4**, 72–93.

Dyer, M. I. (1980). Mammalian epidermal growth factor promotes plant growth. *Proc. Natl. Acad. Sci. U.S.A.* **77**(8), 4836–4837.

Dyer, M. I., and Bokhari, V. G. (1976). Plant–animal interactions: studies of the effects of grasshopper grazing on blue grama grass. *Ecology* **57**, 762–772.

Edson, K. M., Vinson, S. B., Stoltz, D. B., and Summers, M. D. (1981). Virus in a parasitoid wasp: suppression of the cellular immune response in the parasitoid's host. *Science* **211**, 582–583.

Ehrlich, P. R., and Raven, P. H. (1965). Butterflies and plants: a study in coevolution. *Evolution* **18**, 586–608.

Ellis, P. E., Carlisle, D. B., and Osborne, D. J. (1965). Desert locusts: sexual maturation delayed by feeding on senescent vegetation. *Science* **149**, 546–547.

Elton, C., Davis, D. H. S., and Findlay, G. M. (1935). An epidemic among voles (*Microtus agrestis*) on the Scottish border in the spring of 1934. *J. Anim. Ecol.* **4**, 277–288.

Enright, J. T. (1976). Climate and population regulation. *Oecologia* **24**, 295–310.

Evans, W. G. (1971). The attraction of insects to forest fires. *Proc. Tall Timbers Conf. Ecol. Anim. Control by Habitat Manage., 1969* pp. 115–127.

Faeth, S. H., Connor, E. F., and Simberloff, D. (1981). Early leaf abscission: a neglected source of mortality for folivores. *Am. Nat.* **117**, 409–415.

Feeny, P. P. (1970). Seasonal changes in oak leaf tannins and nutrients as a cause of spring feeding by winter moth caterpillars. *Ecology* **51**, 565–581.

Feeny, P. P. (1975). Biochemical coevolution between plants and their insect herbivores. *In* "Coevolution of Animals and Plants" (L. E. Gilbert and P. H. Raven, eds.), pp. 3–19. Univ. of Texas Press, Austin.

Feeny, P. P. (1976). Plant apparency and chemical defense. *Recent Adv. Phytochem.* **10,** 1–40.

Findlay, G. M., and Middleton, A. D. (1934). Epidemic disease among voles *(Microtus)* with special reference to *Toxoplasma. J. Anim. Ecol.* **3,** 150–160.

Fischlin, A., and Baltensweiler, W. (1979). Systems analysis of the larch bud moth system. Part 1. The larch–larch bud moth relationship. *Mitt. Schweiz. Entomol. Ges.* **52,** 273–289.

Fox, L. R. (1981). Defense and dynamics in plant–herbivore systems. *Am. Zool.* **21,** 853–864.

Freeland, W. J. (1974). Vole cycles: another hypothesis. *Am. Nat.* **108,** 238–245.

Fuller, W. A. (1969). Changes in numbers of three species of small rodent near Great Slave Lake, N.W.T., Canada, 1966–1967, and their significance for general population theory. *Ann. Zool. Fenn.* **6,** 113–144.

Fuller, W. A., Stebbins, L. L., and Dyke, G. R. (1969). Overwintering of small mammals near Great Slave Lake, Northern Canada. *Arctic* **22,** 34–55.

Futuyma, D. J. (1976). Food plant specialization and environmental predictability in Lepidoptera. *Am. Nat* **110,** 285–292.

Fye, E. (1974). Populations defined and approaches to measuring population density, dispersal, and dispersion. *Proc. Summer Inst. Biol. Control Plant Insects Dis., 1972* pp. 46–61.

Goodman, R. N. (1980). Defenses triggered by previous invaders: bacteria. *In* "Plant Disease" (J. G. Horsfall and E. B. Cowling, eds.), Vol. 5, pp. 305–317. Academic Press, New York.

Green, T. R., and Ryan, C. A. (1972). Wound-induced proteinase inhibitor in plant leaves: a possible defense mechanism against insects. *Science* **175,** 776–777.

Green, T. R., and Ryan, C. A. (1973). Wound-induced proteinase inhibitor in tomato leaves. *Plant Physiol.* **51,** 19–21.

Greenbank, D. O., Schaefer, G. W., and Rainey, R. C. (1980). Spruce budworm (Lepidoptera: Tortricidae) moth flight and dispersal: new understanding from canopy observations, radar and aircraft. *Mem. Entomol. Soc. Can* **110,** 1–49.

Gruys, P. (1970). Growth in *Bupalus piniarius* (Lepidoptera: Geometridae) in relation to larval population density. *Verh. Rijksnst. Natuurbeheer.* **1,** 1–127.

Gunn, D. L. (1960). The biological background of locust control. *Annu. Rev. Entomol.* **5,** 279–300.

Gustafsson, A., and Gadd, I. (1965). Mutations and crop improvement. II. The genus *Lupinus* (Leguminosae). *Hereditas* **53,** 15–39.

Hamilton, R. I. (1980). Defenses triggered by previous invaders: viruses. *In* "Plant Disease" (J. G. Horsfall and E. B. Cowling, eds.), Vol. 5, pp. 279–303. Academic Press, New York.

Hanover, J. W. (1975). Physiology of tree resistance to insects. *Annu. Rev. Entomol.* **20,** 75–95.

Hanson, C. H., Loper, G. M., Kohler, G. O., Bickoff, E. M., Taylor, K. W., Kehr, W. R., Stanford, E. H., Dudley, J. W., Pedersen, M. W., Sorenson, E. L., Carnahan, H. L., and Wilsie, C. P. (1965). Variation in Coumestrol content of alfalfa as related to location, variety, cutting, year, stage of growth and disease. *U.S. Dep. Agric. Agric. Res. Serv., Tech. Bull.* **1333.**

Hanson, C. H., Pedersen, M. W., Berrang, B., Wall, M. E., and Davis, K. H., Jr. (1973). The saponins in alfalfa cultivars. *Crop Sci. Soc. Am., Spec. Publ.* **4,** 33–52.

Harborne, J . B. (1977). "Introduction to Ecological Biochemistry." Academic Press, New York.

Harborne, J. B., ed. (1978). "Biochemical Aspects of Plant and Animal Coevolution." Academic Press, New York.

Harborne, J. B., and Ingham, J. L. (1978). Biochemical aspects of the coevolution of higher plants with their fungal parasites. *In* "Biochemical Aspects of Plant and Animal Coevolution" (J. B. Harborne, ed.), pp. 343–405. Academic Press, New York.

Haukioja, E. (1980). On the role of plant defenses in the fluctuation of herbivore populations. *Oikos* **35**, 202–213.

Haukioja, E., and Hakala, T. (1975). Herbivore cycles and periodic outbreaks. Formulation of a general hypothesis. *Rep. Kevo Subarct. Res. Stn.* **12**, 1–9.

Haukioja, E., and Neimelä, P. (1976). Does birch defend itself actively against herbivores? *Rep. Kevo Subarct. Res. Stn.* **13**, 44–47.

Haukioja, E., and Niemelä, P. (1977). Retarded growth of a geometrid larva after mechanical damage to leaves of its host tree. *Ann. Zool. Fenn.* **14**, 48–52.

Haukioja, E., and Neimelä, P. (1979). Birch leaves as a resource for herbivores: Seasonal occurrence of increased resistance in foliage after mechanical damage of adjacent leaves. *Oecologia* **39**, 151–159.

Head, G. C. (1974). Shedding of roots. In "Shedding of Plant Parts" (T. T. Kozlowski, ed.), pp. 237–293. Academic Press, New York.

Hedin, P. A., Maxwell, F. G., and Jenkins, J. N. (1974). Insect plant attractants, feeding stimulants, repellents, deterrents, and other related factors affecting insect behavior. *Proc. Summer Inst. Biol. Control Plant Insects Dis., 1972* pp. 494–527.

Hegnauer, R. (1962). "Chemotaxonomie der Pflanzen," Vol. 1. Birkhäuser, Stuttgart.

Higgins, K. M., Browns, J. E., and Haws, B. A. (1977). The black grass bug (*Labops hesperius* Uhler): its effect on several native and introduced grasses. *J. Range Manage.* **30**, 380–384.

Hodson, A. C. (1941). An ecological study of the forest tent caterpillar, *Malacosoma disstria* Hbn. in northern Minnesota. *Minn., Agric. Exp. Stn., Tech. Bull.* **148**, 1–55.

Holling, C. S., Jones, D. D., and Clark, W. C. (1977). Ecological policy design: a case study of forest and pest management. *Proc. Conf. Pest Manage., 1976* pp. 13–91.

Holling, C. S., Dantzig, G. B., Clark, W. C., Jones, D. D., Baskerville, G., and Peterman, G. (1979). Quantitative evaluation of pest management opportunities: the spruce budworm case study. In "Current Topics in Forest Entomology" (W. E. Waters, ed.), *USDA For. Serv. Gen. Tech. Rep.* **WO-8**, 82–102.

Hori, K. (1976). Plant growth-regulating factor in the salivary glands of several heteropterous insects. *Comp. Biochem. Physiol. B* **53**, 435–438.

Hori, K., and Endo, M. (1977). Metabolism of ingested auxins in the bug *Lygus disponsi*: conversion of indole-3-acetic acid and gibberellin. *J. Insect Physiol.* **23**, 1075–1080.

Horn, H. S. (1968). Regulation of animal numbers: a model counterexample. *Ecology* **49**, 776–778.

Horsfall, J. G., and Cowling, E. B., (1980). "Plant Disease," Vol. 5. Academic Press, New York.

Hsiao, T. H. (1969). Chemical basis of host selection and plant resistance in oligophagous insects. *Entomol. Exp. Appl.* **12**, 777–788.

Hsiao, T. H., and Fraenkel, G. (1968). Isolation of phagostimulative substances from the host plant of the Colorado potato beetle. *Ann. Entomol. Soc. Am.* **61**, 476–484.

Huber, D. M. (1980). The role of mineral nutrition in defense. In "Plant Disease" (J. G. Horsfall and E. B. Cowling, eds.), Vol. 5, pp. 381–406. Academic Press, New York.

Iwao, S. (1968). Some effects of grouping in lepidopterous insects. *Colloq. Int. C. N. R. S.* **173**, 185–212.

James, W. D. (1950). Alkaloids in the plant. *Alkaloids (N.Y.)* **1**, 15–90.

Janzen, D. H. (1970). Herbivores and the number of tree species in tropical forests. *Am. Nat.* **104**, 501–528.

Janzen, D. H. (1971). Escape of juvenile *Dioclea megacarpa* (Leguminosae) vines from predators in a deciduous tropical forest. *Am. Nat.* **105**, 97–112.

Janzen, D. II. (1973a). Comments on host-specificity of tropical herbivores and its relevance to species richness. *Syst. Assoc. Spec. Vol.* **5**, 201–211.

Janzen, D. H. (1973b). Community structure of secondary compounds in plants. *Pure Appl. Chem.* **34**, 529–538.

Janzen, D. H. (1974). Tropical blackwater rivers, animals, and mast fruiting by Dipterocarpaceae. *Biotropica* **6**(2), 69–103.

Janzen, D. H. (1977). Why fruits rot, seeds mold and meat spoils. *Am. Nat.* **111**, 691–713.

Jermy, T. (1976). Insect–host-plant relationship—coevolution or sequential evolution. *In* "The Host Plant in Relation to Insect Behavior and Development" (T. Jermy, ed.), pp. 109–113. Plenum, New York.

Johnson, W. T., Lyon, H. H., Koehler, C. S., Johnson, N. E., and Weidhaas, J. A. (1976). "Insects that Feed on Trees and Shrubs." Cornell Univ. Press, Ithaca, New York.

Jung, H. G., Batzli, G. O., Seigler, D. S. (1979). Patterns in the phytochemistry of arctic plants. *Biochem. Syst. Ecol.* **7**, 203–209.

Kalela, O. (1962). On the fluctuations in the numbers of arctic and boreal small rodents as a problem of production biology. *Ann. Acad. Sci. Fenn., Ser. A*4 **66**, 5–38.

Kalkstein, L. S. (1976). Effects of climatic stress upon outbreaks of the southern pine beetle. *Environ. Entomol.* **5**, 653–658.

Kamm, J. A., and Fuxa, J. R. (1977). Management practices to manipulate populations of the plant bug *Labops hesperius* Uhler. *J. Range Manage.* **30**, 385–387.

Kaya, H. K. (1976). Insect pathogens in natural and microbial control of forest defoliators. *In* "Perspectives in Forest Entomology" (J. F. Anderson and H. K. Kaya, eds.), pp. 251–263. Academic Press, New York.

Keith, L. B. (1974). Some features of population dynamic in mammals. *Proc. Int. Congr. Game Biol., 11th, 1973* pp. 17–58.

Kennedy, J. S. (1956). Phase transformation in locust biology. *Biol. Rev. Cambridge Philos. Soc.* **31**, 349–370.

Khasimuddin, S. (1981a). Behavioural ecology of the African armyworm, *Spodoptera exempta* (Walker): observations on population processes during a high-density outbreak. *Insect Sci. Appl.* **1**, 143–146.

Khasimuddin, S. (1981b). Phase variation and "off-season" survival of the African armyworm, *Spodoptera exempta* (Walker) (Lepidoptera: Noctuidae). *Insect Sci. Appl.* **1**, 357–360.

Kimmins, J. P. (1971). Variations in the foliar amino acid composition of flowering balsum fir [*Abies balsamea* (L.) Mill.] and white spruce [*Picea glauca* (Moench) Voss] in relation to outbreaks of the spruce budworm [*Choristoneura fumiferana* (Clem)]. *Can. J. Zool.* **49**, 1005–1011.

Klein, D. R. (1977). Winter food preferences of snowshoe hares *(Lepus americanus)* in Alaska. *Proc. Int. Congr. Game Biol., 13th, 1977* pp. 266–275.

Klomp, H. (1964). Intraspecific competition and the regulation of insect numbers. *Annu. Rev. Entomol.* **9**, 17–40.

Klomp, H. (1968). A seventeen year study of the abundance of the pine looper *Bupalus piniaria* L. (Lepidoptera: Geometridae). *In* "Insect Abundance" (T. R. E. Southwood, ed.), pp. 98–108. Blackwell, Oxford.

Klun, J. A., Tipton, C. L., and Brindley, T. A. (1967). 2,4-Dihydroxy-7-methoxy-1,4-benzoxazin-3-one (DIMBOA) an active agent in resistance of maize to the European corn borer. *J. Econ. Entomol.* **60**, 1529–1533.

Kogan, M. (1977). The role of chemical factors in insect/plant relationships. *Proc. Int. Congr. Entomol., 15th, 1976* pp. 211–227.

Krebs, C. J., and DeLong, K. T. (1965). A *Microtus* population with supplemental food. *J. Mammal.* **46**, 566–573.

Krebs, C. J., Gaines, M. S., Keller, B. L., Meyers, J. H., and Tomarin, R. H. (1973). Population cycles in small rodents. *Science* **179**, 35–40.

Kuć, J., and Caruso, F. L. (1977). Activated coordinated chemical defense against disease in plants. *ACS Symp. Ser.* **62,** 78–89.

Lack, D. (1954). Cyclic mortality. *J. Wildl. Manage.* **18,** 25–37.

Lamb, H. H. (1969). Climatic fluctuations. *In* "General Climatography" (H. Flohn, ed.), Vol. 2, pp. 173–249. Am. Elsevier, New York.

Larsson, S., and Tenow, O. (1982). Local patterns in the distribution of a *Neodiprion sertifer* outbreak. *Proc. IUFRO Work. Party Popu. Dyn. For. Pests, 1980* (in press).

Lawton, J. H., and Strong, D. R., Jr. (1981). Community patterns and competition in folivorous insects. *Am. Nat.* **118,** 317–338.

Leonard, D. E. (1970). Intrinsic factors causing qualitative changes in populations of *Porthetria dispar* (Lepidoptera: Lymantridae). *Can. Entomol.* **102,** 239–249.

Leonard, D. E. (1971). Population quality. *USDA For. Serv. Res. Pap. NE* **NE-194,** 7–19.

Leonard, D. E. (1974). Recent developments in ecology and control of the gypsy moth. *Annu. Rev. Entomol.* **19,** 197–229.

Lessard, E. D. (1974). Climatic, host tree, and site factors affecting the population dynamics of the Douglas-fir tussock moth, *Orgyia pseudotsugata* McDunnough. M.S. Thesis, University of Washington, Seattle.

Levitt, J. (1972). "Responses of Plants to Environmental Stress." Academic Press, New York.

Lewis, A. C. (1979). Feeding preference for diseased and wilted sunflower in the grasshopper *Melanopus differentialis*. *Entomol. Exp. Appl.* **26,** 202–207.

Lloyd, M., and Dybas, H. S. (1966). The periodical cicada problem. II. *Evolution* **20,** 466–505.

Lloyd, M., and White, J. A. (1976). On the oviposition habits of 13 year versus 17 year periodical cicadas of the same species. *J. N. Y. Entomol. Soc.* **84,** 148–155.

Loper, G. M. (1968). Effect of aphid infestation on the coumestrol content of alfalfa varieties differing in aphid resistance. *Crop Sci.* **8,** 104–106.

Loper, G. M., Hanson, C. H., and Graham, J. H. (1967). Coumestrol content of alfalfa as affected by selection for resistance to foliar diseases. *Crop Sci.* **7,** 189–192.

Lorimer, N. (1979). Genetic causes of pest population outbreaks and crashes. *In* "Genetics in Relation to Insect Management" (M. A. Hoy and J. J. McKelvey, Jr., eds.), pp. 50–54. Rockefeller Found., New York.

McFarlane, J. E., and Distler, M. H. W. (1982). The effect of rutin on growth, fecundity and food utilization in *Acheta domesticus* (L.). *J. Insect Physiol.* **28,** 85–88.

McIntyre, J. L. (1980). Defenses triggered by previous invaders: nematodes and insects. *In* "Plant Disease" (J. G. Horsfall and E. B. Cowling, eds.), Vol. 5, pp. 333–343. Academic Press, New York.

McKey, D. (1974). Adaptive patterns in alkaloid physiology. *Am. Nat.* **108,** 305–320.

McKey, D. (1975). The ecology of coevolved seed dispersal systems. *In* "Coevolution of Animals and Plants" (L. E. Gilbert and P. H. Raven, eds.), pp. 159–191. Univ. of Texas Press, Austin.

McKey, D. (1979). The distribution of secondary compounds within plants. *In* "Herbivores: Their Interaction with Secondary Plant Metabolites" (G. A. Rosenthal and D. H. Janzen, ed.), pp. 56–133. Academic Press, New York.

McKey, D., Waterman, P. G., Mbi, C. N., Gartlan, J. S., and Struhsaker, T. T. (1978). Phenolic content of vegetation in two African rain forests: ecological implications. *Science* **202,** 61–64.

McLaughlin, S. B., and Shriner, D. S. (1980). Allocation of resources to defense and repair. *In* "Plant Disease" (J. G. Horsfall and E. B. Cowling, eds.), Vol. 5, pp. 407–431. Academic Press, New York.

McLean, D. L., and Kinsey, M. G. (1968). Probing behaviour of the pea aphid, *Acyrthosiphon pisum* II. Comparisons of salivation and ingestion in host and non-host leaves. *Ann. Entomol. Soc. Am.* **61,** 730–739.

McLeod, J. M. (1979). Discontinuous stability in a sawfly life system and its relevance to pest management strategies. In "Current Topics in Forest Entomology" (W. E. Waters, ed.), pp. 68–81. Sel. Pap. 15th Int. Cong. Entomol. Washington, D.C., USA. 1976.

Mali, P. C., and Mentha, S. L. (1977). Effect of drought on enzymes and free proline in rice varieties. Phytochemistry 16, 1355–1357.

Manville, J. F., Bock, K., and von Rudloff, E. (1977). Occurrence of juvabione-type and epijuvabione-type sesquiterpenoids in Abies alba. Phytochemistry 16, 1967–1971.

Mares, M. A., Enders, F. A., Kingsolver, J. M., Neff, J. L., and Simpson, B. B. (1977). In "Mesquite: Its Biology in Two Desert Scrub Ecosystems" (B. B. Simpson, ed.), pp. 123–149. Dowden, Hutchinson & Ross, Stroudsburg, Pennsylvania.

Markkula, M., Lavrema, S., and Tiittanen, K. (1976). Systemic damage caused by Trioza apicaulis on carrot. In "The Host Plant in Relation to Insect Behavior and Reproduction" (T. Jermy, ed.), pp. 153–155. Plenum, New York.

Mason, R. R. (1981). Numerical analysis of the causes of population collapse in a severe outbreak of the Douglas-fir tussock moth. Ann. Entomol. Soc. Am. 74, 51–57.

Mason, R. R., Beckwith, R. C., and Paul, H. G. (1977). Fecundity reduction during collapse of a Douglas-fir tussock moth outbreak in northeast Oregon. Environ. Entomol. 6, 623–626.

Matches, A. G., Howell, R. W., Fuccillo, D. A., and Paskin, L. H., eds. (1973). Anti-quality components of forages. Crop Sci. Soc. Am., Spec. Publ. 4.

Matsumoto, Y. (1970). Volatile organic sulphur compounds as insect attractants with special reference to host selection. In "Control of Insect Behaviour by Natural Products" (D. L. Wood, R. M. Silverstein, and M. Nakajima, eds.), pp. 133–160. Academic Press, New York.

Mattson, W. J. (1980). Herbivory in relation to plant nitrogen content. Annu. Rev. Ecol. Syst. 11, 119–161.

Mattson, W. J., and Addy, N. D. (1975). Phytophagous insects as regulators of forest primary production. Science 190, 515–522.

Maxwell, F. G., Jenkins, J. N., Keller, J. C., and Parrot, W. L. (1963). An arrestant and feeding stimulant for the boll weevil in water extracts of cotton plant parts. J. Econ. Entomol. 56, 449–454.

Maxwell, F. G., Lafever, H. N., and Jenkins, J. N. (1965). Blister beetles on glandless cotton. J. Econ. Entomol. 58, 792–793.

May, R. M. (1972). Limit cycles in predator–prey communities. Science 177, 900–902.

May, R. M. (1973). Time-delay versus stability in population models with two and three trophic levels. Ecology 54, 315–325.

May, R. M., Conway, G. R., Hassell, M. P. and Southwood, T. R. E. (1974). Time delays, density-dependence and single-species oscillations. J. Anim. Ecol. 43, 747–770.

Miles, P. W. (1968a). Insect secretions in plants. Annu. Rev. Phytopathol. 6, 137–164.

Miles, P. W. (1968b). Studies on the salivary physiology of plant-bugs. Experimental induction of galls. J. Insect Physiol. 14, 97–106.

Miles, P. W. (1978). Redox reactions of hemipterous saliva in plant tissues. Entomol. Exp. Appl. 24, 534–539.

Millburn, P. (1978). Biotransformation of xenobiotics by animals. In "Biochemical Aspects of Plant and Animal Coevolution" (J. B. Harborne, ed.), pp. 35–73. Academic Press, New York.

Miller, C. A. (1963a). The analysis of fecundity proportion in the unsprayed area. Mem. Entomol. Soc. Can. 31, 75–87.

Miller, C. A. (1963b). Parasites and the spruce budworm. Mem. Entomol. Soc. Can. 31, 228–244.

Milne, A. (1957). The natural control of insect populations. Can. Entomol. 89, 193–213.

Mirov, N. T. (1967). "The Genus *Pinus*." Ronald Press, New York.

Mittler, T. E., and Sutherland, O. R. W. (1969). Dietary influences on aphid polymorphism. *Entomol. Exp. Appl.* **12**, 703–713.

Mooney, H. A. (1972). The carbon balance of plants. *Annu. Rev. Ecol. Syst.* **3**, 315–346.

Mooney, H. A., and Chu, C. (1974). Seasonal carbon allocation in *Heteromeles arbutifolia*, a California evergreen shrub. *Oecologia* **14**, 295–306.

Morris, R. F., ed. (1963a). The dynamics of epidemic spruce budworm populations. *Mem. Entomol. Soc. Can.* **31**, 1–332.

Morris, R. F. (1963b). The analysis of generation survival in relation to age-interval survivals in the unsprayed area. *Mem. Entomol. Soc. Can.* **31**, 32–37.

Morris, R. F. (1963c). The development of predictive equations for the spruce budworm based on key-factor analysis. *Mem. Entomol. Soc. Can.* **31**, 116–129.

Morris, R. F. (1963d). Foliage depletion and the spruce budworm. *Mem. Entomol. Soc. Can.* **31**, 223–228.

Morris, R. F. (1963e). The effect of predator age and prey defense on the functional response of *Podisus maculiventris* Say to the density of *Hyphantria cunea* Drury. *Can. Entomol.* **95**, 1009–1020.

Morris, R. F. (1963f). Predation and the spruce budworm. *Mem. Entomol. Soc. Can.* **31**, 244–248.

Morris, R. F. (1967). Influence of parental food quality on survival of *Hyphantria cunea*. *Can. Entomol.* **99**, 24–33.

Morris, R. F., Miller, C. A., Greenbank, D. O., and Mott, D. G. (1958). The population dynamics of the spruce budworm in eastern Canada. *Proc. Int. Congr. Entomol., 10th, 1956* Vol. 4, pp. 137–149.

Moss, R., Watson, A., and Parr, R. (1974). A role of nutrition in the population dynamics of some game birds (Tetraonidae). *Proc. Int. Congr. Game Biol.* **11**, 193–201.

Mothes, K. (1960). Alkaloids in the plant. *Alkaloids (N.Y.)* **7**, 1–29. Academic Press, New York.

Muldrew, J. A. (1953). The natural immunity of the larch sawfly [*Pristiphora erichsonii* (Htg.)] to the introduced parasite *Mesoleius tenthredinis* Morley, in Manitoba and Saskatchewan. *Can. J. Zool.* **31**, 313–332.

Müller, K. O. (1956). Einige Einfache Versuche zum Nachweis von Phytoalexinen. *Phytopathol. Z.* **27**, 237–254.

Müller, K. O., and Börger, H. (1941). Experimentelle Untersuchungen über die *Phytophora*-Resistenz der Kartoffel. *Arb. Biol. Reichsanst. Land-Forstwirtsch. Berlin-Dahlem* **23**, 189–231.

Myers, J. H. (1981). Interactions between western tent caterpillars and wild rose: a test of some general plant herbivore hypotheses. *J. Anim. Ecol.* **50**, 11–25.

Myers, J. H., and Krebs, C. J. (1974). Population cycles in rodents. *Sci. Am.* **230**(6), 38–46.

Nappi, A. J. (1975). Parasite encapsulation in insects. *In* "Invertebrate Immunity" (K. Maramorosch and R. E. Shope, eds.), pp. 293–326. Academic Press, New York.

Naya, J. K., and Fraenkel, G. (1963). The chemical basis of host selection in the Mexican bean beetle *Epilachna varivestis*. *Ann. Entomol. Soc. Am.* **56**, 174–178.

Nichols, J. O. (1968). Oak mortality in Pennsylvania: a ten year study. *J. For.* **66**, 681–694.

Nicholson, A. J. (1954). An outline of the dynamics of animal populations. *Aust. J. Zool.* **2**, 9–65.

Nicholson, A. J. (1957). The self-adjustment of populations to change. *Cold Spring Harbor Symp. Quant. Biol.* **22**, 153–173.

Niemelä, P., Aro, A. M., and Haukioja, E. (1979). Birch leaves as a resource for herbivores. Damage-induced increase in leaf phenols with trypsin-inhibiting effects. *Rep. Kevo Subarct. Res. Stn.* **15**, 37–40.

Nolte, D. J. (1974). The gregarization of locusts. *Biol. Rev. Cambridge Philos. Soc.* **49**, 1–14.

Norris, D. M. (1979). How insects induce disease. *In* "Plant Disease" (J. G. Horsfall and E. B. Cowling, eds.), Vol. 4, pp. 239–255. Academic Press, New York.

Norris, D. M., and Kogan, M. (1980). Biochemicals and morphological bases of resistance. *In* "Breeding Plants Resistant to Insects" (F. G. Maxwell and P. R. Jennings, eds.), pp. 23–61. Wiley, New York.

Nowaki, E., Jurzysta, M., Gorski, P., Nowacka, D., and Waller, G. R. (1976). Effect of nitrogen nutrition on alkaloid metabolism in plants. *Biochem. Physiol. Pflanz.* **169**, 231–240.

Odiyo, P. O. (1981). Development of the first outbreaks of the African armyworm, *Spodoptera exempta* (Walk.), between Kenya and Tanzania during the "off-season" months of July to December. *Insect Sci. Appl.* **1**, 305–318.

Okamoto, H. (1966). Three problems of prey specificity of aphidophagous coccinellids. *In* "Ecology of Aphidophagous Insects" (I. H. Odeck, ed.), pp. 45–46. Academia, Prague, Czechoslovakia.

Olsen, P. (1981). The stimulating effect of a phytohormone, gibberellic acid, on reproduction of *Mus musculus. Aust. Wildl. Res.* **8**, 321–325.

Osborne, D. J. (1973). Mutual regulation of growth and development in plants and insects. *In* "Insect/Plant Relationships" (H. F. Van Emden, ed.), pp. 33–42. Blackwell, Oxford.

Owen, D. F. (1976). Ladybird, ladybird, fly away home. *New Sci.* **71**, 686–687.

Owen, D. F. (1980). How plants may benefit from the animals that eat them. *Oikos* **35**, 230–235.

Owen, D. F., and Wiegert, R. G. (1976). Do consumers maximize plant fitness? *Oikos* **27**, 488–492.

Owen, D. F., and Wiegert, R. G. (1981). Mutualism between grasses and grazers: an evolutionary hypothesis. *Oikos* **36**, 376–378.

Parker, J. (1977). Phenolics in black oak bark and leaves. *J. Chem. Ecol.* **3**, 489–496.

Peacock, J. W., Lincoln, A. C., Simeone, J. B., and Silverstein, R. M. (1971). Attraction of *Scolytus multistriatus* (Coleoptera: Scolytidae) to a virgin female-produced pheromone in the field. *Ann. Entomol. Soc. Am.* **64**, 1143–1149.

Pearson, O. P. (1971). Additional measurements of the impact of carnivores on California voles (*Microtus californicus). J. Mammal.* **52**, 41–49.

Peters, T. M., and Barbosa, P. (1977). Influence of population density on size, fecundity and development rate of insects in culture. *Annu. Rev. Entomol.* **22**, 431–450.

Pitelka, F. A. (1957). Some characteristics of microtine cycles in the arctic. *Annu. Biol. Colloq. Corvallis; 1957* **18**, 73–88.

Pitelka, F. A. (1964). The nutrient-recovery hypothesis for arctic microtine cycles. I. Introduction. *Symp. Br. Ecol. Soc.* **4**, 55–56.

Price, P. W., Bouton, C. E., Gross, P., McPheron, B. A., Thompson, J. N., and Weis, A. E. (1980). Interactions among three trophic levels: influence of plants on interactions between insect herbivores and natural enemies. *Annu. Rev. Ecol. Syst.* **11**, 41–65.

Prokopy, R. J. (1981). Epideictic pheromones that influence spacing patterns of phytophagous insects. *In* "Semiochemicals: Their Role in Pest Control" (D. A. Norlund, R. L. Jones, and W. J. Lewis, eds.), pp. 181–213. Wiley, New York.

Puritch, G. S., and Nijholt, W. W. (1974). Occurrence of juvabione-related compounds in grand fir and pacific silver fir infested by balsam wooly aphid. *Can. J. Bot.* **52**, 585–587.

Rainey, R. C. (1979). Dispersal and redistribution of some Orthoptera and Lepidoptera by flight. *Mitt. Schweiz. Entomol. Ges.* **52**, 125–132.

Reardon, P. O., Leinweber, C. L., Merrill, L. B. (1972). The effect of bovine saliva on grasses. *J. Anim. Sci.* **34**, 897–898.

Reardon, P. O., Leinweber, C. L., and Merrill, L. B. (1974). Responses of sideoats grama to animal saliva and thiamine. *J. Range Manage.* **27**, 400–401.

Rees, C. J. C. (1969). Chemoreceptor specificity associated with choice of feeding site by the beetle *Chrysolina brunsvicensis* on its food plant, *Hypericum hirsutum*. *Entomol. Exp. Appl.* **12,** 565–583.

Rhoades, D. F. (1977). The antiherbivore chemistry of *Larrea*. *In* "Creosote Bush" (T. J. Mabry, J. H. Hunziker, and D. R. DiFeo, Jr., eds.), pp. 135–175. Dowden, Hutchinson & Ross, Stroudsburg, Pennsylvania.

Rhoades, D. F. (1979). Evolution of plant chemical defense against herbivores. *In* "Herbivores: Their Interaction with Secondary Plant Metabolites" (G. A. Rosenthal and D. H. Janzen, eds.), pp. 3–54. Academic Press, New York.

Rhoades, D. F. (1983). Responses of alder and willow to attack by tent caterpillars and webworms: evidence for pheromonal sensitivity of willows. *In* "Mechanisms of plant resistance to insects" (P. Hedin, ed.). *ACS Symp. Ser.* **208,** 55–68.

Rhoades, D. F., and Bergdahl, J. C. (1981). Adaptive significance of toxic nectar. *Am. Nat.* **117,** 798–803.

Rhoades, D. F., and Cates, R. G. (1976). Toward a general theory of plant antiherbivore chemistry. *Recent Adv. Phytochem.* **10,** 168–213.

Root, R. B. (1973). Organization of a plant–arthropod association in simple and diverse habitats: the fauna of collard *(Brassica oleracea). Ecol. Monogr.* **43,** 95–120.

Rosenthal, G. A., and Janzen, D. H., eds. (1979). "Herbivores: Their Interaction with Secondary Plant Metabolites." Academic Press, New York.

Rosenthal, G. A., Janzen, D. H., and Dahlman, D. L. (1977). Degradation and detoxification of canavanine by a specialized seed predator. *Science* **196,** 658–660.

Rothschild, M. (1973). Secondary plant substances and warning colouration in insects. *In* "Insect/Plant Relationships" (H. F. Van Emden, ed.), pp. 59–83. Blackwell, Oxford.

Rudnew, D. F. (1963). Physiologischer Zustand der Wirtsplanze und Massenvermehrung von Forstschädlingen. *Z. Angew. Entomol.* **53,** 48–68.

Ryan, C. A. (1979). Proteinase inhibitors. *In* "Herbivores: Their Interaction with Secondary Plant Metabolites" (G. A. Rosenthal and D. H. Janzen, eds.), pp. 599–618. Academic Press, New York.

Salt, G. (1956). Experimental studies in insect parasitism. IX. The reactions of a stick insect to an alien parasite. *Proc. R. Soc. London, Ser. B* **146,** 93–108.

Salt, G. (1963). The defense reactions of insects to metazoan parasites. *Parasitology* **53,** 527–642.

Salt, G. (1964). The ichneumonid parasite *Nemeritis canaescens* (Gravenhorst) in relation to the wax moth *Galleria mellonella* (L.). *Trans. R. Entomol. Soc.* **116,** 1–14.

Sanders, C. J. (1979). Pheromones and dispersal in the management of eastern spruce budworm. *Mitt. Schweiz. Entomol. Ges.* **52,** 223–226.

Sanders, E. H., Gardner, P. D., Berger, P. J., and Negus, N. C. (1981). 6-Methoxyben-zoxazolinone: A plant derivative that stimulates reproduction in *Microtus montanus*. *Science* **214,** 67–69.

Scheline, R. R. (1978). "Mammalian Metabolism of Plant Xenobiotics." Academic Press, New York.

Schlesinger, W. H. (1976). Toxic foods and vole cycles: additional data. *Am. Nat.* **110,** 315–317.

Schmidt, J. O. (1982). Biochemistry of insect venoms. *Annu. Rev. Entomol.* **27,** 339–368.

Schoeneweiss, D. F. (1967). Susceptibility of weakened cottonwood stems to fungi associated with blackstem. *Plant Dis. Rep.* **51,** 933–935.

Schoonhoven, L. M. (1967). Chemoreception of mustard oil glycosides in larvae of *Pieris brassicae. Proc. K. Ned Akad. Wet. Ser. C* **70,** 556–578.

Schoonhoven, L. M. (1973). Plant recognition by lepidopterous larvae. *In* "Insect/Plant Relationships" (H. F. Van Emden, ed.), pp. 87–97. Blackwell, Oxford.

Schultz, A. M. (1964). The nutrient-recovery hypothesis for arctic microtine cycles. II. Ecosystem variables in relation to arctic microtine cycles. *Symp. Br. Ecol. Soc.* **4**, 57–68.

Schultz, D. E., and Allen, D. C. (1977). Characteristics of sites with high black cherry mortality due to bark beetles following defoliation by *Hydria prunivorata*. *Environ. Entomol.* **6**, 77–81.

Scriber, J. M., and Slansky, F., Jr. (1981). The nutritional ecology of immature insects. *Annu. Rev. Entomol.* **26**, 183–211.

Sequeira, L. (1980). Defenses triggered by the invader: recognition and compatibility phenomena. *In* "Plant Disease" (J. G. Horsfall and E. B. Cowling, eds.), Vol. 5, pp. 179–200. Academic Press, New York.

Shaw, M. R. (1981). Delayed inhibition of host development by the nonparalysing venoms of parasitic wasps. *J. Invertebr. Pathol.* **37**, 215–221.

Shepherd, R. F. (1979). Comparison of the daily cycle of adult behavior of five forest Lepidoptera from western Canada and their response to pheromone traps. *Mitt. Schweiz. Entomol. Ges.* **52**, 157–168.

Shiga, M. (1976). Effect of group size on the survival and development of young larvae of *Malacosoma neustria testacea* Motschulsky (Lepidoptera: Lasiocampidae) and its role in the natural population. *Konchu* **44**(4), 537–553.

Smirnoff, W. A., and Bernier, B. (1973). Increased mortality of the Swain jack-pine sawfly and foliar nitrogen concentrations after urea fertilization. *Can. J. For. Res.* **3**, 112–121.

Smith, B. D. (1966). Effect of the plant alkaloid sparteine on the distribution of the aphid *Acrythosiphon spartii*. *Nature (London)* **211**, 213–214.

Smith, N. G. (1982). Periodic migrations and population fluctuations by the neotropical day-flying moth *Urania fulgens* through the isthmus of Panama. *In* "The Ecology of a Tropical Forest: Seasonal Rhythms and Long-term Changes" (E. G. Leigh, Jr., A. S. Rand, and D. M. Windsor, eds.). Smithsonian Inst. Press, Washington, D.C. (in press).

Smith, R. H. (1961). The fumigant toxicity of three pine resins to *Dendroctonus brevicomis* and *D. jeffreyi*. *J. Econ. Entomol.* **54**, 365–369.

Staedler, E. (1977). Sensory aspects of insect plant interactions. *Proc. Int. Congr. Entomol., 15th, 1976* pp. 228–248.

Staley, J. M. (1965). Decline and mortality of red and scarlet oaks. *For. Sci.* **11**, 2–17.

Stamp, N. E. (1980). Egg deposition patterns in butterflies: why do some species cluster their eggs rather than deposit them singly? *Am. Nat.* **115**, 367–380.

Stark, R. W. (1965). Recent trends in forest entomology. *Annu. Rev. Entomol.* **10**, 303–324.

Stehr, F. W. (1974). Release, establishment and evaluation of parasites and predators. *Proc. Summer Inst. Biol. Control Plant Insects Dis., 1972* pp. 124–136.

Steinhaus, E. A. (1958). Stress as a factor in insect disease. *Proc. Int. Congr. Entomol. 10th, 1956* Vol. 4, pp 725–730.

Stenseth, N. C. (1978). Do grazers maximize individual plant fitness? *Oikos* **31**, 299–306.

Sullivan, C. R., and Green, G. W. (1950). Reactions of larvae of the eastern tent caterpillar *Malacosoma americanum* (F.) and of the spotless fall webworm, *Hyphantria textor* Harr. to pentatomid predators. *Can. Entomol.* **82**, 52.

Sutherland, D. R. W. (1969). The role of the host plant in the production of winged forms by two strains of the pea aphid, *Acrythosiphon pisum*. *J. Insect Physiol.* **15**, 2179–2201.

Suzuki, H. (1980). Defenses triggered by previous invaders: fungi. *In* "Plant Disease" (J. G. Horsfall and E. B. Cowling, eds.), Vol. 5, pp. 319–332. Academic Press, New York.

Swain, T. (1978). Plant–animal coevolution: a synoptic view of the paleozoic and mesozoic. *In* "Biochemical Aspects of Plant and Animal Coevolution" (J. B. Harborne, ed.), pp. 3–19. Academic Press, New York.

Swain, T. (1979). Tannins and lignins. *In* "Herbivores: Their Interaction with Secondary Plant Metabolites" (G. A. Rosenthal and D. H. Janzen, eds.), pp. 657–682. Academic Press, New York.

Swain, T., and Hillis, W. E. (1959). The phenolic constituents of *Prunus domestica*. I. The quantitative analysis of phenolic constituents. *J. Sci. Food Agric.* **10,** 63–68.

Tanada, Y. (1976). Ecology of insect viruses. *In* "Perspectives in Forest Entomology" (J. F. Anderson and H. K. Kaya, eds.), pp. 265–283. Academic Press, New York.

Teivainen, T. (1981). Geographic trends in voles in Finland in the years 1973–80. Herbivore–plant interactions at northern latitudes. A symposium workshop at Kevo, Finland, 14–18 September 1981. *Metsantutkimuslaitoksen Tiedonantoja* **21,** 17 (ISSN 0358-4283).

Thielges, B. A. (1968). Altered polyphenol metabolism in the foliage of *Pinus sylvestris* associated with European pine sawfly attack. *Can. J. Bot.* **46,** 724–726.

Thompson, D. Q. (1955). The 1953 lemming emigration at Point Barrow, Alaska. *Arctic* **8,** 37–45.

Todd, J. G., and Kamm, J. A. (1974). Biology and impact of a grass bug *Labops hesperius* Uhler in Oregon rangeland. *J. Range Manage.* **27,** 453–458.

Uvarov, B. P. (1921). A revision of the genus *Locusta* L. (= *Pachytlus Fieb.)* with a new theory as to the periodicity and migrations of locusts. *Bull. Entomol. Res.* **12,** 135–163.

Uvarov, B. P. (1957). The aridity factor in the ecology of locusts and grasshoppers of the Old World. *Arid. Zone Res.* **8,** 164–198.

van den Bos, J., and Rabbinge, R. (1976). "Simulation of the Fluctuations of the Grey Larch Bud Moth." Cent. Agric. Publ. Doc., Wageningen, Holland.

van den Bosch, R. (1964). Encapsulation of the eggs of *Bathyplectes curculionis* (Thomson) (Hymenoptera: Ichneumonidae) in larvae of *Hypera brunneipennis* (Boheman) and *Hypera postica* (Gyllenhal) (Coleoptera: Curculionidae). *J. Insect Pathol.* **6,** 343–367.

Van Emden, H. F. (1972). Aphids as phytochemists. *In* "Phytochemical Ecology" (J. B. Harborne, ed.), pp. 25–43. Academic Press, New York.

Varley, G. C., Gradwell, G. R., and Hassell, M. P. (1975). "Insect Population Ecology." Blackwell, Oxford.

Vaughan, G. L., and Jungreis, A. M. (1977). Insensitivity of lepidopteran tissues to oubain. Physiological mechanisms for protection from cardiac glycosides. *J. Insect Physiol.* **23,** 585–589.

Vinson, S. B., and Iwantsch, G. F. (1980a). Host regulation by insect parasitoids. *Q. Rev. Biol.* **55,** 143–165.

Vinson, S. B., and Iwantsch, G. F. (1980b). Host suitability for insect parasitoids. *Annu. Rev. Entomol.* **25,** 397–419.

Visscher, S. N.(1980). Regulation of grasshopper fecundity, longevity and egg viability by plant growth hormones. *Experientia* **36,** 130–131.

Vité, J. P. (1961). The influence of water supply on oleoresin exudation pressure and resistance to bark beetle attack in *Pinus ponderosa*. *Contrib. Boyce Thompson Inst.* **21,** 37–66.

Vité, J. P., and Francke, W. (1976). The aggregation pheromones of bark beetles: progress and problems. *Naturwissenschaften* **63,** 550–555.

Wagner, F. H., and Stoddart, L. C. (1972). Influence of coyote predation on black-tailed jackrabbit populations in Utah. *J. Wildl. Manage.* **36,** 329–342.

Wallace, J. W., and Mansell, R. L., eds. (1976). "Biochemical Interaction between Plants and Insects." Plenum, New York.

Wallner, W. E., and Walton, G. S. (1979). Host defoliation: A possible determinant of gypsy moth population quality. *Ann. Entomol. Soc. Am.* **72,** 62–67.

Wangersky, P. J., and Cunningham, W. J. (1958). Time lag in population models. *Cold Spring Harbor Symp. Quant. Biol.* **22,** 329–338.

Wargo, P. M. (1972). Defoliation-induced chemical changes in sugar maple roots stimulate growth of *Armillaria mellea. Phytopathology* **62,** 1278–1283.

Waters, W. E., and Stark, R. W. (1980). Forest pest management: concept and reality. *Annu. Rev. Entomol.* **25,** 479–509.

Watson, A., ed. (1970). "Animal Populations in Relation to Their Food Resources." Blackwell, Oxford.

Watt, K. E. F. (1963). The analysis of the survival of large larvae in the unsprayed area. *Mem. Entomol. Soc. Can.* **31,** 52–63.

Way, M. J. (1977). Control of insect pests. *Science* **198,** 1029.

Way, M. J., and Cammell, M. (1970). Aggregation behaviour in relation to food utilization by aphids. *In* "Animal Populations in Relation to Their Food Resources" (A. Watson, ed.), pp. 229–247. Blackwell, Oxford.

Wellington, W. G. (1957). Individual differences as a factor in population dynamics: the development of a problem. *Can. J. Zool.* **35,** 293–323.

Wellington, W. G. (1960). Qualitative changes in natural populations during changes in abundance. *Can. J. Zool.* **38,** 290–314.

Wellington, W. G. (1964). Qualitative changes in populations in unstable environments. *Can. Entomol.* **96,** 436–451.

Wellington, W. G. (1965). Some maternal influences on progeny quality in the western tent caterpillar *Malacosoma pluviale* (Dyar). *Can. Entomol.* **97,** 1–14.

Wellington, W. G., Fettes, J. J., Turner, K. B., and Belyea, R. M. (1950). Physical and biological indicators of the development of outbreaks of the spruce budworm. *Can. J. Res. Dev.* **28,** 308–331.

Wellington, W. G., Cameron, P. J., Thompson, W. A., Vertinsky, I. B., and Landsberg, A. S. (1975). A stochastic model for assessing the effects of external and internal heterogeneity on insect populations. *Res. Popul. Ecol.* **17,** 1–28.

Wernes, R. A. (1979). Influence of host foliage on development, survival, fecundity and oviposition of the spear-marked black-moth *Rheumaptera hastata* (Lepidoptera: Geometridae). *Can. Entomol.* **111,** 317–332.

Wheelright, N. T., and Orians, G. H. (1982). Seed dispersal by animals: contrasts with pollen dispersal, problems of terminology, and constraints on coevolution. *Am. Nat.* **119,** 402–413.

White, J., and Strehl, C. E. (1978). Xylem feeding by periodical cicada nymphs on tree roots. *Ecol. Entomol.* **3,** 323–327.

White, T. C. R. (1969). An index to measure weather-induced stress of trees associated without breaks of psyllids in Australia. *Ecology* **50,** 905–909.

White, T. C. R. (1974). A hypothesis to explain outbreaks of looper caterpillars with special reference to populations of *Selidosema suavis* in a plantation of *Pinus radiata* in New Zealand. *Oecologia* **16,** 279–301.

White, T. C. R. (1976). Weather, food and plagues of locusts. *Oecologia* **22,** 119–134.

Williams, C. B., Jr., Wenz, J. M., Dahlsten, D. L., and Norick, N. X. (1979). Relation of forest site and stand characteristics to Douglas-fir tussock moth (Lep. Lymantridae) outbreaks in California. *Mitt. Schweiz. Entomol. Ges.* **52,** 297–307.

Wolda, H. (1978). Fluctuations in abundance of tropical insects. *Am. Nat.* **112,** 1017–1045.

Wood, D. L. (1982). The role of pheromones, kairomones and allomones in the host selection and colonization behavior of bark beetles. *Annu. Rev. Entomol.* **27,** 411–446.

Wood, D. L., Silverstein, R. M., and Nakajima, M., eds. (1970). "Control of Insect Behavior by Natural Products." Academic Press, New York.

Wygant, N. D. (1958). Englemann spruce beetle control in Colorado. *Proc. Int. Congr. Entomol.*, *10th*, *1956* pp. 181–192.

David F. Rhoades
Department of Zoology
University of Washington
Seattle, Washington

PART II

Sources of Interplant Variation and Consequences for Herbivores

In addition to the variation in nutritional and defensive chemistry, tissue structure, and density of competitors and predators at the level of the individual plant, interplant variation in these factors further complicates the processes by which herbivores find and utilize suitable resources. Herbivores not only must locate and select appropriate species of host plants from a mosaic of less suitable or unacceptable ones, they also must contend with differences in quality that exist among individuals of the same plant species. Consequently, differences in the abundance and dispersion of host plants in the field, phenological and spatial variation in quality among individuals in a plant population, the nature of the surrounding or intermingled vegetation, and the range of variation in these factors relative to the mobility of the herbivore can all affect the ability of an animal to find and remain on a plant(s) and, subsequently, its fitness.

Rausher (Chapter 7) begins this part by discussing host selection by phytophagous insects, emphasizing that host selection involves a series of "decisions" that eventually lead to the discovery and subsequent acceptance or rejection of a plant. Rausher suggests that there is a decision-making hierarchy in which an ovipositing female first chooses the habitat in which to search, then the species of host(s) that it will accept, and finally the individuals among the acceptable plant species. Rausher discusses the important aspects of the mechanisms by which herbivores execute the decisions of host choice and the evolutionary forces that are thought to shape those mechanisms. Last, Rausher develops a set of rules that apply to the evolution of host searching and oviposition behavior in phytophagous insects, primarily from information on Lepidoptera, including the pipevine swallowtail butterfly, *Battus philenor.*

Different spatial arrangements or combinations of plant species are known to influence patterns of herbivore abundance. As Kareiva points out in Chapter 8, there is little experimental evidence elucidating the relationship among herbivory, plant dispersion, and plant competition. Because theories of the evolution of plant defenses are shaped around plant pattern and abundance, it is essential that we understand the underlying mechanisms contributing to variation in herbivore density. Kareiva reviews tests of the resource-concentration hypothesis in attempting to elucidate why many herbivores achieve different densities on concentrated compared to scattered hosts and suggests that the searching behavior of herbivores plays a primary role in their response to host dispersion; Kareiva provides data in support of that conclusion.

In Chapter 9, Denno shows how spatial and temporal variation in the quality of its host grass (*Spartina*) has a major effect on the metapopulation dynamics of the sap-feeding planthopper, *Prokelisia marginata,* and on the shaping of this insect's life history. *Spartina* occurs as a dynamic network of variable-quality patches, and *Prokelisia* is continuously faced with the decision to remain where it is or migrate to an alternative patch. Denno discusses what factors contribute to variation in host-plant quality, what patterns of patch quality favor migration, what environmental cues are used by planthoppers to measure patch quality and elicit migration, and the ability of planthoppers to select favorable from lesser-quality patches. Denno suggests that an environmentally triggered migration response in *P. marginata* allows this herbivore to track favorable stands of its host grass and cope with a highly variable environment.

In concluding this part, Mitchell (Chapter 10) takes a critical look at what constitutes an adaptation to host variation and whether the advantage gained by an adaptation can be tested and precisely measured. Mitchell discusses seed-size selection by bean weevils, leaf-size selection by gall aphids, and the coevolution of scale insects together with the unique chemistry of individual ponderosa pine trees, in light of increased fitness that these adaptations measurably confer to herbivores.

CHAPTER 7

Ecology of Host-Selection Behavior in Phytophagous Insects

MARK D. RAUSHER

I. INTRODUCTION

It has long been recognized that phytophagous insects can be highly selective with respect to the plants they consume (Brues, 1920, 1924; Dethier, 1941, 1954; Fraenkel, 1956) and that both the degree of selectivity and the identity of preferred plants can change during an individual's lifetime (Jermy *et al.*, 1968; Singer, 1971; Phillips, 1977; Schoonhoven and Meerman, 1978). It is also widely recognized that plant species and individuals can differ in quality or suitability for insect growth, survival, and reproduction (Soo Hoo and Fraenkel, 1966a,b; Dolinger *et al.*, 1973; Slansky and Feeny, 1977; Edmunds and Alstad, 1978; Scriber and Feeny, 1979). Presumably, the behavioral responses of insects that give rise to discrimination are in part an evolutionary response to the existence of variation in plant quality, because individuals that avoid plants of low quality and feed preferentially on plants of high quality will leave more descendants than individuals that do not exhibit such behavior. Simple as this deduction may appear, investigators have only recently begun to explore the relationship between behavioral responses of insects to their food plants and variation in the quality of those plants.

VARIABLE PLANTS AND HERBIVORES
IN NATURAL AND MANAGED SYSTEMS

As Kennedy (1965) has emphasized, host selection by phytophagous insects is a catenary process. It involves a series of "decisions" that ultimately lead to the discovery and subsequent acceptance or rejection of a plant. For ovipositing females, for example, these decisions are of three major types, which can be arranged heuristically into a decision-making hierarchy: an insect first chooses the habitat in which to search, next the species of plants that it will accept, and finally the individuals among the acceptable species (Thorsteinson, 1960; Hassell and Southwood, 1978). In this chapter I describe the most important facets of the mechanisms by which herbivorous insects execute these decisions and discuss the evolutionary forces that are thought to shape those mechanisms. I include in this description the results of my own studies on searching and oviposition behavior of the pipevine swallowtail butterfly, *Battus philenor*.

II. HABITAT SELECTION

Although phytophagous insects are normally found in only a fraction of the habitats that are within flight distance (e.g. Hicks and Tahvanainen, 1974; Ehrlich *et al.*, 1975; Gilbert and Singer, 1975; Wiklund, 1977, 1978), the reasons for habitat restriction are poorly understood. The absence of specialist insects from a particular habitat can often be explained by the absence of suitable host plants. However, the behavioral mechanisms by which insects restrict their searching to habitats containing host plants are not well known. In some cases habitat restriction may be due to intrinsic behavioral barriers to dispersal away from the site of eclosion (Ehrlich, 1961) or to a tendency to modify movement patterns so as to remain in areas in which host plants are abundant (Lewis and Waloff, 1964; Douwes, 1968; Mitchell *et al.*, 1973; Root, 1973; Bach, 1980). The adaptive significance of this type of habitat restriction is almost trivially apparent; individuals that spend much time searching in habitats in which host plants do not grow will have less time for searching in appropriate habitats than will individuals that exhibit habitat restriction. This reduction in time may in turn mean that individuals lay fewer eggs during their lifetime.

Many insects search in only a subset of the habitats that contain acceptable food plants. Several authors have suggested that differential fecundity or offspring survival among habitats is the major selection pressure favoring this type of selective habitat use (Singer, 1972; Ehrlich *et al.*, 1975; Gilbert and Singer, 1975; Wiklund, 1977; Rausher, 1978). For example, by restricting searching and oviposition to habitats in which juvenile survival is greatest, an ovipositing female may maximize her genetic contribution to the following generation. However, in a test using *Battus philenor* and two related *Aristolochia*-feeding swallowtail butterflies, I was unable to confirm this hypothesis (Rausher, 1979a).

In northeastern Mexico, *Battus philenor* and *B. polydamus* females search for and oviposit primarily on larval-food plants in open fields and similar sunny habitats. Only occasionally do they enter shady habitats such as forest edges to search and lay eggs. Nevertheless, experiments have demonstrated that egg, larval, and pupal survival are consistently greater in shady habitats, which are used almost exclusively by a related species, *Parides montezuma*. I therefore suggested that other selection pressures, operating on habitat-selection behavior, may override large differences between sunny and shady habitats in suitability for juveniles. One such additional selection pressure may be the efficacy with which searching females are able to locate host plants in the two types of habitat. Because thermal conditions, host-plant abundance, and other constraints may limit the ability of *Battus* females to locate host plants in shady habitats, they may tend to lay more eggs per unit time, and hence more eggs before dying, when searching in sunny habitats. If the number of additional eggs laid in sunny habitats more than compensates for the lower survivorship of juvenile stages, natural selection will favor the maintenance of behavior that causes females to search primarily in sunny habitats. This hypothesis can obviously be generalized to account for habitat restriction in other phytophagous insects, but it remains untested.

III. DISCRIMINATION BETWEEN HOST SPECIES

A. Mechanisms of Discrimination

Once a female selects a habitat in which to search for larval-host plants, she must then discriminate between "acceptable" and "unacceptable" plant species. Discrimination may be accomplished by a variety of mechanisms, which may be classified according to when during searching they occur: pre- or postalighting.

Prealighting discrimination occurs when individuals selectively approach and alight on certain plants in a habitat. Its existence may be detected experimentally by determining whether individuals alight on plants in proportion to their abundance in the habitat. Using this approach, D. A. MacKay (personal communication) has demonstrated that random alighting occurs in some populations of the butterfly *Euphydryas editha*. At one site in the Sierra Nevada (GH of White and Singer, 1974), host plants (plant species on which *E. editha* eggs can be found and on which females can be observed to oviposit) are segregated spatially. Females searching in areas in which the only host growing is *Collinsia torreyi* alight on *C. torreyi* and on nonhosts in proportion to their abundances in the habitat.

Nevertheless, nonrandom alighting occurs in many searching insects and may actually be the rule. For example, MacKay has found that at the GH site, in an area in which *Pedicularis semibarbata* is the dominant host, female *Euphydryas editha* alight on *P. semibarbata* much more frequently than expected from the relative abundances of *P. semibarbata* and nonhosts. Two behavioral mechanisms may give rise to nonrandom alighting: differential response to olfactory or visual cues and nonrandom movement patterns. An example of the former is provided by pipevine swallowtail females, which normally adopt one of two primary visual search modes when foraging for larval food plants (Rausher, 1978). These modes can be defined by the shape of the leaves of nonhost plants on which females alight and "taste." At any one time a searching female alights predominantly either on plants having narrow leaves or on plants having broad leaves. Moreover, by adopting a particular search mode, a female biases the probability that she will alight on a particular host species. Females responding primarily to narrow leaves alight disproportionately often on *Aristolochia serpentaria*, the narrow-leaved host species, whereas those responding primarily to broad leaves alight disproportionately often on *A. reticulata*, the broad-leaved host. Because the proportion of narrow and broad leaves in the vegetation along flight paths, as well as that of the two host species along those paths, is the same for females in the two search modes (Rausher and Papaj, 1983a), the difference in alighting patterns between females in the two search modes cannot be attributed either to nonrandom movement patterns or to pathiness in the composition of vegetation. The different search modes must therefore reflect differences in response to broad and narrow leaves.

In some species, movement patterns may also contribute to biased encounter of host species, especially when hosts have dissimilar dispersion patterns. Jones (1977a), for example, has suggested that straightline movement will bias alighting in favor of evenly or randomly spaced plant species; periodic turning, by contrast, especially in response to recent host discovery, will favor encounter with clumped host species. Although Jones's arguments were deduced from observations of larval movement patterns, they should apply equally well to searching adult insects. Stanton (1980, 1982) has provided evidence that movement patterns in *Colias* butterflies lead to alighting on host plants in proportions differing from those expected from the relative abundance of leguminous hosts in the habitat. Apparently, *Colias* females search preferentially in microhabitats in which certain host species are disproportionately abundant.

Discrimination that occurs after an insect alights on a plant is believed to be meditated primarily by chemical and tactile stimuli. Two views of the neural mechanisms underlying such discrimination have emerged (Dethier, 1978). On the one hand, detection of generalist receptor cells in a variety of insects has led to the idea of "across-fiber" patterning (Schoonhoven and Dethier, 1966; Dethier and Schoonhoven, 1969). According to this view, although the number of input neurons used for discrimination is often small, the number and complexity of combined signals they can generate are great. Discrimination is thought to result from the interpretation of this complex, across-fiber pattern of inputs, which is presumably matched against an internal template, much as has been hypothesized for recognition of male cricket calls by females (Hoy, 1974, 1978; Hoy *et al.*, 1977). If the pattern matches the template, the host plant is accepted; otherwise, it is not accepted. In species that use several hosts, there are presumably several different templates, and a match with any of them leads to acceptance.

The alternate view is that discrimination and final acceptance of a plant result from the application, either sequentially or simultaneously, of several criteria (Thorsteinson, 1960; Beck, 1965). Each criterion is manifested neurologically by the firing or failure to fire of a single sensory neuron. Failure of all criteria to be met leads to rejection of the plant. For example, in the moth *Plutella maculipennis*, the presence of mustard oils and/or their glucosides is such a criterion. These compounds act as token stimuli that are necessary releasers of oviposition behavior (Gupta and Thorsteinson, 1960b). Although adults have not been examined electrophysiologically, investigations of other specialist insects (e.g., Rees, 1969) suggest that the firing of a specialist receptor cell that detects the token stimuli is necessary for oviposition. For *Pieris brassicae* larvae, the presence of mustard oil glucosides and the absence of deterrent substances such as alkaloids constitute two criteria that must be met in order for feeding to be maintained (Schoonhoven, 1972). In this instance, the criteria are believed to be assayed by individual sensory neurons, though more complex criteria might require several neurons. In general, plants that satisfy all criteria used by an insect will be accepted, wherein those that fail to satisfy one or more will not.

Both of these views are compatible with the two major types of post-alighting discrimination behavior exhibited by phytophagous insects: absolute and graded. Absolute discrimination occurs when the probability of acceptance of a particular plant species is effectively zero and is not a function of an insect's physiological or motivational state. In a sense, absolute discrimination divides plants into two categories: those that are never accepted (nonhosts) and those that may be accepted under some circumstances (hosts). An example of such absolute discrimination is the rejection by the pipevine swallowtail of all plants not in the family Aristolochiaceae. Internally, this rejection may be accomplished either through the presence of templates only for plants in the Aristolochiaceae or by the constitutive use of some criterion that distinguishes aristolochiaceous plants from all others, such as the presence of aristolochic acids. In fact, specific stimuli compatible with the latter mechanism are required to elicit feeding or oviposition behavior in a number of insect species (Verschaffelt, 1910); Dethier, 1954; Gupta and Thorsteinson, 1960a,b; Staedler, 1974; Nishida, 1977; Ichinose and Honda, 1978; Stanton, 1979). Absolute responses may also be produced by deterrent stimuli that are used constitutively, although the deterrent effects of such stimuli can often be overridden by other factors (Dethier, 1970, 1976).

Graded discrimination occurs when insects discriminate against a plant species under some circumstances and accept it under others. Singer (1982, and personal communication) provides an excellent example of such a graded response. The butterfly *Euphydryas editha* oviposits only on plants in the family Scrophulariaceae and in the genus *Plantago*. This restriction is presumably produced by some sort of absolute discrimination against all other plants. Among scrophs and *Plantago*, however, the species that are acceptable to a female at any given time depend upon the time elapsed since last oviposition. For example, a female from the Indian Flat population may accept only *Collinsia tinctoria* when she has recently oviposited. Sometime later she will accept both *C. tinctoria* and *C. bicolor*. At a still later time she will also accept *Castilleja* spp. and *P. erecta*. Similar dependence of diet or host breadth on time since feeding or ovipositing is seen in other insects (Kennedy and Booth, 1963a,b; Kennedy, 1965; Holling, 1966; Mulkern, 1969; Bernays and Chapman, 1970).

Graded discrimination is also compatible with either view of the neural mechanism underlying post-alighting discrimination. On the one hand, graded responses can be produced with the template model by assuming that templates associated with the different host species are available for comparison with sensory input signals only at certain times. Thus, in the case of *Euphydryas editha* from Indian Flat, only the template for *Collinsia tinctoria* would be available immediately after oviposition, whereas those for other plants would become available sequentially as time since oviposition increased. On the other hand, the observed behavior could also be generated by assuming that to each of the four host species there corresponds a single criterion (e.g., presence of a deterrent substance) that can be used to discriminate against that plant species. Immediately after oviposition, all four criteria would be active, and females would reject all three host plants. As time passed, the criterion for *C. tinctoria* would be deactivated, turning off discrimination against that plant. At successively longer times since oviposition, the criteria for the other hosts would be turned off successively, producing a graded response.

Much of this discussion remains speculative. Detailed work on the neurophysiology of discrimination is sorely needed, particularly with respect to the influence of time and deprivation. Too often it is believed that for a particular insect there is a particular magic secondary compound that serves as the single token stimulus necessary for eliciting feeding or oviposition. This view is often probably the result of experiments on caged animals, in which behavior is abnormal and much time elapsed after a previous oviposition or feeding bout. As a consequence, specificity may be quite low, and the presence of a token stimulus that is used in making absolute discriminations may be all that is necessary to bring about oviposition or feeding. However, as I describe later, discrimination in nature is often exceedingly subtle and must be based on many more characteristics that just a few token stimuli.

B. Ecology of Discrimination

Regardless of the mechanisms that produce graded and absolute discriminatory responses, the existence of those responses points out three ways in which natural selection can modify discrimination behavior in phytophagous insects: (1) it may modify host breadth through alteration of the mechanism producing absolute discrimination; (2) it may change the order in which potential hosts are accepted (ranked) as time from oviposition increases; and (3) it may alter the specificity among host plants, that is, the difference between times from oviposition at which two hosts become acceptable may be altered (Singer, 1982).

1. Host Breadth

To some extent the selection pressures that influence absolute responses will be similar to those that influence specificity. For purposes of discussion, however, it is best to ignore preference for different hosts when discussing the evolution of absolute responses. In this subsection, therefore, I shall assume that all potential hosts are equally acceptable and discuss the selection pressures that influence the number of plants that are hosts, that is, host or diet breadth.

In general, diet breadth in phytohagous insects has been viewed as a compromise between two opposing costs: those associated with increasing and those associated with decreasing diet breadth. In the first theoretical discussion of this tradeoff, Levins and MacArthur (1969) suggested that expansion of an insect's host range may tend to decrease fitness because plants less and less suitable for growth, survival, and reproduction would be incorporated successively into the diet or set of acceptable hosts. In contrast, the cost associated with a narrow host range was viewed as an increased probability of failure to reproduce because of rarity of acceptable host plants. An increase in host range would therefore increase the number of host plants available and, hence, decrease the probability of failure or, perhaps more realistically, increase the number of eggs a female may lay before dying. Actual host breadth is, in their view, the one at which the benefit of increased egg production associated with adding another host species is just balanced by the cost associated with a decrease in mean host suitability.

A similar argument has been put forth by Futuyma (1976) and Rhoades and Cates (1976). These authors have argued that insects that feed on early successional plant species should have broader host ranges than species that feed on climax species. According to this argument, because individual species in successional vegetation are often rare and ephemeral, the probability of failure to find a particular successional host species is greater than the probability of failure to locate a generaly more abundant climax host. As long as costs imposed by between-species variability in suitability or quality are similar for successional and climax species, then the balance between the two types of cost will be shifted toward a greater host breadth in species feeding on successional vegetation. Although only limited data are available, Futuyma, Rhoades, and Cates have demonstrated that this prediction is, in general, not realized. Insects feeding on successional species tend, if anything, to have narrower host ranges than those feeding on climax plants.

A second hypothesis that has been put forth to explain the evolution of diet breadth is that polyphagy, or a wide host range, inherently incurs a cost because a generalist insect cannot be simultaneously as proficient at growth and survival on a number of host species as can specialists on their few hosts. Because generalists must maintain a large array of physiological and behavioral mechanisms to circumvent a variety of different plant defenses, it is argued, the costs associated with these mechanisms will reduce growth rates and hence possibly decrease survival or fecundity. The balance between these costs and the benefits associated with an increase in host range will then determine the equilibrium host breadth.

This hypothesis, originally put forth by Dethier (1954), has engendered a considerable amount of both speculation and empirical testing (Waldbauer, 1968; Krieger *et al.*, 1971; Feeny, 1975; Schroeder, 1976, 1977; Janzen, 1978; Smiley, 1978b; Scriber and Feeny, 1979; Fox and Morrow, 1981; Futuyma and Wasserman, 1982). Results, however, are inconclusive. Thus, Smiley (1978b) found that the family generalist *Heliconius cydno* grew more slowly than the specialist *H. erato* on the latter's host, *Passiflora biflora*. In contrast, Futuyma and Wasserman (1982) could detect no differences in measures of feeding efficiency between the generalist moth *Malacosoma disstria* and the family specialist *M. americanum*, when reared on foliage of *Prunus serotina*..

One possible explanation of the contradictory results of these studies may be that they involve comparisons among species rather than among populations within one species or among individuals within a single population. It is well known that within-population or within-species correlations between characters many differ in sign and magnitude from similar between-species correlations (Simpson, 1953; Gould, 1966; Lande, 1979). Consequently, patterns discernible among species can be deceptive regarding the benefits and costs associated with various traits. For making statements about costs and benefits associated with a broad host range, then, it is most useful to examine within one species, and preferably within one population, the trade-offs associated with generalization versus specialization.

Such evolutionary trade-offs are represented by negative genetic correlations between characters (see, e.g., Antonovics, 1976). A negative genetic correlation implies that selection for increased growth performance on one host species leads to a correlated decrease in growth performance on another (Falconer, 1960). The existence of such a negative genetic correlation can reduce the mean fitness of generalist herbivores in the following way. By acting simultaneously to increase survival and fecundity on all host species on which a generalist insect feeds, natural selection will tend to fix all genes that have a positive effect on growth performance on all host species. The only variability that will remain will be due to genes that increase performance on some species while decreasing it on others, giving rise to a negative genetic correlation between performance on two different species (Lerner, 1958; Falconer, 1960; Antonovics, 1976). These negative correlations will in turn constrain improvement of performance on any given host, because selection for improvement on one host would automatically lead to a decrease in performance on others. Specialist insects, however, are not constrained by such negative correlations, because natural selection will act to increase survival and fecundity on only one or, at most, a small number of host species. Consequently, the limits to improvement of growth performance and, presumably, survival and fecundity on a particular host will be lower for generalists than for specialists. The existence of costs associated with being a generalist may thus be revealed by the detection of negative genetic correlations. Absence of such correlations does not imply there is no cost, however, because natural selection may fix all genes conferring increased performance on a particular host, even though this may lead to a decrease in fitness on the other host; once natural selection has fixed all performance on that host, there will be no variation remaining to partake in a genetic correlation.

Experimental evidence suggests that negative genetic correlations in host performance are present in some herbivorous arthropods. Gould (1979) has shown that in an experimental system using the herbivorous mite *Tetranychus urtiae* selection for ability to grow and reproduce on cucumber leaves resulted in a correlated decline in ability to grow and reproduce on lima beans. In another study, Edmunds and Alstad (1978; see also Alstad and Edmunds, Chapter 12) measured the survivorship of scale insects *(Nuculaspis californica)* from different subpopulations on different individual pine trees *(Pinus ponderosa)*. They reported a significant subpopulation × tree interaction for survivorship. The authors interpreted these results as suggesting that some scale genotypes survive well on certain trees but not on others, whereas the reverse is true for other scale genotypes.

Because the presence of genotype × environment (g × e) interactions is a minimal requirement for negative genetic correlations, a survey of examples indicating g × e (host) interactions provides some estimate of the frequency of situations in which evolutionary trade-offs in host specialization are plausible possibilities. In Table I are listed all studies found in a literature search for investigations in which the performance of different insect genotypes or biotypes on different hosts are reported and in which significant g × e interaction was found. Unfortunately, such g × e interactions are not by themselves sufficient for inferring negative genetic correlations. As discussed by Haldane (1946), Allard and Bradshaw (1964), and Cavalli-Sforza and Bodmer (1971), only a few of the many possible types of g × e interactions are indicative of genetic specialization. In the case of two insect genotypes reared on two plant species or varieties, genetic specialization is indicated only if for each insect there is one host plant species or variety on which its fitness is higher than that of the other genotype.

Moreover, demonstration that a g × e interaction is of this "crossing" type does not necessarily imply the existence of negative genetic correlations, hence trade-offs, within the populations from which the tested insects were obtained. As an illustration of this contention, consider a

Table I
Studies Reporting a Significant Interaction between Insect Genotype or Biotype and Larval Host

Insect species	Hosts tested	Characters measured	Interaction of crossing type?	Reference[a]
Rhopalosiphum maidis (Aphidae)	Varieties of sorghum	Fecundity, adult weight	Yes	1
Acyrthosiphum pisum (Aphidae)	Clones of *Medicago sativa*	Survival, fecundity	Yes	2
Myzus persicae (Aphidae)	*Brassica pekinensis, Vicia faba*	Colony size	No	3
Myzus persicae (Aphidae)	Strains of *Beta vulgaris*	Colony size	Yes	4
Euphydryas editha (Lepidoptera)	*Pedicularis densiflora, Collinsia tinctoria*	Survival, growth	Yes	5
Nuculaspis californica (Homoptera)	Individuals of *Pinus ponderosa*	Survival	?	6
Uroleucon rudbeckiae (Aphidae)	Individuals of *Rudbeckia laciniata*	Survival, fecundity	No	7
Macrosiphum pisi (Aphidae)	Varieties of *Pisum sativum*	Adult size, fecundity	No	8
Macrosiphum pisi (Aphidae)	Varieties of *Pisum sativum*	Fecundity	No	9
Toxoptera graminium? (Aphidae?)	Varieties of barley, oats, wheat	Fecundity, longevity	No	10
Brevicoryne brassicae (Aphidae)	Clones of *Brassica oleracea*	Fecundity	Yes	11
Amphorophora rubi (Aphidae)	Varieties of *Rubus idaeus*	Colony size	Yes	12
Schizaphis graminium (Aphidae)	Species of cultivated grasses	Longevity, fecundity	Yes	13
Schizaphis graminium (Aphidae)	Varieties of sorghum	Longevity, fecundity	No	14
Alsophila pometaria (Lepidoptera)	*Acer rubrum, Quercus velutina, Q. prinus*	Survival	No	15

[a] References: 1, Cartier and Painter (1956); 2, Cartier *et al.* (1965); 3, Lowe (1973); 4, Lowe (1974); 5, Rausher (1982); 6, Edmunds and Alstad (1978); 7, P.M. Service and R. E. Lenski (unpublished manuscript); 8, Cartier (1959); 9, Harrington (1945); 10, Dahms (1948); 11, Dunn and Kempton (1972); 12, Briggs (1959); 13, Harvey and Hockerott (1969); 14, Wood (1971); 15, Futuyma *et al.* (1982).

Table II
Selection Regime for Insect Genotypes on Different Hosts[a]

A. Incremental effects on fitness due to alleles at each locus

| | Fitness increment | |
Genotype	On host I	On host II
AA, Aa	$+s$	0
aa	$-s$	0
BB, Bb	0	$+s$
bb	0	$-s$

B. Relative fitnesses of nine possible genotypes on each host.

| | Fitness on | |
Genotype	Host I	Host II
AABB	High	High
AABb	High	High
AAbb	High	Low
AaBB	High	High
AaBb	High	High
Aabb	High	Low
aaBB	Low	High
aaBb	Low	High
aabb	Low	Low

C. Pairs of genotypes producing "noncrossing" genotype × host (g × e) interaction

AABB-AAbb	aabb-aaBb	AABB-aaBB
AABB-aaBb	AABB-Aabb	AABb-Aabb
AABb-aaBB	AABb-AAbb	AaBB-AAbb
AaBB-Aabb	AABb-aaBb	AaBB-aaBb
aabb-AAbb	AaBB-aaBB	aabb-aaBB
	aabb-Aabb	

D. Pairs of genotypes producing a "crossing" genotype × host interaction

AAbb-aaBB	Aabb-aaBb	Aabb-aaBB
	AAbb-aaBb	

[a]Loci A and B act additively. Alleles A and B are dominant to a and b respectively.

hypothetical case in which adaptation to two types of host (I and II) is influenced by variation at two loci (A and B). Locus A governs adaptation to host type I and is neutral with respect to host type II, whereas the opposite is true for locus B. Such a situation is at least approximated by some insect species (Hatchett and Gallun, 1970; Gallun, 1972; Nielson and Don, 1974). Under the selection regime indicated in Table II, A and B, in which alleles A and B are dominant to a and b and in which effects of the two loci are additive, there are 4 pairs of genotypes that yield a crossing g × e interaction (Table II) and a total of 20 pairs that yield any type of interaction (Table II, C and D). Even with no linkage disequilibrium, hence no correlation, between the two loci, with gene frequencies of approximately 0.5 at each locus a random pair of genotypes drawn from the population will be one of the 4 crossing-type pairs 7% of the time. Of the random pairs that show a g × e interaction, crossing-type pairs will occur randomly about 20% of the time. The case in which there is no dominance at either locus is shown in Table III. Here there are 9 pairs of genotypes with a crossing interaction and an additional 18 pairs that have a noncrossing interaction. A random pair of genotypes will be one of the 9 crossing pairs 19.5% of the time and will constitute approximately 34% of all pairs showing a g × e interaction. Thus, even if two biotypes exhibit a crossing type of interaction with respect to growth performance, one is not justified in concluding that adaptation to one host necessitates loss of adaptation to a second, that is, that fitnesses on two different hosts are negatively correlated.

Of the 14 studies in Table I that report the nature of the g × e interaction, 6 (43%) report a crossing interaction. This figure is only slightly greater than the 34% expected under the null hypothesis of variation at two loci with no dominance (Table III). The existence of specialized insect biotypes thus cannot at present be said to provide evidence supporting the hypothesis that adaptation to one host causes loss of adaptation to a second.

Yet other costs may be associated with possessing a broad host range. For example, in many tree-feeding Lepidoptera, a major mortality factor is a mismatch between the timing of egg hatch and phenology of leaf production by the host tree (Varley et al., 1974; Feeny, 1976; Schneider, 1980). Newly hatched larvae are able to feed only on tender, newly produced leaves. Larvae that hatch either before bud burst or after leaves have toughened starve. This heavy mortality presumably leads to selection for traits that improve the synchrony of hatching and bud burst. In fact, Mitter et al. (1979) and Schneider (1980) have shown that clones of the parthenogenetic moth Alsophila pometaria that feed on different host species have diverged with respect to time of adult eclosion, which in turn has led to a divergence in hatching times. Moreover, this divergence is in the direction expected from the leafing phenologies of the different hosts. In a specialist species, such fine tuning of insect phenology to that of the host may be expected to proceed to the limits imposed by genetic variation (ignoring correlations between phenological traits and other traits influencing fitness). In contrast, adaptation by a generalist species to the phenology of one host may be limited by

Table III
Selection Regime for Insect Genotypes on Different Hosts[a]

A. Incremental effects on fitness due to alleles at each locus		
	Fitness increment	
Genotype	On host I	On host II
AA	+s	0
Aa		0
aa	−s	0
BB	0	+s
Bb	0	0
bb	0	−s

B. Relative fitnesses of nine possible genotype on each host		
	Fitness on	
Genotype	Host I	Host II
AABB	High	High
AABb	High	Intermediate
AAbb	High	Low
AaBB	Intermediate	High
AaBb	Intermediate	Intermediate
Aabb	Intermediate	Low
aaBB	Low	High
aaBb	Low	Intermediate
aabb	Low	Low

C. Pairs of genotypes producing "noncrossing" genotype × host (g × e) interaction

AaBB-AABB	AaBB-AaBb	AaBB-aabb
aaBb-AABB	aaBb-AaBb	aaBb-aabb
AABb-AABB	AABb-AaBb	AABb-aabb
Aabb-AABB	Aabb-AaBb	Aabb-AaBb
AAbb-AABB	AAbb-aabb	aaBB-AABB
aaBB-aabb	AaBB-Aabb	AABb-aaBb

D. Pairs of genotypes producing "crossing" genotype × environment interaction

AABb-AaBB	AABb-aaBB	AAbb-AaBB
AAbb-AaBb	AAbb-aaBB	AAbb-aaBb
AaBb-aaBB	Aabb-aaBB	Aabb-aaBb

[a]Loci A and B act additively. No dominance at either locus A or locus B.

negative genetic correlations between traits favoring such adaptation and traits favoring phenological adaptation to other hosts. As a consequence, mortality due to mismatch between insect and host phenologies can be expected to be greater for generalists than for specialists.

Physiological and phenological costs are clearly only two of many types that might be associated with a broad host range. Generalists might also be less efficient searchers than specialists, as the immense literature on search images suggests (e.g., Dawkins, 1971; Pietrewicz and Kamil, 1979); crypsis and other predator-escape adaptations will probably not be as highly developed in generalist herbivores, which will lend to reside on a greater number of background types and encounter a greater variety of predators. Each of these types of cost can generate a trade-off between the costs and benefits associated with a broad host range.

The question of whether such tradeoffs exist and are common will not be settled until genetic correlations between fitness (and its components) on different hosts are measured for a variety of herbivores. Until such time, the contention that there exist costs associated with being a generalist will remain an untested hypothesis.

Interspecific competition is another mechanism that could influence host range in phytophagous insects. Because expansion of an insect species' host range to include plant species on which competitors also feed can lower mean survival or reproductive success (averaged over all hosts used), there may be a cost associated with broadening the host range against against a gradient of competitive intensity. As with other costs associated with being a generalist, a balance between this competitive cost and the benefits associated with increased host availability would determine the equilibrium host range.

Although several authors have suggested that competition is not an important force influencing insect community structure or host range (Hairston *et al.*, 1960; Rathcke, 1976; Lawton and Strong, 1981), several experimental investigations have demonstrated strong competition both between and within herbivorous insect species. The scale insect *Fiorinia externa*, for example, outcompetes another scale, *Tsugaspidiotus tsugae*, on eastern hemlock *(Tsuga canadensis)* and is apparently able to exclude *T. tsugae* from local populations within a period of 3 yr (McClure, 1981; Chapter 5). Whitham (1978, 1980; Chapter 1) has shown that on *Populus angustifolia* there is strong competition among *Pemphigus* aphids for gall sites. Comparison of actual grasshopper communities with neutral models has shown that host-range overlap between species is less than expected in the absence of biotic interactions (Joern and Lawlor, 1980). These kinds of results indicate that competition may in fact be a potent force molding the host range of phytophagous insects; yet, as with other hypotheses about the evolution of host range, compelling evidence that competition has molded the diet breadth of any particular insect species is lacking.

2. Host Ranking

In insects that exhibit graded discrimination among potential host species, the very fact that some species become acceptable before others implies that species are ranked. One important evolutionary question about graded responses is, therefore, What kinds of selection pressures determine the order in which hosts are ranked? Because virtually all investigations that have been designed to answer this question have dealt with host selection by ovipositing females, I restrict discussion to discrimination by ovipositing females.

In analogy with current predictions of foraging theory (MacArthur and Pianka, 1966; Pulliam, 1974; Pyke *et al.*, 1977; Jaenike, 1978), the simplest hypothesis about the evolution of host ranking is that natural selection produces behavior that cause females to rank host species in order of decreasing suitability for offspring survival and reproductive success. The most suitable species thus becomes acceptable again soon after oviposition, whereas the least suitable species becomes acceptable only after a much longer period of time has elapsed since the most recent oviposition (Wiklund, 1974a; Chew, 1975, 1977; Jones *et al.*, 1975; Feeny, 1975; Gilbert and Singer, 1975; Rausher, 1978; Smiley, 1978b; Jaenike, 1978).

Studies designed to test this hypothesis have generally yielded mixed results. Wiklund (1974a, 1975) and Chew (1975, 1977) both reported that postalighting host rankings for ovipositing butterflies correspond roughly to host suitability, but that there are also conspicuous exceptions to this general trend. A partial explanation for these exceptions may be that only indirect measures of host suitability were used in their analyses: laboratory growth rates and survivorship. Because suitability as measured in the laboratory may not be highly correlated with survivorship in the field, inferences based on laboratory measurements must be interpreted with caution. Smiley (1978a) and Gilbert (1978) have also provided indirect evidence in support of the hypothesis. Two species of *Heliconius* butterflies usually oviposit on only two of the several species of *Passiflora* with which they normally cooccur, even though larvae can feed and grow on all species. Moreover, each butterfly lays its eggs on the *Passiflora* species on which ant visitation and, presumably, mortality due to ant predation are lowest. Because ant predation is probably the major source of mortality on the larvae of these butterflies, the host species ranked highest are probably the ones that are most suitable for juvenile survival.

White's (1980) study of oviposition preferences exhibited by periodical cicadas illustrates that it is crucial to examine all components of survivorship when testing the hypothesis that females rank hosts in order of decreasing suitability for offspring. White predicted that egg-hatching success on a host species would be correlated with degree of preference for that species, but no such correlation was found. This result by itself neither refutes nor supports the hypothesis, because oviposition preferences probably influence survivorship after the egg stage as well as during it. Differences in hatching success observed by White may essentially be noise superimposed on much more distinct and stronger differences in survival that occur after nymphs drop to the ground and establish on tree roots. If overall survivorship were examined 17 yr later and compared with oviposition preferences, the correlation White sought might be found. If not, White's prediction could be rejected. On the other hand, if it were reasonable to assume that oviposition site does not affect where a larva becomes established underground, then the influence of oviposition site selection on offspring survival would not be expected to extend beyond the egg stage. The lack of correlation between preference and egg survival found by White would then constitute a valid refutation of White's prediction. Unfortunately, no evidence is available regarding the relationship between larval survival and hatching site.

Most foraging models and the predictions that are derived from them assume that searching is random. When this assumption is valid for searching insects, host discrimination is mediated entirely by postalighting behavior, and the prediction of correspondence between host ranking and suitability is valid. When encounter is not random, however, a searching insect at least partly discriminates between potential host species by adopting a specific searching behavior. The ranking of hosts by this type of prealighting discrimination may be more or less independent of that achieved by postalighting discrimination.

The selection pressures that influence the evolution of nonrandom search and prealighting discrimination are understood even less well than those that influence postalighting responses. Rausher (1980) outlined two possibly opposing forces that act to determine the "optimal" search mode for pipevine swallowtail butterflies. On the one hand, the suitability of different host species for juvenile survival obviously influences the expected success of an individual offspring. All else equal, females that search preferentially for the more suitable host species will lay more eggs on that host then those that search in another manner. Consequently, females searching preferentially for the most suitable host will tend to maximize offspring survival probability. On the other hand, an adult female's life span is often limited to a period lasting from several days to a week or two. This limit may constrain the amount of time available for locating host plants and laying eggs. By searching preferentially for the most abundant host species, a female may lay more eggs before dying than by searching preferentially for a rarer host species.

If the most suitable host differs from the most abundant host, there will necessarily be a trade-off between the number of eggs that a female can lay in her lifetime and the expected survival probability of her offspring. Such tradeoffs may be especially important in species in which time available to adults for oviposition is severely limited by climatic conditions (see, e.g., Ehrlich *et al.*, 1975; Hayes, 1981).

In east Texas, both host abundance and host suitability appear to influence which search mode is adopted by *Battus philenor* females at a particular time (Rausher, 1980). When first-brood adults emerge in the early spring, larval survival is the same on both host species. Most first-brood females adopt the search mode that biases encounter in favor of *Aristolochia reticulata*, the more abundant of the two species. In contrast, larval survival during the second brood is much higher on *A. serpentaria* than on *A. reticulata*. In spite of the fact that *A. serpentaria* is much rarer, most second-brood females adopt the search mode that biases encounter in favor of that species. The difference in suitability of the two host plants for larvae appears to override small but measurable differences in host-discovery rates between females in the two search modes, favoring the observd preferential searching during the second brood. It has not been possible to measure the actual trade-offs involved between searching for the more abundant host and searching for the more suitable host; nor will it always be true that the two factors favor a preference for different host species. Nevertheless, this study does indicate that searching preferences may be correlated with criteria other than host suitability.

When searching behavior leads to nonrandom encounter rates with potential host plants, it is possible for the plant species most suitable for juvenile survival to be effectively excluded from the set of plants on which females lay eggs, a result not predicted by random-encounter models. Even when encounters are not random, however, it seems likely that natural selection will order postalighting preferences in the same manner as occurs when search is random. A female that has alighted on a plant of the most suitable host species "should" lay eggs on it, regardless of how she got there, because she cannot do better by leaving the plant and searching for others (Pyke *et al.*, 1977). Consequently, in insects that search nonrandomly, the host species for which a female searches preferentially may not have the highest postalighting probability of oviposition. Regardless of search method, however, the postalighting preference ranking should always be in order of decreasing suitability for juveniles. Although the behavior of *Battus philenor* females in east Texas is consistent with these predictions (Rausher, 1980), they remain largely untested.

3. Host Specificity

A third way in which natural selection can alter discrimination is by modifying postalighting specificity. An example of this type of alteration is provided by Singer's (1982) elegant experiments on the Checkerspot butterfly, *Euphydryas editha*. As noted previously, Singer ascertained the order in which *E. editha* females rank host plants by offering an array of host plants at various times after an oviposition and noting the times at which each host species became acceptable. Singer measured specificity by the difference between the times two species became acceptable.

By examining the oviposition behavior of females from several populations in this manner, Singer has been able to demonstrate that specificity may differ even though ranking of potential hosts is similar. For example, the two populations SN and IF both rank *Collinsia tinctoria* higher than *Plantago erecta*, because there was a period during testing when females from both populations accepted *C. tinctoria* but not *P. erecta*. However, this period was usually less than 2 hr for SN butterflies, but it lasted for about a day in IF butterflies. When translated into behavior in the field, this difference means that SN females would have to search only a couple of hours without finding their preferred host plant before accepting *Plantago*, whereas IF females would probably have to search for a day or more. It is in this sense that IF females are more specific.

At present, one can only speculate about the types of selection pressures that lead to this type of difference in specificity. Singer has suggested three ways in which specificity may evolve.

1. Selection may cause specificity to increase just to the point at which effective monophagy is ensured, that is, to the point at which the difference in acceptance times between the most preferred species and all others will be great enough under most conditions that the likelihood that sufficient time will elapse during searching to cause acceptance of the less preferred plants will be close to zero. Once this point is reached, there can be only very weak selection acting to increase the thresholds still further.

2. A decrease in suitability of less preferred species relative to the most preferred species may lead to an increase in specificity, because it becomes profitable to continue searching slightly longer than previously before accepting less preferred hosts.

3. A decrease in specificity will be favored whenever the cost to larval survival of prolonged search by females increases. In many *Euphydryas editha* populations, for example, the risk that host plants will senesce and, hence, that larvae will die before they enter diapause increases with

time of oviposition during the season (Ehrlich *et al.*, 1975, 1980). By decreasing specificity, females would presumably lay more eggs earlier in the season and hence decrease the risk of larval death due to senescence.

Jaenike (1978) has provided a model that predicts the optimal specificity of females under a given set of environmental conditions. Only empirical testing will determine whether natural selection molds specificity in ways predicted by Jaenike's model and Singer's hypotheses.

IV. CONSPECIFIC HOST DISCRIMINATION

Numerous investigations of agricultural and forest pests have revealed that ovipositing insects do not accept all individuals of a host-plant species with equal probability. Such conspecific host discrimination may be based on differences in plant size (Everly, 1959), age (Ives, 1978), isolation (Jones, 1977b), texture (Nishijima, 1960), chemistry (Mitchell, 1977), the presence or absence of other eggs or larvae (Prokopy, 1972; Mitchell, 1975; Rothschild and Schoonhoven, 1977; Rausher, 1979b), or other unknown factors that differ among crop varieties (Muller, 1958; Perron *et al.*, 1960; Carlson and Hibbs, 1962). Although it seems likely that conspecific host discrimination is common in natural insect–plant associations, few investigations have dealt specifically with this behavior. Nonrandom patterns of egg and larval distribution (Thompson, 1978; Tilman, 1978; Moore, 1978a,b) may indicate that discrimination may be occurring (e.g., Rausher *et al.*, 1982), but they may be explained equally well by differential offspring survival (e.g., Singer, 1972). In addition, little is known about the behavioral mechanisms that permit discrimination or about the selection pressures that mold those mechanisms (but see Whitham, Chapter 1). The following account is therefore based on information drawn primarily from studies of agricultural pests and from my own observations.

A. Mechanisms of Discrimination

Once again the mechanisms of discrimination may be classified according to whether selectivity occurs prior to or after an insect alights on a host plant. Prealighting discrimination involves some type of nonrandom alighting. Although the aphid *Aphis fabae*, for example, alights indiscriminately on different types of individuals of its preferred host species (Muller, 1958), other insects may exhibit biased-encounter probabilities. The movement patterns of the butterfly *Pieris rapae* cause females to approach and alight preferentially on isolated plants (Cromartie,

1975; Jones, 1977b). My own studies on searching *Euphydryas editha* butterflies demonstrate that females approach and alight upon large, isolated plants more often than expected from their abundance in the habitat (Rausher *et al.*, 1982).

As is true for discrimination between host species, postalighting discrimination between conspecific plants may conceivably be produced either by absolute or graded responses. In virtually all studies that have been performed, however, discrimination against a particular kind of plant is never absolute. Varieties of crops resistant to oviposition, for example, almost always have some eggs laid on them (Horber, 1955; Muller, 1958; Swailes, 1959; Nishijima, 1960; Perron *et al.*, 1960; Carlson and Hibbs, 1962). Similar results have been obtained by other investigators who have examined preferential responses of insects to two or more different host-plant phenotypes (Mitchell, 1977). The deposition of eggs on less preferred varieties indicates that those varieties are acceptable under some circumstances, a result that suggests that postalighting discrimination among conspecific plants is normally produced by a graded response. Whether an individual plant is accepted thus often depends on both the characteristics of that plant and the physiological state of the insect (Jones *et al.*, 1975). The experiments by Kennedy and Booth (1963a,b) on aphids support this conclusion, but whether their results can be extrapolated to other insect species is unknown. Furthermore, it is not known whether the mechanisms that produce graded responses to different host species differ from those that permit graded responses to different plant phenotypes within one host species; indeed, for an insect, taxonomic distinctions may be irrelevant. Finally, the number of different categories of plants within one host species that can be discriminated is unknown for any insect.

B. Ecology of Discrimination

One may reasonably expect that the evolutionary forces that mold mechanisms responsible for conspecific host discrimination are similar to those that shape the behavior underlying discrimination between host species. When host individuals can be classified unambiguously into one of several categories, arguments analogous to those of foraging theory predict that postalighting preferences for a given category will be correlated with the suitability of plants in that category for juvenile survival and subsequent reproductive success. Categories of plants that are most suitable should be most preferred, whereas those least suitable should be least preferred. The most compelling support for this prediction is provided by studies on the responses of ovipositing insects to the presence of eggs or larvae on host plants (Mitchell, 1975; Rausher, 1979b). Females in these studies laid eggs preferentially on hosts on which there were no other conspecific individuals. The probability of survival of eggs and larvae was higher on those plants than on plants on which conspecific individuals were already present.

Investigations purporting to demonstrate a correlation between post-alighting preference and suitability of host phenotypes are few. The best study is that by Blais (1952), who demonstrated in spruce budworm females an oviposition preference for reproductive over nonreproductive balsam fir trees (*Abies balsamea*). Overwinter survival of diapausing larvae was apparently higher on trees that had produced cones during the previous year. As the author admitted, though, the survivorship results could also be explained by preferential overwintering aggregation of small larvae on microsporangiate branches and may thus not truly indicate a greater survival of larvae on the preferred type of tree. Investigations that have examined the relationship between preferences and larval growth rates (Blais, 1952; Perron *et al.*, 1960; Perron and Jasmin, 1963) have often obtained no correlations. Such results do not refute the initial prediction, however, because differences in survival among larvae feeding on different plant phenotypes in the field are not necessarily related in any predictable way to differences in growth rates among larvae feeding on the same phenotypes in the laboratory.

The remarkable studies of Whitham (1978, 1980; Chapter 1) demonstrate that *Pemphigus* gall aphids exhibit selectivity on an even finer scale. Aphids settle and form galls preferentially on large leaves of their host plant, *Populus angustifolia*. This behavior results in maximization of offspring survival and fecundity, because both of these fitness components are positively correlated with leaf size. Although such behavior is not per se discrimination between individuals of the host species, it illustrates a major contention of this chapter, that postalighting discrimination behavior evolves in such a way as to produce a correlation between host ranking and host suitability. That *Pemphigus* obeys this rule when discriminating between leaves of a single tree suggests that other insects should also obey this rule when discriminating between conspecific individuals.

C. Conspecific Host Discrimination by Battus philenor

In several recent experiments, I and my colleagues have attempted to determine whether *Battus philenor* females discriminate between conspecific host plants and whether degree of preference for a particular class of host plants is correlated with suitability of those plants for larval growth and survival. By following searching females in the field, we have been able to mark plants on which each observed female alights. For each plant we removed any eggs laid, recorded whether the female laid eggs and whether eggs were already present on the plant when the female alighted, and then removed all eggs from the plant. At the end of each day of observation we returned to each plant and made several measurements. In 1979 these measurements were number of the *Aristolochia* plants within 1 m and the distance to the three nearest *Aristolochia* plants. In 1980 we measured plant height, terminal bud length, leaf area, and stem diameter. In addition, in 1980 we returned to each plant 7 days later, at the time when larvae would normally hatch from any eggs laid, and remeasured terminal bud length and leaf area. From initial and final leaf-area measurements we estimated change in leaf area. Seven days after a plant was first measured we placed either two or three, depending on the experiment, newly hatched larvae on each plant. At daily censuses we measured larval size and determined whether any larvae had disappeared since the previous census (Rausher and Papaj, 1983b).

Female *Battus philenor* butterflies could discriminate between conspecific host plants by cuing in on at least three different types of ecologically relevant variables: (1) presence versus absence of conspecific eggs or larvae, (2) local host-plant density, and (3) characteristics of individual plants such as size, texture, predator load, or microenvironmental conditions at time of alighting. Each of these possibilities was examined separately.

Females detect the presence of conspecific eggs on a host plant and have a strong tendency to avoid ovipositing when eggs are present (Rausher, 1979b). By doing so, females increase the survival probability of their offspring above that expected if they did not discriminate in this manner, because survivorship on plants with eggs is lower than that on egg-free plants.

Larvae must disperse from their original host plant and find others in order to complete development. Because mortality during dispersal is high (Rausher, 1979b), females could conceivably enhance offspring survival by ovipositing preferentially on host plants growing in locally dense patches (e.g., Thompson, 1978). However, females do not exhibit any apparent postalighting response to plant density. In one experiment conducted in 1979, I compared two measures of local plant density in areas surrounding individual plants on which females alighted (target plants). Accepted and rejected target plants did not differ either in the number of *Aristolochia* plants within a radius of 1 m or in the mean distance of the target plant to its three nearest neighbors (Table IV). Nor

Table IV
Comparison of Local *Aristolochia* Density in Areas Surrounding Accepted and
Rejected *A. reticulata* Plants[a]

Means for accepted and rejected plants		
Female reaction	*Number of plants within 1 m*[b]	*Mean distance (cm) to three nearest neighbors*[b]
Accept	1.14 (± 0.15)	85.4 (± 2.2)
Reject	1.44 (± 0.10)	79.7 (± 1.5)

Analysis of covariance for number of plants within 1 m				
Source	*df*	*MS*	F	P
Slopes	1	1140.7	2.10	NS
Error	341	543.6	—	
Date	1	2187.7	4.01	<0.05
Female reaction	1	821.9	1.51	NS
Error	340	545.4	—	

Analysis of covariance for mean distance to three nearest neighbors				
Source	*df*	*MS*	F	P
Slopes	1	1.27	0.50	NS
Error	341	2.53	—	
Date	1	62.40	24.71	<0.0001
Female reaction	1	0.02	0.01	NS
Error	340	2.53	—	

[a]Because host density increased continually during the study there was a significant correlation between each measure of density and date of observation. Means were therefore compared statistically, using analysis of covariance with date as covariate (Searle, 1971). For each analysis, heterogeneity of slopes was first tested and found to be not significant. Adjusted means were then compared for accepted and rejected plants (female-reaction effect).
[b]Means (± SE) for the two estimates of density used.

do female movement patterns appear to bias overall oviposition probability in favor of plants growing in dense clumps, because the probability that a plant in such a clump will have eggs laid on it does not differ from the probability for plants not growing in clumps (Rausher and Feeny, 1980).

These results do not rule out the possibility that information about host density over much larger areas may influence postalighting oviposition probabilities. One way females could obtain such information would be to monitor the number of host plants encountered per unit time searching (e.g., Charnov, 1976; Waage, 1979). If females use infor-

Table V

Comparison of Prealighting Host Encounter Rates for Accepted and Rejected Plants[a]

K (min)	Female reaction			Reaction × Date		
	df	F	P	df	F	P
2	346	0.07	NS	336	0.45	NS
3	324	0.13	NS	314	1.19	NS
4	301	0.04	NS	291	1.41	NS
5	281	0.00	NS	271	0.56	NS
6	259	0.41	NS	249	0.28	NS
7	242	0.34	NS	232	0.67	NS
8	227	0.03	NS	218	0.82	NS
9	206	0.17	NS	197	0.89	NS
10	186	0.20	NS	177	0.88	NS
11	170	0.10	NS	161	0.46	NS
12	161	0.00	NS	153	0.36	NS
13	149	0.03	NS	141	0.31	NS
14	140	0.01	NS	132	0.12	NS
15	130	0.17	NS	122	0.08	NS
16	123	0.00	NS	115	0.15	NS
17	110	0.01	NS	103	0.18	NS
18	104	0.46	NS	97	0.44	NS
19	95	0.40	NS	88	0.38	NS
20	89	0.39	NS	82	0.63	NS

[a]Analyses compare number of *Aristolochia* plants alighted on in K min prior to alighting on target plant. *F* values are values of *F* statistic in two-way factorial analysis of variance with date of observation and female reaction (accepted versus rejected) as main effects. Indicated degress of freedom correspond to error MS. For female reaction, df of MS is 1. For reaction × date interaction, df of MS is between 7 and 10.

mation of this type in discriminating between conspecific host plants, the rate of host encounter just prior to alighting on a target plant should on average be greater for target plants that are accepted than for target plants that are rejected. I have not been able to detect any difference of this type for intervals up to 20 min prior to a female's alighting on a host plant (Table V). Sample sizes decrease rapidly for longer time periods, making any comparisons of limited value. Recent rate of alighting thus apparently does not influence postalighting responses. Although this evidence is not definitive, it suggests that females do not preferentially select host plants growing in locally dense stands.

Searching females do discriminate between conspecific host plants, using some characteristics of individual plants. Postalighting discrimination is revealed by a comparison of measured characteristics of accepted and rejected *Aristolochia reticulata* plants. Under the hypothesis

Table VI
Comparison of Measured Characteristics for Accepted and Rejected Plants

Multivariate analysis of variance[a]			
Source	df	λ	P
Date (D)	9	0.570	<0.0001
Female reaction (R)	1	0.913	<0.0001
D × R	9	0.853	<0.05
Error	469	—	

Differences in means of individual characters[b]	
Character	Mean of accepted − mean of rejected plants (± 95% confidence interval)
Terminal bud length	
initial (mm)	2.80 (± 2.37)[c]
final (mm)	2.97 (± 2.69)[c]
Height (mm)	−4.40 (± 9.65)
Leaf area, initial (cm^2)	−2.93 (± 1.87)
Change in leaf area (cm^2)	1.95 (± 2.65)
Stem diameter (mm)	0.11 (± 0.12)

[a]Testing for overall difference in measured characteristics between accepted and rejected plants (female-rejection effect). λ, Wilks lambda criterion.
[b]Confidence intervals were calculated using Bonferonni procedure (Timm, 1975).
[c]$P < 0.05$.

of no discrimination, accepted plants should be a random sample of those on which females alight; accepted and rejected plants should therefore not differ from rejected plants. Alternatively, if females do discriminate, accepted and rejected plants should differ in some measurable character.

For females observed during the first brood in 1980, accepted and rejected plants differed overall in the set of characters measured. Accepted plants tended to have larger terminal buds, larger stems, and a smaller total leaf area at time of alighting (Table VI). Because variation in many of these characters is correlated with that in others, differences between accepted and rejected plants for one character may imply that other characters differ as well. Consequently, to determine which of the measured characters contribute to the overall difference detected, the simultaneous confidence-interval procedure outlined by Timm (1975) was used. This procedure revealed that the difference in initial total leaf area and in initial and final terminal bud length contributed significantly to the overall difference (Table VI). Females apparently select small plants with large buds preferentially. This evidence does not necessarily indicate that the cues used by females in "deciding" whether to oviposit include leaf area and bud length. Females probably rely primarily on chemical and tactile cues (see, e.g., Nishida, 1977; Ichinose and Honda, 1978; Stanton, 1979). However, regardless of the identity of the proximate cues used, the end result is preferential selection of certain plants over others.

To test the hypothesis that behavior responsible for conspecific host discrimination by *Battus philenor* females enhances offspring survival, we examined larval growth rates and disappearance rates on accepted and rejected plants (Rausher and Papaj, 1983b). Each larval disappearance was assigned to one of two causes: predispersal mortality or dispersal. We detected no difference between accepted and rejected plants in the proportion of disappearances that were due to predispersal mortality. This result indicated that predator and parasite loads probably do not influence the probability that a female will oviposit on a host plant. We also could detect no differences in larval growth rates in the field.

Discrimination does, however, have an effect on larval demography. Mean size at disappearance was greater for larvae on accepted plants than for larvae on rejected plants. This result held both for all larvae in the experiments and for only those larvae that dispersed from their initial host plants (Rausher and Papaj, 1983b). Discrimination behavior thus appears to cause females to oviposit preferentially on *Aristolochia reticulata* plants on which larvae grow to greater-than-average size prior to dispersal. Because local host-plant density does not influence postalighting oviposition probability, it is unlikely that the influence of discrimination behavior on offspring quality or survival extends beyond the outcome of the first dispersal event. Moreover, previous work on larval dispersal has shown that large larvae are more likely than small larvae to discover a new host plant (Rausher, 1979b). Hence, by increasing larval size at dispersal, discrimination between conspecific host plants would appear to increase overall larval survival above what would occur if females did not discriminate.

V. CONCLUSIONS

Searching and oviposition behavior in phytophagous insects should be viewed as a complex adaptation that enhances the genetic contribution of individuals to succeeding generations. As for any adaptive trait, different searching and oviposition behavior may be selected for in different environments. Nevertheless, there may be certain rules that apply to the evolution of these behaviors in any environment. These rules, if they exist, constitute a set of constraints upon the evolution of insect behavior.

Hence, identification of these constraints should reveal how host selection behavior in general, as opposed to the host selection behavior of a particular species, evolves.

In this review I have suggested three such rules.

1. The number of host species that are under at least some circumstances acceptable to females reflects the balance of a trade-off between costs, measured in terms of decreased mean survivorship and fecundity and associated with increasing an insect's host range, and benefits derived because an increase in host range increases the availability of hosts and hence the number of eggs a female can lay in her lifetime.

2. In an insect's postalighting graded response, host ranking should be correlated with host suitability, where suitability is defined as the expected reproductive success (survivorship times fecundity).

3. Prealighting preferences, which may include habitat preferences, need not be correlated with host suitability. However, prealighting discrimination can be expected to evolve in such a way that the sum over all host species (categories) of the product of encounter rate, oviposition probability, and suitability is maximized.

These rules are analogous to predictions of foraging theory and should apply at all levels of discrimination—among habitats, species, and individuals within a host species. Although these rules appear to be followed by some phytophagous insects, their status as generalizations about insect behavior remains largely untested.

ACKNOWLEDGMENTS

Comments and criticism by May Berenbaum, Frances Chew, Fred Gould, Peter Karieva, Daniel Papaj, and Maureen Stanton greatly improved the manuscript. Many of the ideas expressed here have been developed during numerous discussions with Michael Singer, to whom I am especially indebted. This work was supported in part by NSF grant DEB 8016414 and a grant by the Duke Research Council.

REFERENCES

Allard, R. W., and Bradshaw, A. D. (1964). Implications of genotype–environmental interactions. *Crop Sci.* **4**, 503–508

Antonovics, J. (1976). The nature of limits to natural selection. *Ann. Mo. Bot. Gard.* **63**, 224–247.

Bach, C. E. (1980). Effects of plant density and diversity on the population dynamics of a specialist herbivore, the striped cucumber beetle, *Acalymma vittata* (Fab.). *Ecology* **61**, 1515–1530.

Beck, S. D. (1965). Resistance of plants to insects. *Annu. Rev. Entomol.* **10**, 207–232.

Bernays, E. A., and Chapman, R. F. (1970). Experiments to determine the basis of food selection by *Chorthippus parallelus* (Zetterstedt) (Orthoptera: Acrididae) in the field. *J. Anim. Ecol.* **39**, 761–776.

Blais, J. R. (1952). The relationship of the spruce budworm (*Choristoneura fumiferana*, Clem.) to the flowering condition of balsam fir [*Abies balsaminea* (L.) Mill.]. *Can. J. Zool.* **30**, 1–29.

Briggs, J. B. (1959). Three new strains of *Amphoraphora rubi* (Kalt.) on cultivated raspberries in England. *Bull. Entomol. Res.* **50**, 81–87.

Brues, C. T. (1920). Selection of food plants by insects with special reference to Lepidoptera. *Am. Nat.* **54**, 313–332.

Brues, C.T. (1924). Specificity of food plants in evolution of phytophagous insects. *Am. Nat.* **58**, 127–144.

Carlson, O. V., and Hibbs, E. T. (1962). Direct counts of potato leafhopper, *Empoasca fabae*, eggs in *Solanum* leaves. *Ann. Entomol. Soc. Am.* **55**, 512–515.

Cartier, J. J. (1959). Recognition of three biotypes of the pea aphid from southern Quebec. *J. Econ. Entomol.* **52**, 293–294.

Cartier, J. J., and Painter, R. H. (1956). Differential reactions of two biotypes of the corn leaf aphid to resistant and susceptible varieties, hybrids and selections of sorghum. *J. Econ. Entomol.* **49**, 498–503.

Cartier, J. J., Isaak, A., Painter, R. H., and Sorenson, E. L. (1965). Biotypes of pea aphid. *Acyrthosiphon pisum* (Harris) in relation to alfalfa clones. *Can. Entomol.* **97**, 754–760.

Cavalli-Sforza, L. L., and Bodmer, W. F. (1971). "The Genetics of Human Populations." Freeman, San Francisco.

Charnov, E. L. (1976). Optimal foraging, the marginal value theorem. *Theor. Pop. Biol.* **9**, 129–136.

Chew, F. S. (1975). Coevolution of pierid butterflies and their cruciferous food plants. I. The relative quality of available resources. *Oecologia* **20**, 117–128.

Chew, F. S. (1977). Coevolution of pierid butterflies and their cruciferous food plants. II. The distribution of eggs on potential food plants. *Evolution* **31**, 568–569.

Cromartie, W. J. (1975). The effect of stand size and vegetational background on the colonization of cruciferous plants by herbivorous insects. *J. Appl. Ecol.* **12**, 517–533.

Dahms, R. G. (1948). Comparative tolerance of small grains to greenbugs from Oklahoma and Mississippi. *J. Econ. Entomol.* **41**, 825–826.

Dawkins, M. (1971). Perceptual changes in chicks: another look at the "search image" concept. *Anim. Behav.* **19**, 566–574.

Dethier, V. G. (1941). Chemical factors determining the choice of food plants by *Papilio* larvae. *Am. Nat.* **75**, 61–73.

Dethier, V. G. (1954). Evolution of feeding preferences in phytophagous insects. *Evolution* **8**, 33–54.

Dethier, V. G. (1970). Chemical interactions between plants and insects. In "Chemical Ecology" (E. Sondheimer and J.B. Simeone, eds.), pp. 83–102. Academic Press, New York.

Dethier, V. G. (1976). "The Hungry Fly." Harvard Univ. Press, Cambridge, Massachusetts.

Dethier, V. G. (1978). Other tastes, other worlds. *Science* **201**, 224–228.

Dethier, V. G., and Schoonhoven, L. M. (1969). Olfactory coding by lepidopterous larvae. *Entomol. Exp. Appl.* **12**, 535–543.

Dolinger, P. M., Ehrlich, P. R., Fitch, W. L., Breedlove, D. E. (1973). Alkaloid and predation patterns in Colorado lupine populations. *Oecologia* **13**, 191–204.

Douwes, P. (1968). Host selection and host finding in the egg-laying female *Cidaria albulata* L. (Lep. Geometridae). *Opusc. Entomol.* **33**, 233–279.

Dunn, J. A., and Kempton, D. P. H. (1972). Resistance to attack by *Brevicoryne brassicae* among plants of Brussels sprouts. *Ann. Appl. Biol.* **72**, 1–11.

Edmunds, G. F., and Alstad, D. N. (1978). Coevolution in insect herbivores and conifers. *Science* **199**, 941–945.

Ehrlich, P. R. (1961). Intrinsic barriers to dispersal in checkerspot butterfly. *Science* **134**, 108–109.

Ehrlich, P. R., White, R. R., Singer, M. C., McKechnie, S. W., Gilbert, L. E. (1975). Checkerspot butterflies: a historical perspective. *Science* **188**, 221–228.

Ehrlich, P. R., Murphy, D. D., Singer, M. C., Sherwood, C. B., White, R. R., and Brown, I. L. (1980). Extinction, reduction, stability and increase; the responses of Checkerspot butterfly *(Euphydryas)* populations to the California drought. *Oecologia* **46**, 101–105.

Everly, R. R. (1959). Influence of height and stage of development of dent corn on oviposition by European Corn Borer moths. *Ann. Entomol. Soc. Am.* **52**, 272–279.

Falconer, D. S. (1960). "Introduction to Quantitative Genetics." Ronald Press, New York.

Feeny, P. (1975). Biochemical coevolution between plants and their insect herbivores. *In* "Coevolution of Animals and Plants" (L.E. Gilbert and P.H. Raven, eds.), pp. 3–19. Univ. of Texas Press, Austin.

Feeny, P. (1976). Plant apparency and chemical defense. *Recent Adv. Phytochem.* **10**, 1–40.

Fox, L. R., and Morrow, P. A. (1981). Specialization: species property or local phenomenon. *Science* **221**, 887–893.

Fraenkel, G. (1956). Insects and plant biochemistry: the specificity of food plants for insects. *Proc. Int. Congr. Zool. 14th, 1953* pp. 383–387.

Futuyma, D. F., Leipertz, S. L., and Mitter, C. (1982). Selective factors affecting clonal variation in the fall cankerworm *Alsophila pometaria* (Lepidoptera: Geometridae). *Heredity* (in press).

Futuyma, D. J. (1976). Food plant specialization and environmental predictability in Lepidoptera. *Am. Nat.* **110**, 285–292.

Futuyma, D. J. and Wasserman, S. S. (1982). Food plant specialization and feeding efficiency in the tent caterpillars *Malacosoma disstria* Hubner and *M. americanum* (Fabricus). *Entomol. Exp. Appl.* (in press).

Gallun, R. L. (1972). Genetic interrelationships between host plants and insects. *J. Environ. Qual.* **1**, 259–265,

Gilbert, L. E. (1978). Develoment of theory in the analysis of insect–plant interactions. *In* "Analysis of Ecological Systems" (D. J. Horn, R. Mitchell, and G. R. Stairs, eds.), pp. 117–154. Ohio State Univ. Press, Columbus.

Gilbert, L. E., and Singer, M. C. (1975). Butterfly ecology. *Annu. Rev. Ecol. Syst.* **6**, 365–397.

Gould, F. (1979). Rapid host range evolution in a population of the phytophagous mite *Tetranychus urticae* Koch. *Evolution* **33**, 241–250.

Gould, S. J. (1966). Allometry and size in ontogeny and phylogeny. *Biol. Rev. Cambridge Philos. Soc.* **41**, 587–640.

Gupta, P. D., and Thorsteinson, A. J. (1960a). Food plant relationships of the diamond-back moth *(Plutella maculipennis* (Curt.)). I. Gustation and olfaction in relation to botanical specificity of the larvae. *Entomol. Exp. Appl.* **3**, 241–250.

Gupta, P. D., and Thorsteinson, A. J. (1960b). Food plant relationships of the diamond-back moth [*Plutella maculipenns* (Curt.)]. II. Sensory regulation of oviposition of the adult female. *Entomol. Exp. Appl.* **3**, 305–314.

Hairston, N. G., Smith, F. E., Slobodkin, L. B. (1960). Community structure, population control, and competition. *Am. Nat.* **94**, 421–425.

Haldane, J. B. S. (1946). The interaction of nature and nurture. *Ann. Eugen. (London)* **13**, 197–205.

Harrington, D. D. (1945). Biological races of the pea aphid. *J. Econ. Entomol.* **38**, 12–22.

Harvey, T. L., and Hockerott, H. L. (1969). Recognition of a greenbug biotype injurious to Sorghum. *J. Econ. Entomol.* **62**, 776–779.

Hassell, M. P., and Southwood, T. R. E. (1978). Foraging strategies of insects. *Annu. Rev. Ecol. Syst.* **9**, 75–98.

Hatchett, J. H., and Gallun, R. L. (1970). Genetics of the ability of the Hessian fly, *Mayetiola destructor*, to survive on wheats having different genes for resistance. *Ann. Entomol. Soc. Am.* **63**, 1400–1407.

Hayes, J. L. (1981). The population ecology of a natural population of the pierid butterfly *Colias alexandra*. *Oceologia* **49**, 188–201.

Hicks, K. L., and Tahvanainen, J. O. (1974). Niche differentiation by Crucifer-feeding flea beetles (Coleoptera; Chrysomelidae). *Am. Midl. Nat.* **91**, 406–423.

Holling, C. S. (1966). The functional response of invertebrate predators to prey density. *Mem. Enomol. Soc. Can.* **48**.

Horber, E. (1955). Oviposition preference of *Meromyza americana* for different small grain varieties under greenhouse conditions. *J. Econ. Entomol.* **48**, 426–430.

Hoy, R. R. (1974). Genetic control of accoustic behavior in crickets. *Am. Zool.* **14**, 1067–1080.

Hoy, R. R. (1978). Accoustic communication in crickets: a model system for the study of feature detection. *Fed. Proc., Am. Soc. Exp. Biol.* **37**, 2316–2323.

Hoy, R. R., Hahn, J., and Paul, R. C. (1977). Hybrid cricket auditory behavior: evidence for genetic coupling in animal communication. *Science* **195**, 82–84.

Ichinose, T., and Honda, H. (1978). Ovipositional behavior of *Papilio protenor demetrius* Cramer and the factors involved in its host plants. *Appl. Entomol. Zool.* **13**, 103–114.

Ives, P. M. (1978). How discriminating are cabbage butterflies? *Aust. J. Ecol.* **3**, 261–276.

Jaenike, J. (1978). On optimal oviposition behavior in phytophagous insects. *Theor. Pop. Biol* **14**, 350–356.

Janzen, D. H. (1978). The ecology and evolutionary biology of seed chemistry as relates to seed predation. *In* "Biochemical Aspects of Plant and Animal Coevolution" (J. B. Harborne, ed.), pp. 163–206. Academic Press, New York.

Jermy, T., Hansen, F. E., and Dethier, V. G. (1968). Induction of specific food preference in lepidopterous larvae. *Entomol. Exp. Appl.* **11**, 211–230.

Joern, A., and Lawlor, L. R. (1980). Food and microhabitat utilization by grasshoppers from arid grasslands: comparisons with neutral models. *Ecology* **61**, 591–599.

Jones, J. W., Bowen, H. D., Stinner, R. E., Bradley, J. R., Sowell, S. R., and Bacheler, J. S. (1975). Female boll weevil oviposition and feeding processes: a simulation model. *Environ. Entomol.* **4**, 815–821.

Jones, R. E. (1977a). Search behavior: a study of three caterpillar species. *Behaviour* **60**, 237–259.

Jones, R. R. (1977b). Movement patterns and egg distribution in cabbage butterflies. *J. Anim. Ecol.* **46**, 195–212.

Kennedy, J. S. (1965). Mechanisms of host plant selection. *Ann. Appl. Biol.* **56**, 317–322.

Kennedy, J. S. (1966). The balance between antagonistic induction and depression of flight activity in *Aphis fabae* Scopoli. *J. Exp. Biol.* **45**, 215–228.

Kennedy, J. S., and Booth, C. O. (1963a). Free flight of aphids in the laboratory. *J. Exp. Biol.* **40**, 67–85.

Kennedy, J. S., and Booth, C. O. (1963b). Coordination of successive activities in an aphid. The effect of flight on the settling responses. *J. Exp. Biol.* **40**, 351–369.

Krieger, R. I., Feeny, P. P., and Wilkinson, C. F. (1971). Detoxication enzymes in the guts of caterpillars: an evolutionary answer to plant defenses? *Science* **72**, 579–581.

Lande, R. (1979). Quantitative genetic analysis of multivariate evolution applied to brain: body size allometry. *Evolution* **33**, 402–416.

Lawton, J. H., and Strong, D. R. (1981). Community patterns and competition in folivorous insects. *Am. Nat.* **118**, 317–338.

Lerner, I. M. (1958). "The Genetic Basis of Selection." Wiley, New York..

Levins, R., and MacArthur, R. (1969). An hypothesis to explain the incidence of monophage. *Ecology* **50**, 910–911.

Lewis, C. T., and Waloff, N. (1964). The use of radioactive tracers in the study of dispersion of *Orthotylus virescens* (Douglass and Scott)(Miridae: Heteroptera). *Entomol. Exp. Appl.* **7**, 15–24.

Lowe, H. J. B. (1973). Variation in *Myzus persicae* (Sulz.) (Hemiptera, Aphididae) reared on different host plants. *Bull. Entomol. Res.* **62**, 549–556.

Lowe, H. J. B. (1974). Intraspecific variation of *Myzus persicae* on sugar beet *(Beta vulgaris).* *Ann. Appl. Biol.* **78**, 15–26.

MacArthur, R., and Pianka, E. R. (1966). On optimal use of a patchy environment. *Am. Nat.* **100**, 603–609.

McClure, M. S. (1981). Competition between exotic species: scale insects on hemlock. *Ecology* **61**, 1391–1401.

Mitchell, H. C., Cross, W. H., McGovern, W. L., and Dawson, E. M. (1973). Behavior of the boll weevil on frego bract cotton. *J. Econ. Entomol.* **56**, 677–680.

Mitchell, N. D. (1977). Differential host selection by *Pieris brassicae* (the large white butterfly) on *Brassica oleracea* subsp. *oleracea* (the wild cabbage). *Entomol. Exp. Appl.* **22**, 208–219.

Mitchell, R. (1975). The evolution of oviposition tactics in the bean weevil, *Callosobruchus maculatus* (F.) *Ecology* **56**, 696–702.

Mitter, C. Futuyma, D., Schneider, J., and Hare, J. (1979). Genetic variation and host plant relations in a parthenogenetic moth. *Evolution* **33**, 777–790.

Moore, L. R. (1978a). Seed predation in the legume *Crotalaria*. I. Intensity and variability of seed predation in native and introduced populations of *C. pallida* Ait. *Oecologia* **34**, 185–202.

Moore, L. R. (1978b). Seed predation in the legume *Crotolaria*. II. Correlates of interplant variability in predation intensity. *Oecologia* **34**, 203–223.

Mulkern, G. B. (1969). Behavioral influences on food selection in grasshoppers. (Orthoptera: Acrididae). *Entomol. Exp. Appl.* **12**, 509–523.

Muller, H. J. (1958). The behavior of *Aphis fabae* in selecting its host plants, especially different varieties of *Vicia faba*. *Entomol. Exp. Appl.* **1**, 66–72.

Nielson, M. W., and Don, H. (1974). Interaction between biotypes of the spotted alfalfa aphid and resistance in alfalfa. *J. Econ. Entomol.* **67**, 368–370.

Nishida, R. (1977). Oviposition stimulants of some papilionid butterflies contained in their host plants. *Bochu Kagaku* **42**, 133–140.

Nishijima, Y. (1960). Host plant preference of the soybean pod borer, *Graptolitha glicinivorella* Matsumura (Lep., Eucosmidae). I. Oviposition site. *Entomol. Exp. Appl.* **3**, 38–47.

Perron, J. P., and Jasmin, J. J. (1963). Development and survival of the onion maggot under field and artificial conditions on attractive and unattractive onion varieties. *Can. Entomol.* **95**, 334–336.

Perron. J. P., Jasmin, J. J., Lafrance, J. (1960). Attractiveness of some onion varieties grown in muck soil to oviposition by the onion maggot [*Hylemya atniqua* (Meig.)] (Anthomyiidae: Diptera). *Can. Entomol.* **92**, 765–767.

Phillips, W. M. (1977). Modification of feeding "preference" in the flea beetle, *Haltica lythri* (Coleoptera, Chrysomelidae). *Entomol. Exp. Appl.* **21**, 71–80.

Pietrewicz, A. T., and Kamil, A. C. (1979). Search image formation in the blue jay *(Cyanocitta cristata)*. *Science* **204**, 1332–1333.

Prokopy, R. J. (1972). Evidence for a marking pheromone deterring repeated oviposition in apple maggot flies. *Environ. Entomol.* **1**, 326–332.

Pulliam, H. R. (1974). On the theory of optimal diets. *Am. Nat.* **108**, 59–75.

Pyke, G. H., Pulliam, H. R., and Charnov, E. L. (1977). Optimal foraging: a selective review of theory and tests. *Rev. Biol.* **52**, 137–154.

Rathcke, B. J. (1976). Competition and coexistence within a guild of herbivorous insects. *Ecology* **57**, 76–87.

Rausher, M. D. (1978). Search image for leaf shape in a butterfly. *Science* **200**, 1071–1073.

Rausher, M.D. (1982). Population differentiation in *Euphydryas editha* butterflies: larval adaptation to different hosts. *Evolution* **36**, 581–590.

Rausher, M. D. (1979a). Larval habitat suitability and oviposition preference in three related butterflies. *Ecology* **60**, 503–511.

Rausher, M. D. (1979b). Egg recognition: its advantage to a butterfly. *Anim. Behav.* **27**, 1034–1040.

Rausher, M. D. (1980). Host abundance, juvenile survival and oviposition preferences in *Battus philenor*. *Evolution* **34**, 342–355.

Rausher, M. D., and Feeny, P. (1980). Herbivory, plant density, and plant reproductive success: the effect of *Battus philenor* on *Aristolochia reticulata*. *Ecology* **61**, 905–917.

Rausher, M. D., and Papaj, D. R. (1983a). Host plant selection by *Battus philenor* butterflies: evidence for individual differences in foraging behaviour. *Anim. Behav.* (in press).

Rausher, M. D., and Papaj, D. (1983b). Demographic consequences of conspecific host discrimination by *Battus philenor* butterflies. *Ecology* (in press).

Rausher, M. D., Mackay, D. A., Singer, M. C. (1982). Pre- and post-alighting host discrimination by *Euphydryas editha* butterflies: the behavioral mechanisms causing clumped distributions of egg clusters. *Anim. Behav.* **29**, 1220–1228.

Rees, C. J. C. (1969). Chemoreceptor specificity associated with choice of feeding site by the beetle, *Chrysolina brunsvicensis* on its food plant, *Hypericum hirsutum*. *Entomol. Exp. Appl.* **12**, 565–583.

Rhoades, D. F., and Cates, R. G. (1976). Toward a general theory of plant antiherbivore chemistry. *Recent Adv. Phytochem.* **10**, 168–213.

Root, R. B. (1973). Organization of a plant–arthropod association in simple and diverse habitats: the fauna of Collards *(Brassica oleraceae)*. *Ecol. Monogr.* **43**, 95–124.

Rothschild, M., and Schoonhoven, L. M. (1977). Assessment of egg load by *Pieris brassicae* (Lepidoptera: Pieridae). *Nature (London)* **226**, 352–355.

Schneider, J. C. (1980). The role of parthenogenesis and female aptery in microgeographic, ecological adaptation in the fall cankerworm, *Alsophila pometaria* Harris (Lepidoptera: Geometridae). *Ecology* **61**, 1082–1090.

Schoonhoven, L. M. (1972). Secondary plant substances and insects. *Recent Adv. Phytochem.* **5**, 197–224.

Schoonhoven, L. M., and Dethier, V. G. (1966). Sensory aspects of host-plant discrimination by lepidopterous larvae. *Arch. Neerl. Zool.* **16**, 497–530.

Schoonhoven, L. M. and Meerman, J. (1978). Metabolic cost of change in diet and neutralization of allelochemics. *Entomol. Exp. Appl.* **24**, 489–493.

Schroeder, L. A. (1976). Energy, matter and nitrogen utilization by the larvae of the monarch butterfly *Danaus plexippus*. *Oikos* **27**, 259–264.

Schroedér, L. A. (1977). Energy, matter and nitrogen utilization by the larvae of the milkweed tiger moth *Euchaetias egle*. *Oikos* **28**, 27–31.

Scriber, J. M., and Feeny, P. (1979). Growth of herbivorous caterpillars in relation to feeding specialization and to growth form of their food plants. *Ecology* **60**, 829–850.

Searle, S. R. (1971). "Linear Models." Wiley, New York.

Service, P. M., and Lenski, R. E. (1982). Aphid genotypes, plant phenotypes, and genetic diversity: a demographic analysis of experimental data. *Evolution* **36**, 1276–1282.

Simpson, G. G. (1953). "The Major Features of Evolution." Simon & Schuster, New York.

Singer, M. C. (1971). Evolution of food-plant preference in the butterfly *Euphydryas editha*. *Evolution* **25**, 383–389.

Singer, M. C. (1972). Complex components of habitat suitability within a butterfly colony. *Science* **173**, 75–77.

Singer, M. C. (1982). Quantification of host preference by manipulation of oviposition behavior in the butterfly *Euphydryas edita*. *Oecologia* **52**, 224–229.

Slansky, F. and Feeny, P. (1977). Stabilization of the rate of nitrogen accumulation by larvae of the cabbage butterfly on wild and cultivated food plants. *Ecol. Monogr.* **47**, 209–228.

Smiley, J. (1978a). The host plant ecology of *Heliconius* butterflies in northeastern Costa Rica. PhD. Dissertation, University of Texas, Austin.

Smiley, J. (1978b). Plant chemistry and the evolution of host specificity: new evidence from *Heliconius* and *Passiflora*. *Science* **201**, 745–747.

Soo Hoo, C. F., and Fraenkel, G. (1966a). The selection of food plants in a polyphagous insect, *Prodenia eridania* (Cramer). *J. Insect Physiol.* **12**, 693–709.

Soo Hoo, C. F., and Fraenkel, G. (1966b). The consumption, digestion, and utilization of food plants by a polyphagous insect, *Prodenia eridnia* (Cramer). *J. Insect Physiol.* **12**, 711–730.

Staedler, E. (1974). Host plant stimuli affecting oviposition behavior of the eastern spruce budworm. *Entomol. Exp. Appl.* **17**, 176–188.

Stanton, M. L. (1979). The role of chemotactile stimuli in the oviposition preferences of *Colias* butterflies. *Oecologia* **39**, 79–91.

Stanton, M. L. (1980). The dynamics of search: foodplant selection by *Colias* butterflies. PhD. Dissertation, Harvard University, Cambridge, Massachusetts.

Stanton, M. L. (1982). Searching in a patchy environment: foodplant selection by *Colias p. eriphyle* butterflies. *Ecology* **63**, 839–853.

Swailes, G. E. (1959). Resistance in rutabagas to the cabbage maggot, *Hylemya brassicae* (Bouche) (Diptera: Anthomyiidae). *Can. Entomol.* **91**, 700–703.

Thompson, J. (1978). Within-patch structure and dynamics in *Pastinaca sativa* and resource availability to a specialized herbivore. *Ecology* **59**, 443–448.

Thorsteinson, A. J. (1960). Host selection in phytophagous insects. *Annu. Rev. Entomol.* **5**, 193–218.

Tilman, D. (1978). Cherries, ants and tent caterpillars: timing of nectar production in relation to susceptibility of caterpillars to ant predation. *Ecology* **59**, 686–692.

Timm, N. H. (1975). "Multivariate Analysis with Applications in Education and Psychology." Brooks/Cole, Monterey, California.

Varley, G. C., Gradwell, G. R., and Hassell, M. P. (1974). "Insect Population Ecology: An Analytical Approach." Univ. of California Press, Berkeley.

Verschaffelt, E. (1910). The cause determining the selection of food in some herbivorous insects. *Proc. Acad. Sci. Amsterdam* **13**, 536–542.

Waage, J. K. (1979). Foraging for patchily distributed hosts by the parasitoid, *Nemeritis canescens*. *J. Anim. Ecol.* **48**, 353–371.

Waldbauer, G. P. (1968). The consumption and utilization of food by insects. *Adv. Insect Physiol.* **5**, 229–289.

White, J. (1980). Resource partitioning by ovipositing cicadas. *Am. Nat.* **115**, 1–28.

White, R. R., and Singer, M. C. (1974). Geographical distribution of host-plant choice in *Euphydryas editha* (Nymphalidae). *J. Lepid. Soc.* **28**, 103–107.

Whitham, T. G. (1978). Habitat selection by *Pemphigus* aphids in response to resource limitation and competition. *Ecology* **59**, 1164–1176.

Whitham, T. G. (1980). The theory of habitat selection: examined and extended using *Pemphigus* aphids. *Am. Nat.* **115**, 449–466.

Wiklund, C. (1974a). Oviposition preferences in *Papilio machaon* in relation to the host plants of the larvae. *Entomol. Exp. Appl.* **17**, 189–198.

Wiklund, C. (1974b). The concept of oligophagy and the natural habitats and host plants of *Papilio machaon* L. in Fennoscandia. *Entomol. Scand.* **5**, 151–160.

Wiklund, C. (1975). The evolutionary relationship between adult oviposition preferences and larval host plant range in *Papilio machaon* L. *Oecologia* **18**, 185–197.

Wiklund, C. (1977). Oviposition, feeding and spatial separation of breeding and foraging habitats in a population of *Leptidia sinapis* (Lep., Pieridae). *Oikos* **28**, 56–58.

Wiklund, C. (1978). Host plants, nectar source plants, and habitat selection of males and females of *Anthochris cardamines* (Lepidoptera). *Oikos* **31**, 169–183.

Wood, E. A. (1971). Designation and reaction of three biotypes of the greenbug cultured on resistant and susceptible species of sorghum. *J. Econ. Entomol.* **64**, 183–185.

Mark D. Rausher
Department of Zoology
Duke University
Durham, North Carolina

Influence of Vegetation Texture on Herbivore Populations: Resource Concentration and Herbivore Movement

PETER KAREIVA

I. INTRODUCTION

One of the most central and useful concepts in ecology—certainly one of the most basic—is the idea that the population biology and behavior of consumers depend in some way upon the dispersion of their resources. We usually expect to find consumers concentrated and thriving where their resources are abundant and easy to find. This idea is a prominent component of several ecological theories. For instance, the aggregation of predators in regions of high prey density has received much attention as a potentially stabilizing influence in predator–prey interactions (Hassell, 1978). The concentration of consumers where resources are abundant is also a feature of optimal foraging theory; if searching for resources is costly, then an optimal forager should focus its efforts in regions of high resource density.

This dependence of consumers on the dispersion of their resources plays an especially important role in studies of plant–insect interactions. For example, the argument that plant apparency shapes the evolution of antiherbivore defenses of plants (Feeny, 1975; Rhoades, 1979; Fox, 1981) rests upon the assumption that plant dispersion determines the frequency of encounter between herbivores and their food plants. Agricultural scientists are also beginning to explore the connection between herbivore attack and plant dispersion. There is overwhelming evidence that pest problems in crops are aggravated by the concentration of resources associated with modern agricultural practices (Cromartie, 1981). This evidence has led several authors to take note of the potential for controlling insect pests by manipulating cropping patterns (Perrin, 1977; Perrin and Phillips, 1978; Coaker, 1980; Finch, 1980; Cromartie, 1981; Hare, Chapter 18).

All of these ideas reflect our intuition that an ecosystem's "texture"— the pattern caused by the interweaving of such characteristics as plant density and diversity—should influence patterns of herbivore abundance. Root (1973) was the first to formalize this notion and to emphasize the connection between host-plant dispersion and herbivore community structure. Drawing on his observations of herbivore populations in different experimental plantings of cole crops, Root proposed the *resource-concentration hypothesis*: specialized herbivores are more likely to find and remain in areas where host plants are concentrated, that is, where they grow in pure, large, and/or dense stands. Root's paper inspired a flurry of studies, the goal of which was to discover whether or not the resource-concentration effect could be demonstrated in a variety of agricultural and natural systems. In a relatively short time, Root's resource-concentration effect has become a firmly established part of our ecological folklore. But in spite of the numerous implications it may have for the interpretation of plant–herbivore interactions, its rise to this position has been achieved with a minimum of experimental or theoretical scrutiny. With few exceptions (but see Root's original paper and, more recently, Bach, 1980a,b, 1981, 1983; Risch, 1980, 1981), investigators have been content to describe the existence of a resource-concentration response while neglecting the underlying mechanisms. Before plans for agroecosystem management or theories of coevolution can be based upon the assumption of a resource-concentration response, it is essential that we better understand the causes of that response.

In this chapter, I want to provide some of the scrutiny that has so far been lacking. I will begin by reviewing tests of the resource-concentration hypothesis and will attempt to discover *why* variations in herbivore abundances accompany variations in vegetation texture. My own work (Kareiva, 1981, 1982a,b) has led me to the conclusion that plant dispersion and diversity influence herbivore densities, primarily by altering herbivore movement or searching behavior. In the following sections, I shall attempt to justify that conclusion by examining observations and theories of herbivore searching patterns in textured environments.

II. TESTING THE RESOURCE-CONCENTRATION HYPOTHESIS

Vegetation texture can vary in any of several ways: the distance between individuals of the same species can be altered (density); the areal or geographical extent of a stand of host plants can be altered (patch size); and the frequency and identity of non-host-plant individuals can be altered (stand purity or diversity). Herbivores are likely to have different responses to different aspects of texture. In addition, different species of herbivores can be expected to respond individualistically to changing features of vegetation structure. Root's (1973) resource-concentration hypothesis was specifically intended to explain the accumulation of *specialized* herbivores on a concentrated resource; he pointed out that it was less applicable to herbivores with broad or generalized diets. Most of the studies that have been performed have chosen to focus on abundant, usually specialist, insect species, and most have sensibly considered the effect of a particular aspect of resource concentration (in lieu of trying to investigate the effect of resource concentration in all its possible manifestations). Thus most studies examine a single herbivore species in a natural or experimental setting involving a single host plant. Other plant species, when present, are considered as part of the "background" of diverse vegetation. I shall discuss these studies according to which aspect of resource concentration they chose to focus on: density, patch size, or diversity.

A. Host-Plant Density

By varying the density at which plants are grown in weed-free gardens, several investigators have quantified the relationship between the number of herbivores per plant and host-plant density. In these garden experiments, herbivore number (per plant) invariably declines with increasing host density (Table I). But it is not clear what these results mean

Table I
Herbivore Response to Varying Host-Plant Density[a]

Herbivore	Host plant and its range in density (no./m²)	Change in herbivore abundance (no./plant) with increased host-plant density	Reference
Oscinella frit (Diptera: Chloropidae)	Oats 140–1440	Declined	Adesiyun (1978)
Acalymma vittata (Coleoptera: Chrysomelidae)	Cucumber 1.4–2.9	Declined	Bach (1980a)
Aphis craccivora (Hemiptera: Aphididae)	Groundnuts 0.8–2.4	Declined	Farrell (1976)
Erioischia brassicae (Diptera: Anthomyiidae)	Cauliflower 1.5–83	Declined	Finch and Skinner (1976)
Cephus cinctus (Hymenoptera: Cephidae)	Wheat ?	Declined	Luginbill and McNeal (1958)
Empoasca fabae (Homoptera: Cicadellidae)	Soybeans 28–72	Declined	Mayse (1978)
Frumenta nundinella (Lepidoptera: Gelechiidae)	Horsenettle ?	Declined	Solomon (1981)

[a]All data are from experiments in which plants were grown in weed-free situations so that there was no confounding interaction between increased host density and declining vegetation diversity.

for natural situations or over the long run. One problem is that experimental variations in plant density often alter plant quality. This is true
for at least three of the experiments reported in Table I: sparsely planted
groundnuts were lusher and remained green longer than dense plantings (Farrell, 1976); the height, stem diameter, and stem moisture content
of oats declined with increasing density (Luginbill and McNeal, 1958);
densely planted soybeans grew more slowly and never attained as large
a size as they did when sparsely planted (Mayse, 1978). Apparent reductions in herbivores such as those evident in Table I could represent
a constant density of herbivores per unit weight of plant, but a decline
in plant size with crowding. Only the results of Mayse (1978) include
corrections for plant size, by tabulating herbivore loads (numbers of
herbivores per gram of plant) in lieu of numbers per plant. Even when
plants are widely spaced, they may interact such that foliage quality is
reduced in subtle ways. This is illustrated by experiments that Root
performed, in which collards were planted at 0.35-, 0.70-, 1.4- and 2.8-
m intervals. At the 1.4- and 2.8-m spacing there was no overlap between
the roots or canopy of neighboring collards—in fact, there seemed to
be large zones of untapped soil between plants. Nonetheless, the leaves
of collards planted at 2.8-m intervals were significantly richer in nitrogen
than those of collards at 1.4-m intervals (R. B. Root, unpublished data).
Because plant quality may be altered by crowding, it is misleading to
interpret the results in Table I as a simple direct response to resource
density.

Moreover, all of the studies reported in Table I lasted less than 1 yr.
The brevity of these experiments tends to exaggerate the importance of
colonization as opposed to changes in herbivore mortality or reproduction. If only limited numbers of herbivores are available to colonize
experimental plots, then it may be easy to saturate each herbivore's
colonization potential. In that case, observations of fewer herbivores per
plant at high plant densities (Table I) might reflect nothing more than
a simple saturation effect. Although increases in host-plant density dilute
the number of colonizing herbivores per plant, it remains to be seen
what happens to herbivore numbers after the initial colonization phase.

An alternative approach to studying the consequences of varying plant
density has involved observations or manipulations of plants in natural
communities rather than in cultivated gardens. Studies using this approach have typically investigated herbivore abundances within a much
smaller range of plant densities than those used in the cultivation experiments (cf. Tables I, II). As in the cultivation experiments, plant
quality remains a hidden variable associated with plant density (Thompson and Price, 1977). In natural vegetation, an additional complication

arises because an increase in the density of one host species typically changes the local vegetation diversity. For instance, a host plant might become so dense that it effectively reduces natural mixtures to a monoculture. For that reason, the results in Table II could represent diversity effects as well as density effects. It is worth noting that in only two of six natural systems were herbivores most abundant when their host plants were densest. Because only Thompson and Price (1977; see Table II) reported their data as herbivores per gram of plant food, plant size might present another problem in the interpretation of results in Table II.

Because it is difficult to separate direct consequences of host-plant density from secondary consequences mediated by plant quality, there is no easy resolution to the question of how plant density alters herbivore abundances. Clearly, Tables I and II provide little support for the idea that resource concentration in the form of increased host density enhances herbivore abundance; in only 2 of 13 experiments were the numbers of herbivores per plant higher in the denser stands of host plants.

B. The Size and Isolation of Host-Plant Patches

Both the resource-concentration hypothesis and the equilibrium theory of island biogeography suggest that herbivores should be most abundant in large patches (islands) of host plants. Although there are numerous papers relating herbivore species richness to host-plant area, I found only a few studies that consider how the population densities of herbivores change with the size of host patches (Table III). Of the 19 species reported in Table III, 9 of the herbivores exhibited greater per-plant abundances with increasing patch size, 8 species revealed no effects, and 2 species were less abundant in large patches. Occasionally, the interaction between patch size and herbivore density takes an extreme form; in particular, certain herbivores cannot sustain populations unless their host patches exceed some threshold *critical patch size* (Kareiva, 1981; Bach, 1983; MacGarvin, 1982). For example, MacGarvin (1982) found that *Altica* sp. (Coleoptera: Chrysomelidae) was absent from patches of its host plant covering less than 200 m^2. When I censused collard patches of varying sizes in meadows, single collards by themselves never maintained resident populations of the flea beetles, *Phyllotreta cruciferae* or *P. striolata* (over 50 different single-plant patches were observed; Kareiva, 1981).

On some host plants, herbivore populations may be maintained by repeated colonizations from outside sources (Faeth and Simberloff, 1981).

Table II
Herbivore Response to Varying Host-Plant Density[a]

Herbivore	Host plant and its range in density (no./m²)	Change in herbivore abundance (no./plant) with increased host-plant density	Reference
Tyria jacobaeae (Lepidoptera: Arctiidae)	Ragwort from <0.01 to >10% plant cover	Increased	van der Meijden (1979)
Unidentified curculionid weevil	Astragalus canadensis (milk vetch) 0.01–20	Declined	Platt et al. (1974)
Oncopeltus fasciatus (Hemiptera: Lygaeidae)	Milkweed 1.2–5.8	Increased	Ralph (1977a)
Battus philenor (Lepidoptera: Papilionidae)	Aristolochia reticulata (Dutchman's pipe) 0.33–4	No Change	Rausher and Feeny (1980)
Frumenta nundinella (Lepidoptera: Gelechiidae)	Horsenettle 3.6–20	No Change	Solomon (1981)
Depressaria pastinacella (Lepidoptera: Oecophoridae)	Pastinaca sativa (wild parsnip) <0.2 to 30	Declined	Thompson and Price (1977)

[a]Results are from differing densities of host plants in natural settings. Some of these data may reflect changes in the diversity of vegetation, although that is not the focus of any of the studies below.

Table III
Response of Herbivores to Size of Host-Plant Patches

Herbivore	Host plant	Patch size	Change in herbivore abundance (no./plant) with increasing host-patch size	Reference[a]
Phyllotreta cruciferae (Coleoptera: Chrysomelidae)	Collards	1, 10, 100 plants	Increase	1
Phyllotreta striolata (Coleoptera: Chrysomelidae)	Collards	1, 4, 8, 16 plants	Increase	2
	Collards	1, 10, 100 plants	Increase	1
	Collards	1, 4, 8, 16 plants	Increase	2
Pieris rapae (Lepidoptera: Pieridae)	Collards	1, 10, 100 plants	Decrease	1
	Collards	1, 4, 8, 16 plants	Decrease	2
Depressaria pastinacella (Lepidoptera: Decophoridae)	Wild parsnip	Single, isolated plants versus patch up to 36m in diameter	Increase	3
Thrip sp. (Thysonoptera)	Rosebay willowherb (*Chamerion angustifolium*)	Naturally occurring patches, size 1/4–7050 m^2	Increase	4
Craspedolepta subpuncta (Hemiptera: Psyllidae)	Rosebay willowherb (*Chamerion angustifolium*)	Naturally occurring patches, size 1/4–7050 m^2	Increase	4
Altica sp. (Coleoptera: Chrysomelidae)	Rosebay willowherb (*Chamerion angustifolium*)	Naturally occurring patches, size 1/4–7050 m^2	Increase	4

Species	Host plant	Patch description	Response	Reference
Tenthredo colon (Hymenoptera: Tenthridae)	Rosebay willowherb (*Chamerion angustifolium*)	Naturally occurring patches, size 1/4–7050 m^2	Decrease	4
Dasineura kiefferiana (Diptera: Cecidomyiidae)	Rosebay willowherb (*Chamerion angustifolium*)	Naturally occurring patches, size 1/4–7050 m^2	No change	4
Philaenus spumarius (Hemiptera: Cercopidae)	Rosebay willowherb (*Chamerion angustifolium*)	Naturally occurring patches, size 1/4–7050 m^2	No change	4
Mompha raschkiella (Lepidoptera: Momphidae)	Rosebay willowherb (*Chamerion angustifolium*)	Naturally occurring patches, size 1/4–7050 m^2	No change	4
Macrosiphum euphorbiae (Hemiptera: Ahididae)	Rosebay willowherb (*Chamerion angustifolium*)	Naturally occurring patches, size 1/4–7050 m^2	No change	4
Calocoris norvegicus (Hemiptera: Miridae)	Rosebay willowherb (*Chamerion angustifolium*)	Naturally occurring patches, size 1/4–7050 m^2	No change	4
Delphacodes detecta (Homoptera: Delphacidae)	*Spartina patens*	Naturally occurring patches, size 50–10,000 m^2	No change	5
Tumidagena minuta (Homoptera: Delphacidae)	*Spartina patens*	Naturally occurring patches, size 50–10,000 m^2	Increase	5
Megamelus lobatus (Homoptera: Delphacidae)	*Spartina patens*	Naturally occurring patches, size 50–10,000 m^2	Decrease	5
Amplicephalus simplex (Homoptera: Cicadellidae)	Rosebay willowherb (*Chamerion angustifolium*)	Naturally occurring patches, size 50–10,000 m^2	Increase	5
Destria bisignata (Homoptera: Cicadellidae)	Rosebay willowherb (*Chamerion angustifolium*)	Naturally occurring patches, size 50–10,000 m^2	No change	5
Aphelonema simplex (Homoptera: Cicadellidae)	Rosebay willowherb (*Chamerion angustifolium*)	Naturally occurring patches, size 50–10,000 m^2	Increase	5

[a]References: 1, Cromartie (1975b); 2, Kareiva (1981); 3, Thompson (1978); 4, MacGarvin (1982); 5, Denno *et al.* (1981).

When colonization is important, isolated stands of host plants should contain fewer specialized herbivores. Examples of plants escaping herbivory because of isolation are rare, largely because the appropriate studies have not been performed. Davis (1975) found that when nettles were sown in equal-sized gardens, the most isolated gardens took the longest to be colonized by specialized herbivores. If herbivores are extremely mobile, the effects of host isolation may be apparent only at very large spatial scales, scales which are difficult to work with experimentally. This is well illustrated by a study of cotton boll weevils, in which 26 cotton plants were set out in a tobacco field, with no other cotton within 1.6 mi (Mistric and Mitchell, 1966). In less than 70 days, these "isolated" cotton plants were colonized by 1085 migrating boll weevils. Although there are logistic difficulties associated with studies at such a broad scale, these problems should not deter our attempts to understand the interplay of regional vegetation patterns and herbivore populations. The regional scale (i.e., distances of miles) may well represent the scale at which patch size and patch isolation exert their greatest influence on herbivores in agroecosystems.

C. Vegetation Diversity

Three types of studies have been used to evaluate the effects of vegetation diversity on herbivore populations: (1) cultivating plants in monocultures and polycultures, (2) varying the background in which plants are grown (usually cultivated versus weedy ground), and (3) contrasting herbivore abundances on plants in natural surroundings of differing diversities. Of these approaches, investigations of agricultural cropping systems represent the overwhelming majority of studies. In a review, Risch et al. (1982) summarized the results of 68 published experiments concerning the influence of crop diversity on herbivore populations. The studies that were reviewed contrasted the numbers of herbivores in monocultures with the numbers in weedy or intercropped systems. Seventy-nine herbivore species were more abundant in monocultures, 19 were more abundant in the weedy or intercropped situations, and 17 showed no difference. Unfortunately, few studies successfully isolated crop diversity as an independent variable. For example, intercropped or weedy plantings might reduce herbivore abundances only because they reduce the size or quality of host plants. Because most of the data reviewed by Risch et al. are reported as number of herbivores per host plant, per unit area, or per unit sampling effort, it is impossible to factor out even the simple effect of changing plant size (Risch, 1980). Furthermore, polyculture–monoculture experiments typically involve variations in total plant density and host-plant density, as well as the intended manipulation of diversity. Of these "garden-diversity" experiments, the contributions by Bach (1980a,b, 1981, 1983) and Risch (1980, 1981) best illustrate a more promising and sophisticated model for future research, an approach that addresses the issues of plant size and quality and recognizes the interweaving of density with manipulations of diversity.

Working in Costa Rica, Risch (1980, 1981) investigated the response of six species of chrysomelid beetles (*Acalymma thiemei, Ceratoma ruficornis rogersi, Paranapiacaba waterhousei, Diabrotica viridula, D. balteata, D. adelpha*) to various combinations of corns, beans, and squash. Whenever a beetle species was presented with a polyculture containing at least one nonhost crop, there were fewer beetles (per unit weight of host plant) in that polyculture than in pure stands of the host plant. However, when a beetle fed on all species in a polyculture, this effect was reversed; there were fewer beetles on hosts grown in the monoculture. Thus, as Root originally suggested (1973), the resource-concentration hypothesis best applied when the herbivores were specialized and could not feed on the full spectrum of plants in a diverse polyculture.

Bach (1980a) focused on the response of one specialist herbivore, the striped cucumber beetle (*Acalymma vittata*) to cucumber monocultures versus cucumber–broccoli–maize polycultures. By controlling total plant density, host-plant density, and plant diversity, Bach was able to distinguish the effects of these three confounding variables. Applying a three-way analysis of variance to censuses of beetles per cucumber plant, Bach reported a significant effect of both plant density and diversity on *Acalymma* abundance; but the results only partially support the resource-concentration hypothesis. In particular, although an increase in stand purity yielded the expected increase in beetles per cucumber plant, an increase in cucumber density reduced the number of beetles per plant (Bach, 1980a). Bach (1980a) also found that cucumber plants were on average smaller in polycultures than in monocultures and that beetle density was positively correlated with plant size. There were, however, two polyculture plots with cucumbers equal in size to monoculture cucumbers; in these two thriving polycultures, beetles were still significantly fewer per plant than in monocultures. Thus, it is clear that the reduced beetle numbers in polycultures cannot simply be attributed to smaller cucumber plants. In a later study with *Acalymma vittata*, Bach (1981) provided evidence for a surprising reduction in foliage palatability associated with cucumber–tomato polycultures. Beetles given a laboratory choice between cucumber leaves grown in monoculture and cucumber leaves grown in a tomato–cucumber mixture significantly preferred monoculture leaves. This illustrates the subtle links that are possible between plant diversity and plant quality, quite apart from the conventional ideas concerning the influence of resource concentration on herbivores.

Only a handful of studies concerning vegetation diversity and herbivory have dealt with wild plants (e.g., Futuyma and Wasserman, 1980; Smith and Whittaker, 1980; Rausher, 1981; Solomon, 1981; Bach, 1983). As part of a comprehensive analysis of the pipevine swallowtail's (*Battus philenor*) impact on its primary host plant, *Aristolochia reticulata*, Rausher (1981) clipped to the ground the natural vegetation surrounding 200 isolated host plants, while leaving undisturbed the vegetation surrounding 200 control plants. Fewer *Battus* eggs were laid on the control plants amid the native vegetation, and these control plants also suffered less feeding damage from larvae. Bach (1982) has broadened her analyses of cucurbit–insect systems to include the noncultivated host plant *Cayaponia americana* and its specialized herbivore, *Acalymma innubum* (Coloeoptera: Chrysomelidae). For a wide variety of patch sizes (<0.2 to >24m^2), Bach reported consistently lower levels of herbivory on wild *Cayaponia* vines in habitats with greater vegetation diversity. Another chrysomelid that seems to be sensitive to vegetation diversity is *Gastrophysa viridula*, which feeds mainly on the weed *Rumex obtusifolius*, and it has been extensively studied in England (see Smith and Whittaker, 1980). Smith and Whittaker (1980) found an inverse relationship between the diversity of background vegetation and survivorship in *Gastrophysa*. These changes in beetle survival cannot necessarily be ascribed to changes in vegetation diversity— in the habitats studied by Smith and Whittaker, *Rumex* density also changed concurrently with vegetation diversity (from 1 to 3 plants/m^2). There is a clear need for more studies concerning herbivory and vegetation texture in *natural* as opposed to agricultural communities.

D. Other Features of Vegetation Texture

There are other aspects of vegetation texture that have not been discussed. Structural or physical properties of habitats may influence herbivore abundances as much as or more than the taxonomic composition of plant assemblages. Shade is often avoided by insects (e.g., Cromartie, 1975a; Risch, 1981), regardless of which species casts it. Thus the critical feature of a polyculture might be its shading regime, as opposed to its taxonomic diversity. Risch (1981) demonstrated that beetles were less abundant in maize–bean–squash polycultures, partially because they avoided host plants shaded by corn. Changes in patch size may even alter habitat structure. For example, Rigby and Lawton (1981) discovered a significant correlation between the size of monospecific bracken fern patches and habitat heterogeneity within those patches. They cautioned that the buildup of herbivore species and numbers on larger bracken patches might depend as much on increased habitat heterogeneity as on an increase in island size. In general, tests of the resource-concentration hypothesis can never be straightforward; when the diversity, density, or size of host plant stands is varied, there is much more going on than a simple shift in resource concentration.

E. The Individualistic Response of Herbivores to Vegetation Texture

From the preceding discussion it is obvious that vegetation texture has an important influence on herbivore populations. The nature of that influence, however, varies among herbivore species. At present it is difficult to make sense of the myriad ways in which herbivores respond to vegetation texture. Clearly, the resource-concentration hypothesis does not hold up as a robust generalization; it seems to fail about as often as it succeeds. Root (1975) noted this with his own experiments, concerning cole-crop herbivores, and suggested that the individualistic responses of herbivores should not be a surprise; in particular, Root argued that we should expect such a diversity of responses to vegetation texture because evolution will shape the behavior of herbivores to meet the challenges provided by different arrangements of host plants. In subsequent research we need to identify species-specific traits (e.g., diet specialization, mobility, range at which hosts can be detected, etc.) that govern the responses of herbivores to vegetation textures.

At this point, diet breadth is the one trait that seems to be most important in determining an herbivore's reaction to vegetation texture. Because species-specific feeding habits determine an herbivore's perception of vegetation texture (e.g., food versus nonfood), it follows that diet breadth shapes each herbivore's relationship with vegetation texture. For example, in contrast to the expectation that herbivory increases in pure stands, some plant species suffer greater herbivore loads when they are the *rarer* species in a stand (Futuyma and Wasserman, 1980; Parket and Root, 1981). Notably, these instances of a *reverse* resource-concentration effect all involve polyphagous herbivores that feed on the surrounding "diverse" vegetation and spill over onto the rarer plant. In a similar vein, as mentioned earlier, Risch (1981) has reported herbivores to be more abundant in polycultures than in monocultures when those herbivores feed on all plant species in the polyculture.

The individualistic responses of herbivores to plant dispersion have important consequences for the organization of herbivore guilds. Imagine several different herbivores that exploit the same host-plant species. If the herbivores respond individualistically to vegetation textures, each herbivore may thrive and prevail in different circumstances, depending on where and how the plant is growing. Often, entirely different herbivores are associated with the same host plant, depending on the spatial dispersion of the host (Cromarite, 1975b; Denno *et al.*, 1981; Kareiva, 1981; McLain, 1981a,b; MacGarvin, 1982). This suggests that herbivores might avoid competition by each using host plants that grow in different densities, patch sizes, or background vegetation. Thus a complex pattern of host plant dispersion could permit a high diversity of herbivores to share the same taxonomic resource (Cromartie, 1975b). It should be noted, however, that observations of different herbivores using plants in different-sized patches do not guarantee that interspecific competition among herbivores is avoided. If those herbivores use plants that originate from a common seed pool, they may reduce that seed pool and thus compete without ever occupying the same individual plants. As yet, there is no experimental evidence to support the tempting idea that, by partitioning plants according to their dispersion, herbivores enhance their opportunities for coexistence.

III. MECHANISMS THAT UNDERLIE THE RESPONSES OF HERBIVORES TO VEGETATION TEXTURE

The experiments summarized in Tables I–III allow us to conclude only that *some* herbivore species increase in abundance when their host plants become more concentrated. Even if we narrow our focus to a single herbivore species, it is difficult to make robust predictions; each herbivore's interplay with plant dispersion may depend on factors such as the size and permanence of experimental plots, the taxonomic identity or growth form of host and nonhost vegetation, and the fertility of the soil. To avoid merely cataloging endless possibilities, we need to examine the mechanisms that determine shifts in herbivore abundance with changes in plant dispersion. Only by better understanding mechanisms can we hope to explain why different species respond differently to resource concentration, why one particular species might be so sensitive to growth form of nonhost vegetation, and so on.

There are three primary routes by which vegetation texture might influence herbivore numbers.

1. Vegetation texture may limit the numbers of parasites and predators in a habitat and, consequently, determine the degree of regulation of herbivores by their natural enemies.
2. Changes in vegetation texture might alter the suitability of individual food plants for herbivore growth and reproduction.
3. Vegetation texture may shape the movement and searching behavior of herbivores and affect their host-finding success.

The data are too sparse to draw conclusions about which of these processes is most important. For instance, although host-plant quality commonly varies in concert with vegetation texture, only the studies by Bach (1980a,b, 1981) and Risch (1980, 1981) have explicitly examined the consequences of such variation.

The effects of vegetation texture on the natural enemies of herbivores have not been ignored, as has plant quality, but critical data are lacking. It is widely accepted that diverse vegetation can be an asset to pest control, because it harbors large numbers of predators and parasites (e.g., Huffaker and Messenger, 1976; Speight and Lawton, 1976). Numerous studies have shown that populations of insect predators and parasites are directly influenced by vegetation texture (see discussion in Root, 1973). There is, however, very little evidence that natural enemies are responsible for lower herbivore numbers in polycultures; most data are in the form of correlations between some aspect of vegetation texture and predator or parasite density. The actual *impacts* of these natural enemies on herbivores are undocumented. Of the 68 agricultural studies reviewed by Risch *et al.* (1983), less than 10 explored the ecological factors underlying changes in herbivore abundance; and of this small subset even fewer studies discussed the relative importance of natural enemies versus herbivore-movement in explaining observed patterns. When the relevant comparisons are made, the impact of natural enemies is negligible (Risch *et al.*, 1983). Similarly, I have found no evidence that natural enemies account for any of the results presented in Tables I–II (but again, rarely has any attempt been made to look for such evidence).

The one mechanism connecting herbivore abundance to vegetation texture for which there is a surplus of data is herbivore movement. Of the three routes listed previously, movement is probably the best quantified, because it is easier to measure than plant quality or mortality due to predation. Several investigations have related the changes in herbivore number that occur with various arrangements of host plants to simple shifts in herbivore-movement patterns (Bach, 1980a,b, 1983; Risch,

1980, 1981; Kareiva, 1981). Because herbivores must move in order to locate their food plants, their patterns of movement determine their success at searching out host plants. Diverse vegetation appears to disrupt the searching process of many different herbivores and may thereby reduce herbivore survival (Dethier, 1959; Ralph, 1977a,b; Kemp and Simmons, 1979; Rausher, 1981). More evidence for herbivore movement as a key process can be found in the comprehensive review by Risch *et al.* (1983), which concludes that, for annual cropping systems, herbivore movement is the most important factor underlying reduced herbivore populations in diverse vegetation. In the following subsections I shall address the different ways in which herbivore movement mediates the interaction of herbivore density with host-plant dispersion.

A. Problems of Locating Host Plants: Consequences for Herbivore Populations

Herbivores with narrow host ranges frequently have difficulty locating food plants, especially if those food plants are scarce or are hidden amid unsuitable vegetation. Because vegetation texture influences the likelihood that herbivores will find host plants, it will in turn influence the relative abundances of herbivores in different situations. This intuitively appealing idea is central to the resource-concentration hypothesis. Food plants may often appear abundant to us yet represent a scarce and unapparent resource, relative to an herbivore's searching abilities. Although many airborne insects can use visual or olfactory cues to locate host plants (e.g., Finch, 1980), this sensory sophistication is by no means a general phenomenon in phytophagous insects. Specialized herbivores, especially crawling stages or species, can be remarkably inept at searching for host plants. For instance, the larvae of several species wander about randomly and cannot identify a host plant until they physically bump into it or, even worse, until they climb the stem and "taste" the foliage (Dethier, 1959; Rausher, 1981; Messina, 1982).

1. Hidden Host Plants and Confused Herbivores

According to ecological folklore, individual host plants may be hidden from herbivores if they are surrounded by nonhost vegetation (see Tahvanainen and Root, 1972; Feeny, 1975; Atsatt and O'Dowd, 1976). It is easy to imagine a plant hiding from a visually searching herbivore—surrounding vegetation may inhibit discovery by simply blocking the view of searching insects. The reduced oviposition of *Battus philenor* (Lepidoptera: Papilionidae) on host plants amid uncut vegetation appears to reflect such hiding (Rausher, 1981). When an herbivore finds its host plants via olfaction, the concept of a hidden plant is less straight-forward. How is an odor hidden? There are two standard explanations for how host plants hide from olfactory searchers: (1) surrounding vegetation may emit odors that somehow mask the host plant's odors; (2) a neighboring nonhost species may produce repellent volatile compounds. Although data from several field experiments support the idea of chemical hiding (see Tahvanainen and Root, 1972), Finch (1980) has cautioned that many of these results are subject to alternative explanations.

Only direct behavioral observations of searching herbivores can demonstrate that a host plant is hidden by surrounding vegetation. Such observations are difficult to make in the field. Consequently, the relative frequency with which host plants are discovered by an herbivore is often estimated by censusing that herbivore's abundance or tabulating the rate at which its eggs appear on host plants. These data do not necessarily reflect discovery rates. For example, cabbage-root flies (*Delia brassicae*) lay fewer eggs on *Brassica* hosts that are intercropped with clover than on host plants grown in monocultures (Hawkes and Coaker, 1976; Ryan *et al.*, 1980). Yet laboratory experiments using large flight chambers indicate that the same number of root flies arrive at trays of *Brassica* mixed with clover as at trays of *Brassica* alone (Hawkes and Coaker, 1976; Coaker, 1980). Clover did not disrupt normal host plant finding in these experiments, but it did increase fly activity upon arrival at the intercropped trays. Flies in the presence of clover and *Brassica* spent more time moving and less time laying eggs than flies at pure *Brassica* trays; they also emigrated at a higher rate when in the presence of clover (Coaker, 1980). This example illustrates how difficult it can be to resolve whether nonhost vegetation interferes with an herbivore's host-finding behavior or disturbs and agitates the herbivore after it has found its host.

Many insects seem to have problems locating their host plants if those hosts blend into their background (Cromartie, 1981). For example, experiments have shown that several aphid species colonize their host plants at significantly lower rates when those hosts are surrounded by weeds, a nonhost crop, or even green burlap, as opposed to bare brown ground (see Smith, 1976; Horn, 1981). At present, we don't know what it is about the plant–background contrast (or lack thereof) that insects perceive and respond to, although color clearly plays some role.

Because so little is known about herbivore sensory skills, we don't really understand how plants might "hide" from herbivores. This ignorance limits our ability to explain the different responses of herbivores to vegetation texture. We need to complement our population-level studies of herbivory and vegetation texture with behavioral investigations of herbivore perception and orientation. For instance, each plant–herbivore interaction can be characterized by a zone of detection (that is, the maximum distance from which an herbivore can detect, orient toward, and ultimately land on an individual target plant). A plant within its herbivore's zone of detection can be considered "found" by that herbivore. It would be interesting to quantify the extent to which nonhost vegetation reduces the zone of detection for various insect–plant associations. Even though we have identified numerous volatile plant compounds that act as attractants for herbivores, we have little information about the distances over which these compounds can act (Finch, 1980).

2. Mortality while Searching for Food Plants

Because they are exposed, vulnerable, or run out of energy, plant-feeding insects often suffer increased mortality while searching for food plants. After defoliating their intitial food plants (*Aster*), larval *Melitaea harrisii* (Lepidoptera: Nymphalidae) must locate additional hosts in order to complete development. Dethier (1959) estimated that these larvae suffered up to 80% mortality while searching for their required second plant, and this was in a field that averaged 2.36 food plants/m². Dethier emphasized that a superficial examination of such a field suggested that *Aster* was plentiful and that larvae unerringly located their host plants. Only by following the fates of individual larvae was Dethier able to detect the enormous losses *M. harrisii* suffered in search of food. Ralph (1977a,b) quantified the behavior and mortality of milkweed bugs (*Oncopeltus fasciatus*) that were searching for host plants growing in different spatial arrangements and found that *Oncopeltus* nymphs were less abundant (fewer individuals per host plant) in sparse stands of milkweed, partly because these nymphs suffered their highest mortality while searching for milkweed in these sparse stands (Ralph, 1977b). Mortality during the dispersal phase appears to be an important factor in the population dynamics of many forest lepidoptera. For example, outbreaks of spruce budworms are typically associated with forests in which preferred food plants occur in dense pure stands (Crook *et al.*, 1979; Kemp and Simmons, 1979). Kemp and Simmons have reported that the presence of nonhost trees significantly increases the mortality rates of dispersing budworms. This effect of nonhost trees may explain the tendency of budworm outbreaks to be restricted to denser, purer stands of host trees (Kemp and Simmons, 1979).

In general, the interplay of plant dispersion and the mortality suffered by a dispersing herbivore will depend on the insect's innate host-finding skills. Herbivores that are passive dispersers (e.g., spruce budworms,

Has anybody critically examined interaction between resource conc. and natural enemies?

gypsy moths) or that lack the ability to detect hosts from afar (e.g., larval *Melitaea harrisii*) will run the greatest risk of dying before they locate their food plants. In these situations, herbivore population dynamics should be tightly coupled to changes in host-plant density.

B. Herbivore Loads and Equilibrium Island Biogeography: A Balance between Immigration and Emigration

Janzen (1968) pointed out that interactions between insects and their host plants could be viewed from the perspective of island biogeography. In particular, Janzen emphasized that the number of insects on individual plants represents a balance between immigration and emigration rates and that these rates will vary with factors such as host patch size or isolation. Plants might escape from herbivory because they are rarely found or because emigration from them exceeds immigration. To better understand long-term consequences of vegetation texture, it is essential that we quantify the relative contributions of these two processes. If herbivore densities are governed primarily by colonization events, then rare or stochastic invasions of host patches will have persistent consequences. In contrast, if high emigration rates are responsible for low herbivore abundances on unapparent hosts, then those hosts will be only briefly affected by a chance surplus of colonizing herbivores.

I first became interested in the emigration response of herbivores as a result of casual field observations of insect behavior. I noticed that two species of crucifer-feeding flea beetles (*Phyllotreta cruciferae* and *P. striolata*) were incorrigibly nomadic—they eventually abandoned the best possible patches of host plants, even if those patches were surrounded by a large expanse of nonhost vegetation (Kareiva, 1981). To quantify the relative importance of emigration and immigration behavior in these species, I followed their population dynamics in experimental archipelagoes of different-sized collard patches. By placing known numbers of marked beetles on different patches and then repeatedly censusing each patch, I was able to distinguish and estimate patch-specific immigration and emigration rates. After 2–3 weeks, beetles had attained densities that were independent of the initial numbers placed on patches; at that time patch size and vegetation background significantly affected beetle density (Fig. 1). Moreover, the number of beetles initially placed on each patch had no effect on the ultimate density of beetles; the patterns in Fig. 1 reflect an "equilibrium," balancing immigration and emigration. Thus, when I placed flea beetles on single, isolated collards, those collards escaped herbivory because the beetles quickly wandered off the

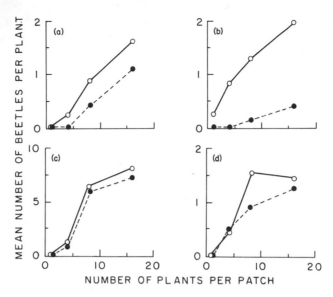

Fig. 1. The response of flea beetles to host-plant (collard) patch size and background vegetation. These abundances are densities, attained 2–3 weeks after the experiment was initiated. By that time the density was independent of the initial number of beetles placed on each patch. Each point represents a mean of eight patches for the one-plant patch size and four patches for all other patch sizes. (a,b) July experiment (○, cultivated; ●, goldenrod background): *Phyllotreta cruciferae* (a); *P. striolata* (b). (c,d) August experiment (○, cultivated; ●, green meadow): *P. cruciferae* (a); *P. striolata* (b).

plants and never returned. By independently estimating both emigration and immigration rates, I found that emigration rates varied much more with patch size than did immigration rates (Kareiva, 1981).

Within the last few years, field experiments with several plant–insect systems have indicated that herbivore emigration is extremely sensitive to vegetation texture (see Bach, 1980a; Risch, 1981; Risch *et al.*, 1983). The studies by Bach (1980a) and Risch (1981) are especially noteworthy because they examined the relative contributions of immigration, emigration, and natural enemies to changes in herbivore abundances associated with polyculture versus monoculture cropping patterns. They found no evidence for differences in immigration rates or natural enemies between mono- and polycultures and concluded that increased emigration was the primary factor underlying reduced herbivore loads in polycultures.

Most theoretical discussions of herbivory and vegetation texture bring to mind visions of plants "hiding" from their herbivores (see Atsatt and O'Dowd, 1976). Phrases such as "plant apparency, escape in space, and bound to be found" all emphasize the problems herbivores have discovering food plants. To accommodate new data concerning the importance of emigration, we will have to recognize that being "easy to lose" is just as effective an escape route for a plant as being "hard to find."

C. Plant Dispersion and the Effectiveness of Herbivores at Choosing the Best Diet

An important theme throughout this book is that plants differ greatly in quality and that these differences affect growth, survivorship, and reproduction in herbivorous insects. By discriminating between food plants, herbivores may enhance their net replacement rate. This interaction between an individual's foraging behavior and its demographic performance provides yet another mechanism by which vegetation texture may determine herbivore abundance. In particular, I argue that

1. Vegetation texture influences herbivore mobility.
2. An herbivore's mobility constrains its opportunities for finding and selecting the "best" food plants.
3. Therefore, vegetation texture may indirectly determine herbivore abundance through its influence on herbivore foraging decisions.

Although there is not field evidence to support the final step in this argument, there are data to support steps 1 and 2.

Numerous studies document changes in herbivore-movement patterns as a result of shifts in plant dispersion (Douwes, 1968; Jones, 1977a; Ralph, 1977a; Bach, 1980a; Risch, 1981; Kareiva, 1982a; Parker, 1982). For example, there is generally more movement on the part of foraging herbivores when food plants or food-plant patches are close together (Kareiva, 1982a; Parker, 1982). The type of vegetation between food plants can also influence movement (see Kareiva, 1982a), and in some cases certain habitats or vegetation act as effective dispersal barriers to specialized herbivores (see Cromartie, 1975a). The importance of movement in providing opportunities for selective feeding is illustrated by experiments I performed with flea beetles (*Phyllotreta cruciferae* and *P. striolata*) and their collard food plants. To determine the influence of patch dispersion on foraging selectivity, I varied the distance between collard patches of differing qualities. The degree of foraging discrimination exhibited by both beetles was greatest when host patches were closest together, declining as distance between patches increased. The dependence of beetle foraging discrimination on patch dispersion was shown to be a product of varying movement rates; when patches were widely spaced and interpatch movement low, beetles selected their food-plants almost randomly with respect to patch quality (Kareiva, 1982a). It remains to be seen whether such shifts in foraging discrimination translate into shifts in total populations of herbivores.

IV. QUESTIONS OF SCALE AND SOME ISSUES IN EXPERIMENTAL DESIGN

A crucial feature of experiments concerned with vegetation texture is the scale (both temporal and spatial) at which manipulations are per-formed. The key decisions concern the sizes of experimental plots, dis-tances between different treatments (such as polyculture versus monoculture), and duration of the experiment. It is easiest to appreciate the importance of these decisions by imagining a particular example. Suppose we wish to compare herbivore loads in poly- versus monocul-tures, with the ultimate goal of recommending agricultural practices. The outcome of any experiment is likely to be sensitive to the exact spatial layout of the poly- and monocultures. An experiment that in-volves several 10 × 10 m replicates of poly- and monocultures in close proximity may not be suitable for predictions about agroecosystems. For instance, assume that such an alternating series of poly- and monocul-ture gardens revealed significantly fewer herbivores in the polycultures. The scarcity of herbivores in polycultures might result from a preference of mobile herbivores for neighboring monoculture "sinks." If experi-mental polycultures did, in fact, escape herbivory because they were bordered by more attractive monocultures, there is no reason to expect large-scale polycultural agroecosystems to also escape herbivory. A crop available *only in large polycultures* might accumulate just as many her-bivores as if it were growing *only in large monocultures* (regardless of the results of experiments involving small alternating poly- and monoculture gardens). This hypothetical example points out the importance of iden-tifying the mechanism behind an herbivore's response to vegetation texture and illustrates the limitations of alternate-plot experiments. Most of the experiments discussed in the preceding sections manipulate veg-etation texture over small spatial scales relative to the mobilities of the associated herbivores. Consequently, many of the reported changes in herbivore density may reflect nothing more than choices of particular habitats over neighboring habitats. These behavioral responses are in-formative, but they do not lead to predictions about herbivore population dynamics at the scale of ecosystems.

A recurring problem in studies of herbivory and vegetation texture is the brevity of observations. If vegetation texture alters the survivorship or fecundity of herbivores, these effects may be negligible when experimental plots are first colonized but may become striking in subsequent herbivore generations. Most experimental manipulations of vegetation texture have been observed only during the early colonization stages; rarely is more than one generation of herbivores included in the experimental interval. Suppose herbivore fecundity is dramatically reduced in diverse vegetation because females waste so much time and energy searching for oviposition sites. The consequences of such an effect could not be observed over the time period that typifies past studies of vegetation texture. There is much information to be gained simply by repeating experimental manipulations of plant dispersion in the same positions, year after year.

In reviewing vegetation texture experiments, I was frequently frustrated by the failure of investigators to adequately describe their experimental layouts. Too often I was unable to answer key questions such as

1. How big were the experimental plots?
2. How widely separated were different experimental treatments?
3. Were alternative host plants (e.g., plants in the same genus or family) present in the surrounding vegetation (i.e., the vegetation that was not explicitly part of the experiment)?
4. If the experiment was continued for more than one field season, did each experimental treatment remain in the same position from year to year?
5. Did the quality of host plants vary in any consistent pattern?

There is good reason to believe that the answer to these questions are just as likely to influence the outcome of experiments as controlled experimental factors such as density, patch size, or diversity. By paying closer attention to the sorts of auxiliary variables addressed in these questions, we may better interpret the response of herbivores to traditionally investigated aspects of vegetation texture.

V. A PLEA FOR A THEORY OF HERBIVORE SEARCH

Because insect searching behavior is often the key process underlying the response of herbivores to vegetation texture, it is essential that we quantitatively explore the consequences of different searching patterns and how these patterns might be influenced by vegetation texture. In this section I sketch three theoretical approaches for connecting herbivore movement to vegetation texture. Because results are scanty, my intent is to interest researchers in these different approaches, to stimulate future empirical and theoretical inquiry.

A. Modeling Herbivore Movements as Diffusion Processes

Diffusion (random-walk) models have aptly described the foraging movements of several herbivorous insects (Okubo, 1980; Kareiva, 1981, 1982a). One result from diffusion theory that is especially relevant to plant–insect systems is the notion of critical patch size. If herbivores diffuse from host-plant patches, the magnitude of that loss should be proportional to the perimeter (or boundry across which the emigration takes place) of the host patch. The potential carrying capacity of a host patch for herbivores should be proportional to the total number of food plants in the patch or host patch area. Consequently, emigration losses *per host plant* will tend to be greater in host patches with larger ratios of perimeter to host plant (i.e., larger ratios of perimeter to area). This means that as the size of host patches declines, the relative importance of emigration losses (per plant) increases. Ultimately, below a certain critical patch size it may be impossible to maintain an herbivore population because diffusive losses outweigh colonization and internal birth. A rigorous development of these arguments has been presented by Okubo (1980), and the exact consequences of changing perimeter/area ratios depend on the dynamics of herbivores within patches as well as the nature of population flux across patch boundaries. In general, perimeter/area ratio of host patches will influence herbivore abundance for a wide variety of emigration behaviors in addition to simple passive diffusion. In an elegant paper, Ludwig *et al.* (1979) used diffusion models to explore the role of forest spatial patterning in spruce budworm outbreaks. In addition to the critical size of a forest patch, they also investigated the potential of dispersal barriers for containing budworm outbreaks (Ludwig *et al.*, 1979). The approach adopted by Ludwig *et al.* may be broadly applicable to questions of vegetation texture at the ecosystem (as opposed to experimental garden) scale.

B. Borrowing Ideas from Theories about the Adaptive Significance of "Prey" Clumping

The spatial arrangement of food plants will influence the success or fitness of both individual plants and individual herbivores. In a general setting, several models have explored adaptationist explanations for different strategies of prey spacing or clumping (see Taylor, 1979; Kiltie, 1980). Ideas regarding the adaptive significance of prey aggregation may be applied to questions of herbivory and host-plant dispersion. For example, one hypothesis for the advantage of clumping of prey is that, by occurring in aggregations, an individual reduces its chances of falling victim to predators (Taylor, 1979; Kiltie, 1980). This hypothesis arises from models that use the theory of random search (see Stone, 1975; Haley and Stone, 1980) to make quantitative statements about per capita risk of gregarious versus solitary victims (Kiltie, 1980). Although details vary, a key feature of all of these models is some function that relates the radius of detection for a prey aggregation to the size of the prey aggregation (for convenience referred to as detection–aggregation functions). In general, the less detectability increases with prey clump size, the more likely a victim is to enjoy a reduced threat of predation by occuring in aggregations (Kiltie, 1980). Because analogous arguments should hold for herbivores searching for plants, it would be valuable to apply prey-aggregation theory to data concerning herbivore loads and host-plant patch size. Perhaps the individualistic responses of herbivores to patch size can be traced in part back to species-specific variation in detection–aggregation functions. After finding that isolated *Astragalus* plants had greater weevil loads than clumped plants, Platt *et al.* (1974) presented a graphical model for the advantage of plant clumping, based on overlapping ranges of detection in plant clumps. Their argument regarding overlapping ranges of detection is another form (albeit more intuitive and less mathematical) of the theory of random search and detection–aggregation functions. The key idea emerging from these speculations is that it is essential to quantify how the radius at which herbivores can detect host plants varies with host patch size.

C. Simulating the Search Process in Herbivores

Both diffusion theory and random-search models sacrifice details of individual behavior in order to obtain powerful generalizations. A complementary approach involves computer simulations of searching by individual herbivores. Although simulations forgo generality, they facilitate direct incorporation of field data (see Jones, 1977a,b, 1980). All simulations of movement begin by decomposing the process into elements such as move lengths, turning angles, autocorrelation between moves, and so on. There are many possible options for simulating movement (see Siniff and Jessen, 1969; Kitching, 1971; Jones, 1977a; Okubo, 1980; Kareiva, 1982a; Parker, 1982; Root and Kareiva, 1983), and it is not known to what extent the outcomes of these models are sensitive to the manner in which movement is represented in the simulation.

The work of Jones and colleagues on cabbage butterfly oviposition (Jones, 1977a; Jones *et al.*, 1980) includes an exemplary application of simulation modeling to herbivore movement. By observing the behavior of ovipositing females in experimental gardens, Jones (1977a) deduced rules of movement for cabbage butterflies. These rules governed stochastic decisions such as, Stop or move another unit distance? Lay or not lay eggs? and Change flight direction? Simulations that incorporated these rules of movement correctly predicted observed field patterns of egg dispersion. Moreover, the models enabled Jones to identify the features of flight behavior that were responsible for differences in patterns of egg laying between Canadian and Australian butterfly populations. Jones' rules of movement applied to flying and egg laying over short distances (<100 m) and short intervals of time; simulations using these rules were initially used only to predict oviposition patterns at these scales in small cabbage gardens (Jones, 1977a). The most impressive accomplishment of Jones *et al.* (1980) was to take these short-range rules of movement and run the simulation for enough time that movement occurred at the scale of a kilometer. To test the long-running simulation, several different arrangements of potted cabbage were set out on a 1-km^2 grid. The egg deposition of cabbage butterfiles was then observed in these large study grids (see Jones *et al.*, 1980, for special techniques). The match between observed placement of eggs and the placement predicted by the simulation was remarkably and consistently good (Jones *et al.*, 1980). Thus, by studying short-range patterns of movement (at the scale of meters), Jones *et al.* extrapolated these data with a simulation model and successfully predicted egglaying behavior at the scale of kilometers.

In addition to describing and extrapolating movement, simulations can also allow us to examine "strategies" of movement. For example, given a particular dispersion of host plants, we might use simulations to determine the success of herbivores at locating food plants as a function of radius of detection, move velocity, turning angle between moves, etc. Conversely, for any given suite of herbivore searching parameters (probability distribution of move lengths, turning angle, mortality rate while searching, etc.), simulations could be used to quantify the "escape" of food plants as a function of different spatial arrangements. The interpretation of such simulations requires caution because the results often depend on external parameters such as size of area in which search is simulated and how long the simulation is run. As an example, consider two bounded areas with the *same total number of host plants*, but one area has the plants occurring in clumps and the other area has the plants scattered randomly about the space. Under a variety of simulation schemes, differences in the number of herbivores discovering clumped versus scattered plants depends largely on how long herbivores are allowed to search for food plants (P. Kareiva, unpublished observations). As long as we remain aware of their limitations, simulations may help us predict the response of different herbivores to different manipulations of vegetation texture, by connecting searching behavior to plant dispersion. There are already empirical results indicating that herbivore species engage in searching behavior that is adapted to the specific circumstances in which they typically seek food plants (see Jones, 1977b). Perhaps the biggest point in favor of the simulation approach is that searching models may be designed so that their parameters can be directly obtained from field observations. Consequently, predictions about optimal searching strategies (for insects) or optimal escape strategies (plant arrangements) should be readily testable.

VI. FINAL REMARKS

In this chapter I have explored the influence of vegetation texture on herbivore populations. The variety of herbivore responses that I have reported dissolves any hope for easy generalizations such as a resource-concentration effect. Now the challenge is to understand why herbivores react so individualistically to changes in vegetation texture. Much of the answer involves differences between species, in their mobility and searching behavior. A more satisfying resolution awaits observations of herbivore foraging that quantify parameters such as mortality while searching and radius of detection.

Most studies of herbivory and vegetation texture have censused small experimental gardens over a 3- to 5-month period. As a consequence of the brevity of these experiments, the data primarily reflect the immediate behavioral responses (especially colonization) of herbivores to vegetation texture. Little is known about the influence of plant dispersion on patterns of herbivore survivorship or reproduction. The small scale at which experiments typically have been performed may be inappropriate for extrapolations to agroecosystem design—it may even be too restricted for inferences about herbivore populations.

Since Root first proposed the resource-concentration hypothesis in 1973, we have learned much about what can happen to herbivore abundances as a result of changes in food-plant dispersion. But until we have a better mechanistic understanding of the interaction between herbivores and vegetation texture, there is little hope for making useful predictions about the consequences of vegetation texture.

ACKNOWLEDGMENTS

Preparation of the manuscript was supported by a BRSG grant to Brown University. Catherine Bach, Matt Parker, Richard Root, and Steve Risch shared unpublished data and ideas. I thank N. Cappuccino and S. Levin for numerous editorial suggestions. Several colleagues helped by answering correspondence or sending much needed preprints: P. Atsatt, C. Bach, T. Coaker, S. Finch, J. Lawton, M. MacGarvin, M. Mayse, K. McLain, M. Perrin, S. Risch, and M. Stanton. Finally, I am especially grateful to Paulette Bierzychudek for commenting on an early draft.

REFERENCES

Adesiyun, A. (1978). Effects of seeding density and spatial distribution of oat plants on colonization and development of *Oscinella frit* (Diptera: Chloropidae). *J. Appl. Ecol.* **15**, 797–808.

Atsatt, P., and O'Dowd, D. (1976). Plant defense guilds. *Science* **193**, 24–29.

Bach, C. E. (1980a). Effects of plant density and diversity in the population dynamics of a specialist herbivore, the striped cucumber beetle, *Acalymma vittata*. *Ecology* **61**, 1515–1530.

Bach, C. E. (1980b). Effects of plant diversity and time of colonization on an herbivore–plant interaction. *Oecologia* **44**, 319–326.

Bach, C. E. (1981). Host plant growth form and diversity: effects on abundance and feeding preference of a specialist herbivore *Acalymma vittata* (Coleoptera: Chrysomelidae). *Oecologia* **50**, 370–375.

Bach, C. E. (1983). Plant spatial pattern and herbivore population dynamics: factors affecting the abundance of a tropical cucurbit specialist *(Acalymma innubum)*. *Ecology* (in press).

Coaker, T. H. (1980). Insect pest management in *Brassica* crops by intercropping. *Integr. Control* Brassica Crops, *I.O.B.C. WPRS Bull.* **3**, 117–125.

Cromartie, W. J. (1975a). Influence of habitat on colonization of collard plants by *Pieris rapae*. *Environ. Entomol.* **4**, 783–784.

Cromartie, W. J. (1975b). The effect of stand size and vegetational background on the colonization of cruciferous plants by herbivorous insects. *J. Appl. Ecol.* **12**, 517–533.

Cromartie, W. J. (1981). The environmental control of insects using crop diversity. *In* "Handbook of Pest Management" (D. Pimentel, ed.), pp. 223–251. Chemical Rubber Company in Agriculture, Boca Raton, Florida.

Crook, G., Vezina, P., and Hardy, Y. (1979). Susceptibility of balsam fir to spruce budworm defoliation as affected by thinning. *Can. J. For. Res.* **9**, 428–435.

Davis, B. N. K. (1975). The colonization of isolated patches of nettles *(Urtica dioica)* by insects. *J. Appl. Ecol.* **12**, 1–14.

Denno, R., Raupp, M., and Tallamy, D. (1981). Organization of a guild of sap-feeding insects: equilibrium versus nonequilibrium coexistence. *In* "Insect Life History Patterns: Habitat and Geographic Variation" (R. F. Denno and H. Dingle, eds.), pp. 151–181. Springer-Verlag, Berlin and New York.

Dethier, V. G. (1959). Food-plant distribution and density and larval dispersal as factors affecting insect populations. *Can. Entomol.* **88**, 581–596.

Douwes, P. (1968). Host selection and host finding in the egg-laying female *Cidaria albulata* L. (Lep. Geometridae). *Opusc. Entomol.* **33**, 233–279.

Faeth, S., and Simberloff, D. (1981). Experimental isolation of oak host plants: effects on mortality, survivorship, and abundances of leaf-mining insects. *Ecology* **62**, 625–635.

Farrell, J. A. K. (1976). Effects of groundnut crop density on the population dynamics of *Aphis craccivora* Koch (Hemiptera, Aphididae) in Malawi. *Bull. Entomol. Res.* **66**, 317–329.

Feeny, P. (1975). Biochemical coevolution between plants and their insect herbivores. *In* "Coevolution of Animals and Plants" (L. E. Gilbert and P. H. Raven, eds.), pp. 3–19. Univ. of Texas Press, Austin.

Finch, S. (1980). Chemical attraction of plant-feeding insects to plants. *Appl. Biol.* **5**, 67–143.

Finch, S., and Skinner, G. (1976). The effect of plant density on populations of the cabbage root fly *(Erioischia brassicae)* and the cabbage stem weevil *(Ceutorhynchus quadridens)* on cauliflowers. *Bull. Entomol. Res.* **66**, 113–123.

Fox, L. R. (1981). Defense and dynamics in plant–herbivore systems. *Am. Zool.* **21**, 853–864.

Futuyma, D., and Wasserman, S. (1980). Resource concentration and herbivory in oak forests. *Science* **210**, 920–922.

Haley, K., and Stone, L. D., eds. (1980). "Search: Theory and Applications." Plenum, New York.

Hassell, M. P. (1978). "The Dynamics of Arthropod Predator–Prey Systems." Princeton Univ. Press, Princeton, New Jersey.

Hawkes, C., and Coaker, T. H. (1976). Behavioral responses to host plant odours in adult cabbage rootfly *(Erioischia brassicae)*. *In* "The Host Plant in Relation to Insect Behavior and Reproduction" (T. Jermy, ed.), pp. 85–89. Plenum, New York.

Horn, D. J. (1981). Effect of weedy backgrounds on colonization of collards by green peach aphid, *Myzus persicae*, and its major predators. *Environ. Entomol.* **10**, 285–289.

Huffaker, C. B., and Messenger, P. S., eds. (1976). "Theory and Practice of Biological Control." Academic Press, New York.

Janzen, D. (1968). Host plants as islands in evolutionary and contemporary time. *Am. Nat.* **102**, 592–595.

Jones, R. E. (1977a). Movement patterns and egg distribution in cabbage butterflies. *J. Anim. Ecol.* **46**, 195–212.

Jones, R. E. (1977b). Search behavior: a study of three caterpillar species. *Behaviour* **60**, 237–259.

Jones, R. E., Gilbert, N., Guppy, M., and Nealis, V. (1980). Long-distance movement of *Pieris rapae*. *J. Anim. Ecol.* **49**, 629–642.

Kareiva, P. (1981). Non-migratory movement and the distribution of herbivorous insects: experiments with plant spacing and the application of diffusion models to mark–recapture data. Ph.D. Dissertation, Cornell University, Ithaca, New York.

Kareiva, P. (1982a). Experimental and mathematical analyses of herbivore movement: quantifying the influence of plant spacing and quality on foraging discrimination. *Ecol. Monogr.* **52**, 261–282.

Kareiva, P. (1982b). Exclusion experiments and the competitive release of insects feeding on collards. *Ecology* **63**, 696–704.

Kemp, W. P., and Simmons, G. A. (1979). Influence of stand factors on survival of early instar spruce budworm. *Environ. Entomol.* **8**, 993–996.

Kiltie, R. A. (1980). Application of search theory to the analysis of prey aggregation as an antipredation tactic. *J. Theor. Biol.* **87**, 201–206.

Kitching, R. (1971). A simple simulation model of dispersal of animals among units of discrete habitats. *Oecologia* **7**, 95–116.

Ludwig, D., Aronson, D., and Weinberger, H. (1979). Spatial patterning of the spruce budworm. *J. Math. Biol.* **8**, 217–258.

Luginbill, P., and McNeal, F. (1958). Influence of seeding density and row spacings on the resistance of spring wheats to the wheat stem sawfly. *J. Econ. Entomol.* **51**, 804–808.

MacGarvin, M. (1982). Species-area relationships of insects on host plants: herbivores on rosebay willowherb. *J. Anim. Ecol.* **51**, 207–223.

McLain, D. K. (1981a). Resource partitioning by three species of hemipteran herbivores on the basis of host plant density. *Oecologia* **48**, 414–417.

McLain, D. K. (1981b). Numerical response of *Murgantia histrionica* to concentrations of its host plant. *J. Ga. Entomol. Soc.* **16**, 257–260.

Mayse, M. (1978). Effects of spacing between rows on soybean arthropod populations. *J. Anim. Ecol.* **15**, 439–450.

Messina, F. J. (1982). Food plant selection by goldenrod leaf beetles: beetle foraging in relation to plant quality. Ph.D. Thesis, Cornell University, Ithaca, New York.

Mistric, W., and Mitchell, E. (1966). Attractiveness of isolated groups of cotton plants to migrating boll weevils. *J. Econ. Entomol.* **59**, 39–41.

Okubo, A. (1980). "Diffusion and Ecological Problems: Mathematical Models." Springer-Verlag, Berlin and New York.

Parker, M. (1982). Herbivore foraging movements and plant population dynamics: the impact of a specialist grasshopper on two arid grassland composites. Ph.D. Dissertation, Cornell University, Ithaca, New York.

Parker, M., and Root, R. B. (1981). Insect herbivores limit habitat distribution of a native composite, *Machaeranthera canescens*. *Ecology* **62**, 1390–1392.

Perrin, R. M. (1977). Pest management in multiple cropping systems. *Agro-Ecosystems* **3**, 93–118.

Perrin, R. M., and Phillips, M. (1978). Some effects of mixed cropping on the population dynamics of insect pests. *Entomol. Exp. Appl.* **24**, 385–393.

Platt, W., Hill, G., and Clark, S. (1974). Seed production in a prairie legume (*Astragalus canadensis* L.). *Oecologia* **17**, 55–63.

Ralph, C. P. (1977a). Search behavior of the large milkweed bug, *Oncopeltus fasciatus* (Hemiptera: Lygaeidae). *Ann. Entomol. Soc. Am.* **70**, 337–342.

Ralph, C. P. (1977b). Effect of host plant density on populations of a specialized, seed-sucking bug, *Oncopeltus fasciatus*. *Ecology* **58**, 799–809.

Rausher, M. (1981). The effect of native vegetation on the susceptibility of *Aristolochia reticulata* (Aristolochiaceae) to herbivore attack. *Ecology* **62**, 1187–1195.

Rausher, M., and Feeny, P. (1980). Herbivory, plant density, and plant reproductive success: the effect of *Battus philenor* on *Aristolochia reticulata*. *Ecology* **61**, 905–917.

Rhoades, D. F. (1979). Evolution of plant chemical defense against herbivores. *In* "Herbivores: Their Interaction with Secondary Plant Metabolites" (G. A. Rosenthal and D. H. Janzen, eds.), pp. 3–54. Academic Press, New York.

Rigby, C., and Lawton, J. (1981). Species–area relationships of arthropods on host plants: herbivores in bracken. *J. Biogeogr.* **8**, 125–133.

Risch, S. (1980). The population dynamics of several herbivorous beetles in a tropical agroecosystem: the effect of intercropping corn, beans and squash in Costa Rica. *J. Appl. Ecol.* **17**, 593–612.

Risch, S. (1981). Insect herbivore abundance in tropical monocultures and polycultures: an experimental test of two hypotheses. *Ecology* **62**, 1325–1340.

Risch, S., Altieri, M., and Andow, D. (1983). Agroecosystem diversity and pest control: data, tentative conclusions and new research directions. *Environ. Entomol.* (in press).

Root, R. B. (1973). Organization of a plant–arthropod association in simple and diverse habitats: the fauna of collards (*Brassica oleracea*). *Ecol. Monogr.* **43**, 95–124.

Root, R. B. (1975). Some consequences of ecosystem texture. *In* "Ecosystem Analysis and Prediction" (S. A. Levin, ed.), pp. 83–95. Soc. Ind. Appl. Math., Philadelphia.

Root, R. B., and Kareiva, P. (1983). The search for resources by cabbage butterflies *(Pieris rapae):* ecological consequences and adaptive significance of markovian movements in a patchy environment. *Ecology* (in press).

Ryan, J., Ryan, M., and McNaeidhe, F. (1980). The effect of interrow plant cover on populations of the cabbage root fly, *Delia brassicae. J. Appl. Ecol.* **17,** 31–40.

Siniff, D., and Jessen, C. (1969). A simulation model of animal movement patterns. *Adv. Ecol. Res.* **6,** 185–219.

Smith, J. (1976). Influence of crop background on aphids and other phytophagous insects on Brussels sprouts. *Ann. Appl. Biol.* **83,** 1–13.

Smith, R., and Whittaker, J. (1980). The influence of habitat type on the population dynamics of *Gastrophysa viridula* Degeer (Coleoptera: Chrysomelidae). *J. Anim. Ecol.* **49,** 225–236.

Solomon, B. P. (1981). Response of a host-specific herbivore to resource density, relative abundance, and phenology. *Ecology* **62,** 1205–1214.

Speight, M., and Lawton, J. (1976). The influence of weed-cover on the mortality imposed on artificial prey by predatory ground beetles in cereal fields. *Oecologia* **23,** 211–223.

Stone, L. D. (1975). "Theory of Optimal Search." Academic Press, New York.

Tahvanainen, J., and Root, R. B. (1972). The influence of vegetational diversity on the population ecology of a specialized herbivore, *Phyllotreta cruciferae* (Coleoptera: Chrysomelidae). *Oecologia* **10,** 321–346.

Taylor, R. J. (1979). The value of clumping to prey when detectability increases with group size. *Am. Nat.* **113,** 299–301.

Thompson, J. (1978). Within-patch structure and dynamics in *Pastinaca sativa* and resource availability to a specialized herbivore. *Ecology* **59,** 443–448.

Thompson, J., and Price, P. (1977). Plant plasticity, phenology, and herbivore dispersion: Wild parsnip and the parship webworm. *Ecology* **58,** 1112–1119.

van der Meijden, E. (1979). Herbivore exploitation of a fugitive plant species: local survival and extinction of the cinnabar moth and ragwort in a heterogeneous environment. *Oecologia* **42,** 307–323.

Peter Kareiva
Division of Biology
Brown University
Providence, Rhode Island

CHAPTER 9

Tracking Variable Host Plants in Space and Time

ROBERT F. DENNO

I. INTRODUCTION

Data from various systems suggest that the host plants herbivorous insects exploit are extremely variable (Roeske *et al.*, 1976; Denno, 1978, 1979; Edmunds and Alstad, 1978, 1981; Jones *et al.*, 1979; McNeill and Southwood, 1978; Whitham, 1978, 1980, 1981; Chapter 1; Denno and Grissell, 1979; Denno *et al.*, 1980; Alstad and Edmunds, Chapter 12; Krischik and Denno, Chapter 14). When referring to variable host plants, I speak of variation in nutrition and allelochemistry (see Roeske *et al.*, 1976; Ikeda *et al.*, 1977; McNeill and Southwood, 1978; Haukioja and Niemelä, 1979; Scriber and Feeny, 1979; Mattson, 1980; Scriber, 1982; Scriber and Slansky, 1981; Berenbaum, 1981; Ryan, Chapter 2; Rhoades,

Chapter 6; Jones, Chapter 15), in predator and competitor density on plants (see Whitham, 1978, 1979, 1981; Chapter 1; McClure, 1979; Chapter 5; Williams and Gilbert, 1981), as well as in the favorableness of overwintering and diapause sites provided by vegetation (see Denno *et al.*, 1981). As a result, insects are faced with locating and using suitable resources amid a complex mosaic of less favorable and unacceptable ones. The consequences for herbivores of choosing or being relegated to poor-quality hosts can be drastic (Mittler, 1958; Auclair, 1966; Dixon, 1970, 1971; White, 1969; van Emden 1972; Horsfield, 1977; McClure, 1977, 1979, 1980; Whitham, 1978, 1979, 1980, 1981; Denno *et al.*, 1980; Raupp and Denno, Chapter 4). It can be as important for a species to place offspring appropriately on a favorable resource as it is to reproduce at all, and the ability to track suitable resources in time and space can be an important factor in the shaping of insect life histories (Southwood 1962, 1977; Dingle, 1972, 1974, 1978, 1979, 1981; Solbreck, 1978; Denno and Grissell, 1979; Denno, *et al.*, 1980; Price, 1980; Denno and Dingle, 1981). In insects, migration and diapause synchronize reproduction with resources in space and time, respectively. Consequently, these behaviors can be viewed as important elements of herbivore life histories, and examples of how they integrate reproduction with appropriate resources have been provided by Blau (1981), Denno *et al.* (1980, 1981), Derr (1980), Dingle (1981), Kennedy (1975), and Solbreck (1978).

Southwood (1962, 1977) has suggested the evolutionary advantage of migration is that it allows organisms (herbivorous insects in this case) to keep pace with changing resources, enabling the escape from deteriorating conditions on current resources and the colonization of more favorable habitats elsewhere. Whitham (1980) has emphasized that increased individual fitness must form the basis for migration and habitat selection. Thus in the course of evolution the members of a species will evolve those life history traits that maximize the number of their descendents in the habitat, which must be viewed in two "dimensions", namely, *time* and *space* (Southwood, 1977). An organism must choose between reproducing "now" and "later" in time, and between "here" and "elsewhere" in space. Each of these choices offers a level of favorableness for reproduction, where favorableness is expressed in terms of r, the mean intrinsic rate of increase, or other measures of fitness such as fecundity (Southwood, 1977). The favorableness of a habitat is dictated by the quantity and quality of resources, the density of predators, parasites, pathogens, intra- and interspecific competitors, and physical factors. However, as Southwood (1977) has pointed out, this is not a complete expression of the probability of reproductive success in relation to the various life history options (reproduction now, later, here, or elsewhere).

Consequently, the chances of surviving diapause and, in the case of migration, successfully finding a new habitat and breeding (the expectancy of "being there") must be considered. Also, variations in the favorableness of habitats in time and space must be taken into account. A complete picture of reproductive success for each life history option is obtained by combining the favorableness of habitats, its variance, and the expectancy of being there (Southwood, 1977).

Often, the contingencies associated with tracking variable resources are very different, particularly to small animals like insects, and cannot be accomplished by a single phenotype (see Levins, 1968; Vepsäläinen, 1974, 1978; Jarvinen and Vepsäläinen, 1976; Denno, 1979; Denno et al., 1980; Harrison, 1980). Consequently, selection may favor a polymorphism in which one morph is more successful under one set of conditions and a different morph(s) thrives under others. Examples include the long-winged (macropters) migrants and flightless forms (short-winged brachypters and apters) of planthoppers and aphids (Lees, 1961, 1966, 1967; Denno, 1976, 1978, 1979) and the migratory and non-migratory forms of milkweed bugs (Dingle, 1978, 1981). The partitioning of individuals between migrants and nonmigrants or between diapausing and nondiapausing individuals will be a reflection of the relative frequencies of reproductive success for each morph (Southwood, 1977). Thus the intensity of migration (proportion of migrants to nonmigrants) exhibited by a population depends on the relative favorableness, permanence, predictability, and isolation of the resource patches it exploits (Southwood, 1962, 1977; Johnson, 1969; Dingle, 1972, 1974, 1978, 1981; Southwood et al., 1974; Denno, 1976, 1978, 1979; Solbreck, 1978; Denno and Grissell, 1979; Denno et al., 1980).

If changes in resource favorability mimic each other in patches here and elsewhere, then diapause rather than migration should be favored when all patches simultaneously deteriorate (Fig. 1A). However, if changes in resource abundance here and elsewhere are not in phase, migration should be favored because as conditions deteriorate here they are improving elsewhere (Fig. 1B). Migration will also be favored where an insect inhabits a relatively persistant habitat here, but changes in conditions elsewhere provide additional but temporary resources for exploitation (Fig. 1C). Solbreck (1978) has suggested this is the case for species that continuously reproduce in a source area but that exploit new habitats during summer when they become available with the seasonal expansion of the resource base.

Denno (1979), Gadgil (1971), Levins (1961, 1962, 1964, 1968), Solbreck (1978), Southwood (1977), and Vepsäläinen (1974, 1978) have provided theoretical models predicting when it is adaptive to migrate, based on

Fig. 1. Predicted life-history responses of herbivorous insects to spatial and temporal changes in the favorableness of resources in patches "here" (——) and "elsewhere" (‑‑‑). (A) Where changes in the favorableness of patches here and elsewhere are similar, better alternatives are not available, and diapause rather than migration should be favored when the quality of all patches is low. (B) In contrast, if the favorableness of patches elsewhere improves while the current patch deteriorates, migration should be favored. (C) If resources are permanently available in one habitat here yet fluctuate seasonally elsewhere, migrations to and from the temporary habitat can occur. From Solbreck (1978).

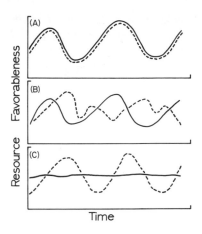

relative patch characteristics. However, little is known for a single species about (1) how host-plant quality, competitor, predator, and parasite density integrate to dictate patch quality and deterioration; (2) what effect a deteriorating patch has on the reproductive success of a herbivore and, subsequently, what the success of the herbivore might be in an alternative newly colonized patch; (3) what environmental cues are used by herbivores to measure patch deterioration and trigger migration; (4) if indeed there are identifiable patches with spatial and temporal differences in favorableness and what the long-term dynamics of these patches are; and (5) how well herbivores track variable hosts by leaving poor-quality patches and moving to better-quality ones. The integration of these factors is central to understanding the tracking problems variable host plants pose for herbivorous insects and to elucidating what combinations of life-history traits allow herbivores to cope with their patchy resources.

In addressing these queries for this chapter, I have chosen to draw primarily on what is known about one plant–herbivore system. The ultimate advantage of this approach is to gain a clearer understanding of the metapopulation dynamics of a single herbivore. The herbivore is a host specific planthopper, *Prokelisia marginata* (Van Duzee), that feeds on *Spartina alterniflora* Lois., an intertidal grass that dominates the vegetation of salt marshes along the eastern and Gulf (of Mexico) coasts of North America. This plant–insect system is particularly attractive for studying the role of migration in population dynamics because (1) both the planthopper and its host grass are abundant (Mobberley, 1956; Blum, 1968; Denno, 1976, 1977; Redfield, 1972); (2) much is known about the natural history and enemies of *P. marginata* (Denno, 1976, 1977); (3), *P. marginata* is dimorphic for wing length [there are both macropters that can fly and flightless, brachypters, facilitating the identification of potential migrants (Denno, 1976, 1977, 1978, 1979)]; (4) the relative dispersal abilities of wing forms are documented (Denno and Grissell, 1979, Tallamy and Denno, 1979; Denno *et al.*, 1980); and (5) the structure and growth dynamics of *S. alterniflora* are diverse (because of a relatively large tidal range on many Atlantic coastal marshes), resulting in an expansive mosaic of variable-quality patches, a situation ideal for the study of how migration allows organisms to cope with changing resources (see Denno and Grissell, 1979; Denno *et al.*, 1980).

In the sections that follow I shall discuss the natural history of the (*Prokelisia marginata–Spartina* system, what constitutes a favorable food item for the planthopper, how food items are organized into patches, how patch favorableness varies in space and time, and how *P. marginata* tracks suitable resources in its harlequin environment.

II. NATURAL HISTORY, DISTRIBUTION, AND ABUNDANCE OF *PROKELISIA MARGINATA*

Prokelisia marginata is by far the most abundant herbivore throughout most of the Atlantic and gulf coast distribution of its host grass, *Spartina alterniflora*. On mid-Atlantic marshes it constitutes 95–99% of all herbivores sampled and is similarly dominant along the gulf coast (Denno, 1976, 1977, 1979; Tallamy and Denno, 1979; Vince *et al.*, 1981). In New Jersey, *P. marginata* is trivoltine, with peaks of adult abundance during May, July, and September (Fig. 2A); adults are absent on the marsh from December through March (Denno, 1976, 1977). At Cedar Key, Florida, the phenology of *P. marginata* is quite different. Adults are present year-round on the marsh, and there are at least six broadly overlapping generations per year, and possibly twice that number (Fig. 2B). Another striking difference between mid-Atlantic and gulf coast locations is the density of *P. marginata* The average number of individuals in a 30-sweep sample taken on the high marsh in New Jersey is 1000 (annual average based on 12 samples taken at monthly intervals) whereas at Cedar Key the same sample contains only 225 planthoppers. The density discrepancy is even greater when one corrects for differences in the standing-crop biomass of *S. alterniflora* between locations. When this is done, the load of *P. marginata* (number of planthoppers per gram dry weight of *Spartina* leaf blade) is on the average 10 times greater on mid-Atlantic compared to gulf coast sites.

Nymphs (there are five instars) and adults feed on the phloem sap of *Spartina alterniflora*. Females insert their eggs between the blade ridges

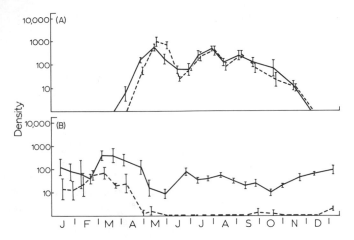

Fig. 2. Seasonal density (no. individuals/30 sweeps) of the wing forms of *Prokelisia marginata* in stands of short-form *Spartina alterniflora* in Manahawkin, New Jersey (A) and Cedar Key, Florida (B). *Prokelisia marginata* is trivoltine in New Jersey, with adults absent during winter. In Florida there are at least six generations annually, and adults are present year-round. Brachypters (——); macropters (– – –).

on adaxial leaf surfaces. Most planthoppers feed and oviposit toward the axil and central portion of the blade, although feeding scars and oviposition punctures can be found throughout the blade. For the most part, the stem, leaf sheath, and central furled blade are not used for either feeding or oviposition. Active nymphs overwinter in litter or rolled, dead leaves of standing vegetation (Denno, 1977). Tallamy and Denno (1979) showed that, if litter is removed in autumn, significantly smaller populations occur the following season, suggesting that litter is a critical resource for winter survival.

On the salt marsh, planthoppers must contend with rising tidewaters, which occasionally inundate the entire grass system. As tidewaters rise, nymphs and adults retreat up the culms of the grass (Denno and Grissell, 1979). Davis and Gray (1966) observed similar behavior in the laboratory. When dislodged from their holds in the field, individuals hop along the surface film toward a culm and leap onto it. Younger nymphs are less effective than older nymphs or adults at relocating plants. When Davis and Gray (1966) artificially submerged individuals in the laboratory, they found none surviving beyond 5 hr. Furthermore, I have slowly drawn small grass blades containing adult planthoppers under the water in the field and watched them pop to the surface almost immediately. However, while snorkeling along tidal creek banks, Vince *et al.* (1981) observed *Prokelisia marginata* trapped in air bubbles under water during high tide. It may be that the channel of air that becomes trapped in the concavity of large, submerged grass blades provides sufficient oxygen for some individuals to withstand an inundation. Regardless, the point is that the larger the plant, either by virtue of its height or by the size of the meniscus of air it provides, the greater the refuge it offers to planthoppers as the tidewaters rise.

III. WING DIMORPHISM IN *PROKELISIA MARGINATA*, MECHANISMS OF ITS DETERMINATION, AND CORRELATES WITH REPRODUCTION

Populations of planthoppers contain two discrete wing forms (Kisimoto, 1965; Raatikainen, 1967; Denno, 1976, 1978). There are long-winged macropters, which can fly, and flightless, short-winged brachypters. Macropters are effective at colonizing new resources and escaping deteriorating ones, because of their ability to fly (Denno and Grissell, 1979; Denno et al., 1980). Brachypters do not have this capability except over very short (<5 m) distances (see Raatikainen, 1967; Denno et al., 1980). Thus macropters are the adaptive morph in temporary habitats (Denno, 1978, 1979).

Although it is not currently known for *Prokelisia marginata*, brachypters of several other planthopper species have a higher fecundity and/or oviposit at an earlier age compared to macropters (Tsai et al., 1964; Kisimoto, 1965; Nasu, 1969; May, 1971; Mochida, 1973). As a result, the reproductive potential of brachypters is greater than that of macropters. Also, because of their flightlessness, brachypters are more likely to remain on the immediate resource. Laboratory observations show that during a disturbance brachypters are much more sessile, unresponsive, and more reluctant to jump from a blade than their long-winged counterparts. For these reasons, brachypters can more effectively exploit the current patch (Denno and Grissel, 1979), particularly if it occurs in a climatically harsh habitat, where it is adaptive to balance high mortality with increased reproductive effort.

Based on reciprocal crosses between brachypters and macropters of several economic-pest species of planthoppers, Kisimoto (1956, 1965) and Raatikainen (1967) concluded that wing form is not inherited by any simple genetic rule. Wing form is mediated by an individual's response during the nymphal stage to various proximate environmental cues (e.g., host-plant quality) that measure the probability of current resource deterioration (Kisimoto, 1956, 1965; Mochida, 1973). As long as conditions remain favorable on the current resource, the developmental switch responds with the production of a short-winged adult. Environmental cues associated with deteriorating patch quality result in the production of a long-winged individual (see Denno and Grissell, 1979; Denno et al., 1980).

For several species of planthoppers poor plant nutrition and crowded conditions incurred during the nymphal stage lead to the production of macropters (Kisimoto, 1956; Johno, 1963; Raatikainen, 1967; Mochida and Kisomoto, 1971; Mochida, 1973; Drosopolous, 1977). Johno (1963), Mochida and Kisimoto (1971); and Mochida (1973) have shown that high densities of nymphs lower the nutritional quality of host plants, indirectly resulting in long-winged forms. Johno (1963) suggested that physical stimulation alone among nymphs can alter wing form and also showed that adults of *Laodelphax striatellus* have an effect on the determination of the wing form of another species, *Nilaparvata lugens*, when they are reared together. Photoperiod as a proximate environmental cue has been shown to have major effects on the determination of wing form in certain species (Drosopolous, 1977), yet not in others (Kisimoto, 1956). Due to the lack of consistant generational differences in the proportion of wing forms on the same marsh, where photoperiod changes drastically throughout the year (Fig. 2A), as well as major differences in the wing-form compositon of planthopper populations on marshes that share the same photoperiod (see Denno and Grissell, 1979), I suggest that photoperiod very likely plays little or no role in the determination of wing form in *Prokelisia marginata*.

Denno (1976) and Denno and Grissell (1979) have strongly implicated crowding as an environmental cue used to predict habitat deterioration and determine wing form in *Prokelisia marginata*. There is a positive relationship between the proportion of macropterous adults in New Jersey and Florida populations and the level of crowding they incur during the nymphal stage (Fig. 3). These correlations suggest that crowding either directly or indirectly by influencing host-plant quality, is an important determinant of wing form throughout the geographic range of *P. marginata*. Differences in the slopes of the New Jersey and Florida regressions may suggest that a genetic difference exists between populations, because for the same increment increase in crowding, proportionately more macropters are produced in New Jersey (see Denno and Grissell, 1979).

IV. POTENTIAL COMPETITORS, PREDATORS, AND PARASITES OF *PROKELISIA MARGINATA*

In addition to host plants, the competitors and enemies of *P. marginata* may contribute to patch quality; consequently, a bit about their life history is appropriate. Four other sap-feeding insects feed on *Spartina alterniflora* on mid-Atlantic marshes, but together they represent less than

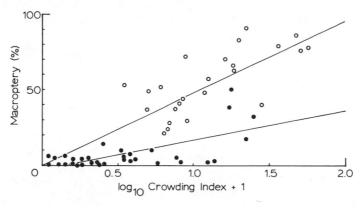

Fig. 3. Relationship between the intensity of crowding incurred as nymphs and macroptery in populations of *Prokelisia marginata* at Tuckerton, New Jersey (○, *r* = 0.739**) and Cedar Key, Florida (●, *r* = 0.683**). From Denno and Grissell (1979). Copyright 1979, the Ecological Society of America.

5% of the annual total of sap-feeders (Denno, 1976, 1977, 1979; Tallamy and Denno, 1979). Two trivoltine, wing-dimorphic planthoppers, *Delphacodes detecta* (Van Duzee) and *Megamelus lobatus* Beamer, occur frequently on the marsh, particularly during fall. Both embed their eggs in the grass with saw-like ovipositors. *Megamelus lobatus* overwinters as eggs (Denno *et al.*, 1981) and *D. detecta* overwinters as nymphs. The leafhopper *Sanctanus aestuarium* (D. & S.), is bivoltine, monomorphic (macropterous) for wing length, embeds its eggs in vegetation, and overwinters as eggs. *Trigonotylus uhleri* (Reuter), a mirid bug, is also bivoltine, macropterous, inserts its eggs in the furled central blades of the grass, and overwinters as eggs. At Cedar Key, Florida, all of these sap-feeders are present, but *M. lobatus* and *S. aestuarium* are rare. Two other sap-feeders, a leafhopper, *Carneocephala floridana* (Ball), and the lygaeid bug *Ischnodemus badius* Van D. join the herbivore community on *S. alterniflora*, but they too are overshadowed by the dominant *P. marginata*.

Four species of spiders are abundant on mid-Atlantic and New England intertidal marshes and are predators on *Prokelisia marginata*. *Pardosa floridana* Banks (Lycosidae) and *Clubiona littoralis* Banks are large (≤1 cm), free-roaming animals, and *Dictyna roscida* (Hentz) (Dictynidae) and *Grammonota inornata* Emerton (Linyphiidae) are very small (≤3 mm), web-building predators. Delphacids, particularly macropters of *Prokelisia marginata*, are commonly captured in the webs of *G. inornata* in New Jersey, and Vince *et al.* (1981) have made the same observation on Massachusetts marshes. Pooled spider density is greatest during late summer, and *Pardosa floridana* produces two generations per year (Fig. 4).

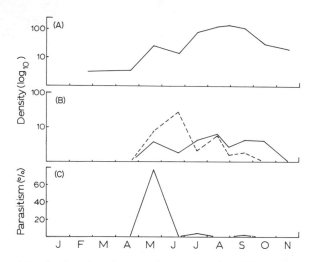

Fig. 4. Seasonal distribution of predators and parasitism of *Prokelisia marginata* at Tuckerton, New Jersey. (A) Density (no./30 sweeps) of spiders. (B) Density (no./30 sweeps) of *Tytthus vagus*, an egg predator. – – –, Nymphs; ——, adults. (C) Parasitism of nymphs by *Elenchus koebelei* and *Haplogonatopus americanus*.

Tytthus vagus (Knight), a mirid bug, feeds on the eggs of *Prokelisia marginata* and is particularly abundant in May (Fig. 4B). Two nymphal parasitoids, the strepsipteran *Elenchus koebelei* Pierce (Elenchidae) and the wasp *Haplogonatopus americanus* Perkins (Dryinidae) together can account for approximately 80% of the parasitism (Fig. 4C). Parasitism by these animals results in deformed external genitalia, rudimentary gonads, and loss of reproductive capability in adult planthoppers (Kathirithamby, 1977). Despite this, nymphal parisitism is high for only a short time during May, and its importance as a mortality factor seems small compared to predation.

At Cedar Key, Florida, the community of predators in *Spartina alterniflora* is similar to that on mid-Atlantic marshes; it is dominated by spiders and the egg predator *Tytthus vagus* (R.F. Denno, unpublished data). However, the average load of predators is much greater at Cedar Key. The number of spiders per 1000 sap-feeders is $\bar{x} = 181$ in New Jersey, compared to $\bar{x} = 402$ in Florida ($P < 0.01$, F test). Similarly, the number of *T. vagus* per 1000 sap-feeders is $\bar{x} = 22$ and 71 for New Jersey and Florida marshes, respectively ($P < 0.01$, F test). Stiling and Strong (1982) studied the intensity of *Prokelisia marginata* egg parasitism by the parasitoid *Anagrus delicatus* at Oyster Bay, Florida, on the gulf coast. They found an inverse density-dependent response and suggested that fluctuating tidewaters limited parasitoid search, resulting in the inverse pattern. They also suggested that a weak numerical response on the part of the parasitoid population could yield a similar inverse density-dependent response. Regardless, the feeling that one gets with what little data are available is that predation more than parasitism is an important mortality factor.

Vince *et al.* (1981) have suggested that delphacids are more susceptible to spider predation than other salt-marsh herbivores, due to their small size and more conspicuous feeding position (recall that they feed in the blade axils). Vince *et al.* also reported that numerical increases in populations of *Prokelisia marginata* can be checked by spider predation. These data strongly suggest that predation is an important mortality factor in northern marshes and that, coupled with my data on predator loads, predation may be even more important in Florida.

V. DISTRIBUTION, STRUCTURE, AND GROWTH DYNAMICS OF *SPARTINA ALTERNIFLORA*

Along most of the Atlantic coast, *Spartina alterniflora* dominates the vegetation of the intertidal marsh, where it commonly occurs as extensive pure stands (Adams, 1963; Duncan, 1974). On the north-central Atlantic coast of Florida, salt-marsh vegetation rapidly grades into mangrove. Here, *S. alterniflora* occurs as a narrow fringe of vegetation on the seaward edge of the mangrove (Turner, 1976). On the gulf coast, large stands of *S. alterniflora* are uncommon, and the grass is usually confined to a narrow but extensive strip of streamside vegetation that borders the bay and tidal creeks in the marsh (Turner and Gosselink, 1975; Turner, 1976).

Within the intertidal zone, *Spartina alterniflora* occupies a rather wide elevation range of sites from approximately mean high water level (MHW) to as much as 2 m below MHW (Blum, 1968; Redfield, 1972). The plant structure of *S. alterniflora* changes dramatically with marsh elevation, and two forms (tall and short) are commonly recognized at most Atlantic coast localities (Miller and Egler, 1950; Teal, 1962; Adams, 1963; Blum, 1968; Redfield, 1972; Squiers and Good, 1974; Hatcher and Mann, 1975; Denno and Grissell, 1979; Denno *et al.*, 1980). Along the depressed margins of regularly flooded creek banks, the vegetation is composed of robust plants reaching heights well over 2 m (Redfield, 1972; Squiers and Good, 1974). However, at approximately MHW, the plants occur as a dense bed of short rosettes that attain heights of only 10–40 cm (Blum, 1968). Many of the salt marshes of the Atlantic coast are characterized by large expanses of the short form on the high marsh, which abruptly intergrade into a fringe of tall form that borders the serpentine array of tidal creeks.

New shoots of both growth forms appear during spring, and by summer or early fall maximum live standing crop is attained. Rosettes of the short form senesce during late fall, but they remain in place over winter and then decay over the course of the next season (Squiers and Good, 1974). Subsequently, there is a loose lattice of dead culms and blades permanently associated with the short-form habitat. Contrarily, the action of winter tides, winds, and ice shear off the culms of the tall form, often leaving exposed creek banks free of litter. Debris from primarily tall-form sites is carried out to sea or transported by tides around the marsh where it often accumulates as mats. Squiers and Good (1974) and Teal (1962) reported that both growth forms follow this pattern in New Jersey and Georgia, respectively, and it is probably safe to assume that these grass dynamics are representative of most Atlantic coastal marshes.

On gulf coast marshes, stream-side plants are generally shorter, and the gradient in grass structure from creek-side to high-marsh sites is far less pronounced than in Atlantic marshes (Turner and Gosselink, 1975). Turner (1976) has suggested that the low tidal amplitude along the gulf coast may partially explain the difference in grass structure, particularly the reduced stream-side productivity, between gulf and Atlantic populations of *Spartina alterniflora*.

The growth dynamics of the grass on the gulf coast contrasts with that in Atlantic marshes because the nearly subtropical climate allows for continuous growth throughout the year, although there are certainly seasonal cycles (Kirby and Gosselink, 1976; Turner, 1976). Also, probably for reasons concerning reduced tidal energy and the absence of ice, the destruction of stream-side vegetation during winter is minor, as evidenced by the large amounts of litter or standing dead culms at that time (Kirby and Gosselink, 1976; Denno and Grissell, 1979).

On most Atlantic coastal marshes *Spartina alterniflora* occurs in two dynamically different habitats. In one (high marsh), grass persists and provides requisites for planthoppers year round. In the other (stream side), resources do not remain during winter because vegetation is sheared off by the action of winds, waves, and ice and is carried away by tidewaters. However, during June, the resource base expands with the proliferation of stream-side vegetation, which provides vacant and more abundant resources (Denno and Grissell, 1979; Denno et al., 1980).

Changes in the live biomass, stand height, leaf surface area, culm density, and litter biomass of *Spartina alterniflora* along an elevational gradient from stream side to high marsh in New Jersey and Florida marshes are compared in Figs. 5 and 6, emphasizing the habitat differences in structure and growth dynamics of *S. alterniflora* on Atlantic coastal marshes and the relative homogeneity of gulf coast grass.

VI. FOOD ITEMS, PATCHES, AND HABITATS AS LEVELS OF RESOURCE ORGANIZATION

In order to understand the problems variable resources pose for herbivores, it is essential to know what a favorable resource is and how it is dispersed among less suitable and unacceptable ones. The problem of resource definition is in no way straightforward, as is evidenced by discussions of patch and habitat in the foraging-theory literature (see Hassell and Southwood, 1978; Krebs and Davies, 1978; Morse, 1980). For consistency I have chosen to follow the resource hierarchy proposed by Hassell and Southwood (1978) of *food item, patch,* and *habitat.* For caterpillars, Hassell and Southwood proposed that leaves are food items, yet we know that not all leaves on a plant are suitable for herbivore development (Denno *et al.,* 1980; Whitham, 1981). The definition of food item is even more difficult for sap-feeding herbivores, like planthoppers, that feed on the constantly changing and chemically complex contents of the phloem under certain conditions yet change their fidelity to other plant cells (e.g., parenchyma) under other conditions (Chang, 1978; Chang and Ota, 1978). As Hassell and Southwood (1978) have pointed out, we must look to the *forager* and its behavior to identify food items. Consequently, the larger leaves of cottonwood trees serve as favorable food items for *Pemphigus* gall aphids because colonizing stem mothers selectively initiate gall formation on large leaves, where their fitness is maximized compared to small leaves (Whitham, 1980, 1981; Chapter 1). Similarly, other aphid species (Dixon, 1970; McNeill and Southwood, 1978), planthoppers (Denno *et al.,* 1980, 1981), spittlebugs (Horsfield, 1977), and scale insects (McClure, 1980; Chapter 5) all select to feed on a subset of plant parts from an array of those availiable on a single plant or culm. Thus, despite changes in the probing behavior of sap-feeders among plant cells within a leaf, there is strong behavioral selection taking place at the level of the plant part, and it seems realistic to consider favorable plant parts (e.g., terminal young leaves of a suitable host) as food items for herbivorous insects. This is with the understanding that the favorableness of food items may vary as a result of intrinsic and herbivore-induced changes in plant allelochemistry and nutrition (Dixon, 1970; Way and Cammell, 1970; McClure, 1977, 1979; Haukioja and Niemelä, 1979; McKey, 1979; Rhoades, 1979; Chapter 6), competitors (Whitham, 1978, 1980; Williams and Gilbert, 1981; Raupp and Denno, Chapter

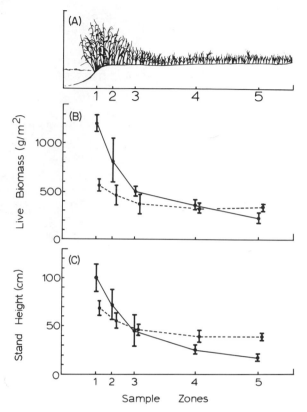

Fig. 5. (A) Stylized profile of the structure of *Spartina alterniflora* along an elevational gradient from creek bank (zone 1) to high marsh (zone 5) at Tuckerton, New Jersey. The centers of the five zones of vegetation are depicted. Comparative July profiles of the live standing-crop biomass (B) and absolute stand height (C) of *S. alterniflora* in each of the vegetation zones at Tuckerton, New Jersey (——) and Cedar Key, Florida (–––). Intervals around means are 1 SD (standard deviation). From Denno and Grissell (1979). Copyright 1979, the Ecological Society of America.

4; McClure, Chapter 5), predators and parasites (Herrebout *et al.*, 1963; Herrebout, 1969; Hassell and Southwood, 1978), and physical factors (Dixon, 1970). As a consequence of such factors, herbivores may switch food items, as is the case when colonies of *Aphis fabae* move from terminals to the flower shoots and pods of bean plants, are relegated to poorer quality food items (see Whitham, 1978), or lose food items altogether (Dixon, 1970). The ultimate result of the combined actions of these factors is almost invariably a heterogeneous spatial distribution of

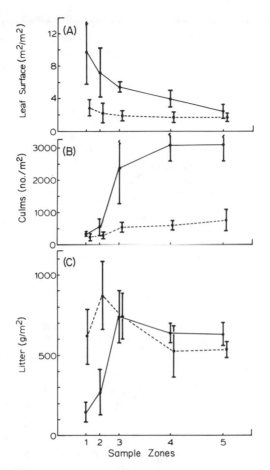

Fig. 6. Comparative July profiles of the ratio of adaxial leaf surface to ground surface area (A), culm density (B), and February profiles of litter biomass (both standing and fallen) (C) of *Spartinia alterniflora* in each of the five vegetation zones at Tuckerton, New Jersey (——) and Cedar Key, Florida (–––). Intervals around means are 1 SD. From Denno and Grissell (1979). Copyright 1979, the Ecological Society of America.

food items. Thus aggregations of food items allow for the identification of patches, the next level in the hierarchy of resource organization (see Hassell and Southwood, 1978).

Patches can be readily identified if food items are distributed as discrete units. For instance, if a mosaic of grass stands is composed of some stands entirely in flower and others totally vegetative, those in flower may be recognized as patches to an herbivore that feeds selectively on seed heads. Identifying patches is often not as easy as this. In pure expanses of native grass species, flowering frequency often varies tremendously along a line transect (e.g., Denno *et al.*, 1980). Does a stand in which only 10% of the culms flower cease to be a patch because favorable food items are rare and difficult to find? Again, the herbivore itself defines the patch, and we must look for changes in its behavior to identify patch boundaries (Hassell and Southwood, 1978). Thus, as Hassell and Southwood have pointed out, a patch is an area containing a stimulus or simuli that at the appropriate intensity elicit a characteristic foraging activity in a responsive herbivore.

Patches themselves are not uniformly distributed in the environment (Hassell and Southwood, 1978). They tend to be aggregated like food items, which allows us to define the habitat, the third level in the organizational hierarchy of resources, as an aggregation of patches. A straightforward example of how patches of food items can be aggregated in different habitats is provided by aphids (e.g., *Hyalopterus pruni* and *Pemphigus trehernei*) that fly between alternate host plants seasonally (see Johnson, 1969; Foster, 1975a,b; Foster and Treherne, 1978). *Pemphigus trehernei* forms galls on its upland, overwintering host *(Populus)* yet undergoes annual interhabitat migrations to and from its summer host, *Aster tripolium*, a salt-marsh halophyte (Foster, 1975a). Thus locating appropriate alternate hosts during interhabitat flights of *P. trehernei* (Foster and Treherne, 1978) poses resource-tracking problems of a scale different from the within-habitat obstacles that individual variable poplar trees present to colonizing *Pemphigus betae*, a closely related aphid (see Whitham, 1978, 1979, 1981).

In Sections VII–IX, I define what a favorable food item is for the planthopper *Prokelisia marginata*, show that food items are heterogeniously distributed at the level of the patch as well as between habitats, and discuss the set of life-history traits that have evolved, allowing these animals to cope with variable host plants.

VII. MICROHABITAT DISTRIBUTION OF PLANTHOPPERS ON GRASS ROSETTES AND THE DEFINITION OF FAVORABLE FOOD ITEMS

Adults of *Prokelisia marginata* (both wing forms) occur most abundantly on the seed heads of flowering rosettes (Fig. 7) and the subterminal, unfurled leaf blades of nonflowering rosettes (Fig. 8). The apical, furled blade of nonflowering plants does not have the adaxial surface exposed and is thereby not available for feeding and oviposition until it uncoils. The general trend is for planthopper density to decline along a gradient

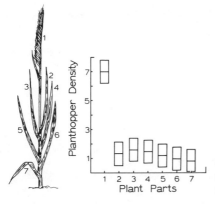

Fig. 7. Number of adult planthoppers on the individual plant parts of a flowering short-form *Spartina alterniflora* rosette. Numbers along the abscissa rank plant parts from seed head (1) to basal leaf (7) and correspond to the labeled parts on the stylized rosette to the left. Intervals around means are least significant differences (LDSs). Means with non-overlapping LSDs are significantly different ($P < 0.05$). From Denno *et al.* (1980). Copyright 1980, the Ecological Society of America.

of available leaves, from the top to the base of culms. This trend is particularly clear on nonflowering rosettes (Fig. 8) but breaks down on flowering ones, because seed heads are apparently so attractive for feeding. When adjacent rosettes from a mixed stand are compared, flowering rosettes support a mean of 13.57 planthopper adults per plant and nonflowering ones only 3.57 ($t_{58} = -6.276$, $P < 0.001$; Denno *et al.*, 1980).

Undehisced seed heads of *Spartina alterniflora* contain the highest amount of crude protein (12.20%), and crude protein per leaf decreases along a gradient from the apex to the base in both flowering (9.26–6.36%) and nonflowering (9.43–6.03%) rosettes. The relationship between crude protein per plant part and the position of the plant part along the vertical axis of the plant is significant ($r^2 = 0.896$, $P < 0.01$; Fig. 9). The relationship between the number of adult planthoppers per plant part and the crude protein (%) in plant parts is significant ($r^2 = 0.931$, $P < 0.01$; Fig. 10). Most of the points for flowering plants fall above the regression line, whereas those for nonflowering ones fall below, suggesting that flowering plants are more attractive to planthop-

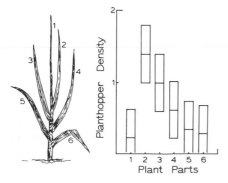

Fig. 8. Number of adult planthoppers on the individual plant parts of a nonflowering short-form *Spartina alterniflora* rosette. Numbers along the abscissa rank plant parts from terminal (1) to basal leaf (6) and correspond to the labeled parts on the stylized rosette to the left. LSDs as in Fig. 7. From Denno *et al.* (1980). Copyright 1980, the Ecological Society of America.

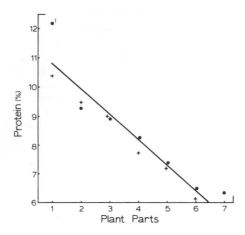

Fig. 9. Relationship between mean crude-protein content in individual plant parts and the position of plant parts along the vertical axis of the plant from the apex (1) to the base (7). ●, Flowering; +, nonflowering. The seed head is designated with a 1. Means are based on three observations; the regression equation is $y = -0.850x + 11.541$, $r^2 = 0.896$, $P < 0.01$. From Denno *et al.* (1980). Copyright 1980, the Ecological Society of America.

pers. The furled central blade (Fig. 10, point 2) of nonflowering plants is excluded from the regression because it is not accessible to planthoppers for feeding. The upshot of these patterns is that individuals of *Prokelisia marginata* feed on the most nutritious available rosette and plant tissue, and mean crude protein content appears to play a major role in their choice of microhabitat (see also Denno *et al.*, 1980).

Vince *et al.* (1981) found that females of *Prokelisia marginata* were larger and much more fecund when fed on fertilized compared to nonfertilized *Spartina alterniflora*. Densities of nymphs greater by factors of 5–10 resulted from females fed fertilized grass (2.4% nitrogen = 15.0% crude protein) compared to those fed normal grass (1.2% nitrogen = 7.5% crude protein). Thus the fitness of *P. marginata* is increased greatly by feeding on high-quality rosettes or tissues, as has been shown for many other sap-feeding insects (Mittler, 1958; van Emden, 1966; White, 1969; Dixon, 1970; Auclair, 1976; Horsfield, 1977; McClure, 1977, 1979; Slansky and Feeny, 1977; McNeill and Southwood, 1978).

Once on a *Spartina* culm, both nymphs and adults are able to move and select the most favorable plant part. Even the very sessile first-instar nymphs can be seen moving from the subterminal to the terminal blade as it uncoils and becomes available for feeding (observed in small lab cages). However, early instars, because of their sessility and the distance between culms, are relegated to the culm in which their mother ovi-

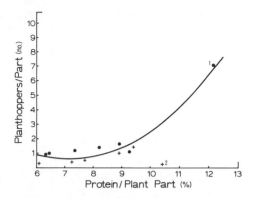

Fig. 10. Relationship between mean ($n = 3$) crude-protein content in individual plant parts and the mean ($n = 30$) density of adult planthoppers on plant parts for flowering (●) and nonflowering (+) rosettes of *Spartina alterniflora*. The number 1 identifies the seed head of flowering plants, and 2 identifies the furled blade of nonflowering rosettes, which was omitted from the regresson because it is not available to planthoppers. $y = 0.249x^2 - 3.575x + 13.394$, $r^2 = 0.931$, $P < 0.01$. From Denno *et al.* (1980). Copyright 1980, the Ecological Society of America.

posited. As older instars (≥third) and adults, individuals can easily move among adjacent culms. Consequently, once colonized, microhabitat variation on a culm and among adjacent culms (early instars excepted) does not pose tracking problems for *Prokelisia marginata*, as it might for less mobile insects like scales.

Even with this information at hand it is not easy to define a favorable food item for *Prokelisia marginata*. The behavioral responses of *P. marginata*, coupled with a strong precedent in the literature (Dixon, 1973; Southwood and McNeill, 1978; Mattson, 1980; Bernays, 1981; Scriber, 1982; Scriber and Slansky, 1981), suggest that plant tissues high in crude protein or nitrogen (6.25 × nitrogen content = crude-protein content) are critical to the development of phytophagous intects. This is not to suggest that nitrogen content is the only feature of host plants that is important and that the nutrition and allelochemistry of plants are in any way simple, only that nitrogen or crude protein are often good predictors of plant-part favorableness. Based on the behavioral and fecundity responses of *P. marginata* (Denno *et al.*, 1980, in prep.; Vince *et al.*, 1981), plant parts containing 10% or more crude protein are probably very favorable for development, whereas those containing less than 7% crude protein are not likely to be suitable for development. Thus favorable food items for *P. marginata* are for the most part restricted to the seed heads, terminal blades (*if* they are unfurled), and subterminal blades of *Spartina alterniflora*.

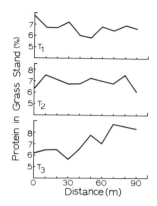

Fig. 11. Three 90-m transects (T₁–T₃) showing spatial variation of crude-protein content in a stand of short-form *Spartina alterniflora*, during early September at Tuckerton, New Jersey. From Denno *et al.* (1980). Copyright 1980, the Ecological Society of America.

VIII. WITHIN-HABITAT VARIATION IN THE FAVORABLENESS OF *SPARTINA ALTERNIFLORA*: DIFFERENCES IN PATCH SELECTION BETWEEN WING FORMS

In this section evidence is provided showing that (1) the quality of *Spartina alterniflora* in the high marsh habitat alone is highly variable; (2) the distance between high-quality patches is beyond the ambit of brachypters but not macropters; (3) macropters are able to select favorable patches over less suitable ones; and (4) migration (macroptery) should be favored under these conditions.

I used the crude protein (%) in short-form *Spartina alterniflora* as an indicator of stand quality. Measured at 10-m intervals in the high marsh habitat in September, there is considerable variability in crude protein (three 90-m transects are shown in Fig. 11). Also, the frequency of flowering culms on the high marsh is highly variable (Fig. 12), and there is a significant positive relationship ($r^2 = 0.388$, $P < 0.01$) between the crude protein in the stand of grass and flowering frequency in the local area (Denno *et al.*, 1980). Together, these data suggest that favorable food items are patchy in their distribution.

Several pieces of information support the contention that macropters are much better than brachypters at locating high-quality patches of vegetation. First, although there is a significant positive relationship between the density of both wing forms and the concentration of crude protein in local stands of grass (also frequency of flowering rosettes), the slope of the regression line is much steeper for macropters than brachypters (Fig. 13). This suggests that macropters are more successful at moving from low- to high-quality vegetation. The significant rela-

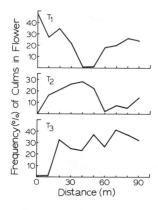

Fig. 12. Three 90-m transects (T_1–T_3) showing spatial variation in the frequency of flowering in a stand of short-form *Spartina alterniflora*, during early September at Tuckerton, New Jersey. From Denno *et al.* (1980). Copyright 1980, the Ecological Society of America.

tionship between grass quality and brachypter density suggests that brachypters are not entirely inept colonizers of high-quality patches, but this is probably the result of short-distance (<10 m) movements from adjacent areas of lower-quality grass. However, the effective area in which brachypters are able to select habitats is probably infinitesimal compared to macropters.

A set of field manipulations further documents the differential colonizing abilities of the two wing forms. Small field plots (100 m²) were established in the high-marsh habitat, and four different treatments were applied. Two highly favorable plots were artificially created by fertilizing them biweekly from May through September (see Denno *et al.*, in prep.). The crude-protein content of *Spartina alterniflora* can be significantly elevated and sustained above ambient levels throughout summer by fertilization (Valiela *et al.*, 1978; Denno *et al.*, in prep.). Two other plots were chronically defaunated with biweekly applications of the short-lived, systemic insecticide Orthene (Willcox and Coffey, 1977). Orthene has a half-life of about 5 days in the plant. Consequently, reproduction and development on the grass were drastically reduced, but colonization and establishment by adults were not affected that much during the last half of the 2-week sampling interval, when plants were not toxic. Thus the relative colonizing abilities of morphs could be studied. Two other plots were both chronically fertilized and sprayed with Orthene, and four others were untreated and left as controls (see Denno *et al.*, in prep., for details on methods).

The relative colonizing abilities of the two wing forms are shown in Fig. 14. Macropters colonized chronically defaunated, fertilized plots with two bouts of immigration, once in May–June and again in July. These colonization bouts correspond to peak abundances of first- and

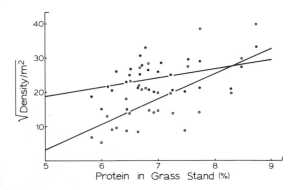

Fig. 13. Relationship between crude-protein content of the stand and the density of macropters [○; $y = -33.959 + 7.439x$ ($r^2 = 0.419$, $P < 0.01$)] and brachypters [●; $y = 5.478 + 2.681x$ ($r^2 = 0.162$, $P < 0.05$)] of *Prokelisia marginata* at Tuckerton, New Jersey. The slopes of the regressions are significantly different ($t_{52} = 2.272$, $P < 0.05$). From Denno *et al.* (1980). Copyright 1980, the Ecological Society of America.

second-generation adults (see Fig. 2A). In contrast, following the first application of Orthene, brachypters were rare in the fertilized *Spartina alterniflora*, demonstrating their poor colonizing ability (Fig. 14). The combined effects of colonization, accumulation, and reproduction on the density of the two wing forms are shown in plots that were fertilized but not sprayed with Orthene (Fig. 15). The first peak of adults following the fertilization treatment was dominated by colonizing macropters, which accumulated at a faster rate than brachypters. Notice too that prior to fertilization the trend was reversed, with brachypters the more abundant morph. Furthermore, nymphs were not molting to adults at this time (Denno *et al.*, in prep.), substantiating the fact that differential colonization by macropters rather than on-site reproduction was responsible for their abundance in May. By July brachypters were nearly as abundant as macropters (Fig. 15). This is attributable in large part to on-site reproduction, because nymphs that peaked in abundance in June molted to both brachypters and macropters.

The fitness payoffs of colonizing high-quality (fertilized) patches can be realized by significantly higher densities ($P < 0.01$, F test) of nymphs (Fig. 16A) and brachypters (Fig. 16B) there, compared to normal (unfertilized) control vegetation. Vince *et al.* (1981) found a similar response by *Prokelisia marginata*, in some of their fertilized *Spartina* plots on a Massachusetts marsh. I omitted macropters in support of this argument because their desities can be strongly governed by immigration and emigration, whereas the densities of sessile nymphs and brachypters are much more likely to reflect differences in survivorship and fecundity.

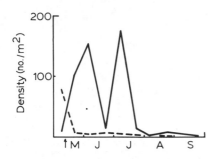

Fig. 14. Relative colonizing abilities of the macropters (——) and barachypters (– – –) of *Prokelisia marginata*. Seasonal densities of wing forms in chronically fertilized and defaunated (Orthene) plots of short-form *Spartina alterniflora* during 1981 at Tuckerton, New Jersey. Arrow on the abscissa indicates first treatment. Wing-form abundance is the result of colonization only; development is prevented by chronic defaunation.

Another question central to understanding the population dynamics of *Prokelisia marginata* on *Spartina* concerns the ability of macropters to discirminate and select high-quality patches over those of lesser quality. In answer to this question I turn again to the densities of wing morphs in small field plots, half of which were chronically treated with Orthene and fertilized (high quality) and the other half chronically treated with Orthene only (normal quality). The densities of macropters were significantly higher ($P < 0.01$, F test) on fertilized *Spartina* compared to unfertilized grass during both May–June and July, when first- and second-generation adults were, respectively, most abundant (Fig. 17A). In contrast, there were no significant differences ($P > 0.05$, F test) in the density of brachypters in fertilized and unfertilized plots (Fig. 17B). These data strongly suggest that macropters are able to identify and select high-quality patches from those of lesser quality, but that brachypters are unable to do so efficiently, probably because of their relative immobility.

There are several reasons for believing that the occurrence of high-quality flowering patches of vegetation in the high marsh includes elements of uncertainly in time and space. In the Tuckerton study marsh in New Jersey, flowering and seed set of *Spartina alterniflora* occur during August and early September, and most plants shed their seed by mid-September (Squiers and Good, 1974). However, there are phenological differences in flowering among patches of grass (Squiers and Good, 1974), as well as the spatial differences that I have pointed out. These probably result from subtle environmental differences or genetic differences between parapatric clones (*S. alterniflora* spreads vegetatively by rhizomes as well as reproducing sexually; see Redfield, 1972). That the amount of crude protein (%) explains only 38% of the variability in the frequency of flowering ($r^2 = 0.384$) is consistent with the argument that some patches flower before others (Denno et al., 1980).

Also, there are several reasons for believing that the planthoppers themselves may contribute to the unpredictable demise of local patches

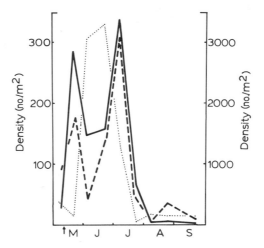

Fig. 15. Seasonal densities of macropters (——) and brachyters (– – –) (left ordinate) and nymphs (·······; right ordinate) of *Prokelisia marginata* in chronically fertilized plots of short-form *Spartina alterniflora* during 1981 at Tuckerton, New Jersey. Because plots were not defaunated, abundances are the result of the combined effects of colonization and reproduction. Arrow on the abscissa indicates first fertilization treatment.

of grass. Under conditions of heavy feeding and oviposition by plant-hoppers, patches of vegetation yellow and die (Mochida *et al.*, 1977). I observed large intermittent patches of chloroitic vegetation (>50 m²) and associated feeding and oviposition scars in the New Jersey marsh. For other sap-feeding insects, Franz (1958) and McClure (1977) have shown how previous feeding by woolly aphids and scale insects reduces host-plant quality, making it less suitable for subsequent attack.

Predators (spiders), too, may indirectly influence patch quality and affect the population dynamics of *Prokelisia marginata*. Vince *et al.* (1981) found a negative relationship between the total number of *P. marginata* (nymphs and adults) caught over the season and the seasonal total of spiders in 11 field plots. *Prokelisia marginata* was most abundant in plots that showed a delayed numerical response of spiders to increased prey density. Vince *et al.* (1981) concluded that potential increases in the number of *P. marginata* in response to fertilized *Spartina* can be checked by the increased abundance of spiders. Because predaceous spiders can influence planthopper abundance, and if it is true that at high densities planthoppers may reduce the nutritional quality of *Spartina*, then spiders may indirectly mediate host plant quality.

The general pattern in the high marsh is for the crude-protein content of *Spartina alterniflora* to decrease throughout the season, from a high of

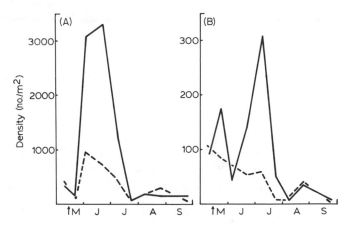

Fig. 16. Differences in the densities of the nymphs (A) and brachypters (B) of *Prokelisia marginata* in chronically fertilized (——) and control (– – –) plots of short-form *Spartina alterniflora* during 1981 at Tuckerton, New Jersey. Arrow on the abscissa indicates first treatment with fertilizer.

12% in May to about 6% in November (Fig. 18; Squiers and Good, 1974). This is certainly the case for stands of grass that fail to flower. However, in September, highly nutritious food items (12% crude protein; see Fig. 9) are locally available as seed heads in patches of flowering grass. We can construct seasonal patterns of patch favorableness (crude-protein content), for flowering and nonflowering stands of *Spartina* (Fig. 19), that are reminiscent of those in the general model (Fig. 1B), which predicts migration will be adaptive when there is asynchrony in patch qual-

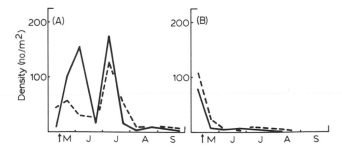

Fig. 17. Differences in the ability of the wing forms of *Prokelisia marginata* to select high-quality patches over less favorable patches. Seasonal densities of macropters (A) and brachypters (B) in plots of short-form *Spartina alterniflora* fertilized and defaunated with Orthene (——) and plots only defaunated with Orthene (– – –) during 1981 at Tuckerton, New Jersey. Arrows on abscissas indicate first treatment.

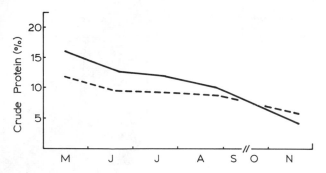

Fig. 18. Seasonal changes in the crude-protein content of *Spartina alterniflora* in stream-side (——) and high-marsh (–––) habitats at Tuckerton, New Jersey.

ity. Migration allows insects to leave deteriorating patches and colonize those that are improving (flowering, in this case).

Spartina patch dynamics are not quite this simple. However, I would argue that other factors (the planthoppers themselves, predators, the differential effects of tidewaters, and asynchrony in flowering among stands) also add to the spatial variation in patch favorableness that already exists, further promoting migration.

This information suggests that there is dramatic variation in the nutritional quality of *Spartina alterniflora* in the high-marsh habitat (Figs. 11 and 12), that favorable patches are often separated by distances greater than the ambit of brachypters (Figs. 13–15), that macropters are clearly the colonizing morph (Figs. 13–15), that macropters select more favorable over less favorable patches (Fig. 17), and that when patches "here" deteriorate, others "elsewhere" improve (Fig. 19), a situation that favors migration.

IX. BETWEEN-HABITAT VARIATION IN THE FAVORABLENESS OF *SPARTINA ALTERNIFLORA:* DIFFERENCES IN HABITAT SELECTION BETWEEN WING FORMS

This section elucidates the various factors that contribute to temporal differences in the favorableness (abundance and quality of food items and predator density) of the two habitat types of *Spartina alterniflora* (stream side and high marsh) and illustrates that migration allows *Prokelisia marginata* to track spatial changes in suitable resources at the habitat level.

With the general knowledge of the life history of *Prokelisia marginata* available, several discrete resource variables can be defined and used to

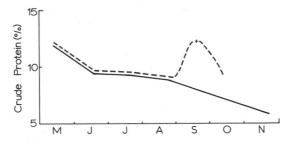

Fig. 19. Seasonal changes in the crude-protein content of flowering (– – –) and nonflowering (——) stands of *Spartina alterniflora* on the high marsh at Tuckerton, New Jersey. The cross indicates the high crude-protein content that can be locally available in the seed heads during late summer and fall.

predict the most favorable habitat (stream side or high marsh) for plant-hopper survival. First, I use live standing-crop biomass as a measure of the availability of food and oviposition space. Second, stand height, referenced to MHW, is used as an index of the refuge potential the vegetation offers in the intertidal habitat during inundation. Last, I use litter biomass (dead culms and blades) as a measure of the protective substrate necessary for winter survival.

In the forthcoming simple model I use these resource variables to predict temporal (seasonal) differences in the favorableness of *Spartina alterniflora* between steam-side (tall-form) and high-marsh (short-form) habitats for *Prokelisia marginata* (see Denno and Grissell, 1979). The model assumes that habitats that supply more of one resource or combination of resources are more suitable than those habitats offering less.

In New Jersey, living grass occurs in both stream-side and high-marsh habitats from April through early December, but biomass is generally greater in the stream-side habitat, with the greatest difference occurring from late July through September (Fig. 20). However, because the streamside habitat is approximately 50 cm below MHW, it is not until June that the grass culms grow to a height ($\approx$ MHW) at which they are not inundated by tidewaters (Fig. 21). During June and July in the stream-side habitat, the culms and blades undergo rapid elongation and proliferation and soon offer many refuges to planthoppers that they previously did not provide. During winter, all requisites are lost when stream-side vegetation is destroyed. At this point, I emphasize that although the refuge potential of *Spartina alterniflora* on the high marsh is less than that in the stream-side habitat during summer and fall, some refuge is provided year-round in the high-marsh habitat because of the relatively high elevation there and culms that stand through winter.

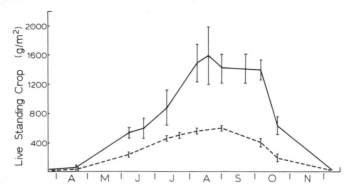

Fig. 20. Seasonal changes in live standing-crop biomass of *Spartina alterniflora* in stream-side (——) and high-marsh (– – –) habitats at Tuckerton, New Jersey. From Denno and Grissell (1979). Copyright 1979, the Ecological Society of America.

To generate a trend of resource favorableness based on food, oviposition space, and refuge from tidewater for *Spartina alterniflora* in stream-side and high-marsh habitats at Tuckerton, in New Jersey, I multiplied together monthly values for live biomass (data from Fig. 20) and stand height above the marsh surface at the stream-side site (data from Fig. 21) for both growth forms. A relative favorableness trend for each growth form resulted (Fig. 22), showing that (1) short-form *S. alterniflora* is the more favorable of the two habitats from December through late April, primarily because the tall form is sheared off during the winter and offers little refuge; and (2) during summer and fall, the tall form proliferates to offer more food, oviposition space, and refuge than the short form. Notice the resemblance between this model (Fig. 22) and Solbreck's (Fig. 1C), where continuous reproduction is possible "here" on the high marsh, but stream-side vegetation proliferates "elsewhere," allowing for seasonal exploitation.

The results of the two-factor model allow us to define two somewhat distinct periods for the Tuckerton marsh. There is a warm-season "feeding" period (April–September), when food, oviposition space, and refuge from tidewaters are important, and a cold-season "overwintering" period (October–March), when refuge continues to be a critical resource. Additional data collected in both habitats during the "feeding" period at Tuckerton reinforces the prediction that tall-form *Spartina alterniflora* should be the more favorable habitat at this time (Fig. 23A).

Because both resources (food and refuge) are necessary for survival, an excess of one does not completely compensate for a deficit in the other. Also, these resources are not entirely independent, and it is there-

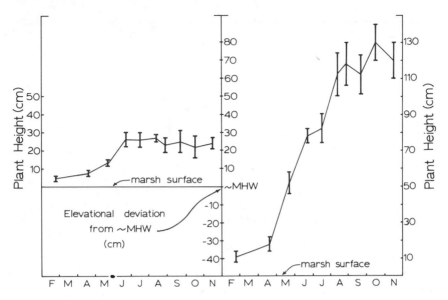

Fig. 21. Seasonal changes in stand height (live vegetation) of *Spartina alterniflora* referenced to mean high water level (MHW) in high-marsh (left) and stream-side (right) habitats at Tuckerton, New Jersey. The average elevation of the marsh surface in the creek-bank, habitat is 50 cm lower than the high marsh. From Denno and Grissell (1979). Copyright 1979, the Ecological Society of America.

fore not possible for biomass to exist without some refuge potential and vice versa. For these reasons, the functions that best describe patches of equal favorableness are a family of parabolic curves, the tails of which approach the axes asymptotically (see Vepsäläinen, 1978; Denno and Grissell, 1979). The most favorable habitat is that lying nearest the curve, farthest from the origin.

Clearly, however, litter (overwintering substrate) is as important a requisite as stand height (refuge) during the "overwintering" period. These two variables have been combined in Fig. 23B and further emphasize the favorableness of the high-marsh habitat throughout winter.

So far, I have emphasized differences in the abundance of resource items between the two habitats; there are differences in the quality of resources as well. The crude-protein content of stream-side vegetation is higher than that for high-marsh grass, particularly during May and June (Fig. 18). Representative profiles of spider density, measured several times throughout the season, show that spiders are relatively rare in the stream-side habitat (zone 1) compared to transitional (zones 2 and 3) and high-marsh (zones 4 and 5) habitats (Fig. 24). The pattern is

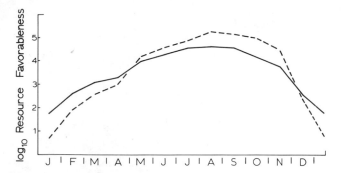

Fig. 22. Seasonal changes in the favorableness of *Spartina alterniflora* in stream-side (– – –) and high-marsh (——) habitats at Tuckerton, New Jersey. The index of habitat favorableness is the product of the refuge potential (grass height in centimeters above marsh surface at stream-side zone) and the available feeding and oviposition space (live grass standing crop in grams per square meter) provided by the grass in both habitats.

similar for a potential competitor, *Trigonotylus uhleri*; it, too, is more abundant in transitional vegetation (Fig. 25). The paucity of predacious spiders and mirid bugs in stream-side vegetation is likely the result of the violently fluctuating tidewaters in that habitat. On northern marshes, from June through October the stream-side habitat provides more

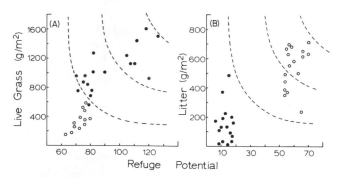

Fig. 23. Relative favorableness of stream-side (●) and high-marsh (○) habitats during the feeding (A; April–September) and overwintering period (B; October–March) for *Prokelisia marginata* at Tuckerton, New Jersey. Resource favorableness during the feeding period is based on the refuge potential and available feeding and oviposition space (as in Fig. 22) provided by *Spartina alterniflora* in both habitats. Habitat favorableness during winter is a function of refuge potential (as in Fig. 22) and available overwintering sites (biomass of litter) provided by *S. alterniflora* in both habitats. Parabolic curves define habitats of equal favorableness, and the optimum habitat lies on the curve farthest from the origin. Note that streamside vegetation is more favorable during the feeding period, whereas the high marsh is more favorable in winter. From Denno and Grissell (1979). Copyright 1979, the Ecological Society of America.

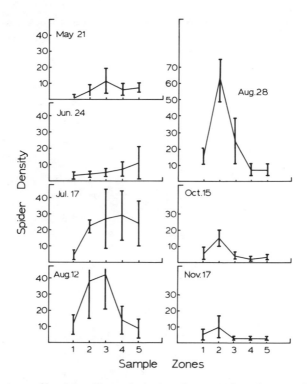

Fig. 24. Density profiles (May–November) of predatory spiders along an elevational gradient from stream side (zone 1) to high marsh (zone 5) at Tuckerton, New Jersey (no. individuals/10 sweeps). 1 SD surrounds each mean.

abundant feeding, oviposition, and refuge sites, more nutritious food, and is relatively devoid of predacious spiders and potential interspecific competitors.

At Cedar Key, Florida the seasonal pattern of resource favorableness is quite different. The reduced tidal energy and absence of winter ice allow for standing vegetation and litter development along creek banks. The subtropical climate allows for grass growth year-round, providing food, oviposition sites, and refuge, and eliminates any apparent need for overwintering sites. For these reasons, the division of the season into "feeding" and "overwintering" periods is not justifiable. However, I have compared the amount of food, refuge potential and litter development between tall- and short-form habitats when maximum (April–September) and minimum (October–March) live biomass occurs on the Cedar Key marsh. These times were roughly synchronous with the overwintering and feeding periods defined for Tuckerton.

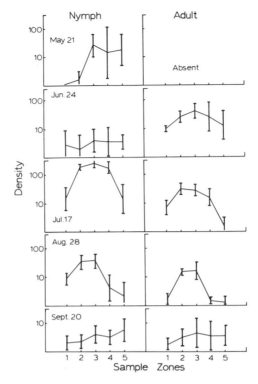

Fig. 25. Density profiles (May–September) of the nymphs and adults of *Trigonotylus uhleri* along an elevational gradient from stream side (zone 1) to high marsh (zone 5) at Tuckerton, New Jersey (no. individuals/10 sweeps). 1 SD surrounds each mean.

A two-factor model based on refuge potential and food shows the stream-side habitat is more favorable than the high marsh, during both the hot and cool seasons at Cedar Key (Fig. 26A,B). However, the difference between the favorableness of the two habitats is much less than that occurring during the feeding period on the Tuckerton marsh. Although it is unlikely that litter is an often-used resource along the Gulf of Mexico, I combined litter and refuge potential, the two critical resources used during winter at Atlantic coast locations, into a model (Fig. 26C) that also predicts the stream-side habitat as the most favorable. Again, the difference in favorableness between both habitats is minimal, and both habitats are relatively persistent due to the absence of winter shearing of stream-side vegetation. Thus there is very little evidence for two dynamically different habitat types at Cedar Key. Consequently, *Spartina alterniflora* "here" (high marsh) and "elsewhere" (steam side) is similarly favorable year-round, and migration should not be favored (see Fig. 1A).

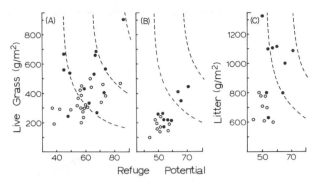

Fig. 26. Relative favorableness of stream-side and high-marsh habitats from June through September (A) and October through March (B), based on the refuge potential (as in Fig. 22) and available feeding and oviposition space provided by *Spartina alterniflora* in both habitats at Cedar Key, Florida. (C) Favorableness of stream-side and high-marsh habitats from October through March based on the refuge potential and availability of overwintering sites in the litter. Parabolic curves define habitats of equal favorableness. Note that in contrast to Tuckerton (Fig. 23), stream-side vegetation is slightly the more favorable of the two habitats year-round. From Denno and Grissell (1979). Copyright 1979, the Ecological Society of America.

Now I proceed to examine the migration response of *Prokelisia marginata*, as predicted by between-habitat variation in the favorableness of *Spartina alterniflora* in New Jersey and Florida. The colonization and utilization of habitats by *P. marginata* in New Jersey were determined by measuring wing-morph and nymphal densities along a gradient from stream-side to high-marsh sites throughout the year (Denno and Grissell, 1979; Fig. 27). These density profiles show that (1) overwintering nymphs occur only on the high marsh (Feb. 26); (2) proliferating, previously unexploited stream-side vegetation is colonized by macropterous adults in late spring (May 21) and again in early summer (June 24); (3) nymphs increase dramatically in the stream-side vegetation during early August; (4) macropterous adults move from stream-side to high-marsh habitats in late August and September; and (5) brachypterous adults maintain fidelity to the high-marsh habitat throughout the year. Fluctuations in the density of macropters in *Distichlis spicata*, a nonhost grass growing in large, pure stands in the same marsh, further document the spring, early summer, and fall migrations of *P. marginata* (Fig. 28). These data are consistent with the predictions of the models (Figs. 1C, 22, and 23) that migration should be favored when high-quality resources "elsewhere" (stream-side vegetation) become available for exploitation. The high level of migration in this marsh is documented by the fact that 78% of all adults are macropterous.

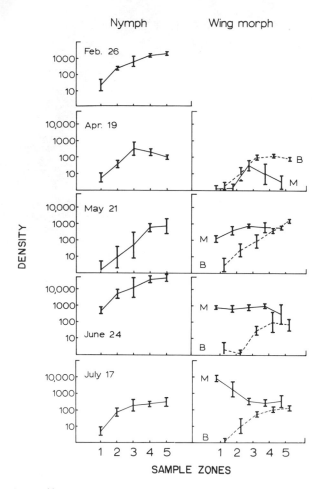

Fig. 27. Density profiles (February–November) of the nymphs and wing morphs (B, bracypter; M, macropter) of *Prokelisia marginata* along an elevational gradient from stream side (zone 1) to high marsh (zone 5) at Tuckerton, New Jersey (no. individuals/10 sweeps).

In contrast, where resources "here" (high marsh) and "elsewhere" (stream side) are similarly favorable, as is the case at Cedar Key (Figs. 1A and 26), migration should not be adaptive. This prediction is supported by (1) the rarity of macropters (only 10% of all adults) and (2) the equitable distribution of nymphs, brachypters, and macropters along the grass gradient (Fig. 29). Recall that brachypters are limited in their distribution to the "high marsh" and that macropters and nymphs undergo dramatic seasonal shifts in density between stream-side and high-marsh habitats in New Jersey.

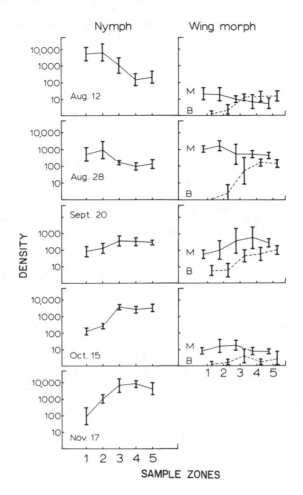

Vegetation zones correspond to those in Fig. 5A. 1 SD surrounds each mean. From Denno and Grissell (1979). Copyright 1979, the Ecological Society of America.

X. GEOGRAPHIC DIFFERENCES IN THE WING-FORM COMPOSITION OF *PROKELISIA MARGINATA* POPULATIONS

Denno (1979) predicted that the number of each wing form in the meta-population should occur in proportion to the abundance of the persistent ("high-marsh") and temporary ("stream-side") habitats in the local area. From Section IX recall that brachypters are the successful morph in

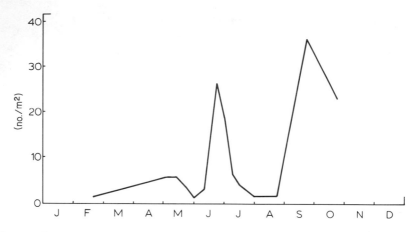

Fig. 28. Spring, summer, and fall migrations of *Prokelisia marginata*, measured as the number of macropterous adults per square meter that settled on *Distichlis spicata*, a nonhost grass growing in large, pure stands on the high marsh at Tuckerton, New Jersey. From Denno and Grissell (1979). Copyright 1979, the Ecological Society of America.

habitats that are persistantly favorable and that macropters are successful in temporary habitats.

To test this contention, Denno and Grissell (1979) adopted one easily measured property of grass vegetation that estimated the relative frequency of persistent (high-marsh) and temporary (stream-side) habitats in *Spartina alterniflora* marshes at various gulf and Atlantic coast locations and then used that property to predict in a general way the wing-morph structure of planthopper populations. Their rationale for using the coefficient of variation in grass stand height (CVSH) is as follows.

Where very tall, stream-side grass grades into short vegetation in the high marsh, two dynamically different habitats occur, one persistent and the other not. The CVSH for such a marsh should be high if measurements are made when standing biomass is near its maximum. For example, the CVSH for the Tuckerton, New Jersey, marsh in July (Fig. 5C; based on five measurements in each of the five zones) is 63%. In contrast, for marshes such as Cedar Key, Florida, in which stand height is more uniform and there is little evidence for the existence of extensive temporary habitats, the CVSH is 26%. Consequently, the largest CVSHs should occur in marshes with similar proportions of persistent and temporary habitats. Planthoppers occuring on marshes with a high CVSH should be largely macropterous in order to colonize and escape the extensive temporary habitat, whereas on marshes with a low CVSH (mostly persistent) macropters should be rare.

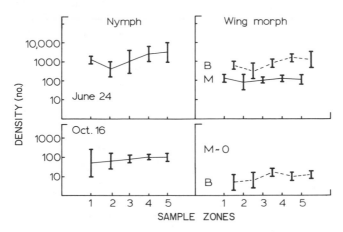

Fig. 29. Representative density profiles (June and October) of the nymphs and wing forms (B, brachypter; M, macropter) of *Prokelisia marginata* along an elevational gradient from stream side (zone 1) to high marsh (zone 5) at Cedar Key, Florida (no. individuals/10 sweeps). Vegetation zones correspond to those in Fig. 5A. 1 SD surrounds each mean. From Denno and Grissell (1979). Copyright 1979, the Ecological Society of America.

Denno and Grissell (1979) determined the CVSH of *Spartina alterniflora* and sampled the wing-morph composition of *Prokelisia marginata* populations at 19 locations along the Atlantic and gulf coasts. Eleven of the study areas were located on Atlantic coast marshes characterized in general by large expanses of *S. alterniflora* (>5 ha). Two samples were taken on the central Atlantic coast of Florida, where *S. alterniflora* fringes the mangrove zone. The remaining 6 sites were situated along the gulf coast of Florida and supported at least a 1-ha stand of the host grass.

The positive correlation between CVSH and macroptery (%) in populations of *Prokelisia marginata* was highly significant ($r = 0.943$; Fig. 30), substantiating the notion that the population structure of a planthopper can be dictated in large part by the persistence relationships of the habitats it exploits.

We may now ask what environmental factor(s) is responsible for such geographic variation in the height of *Spartina* between stream-side and high-marsh habitats. Tidal range (difference between mean high and low tides) may be an important factor. Johnson and York (1915) and Adams (1963) have suggested that the relative time of submergence and exposure of a plant at its upper and lower limit in a tidal marsh will make it possible to predict the vertical range of that plant taxon throughout its distribution. Adams (1963) demonstrated a strong positive relationship between the elevational range (ft) occupied by *S. alterniflora* and

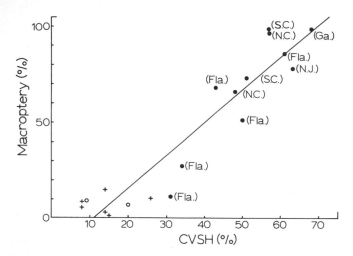

Fig. 30. Relationship ($r = 0.943^{**}$) between the coefficient of variation in stand height (CVSH) of *Spartina alterniflora* and macroptery in populations of *Prokelisia marginata* at various Atlantic and gulf coast locations. Fla., Florida; Ga., Georgia; N.C., North Carolina; N.J., New Jersey; S.C., South Carolina. From Denno and Grissell (1979). Copyright 1979, the Ecological Society of America.

the tidal range (ft) measured at ten widely separate locations along the eastern seaboard. Furthermore, Steever *et al.* (1976) and Bowman (1977) found a strong positive relationship between the standing crop of *S. alterniflora* and tital range ($r = 0.95$, Bowman data). Increased standing crop may result from greater oxygenation of intertidal peat (Romig, 1973; Woodfin, 1976; Linthurst, 1979, 1980), along with the circulation and replenishment of nutrients (Niering and Warren, 1980) that are associated with high tital range. Together, these data sets suggest that tidal range may be important in dictating the elevational distribution as well as the above-ground standing crop of *S. alterniflora*.

I found a positive relationship between tidal range (Tide Tables, 1977) and the CVSH of *Spartina alterniflora*, measured at the Atlantic and gulf coast locations shown in Fig. 30 ($r = 0.714$, $P < 0.01$). This relationship suggests that the low tidal range along the gulf coast may be responsible for the similarity in height and structure of *S. alterniflora* in stream-side and high-marsh habitats. The high tidal ranges at some Atlantic locations may be responsible for the striking differences in *Spartina* growth form seen there and, ultimately, the high proportion of macropters in those planthopper populations.

Other factors may also contribute to variation in the proportion of wing forms in populations. McCoy and Rey (1981) studied the wing-

Table I

Flightlessness in Populations of Planthoppers on *Spartina patens*
at Tuckerton, New Jersey

Species	Brachyptery (%)
Delphacodes detecta	86
Neomegamelanus dorsalis	88
Megamelus lobatus	97
Tumidagena minuta	>99

morph composition of *Prokelisia marginata* on *Spartina alterniflora* at St. Marks, Florida (gulf coast), where *Spartina* occurs as small, infrequent, isolated stands, and concluded that macropters were rare (10% of adults), because the probability of finding a more favorable stand was low. In my analysis (Fig. 30), I tried to minimize the effects of resource isolation by sampling planthoppers only at locations characterized by large expanses of *S. alterniflora*.

Yet another factor that could influence population differences in wing-form composition is planthopper density. *Prokelisia marginata* is more abundant in New Jersey than Cedar Key, Florida, by a factor of 10, and predacious spiders and egg predators are more abundant in Florida than New Jersey by a factor of 2. One could argue that the equable climate on the gulf allows spiders to more effectively check planthopper population increases. Consequently, planthoppers seldom reach densities at which they contribute to the demise of the local patch or at which the developmental switch is triggered, resulting in a macropter.

When one looks to other similar intertidal planthopper–grass systems, it is difficult to see how density alone can explain (1) the high proportion of macropters in some Atlantic coast populations of *Prokelisia marginata* and (2) the large geographic variance in wing-form composition of populations.

Spartina patens (Ait.) Muhl., another grass, occurs as immense, pure stands from MHW to approximately 0.5 m above MHW on most Atlantic coast tidal marshes (Blum, 1968; Redfield, 1972). At about MHW, pure stands of *S. patens* often abut pure stands of *S. alterniflora*, and the line of demarcation can be remarkable. Associated with *S. patens* is a larger assemblage of wing-dimorphic planthoppers (Denno, 1977, 1980; Denno et al., 1981). At Tuckerton, New Jersey, four species are abundant, and their populations contain from 86 to nearly 100% brachypters (Table I). Furthermore, two species are as individually abundant (no. individuals/ m²) as *Prokelisia marginata*, and the combined density of planthoppers on *S. patens* is consistently much higher (2–3×) than on *S. alterniflora*

(R. F. Denno, unpublished data). If density alone dictated wing-form composition of planthoppers, one would expect those populations on *S. patens* to contain more macropters than those on *S. alterniflora*. Yet the trend is strongly reversed in New Jersey, with populations of *P. marginata* containing 78% macropters and populations of *S. patens* containing 1–14% macropters.

I contend that large tidal range and climate act in a profound way on the growth and dynamics of *Spartina alterniflora* at many Atlantic coast locations (e.g., Tuckerton, New Jersey), promoting the occurrence of lush stream-side vegetation that becomes seasonally available for colonization by *Prokelisia marginata*. Also, flooding of the high marsh results in reduced *S. alterniflora* growth or dieback there (Mendelssohn *et al.*, 1981). The differential effects of tidewaters and soil properties that lead to waterlogging may likely explain much of the variation in crude-protein content and flowering that we see in stands of *S. alterniflora* in the high marsh (see Mendelssohn *et al.*, 1981). The point to be made is that, in many Atlantic marshes, tidal conditions are likely responsible for creating a mosaic of patches (both within and between habitats), some of which deteriorate or remain the same while others improve. Better alternatives are available elsewhere, and migration (macroptery) provides a mechanism for colonization. Consequently, selection may have favored a low threshold at which the developmental switch responds to density or host-plant quality and a nymph molts to a macropter (Denno, 1976; Denno and Grissell, 1979).

For planthoppers on *Spartina patens* the situation is very different. *Spartina patens* occupies a much narrower elevation range than does *S. alterniflora*, is flooded less frequently, and occurs on better drained soil (Blum, 1968; Redfield, 1972). Consequently, the tidal range and waterlogging factors that contribute significantly to variation in growth form and flowering in *S. alterniflora* do not have this effect on *S. patens*. Its growth form is much more uniform, and there is nothing comparable to the ephemeral stream-side vegetation of *S. alterniflora*. Also, seasonal changes in the protein content of five very different sizes stands of *S. patens* reveal remarkable uniformity (Fig. 31). I contend that, unlike *S. alterniflora*, *S. patens* does not provide better alternatives elsewhere very frequently, that patches usually fluctuate in favorableness together, and that migration is not favored under these conditions (see Fig. 1A).

The high proportion of brachyters in *Spartina patens*-inhabiting planthoppers is consistent with this argument (Denno, 1976, 1978; Denno *et al.*, 1981). Selection has apparently favored a high threshold at which the developmental switch responds to density or host-plant quality and nymphs molt to brachypters (Denno, 1976). On occasion, densities may

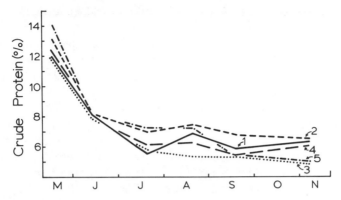

Fig. 31. Seasonal changes in the crude-protein content of five different sized "islands" (stands) of *Spartina patens* during 1979 at Tuckerton, New Jersey. "Island" size (m²): 1, <50; 2, 51–100; 3, 101–1000; 4, 1001–10,000; 5, 10,001–100,000. From Denno *et al.* (1981).

become so high locally and/or host-plant quality so low that the switch is triggered and macropters are produced, but only under these conditions is there a "better" alternative predictably available elsewhere. Populations of eight other species of planthoppers inhabiting six species of intertidal grasses, rushes, and shrubs are also composed of mostly ($\bar{x}$ = 96%) brachypterous adults (Denno, 1978).

Prokelisia marginata, mostly macropterous on many Atlantic coast marshes, is truly exceptional. However, most gulf coast populations of *P. marginata*, with only 10% macropters, are very similar in wing-morph composition to other salt-marsh-inhabiting species (see Denno, 1976, 1978; Denno and Grissell, 1979). Along the Gulf of Mexico, 10% macroptery may result from occasional local population increases or the advantages accrued by colonizing flowering stands of *Spartina alterniflora*. However, to be brachypterous is usually advantageous because better alternatives are not common, and because predator loads are high it would seem advantageous to offset this potential mortality with increased fecundity or early age to first reproduction, characteristic of the brachypterous but not macropterous morph. Thus in gulf coast populations selection has apparently favored a high threshold at which the developmental switch responds to crowding and most nymphs molt to short-winged adults (see Fig. 3).

The single factor that appears to explain geographic variation in the wing-form composition of *Prokelisia marginata* populations is the proportion of ephemeral stream-side vegetation to persistent high-marsh habitat. The difference in the dynamics of these two habitats is maximized when tidal range is great and winters are harsh.

XI. CONCLUSIONS AND GENERAL CONSIDERATIONS

In this chapter I have presented data showing that *Spartina alterniflora* is an extremely variable resource for the host-specific planthopper, *Prokelisia marginata*, which occurs so abundantly on this intertidal marsh grass. Tidal patterns dictate tremendous differences in the structure and persistence of this grass between high-marsh and stream-side habitats. Furthermore, within a habitat (e.g., high marsh), there is extreme intrinsic variation in the protein content and flowering frequency of *Spartina*, and high densities of planthoppers may reduce the protein content of the grass, rendering it less suitable for subsequent generations, as has been shown for other sap-feeding insects (McClure, 1980; Chapter 5). The result is tremendous spatial and temporal variation in the quantity and quality of *Spartina* resources that are essential for the survival of *P. marginata*. On the high marsh alone there is a mosaic of *Spartina* patches, which behave asynchronously; resources may be deteriorating in some patches yet improving (e.g., flowering) in others. Moreover, the spatial scale of host-plant variation both within and between habitats is such that small, wingless, sessile insects often are stranded on deteriorating vegetation and fail to colonize a more suitable patch elsewhere. Because the nymphs of planthoppers have such limited ability to move among patches, it is the adult that must place its offspring on favorable vegetation. Consequently, the winged adult must be able to move among patches, discriminating favorable ones from those less suitable. However, as the body size of winged insects becomes small, they become more subject to physical forces that could remove them from their host (Denno, 1976). Berland (1935) reported that "aerial plankton" (insects carried aloft by ascending air currents) is composed primarily of small, light, weakly flying insects with a large wing surface to body weight ratio. Thus the same feature, namely, wings, that allows small insects to escape deteriorating patches and colonize better ones may predispose them to being swept from a favorable patch.

With small insects like planthoppers and aphids, environmental contingencies imposed by host plants are apparently too extreme to be solved by a single phenotype, and selection has favored a dimorphism in which the functions of (1) remaining on and utilizing the current patch and (2) colonizing other patches are discretely partitioned between flightless and winged morphs, respectively. Control of the dimorphism may be environmental, genetic, or a combination of the two for most insects (Harrison, 1980), but for planthoppers and aphids most evidence points to a developmental "switch" that is triggered by environmental cues to determine wing form (Denno, 1976; Harrison, 1980).

Although variation in wing length provides a very obvious example of dispersal polymorphism, other mechanisms produce the same result. For instance, variation in flight-muscle development is common (Harrison, 1980). Wing-muscle formation may be arrested during development, as is the case with corixids (Scudder, 1971), or functional flight muscles may degenerate, resulting in flightlessness, as occurs in some aphids and *Dysdercus* bugs (Johnson, 1959; Edwards, 1969). Also, extensive variation in flight behavior can occur among individuals in a population completely capable of flight (Harrison, 1980). Dingle (1978, 1981) has described differences in the proportion of long- and short-duration flyers between milkweed bug populations. Thus wing dimorphism lies at one end of a morphological–behavioral spectrum that affects the dispersal capability of insects.

Although wing dimorphism clearly allows planthoppers to better track their variable host plants, we may ask why such dimorphisms are so infrequent in the insect world, and, subsequently, whether the information we gain by studying them is applicable to understanding how herbivores in general cope with their changing hosts. Though many planthoppers and aphids exhibit wing dimorphism (Denno, 1978; Harrison, 1980), there are thousands of species of sap-feeders with similar life histories, including most leafhoppers (Cicadellidae), psyllids, treehoppers, froghoppers, and fulgoroids, that do not. It may be that there is indeed variation in the function of wing muscles or in behavior resulting in flight polymorphism that is obscured only by our lack of knowledge about these groups. However, the apparent lack of a flight dimorphism may be real as well. Most dimorphic planthoppers feed on grasses and other low-profile vegetation. They essentially inhabit two-dimensional systems. Planthoppers and aphids as well often avoid predators by quickly leaping or falling from their holds (Dixon, 1958; Denno, 1979; Nault and Montgomery, 1979). In low-profile, dense vegetation, an escaping or dislodged planthopper usually lands on or near a suitable culm or blade. However, if the host plant is a large tree and the planthopper brachypterous, it may be virtually impossible to relocate a suitable host. For a macropter, relocating an acceptable host would be much more likely. Consequently, as host plants become three-dimentional, the advantages of brachyptery may wane, and selection may favor monomorphic populations composed of macropters, regardless of the persistence of the resource. Leafhoppers span a much greater diversity of habitats than do planthoppers, and their wing-morph pattern is consistent with the argument that the brachypterous morph is disadvantaged in three-dimensional vegetation. For instance, the leafhopper fauna of temperate and tropical trees is composed of species that are monomorphically macropterous. Of the leafhoppers that do exhibit flight dimorphism, most occur in low-profile vegetation like grasses (see Rose, 1972; Denno, 1978; Denno *et al.*, 1981).

Although the vertical structure of vegetation may dissuade the evolution of wing dimorphisms, other factors such as body size, which I have already alluded to, may play a role as well. Generally, as the size of an insect increases, so too does its ambit. The scale of host-plant heterogeneity that precludes an aphid from moving from a low- to a high-quality plant may pose no problem whatsoever for a large coreid bug. Also, larger winged insects, with greater wing loading, wings that can be folded or housed under hemielytra or elytra, and more-directed flight capability, are much less likely to be swept from a suitable host than a small insect with the opposite set of features. Thus with large insects, by virtue of their size and, consequently, mobility and control, the environmental contingencies of finding and remaining on host plants are more likely to be solved by a single phenotype. This is not to say that wing dimorphisms do not occur in larger insects, because they do (see Vepsäläinen, 1974, 1978; Slater, 1977), only they are less likely.

Simple systems like the *Spartina alterniflora–Prokelisia maginata* one contain all the essentials for studying the problems that variable hosts pose for herbivores and the life-history traits of herbivores that allow them to track favorable hosts. *Spartina* is highly variable yet occurs in pure stands of two-dimensional vegetation, in which the effects of mixed vegetation and complex vegetational structure can be eliminated. Being small and exhibiting wing dimorphism, *P. marginata* facilitates our understanding of the population dynamics of herbivores in patchy environments.

To date the following key points surface from this study.

1. The fitness of *Prokelisia marginata* is positively correlated with crude-protein content of the *Spartina* on which it feeds.

2. The brachypter is the adaptive morph in a high-quality patch by virtue of its ability to remain there and its higher fecundity and/or earlier age to first reproduction.

3. The macropter is the adaptive morph for escaping deteriorating patches and colonizing favorable ones. Its ambit is great compared to that of the brachypter, and it can discriminate and select high- versus lesser quality (on the basis of protein content) patches.

4. Many Atlantic coast marshes are characterized by two dynamically different *S. alterniflora* habitats. There is persistent vegetation on the high-marsh and stream-side vegetation that is temporarily available during summer. Brachypters remain in the persistent vegetation, and macropters colonize the temporary habitat. High incidences of migration

(e.g., 70% macropters) occur in such marshes, which is consistent with theoretical predictions.

5. Some Atlantic and many Gulf of Mexico coastal marshes are characterized by only persistent vegetation and the absence of temporary habitats. Here, as predicted, planthopper populations are composed mostly (90%) of brachypters.

6. The proportion of macropters in *P. marginata* populations is positively correlated with the relative abundance of temporary stands of vegetation in the local marsh.

7. Within the high-marsh habitat there are asynchronous changes in the favorableness of patches, resulting from differences in flowering frequency and the density of planthoppers, which may lower the protein content of the vegetation. Because favorable patches lie beyond the ambit of brachypters, macroptery is favored.

8. Locating and exploiting favorable resources amid a changing mosaic of alternatives has been partially overcome in *P. marginata* by employing two wing morphs.

Spatial and temporal variation in the favorableness of *Spartina alterniflora* presents a dynamic patchwork of alternatives to herbivores. The planthopper *Prokelisia marginata* has partially solved the problem of tracking favorable stands of grass with an environmentally induced wing dimorphism that allows for exploitation of the patch as long as conditions remain suitable yet escape to better alternatives elsewhere if local conditions deteriorate.

ACKNOWLEDGMENTS

Barbara Denno, Vera Krischik, Mike Raupp, and Doug Tallamy have assisted with many aspects of this work over the course of the last 8 yr. Their input has been invaluable. Mark McClure reviewed an earlier draft of this chapter. I am most grateful to all of these people.

Scientific Article no. A-3172, Contribution no. 6241 of the Maryland Agricultural Experimental Station, Department of Entomology.

REFERENCES

Adams, D. A. (1963). Factors influencing vascular plant zonation in North Carolina salt marshes. *Ecol. Monog.* **44**, 445–456.

Auclair, J. L. (1976). Feeding and nutrition of the pea aphid, *Acyrthosipon pisum* (Harris), with special reference to amino acids. *Symp. Biol. Hung.* **16**, 29–34.

Berenbaum, M. (1981). Patterns of furanocoumarin distribution and insect herbivory in the Umbelliferae: plant chemistry and community structure. *Ecology* **5**, 1254–1266.

Berland, L. (1935). Premiers résultats de mes recherches en avion sur la faune et la flore atmosphériques. *Ann. Entomol. Soc. Fr.* **104**, 73–96.

Bernays, E. A. (1981). Plant tannins and insect herbivores: an appraisal. *Ecol. Entomol.* **6**, 353–360.

Blau, W. S. (1981). Latitudinal variation in the life histories of insects occupying disturbed habitats: a case study. *In* "Insect Life History Patterns: Habitat and Geographic Variation" (R. F. Denno and H. Dingle, eds.), pp. 75–95. Springer-Verlag, Berlin and New York.

Blum, J. L. (1968). Salt marsh spartinas and associated algae. *Ecol. Monog.* **38**, 199–221.

Bowman, M. J. (1977). Nutrient distributions and transport in Long Island Sound. *Estuarine Coastal Mar. Sci.* **5**, 531–548.

Chang, V. C. (1978). Feeding activities of the sugarcane leafhopper: identification of electronically recorded waveforms. *Ann. Entomol. Soc. Am.* **71**, 31–36.

Chang, V. C., and Ota, K. (1978). Feeding activities of *Perkinsiella* leafhoppers and Fiji disease resistance of sugarcane. *J. Econ. Entomol.* **71**, 297–300.

Davis, L. V., and Gray, I. E. (1966). Zonal and seasonal distribution of insects in North Carolina salt marshes. *Ecol. Monog.* **36**, 275–295.

Denno, R. F. (1976). Ecological significance of wing-polymorphism in Fulgoroidea which inhabit salt marshes. *Ecol. Entomol.* **1**, 257–266.

Denno, R. F. (1977). Comparison of the assemblages of sap-feeding insects (Homoptera–Hemiptera) inhabiting two structurally different salt marsh grasses in the genus *Spartina*. *Environ. Entomol.* **6**, 359–372.

Denno, R. F. (1978). The optimum population strategy for planthoppers (Homoptera: Delphacidae) in stable marsh habitats. *Can. Entomol.* **110**, 135–142.

Denno, R. F. (1979). The relation between habitat stability and the migration tactics of planthoppers. *Misc. Publ. Entomol. Soc. Am.* **11**, 41–49.

Denno, R. F., and Dingle, H. (1981). Considerations for the development of a more general life history theory. *In* "Insect Life History Patterns: Habitat and Geographic Variation" (R. F. Denno and H. Dingle, eds.), pp. 1–6. Springer-Verlag, Berlin and New York.

Denno, R. F., and Grissell, E. E. (1979). The adaptiveness of wing-dimorphism in the salt marsh-inhabiting planthopper, *Prokelisia marginata* (Homoptera: Delphacidae). *Ecology* **60**, 221–236.

Denno, R. F., Raupp, M. J., Tallamy, D. W., and Reichelderfer, C. F. (1980). Migration in heterogeneous environments: differences in habitat selection between the wing-forms of the dimorphic planthopper, *Prokelisia marginata* (Homoptera: Delphacidae), *Ecology* **61**, 859–867.

Denno, R. F., Raupp, M. J., and Tallamy, D. W. (1981). Organization of a guild of sap-feeding insects: equilibrium vs nonequilibrium coexistence. *In* "Insect Life History Patterns: Habitat and Geographic Variation" (R. F. Denno and H. Dingle, eds.), pp. 151–181. Springer-Verlag, Berlin and New York.

Denno, R. F., Krischik, V. A., Raupp, M. J., and Tallamy, D. W. Population dynamics of a salt marsh-inhabiting planthopper on host plants of variable nutritional quality: an experimental study. In preparation.

Derr, J. A. (1980). The nature of variation in life history characters of *Dysdercus bimaculatus* (Heteroptera: Pyrrhocoridae), a colonizing species. *Evolution* **34**, 548–557.

Dingle, H. (1972). Migration strategies of insects. *Science* **175**, 1327–1335.

Dingle, H. (1974). The experimental analysis of migration and life-history strategies in insects. *In* "Experimental Analysis of Insect Behavior" (L. Barton Browne, ed.), pp. 329–342. Springer-Verlag, Berlin/New York.

Dingle, H. (1978). Migration and diapause in tropical, temperate, and island milkweed bugs. *In* "The Evolution of Insect Migration and Diapause" (H. Dingle, ed.), pp. 254–276. Springer-Verlag, Berlin/New York.

Dingle, H. (1979). Adaptive variation in the evolution of insect migration. *In* "Movement of Highly Mobile Insects: Concepts and Methodology in Research" (R. L. Rabb and G. G. Kennedy, eds.), pp. 64–87. North Carolina State Univ. Press, Raleigh.

Dingle, H. (1981). Geographical variation and behavioral flexibility in milkweed bug life histories. *In* "Insect Life History Patterns: Habitat and Geographic Variation" (R. F. Denno and H. Dingle, eds.), pp. 57–74. Springer-Verlag, Berlin and New York.

Dixon, A. F. G. (1958). The escape responses shown by certain aphids to the presence of the coccinellid, *Adalia decempunctata* (L.) *Trans. R. Entomol. Soc. London* **110**, 319–334.

Dixon, A. F. G. (1970). Quality and availability of food for a sycamore aphid population. *In* "Animal Populations in Relation to their Food Resources" (A. Watson, ed.), pp. 271–287. Blackwell, Oxford.

Dixon, A. F. G. (1971). The role of aphids in wood formation. I. The effect of the Sycamore Aphid, *Drepanosiphum platanoides* (Schr.) (Aphididae), on the growth of sycamore, *Acer pseudoplatanus* (L.). *J. Appl. Ecol.* **8**, 165–179.

Dixon, A. F. G. (1973). "Biology of Aphids." Camelot Press, London.

Drosopoulos, S. (1977). Biosystematic studies on the *Muellerianella* Complex (Delphacidae, Homoptera, Auchenorrhyncha). *Meded. Landbouwhogesch. Wageningen* No. 284, pp. 77–114.

Duncan, W. H. (1974). Vascular halophytes of the Atlantic and Gulf Coasts of North America north of Mexico. *In* "Ecology of Halophytes" (R. J. Reimold and W. H. Queen, eds.), pp. 23–50. Academic Press, New York.

Edmunds, G. F., and Alstad, D. N. (1978). Coevolution in insect herbivores and conifers. *Science* **199**, 941–945.

Edmunds, G. F., and Alstad, D. N. (1981). Responses of black pineleaf scales to host plant variability. *In* "Insect Life History Patterns: Habitat and Geographic Variation" (R. F. Denno and H. Dingle, eds.), pp. 29–38. Springer-Verlag, Berlin and New York.

Edwards, F. J. (1969). Development and histolysis of the indirect flight muscles in *Dysdercus intermedius*. *J. Insect. Physiol.* **15**, 1591–1599.

Foster, W. A. (1975a). The life history and population biology of an intertidal aphid, *Pemphigus trehernei* Foster. *Trans. R. Entomol. Soc. London* **127**, 193–207.

Foster, W. A. (1975b). A new species of *Pemphigus* Hartig (Homoptera: Aphidoidea) from Western Europe. *J. Entomol. Ser. B* **44**, 255–263.

Foster, W. A., and Treherne, J. E. (1978). Dispersal mechanisms in an intertidal aphid. *J. Anim. Ecol.* **47**, 205–217.

Franz, J. M. (1958). The effectiveness of predators and food in limiting gradations of *Adelges (Dreyfusia) piceae* (Ratz.) in Europe. *Proc. Int. Congr. Entomol, 10th, 1956* Vol. 4, pp. 781–787.

Gadgil, M. (1971). Dispersal: population consequences and evolution. *Ecology* **52**, 253–261.

Harrison, R. G. (1980). Dispersal polymorphisms in insects. *Annu. Rev. Ecol. Syst.* **11**, 95–118.

Hassell, M. P., and Southwood, T. R. E. (1978). Foraging strategies of insects. *Annu. Rev. Ecol. Syst.* **9**, 75–98.

Hatcher, B. G., and Mann, K. H. (1975). Above-ground production of marsh cordgrass (*Spartina alterniflora*) near the northern end of its range. *J. Fish. Res. Board Can.* **32**, 83–87.

Haukioja, E., and Niemelä, P. (1979). Birch leaves as a resource for herbivores: seasonal occurrence of increased resistance in foliage after mechanical damage of adjacent leaves. *Oecologia* **39**, 151–159.

Herrebout, W. M. (1969). Some aspects of host selection in *Eucarcelia ratilla* Vill. (Diptera, Tachinidae). *Neth. J. Zool.* **19**, 1–104.

Herrebout, W. M., Kuyten, P. J., and DeRuiter, L. (1963). Observations on colour patterns and behavior of caterpillars feeding on Scots pine. *Arch. Neth. Zool.* **15**, 315–357.

Horsfield, D. (1977). Relationships between feeding of *Philaenus spumarius* (L.) and the amino acid concentration in the xylem sap. *Ecol. Entomol.* **2**, 259–266.

Ikeda, T., Matsumura, F., and Benjamin, D. M. (1977). Mechanisms of feeding discrimination between matured and juvenile foliage by two species of pine sawflies. *J. Chem. Ecol.* **3**, 677–694.

Jarvinen, O., and Vepsäläinen, K. (1976). Wing dimorphism as an adaptive strategy in water-striders (Gerris). *Hereditas* **84**, 61–68.

Johno, S. (1963). Analysis of the density effect as a determining factor of the wing-form in the brown planthopper, *Nilaparvata lugens*. *Jpn. J. Appl. Entomol. Zool.* **7**, 45–48.

Johnson, B. (1959). Studies on the degeneration of the flight muscle of alate aphids. II. Histology and control of muscle breakdown. *J. Insect Physiol.* **3**, 367–377.

Johnson, C. G. (1969). "Migration and Dispersal of Insects by Flight." Methuen, London.

Johnson, D. S., and York, H. H. (1915). "The Relation of Plants to Tide Levels," Publ. 206. Carnegie Institution, Washington, D.C.

Jones, S. B., Burnett, W. C., Coile, N. C., Mabry, T. J., and Betkouski, M. F. (1979). Sequiterpene lactones of *Vernonia*. Influence of glaucolide-A on the growth rate and survival of lepidopterous larvae. *Oecologia* **39**, 71–77.

Kathirithamby, J. (1977). The effects on stylopisation on the sexual development of *Javesella dubia* (Kir.) (Homoptera: Delphacidae). *Biol. J. Linn. Soc.* **10**, 163–179.

Kennedy, J. S. (1975). Insect dispersal. *In* "Insects, Science and Society" (D Pimentel, ed.), pp. 103–109. Academic Press, New York.

Kirby, C. J., and Gosselink, J. G. (1976). Primary production in a Louisiana Gulf Coast *Spartina alterniflora* marsh. *Ecology* **57**, 1052–1059.

Kisimoto, R. (1956). Factors determining the wing-form of adult, with special reference to the effect of crowding during the larval period of the brown planthopper, *Nilaparvata lugens* Stal. Studies of the polymorphism in the planthoppers (Homoptera, Araeopidae). I. *Oyo Kontyu* **12**, 105–111.

Kisimoto, R. (1965). Studies on the polymorphism and its role playing in the population growth of the brown planthopper, *Nilaparvata lugens* Stal. *Bull. Shikoku Agric. Exp. Stn.* **13**, 1–106.

Krebs, J. R., and Davies, N. B. (1978). "Behavioral Ecology." Sinauer Associates, Sunderland, Massachusetts.

Lees, A. D. (1961). Clonal polymorphism in aphids. *Symp. R. Entomol. Soc. London* **1**, 68–79.

Lees, A. D. (1966). The control of polymorphism in aphids. *Adv. Insect Physiol.* **3**, 207–277.

Lees, A. D. (1967). The production of the apterous and alate forms in the aphid, *Megoura viciae* Buckton, with special reference to the role of crowding. *J. Insect Physiol.* **13**, 289–318.

Levins, R. (1961). Mendelian species as adaptive systems. *Gen. Syst.* **6**, 33–39.

Levins, R. (1962). Theory of fitness in a heterogeneous environment. I. The fitness set and adaptive function. *Am. Nat.* **96**, 361–378.

Levins, R. (1964). The theory of fitness in a heterogeneous environment. IV. The adaptive significance of gene flow. *Evolution* **18**, 635–638.

Levins, R. (1968). "Evolution in Changing Environments: Some Theoretical Explorations." Princeton Univ. Press, Princeton, New Jersey.

Linthurst, R. A. (1979). The effect of aeration on the growth of *Spartina alterniflora* Loisel. *Am. J. Bot.* **66**, 685–691.

Linthurst, R. A. (1980). A growth comparison of *Spartina alterniflora* Loisel. ecophenes under aerobic and anaerobic conditions. *Am. J. Bot.* **67**, 883–887.

McClure, M. S. (1977). Population dynamics of the red pind scale, *Matsucoccus resinosae* (Homoptera: Margarodidae): the influence of resinosis. *Environ. Entomol.* **6**, 789–795.

McClure, M. S. (1979). Self-regulation in hemlock scale populations: role of food quantity and quality. *Misc. Publ. Entomol. Soc. Am.* **11**, 33–40.

McClure, M. S. (1980). Foliar nitrogen: a basis for host suitability for Elongate Hemlock Scale, *Fiorinia externa* (Homoptera: Diaspididae). *Ecology* **61**, 72–79.

McCoy, E. D., and Rey, J. R. (1981). Patterns of abundance, distribution, and alary polymorphism among the salt marsh Delphacidae (Homoptera: Fulgoroidea) of northwest Florida. *Ecol. Entomol.* **6**, 285–291.

McKey, D. (1979). The distribution of secondary compounds within plants. *In* "Herbivores: Their Interaction with Secondary Plant Metabolites" (G. A. Rosenthal and D. H. Janzen, eds.), pp. 56–134. Academic Press, New York.

McNeill, S., and Southwood, T. R. E . (1978). Role of nitrogen in the development of insect–plant relationships. *In* "Biochemical Aspects of Plant and Animal Coevolution" (J. B. Harborne, ed.), pp. 77–98. Academic Press, New York.

Mattson, W. J. (1980). Herbivory in relation to plant nitrogen content. *Annu. Rev. Ecol. Syst.* **11**, 119–161.

May, Y. Y. (1971). The biology and population ecology of *Stenocranus minutus* (Fab.) (Delphacidae: Hemiptera). Ph.D. Dissertation, University of London, London, England.

Mendelssohn, I. A., McKee, K. L., and Patrick, W. H. (1981). Oxygen deficiency in *Spartina alterniflora* roots: metabolic adaptation to anoxia. *Science* **214**, 439–441.

Miller, W. R., and Egler, F. E. (1950). Vegetation of the Wequetequockpawcatuck tidemarshes, Connecticut. *Ecol. Monog.* **20**, 143–172.

Mittler, T. (1958). Studies on the feeding and nutrition of *Tuberolachnus salignus* (Gmelin) (Homoptera: Aphididae). II. The nitrogen and sugar composition of ingested phloem sap and excreted honeydew. *J. Exp. Biol.* **35**, 74–84.

Mobberley, D. G. (1956). Taxonomy and distribution of the genus *Spartina. Iowa State Coll. J. Sci.* **30**, 471–574.

Mochida, O. (1973). The characters of the two wing-forms of *Javesella pellucida* (F.) (Homoptera: Delphacidae), with special reference to reproduction. *Trans. R. Entomol. Soc. London* **125**, 177–225.

Mochida, O., and Kisimoto, R. (1971). A review of the studies on *Javesella pellucida* (F.) (Homoptera, Delphacidae) and associated subjects. *Rev. Plant Prot. Res.* **4**, 1–59.

Mochida, O., Suryana, T., and Wahyu, A. (1977). Recent outbreaks of the brown planthopper in Southeast Asia (with special reference to Indonesia). *Proc. Int. Semin., Food Fert. Technol. Cent. Asian Pac. Reg.* **1**, 170–191.

Morse, D. H. (1980). "Behavioral Mechanisms in Ecology." Harvard Univ. Press, Cambridge, Massachusetts.

Nasu, S. (1969). "The Virus Diseases of the Rice Plant." Johns Hopkins Press, Baltimore, Maryland.

Nault, L. R., and Montgomery, M. E. (1979). Aphid alarm pheromones. *Misc. Publ. Entomol. Soc. Am.* **11**, 23–31.

Niering, W. A., and Warren, R. S. (1980). Vegetation patterns and processes in New England salt marshes. *BioScience* **30**, 301–307.

Price, P. W. (1980). "Evolutionary Biology of Parasites." Princeton Univ. Press, Princeton, New Jersey.

Raatikainen, M. (1967). Bionomics, enemies and population dynamics of *Javesella pellucida* (F.) (Homoptera, Delphacidae). *Ann. Agric. Fenn.* **6**, 1–149.

Redfield, A. C. (1972). Development of a New England salt marsh. *Ecol. Monog.* **42**, 201–237.

Rhoades, D. F. (1979). Evolution of plant chemical defense against herbivores. *In* "Herbivores: Their Interaction with Secondary Plant Metabolites" (G. A. Rosenthal and D. H. Janzen, eds.), pp. 4–54. Academic Press, New York.

Roeske, C. N., Sieber, J. N., Brower, L. P., and Moffitt, C. M. (1976). Milkweed cardenolides and their comparative processing by monarch butterflies (*Danaus plexippus* L.). *In* "Biochemical Interaction Between Plants and Insects" (J. W. Wallace and R. L. Mansell, eds.), pp. 93–167. Plenum, New York.

Romig, R. F. (1973). Growth and reproduction of *Spartina*. Ph.D. Dissertation, University of Delaware, Newark.

Rose, D. J. W. (1972). Dispersal and quality in populations of *Cicadulina* species (Cicadellidae). *J. Anim. Ecol.* **41,** 589–609.

Scriber, J. M. Nitrogen nutrition of plants and insect invasion. *In* "Nitrogen in Crop Protection" (R. F. Hauck, ed.). Am. Soc. Agron., Madison, Wisconsin (in press).

Scriber, J. M., and Feeny, P. P. (1979). Growth of herbivorous caterpillars in relation to feeding specialization and to growth form of their food plants. *Ecology* **60,** 828–850.

Scriber, J. M., and Slansky, F. (1981). The nutritional ecology of immature insects. *Annu. Rev. Entomol.* **26,** 183–211.

Scudder, G. G. E. (1971). The postembrionic development of the indirect flight muscles in *Cenocorixa bifida* (Hung.) (Hemiptera: Corixidae). *Can. J. Zool.* **49,** 1387–1398.

Slansky, F., and Feeny, P. P. (1977). Stabilization of the rate of nitrogen accumulation by larvae of the cabbage butterfly on wild and cultivated food plants. *Ecol. Monogr.* **47,** 209–228.

Slater, J. A. (1977). The incidence and evolutionary significance of wing polymorphism in lygaeid bugs with particular reference to those of South Africa. *Biotropica* **9,** 217–229.

Solbreck, C. (1978). Migration, diapause, and direct development as alternative life histories in a seed bug, *Neacoryphus bicrucis*. *In* "The Evolution of Insect Migration and Diapause" (H. Dingle, ed.), pp. 195–217. Springer-Verlag, Berlin/New York.

Southwood, T. R. E. (1962). Migration of terrestial arthrophods in relation to habitat. *Biol. Rev. Cambridge Philos. Soc.* **37,** 171–214.

Southwood, T. R. E. (1977). Habitat, the templet for ecological strategies? *J. Anim. Ecol.* **46,** 337–465.

Southwood, T. R. E., May, R. M., Hassell, M. P., and Conway, G. R. (1974). Ecological strategies and population parameters. *Am. Nat.* **108,** 791–804.

Squiers, E. R., and Good, R. E. (1974). Seasonal changes in the productivity, caloric content and chemical composition of a population of salt marsh cord-grass (*Spartina alterniflora*). *Chesapeake Sci.* **15,** 63–71.

Steever, E. Z., Warren, R. S., and Niering, W. A. (1976). Tidal energy subsidy and standing crop production of *Spartina alterniflora*. *Estuarine Coastal Mar. Sci.* **4,** 473–478.

Stiling, P. D., and Strong, D. R. (1982). Egg density and the intensity of parasitism in *Prokelisia marginata* (Homoptera: Delphacidae). *Ecology* **63,** 1630–1635.

Tallamy, D. W., and Denno, R. F. (1979). Responses of sap-feeding insects (Homoptera–Hemiptera) to simplification of host plant structure. *Environ. Entomol.* **8,** 1021–1028.

Teal, J. M. (1962). Energy flow in the salt marsh ecosystem of Georgia. *Ecology* **4,** 614–624.

Tide Tables (1977). "East Coast of North and South America." U.S. Dept. of Commerce, National Oceanic and Atmospheric Administration, National Ocean Survey, Rockville, Maryland.

Tsai, P., Hwang, F., Feng, W., Fu, Y., and Dong, Q. (1964). Study on *Delphacodes striatella* Fallen (Homoptera, Delphacidae) in north China. *Acta Entomol. Sin.* **13,** 552–571.

Turner, R. E. (1976). Geographic variations in salt marsh macrophyte production: a review. *Contrib. Mar. Sci.* **20**, 47–68.

Turner, R. E., and Gosselink, J. G. (1975). A note on standing crops of *Spartina alterniflora* in Texas and Florida. *Contrib. Mar. Sci.* **19**, 113–118.

Valiela, I., Teal, J. M., and Dueser, W. G. (1978). The nature of growth forms in the salt marsh grass *Spartina alterniflora. Am. Nat.* **112**, 461–470.

van Emden, H. F. (1966). Studies on the relations of insect and host plant. III. A comparison of the reproduction of *Brevicoryne brassicae* and *Myzus persicae* (Hemiptera: Aphididae) on Brussels sprout plants supplied with different rates of nitrogen and potassium. *Entomol. Exp. Appl.* **9**, 444–460.

Vepsäläinen, K. (1974). The life cycles and wing lengths of Finnish *Gerris* Fab. species (Heteroptera: Gerridae). *Acta Zool. Fenn.* **141**, 1–73.

Vepsäläinen, K. (1978). Wing Dimorphism and diapause in *Gerris:* determination and adaptive significance. *In* "The Evolution of Insect Migration and Diapause" (H. Dingle, ed.), pp. 218–253. Springer-Verlag, Berlin and New York.

Vince, S. W., Valiela, I., and Teal, J. M. (1981). An experimental study of the structure of herbivorous insect communities in a salt marsh. *Ecology* **62**, 1662–1678.

Way, M. J., and Cammell, M. (1970). Aggregation behavior in relation to food utilization by aphids. *Symp. Br. Ecol. Soc.* **10**, 229–247.

White, T. C. R. (1969). An index to measure weather-induced stress of trees associated with outbreaks of psyllids in Australia. *Ecology* **50**, 905–909.

Whitham, T. G. (1978). Habitat selection by *Pemphigus* aphids in response to resource limitation and competition. *Ecology* **59**, 1164–1179.

Whitham, T. G. (1979). Territorial behavior of *Pemphigus* gall aphids. *Nature (London)* **279**, 324–325.

Whitham, T. G. (1980). The theory of habitat selection: examined and extended using *Pemphigus* aphids. *Am. Nat.* **115**, 449–466.

Whitham, T. G. (1981). Individual trees as heterogeneous environments: adaptation to herbivory or epigenetic noise? *In* "Insect Life History Patterns: Habitat and Geographic Variation" (R. F. Denno and H. Dingle, eds.), pp. 9–27. Springer-Verlag, Berlin and New York.

Willcox, H., and Coffey, T. (1977). "Forest Insect and Disease Management: Environmental Impacts of Acephate Insecticide (Orthene)," USDA sponsored program report, USFS Coop. Agreement No. 42–197. USDA, Washington, D.C.

Williams, K. S., and Gilbert, L. E. (1981). Insects as selective agents on plant vegetation morphology: egg mimicry reduces egg laying by butterflies. *Science* **212**, 467–469.

Woodfin, F. S. (1976). Soil oxygen diffusion and photosynthetic rates of *Spartina alterniflora* in Connecticut salt marshes. M.A. Thesis, Connecticut College, New London.

Robert F. Denno
Department of Entomology
University of Maryland
College Park, Maryland

CHAPTER 10

Effects of Host-Plant Variability on the Fitness of Sedentary Herbivorous Insects

RODGER MITCHELL

I. INTRODUCTION

Very nearly all the phenomena considered in this book are explained as adaptations of either plants or insects. The advances in studies of how host-plant variation affects insects provide data for a fresh look at the vexing puzzle of what constitutes an adaptation and the critical problem of whether the advantage gained by an adaptation can be tested and precisely measured. I shall consider a general scheme for measuring the value of three purported adaptations.

1. Selective oviposition by the bean weevil *Callosobruchus maculatus,* which is claimed to be an adaptation increasing survival (Mitchell, 1975). (The analysis of oviposition behavior will be compared with the effects of food quality on fitness.)

2. The selection of leaves by the aphid *Pemphigus betae,* which alters the fecundity and survivorship of stem mothers (Whitham, 1978; Chapter 1)

3. *Nuculaspis californica,* a scale insect, which has been said to evolve physiological adaptations for dealing with the chemical peculiarities of individual hosts of ponderosa pine (Edmunds and Alstad, 1978; Alstad and Edmunds, Chapter 12).

VARIABLE PLANTS AND HERBIVORES
IN NATURAL AND MANAGED SYSTEMS

Will a general test prove that these adaptations measurably increase the fitness of the organisms, or are these just three more idiosyncratic adaptationist stories that Gould and Lewontin (1979) would castigate as Panglossian paradigms? Too many of those who try to understand the traits of organisms have followed the example of George Williams (1966): "I have assumed, as is customary, that functional design is something that can be intuitively comprehended by an investigator and convincingly communicated to others [p.260]." Such advice is appropriate when a suite of interacting morphological and physiological traits are considered, but it is not appropriate in dealing with traits that are claimed to have a unitary effect on fitness. Intuitively appealing phrases have become a current fetish among adaptationists. Cute phrases like "evolutionary arms races" (Dawkins and Krebs, 1979), "sexy son hypothesis" (Weatherhead and Robertson, 1979), and the ominous "underworld" in sparrow populations (Smith, 1978) have great appeal as long as no one convincingly consigns an idea to the purgatory of counterintuitive ideas. An anlytical approach, not intuition, should be expected when adaptationists assert that a trait has a unitary effect on fitness, yet Gould and Lewontin (1979) appear to have stopped short of condemning the unscientific reliance of adaptationists for exaggerating the value of selectionist models and would appear to accept intuitive persuasions of adaptationists just as long as it is only a part of a pluralistic view of evolution.

Some of the adaptationist's explanations in the literature are Panglossian nonsense. Other studies are rigorous interpretations of reliable data on fecundity and survivorship in nature that establish differences in fitness between the phenotypes in natural populations. Such studies of the components of fitness and the examples used to erect the Panglossian paradigm are profoundly different, but they do share an important attribute. Almost without exception, field studies are at a new level of sophistication in demanding quantifiable observations and devising more-appropriate statistical analyses. More and more field studies are buttressed by experiments in the field and laboratory. Whatever one thinks about interpretations, these technical changes have moved natural history from a descriptive to an analytical science. The criticisms of Gould and Lewontin (1979) can be relished for their style and imagination, but the pluralistic view they advocated will be flawed unless the emerging rigor in field studies of the mechanisms of adaptation is distinguished from superficial stories about adaptations.

The pluralistic view should not be a compromise, as implied by Gould and Lewontin (1979). It should be based on the explicit recognition that research on the evolution of complex interactive systems involving compromises and constraints must be done quite differently than research on traits that have an independent unitary effect on fitness. The latter can be precisely measured by an adaptationist, whereas the interactions of complex systems can only be described and functional compromises and constraints explained. Studies of interacting systems have used the concept of a body plan and have applied it to systems that cannot be separated into a set of independent adaptations. It may be possible to account for the origin of a given body plan from antecedant systems, but it is not possible to evaluate the gain of fitness because a question like, How much does flight contribute to the fitness of an insect? has no answer. At best we can explain how flight works and what its metabolic cost is.

Given an insect that can fly, then alternative flight patterns represent independent modes of behavior, and the adaptive value of a random-flight pattern versus a flight pattern modified by the discovery of food can be measured as a yield of food. If the way that food alters survival or fecundity can be determined, then explicit measures of fitness can be obtained for the two modes of flight and used to measure the gain in fitness that results from nonrandom flight.

The pluralist, then, will seek to explain how systems operate when dealing with complex interactive sets of traits and, in dealing with non-interacting unitary traits, will go beyond intuitive explanations to prove a measurable alteration of fitness. Alterations of survival or fecundity, or both, change fitness so that measurements of fitness must rest on the determination of net reproductive rates (R_0) or intrinsic rates of growth (r_m) from the analysis of life tables (Istock, 1970; Mitchell and Williams, 1979).

II. MEASURING THE EFFECT OF ADAPTATIONS ON FITNESS

If alternative traits are found in nature, then it may be possible to measure the fecundity and survival of each phenotype to compare the fitness of the phenotypes. The traditional examples of empirical proof for the value of adaptations, industrial melanism (Kettlewell, 1956, 1965), snail colors (Cain and Sheppard, 1954), and sickle-cell anemia (Allison, 1964), rest on evidence of differential mortality rather than detailed life tables. It is assumed, with good reason, that other modifiers of fitness, environmental and biotic interactions with survival and fecundity, could not reverse the effects on fitness inferred in the original studies. In addition to these studies of polymorphisms in nature, the value of an adaption can be measured against a synthesized antecedent phenotype, as in disrupting a mimic or aposematic color pattern (Brower et al., 1971) or considering how the result of a random search differs from the observed fitness with nonrandom foraging (Mitchell, 1975). Laboratory experiments paralleling field studies can also be used to measure components of fitness (Istock *et al.*, 1976).

If measures of survival and fecundity are complete enough to provide a life-table schedule for the life cycle or some segment of the life cycle, then a measure of fitness can be obtained. Fitness is a complex function in animals with overlapping and interacting cohorts, but such complications are avoided in the calculation of fitness for insects having a synchronized succession of year-long generations. In such insects, R_0 is a direct measure of the contribution to the next generation. Comparisons of R_0 for alternative phenotypes provide quantitative measures that fit M. William's (1970) axiomatization of natural selection and other models for fitness (Istock, 1970; Mitchell and Williams, 1979).

The examples used here provide data for the calculation of R_0 that is a measure of fitness (w). The relative value of a trait will be determined as the difference between the fitness of the original or antecedent trait (w_0) and the phenotype with the derived adaptation (w_a). It is convenient to express this as a ratio:

$$\text{value of a trait} = w_a/w_0, \tag{1}$$

with 1.0 indicating equal value. Ratios other than 1.0 define the differential in contributions to the next generation. This will be the measure of relative fitness applied here.

It is not a matter of chance that sedentary insects are selected for analysis. These insects spend a major segment of their life attached to one site on the host. They leave a record of mortality and, in some cases, fecundity at the attachment site. Of the 21 reasonably complete life tables of insects reviewed by Price (1975), most (13/21) are sedentary herbivores such as leaf miners, gall formers, bean weevils, scale insects, and stem borers. The attachment site defines the resource; hence, the record of resource-related fecundity and survival can be read from remains at the attachment site. Consequently, sedentary insects are ideal subjects for determining the way resources can affect survival and fecundity in nature and how this, in turn, determines fitness.

Stearns (1977) specified what one must know about a population in order to establish the basic facts about life history phenomena and define an adaptation. Stearns' criteria are

1. Was the genetic basis for variability identified?
2. Were the environmental factors used in the explanation measured?
3. Was the pattern of population regulation measured?
4. Was year-to-year variability in mortality measured?
5. Were the data used in the explanation verified with statistical tests?
6. Was the reproductive effort measured and its variance explained?

Perhaps few of these criteria can be satisfied in field studies, but the studies of the three sedentary herbivores considered here can meet more criteria than are met in the most complete studies cited by Stearns (1977). All criteria but number 1 are met in the most complete studies cited by Stearns (1977). All criteria but number 1 are met in the case of *Pemphigus* (Whitham, 1978; Chapter 1). For *Callosobruchus* 5 criteria are met (Mitchell, 1975), and the genetic data can be obtained (Utida, 1972). All criteria could be met in studies of *Nuculaspis* (Edmunds and Alstad, 1978). The 34 studies cited by Stearns (1977) met an average of 1.8 criteria and only 5 studies satisfied 4 criteria.

Evolutionary explanations are developed in two steps that are analogous to defining a line in geometry. If the criteria just enumerated are satisfied, then phenotypes with the adaptive trait can be compared to phenotypes without the trait. Evolutionary models may use contemporary estimates of adaptations to make projections backward over evolutionary time. This second step of asserting how the environment and the biota interacted to affect survivorship and fecundity over evolutionary time is pure speculation. There is rarely any alternative to the argument that the selective differentials existing at this time are representative of the evolutionary forces that operated over evolutionary time. Assertions about the patterns of survival and fecundity over many generations may be less outrageous presumptions for the sedentary herbivores considered here. The evolution of seed selection by *Callosobruchus* presumes that legume seeds always varied in size and that size itself independently affects fitness in several ways. *Pemphigus* is presumed to have responded to an association of photosynthate quantity with the area of a leaf, and the scale insets are thought to be faced with trees, each of which has a characteristic chemical phenotype throughout its life. These kinds of relations do seem likely to have persisted over evolutionary time spans.

Each of the three examples will be evaluated for the way in which the criteria for defining adaptations from data on resources and life history (Stearns, 1977) are met, and then the problem of projecting events over evolutionary time will be reviewed.

III. EXAMPLES

A. Callosobruchus maculatus

This beetle has been a pest in stored beans, principally species of *Vigna* (Larson, 1927; Balachowski, 1962), for several thousand years. With eight to ten generations a year in the warm climates where it flourishes, the beetles may well have experienced tens of thousands of generations as a domestic pest. *Callosobruchus maculatus* seems likely to be as well adapted to life in bean stores, just as wild species are adapted to their present environment. Most laboratory experiments match storage conditions, and these reveal a great deal about the patterns of survivorship and fecundity.

Physical factors (temperature and humidity) and host quality have physiological effects that alter mortality, development time, and fecundity. Such alterations are the consequences of a set of physiological compromises and constraints that are the physiological equivalent of a body plan. It is most unlikely that there will be one simple unitary response to temperature, another to humidity, with a third independent response to food quality.

The physiological responses will be used to illustrate the problems of dealing with a complex interactive set of adaptations. Oviposition behavior will be used as an example of an independent unitary trait that can be analyzed for its direct effect on fitness.

1. Physiological Response to Resources

As a species, *Callosobruchus maculatus* is polyphagous, but larvae cannot move from one bean to another, so every individual is obligately monophagous. Each individual must develop in the bean on which its mother attached an egg. The various beans on which *C. maculatus* will oviposit are known to affect mortality, developmental patterns, and fecundity (Larson, 1927; Howe and Curry, 1964; Nwanze and Horber, 1975a). Oviposition follows development, and females will lay a complement of eggs in 10 days, even if they have no water or food. This is the resource-determined fecundity. When given water, fecundity rose from 88.5 to 114.9 eggs, with honey, females laid 119.9 eggs (not significantly different from water), and with sugar water, fecundity was significantly increased to 127.5 eggs (Larson and Fisher, 1927). Because beetles in storage conditions rarely have access to water or food, it is appropriate to use the egg production of females without food or water as a measure of the effect of food resources on fecundity.

Fecundity, physiological deaths, and development time are the physiological determinants of fitness, and all must be measured to determine fitness differentials. All three are affected by food quality (Larson, 1927; Howe and Curry, 1964, Nwanze and Horber, 1975a), but it is not known if the responses are so closely correlated that one physiological response will be an index of the effect of host quality.

To determine the interactions among the physiologial factors, a set of newly emerged females from a stock maintained on the Oriental variety of mung beans *(Vigna radiata)* were provided with four commonly attacked host beans for 72 hr. Beans with one egg on them were isolated and the fate of each egg determined. This cohort of similarly aged (± 36 hr) eggs were held under identical ambient conditions (21–23°C), and emerging females were mated within 24 hr and isolated to oviposit on 150 beans of the type from which they emerged. Females had neither food nor water.

The sex ratio of the emerging beetles was 1:1, so R_0 could be calculated as one-half of the product of survival and fecundity, and r_m was obtained as $(\ln R_0)/T$, where T is development time (Istock, 1970). These estimates of physiologically determined fitness show that two hosts, moth (*Vigna acontifolia*) and Oriental mung beans, are favorable, whereas black-eye peas (*V. unguiculata*) and adzuki (*V. angularis*) are unfavorable (Table I). The low egg mortality is characteristic of the entire cohort and independent of bean type. All other life-table components were similar in moth and oriental except fecundity, which was slightly lower for females from moth beans. Moth beans are very small, and the fecundity of females emerging from moth beans is correlated with the weight of the bean on which they fed ($r_{20} = 0.50$, $P < 0.05$): eggs = 36.9 + (1.37 × milligrams of bean).

Weevils growing in adzuki and black eye have a sharply reduced fitness. Nearly half of the larvae in adzuki and a quarter of those in black eye die during the larval stage. All surviving larvae pass through the pupal stage to emerge as normal-appearing adults, but the adult can exit only if the larva prepared an exit prior to pupation. The last acts of a normal larva are to excavate the endosperm from under a circular window of the seed coat and weaken the margins of that window so that the adult can push its way out. In adzuki, 27% of the larvae either failed to cut an exit or cut a faulty exit. These larvae nevertheless completed pupation normally, but the adults from these pupae died entombed by their own aberrant behavior as larvae. This is also true for larvae in black eye. Because the proportions of larvae dying and misbehaving are closely correlated in a given host (Table I), the two physiological responses may be caused by the same deficiency in resources.

Resource quality also affects fecundity and development time. These physiological responses appear to be independent of larval mortality and behavior because development time is significantly longer in adzuki but not in black eye, whereas fecundity is significantly lower in black eye and normal in adzuki. Because survival, development time, and fecundity vary independently of each other, fitness estimates will require complete life-table data, as in Table I.

The fine work of Howe and Curry (1964) gives an idea of how this complex of physiological responses to host quality may interact with temperature and humidity. Their data can be projected as surfaces describing the patterns of survival and fecundity with respect to climate

Table I

Life-Table Statistics for a Cohort ($\pm$36 hr) of *Callosobruchus maculatus* Eggs Developing under Identical Ambient Conditions on Four Different Hosts[a]

Bean	Stage of death				Adult survival	Fecundity[b]	R_o	Development time[b]	r^m $[(\ln R_o)/t]$
	No eggs	Eggs	Larvae	Exiting					
Moth (28.8 mg) (*Vigna acontifolia*)	135	0.044[a]	0.141[a]	0.000[a]	0.815[a]	74.3 (66–82)	30.3	45.2 (45–46)	0.0754
Oriental (44.0 mg) (*Vigna radiata*)	146	0.089[a]	0.082[a]	0.000[a]	0.829[a]	89.7 (82–97)	37.2	46.8 (46–48)	0.0773
Adzuki (94.3 mg) (*Vigna angularis*)	135	0.030[z]	0.430[b]	0.274[b]	0.267[b]	82.6 (67–98)	11.0	54.2 (51–58)	0.0443
Black-eye pea (248.1 mg) (*Vigna unguiculata*)	141	0.050[a]	0.255[c]	0.199[c]	0.496[c]	57.2 (48–67)	14.2	48.0 (47–49)	0.0552

[a] $T = 21$–24°C. Death rates and survival rates that differ from the others at a 0.01 level are given the different letter subscript (there were no differences at the 0.05–0.01 level based on the confidence limits for percentages).
[b] Confidence limits are 95% for fecundity and development time.

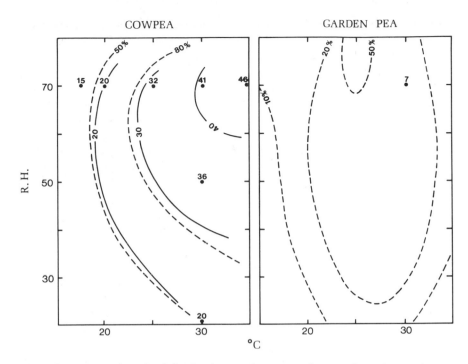

Fig. 1. Response surfaces for *Callosobruchus maculatus* on two hosts under various regimens of climate. The dashed lines join points of equal percentage of survival as a function of temperature (°C) and relative humidity (R.H.). Solid lines are fecundity, and the points indicate net reproductive rate (R_0) at particular combinations of humidity and temperature. Based on data from Howe and Curry (1964).

for beetles feeding on two hosts, cowpeas *(Vigna unguiculata)* and garden peas *(Pisum sativum).*

When grown in cowpeas, *Callosobruchus maculatus* is most successful at high temperatures and moderate humidities, but when feeding on garden peas *C. maculatus* is most successful at high humidities and moderate temperatures. The interaction between climate and host quality produces profoundly different patterns of survival and fecundity (Fig. 1), just as host quality alone produces large uncorrelated differences in life-table components (Table I). It would appear that physiological responses may well be unique for each combination of climate and host, which suggests a very complex interactive set of physiological constraints.

Still another physiological response is seen at times of crowding. When an outbreak population is at the point of destroying a clump of beans, the metabolic heat from dense concentrations of larvae may trigger the appearance of the active morph. Temperature (Sano, 1967) and, possibly, other cues associated with crowding (Taylor, 1974; Nwanze and Horber, 1975b) induce a switch in development so that small, more active, flying adults of reduced fecundity appear. The active forms live 10–20 days in the laboratory, twice as long as normal morphs. In addition to fully developed wing muscles, they have 70% more fat stores and a partially developed ovary, with only a few fully developed eggs. Active morphs produce an average of 38 eggs, 27 less than normal morphs (Utida, 1972).

The body plan of the active and the normal morph may represent a compromise, with the loss of 27 eggs in fecundity representing the cost of developing and of fueling flight. This can be looked on as a measure of the cost of dispersal, but it cannot be taken as a basis for comparing the fitness of the two morphs. If active morphs appeared when the local resources were destroyed, then the normal morphs would have zero fitness because there would be no resources. All active morphs producing more than 0 eggs would have a greater potential fitness. The dimorphic species is adapted for discontinuous arrays of resources, in which several generations can be passed in most resource patches. The relative advantage of one morph over the other changes with the resource density.

The physiological responses just reviewed are the outcome of processes regulating growth, metabolism, and water balance. If the species has a general pattern of response, then the physiological aspects of fitness, survival and fecundity, can be expressed as

$$r_m = f(T,H,Q,D). \tag{2}$$

The data at hand (Table I; Fig. 1) establish that there is not an orderly relation of survival and fecundity with temperature (T), humidity (H), resource quality (Q), and density (D). The interactions are complex and have major effects on components of fitness. As a result, there may be no optimal adaptive response for a population using a variety of hosts in a variable climate and little hope of accounting for the observed physiological traits as adaptations.

2. Oviposition Strategy

Females make choices as they deposit a physiologically determined complement of eggs. Each egg is firmly glued to a bean, and eggs will be attached to any kind of surface if females are confined at artificially high densities. However, such densities are not found when females are allowed to disperse. In nature, and in all experiments in which the potential fecundity of females is no more than two or three times the number of available beans, there is a consistent pattern of selective oviposition in response to three factors.

Females prefer smooth beans over beans that have a rough or irregular surface or any kind of physical damage (Larson, 1927; Nwanze and Horber, 1975a). When given one kind of bean, females will oviposit on the largest beans first and then add eggs to smaller and smaller beans (Utida, 1943; Avidov *et al.*, 1965a; Mitchell, 1975; Nwanze and Horber, 1975a). Finally, females will avoid adding a second egg to a bean until nearly all available beans have one egg on them, and this may be due to a pheromone (Oshima *et al.*, 1973).

The roughness, size, and density of eggs on a bean are unrelated cues that correlate with a variety of factors determining the prospective survival, fecundity, or both. The three oviposition responses and the prospective fitness of eggs are independent functions. The consequences of any nonrandom pattern of oviposition can be measured against the fitness of randomly dispersed sets of eggs. Such measures of the advantages or disadvantages of specialized behavior can be used to explore the problems of validating rigorous adaptationist explanations for each kind of nonrandom oviposition.

a. Density.   Egg density is critical when eggs are placed on host seeds that are not large enough to feed two larvae. Moth beans are too small to support two larvae and some mung beans are too small for the development of two larvae (Mitchell, 1975). It is rare to find two exits on a bean large enough to support two larvae until a second generation is grown on a set of beans. In a sample of 250 beans carrying two equal-aged eggs, there were 21 double exits and 207 single exits. Development for beetles in all beans with two eggs was 30% longer than development in beans with single eggs (Mitchell, 1975). In the experiment cited in Table I, females deposited two eggs on 29 black-eye peas, which are nine to ten times the size of mung beans, and all black-eye peas had only single exits. Some kind of interference competition must have eliminated one larva and delayed the survivor's development. Perhaps interference competition evolved to insure the success of at least one larva from smaller beans. In exploitive competition both larvae would die when the resources of the bean were used up.

Interference competition sharply increases the advantage gained from minimizing the eggs on a bean.

If females are presumed to search in a fashion that resembles random movement, then the effort, expressed as the number of contacts per bean, needed to achieve an observed level of dispersion can be deter-

Table II
Dispersion of Eggs on Beans in the Experiments, Tested against the Poisson[a]

| | Beans with n eggs [mean weight (mg) of beans] | | | | | | Mean contacts/bean |
Bruchid	n = 0	1	2	3	χ^2	Eggs/Bean	$[ln(N_0/N)]$
Callosobruchus	26	117	35	1	24.72^b	1.06	1.93
maculatus	[46]	[52]	[57]	[88]			
Stator	42	16	7	3	3.22	0.57	0.48
limbatus	[242]	[256]	[270]	[288]			
Mimosestes	10	38	12	0	18.84^b	1.03	1.79
amicus	[190]	[221]	[218]	—			

[a]The contacts indicate the average number of times each bean would have to be encountered in a random search to discover the number of beans with eggs on them. Dry beans were presented to females in flat 9-cm diameter dishes.
[b]$P < 0.001$.

mined. If beans with no eggs are presumed to be undiscovered (N_0), then the average contacts per bean ($\bar{c}$) can be obtained by solving for $\bar{c}$ in the Poisson term for zero contacts when N_0 and the number of beans (N) are known:

$$N_0 = N e^{-\bar{c}}, \text{ therefore, } \bar{c} = \ln(N_0/N). \tag{3}$$

Table II gives the cost of dispersion for *Callosobruchus maculatus* and two other bruchids. *Stator limbatus* distributes its eggs as a Poisson, with the ratio of contacts to eggs per bean insignificantly different from 1.0; hence, this beetle does not expend extra effort in dispersing eggs. Both *C. maculatus* and *Mimosestes amicus* disperse eggs significantly more uniformly than a Poisson and can achieve this by having the ratio of contacts to eggs per bean increased to 1.93 and 1.79, respectively (Table II). This is the behavioral cost of dispersion.

The dispersion of eggs by *Callosobruchus maculatus* increases the number of beans with one egg from 65.7 expected under the Poisson to 117 and decreases the beans with two or more eggs from 51.3 to 35. When multiple eggs are on a bean, interference competition may eliminate surplus larvae; the dispersion by *C maculatus* reduced interference competition by 42%. The yield of offspring, which is proportional to beans with single eggs on them, is 31% above that expected under a Poisson. That is the benefit gained from the extra effort invested in searching.

Presumably, exploitative competition in beans too small for two larvae could favor the evolution of both dispersion of eggs and interference competition. Interference competition may have developed first. In either case, interference competition greatly increases the advantages of dispersing eggs, to the extent that large beans that could support two or more larvae are limited to production of one beetle. An adaptationist explanation for the trait of dispersing eggs depends on answers to two questions: (1) Did egg dispersion evolve in response to exploitative competition or as a consequence of the evolution of interference competition? (2) Could a majority of the beans support two or more larvae without serious exploitative competition? The answer to the first question is lost in history. Most certainly a majority of the beans attacked have much more than twice the 15 mg of endosperm needed by one *Callosobruchus maculatus* (Mitchell, 1975). If females deposited eggs in proportion to food resources, they would be much more efficient exploiters of resources than *C. maculatus* is now. Beans large enough to support two or more larvae are, with only rare exceptions (Mitchell, 1975), under-exploited. The greater success of females that disperse eggs is not presently due to an adaptation to bean size; instead, it is a trait maintained as the result of an evolved larval behavior. This trait of dispersing eggs leaves large quantities of potential food resources unused.

b. Bean Size.   *Callosobruchus maculatus* can distinguish bean size on the basis of cues associated with the curvature of the surface (Avidov *et al.*, 1965b). There are several instances of survival and fecundity increasing with bean weight. In cowpeas (Nwanze and Horber, 1975a) and some varieties of mung bean (Mitchell, 1975), survival is linearly related to bean size (Fig. 2), but food quality evidently acts to make the intercept for mung bean higher than that for cowpea. It is now known that size-related survival on mung bean is a characteristic peculiar to a commercial stock of beans (Mitchell, 1975) that may have been imported from Thailand. That relation is not seen in the common cultivars (Berkin and Oriental) grown in the United States.

The benefits of selecting larger beans are maximal at low densities. To measure empirically the potential gain on the commercial stock of mung bean, freshly emerged and mated females were isolated with 100 beans (averaging 42.2 mg) and interrupted before they had deposited more than 10 eggs. Eggs were placed on beans averaging 59.9 mg, and they would be expected to have had a survival of 0.614, based on the regression from Fig. 2. Eggs on beans averaging 42.2 mg would be expected to have a survival of 0.579. Fecundity is not affected by bean weight. Because survival is the only variable component of fitness (Fig. 3), the difference in fitness resulting from selective oviposition (Fig. 3) is

$$w_a/w_0 = l_a/l_0 = 0.614/0.597 = 1.061. \qquad (4)$$

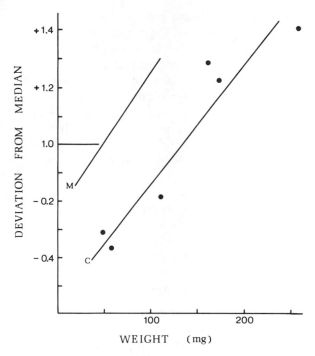

Fig. 2. Curves for the survival of *Callosobruchus maculatus* on mung beans (M, *Vigna radiata*), from Mitchell (1976), and several varieties of cowpeas (C, *Vigna unguiculata*), from Nwanze and Horber (1975a), as a function of bean weight. Survival (*l*) is given as deviations from the survival on a median sized bean: M, $l = 0.368 + (0.005 \text{ mg})$; C, $l = 0.250 + (0.002 \text{ mg})$. The points for survival refer to cowpea data.

The fitness gained by selective oviposition is highest at low egg densities and falls as egg densities increase.

It was shown earlier that females emerging from moth beans (Table I), have fecundity significantly ($r_{20} = 0.499$, $P < 0.05$) correlated with bean weight: eggs $= 36.90 + (1.37 \times \text{milligrams of bean})$. Again, empirical estimates of differential oviposition were obtained from three freshly emerged and mated females isolated on 150 moth beans for 48 hr. They each deposited 8–10 eggs, and the 28 beans with eggs (35.28 mg) would be expected to produce females with an expected fecundity of 85.2, whereas eggs laid on a random sample of beans (30.77 mg) would produce females with a fecundity of 79.0. Survival is constant over bean size; consequently, the difference in fitness due to selection of larger beans (Fig. 4) will be

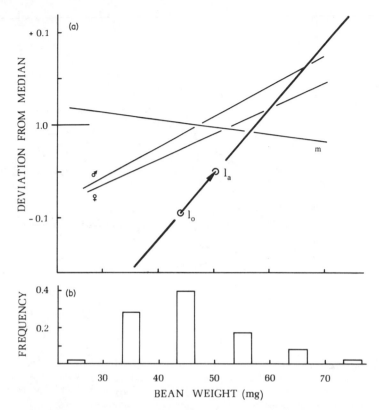

Fig. 3. (a) Weight of mung beans (*Vigna aureus*) and its effect on the fitness of *Callosobruchus maculatus*. (b) Relative abundances of beans. If eggs were dispersed at random, the survivorship from egg to adult would be l_0, but selection of large beans is an adaptation that increases survivorship to l_a. The slopes of the regression lines for survivorship ($l = 0.007$, $r = 0.98$) and weights ($\male = 0.03$, $r = 0.60$; $\female = 0.03$, $r = 0.50$) are shown as deviations from performance on beans of median weight. The relation of fitness to body weight is not known.

$$w_a/w_0 = m_a/m_0 = 85.2/79.0 = 1.08. \qquad (5)$$

Survival on certain mung-bean cultivars increases with weight, and on moth beans it is fecundity, not survival, that increases with weight. There are two other known ways in which bean size can affect survival. Bruchids always encounter a few stunted or aborted seeds. In the case of *Callosobruchus maculatus*, certain species of hosts are smaller than the stunted seeds of larger hosts. Absolute size cannot be used to reject the stunted and aborted seeds in which larvae die, but females can avoid placing eggs on such seeds if they select the largest seeds first.

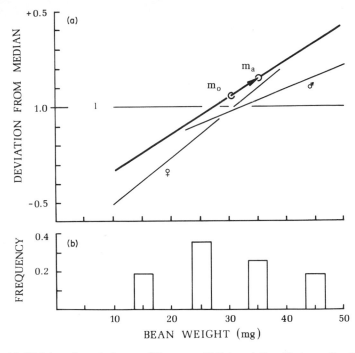

Fig. 4. (a) Weight of moth beans *(Vigna acontifolia)* and its effect on the fitness of *Callosobruchus maculatus.* (b) Relative abundances of beans. If eggs were dispersed at random, the fecundity of emerging females would be m_0, but selection of larger beans is an adaptation that increases fitness to m_a. The slopes of the regression lines for fecundity (m = 0.018, r = 0.499) and weight ($\male$ = 0.020, r = 0.615; $\female$ = 0.024, r = 0.499) are shown as deviations from the performance on median-weight beans. Only survivorship (l) is not significantly correlated with bean weight.

Another possible explanation is that larger seeds allow the larvae to bore deeply, and, if the entrance passage is longer than the ovipositor of parasitoids, the larva can escape parasitism. This may have happened in the experiments of Utida (1955).

Thus there are four independent effects on fitness, each of which would give an advantage to females that discriminate bean size: avoidance of stunted beans, escape from parasites, and bean-weight–survival or bean-weight–fecundity relations. Any one or a combination of these factors could favor the evolution of bean-size discrimination. It is possible to measure how these factors affect fitness in a particular population at the present time, but proof of the way a trait is currently maintained is not proof that these same factors operated as the trait evolved. Each of the four different factors could act independently or in any combination to produce the same outcome. Because discrimination of bean size can be advantageous under many circumstances, one might expect it to be a common trait of bruchids.

The two bruchids attacking *Cercidium floridum* (palo verde), *Mimosestes amicus* and *Stator limbatus*, have sharply contrasting habits in nature (Mitchell, 1976). As defined by Johnson (1981), *M. amicus* belongs to the mature-pod guild that oviposits only on pods. *Stator limbatus* is of the mature-seed guild and must gain access to the seeds in the pod in order to oviposit. *Callosobruchus maculatus* belongs to the third guild, the scattered-seed guild.

When presented with loose beans in the laboratory, the three species, representing different guilds, selected the larger beans for oviposition, despite the artificiality of the experimental system (Table II). The system is most unrealistic for *Mimosestes amicus*, which normally oviposits only on pods just beginning to dry out, but which was forced to oviposit on exposed, dry seeds in the laboratory. The oviposition pattern of *M. amicus* in nature can be determined from the eggs stuck to the pod (Mitchell, 1976), and the ability of *M. amicus* to discriminate size in nature can be tested because seed position is not a cue to seed size. In a sample of 25 two-seeded palo verde pods with eggs but no seed damage, the basal seed was larger in 13 cases and the distal seed larger in the other 12. An average of 4.3 ± 1.3 eggs were attached over the larger seed, and 1.0 + 0.4 eggs over the smaller. *Mimosestes amicus* does discriminate the size of seeds in the pods in nature.

By following the advice of Sih and Dixon (1981), "Thus, it is very important that one consider all reasonable alternate hypotheses and then try to create tests that can unambiguously rule out hypotheses [p. 558]", four completely independent explanations for the advantage of selecting larger seeds have been demonstrated (Figs. 3 and 4) or strongly implied. It may well be impossible to account for the advantage of selective oviposition for a contemporary *Callosobruchus maculatus* population, because a set of advantages may change with the abundances of alternative hosts, or parasites, or with the weather (which affects the frequencies of stunted or aborted seeds). Each advantage can be measured with precision, but these measures will not lend support to adaptationist explanations when a variety of independent factors simultaneously affect the components of fitness.

c. Surface Texture. In mixtures of beans with different surface textures, the rougher seeds are rejected. This discrimination disappears, however, if the seed coat is removed. Among 2301 eggs on smooth beans, 93% of the larvae penetrated the bean, but only 89% of the larvae from 2578 eggs on rough seeds penetrated the bean (Nwanze and Horber, 1976). The 4% advantage of smooth beans is attributed to the ability of larvae to chew through the loosely arranged ridges of macrosclereids in the seed coat of smooth seeds and the fact that newly hatched larvae have more leverage, because the egg shell is more firmly attached to smooth surfaces. The cues used to distinguish roughness may also serve as the basis for rejecting cracked and broken seeds, in which the larvae often die of exposure. An adaptionist explanation for the rejection of cracked beans and varieties with rough surfaces is not confounded by interacting constraints, but it is ambiguous because one set of cues may identify two different sources of larval mortality, seed-coat morphology and breaks in seeds. These two mortality factors may have acted independently or together in the evolution of responses, for rejecting all beans with irregular surfaces.

B. Aphids and Resources

A stem mother of *Pemphigus* attaches to a leaf and remains at one position. The environmental factors affecting each female are fixed by her position, and the resources she can use are related to the surface area of the leaf. Leaves collected at the end of the season carry a record of the level of infestation, stem-mother mortality, and fecundity. The density of aphids on the leaf and the regulation of the densities of aphids on leaves have been analyzed in great detail (Whitham, 1980). The genetic basis for the behavior and variation in life-history traits is not known, and it may be impractical to measure the effects of genetic variance for aphids with a complex annual life cycle. Thus all the criteria specified by Stearns (1977), except heritability, are fully satisfied.

The newly hatched stem mother selects the resources she and her daughters will use. Leaves at the base and tip of a twig are smaller than those in the middle; thus selection of the middle leaves along the twig would put aphids on the largest leaves. The smaller leaves at the base and tip are less frequently occupied, and the orienting behavior is so strong that there is competition for potentially larger leaves (Whitham, 1978, 1980). Chemical cues may identify larger leaves (Whitham, Chapter 1).

All leaves appear to provide similar environments, but they provide different quantities of resources. Photosynthate production of a leaf is proportional to the leaf area, which ranges from 5.0 to 17.5 cm^2, a threefold range. The assertion that the photosynthate from a leaf determines the performance of a stem mother is supported by experiments in which aphids on fertilized trees have been shown to have higher fecundities

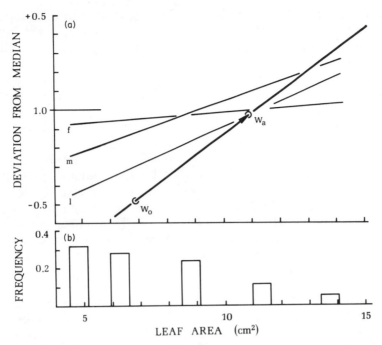

Fig. 5. (a) Leaf area and its effect on the components of fitness in *Pemphigus betae*. (b) Relative abundances of leaf-size classes. If aphid stem mothers were dispersed at random over the leaves, they would have a fitness of w_0 (Table III). Larger leaves are selected for settling, and so the observed fitness due to the adaptive discrimination of leaves is wa. Slopes of the regression lines for fitness ($w = 0.11$) and its components, survival of stem mothers ($l = 0.06$) and fecundity of steam mothers ($m = 0.05$) and embryos (granddaughters) in the bodies of dispersing daughters ($f = 0.01$), are all shown as deviations from the performance of stem mothers on median-sized leaves. All slopes have $r > 0.95$. Data from Whitham (1978; and personal communication).

(Whitham, 1978). The direct association of each aphid with one leaf provides one of the simplest and most direct ways to measure how the quantity of resources can determine fitness in nature.

The survival, number of daughters, and potential of those daughters can be measured for individual stem mothers. The only component of fitness that has not been measured is the probability of a daughter dispersing to an alternative host and surviving. Consequently, this is not a complete measure of fitness over the life cycle, but it is an exact measure of all the components of fitness during the entire segment of the life cycle spent on the primary host.

The positive correlation of these components of fitness with leaf surface area (Fig. 5) is the sort of outcome expected if the leaves differed only in the quantity of resources available to the stem mother. Stem-mother survival contributes the most to stem-mother fitness. There is a 6% increase in survival for each square centimeter of leaf, whereas fecundity (number of daughters maturing) increases by 5%. The three multiplicative components of fitness combine to give a slope of 11% (Fig. 5). Fitness is a joint function of three components that have different response rates to resources. The trade-off between survival and fecundity with respect to resources is: survival : fecundity = 1.2:1.0. This means that as females gain more resources, both components of fitness show a linear increase. Survival increases most rapidly, whereas embryos per daughter increases at a significant ($P < 0.05$) but slow rate. The different rates might be interpreted in two ways. The slopes might represent the cost in resources of survival versus reproduction, or it could be an adaptive response that divides resources between production and survival, perhaps to maximize the number of daughters. The number of daughters determines the chances of successful dispersal to a secondary host, and dispersal may be more important than the subsequent fecundity of the dispersing daughters.

The relative value of the ability of *Pemphigus* to select leaves can be measured from the data of Table III. The fitness of females is taken as the product of survivorship and yields of daughters and embryos in daughters, as determined from the data of Whitham (1978, also personal communication), used by Mitchell (1981). The sum of the products of leaf-specific fitness and the frequencies for each leaf-size class on the tree is the presumed performance of females without the ability to discriminate leaves, whereas the sum of products using the observed frequency of aphid galls gives the performance with discrimination: Equation (1) gives

$$w_a/w_0 = 1340.3/737.1 = 1.82 \tag{6}$$

as the gain in relative fitness with the trait.

This is a very large gain, which seems to be a general trait despite the tree-to-tree and branch-to-branch variation discussed by Whitham (1981). Combining the data from Tables I and II of Whitham (1981) with the specific values based on Whitham (1978) gives a relation of survival to leaf size (cm^2):

$$\text{survival} = 0.136 + (0.054 \times cm^2). \tag{7}$$

The correlation coefficient ($r_{11} = 0.879$) is significant at the 1% level, and the slopes for the three data sets are not significantly different from that of the pooled data.

Table III
Calculation of the Fitness of *Pemphigus* without Leaf-Size Discrimination, in Contrast to the Observed Selection of Leaves[a]

Leaf area (cm²)	Offspring	Leaf frequency		Yields of aphids	
		On tree	With galls	Random dispersion	Observed dispersion
5.1	209.4	0.317	0.000	66.4	0.0
5.1–7.5	633.2	0.275	0.045	174.1	28.5
7.6–10.0	846.3	0.235	0.394	198.9	333.4
10.1–12.5	1631.1	0.106	0.283	172.9	461.6
12.6–15.0	1740.1	0.052	0.202	90.5	351.5
15.1–17.5	2146.5	0.016	0.077	34.3	165.3
				737.1	1340.3

[a]Data from Whitham (1978; and personal communication), used as explained in the text and by Mitchell (1981).

Perhaps it is impossible to prove that the differences in female performance are the simple consequences of the quantity of photosynthate per leaf, but I can think of no alternative explanation. One might argue that the behaviorial discrimination resulting in the colonization of leaves, even if it is based on the secondary cue of leaf position, could have evolved under some other conditions, but again I can think of no alternative.

The behaviorial discrimination that puts *Pemphigus* on larger leaves results in almost doubling female fitness. The argument that the contemporary relationship of leaf area to female fitness is representative of conditions that have persisted over revolutionary time is persuasive for two reasons. (1) The increase of photosynthate yields with leaf area is a fundamental property of all plants. (2) The fitness differentials are large, and the correlations are significant, but the strongest arguments lie in the fact that alternative explanations seem to be excluded in this case because both the leaf selection and the resource–leaf-area relation seem to be independent unitary traits that do not interact with each other and that are not part of a more inclusive adaptive system.

C. Black Pineleaf Scale

The scale insect *Nuculaspis californica* appears to be the best example of how the evolution of adaptations in sedentary insect herbivores can be traced and quantified. All the feeding of a scale insect is done at one site, so the history of each scale can be traced from the time a dispersant, the *crawler*, attaches (Edmunds, 1973). Estimates of fecundity can be obtained in the field, although there is some uncertainty because females produce a sequence of eggs over a period of about 2 weeks. The relative density of a scale population at maturity, July, can be easily obtained from samples of needles, which also bear the remains of the scales that died.

That the density of scale populations increases with the age of the host tree led Edmunds (1973) to suggest that the scales on an older tree are predominantly a lineage that has evolved adaptations to the chemical signature of their host. Populations on a mature (180 yr) host presumably reflect the outcome of nearly 180 generations of selection. The outcome evidently differs from tree to tree because each tree has a characteristic density of scales, and most attempts to transfer scales from tree to tree fail (Edmunds and Alstad, 1978; Alstad and Edmunds, Chapter 12).

Winged males and crawlers do disperse to other trees, so the populations are not isolated. Still, there is stringent selection, so the population is most likely to be predominantly descended from the previous year's population on the tree. The mechanisms of adaptation and the problems of maintaining colonizing ability and evolving adaptations to the host have been discussed (Alstad and Edmunds, Chapter 12).

The available data are incomplete and, in some ways, inappropriate for critical measures of adaptations to host chemistry, yet some preliminary estimates can be made. This approximation is an important exercise because it illustrates an extension of the analysis developed here and is put forth here in spite of reservations held by G. F. Edmunds, Jr. and D. N. Alstad (personal communication) and myself.

Scales from different trees differ in their adaptations, and trees differ in their suitability, so the antecedent state (no host-specific adaptation) must be taken as the average performance of colonizing crawlers from many donor trees on a large and representative sample of recipient trees. In 271 transfer experiments (Edmunds and Alstad, 1978) the scales established in 29% of the experiments but only 10% reproduced, and only in 2 cases was the level of reproduction high enough to replace the population with young ($R_0 > 1.0$). Earlier, it was noted that only 10% of the young trees (<2 m) carried populations of at least 1.4 scales per needle, and that would be the result of multiple colonizations and several generations of selection.

The frequency of populations establishing in these transfer experiments, 0.0074 (= 2/271), can be taken as a measure of the incidence of colonization. Colonization and selection act on resident populations over many generations. Although 10% of the trees under 2 m have large populations, 67% of those over 9 m do. These scale populations may have had 25–175 generations to adapt to their host (Edmunds, 1973). The densities of scale populations also appear to be greater on older trees.

By making the reasonable assumption of uniformitarianism, the populations on young trees at the present time can be taken as representative of the situation at the time of establishment of the populations we now see on old trees. Hence, contemporaneous observations can be used as if they represented the beginning and the end of a 200-generation selection experiment. The value of the adaptation to a single host might be most appropriately measured as some joint function of the frequency of trees with scales and the density of scales on a large number of aged trees. To illustrate the calculation, the success of transfers (0.0074) can be taken as representing the frequency of scales establishing on young trees. This measure of the antecendent trait (t_0) can be compared to the frequency of denser scale populations in a large sample of older trees, as the adapted trait (t_a). Hence, the value of adaptation to a host would be, on the average,

$$t_a/t_0 = 0.67/0.0074 = 90.5. \tag{8}$$

This represents the incidence of large, stable populations on older trees, relative to the frequency of successful colonizations on younger trees. Each large population on an older tree will presumably have a unique evolutionary history of adaptation to the peculiar chemistry of its host tree. This ratio approximates the frequency with which host tolerance may evolve over time, but the calculations are illustrative only. There are substantial reservations about the validity of this exercise as anything other than an illustration of techniques (G. F. Edmunds, Jr. and D. N. Alstad, personal communication).

Tolerance must evolve in many different ways, and all components of fitness must be pooled, as they are here ($R_0 \geq 1.0$), to compare a large sample of evolutionary outcomes. It may be possible to determine how the outcomes differ. Because the fates of established crawlers and, probably, fecundity can be obtained in the field, it should be possible to see if the components of fitness, the mortality schedule, and fecundity differ from one scale population to another.

It would appear that a system such as this could be used to generalize about the process of adaptation, its rates and the variety of pathways of adaptation (from a vast number of replicated natural experiments).

IV. DISCUSSION

The adaptations of these three sedentary herbivores to host-plant variability span the full range of evolutionary viewpoints embraced by the pluralistic approach of Gould and Lewontin (1979). The choice of feeding sites by female aphids and bruchids are noninteracting, unitary traits that independently alter fitness in a measurable way and that are appropriate for an adaptationist approach. Physiological responses to food quality lie at the opposite extreme. They are interacting systems in which an evolutionary response is governed by many intrinsic limits and constraints as well as by external modifiers of survival and fecundity.

The choice of leaves by female *Pemphigus* involves a behavioral repertoire that is independent of other systems, and the benefits of leaf selection can be precisely measured as deviations from the performance of nonselective females (Fig. 5). The benefits gained by the selective oviposition of *Callosobruchus maculatus* (Figs. 3 and 4) can be measured in exactly the same way. This illustrates that adaptationist explanations can be expected to be supported by analytical proof, and they cannot be dismissed as "Panglossian paradigms" (Gould and Lewontin, 1979), supported only by persuasive stories.

Contemporaneous fitness differentials can account for the maintenance of a trait and yet fail to be the basis for explaining the evolutionary history of a trait. The facts necessary for an evolutionary explanation are usually lost in the past, but Whitham's *Pemphigus* studies (Chapter 1) may be the exception. The fitness gained by selecting the larger leaves on a twig (Fig. 5) is almost certainly due to the quantity of photosynthate fixed by a leaf, and that is determined by leaf size now, just as it must have been over evolutionary time. This is the only relation needed to explain the evolutionary outcome, and the measured advantage is so large that selection would move rapidly. No alternative explanation seems possible, so this stands as the most comprehensive and convincing proof for an adaptationist account of the evolution of a trait.

The proof for contemporaneous gains in fitness as *Callosobruchus maculatus* selects larger beans (Figs. 3 and 4) is equally clear, but the search for alternative explanations (Dayton, 1973; Sih and Dixon, 1981) produces an array of factors affecting fitness. The selection of large beans may increase the realized fecundity of females in four ways. (1) It may reduce the loss of young in stunted or aborted seeds. (2) On cultivars with very small beans the fecundity, but not survival, of females from larger beans may be higher (Fig. 4). (3) On other hosts survival, but not fecundity, of daughters will be higher on larger beans. (4) Larvae may be able to be out of the reach of a parisitoid's ovipositor in larger beans.

These various factors act in different combinations over the range of C. *maculatus*. The multiple causes for higher fitness of eggs on larger beans makes it easy to understand why size selection may be a widespread trait among bruchids, but it also makes it impossible to believe that there is any hope of specifying which factors acted in the evolution of the trait.

Beans with rough surfaces and physical damage are rejected by *Callosobruchus maculatus*, and larvae on both of these sorts of beans have higher mortality. Multiple causation also confounds the problem of explaining how this discrimination could have evolved.

Egg dispersion may have evolved in *Callosobruchus maculatus* as a way to avoid the loss of larvae due to exploitative competition in beans too small for two larvae to develop. If egg dispersion did evolve first, there must have been enough exploitative competition that there was an advantage gained by interference competition, in which at least one larva would survive. Regardless of whether interference competition was first or second to evolve, it is now the major factor determining the benefits of placing one egg on a bean. Egg dispersion is, therefore, a trait of ovipositing females that is advantageous because of interference competition among her own offspring. The oviposition traits that have evolved in response to larval interference competition reduce success in multiply attacked beans and result in underexploitation the large portion of beans that have sufficient food for two or more larvae.

All of these independent adaptations are instances in which explicit measures of fitness differentials are possible, but, with one exception, multiple causation reduces any unraveling of the past evolutionary history of the traits to speculative guesses.

At the other extreme, the pluralist approach considers adaptations to external factors affecting fitness in which intrinsic constraints and tradeoffs limit the response to external factors. The physiological determinants of fitness in *Callosobruchus maculatus* illustrate the complex responses of interactive systems (Fig. 1 and Table I). The effects of food quality, temperature, and humidity act through a variety of physiological pathways to alter survival, development time, and fecundity. Each combination of food quality with climate seems to produce a different set of responses, with no trend along axes of temperature, humidity (Fig. 1), or food quality (Table I). Although the variation in potential fitness is immense, there is, for example, no apparent way to divide this into a temperature response independent of other factors affecting physiology.

It may be that the qualitative intraspecific chemical variation among hosts of *Nuculaspis* could have quite different effects on the scale life table, producing something as complex but probably less extensive than the interspecific effects of the *Callosobruchus* hosts (Table I). If it is established that the large *Nuculaspis* populations on old trees have indeed evolved physiological adaptations, then both measures of the outcomes of many parallel evolutionary events, such as those illustrated in this chapter, and analyses of individual populations will show whether the outcomes of many replicated evolutionary processes are uniform or not.

Experimental manipulations may well help clarify the constraints and some of the interactions within the system, but the system cannot be broken down into a set of independent factors, as is sometimes possible for behavioral and life-history traits. Although the independent adaptive factors discussed here can be precisely evaluated for their contemporary advantage, multiple factors are usually at work, and secondary interactions may have evolved. Either of these phenomena may make evolutionary reconstructions impossible.

REFERENCES

Allison, C. (1964). Polymorphism and natural selection in human populations. *Cold Spring Harbor Symp. Quant. Biol.* **29**, 137–149.

Avidov, Z., Applebaum, S. W., and Berlinger, M. J. (1965a). Aspects of host specificity in the Bruchidae. II. Ovipositional preference and behavior of *Callosobruchus chinensis* L. *Entomol. Exp. Appl.* **8**, 96–106.

Avidov, A., Berlinger, M. J., and Applebaum, S. W.(1965b). Physiological aspects of host specificity in the Bruchidae. III. Effect of curvature and surface area on oviposition of *Callosobruchus chinensis* L. *Anim. Behav.* **13**, 178–180.

Balachowsky, A. S., ed. (1962). "Entomologie appliquée à lágriculture," Vol. I. Masson, Paris.

Brower, L. P., Alcock, T., and Brower, T. V. Z. (1971). Avian feeding behaviour and the selective advantage of incipient mimicry. *In* "Ecological Genetics and Evolution" (R. Creed, ed.), pp. 261–274. Blackwell, Oxford.

Cain, A. J., And Sheppard, P. M. (1954). Natural selection in *Cepea*. *Genetics* **39**, 89–116.

Dawkins, R., and Krebs, J. R. (1979). Arms races between and within species. *Proc. R. Soc. London, Ser. B* **205**, 489–511.

Dayton, P. K. (1973). Two cases of resource partitioning in an intertidal community: making the right predition for the wrong reason. *Am. Nat.* **107**, 663–670.

Edmunds, G. F. (1973). Ecology of black pineleaf scale (Homoptera: Diapsidae). *Environ. Entomol.* **2**, 765–777.

Edmunds, G. F., and Alstad, D. N. (1978). Coevolution in insect herbivores and conifers. *Science* **199**, 941–945.

Gould, S. J., and Lewontin, R. C. (1979). The spandrels of San Marco and the Panglossian paradigm: a critique of the adaptationist programme. *Proc. R. Soc. London, Ser. B* **205**, 581–598.

Howe, R. W., and Curry, J. E. (1964). Some laboratory observations on the rates of development, mortality and oviposition of several species of Bruchidae breeding in stored pulses. *Bull. Entomol. Res.* **55**, 437–477.

Istock, C. A. (1970). Natural selection in ecologically and genetically defined populations. *Behav. Sci.* **15,** 101–115.

Istock, C. A., Zisfein, J., and Vavra, K. J. (1976). Ecology and evolution of the pitcher-plant mosquito. 2. The substructure of fitness. *Evol.* **30,** 535–547.

Johnson, C. D. (1981). Interactions between bruchid (Coleoptera) feeding guilds and behavioral patterns of pods of the Leguminosae. *Environ. Entomol.* **10,** 249–253.

Kettelwell, H. B. D. (1956). Further selection experiments on industrial melanism in the lepidoptera. *Heredity* **10,** 287–301.

Kettelwell, H. B. D. (1965). Insect survival and selection for patterns. *Science* **148,** 1290–1296.

Larson, A. O. (1927). The host-selection principle as applied to *Bruchus quadrimaculatus* Fab. *Ann. Entomol. Soc. Am.* **20,** 37–80.

Larson, A. O., and Fisher, C. K. (1927). Longevity and fecundity of *Bruchus quadrimaculatus* Fab. as influenced by different foods. *J. Agric. Res.* **29,** 297–305.

Mitchell, R. (1975). The evolution of oviposition tactics in the bean weevil, *Callosobruchus maculatus* (F.) *Ecology* **56,** 696–702.

Mitchell, R. (1976). Bruchid beetles and seed packaging by palo verde. *Ecology* **58,** 644–651.

Mitchell, R. (1981). Insect behavior, resource exploitation, and fitness. *Annu. Rev. Entomol.* **26,** 373–396.

Mitchell, R., and Williams, M. B. (1979). Darwinian analyses: the new natural history. *In* "Analysis of Ecological Systems" (D. J. Horn, R. Mitchell, and G. R. Staris, eds.), pp. 23–50. Ohio State Univ. Press, Columbus.

Nwanze, K. F., and Horber, E. (1975a). Laboratory techniques for screening cowpeas for resistance to *Callosobruchus maculatus* (F.). *Environ. Entomol.* **4,** 415–419.

Nwanze, K. F., and Horber, E. (1975b). How seed size affects the occurrence of "active" and "miniature" forms of *Callosobruchus maculatus* in laboratory populations. *Environ. Entomol.* **4,** 729–732.

Nwanze, K. F., and Horber, E. (1976). Seed coats of cowpeas affect oviposition and larval development of *Callosobruchus maculatus*. *Environ. Entomol.* **5,** 213–218.

Oshima, K., Honda, H., and Yamamoto, T. (1973). Isolation of an oviposition marker from the azuki bean weevil, *Callosobruchus chinensis* (L.) *Agric. Biol. Chem.* **37,** 2679–2680.

Price, P. (1975). "Insect Ecology." Wiley, New York.

Sano, I. (1967). Density effect and environmental temperature as the factors producing the active form of *Callosobruchus maculatus*. *J. Stored Prod. Res.* **2,** 187–195.

Sih, A., and Dixon, J. (1981). Tests of some predictions from MacArthur–Levins competition models: a critique. *Am. Nat.* **117,** 550–559.

Smith, S. M. (1978). The "underworld" in a territorial sparrow: adaptive strategy for floaters. *Am. Nat.* **112,** 571–582.

Stearns, S. C. (1977). The evolution of life history traits: a critique of the theory and a review of the data. *Annu. Rev. Ecol. Syst.* **8,** 145–171.

Taylor, T. A. (1974). Observations on the effects of initial population densities in culture, and humidity on the production of "active" females of *Callosobruchus maculatus* (F.) (Coleoptera, Bruchidae). *J. Stored Prod. Res.* **10,** 113–122.

Utida, S. (1943). Studies on the experimental population of the azuki bean weevil, *Callosobruchus chinensis* (L.). VIII. Statistical analysis of the frequency distribution of the emerging weevils on beans. *Kyoto Imp. Univ. Coll. Agric., Mem.* **54,** 1–22.

Utida, S. (1955). Population fluctuation in the system of host–parasite interaction. *Mem. Coll. Agric., Kyoto Univ.* **71,** 1–31.

Utida, S. (1972). Density dependent polymorphism in the adult of *Callosobruchus maculatus* (Coleoptera, Bruchidae). *J. Stored Prod. Res.* **8,** 111–126.

Weatherhead, P. J., and Robertson, R. J. (1979). Offspring quality and the polygyny threshold: "the sexy son hypothesis." *Am. Nat.* **113,** 201–208.

Whitham, T. G. (1978). Habitat selection by *Pemphigus* aphids in response to resource limitations and competition. *Ecology* **59,** 1164–1178.

Whitham, T. G. (1980). The theory of habitat selection: examined and extended using *Pemphigus* aphids. *Am. Nat.* **115,** 449–466.

Whitham, T. G. (1981). Individual trees as hetergeneous environments: adaptation to herbivory or epigenetic noise? *In* "Insect Life History Patterns: Habitat and Geographic Variation" (R. F. Denno and H. Dingle, eds.), pp. 9–27. Springer-Verlag, Berlin and New York.

Williams, G. C. (1966). "Adaptation and Natural Selection." Princeton Univ. Press, Princeton, New Jersey.

Williams, M. (1970). Deducing the consequences of evolution: a mathematical model. *J. Theor. Biol.* **29,** 343–385.

Rodger Mitchell
Department of Zoology
The Ohio State University
Columbus, Ohio

PART III

Host Plants and Genetic Variation in Herbivore Populations

The preceding chapters have emphasized the various sources and levels of host-plant variation and the effects of variation on the fitness, distribution, and abundance of herbivores. The responses of herbivores discussed so far have been measured in terms of mean values such as the average fecundity of aphids at different positions on leaves or the mean density of flea beetles in collard patches of different sizes. Furthermore, resource optima have been defined and used to predict the average abundance of phenotypes. The density of scale insects on pine branches of known nitrogen content and the abundance of winged and flightless forms of planthoppers in persistent and ephemeral stands of vegetation are examples. Of equal importance to the effect of plant variation on herbivore distribution and abundance is how the genetic variation of herbivores changes when these animals are confronted with heterogeneous host plants. The chapters in this part emphasize that genetic variation itself may be a herbivore's "optimal strategy" when it is faced with tracking and utilizing its variable hosts.

In Chapter 11, Scriber considers the relationships among feeding specialization, physiological efficiency, and host-race formation in geographically distant populations of swallowtail butterflies (Papilionidae) and silk moths (Saturniidae). Scriber attempts to segregate the influences of host-plant chemistry, the environment, and feeding specialization on the growth of phytophagous Lepidoptera. Scriber also discusses whether feeding specialization results in improved physiological efficiency or growth of herbivores and emphasizes that changes in the ability of insects to effectively process some of their hosts could result in various degrees of obligate monophagy and, subsequently, have a dramatic impact on the coevolution of plants and herbivores.

Alstad and Edmunds (Chapter 12) suggest that ponderosa pine trees display great intertree variability in their allelochemistry. Natural selection results in genetically differentiated demes of black pineleaf scale insects on individual ponderosa pine trees. Concurrent with genetic differentiation and increasing scale-insect density, there is a probable reduction in the genetic variance of the deme. The authors suggest that demes with reduced genetic variance are less likely to produce colonists that can survive on new hosts. They discuss changes in the size, genetic structure, and sex ratio of scale-insect populations following colonization, in the context of an evolutionary dilemma that intraspecific variability among trees poses for these herbivores.

An evolutionary–genetic viewpoint of the consequences of variable hosts for their herbivores is taken by Mitter and Futuyma in Chapter 13. The origin and maintenance of genetic variation within herbivore populations are central issues, as is the role of host plants in the promotion of such variability. Mitter and Futuyma consider geographic variation in host preference and physiological adaptation to hosts, the relationship between host-associated genetic differentiation and the mobility of herbivores, the existence of host-associated polymorphisms, the relationship between genetic variation and feeding specialization in herbivores, and the role of host plants in race and species formation in herbivores. The authors also underscore the rather primitive state of affairs of a genetic analysis of adaptation to host plants, but they emphasize that such an approach is essential to our understanding of the reciprocal genetic and ecological effects that herbivores and plants have on each other.

CHAPTER 11

Evolution of Feeding Specialization, Physiological Efficiency, and Host Races in Selected Papilionidae and Saturniidae

J. MARK SCRIBER

I. INTRODUCTION: THE FEEDING-SPECIALIZATION HYPOTHESIS

The *feeding-specialization hypothesis* is based on the presumption that diet specialization mediates an ecologically or metabolically more efficient utilization of food resources than does polyphagy (Brues, 1924; House, 1962; Emlen, 1973; Gilbert, 1979). Although Dethier (1954) suggested that polyphagous and monophagous insect herbivores would reflect quantitative differences in the efficiencies of utilizing available materials, few empirical data of this nature exist, even at this time. Scriber and Feeny (1979) bioassayed 20 species of Lepidoptera on a variety of plant species and found no consistent trend in efficiency of biomass or nitrogen use for those species feeding on one plant family (arbitrarily called *specialists*) versus those feeding on 2–10 *(intermediates)* or more than 10 families *(generalists)*. The conclusion presented by Scriber and Feeny (Fig. 1; see also Scriber, 1982a) is that chemical factors correlated with plant growth form account for the major portion of the variation in larval efficiency and/or rate of growth (see also Schroeder, 1976, 1977; Futuyma and Wasserman, 1981). Because particular exceptions do exist, more information will be required concerning local specialization by populations of generalist species before this feeding-specialization hypothesis can be completely rejected. This chapter will address differential food-plant utilization abilities of geographically distant populations of selected silk moths (Saturniidae) and swallowtail butterflies (Papilionidae) in the hope of better understanding the relationships among feeding specialization, physiological efficiency, and host-race formation.

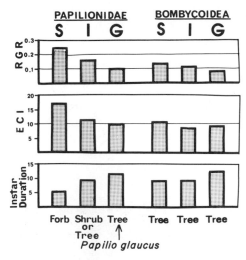

Fig. 1. Larval growth performance of 10 species of Papilionidae and 9 species of Bombycoidea [RGR, relative growth rate; ECI, efficiency of conversion of ingested food (%); duration in days]. Classification of degree of species feeding specialization as specialist (S, 1 plant family), intermediate (I, 2–20 families), or generalist (G, more than 10 families). Adapted from Scriber and Feeny (1979).

The importance of understanding feeding ecology at each of three levels—individual, population, and species—has been stressed by Dethier (1954). Dethier stressed that it is critical to our understanding of the evolution of feeding preferences in phytophagous insects (and therefore also to understanding insect–plant coevolution) that we have careful studies of feeding-habit variability among populations of monophagous, oligophagous, and polyphagous species of insects. Without such information, ecological conclusions about the significance of feeding specialization are necessarily restricted (Scriber and Feeny, 1979; Fox and Morrow, 1981).

The role that feeding specialization has played in the formation of geographic races or incipient species is basically unknown (but see Dethier, 1954; Bush, 1975; White, 1979; and Futuyma and Mayer, 1980, for syntheses of present information). More than a quarter of a century ago, Dethier (1954, p. 43) implored researchers to "undertake crucial experiments which would identify genetic and phenotypic races" of phytophagous insects. During the fourth Insect and Host Plant symposium, Dethier pointed out the continuing lack of genetic considerations (pp. 759–766, in Chapman and Bernays, 1978). Our understanding of the mechanisms of feeding-niche expansion (generalization) or contraction (specialization) may depend largely upon our ability to distinguish between individual and population heterogeneity (McNaughton and Wolf, 1970; Dethier, 1978; Smiley, 1978; Fox and Morrow, 1981). Criteria for distinguishing true host races and sympatric host-associated sibling species have been presented by Jaenike (1981). Also, the magnitude and relative importance of phenotypic variability (behavioral and physiological induction and flexibility) must be understood at the level of the individual (Scriber, 1981, 1982b; Grabstein and Scriber, 1982) before the significance of species differences in feeding ecology (i.e., specialization, efficiency, and/or growth rates) can be fully understood. Gilbert (1979, p. 145) has suggested that tests of ecological generalities in this regard should be carefully made "within guilds defined by host plant preferences, between local habitats within which actual resource patterns are known and with the overall life cycle of the insect fully considered."

The difficulties in properly classifying individuals or populations with regard to local food-plant favorites (i.e., actual degree of feeding specialization) has been reviewed by Fox and Morrow (1981). Distinguishing a polymorphic population of specialist individuals from a monomorphic population of generalists cannot be done from a literature survey of food plants used by the species. Among the other problems involved in properly classifying an insect as specialist, generalist, or intermediate in feeding specialization is the possibility that use of resource types (e.g., food-plant species or food-plant parts) by individuals or populations may be dynamic and in constant flux (Gould, 1979). It is also likely that an insect may be a chemical specialist yet use taxonomically diverse hosts. Actual feeding specialization that is observed (even on a local level) is determined by a variety of factors. The availability, acceptability, and suitability of a plant for a herbivore is influenced by biotic as well as abiotic environmental factors, which directly and indirectly alter the plant-quality or insect utilization patterns (see Table I; Gilbert, 1979; Atsatt, 1982; Miller and Strickler, 1982; Scriber, 1982a).

Once local feeding specialization has been identified, it is then possible to test for improved physiological efficiency and/or growth rates for those insects, relative to other populations. Conversely, it is also of interest whether there is a loss of ability to efficiently ingest and metabolize ancestral hosts (i.e., those plant species that are currently peripheral or unused) following specialization for one particular host. If such a biochemical ability is really lost, varying degrees of obligate monophagy might result. It is difficult to know how long local specialization might have existed, although inferences can sometimes be made from biogeographical evidence such as probable range changes in response

Table I

Determinants of *Local Specialization* in Herbivorous Insects

Physiologically acceptable and suitable plant is not used by ovipositing adult
  Unavailable geographically
  Unavailable temporally
  Not preferred (in a choice situation)
Plant characteristics affecting acceptability and/or suitability
  Plant abundance (absolute and/or relative basis)
  Plant chemistry (nutrients, allelochemics)
  Plant microclimates
  Associated insect community (parasites, predators, competitors)
Insect characteristics affecting acceptability and/or suitability of the plant
  Genetically fixed characteristics
    Antixenosis (nonpreference)
    Antibiosis
  Flexible (inducible) characteristics
    Feeding preferences (behavioral)
    Digestive enzymes (physiological)
    Detoxification activity (toxicological)
    Oviposition choices (by the adult; see reasons for failure to use plant for oviposition
      above)

to glaciation. Smiley (1978) has suggested that biochemical food-plant specialization may have played a major role in insect–plant coevolution (Ehrlich and Raven, 1964, 1969; Feeny, 1975; Starmer *et al.*, 1980; Berenbaum and Feeny, 1981). In most cases it is uncertain whether reproductive isolation and subsequent divergence (i.e., host races) are due solely to different host preferences (Endler, 1977; Atchley and Woodruff, 1981; Menken, 1981; Tauber and Tauber, 1981; Templeton, 1981; Turner, 1981) or are the result of other factors as well (e.g., host-associated sibling species; see Futuyma and Mayer, 1980; Jaenike, 1981). Species-level comparisons of biochemical-processing abilities are nonetheless useful for understanding the processes involved in specialization, especially if geographic variability within a species is carefully considered.

Perhaps the most profitable methods of investigation of the evolutionary role of host adaptations are those that consider food-plant specialization in comparison with other aspects of regional population divergence, such as morphology (including allelomorphic differences), phenology, and overall genetic compatibility (as revealed by hybridization). Among a series of sample populations connecting the center of a species' range with outlying subspecies, the severity of change within and degree of concordance within and between each of these four parameters (i.e., clinal variation) might indicate the role each has played in restricting gene flow and, consequently, promoting evolutionary divergence. Such evidence would be useful in considering modes of speciation. For example, Are regional host adaptations a cause or an effect of overall genetic divergence?

I will now describe some preliminary attempts to discriminate between host-plant chemistry, environmental factors, and insect adaptations (particularly feeding specializations) as factors influencing the postingestive growth performance of selected Lepidoptera. Emphasis will be placed on interspecific and regional intraspecific comparisons.

A. Preliminary Evidence at the Species Level

Selected species comparisons of postingestive larval-growth performance might, at first, also be viewed as support for the feeding-specialization hypothesis. For example, the tulip-tree (*Liriodendron tulipifera* L.) specialist *Callosamia angulifera* (Saturniidae) converts leaves into larval biomass with an efficiency of 13.9% for an average larval growth rate of 27 mg/day/g, which is nearly twice that of its more polyphagous relative, *C. promethea* (with an efficiency of only 7.9% and a growth rate of 17 mg/day/g). However, larvae of one local population of tulip-tree-feeding *C. promethea* were equal in efficiency and growth rate to that of the tulip-tree specialist, suggesting that local adaptation in physiological processing abilities is a reality (Scriber and Feeny, 1979). This result raises the possibility that many so-called generalists may be regional specialists.

The spice-bush swallowtail, *Papilio troilus* L., occurs throughout the eastern half of the United States, where it predominantly (if not exclusively) uses spice bush, *Lindera benzoin* (L.) Blume, and/or sassafras, *Sassafras albidum* (Nutt.) Nees, as its larval food plants. In fact, the range of *P. troilus* is essentially delineated by the ranges of these two plant species (both of the Lauraceae). Larval survival and growth performance of this stenophagous swallowtail is exceptionally good on spice bush, especially when compared to larvae of the generalized eastern tiger swallowtail, *Papilio glaucus glaucus* L. (Scriber *et al.*, 1975; Scriber and Feeny, 1979). In New York state (Tompkins County), *P. troilus* larvae (penultimate and final instars) consume spice bush at 3 times the rate, convert it with 2 times the efficiency, and grow 5 times as fast as *P. glaucus* larvae (Table II). A parallel in performance has been observed for Ohio populations of *P. troilus* (Green County) on spice bush. A similar pattern of postingestive processing abilities has also been observed for *P. troilus* and *P. glaucus* fed sassafras (Table III).

Table II
Nutritional Indices[a] of *Papilio troilus* and *P. glaucus* Fed Spice Bush (*Lindera benzoin*)

Papilio *species*	*Location*	n	RCR[b] (mg/day/g)	ECI[c] (%)	RGR[d] (mg/day/g)
Penultimate instar					
P. troilus	New York	5	229 ± 17	22.4 ± 2.1	51 ± 5
	Ohio	6	96 ± 9	25.1 ± 1.6	24 ± 1
P. glaucus	New York	4	81 ± 6	10.8 ± 0.3	9 ± 1
Final instar					
P. troilus	New York	5	163 ± 9	20.6 ± 1.1	33 ± 2
	Ohio	6	68 ± 4	21.1 ± 1.4	14 ± 1
P. glaucus	New York	2	54 ± 5	11.6 ± 1.3	6 ± 1

[a]Data are presented as a mean ± SE. Ithaca, New York, 1972; Dayton Ohio, 1977. Identical experimental conditions.
[b]RCR (relative consumption rate) = food ingested divided by mean larval weight times days.
[c]ECI (efficiency of conversion of ingested food) = larval weight gain divided by food ingested.
[d]RGR (relative growth rate) = larval weight gain divided by mean larval weight times days. Note that RGR = RCR × ECI (for further details see Scriber and Slansky, 1981).

Although the poor abilities of penultimate- and final-instar *Papilio glaucus* larvae for utilizing these two lauraceous plant species are dramatically evident when compared to that of the specialist (Tables II and III), another (perhaps more significant) factor is the differential survival abilities of earlier instars. The only documented report of *P. glaucus* using spice bush for oviposition and/or as a larval food plant is that in New York state (Scriber *et al.*, 1975). Preliminary studies, in 1980 and 1981 (J. M. Scriber, unpublished), indicate that Wisconsin populations are both ecologically (spice bush does not naturally occur in the state) and physiologically (no-choice lab studies) unable to utilize this host plant. None of the larvae from 20 *P. glaucus canadensis* females from northern Wisconsin counties survived the first instar on spice bush in no-choice situations (Scriber *et al.*, 1982). Similarly, no larvae from either dark- or yellow-morph *P. glaucus glaucus* females from southern Wisconsin, Alabama, and Florida survived the first instar on spice bush. In contrast, *P. glaucus* stock (obtained from William Houtz) from Pennsylvania, where *Lindera* is abundant, exhibited a greater tolerance for spice bush; the first-instar survival of larvae from 13 different yellow-morph females (*n* = 190 larvae) was 33.7%. All of this suggests considerable variation and perhaps differential adaptation within a single insect species (see section II, B, 3 for further discussion regarding *P. glaucus*). However, it was only a rare few *P. glaucus* that survived to pupation, and these required abnormally long periods of time to complete development (most in excess of 80 days).

Table III
Nutritional Indices[a] of *Papilio troilus* and *P. glaucus* Fed Sassafras (*Sassafras albidum*)

Papilio species	Location	n	RCR (mg/day/g)	ECI (%)	RGR (mg/day/g)
Penultimate instar					
P. troilus	New York	6	91 ± 4	23.0 ± 0.7	21 ± 1
	Ohio	6	104 ± 9.5	23.8 ± 1.5	23 ± 1
P. glaucus	New York	3	31 ± 10	12.2 ± 2.0	4 ± 2
Final instar					
P. troilus	New York	4	112 ± 4	13.4 ± 0.5	15 ± 1
	Ohio	6	93 ± 5	14.1 ± 1.0	13 ± 1
P. glaucus	New York	1	104	7.8	9

[a] Data are presented as a mean ± SE. Ithaca, New York, 1972; Dayton, Ohio, 1977. RCR, ECI, and RGR as in Table II.

This *Papilio troilus–P. glaucus* comparison is exceptional in illustrating the magnitude of differences in survival, consumption, efficiency, and growth rate that have evolved between a Lauraceae specialist and a closely related, sympatric, polyphagous species of the same genus. The roles that differential survival and host-utilization abilities have played in speciation processes of *P. troilus* and *P. glaucus* are unknown, although it is generally agreed that Lauraceae is a key food-plant family for *Papilio* and other genera of Papilionidae (Munroe, 1960; Scriber, 1973; Scriber et al., 1975).

B. Evidence from Geographically Separate Populations

1. The *Callosamia promethea* Group

The genus *Callosamia* Packard is comprised of three species of closely related moths. *Callosamia securifera* (Maassen) is found only in swamps and certain pine woods of the southeastern United States (Peigler, 1975) and normally feeds only on sweet bay (*Magnolia virginiana* L.). *Callosamia angulifera* (Walker) feeds exclusively on tulip tree (*Liriodendron tulipifera*) and occurs throughout the general range of this plant (i.e., east of the Mississippi River from Michigan and Pennsylvania to northern Florida). *Callosamia promethea* (Drury) exhibits both a wider range of hosts and a more extensive geographic distribution than its two congeners (from Canada to Florida and west to the Great Plains; Fig. 2). Among its favorites over much of its range are sassafras (*Sassafras albidum*), spice bush (*Lindera benzoin*), sweet gum (*Liquidambar styraciflua* L.), and tulip tree (*Liriodendron tulipifera*). At the northern limits of its range, where the Magnoliaceae, Lauraceae, and hosts of more tropical affinities do

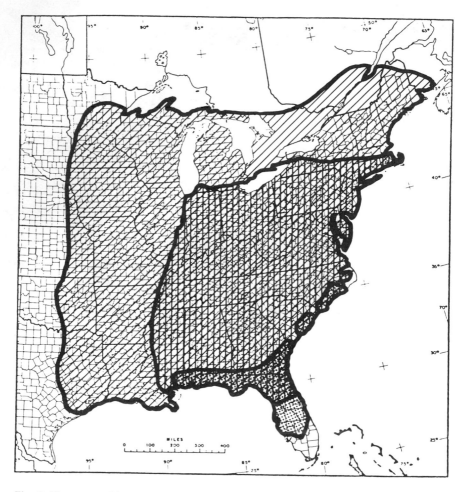

Fig. 2. The geographic range of *Callosamia securifera* (▦), *C. angulifera* (▥), and *C. promethea* (▨). (Range distributions are very strongly correlated with favored food plants: sweet bay, tulip tree, and wild black cherry, respectively).

not occur, wild black cherry (*Prunus serotina* Ehrhart), white ash (*Fraxinus americana* L.), and lilac (*Syringa vulgaris* L.) are the predominant favorites, with other, somewhat marginal hosts requiring additional documentation (e.g., paper birch, *Betula papyrifera* Marshall; see Packard, 1914; Collins and Weast, 1961; Ferguson, 1972; Peigler, 1976; Wagner *et al.*, 1981).

It has been suggested that reproductive isolation between these species is due in large part to different circadian mating activities of each (Table IV). Other prezygotic and postzygotic isolating mechanisms in

Table IV
Comparison of the Three Species of *Callosamia* Silk Moths (Saturniidae)[a]

Insect species	Peak flight (mating) time	Cocoon type	Normal food-plant species
C. securifera (Sweet-bay silk moth)	10 AM–3 PM	Attached	Sweet bay (Magnoliaceae)
C. angulifera (Tulip-tree silk moth)	8 PM–Midnight	Unattached	Tulip tree (Magnoliaceae)
C. promethea (Promethea silk moth)	4 PM–8 PM	Attached (on tree)	Sassafras, spicebush (Lauraceae); black cherry (Rosaceae); tulip tree (Magnoliaceae); sweet gum (Hamamelidaceae); sweetleaf (Symplocaceae); ash, lilac (Oleaceae)

[a]Data from Haskins and Haskins (1958), Collins and Weast (1961), Brown (1972), Ferguson (1972), Peigler (1976, 1981).

this group have been reviewed by Peigler (1981). The structuring of the cocoons (i.e., method of attachment to the leaves) is different among the species and is apparently controlled by multiple genes (Haskins and Haskins, 1958). The result is that *Callosmia securifera* and *C. promethea* cocoons remain attached to the tree via leaf petioles, whereas cocoons of *C. angulifera* fall to the ground litter, but the ecological significance of these differences is unknown. In addition to cocoon-spinning behavior and food-plant utilization abilities, it would also be enlightening to determine the inheritance of flight (mating) times, ovipositional preferences, larval preferences, and fertilities of backcrosses of artificially hybridized *Callosamia* species (see Peigler, 1977).

Food-plant utilization abilities for larvae of the tulip-tree silk moth (*Callosamia angulifera*) and the sweet-bay silkmoth *(C. securifera)* are generally very poor (especially in the first larval instar) on any but their own host (Haskins and Haskins, 1958; Remington, 1958; Brown, 1972; Ferguson, 1972; Peigler, 1976). Although *C. promethea* larvae do occasionally use sweet bay as a host, their survival and growth are poor (Peigler, 1976). Use of tulip tree by *C. promethea* is common, and larval survival and growth performances are excellent (Scriber and Feeny, 1979). If the tulip tree is in fact the ancestral host, it seems that *C. promethea* has retained the ability to biochemically process this host as efficiently and effectively as the specialist.

Strong induction of larval host preference has been observed for *Callosamia promethea* on each of several plants (Hanson, 1976), which contrasts with the rather rigid behavioral choices of *C. angulifera* and *C. securifera*. Although some *C. angulifera* will accept spice bush, sassafras and black cherry, it is expected that larval growth will be much inferior to that on tulip tree (Peigler, 1976). It is interesting that F_1 hybrid larvae from different sources (*C. promethea* ♀ × *C. angulifera* ♂) preferred tulip tree and sassafras to black cherry in some cases (see Haskins and Haskins, 1958), with the reverse being true in other cases (Remington, 1958). None of the F_2 or backcross ova produced larvae (but see Peigler, 1977 and 1981). In general, tulip tree is the best host for hybrids of any *Callosamia* cross, and it is apparently the only host common to all three species (Peigler, 1976).

In order to assess the degree to which local feeding specialization would alter the survival and growth performance of *Callosamia promethea* larvae on various reported hosts, we first obtained overwintering *C. promethea* cocoons from various locations throughout the geographic range of the insect species (see Fig. 2). Emerging adults were paired, resulting larvae were distributed (immediately after eclosion) evenly across the various food plants, and survival (especially through the first instar) was monitored under controlled-environment conditions. Feeding experiments were also performed on larvae surviving to the penultimate instar, to determine the consumption rate and efficiencies of digestion and conversion of the various plant tissues for larval growth. The overall objective was to determine if poorer survival and/or loss of biochemical-processing abilities correlated with geographical distance of a given *C. promethea* population from a particular food-plant species.

During 1980 and 1981 a total of 11,500 individual larvae from 10 major geographic sites in nine states (see Fig. 3) were monitored on 10 different food plants under the same controlled-environment conditions. Because the geographic range of *Callosmia promethea* is virtually identical to the main eastern range of wild black cherry, it is perhaps not surprising that overall survival (Table V) was excellent (81.4%), with no unusually poor survival from any of the particular locations that were tested (Fig. 3). Similarly, excellent overall survival was observed through the critical first instar on sassafras and tulip tree (Table V). The survival of Wisconsin, northern Illinois, and Maine larvae on sassafras (Fig. 4) and on tulip tree (Fig. 5) were unexpectedly high, considering their geographic distance from these host plants. Thus, in these two cases, differential adaptation to food plants is not necessarily reflected by geographical proximity to the host. On the other hand, *C. promethea* larvae from Wisconsin and Maine exhibited excellent survival on paper birch (94 and 86%, respectively) compared to other populations. In fact, preliminary data (Fig. 6) suggest declining survival with increasing geographic dis-

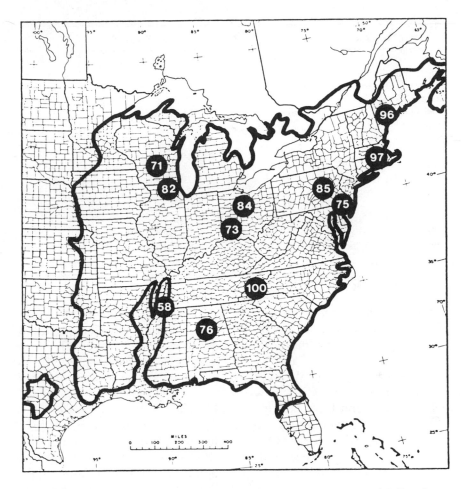

Fig. 3. First-instar larval survival (%) on black cherry *(Prunus serotina)* of *Callosamia promethea* from various geographic locations. The initial number of larvae tested from each location was: 438, WI; 165, IL; 105, N OH; 78, S OH; 36, TN; 196, ME; 29, MA; 490, PA; 53, NJ; 65, NC, 59, AL.

tance from the paper birch, with Ohio populations (farthest from the host plant) doing poorest (26 and 55%). Populations on the range edge of paper birch (i.e., Illinois in the West and New Jersey, Pennsylvania, and Massachusetts in the East) were intermediate in survival abilities (ranging from 69 to 79%; see Fig. 6). Tennessee survival was relatively poor (42%), and Alabama was unexpectedly high (73%), however, in both of these cases the sample sizes were small (i.e., less than 50 total larvae from one or two different female parents). In contrast to paper

Table V
Survival of Lab-Reared *Callosamia promethea* on 10 Food Plants[a]

Food plant	First instar survival (%)	Starting number	Number of female parents
Sassafras	82.0	1,690	96
Black cherry	81.4	1,882	96
Tulip tree	79.0	1,807	98
Paper birch	76.6	1,629	95
Spice bush	74.9	847	39
White ash	57.9	883	40
Choke cherry	57.3	735	50
Lilac	42.5	1,162	77
Quaking aspen	0	737	51
Mountain ash	0	338	24
		11,500	
		5,828 (1980)	
		5,672 (1981)	

[a]Madison, Wisconsin, 1980, 1981.

birch, quaking aspen (*Populus tremuloides* Michx.) and mountain ash (*Sorbus*) were totally unacceptable for all *C. promethea* populations tested (including those from the northernmost parts of the range, which do have potential contact; Table V; Fig. 7). Lilac, reported as a favorite in Wisconsin (Collins and Weast, 1961), warrants particular study in view of the extreme differences between lab and field growth and survival (M. H. Evans and J. M. Scriber, unpublished).

The relative consumption rates (RCRs), conversion efficiencies [ECI = approximate digestibility (AD) × efficiency of conversion of digested food (ECD)] and relative growth rates (RGRs) of penultimate-instar *Callosmia promethea* larvae from various geographic sites were monitored on various food plants under controlled-environment conditions, using the methods described by Scriber and Feeny (1979). The results of these feeding studies (J. M. Scriber, J. Potter, M. Evans, E. Grabstein, and M. Finke, unpublished data) suggest that once a food plant is accepted by a young larva, subsequent growth rates and efficiencies are determined largely by the plant nutritional quality. Scriber (1982a) described a *physiological-efficiency model* based on leaf water and nitrogen contents as an index of plant quality (see also Scriber and Slansky, 1981). This model is based on hundreds of separate feeding experiments, incorporates seasonal trends in leaf chemistry, and predicts the upper limits for physiological efficiency and growth rates of Lepidoptera. It is, in fact, a necessary starting point for interpretations of tests of the feeding-specialization hypothesis.

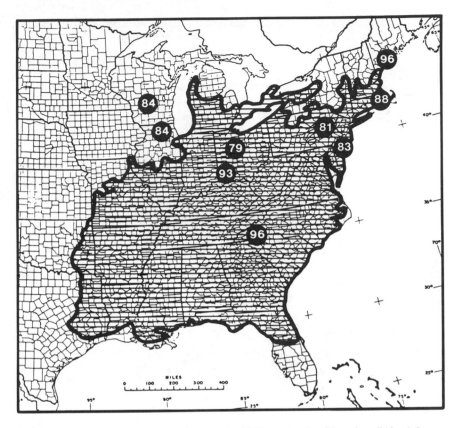

Fig. 4. First-instar *Callosamia promethea* survival (%) on sassafras (*Sassafras albidum*). Larvae tested from each location: 361, WI; 165, IL; 105, N OH; 59, S OH; 186, ME; 26, MA; 414, PA; 58, NJ; 54, NC.

The efficiencies and growth rates of *Callosamia promethea* are poorest on plant species with low leaf water and nitrogen contents (e.g., paper birch and white ash), whereas plants with higher leaf water and nitrogen contents (e.g., spice bush and sassafras) are much superior in their support of efficient and/or rapid growth. The predominant significance of plant quality (as indexed by leaf water and nitrogen contents) is illustrated using total larval developmental period (egg eclosion to cocoon; Fig. 8; see Scriber and Slansky, 1981). Irrespective of the original geographic source or the actual food-plant utilization history of the *C. promethea* populations tested, growth performance (of surviving larvae) on any given plant (various plant species separate fairly distinctly on the two axes of Fig. 8) was observed to be within the upper limits dictated

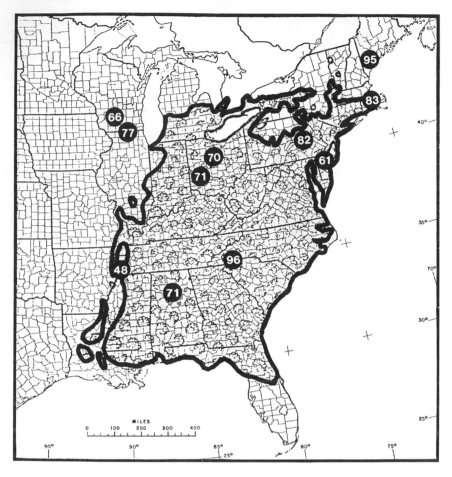

Fig. 5. First-instar *Callosamia promethea* survival (%) on tulip tree *(Liriodendron tulipifera)*. Initial number of larvae tested from each location: 417, WI; 161, IL; 105, N OH; 93, S OH; 29, TN; 192, ME; 29, MA; 499, PA; 49, NJ; 50, NC; 51, AL.

by this physiological efficiency model of plant quality. Although the lower limits on larval growth performance cannot be predicted using this model, seasonal declines in leaf quality, which affect consumption and conversion of plant biomass for larval growth, can be predicted. This narrowing of the variation introduced by extrinsic factors (i.e., environmental and food-plant influences on larval performance) provides a means by which more realistic assessments can be made of the intrinsic variables (i.e., differential physiological adaptations of the larvae) that influence the postingestive utilization of food.

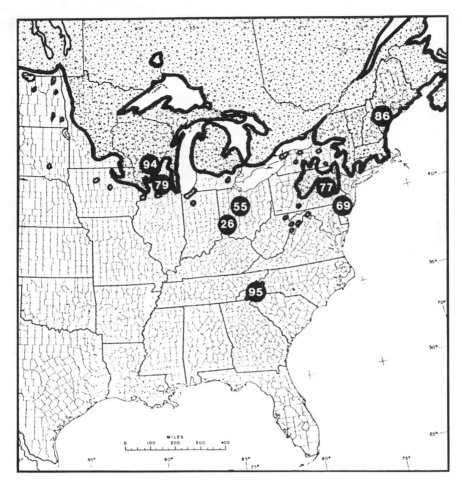

Fig. 6. First-instar *Callosamia promethea* survival (%) on paper birch *(Betula papyrifera)*. Initial number of larvae tested from each location: 286, WI; 161, IL; 89, N OH; 70, S OH; 191, ME; 473, PA; 58, NJ; 49, NC (the NC populations are very near paper birch).

2. The Giant Swallowtail *(Papilio cresphontes)*

The giant swallowtail, *Papilio cresphontes* Cramer, seems to exhibit considerable geographic variability in growth performance on various food plants, unlike *Callosamia promethea*, which has shown little evidence of any major geographic differences. The giant swallowtail is basically a Rutaceae specialist; however, the various populations utilize different food-plant species in different parts of their range. *Citrus* species are favorites in Florida, although the native lime prickly ash, *Zanthoxylum*

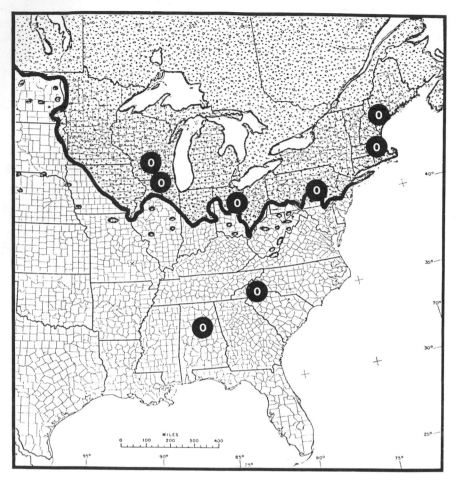

Fig. 7. First-instar *Callosamia promethea* survival on quaking aspen *(Populus tremuloides)* was 0% for all populations tested.

fagara L., is also used frequently. In the extreme northern limits of the giant swallowtail's range (i.e., Wisconsin, Michigan, and parts of New England), the northern prickly ash, *Z. americanum* Mill., is the primary host plant, whereas hop tree, *Ptelea trifoliata* L., is also frequently used between these northern and southern areas.

Giant swallowtail stocks were obtained from Florida (Broward County), Ohio (Preble County), and Wisconsin (Richland, Iowa, and Dane Counties) in order to determine if differential food-processing abilities (under controlled-environment conditions) exist between these geographically

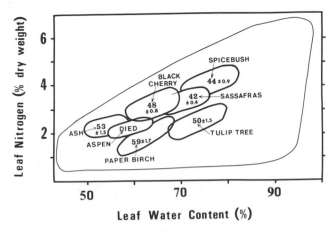

Fig. 8. Total larval developmental time (days) of *Callosamia promethea* on various species of trees, presented as a function of leaf water and nitrogen contents of mature leaves. Surviving larvae (see Table V) from all geographic locations (1980) were used in mean-duration calculations. Seasonal trends in leaf water and nitrogen during the rearing period are encompassed by the enclosure curve for each plant species. Controlled-environment conditions were maintained at 16/8 photo/scotophase, with corresponding temperatures of 23.5/19.5°C.

distant populations. Certain comparisons of final-instar larval growth performances do indeed support the supposition that *Papilio cresphontes* populations are biochemially well adapted to what they have locally adopted as a food plant. The Ohio and Wisconsin populations physiologically processed northern (common) prickly ash with twice the efficiency (ECI) of the southern Florida populations, and their larval growth (RGR) was also faster than that of Florida populations (Fig. 9). The Ohio population was more efficient and grew even faster on its local favorite (hop tree) than on prickly ash, and the Wisconsin populations grew more slowly and less efficiently on hop tree (Fig. 10) than on their favorite (prickly ash) (cf. Figs. 9 and 10). Florida populations have not been tested on hop tree; however, a simultaneous comparison of performance of Florida larvae on lime prickly ash with Ohio larvae suggests that differential biochemical adaptation exists. Although growth on lime prickly ash is generally poor compared to other rutaceous foods, the Florida populations were 4 times as efficient and exhibited 2 times the growth rate of their Ohio relatives (Fig. 11).

It is intriguing to observe differences of the magnitude described in Figs. 7–9; however, these data must be regarded with considerable caution before concluding that they support the feeding-specialization hypothesis for local specialists. First among such considerations is the fact

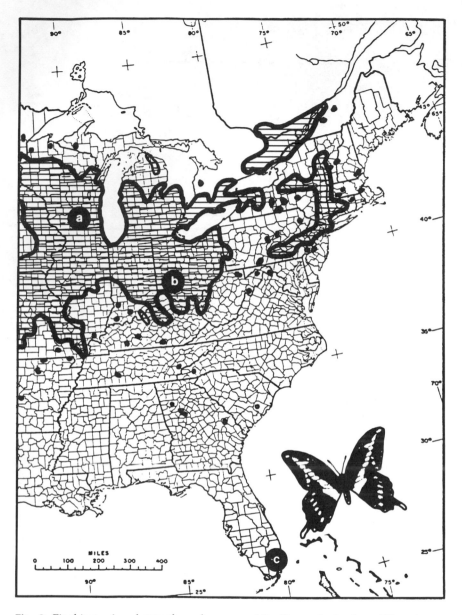

Fig. 9. Final-instar larval growth performance of *Papilio cresphontes* from different geographic populations on common prickly ash *(Zanthoxylum americanum)*. Relative growth rate (RGR = mg gain/day/mg average weight during the instar) and overall conversion efficiency (ECI = percentage of ingested food converted into larval biomass) are mean values of replicated feeding experiments under controlled conditions (16/8 photo/scotophase, corresponding temperatures 23.5/19.5°C). (a) RGR = 0.123 ± 0.008; ECI = 11.1% ± 1.2%; n = 9. (b) RGR = 0.160 ± 0.005; ECI = 12.6% ± 0.4%; n = 4. (c) RGR = 0.100 ± 0.009; ECI = 6.3% ± 0.7%; n = 6.

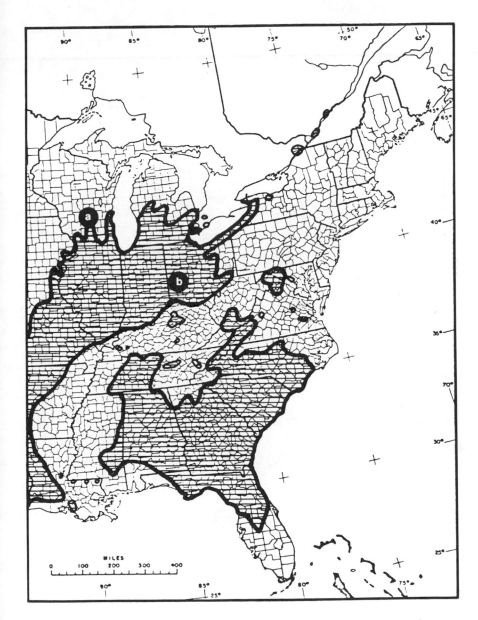

Fig. 10. Final-instar larval growth performance of *Papilio cresphontes* on common hop tree (*Ptelea trifoliata*). (a) RGR = 0.066 ± 0.009; ECI = 8.4% ± 0.3%; *n* = 8. (b) RGR = 0.215 ± 0.005; ECI = 18.8% ± 0.3%; *n* = 4. (See legend of Fig. 9 for explanation.)

Fig. 11. Final-instar larval growth performance of *Papilio cresphontes* on lime prickly ash (*Zanthoxylum fagara*). (a) RGR = 0.032 ± 0.003; ECI = 1.7% ± 0.1%; *n* = 3. (b) RGR = 0.084 ± 0.006; ECI = 7.5% ± 2.8%; *n* = 3. (See legend of Fig. 9 for explanation.)

that only surviving final instars were bioassayed (i.e., there was no measure of first-instar survival for these different populations on the various rutaceous hosts, and we have already seen how significant this can be with *Callosmia promethea*; Section II,B,1). Second, penultimate-

Table VI
Food-Plant Quality and Pupal Weights of *Papilio cresphontes* from Ohio[a]

Food plant	n	Pupal weight (mg dry wt)	RGR[b]	Leaf nitrogen (% dry wt)	Leaf water (% fresh wt)
Hop tree (*Ptelea trifoliata*)	4	361.7 ± 29.5	21.5 ± 0.5	3.65 ± 0.09	72.3 ± 0.5
Common prickly ash (*Zanthoxylum americanum*)	4	198.0 ± 0.5	16.0 ± 0.5	2.84 ± 0.01	73.2 ± 0.9
Lime prickly ash (*Zanthoxylum fagara*)	3	95.6 ± 3.3	3.2 ± 0.3	1.54 ± 0.28	66.7 ± 1.7

[a]Data are presented as a mean ± SE.
[b]RGR = relative growth rate (average weight gain; mg/day/g) for final-instar larvae.

instar growth performances of *Papilio cresphontes* do not always follow the same patterns as do those of the final instars (J. M. Scriber, unpublished data). Also, even simultaneous-feeding experiments, using leaves from the same tree, may nonetheless (unavoidably) introduce slight differences in nutritional quality, which will partially obscure intrinsic (i.e., larval) characteristics (i.e., behavioral or physiological adaptations; Scriber, 1982a). Finally, it is possible that efficiencies (ECIs) and growth rates (RGRs) may not reflect the real "fitness" or degree of biochemical adaptation to particular host plants. Although it happens that pupal sizes in Ohio *P. cresphontes* are positively correlated with ECI and RGR (Table VI), this is not a prerequisite (because identical efficiencies and growth rates could yield different-sized pupae simply by cessation of growth at different times). Finally, the bigger Ohio pupae observed on hop tree (361.7 ± 29.5 mg dry weight) and common prickly ash (198.0 ± 5.0 mg dry weight) compared to lime prickly ash (95.6 ± 3.3 mg dry weight) may simply be related to differential nutritional quality of the leaf tissues (Table VI) and may not necessarily reflect any biochemical adaptation in regard to frequency of host-plant use through evolutionary time.

3. The *Papilio glaucus* Species Group

The poor survival and low consumption and conversion efficiencies of *Papilio glaucus* larvae on spice bush and sassafras compared to *P. troilus* have already been described (Section II,A). The evolutionary divergence between these two sympatric eastern insect species is considerably greater than is that of *P. glaucus* compared to its three western *Papilio* relatives (*P. multicaudatus*, *P. rutulus*, and *P. eurymedon*; see Fig. 12 and Brower, 1959a,b). These three sympatric western *Papilio* species have

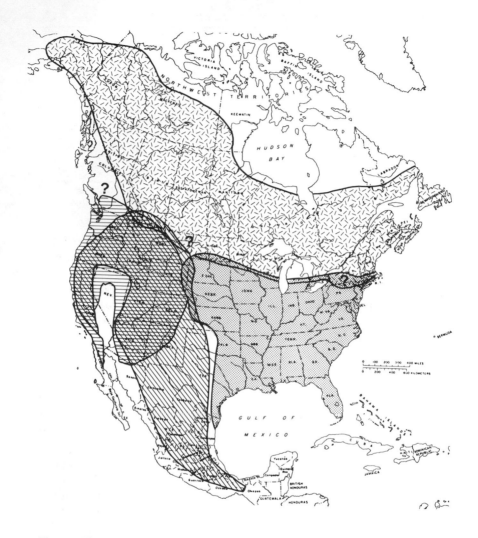

Fig. 12. The geographic ranges of the subspecies of *Papilio glaucus* (*P. glaucus canadensis* ⊡ and *P. glaucus glaucus* ▨) and the related western species group (*P. eurymedon* ▤, *P. rutulus,* ▤ and *P. multicaudatus* ▨). Distribution records are from Brower (1957), Ferris and Brown (1981), and Scriber *et al.* (1982).

apparently subdivided the various food-plant families utilized by the polyphagous *P. glaucus* in such a way that each of the western *Papilio* species feeds on two or three mutually exclusive families of plants, although none utilizes the Magnoliaceae or Lauraceae, as does *P. glaucus glaucus* (see Brower, 1958). Speciation processes since the Pleistocene glaciation in the western United States may have been aided by the mountainous terrain, whereas east of the Rocky Mountains a single species, *P. glaucus*, occupies a geographic range of approximately 4 × 10^6 mi^2 (Fig. 12). In addition, the Pleistocene refugia of *P. glaucus* were very rich in plant species, unlike the West (Watts, 1980).

Although numerous reproductive isolating mechanisms are likely to be involved between each pair of these three western species (Brower, 1959a,b) and also in areas where their ranges contact that of *Papilio glaucus*, the role of food plants in this speciation process is still basically unknown. The penultimate- and final-instar larval growth performance of *P. multicaudatus* was virtually identical to that of its more polyphagous eastern relative, *P. glaucus*, when both were fed hop tree (*Ptelea trifoliata*, Rutaceae), white ash (*Fraxinus americana*, Oleaceae), and choke and black cherry (*Prunus virginiana* and *P. serotina*, Rosaceae) under controlled conditions (Scriber, 1975; Scriber and Feeny, 1979). Nothing is presently known of the food-plant processing abilities of *Papilio rutulus* and *P. eurymedon*.

In the eastern half of the North American continent, the degree of reproductive isolation between the two subspecies, *Papilio glaucus glaucus* and *P. glancus canadensis*, is uncertain. A major change in potential host-plant availability occurs between 40 and 45° N latitude, from Minnesota and Wisconsin eastward through Michigan, New York, and New England, in what might be called a plant transition (or tension) zone (see Fig. 12, and Scriber, 1982a). Curtis (1959) has described this situation in detail for Wisconsin vegetation, and it appears significant that the zone of overlap of *P. glaucus glaucus* and *P. glaucus canadensis* corresponds almost identically to this plant transition zone (Fig. 13; see also Scriber *et al.*, 1982).

In addition to the morphological (color patterns and size) differences that have traditionally been used to distinguish *Papilio glaucus glaucus* and *P. glaucus canadensis* (see Fig. 13, and Ebner, 1970; Shapiro, 1974; Tyler, 1975), there are in Wisconsin (and elsewhere) several interesting biological differences between these two subspecies. The northern subspecies *(P. glancus canadensis)* is believed to be univoltine, not only in Wisconsin but throughout its range (Fig. 12). Individuals of *P. glaucus glaucus*, on the other hand, are multivoltine (bivoltine in Wisconsin; Fig. 13). Thus, although there is certainly a strong genetic basis, it may be

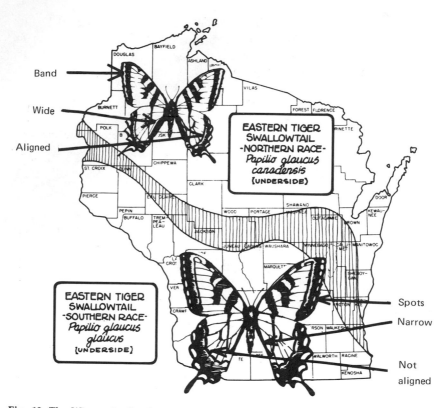

Fig. 13. The Wisconsin distribution and features of the subspecies of *Papilio glaucus: canadensis*, univoltine, monomorphic ♀♀ (yellow), wingspan 50–105 mm; *glaucus*, multivoltine, polymorphic ♀♀ (dark and yellow), wingspan 85–140mm. The shaded area on the map represents the plant tension zone (Curtis, 1959) and also delineates the approximate distribution and overlap of these butterfly subspecies (see Scriber *et al.*, 1982).

that environmental factors are more directly involved in determining the precise northern geographic limits of multivoltinism (Beck and Apple, 1961; Tauber and Tauber, 1981; cf. Shapiro, 1976). The thermal-unit accumulations necessary to complete one generation (from egg to adult) will vary considerably with the food-plant species, but in Wisconsin (using a conservative developmental threshold temperature of 11°C) they range from approximately 600 degree days (day • °C) on black cherry to 800 or more on ash and certain marginal food plants (Scriber *et al.*, 1982, and unpublished). It can be seen from a comparison of a 20-yr average thermal-unit accumulation in Wisconsin (Fig. 14) that, even on the very best food plants in a warm year, a second generation of *P. glaucus* could not be completed in the northern third of Wisconsin. In fact, the precise

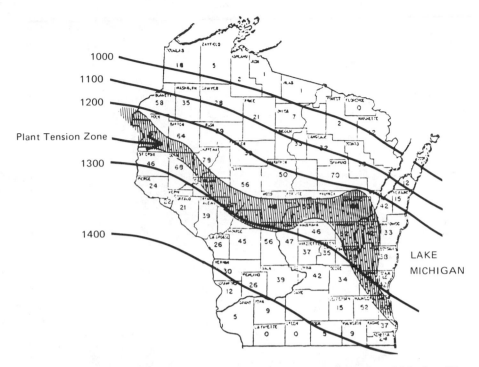

Fig. 14. Seasonal degree-day accumulation (above 10°C) in Wisconsin from 1 March to 27 September. Values are calculated as means over a 20-yr period (Wisconsin Statistical Reporting Service, Madison). Note that the plant tension zone very closely approximates the northern limit of bivoltine potential of *Papilio glaucus* (one generation, egg to adult, requires 600 day·°C on the best food plant, black cherry, and up to 800 day·°C on ash).

northern limits of double-brood potential (based on the thermal-unit map) corresponds very closely to the subspecies separation zone (Fig. 13).

Finally, it is now evident that major differences in survival and utilization of certain food plants exist between *Papilio glaucus canadensis* and *P. glaucus glaucus*. All *P. glaucus canadensis* larvae tested from Wisconsin and the adjacent upper penninsula of Michigan died during the first instar when offered tulip tree in a no-choice situation (Scriber *et al.*, 1982). In contrast, all individuals of *P. glaucus* tested throughout its range (including those from southern Wisconsin) survived and grew well on tulip tree (Fig. 15). This inability of *P. glaucus canadensis* to survive on tulip tree is shared by *P. multicaudatus* and *P. eurymedon* (of the western group). The genetics involved in *Liriodendron* suitability are intriguing and perhaps relatively uncomplicated, because *P. glaucus glaucus* can be

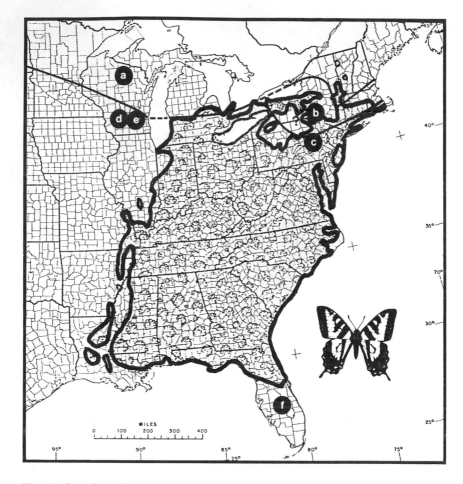

Fig. 15. Growth performance of penultimate-instar larvae of *Papilio glaucus* from different geographic populations (and also F₁ hybrids of a hand-paired subspecies cross; see Tables VII and VIII). Distribution of tulip tree *(Liriodendron tulipifera)* is shown. Relative growth rate (RGR = mg gain/day/mg average larval weight) and overall conversion efficiency (ECI = percentage of ingested food converted into larval biomass) for descendant larvae of yellow- and dark-color-morph females: (a) *P. glaucus canadensis;* all died in first instar (88 larvae, 21 females, 6 counties). (b) *P. glaucus glaucus* or *P. glaucus canadensis* (actual taxonomic status uncertain), RGR = 0.21, ECI = 13%. (c)–(f) *P. glaucus glaucus.* (c) Dark morph, RGR = 0.22, ECI = 15%; yellow morph, RGR = 0.23, ECI = 18%. (d) Dark morph, RGR = 0.23, ECI = 20%. (e) Dark morph, RGR = 0.30, ECI = 20%. (f) Dark morph, RGR = 0.17, ECI = 23%; yellow morph, RGR = 0.16, ECI = 18%. In 29 fertile laboratory hybrids of *P. glaucus glaucus* × *P. glaucus canadensis,* 81% of F₁s survived in first instar.

hand-mated with *P. eurymedon* (Clarke and Sheppard, 1957), with *P. rutulus* (Clarke and Sheppard, 1955), and with *P. glaucus canadensis* (J.M. Scriber, unpublished data) to give F_1 larvae that are able to consume, survive, and grow well on *L. tulipifera* leaves (Scriber, 1982c; Table VII).

In direct contrast to the situation observed with tulip tree, all but a very few individuals of *Papilio glaucus glaucus* populations tested died in the first instar on quaking aspen, which is one of the best foodplants for *P. glaucus canadensis* across North America (Fig. 16). Here again F_1 hybrids of the subspecies survived and grew well on *P. tremuloides* (Table VIII).

With paper birch, we observed excellent survival within the range of *Papilio glaucus canadensis*, with an apparent decline when moving southward (Fig. 17). This situation is analogous with that observed with *Callosamia promethea* on paper birch (i.e., poorer survival with greater allopatry; Fig. 6).

Although the food-plant species is fundamental in determining the final size of *Papilio glaucus glaucus* and *P. glaucus canadensis* pupae (on a given plant species, *P. glaucus canadensis* pupae are 30–60% smaller than those of *P. glaucus glaucus*; Scriber *et al.*, 1982), the role played in reproductive isolation between the two subspecies is unknown. *Fraxinus americana* and *Prunus serotina* are frequently utilized as food plants for both subspecies of *Papilio glaucus*. The reasons for the geographic restriction of *P. glaucus canadensis* individuals north of 40° latitude are therefore not simply host related. In fact, *P. glaucus canadensis* larvae from northern Wisconsin surviving the first instar do fairly well on *Ptelea trifoliata*, *Sassafras albidum*, and *Magnolia acuminata*, plants which they are extremely unlikely to have ever encountered (Scriber *et al.*, 1982). As described in Section II,A, all Wisconsin *P. glaucus* fail to survive the first instar on *Lindera benzoin*. Although this is true also for Florida and Alabama populations, it is not for New York and Pennsylvania populations (Fig. 18).

Choke cherry *(Prunus virginiana* L.*)* is an interesting and unique plant in regard to the geographic distribution of the *Papilio glaucus* species (and subspecies) complex. It is trans-Canadian and extends southward throughout the Rockies and the Pacific coast as well as projecting southward somewhat into Tennessee and North Carolina in the eastern United States. [The western form, *Prunus demissa* (Nutt.) Walp., was once considered a subspecies of *P. virginiana*, but it is now considered by some a separate but closely related species.] It thus forms a coarsely contiguous, potential food-plant bridge between all current species of presumed post-Pleistocene-glaciation isolates (i.e., the ancestral southeastern and southwestern populations of this *Papilio glaucus* species complex). In fact, choke cherry is one of only four or five potential hosts for *P.*

Table VII
Larval Survival to Second Instar on Three Key Food Plants[a]

Insect	Black cherry (Prunus serotina)	Tulip tree (Liriodendron tulipifera)	Quaking aspen (Populus tremuloides)
Papilio glaucus glaucus[b]			
With dark-morph mothers	79%	76%	0%
	(43)	(67)	(64)
With yellow-morph mothers	84%	78%	8%
	(61)	(76)	(80)
Papilio glaucus canadensis[c]	88%	0%	86%
	(73)	(88)	(80)
F₁ Hybrids[d]	77%	82%	73%
	(39)	(44)	(44)

[a]Initial numbers are indicated in parentheses.
[b]From Pennsylvania (Schuylkill County, 1980) and Wisconsin (Richland County, 1979; Dane County, 1981).
[c]From six counties on northern Wisconsin, 1980; see Scriber et al., (1982).
[d]*Papilio glaucus canadensis* × *P. glaucus glaucus*. Hand-paired in the laboratory in 1981.

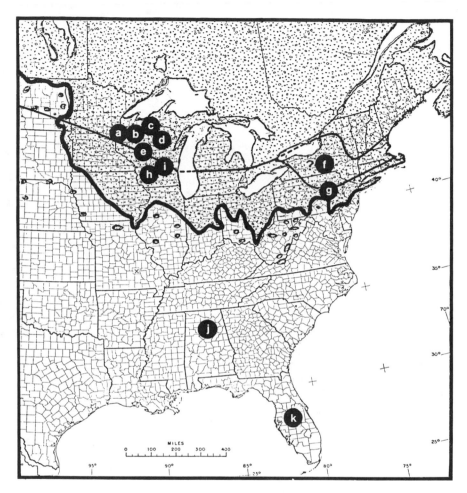

Fig. 16. Growth performance of penultimate-instar larvae of *Papilio glaucus* from different geographic populations on quaking aspen *(Populus tremuloides)*. (See Fig. 15 legend for further explanation.) (a)–(e) *P. glaucus canadensis;* 86% survival in first instar (20 females, 5 counties). (a) RGR = 0.15, ECI = 11%. (b) RGR = 0.10, ECI = 7%. (c) RGR = 0.14, ECI = 11%. (d) RGR = 0.12, ECI = 8%. (e) RGR = 0.14, ECI = 9%. (f) Yellow morph; <25% survival in first instar, RGR = 0.09, ECI = 7%. (g) 197 of 204 larvae from 17 yellow-morph females died in first instar; all larvae of dark-morph female parentage died in first instar. (h)–(i) All larvae of dark-morph female parentage died in first instar. (j)–(k) All larvae of both dark- and yellow-morph female parentage died in first instar. The taxonomic status of (f) is uncertain.

Table VIII
Total Larval Duration on Three Key Food Plants.[a]

Insect	Black cherry (Prunus serotina)	Tulip tree (Liriodendron tulipifera)	Quaking aspen (Populus tremuloides)
Papilio glaucus glaucus			
With dark-morph mothers	31.2 ± 0.4 (13)	28.6 ± 0.5 (29)	None survived
With yellow-morph mothers	31.9 ± 1.0 (12)	27.5 ± 0.4 (36)	None survived
Papilio glaucus canadensis	32.0 ± 0.7	None survived	38.7 ± 0.8 (36)
F₁ Hybrids[b]	26.2 ± 0.6 (21)	26.6 ± 0.5 (21)	35.4 ± 0.9 (25)

[a]In days. Data are presented as a mean ± SE. Initial numbers are indicated in parentheses. Sources as in Table VIII.
[b]*Papilio glaucus canadensis* × *P. glaucus glaucus*.

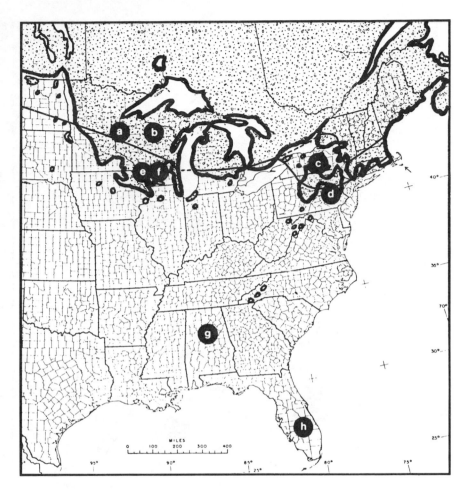

Fig. 17. First-instar survival and penultimate-instar growth performance of *Papilio glaucus* from different geographic populations on paper birch *(Betula papyrifera)*. (See Fig. 15 legend for further explanation.) (a)–(b) *P. glaucus canadensis*. (a) RGR = 0.178. ECI = 13.8%. (b) RGR = 0.159, ECI = 13.7%. (c) RGR = 0.140, ECI = 15.9%. (d)–(h) *P. glaucus glaucus*. (d) Dark morph, RGR = 0.163, ECI = 16.8%; yellow morph, RGR = 0.108, ECI = 11.3%. (e) Dark morph, RGR = 0.126, ECI = 17.4%. (f) Dark morph, RGR = 0.244, ECI = 16.8%. (g)–(h) All larvae died in first instar. The taxonomic status of (c) is uncertain.

glaucus canadensis north of 50° N latitude (see Scriber, 1982a). It is interesting in this regard that choke cherry is the only plant (of 12 tested) for which the mean larval duration of *Papilio glaucus canadensis* was significantly less than that for adjacent Wisconsin *P. glaucus glaucus* (Scriber *et al.*, 1982). More discussion of the potentially key biogeographic role

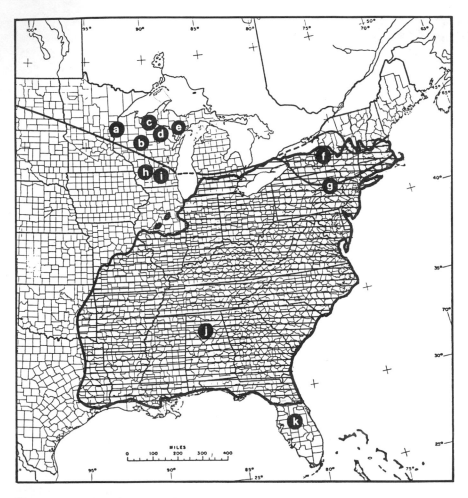

Fig. 18. Growth performance of *Papilio glaucus* from different geographic populations on spice bush *(Lindera benzoin)*. First-instar survival: (a)–(e) *P. glaucus canadensis*; all larvae died in first instar. (f) *P. glaucus glaucus* yellow morph, RGR = 0.09, ECI = 11%. (g) *P. glaucus glaucus*: dark morph, 14%; yellow morph, 34%. *P. glaucus canadensis* × *P. glaucus glaucus* F₁ "hybrid"; 17%. (h)–(k) *P. glaucus glaucus*. (h)–(i) Dark- and yellow-morph ♀♀, 0%. (j)–(k) 0%.

played by choke cherry for another group of Lepidoptera is described in the following subsection. Genetic and comparative host-plant studies should reveal the degree of concordance of adult phenotype, phenology, and host-plant adaptations exhibited by various populations now tentatively included in the rubric *"canadensis."*

4. The *Hyalophora* Species Group

As with the *Papilio glaucus* group (Section II,B,3), the genus *Hyalophora* (Saturniidae) is comprised of a polyphagous eastern species *(H. cecropia* L.)* and three somewhat more stenophagous species, *H. euryalus* Bois-duval along the western coast of the United States, *H. gloveri gloveri* (Strecker) in the Rockies;, *H. gloveri nokomis* (Brodie) eastward in Canada to Manitoba, and the larch- (i.e., tamarack)-feeding specialist, *H. columbia* (S. I. Smith), which is restricted geographically to acidic bog-type areas in the eastern half of Canada, in Maine, and in the northern parts of Great Lakes states, particularly Wisconsin and Michigan (Fig. 19). Al-though larval and adult characteristics are rather distinct among the four species, considerable hybridization may exist where the ranges overlap (Sweadner, 1937; Weast, 1959; Wright, 1971; Collins, 1973, 1981; L. Ferge, unpublished data). In fact, Collins (1973) has suggested that *H. columbia* may only be a melanic subspecies of *H. gloveri*.

The generalized *Hyalophora cecropia* uses a very large variety of food plants throughout the eastern half of the United States (Scarbrough *et al.,* 1974). It is interesting that the geographically adjacent species (or subspecies) are more specialized in their diet. *Hyalophora columbia* is generally believed to feed exclusively on tamarack, *Larix laricina* (DuRoi) Koch, whereas *H. gloveri nokomis*, across the plains from Alberta to Man-itoba, feeds primarily on the Elaeagnaceae (wolf willow, *Elaeagnus ar-gentea* Pursh, and buffalo berry, *Shepherdia* spp.). *Hyalophora gloveri gloveri* in the Rockies also utilizes western choke cherry *(Prunus demissa)* and willow *(Salix* supp.)* as well as the introduced Russian olive *(E. angustifolia* L.)* (Collins, 1973). *Hyalophora euryalus* in California (Sierra Nevada and northward) frequently uses plants of the Rhamnaceae (e.g., *Ceanothus* spp. and *Rhamnus* spp.), Ericaceae *(Arctostaphylos* spp. and *Arbutus men-ziesii* Pursh *)*, and Rosaceae [*Prunus emarginata* (Douglas) Walp.] as well as others (e.g., "birch") that have been reported (Ferguson, 1972; see also Collins, 1981).

In addition to geographic distribution, a striking similarity also exists in food-plant use between members of the *Hyalophora* group and the *Papilio glaucus* group (see Section II,B,3). Similar ranges and food-plant favorites are shared by *P. glaucus* and *H. cecropia*, *P. rutulus* and *H. gloveri gloveri*, and *P. eurymedon* and *H. euryalus* (cf. Figs. 12 and 19). It is also interesting that choke cherry is one of the very few plant species (also *Salix* spp.) that occur within the present geographic range of all species (and subspecies) of both the *Hyalophora* group (Saturniidae) and the *Papilio glaucus* group (Papilionidae). As such, these plants provide a potential food-plant bridge connecting the Great Lakes species and the Rocky Mountains species across Canada. Preliminary studies (J.M. Scri-

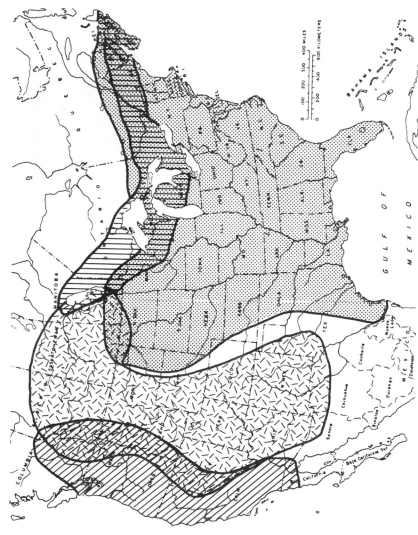

Fig. 19. Geographic ranges of the North American species of *Hyalophora*: *H. cecropia* (▦), *H. columbia* (▨), *H. gloveri* (▣; *H. gloveri nokomis* in the northern part of the range, *H. gloveri gloveri* in the southern part), and *H. euryalus* (▥). Distribution records are from Sweadner (1937), McGugan (1958). Ferguson (1972), Collins (1973, 1981), Kohalmi and Moens (1975), and L. Ferge (unpublished information).

Table IX

Utilization[a] of Choke Cherry *(Prunus virginiana)* by Penultimate-Instar Larvae of Four Species of *Hyalophora* (Saturniidae)

Hyalophora *species* (reported food-plant use)	n	RCR (mg/day/g)	ECI (%)	RGR (mg/day/g)
H. euryalus (occasional)	3	73.4 ± 3.1	16.6 ± 0.7	12.1 ± 0.7
H. gloveri (occasional)	3	89.6 ± 8.4	12.8 ± 0.3	10.9 ± 1.2
H. cecropia (marginal)	10	68.0 ± 2.2	14.9 ± 0.2	10.1 ± 0.2
H. columbia[b] (rare or never)	1	110.5	8.6	9.5

[a]Data (for penultimate instar) are presented as a mean ± SE. Madison, Wisconsin, 1980.
[b]RCR, ECI, RGR as in Table II. *Hyalophora columbia* larvae initially believed to be penultimate died or spun cocoons and were, in fact, final instars. This survivor is included here because it was virtually identical in size to the penultimate instar of the three larger species.

ber, E.M. Grabstein, and L. Ferge, unpublished) indicate that some individuals of all species of the *Hyalophora* group can, in fact, survive and successfully reach the pupal stage when fed only choke cherry. Penultimate-instar performances are similar for those larvae tested on choke cherry (Table IX).

The possibility of improved biochemical adaptation with food-plant specialization (as evidenced by increased larval food-processing efficiencies and/or growth rates) in *Hyalophora euryalus*, *H. gloveri*, and *H. columbia* has yet to be adequately assessed. However, preliminary feeding studies suggest that *H. gloveri* larvae do consume and process *Elaeagnus angustifolia* more efficiently and more rapidly than do larvae of its more polyphagous relative, *H. cecropia* (Table X). Survival and food-processing abilities of *H. columbia* on *Larix* spp. are not significantly better than those of *H. cecropia* larvae (J. M. Scriber and L. Ferge, unpublished data; see also Scarbrough *et al.*, 1974). *Larix* is also a suitable foodplant for *H. gloveri* and perhaps *H. euryalus*, which does feed in nature on Douglas fir [*Pseudotsuga menziesii* (Mirbel) Franco] (Collins, 1973, and personal communication).

Subspecies crosses or artificial-hybridization studies of the various *Hyalophora* populations would provide an excellent experimental system for judging differential food-plant acceptance and physiological processing abilities. The inheritance of food-plant preferences or utilization abilities in the *Hyalophora* group is basically unknown, despite the popularity of this group with lepidopterists (but see Wright, 1971; Collins, 1981). It has been suggested (Weast, 1959) that the range of acceptable

Table X
Nutritional Indexes of Penultimate-Instar Larvae of *Hyalophora gloveri gloveri* and *H. cecropia* Fed Russian Olive *(Elaeagnus angustifolia)*[a]

Hyalophora species	n	RCR (mg/day/g)	ECI (%)	RGR (mg/day/g)
H. cecropia	11	58.5 ± 3.1	13.6 ± 0.8	7.9 ± 0.5
H. gloveri	6	89.2 ± 6.0	16.5 ± 0.6	14.6 ± 0.7

[a]RCR, ECI, and RGR as in Table II.

foods of the more stenophagous feeders (such as *H. euryalus, H. gloveri,* and *H. columbia*) is increased by crossings with *H. cecropia,* but not to as great a degree as for *H. cecropia* itself.

The role of food plants in the speciation of this *Hyalophora* group is still basically unknown. Understanding the geographic differences in actual and potential host-plant-utilization abilities might help clarify certain aspects of their feeding ecology; however, any conclusions in regard to phylogenetic relationships must be made with extreme caution, considering the various nongenetic factors (whether environmental or behavioral, or physiological or ecological) that influence food-plant acceptability and suitability for a population or an individual (Scriber and Slansky, 1981; Miller and Strickler, 1982; Scriber, 1982a).

II. CONCLUSION

Feeding specialization conveys different concepts to different researchers. It has become evident that the relationships of selective feeding in field situations can be due to a variety of ecological factors, many of which may have little to do with improved biochemical adaptation to the plant. Survival and physiological rates and/or efficiencies of a phytophagous insect on a given species, individual, or part of the plant will be influenced greatly by variable plant quality; however, we must also consider variability in the insect species, population, and individual instar adaptations as well.

Geographic differences in detoxification and physiological processing abilities of Papilionidae and Saturniidae are significant. Analysis of the specific biochemical mechanisms of adaptation is needed to evaluate the physiological-efficiency hypothesis in proper fashion. Determining the biochemical and genetic bases of these differential abilities will contribute greatly to our understanding of the processes involved in host-race formation and coevolution between insect herbivores and plants. Additional studies designed to determine whether clines exist in genetic compatibility (and also in morphological, alleolmorphic, phenological, and host-preference characters; see, e.g., Wiklund, 1982) would be extremely valuable in assessing regional genetic differentation.

ACKNOWLEDGMENTS

This research was supported by the National Science Foundation (DEB-7921749) and the College of Agricultural and Life Sciences of the University of Wisconsin at Madison (Hatch Project 5134). I am grateful to Lincoln Brower, Michael Collins, Doug Futuyma, Fred Gould, Ric Peigler, and Art Shapiro for their contributions toward improvement of the text. I would also like to thank the following people for their assistance in obtaining living specimens for these studies: Michael Collins, Robert Dowell, Mark Evans, Les Ferge, Mark Finke, Mecky Furr, William Houtz, Phil Kingsley, Greg Lintereur, Bruce Pulsifer, Dave Ritland, Bryan Steinberg, and Ken Thorne. Thanks and congratulations are extended to Jerry Bentz, Mark Evans, Eric Grabstein, Susan Heg, Syafrida Manuwoto, Brian Mohr, Julianna Potter, and Tom Ulhman for successfully enduring the mass-rearing processes.

REFERENCES

Atchley, W. R., and Woodruff, D. (1981). "Evolution and Speciation." Cambridge Univ. Press, London.

Atsatt, P. R. (1981). Lycaenid butterflies and ants: selection for enemy free space. *Am. Nat.* **118,** 638–654.

Beck, S. D., and Apple, J. W. (1961). Effects of temperature and photoperiod on voltinism of geographical populations of the European corn borer, *Pyrausta nubilalis. J. Econ. Entomol.* **54,** 550–558.

Berenbaum, M., and Feeny, P. (1981). Toxicity of angular furanocoumarins to swallowtail butterflies: escalation in a coevolutionary arms race? *Science* **212,** 927–929.

Brower, L. P. (1957). Speciation in the *Papilio glaucus* group. Ph.D. Dissertation, Yale University, New Haven, Connecticut.

Brower, L. P. (1958). Larval foodplant specificity in butterflies of the *P. glaucus* group. *Lepid. News* **12,** 103–114.

Brower, L. P. (1959a). Speciation in butterflies of the *Papilio glaucus* group. I. Morphological relationships and hybridization. *Evolution* **13,** 40–63.

Brower, L. P. (1959b). Speciation in butterflies of the *Papilio glaucus* group. II. Ecological relationships and interspecific sexual behavior. *Evolution* **13,** 212–228.

Brown, L. N. (1972). Mating behavior and life habits of the sweet-bay silk moth (*Callosamia carolina*). *Science* **176,** 73–75.

Brues, C. T. (1924). The specificity of foodplants in the evolution of phytophagous insects. *Am. Nat.* **58,** 127–144.

Bush, G. L. (1975). Modes of animal speciation. *Annu. Rev. Ecol. Syst.* **6,** 339–364.

Chapman, R., and Bernays, E. A., eds. (1978). "Insect and Host Plant." Nederlandse Entomologische Vereiniging.

Clarke, C. A., and Sheppard, P. M. (1955). The breeding in captivity of the hybrid *Papilio rutulus* female × *P. glaucus* male. *Lepid. News* **9,** 46–48.

Clarke, C. A., and Sheppard, P. M. (1957). The breeding of the hybrid *Papilio glaucus* female × *P. eurymedon* male. *Lepid. News* **11**, 201–205.

Collins, M. M. (1973). Notes on the taxonomic status of *Hyalophora columbia* (Saturaniidae). *J. Lepid. Soc.* **27**, 225–235.

Collins, M. M. (1981). Genetics and ecology of a hybrid zone in *Hyalophora*. Ph.D. Thesis, University of California, Davis.

Collins, M. M., and Weast, R. D. (1961). "Wild Silk Moths of the United States." Collins, Cedar Rapids, Iowa.

Curtis, J. T. (1959). "The Vegetation of Wisconsin." Univ. of Wisconsin Press, Madison.

Dethier, V. G. (1954). Evolution of feeding preferences in phytophagous insects. *Evolution* **8**, 33–54.

Dethier, V. G. (1978). Studies on insect/plant relations—past and future. *Entomol. Exp. Appl.* **24**, 759–766.

Ebner, J. A. (1970). "Butterflies of Wisconsin," Pop. Sci. Handb. No. 12. Milwaukee Public Mus., Milwaukee, Wisconsin.

Ehrlich, P. R., and Raven, P. H. (1964). Butterflies and plants: a study in coevolution. *Evolution* **18**, 586–608.

Ehrlich, P. R., and Raven, P. H. (1969). Differentiation of populations. *Science* **165**, 1228–1232.

Emlen, J. M. (1973). Feeding ecology. "Ecology: An Evolutionary Approach," pp. 157–185. Addison-Wesley, Reading, Massachusetts.

Endler, J. A. (1977). "Geographic Variation, Speciation and Clines." Princeton Univ. Press, Princeton, New Jersey.

Feeny, P. P. (1975). Biochemical coevolution between plants and their insect herbivores. *In* "Coevolution of Animals and Plants" (L. E. Gilbert and P. R. Raven, eds.), pp. 3–19. Univ. of Texas Press, Austin.

Ferguson, D. C. (1972). Bombycoidea, Saturniidae (in part) *In* "The Moths of America North of Mexico," (R. B. Dominick, ed.), Fasc. 20.2B.

Ferris, C. D., and Brown, F. M. (1981). "Butterflies of the Rocky Mountain States." Univ. of Oklahoma Press, Norman.

Fox, L. R., and Morrow, R. A. (1981). Specialization: species property or local phenomenon? *Science* **211**, 887–883.

Futuyma, D. J., and Mayer, G. C. (1980). Non-allopatric speciation in animals. *Syst. Zool.* **29**, 254–271.

Futuyma, D. J., and Wasserman, S. S. (1981). Foodplant specialization and feeding efficiency in the tent caterpillars *Malacosoma disstria* and *M. americanum*. *Entomol. Exp. Appl.* **30**, 106–110.

Gilbert, L. E. (1979). Development of theory in the analysis of insect–plant interactions. *In* "Analysis of Ecological Systems" (D. J. Horn, G. S. Stairs, and R. D. Mitchell, eds.), pp. 117–154. Ohio State Univ. Press, Columbus.

Gould, F. (1979). Rapid host range evolution in a population of the phytophagous mite *Tetranychus urticae* Koch. *Evolution* **33**, 791–802.

Grabstein, E. M., and Scriber, J. M. (1982). The relationship between restriction of host plant consumption, and post-ingestive utilization of biomass and nitrogen in *Hyalophora cecropia*. *Entomol. Exp. Appl.* **31**, 202–210.

Hanson, F. E. (1976). Comparative studies on induction of food choice preferences in lepidopterous larvae. *Symp. Biol. Hung.* **16**, 71–77.

Haskins, C. P., and Haskins, E. F. (1958). Note on the inheritance of behavior patterns for food selection and cocoon spinning in F_1 hybrids of *Callosamia promethea* × *C. angulifera*. *Behaviour* **13**, 89–95.

House, H. L. (1962). Insect nutrition. *Annu. Rev. Biochem.* **31**, 653–672.

Jaenike, J. (1981). Criteria for ascertaining the existence of host races. *Am. Nat.* **117**, 830–834.

Köhalmi, L., and Moens, P. (1975). Evidence for the existence of an intergrade population between *Hyalophora gloveri nokomis* and *H. columbia* in northwestern Ontario (Lepidoptera: Saturniidae). *Can. Entomol.* **107**, 793–799.

McGugan, B. M. (1958). "Forest Lepidoptera of Canada Recorded by the Forest Insect Survey," Vol. 1, Publ. 1034. Can. Dept. Agric. (For. Biol. Div.),

McNaughton, S. J., and Wolf, L. L. (1970). Dominance and the niche in ecological systems. *Science* **167**, 131–139.

Menken, S. B. (1981). Host races and sympatric speciation in small ermine moths, Yponomeutidae. *Entomol. Exp. Appl.* **30**, 280–292.

Miller, J., and Strickler, K. (1983). Foodplant location and assessing. *In* "Chemical Ecology of Insects" (W. Bell and R. Carde, eds.), Chapter 5. Chapman & Hall, London (in press).

Munroe, E. (1960). The generic classification of the Papilionidae. *Can. Entomol. Suppl.* **17**, 1–51.

Packard, A. S. (1914). Monograph of the bombycine moths of North America. Part 3. *Mem. Natl. Acad. Sci.* **12**, 1–516.

Peigler, R. S. (1975). The geographical distribution of *Callosamia securifera* (Saturniidae). *J. Lepid. Soc.* **29**, 188–191.

Peigler, R. S. (1976). Observations on host plant relationships and larval nutrition in *Callosamia* (Saturniidae). *J. Lepid. Soc.* **30**, 184–187.

Peigler, R. S. (1977). Hybridization of *Callosamia* (Saturniidae). *J. Lepid. Soc.* **31**, 23–34.

Peigler, R. S. (1981). Demonstration of reproductive isolating mechanisms in *Callosamia* (Saturniidae) by artificial hybridization. *J. Res. Lepid.* **19**, 72–81.

Remington, C. L. (1958). Genetics of populations of Lepidoptera. *Proc. Int. Congr. Entomol.*, *10th, 1956* Vol. 2, pp. 787–805.

Scarbrough, A. G., Waldbauer, G. P., and Sternburg, J. G. (1974). Feeding and survival of *cecropia* (Saturniidae) larvae on various plant species. *J. Lepid. Soc.* **28**, 212–219.

Schroeder, L. A. (1976). Effect of food deprivation on the efficiency of utilization of dry matter, energy, and nitrogen by larvae of the cherry scallop moth, *Calocalpe undulata*. *Ann. Entomol. Soc. Am.* **69**, 55–58.

Schroeder, L. A. (1977). Energy, matter, and nitrogen utilization by larvae of the milkweed tiger moth. *Euchaetias egle*. *Oikos* **28**, 27–31.

Scriber, J. M. (1973). Latitudinal gradients in larval feeding specialization of the world Papilionidae (Lepidoptera). *Psyche* **80**, 355–373.

Scriber, J. M. (1975). Comparative nutritional ecology of herbivorous insects: generalized and specialized feeding strategies in the Papilionidae and Saturniidae (Lepidoptera). Ph.D. Thesis, Cornell University, Ithaca, New York.

Scriber, J. M. (1981). Sequential diets, metabolic costs, and growth of *Spodoptera eridania* (Lepidoptera: Noctuidae) feeding upon dill, lima bean, and cabbage. *Oecologia* **51**, 175–180.

Scriber, J. M. (1982a). Foodplant suitability. *In* "Chemical Ecology of Insects" (W. Bell and R. Carde, eds.), Chapter 6. Chapman & Hall, London (in press).

Scriber, J. M. (1982b). The behavior and nutritional physiology of southern armyworm larvae as a function of plant species consumed in earlier instars. *Entomol. Exp. Appl.* **31**, 359–369.

Scriber, J. M. (1982c). Foodplants and speciation in the *Papilio glaucus* group. *Proc. Int. Symp. Insect–Plant Relationships, 5th*, pp. 307–314.

Scriber, J. M., and Feeny, P. P. (1979). The growth of herbivorous caterpillars in relation to degree of feeding specialization and to growth form of their foodplants. (Lepidoptera: Papilionidae and Bombycoidea). *Ecology* **60**, 829–850.

Scriber, J. M., and Slansky, F., Jr. (1981). The nutritional ecology of immature insects. *Annu. Rev. Entomol.* **26**, 183–211.

Scriber, J. M., Lederhouse, R. C., and Contardo, L. (1975). Spicebush, *Lindera benzoin,* a little known foodplant of *Papilio glaucus* (Papilionidae). *J. Lepid. Soc.* **29**, 10–14.

Scriber, J. M., Lintereur, G. L., and Evans, M. H. (1982). Foodplant utilization and a new oviposition record for *Papilio glaucus canadensis* R & J (Papilionidae: Lepidoptera) in northern Wisconsin and Michigan. *Great Lakes Entomol.* **15**, 39–46.

Shapiro, A. M. (1974). Butterflies and skippers of New York state. *Search* **4**, 1–59.

Shapiro, A. M. (1976). Seasonal polyphenism. *Evol. Biol.* **9**, 259–263.

Smiley, J. (1978). Plant chemistry and the evolution of host specificity: new evidence from *Heliconius* and *Passiflora. Science* **201**, 745–747.

Starmer, W. T., Kircher, H. W., and Phaff, H. J. (1980). Evolution and speciation of host plant specific yeasts. *Evolution* **34**, 137–146.

Sweadner, W. R. (1937). Hybridization and the phylogeny of the genus *Platysamia. Ann. Carnegie Mus.* **25**, 163–242.

Tauber, C. A., and Tauber, M. J. (1981). Insect seasonal cycles: genetics and evolution. *Annu. Rev. Ecol. Syst.* **12**, 281–308.

Templeton, A. R. (1981). Mechanisms of speciation—A population genetic approach. *Annu. Rev. Ecol. Syst.* **12**, 23–48.

Turner, J. R. G. (1981). Adaptation and evolution in *Heliconius:* a defense of neo-Darwinism. *Annu. Rev. Ecol. Syst.* **12**, 99–121.

Tyler, H. (1975). "The Swallowtail Butterflies of North America." Naturegraph, Healdsburg, California.

Wagner, W. H., Hansen, M. K., and Mayfield, M. R. (1981). True and false foodplants of *Callosamia promethea* (Lepidoptera: Saturniidae) in southern Michigan. *Great Lakes Entomol.* **14**, 159–165.

Watts, W. A. (1980). Late Quarternary vegetation history of the southeastern U.S. *Annu. Rev. Ecol. Syst.* **11**, 387–409.

Weast, R. D. (1959). Isolation mechanisms in populations of *Hyalophora* (Saturniidae). *J. Lepid. Soc.* **13**, 213–216.

White, M. D. (1979). "Modes of Speciation." Freeman, San Francisco.

Wiklund, C. (1982). Generalist versus specialist utilization of host plants among butterflies. *Proc. Int. Symp. Insect–Plant Relationships, 5th,* pp. 181–191.

Wright, D. A. (1971). Hybrids among species of *Hyalophora. J. Lepid. Soc.* **25**, 68–73.

J. Mark Scriber
Department of Entomology
University of Wisconsin
Madison, Wisconsin

CHAPTER 12

Adaptation, Host Specificity, and Gene Flow in the Black Pineleaf Scale

D. N. ALSTAD

G. F. EDMUNDS, JR.

I. INTRODUCTION

The black pineleaf scale insect, *Nuculaspis californica* Coleman, is a sedentary herbivore with host records from 11 North American pine *(Pinus)* species and Douglas fir *(Pseudotsuga menziesii)* (Edmunds, 1973). It occurs on western yellow pine *(Pinus ponderosa* Lawson*)* over much of its range, but populations are typically regulated at very low density by natural enemies. Although predation by coccinelid larvae is important, the principle agent of mortality is a eulophid parasitoid [*Encarsia (= Prospaltella*) n. sp., near *E. aurantii*]. In addition, a significant number of black pineleaf scales die during the molt between instars, without evidence of an external agent, and at the initial settlement period of first-instar larvae, when large numbers die in the crawler stage. These deaths may reflect the difficulty of accomodating the diverse chemical defenses of the host pine, but in circumstances that eliminate predators, especially parasitoids, the black pineleaf scale produces outbreak densities that cause severe damage and tree death in affected pine stands. The wasps are especially sensitive to dust pollution and insecticide drift from pest-spraying operations, and gradients of declining black pineleaf scale density and increasing frequency of parasitism can be observed on transects away from these pollution sources. We have studied the interaction of pines and black pineleaf scale in polluted areas where the parasitoid density is low. Under these conditions, variations in the abundance of black pineleaf scale reflect interactions of the herbivore and its host. Our present understanding of this system is based on continuous annual observation of numbered pines, beginning in 1953 (Edmunds, 1973), and on collaborative field experiments, performed each summer since 1973 (Edmunds and Alstad, 1978, 1981; Alstad et al., 1980).

Long-term observation of the black pineleaf scale–ponderosa pine interaction has uncovered two important patterns. First, there is great variance in the intensity of insect attack from one tree to the next within an infested stand of pines, even though the trees stand on uniform sandy soils. Trees that are completely free of scale insects can often be found touching branches with heavily damaged individuals carrying 10 insects/cm of needle throughout their crown. Such scale-free trees withstand annual colonization from infested neighbors. This pattern suggests that there are important genetic differences between the pines and that some individuals are "resistant" to the black pineleaf scale.

The second pattern of interest comes from the continuous observation of individually numbered trees. "Resistant" trees are not immune to insect attack. Repeatedly, trees that had remained scale free have been observed to suffer successful scale colonization. The course of the infestation on that host tree then follows a characteristic ontogeny. The population of successfully reproducing colonists remains at a low density for many insect generations, with gradual annual increases that result in a high scale density on the pine. We suggest that this pattern represents the establishment of a marginally preadapted insect genotype on the host tree and an interval of selection and adaptation.

In field transfer experiments, we have demonstrated that individual pines differ in phenotypic characteristics that significantly affect insect survivorship. Insects that are artificially moved from tree to tree show reduced survival in comparison to controls moved from branch to branch on the original host. Trees differ significantly in their "resistance," and insect populations that originated on different host individuals differ significantly in their ability to colonize new trees. These patterns represent features of each pine and each scale population, respectively, which all the interacting groups experience in a similar way. They contribute significant main treatment effects to the variance of the experimental results. In addition, a two-way analysis of variance shows significant interaction among these main treatment effects. Thus poor colonists occasionally do well on a highly "resistant" tree. This means that some components of the "resistance" of each individual tree have different effects on individual insect populations from different hosts. Such an outcome would be predicted if the criterion of insect success involved the similarity of the original host and the new tree into which the transfer was artificially moved. These results led us to conclude that any ponderosa pine genotype may ultimately be vulnerable to black pineleaf scale attack, and that, with respect to this interaction, the phenomenon of resistance per se has little meaning. Rather, it must be quantified in the context of the insect genotypes against which the defense is mounted (Edmunds and Alstad, 1978), and it essentially offers an inverse index of their adaptation to the host. Clonal propagation of "resistant" trees results in a type of resistance that is soon ineffective in natural tree stands. Some forest-tree breeders refer to this as "soft" resistance. After 35 yr of high-level infestation, scale-free trees have almost totally disappeared from our study areas; this suggests that interaction plays a large role in the scale–pine relationship.

We intend in this chapter to offer data characterizing the ontogeny of a scale attack on an individual host and, specifically, to address the question, What ontogenetic changes in the scale deme on an individual tree characterize the adaptive process? Because this ontogeny occurs over an interval of many years, it is not possible to follow the entire time sequence with data collection and experimental manipulations. We have chosen to sample trees representing the range of this infestation ontogeny from an infested stand at one particular time. In practice, this involves the examination of trees that carry different densities of scale insects and the assumption that insect density represents the adaptation of populations on individual trees to the defensive character of their host.

II. DENSITY DEPENDENCE

The feeding activity of a scale insect on the needle of a ponderosa pine produces a chlorotic lesion around the inserted stylet. The stylet terminates in palisade cells of the needle mesophyll rather than in conductive tissue, and it is situated far from the resin ducts at the perimeter of the needle's cross section. A fully developed female scale produces a yellowed diffusion lesion on the needle that stretches for 3–5 mm of its length. Inevitably, at high densities the insects seriously affect tree condition; length and weight of needles produced by such trees decline. Thus the quality of the tree as a growth substrate for insects declines as insect density increases. In addition, at high density the chlorotic lesions produced by individual insects on the needle begin to overlap. For these reasons, which have little to do with scale-insect adaptation, there will

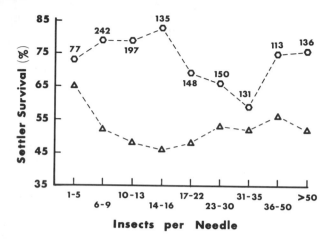

Fig. 1. Density dependence of black pineleaf scale survivorship. Numbered pine needles were divided into density classes after counting the number of settling scale crawlers. Subsequent recounts during the second and third instars allowed a percentage of survivorship to be calculated. **O**, Second-instar data; **▲**, third instar. The number of insects at risk in each size class of the original sample is indicated with the second-instar data.

be density-dependent changes in the performance and population biology of the insects which must be understood if we are to assess other density correlates.

We have followed the density dependence of both survivorship and fecundity of the black pineleaf scale on ponderosa pines by censusing first-instar crawlers that settle on individually numbered needle fascicles. By clipping 2 mm from the tip of one fascicle member, each needle can be identified during later samples to determine the survivorship of the initial colonists, and, at the end of their maturation, egg counts can be made from dissected females. The resulting patterns are illustrated in Fig. 1 and Table I. Survivorship data show that the number of initial colonists that persist into the third larval instar (overwintered) is considerably less than the number of second-instar survivors in the fall; although considerable mortality has occurred, the pattern of density dependence in the data is absent. This suggests that most of the mortality represented in Fig. 1 results from agencies other than competition and resource depression, that is, chlorosis and reduction of tree quality are not principle factors in the early-survival pattern. Predation, parasitism, and the host's defensive chemistry are potential agents that may yield this pattern. The relative density independence of mortality also fits with our observations of the settling behavior of first-instar crawlers. Black pineleaf scale insects take clumped positions on the pine needle. They

Table I
Density-Dependent Fecundity of the Black Pineleaf Scale on Ponderosa Pine[a]

Females per 10 cm (no.)	Sample size	Mean no. of eggs/female	Standard deviation
<1	50	36.9	8.5
1<2	70	35.4	9.2
2<3	63	30.4	10.7
3<4	42	25.9	10.7
4<5	44	27.1	12.7
5<6	58	23.0	12.1
>6	53	22.9	12.5

[a]Density is indicated as the number of insects per 10-cm section of pine needle.

may settle almost anywhere in the proximal three-fifths of a pine needle, but within this range individuals are most often contagiously distributed. This behavior would be unlikely if density-dependent destruction of the host substrate were an important source of mortality.

Fecundity is a full-performance measure spanning the late-development period, when feeding lesions become quite large. A more density-dependent pattern is thus understandable. The mean egg number per female falls by about one-third from 37 at a density of 0.1 insect/cm of needle to 23 eggs at 1.0 insect/cm of needle (Table I). The patterns of variance in fecundity and density are also very interesting. The data show that variance in fecundity rises while the mean egg number falls. Variance in the degree of crowding experienced by clumped insects must rise as a simple statistical correlate of density. The variance pattern suggests that declining fecundity is not a characteristic of the insects per se, but of their density and its effect on the quality of the host tree as a substrate. In fact, a decline in fecundity of one-third is small relative to the 10-fold density range of the samples.

III. HOW DOES COLONIZING ABILITY VARY WITH DENSITY?

Our early transfer experiments were designed to illustrate the differentiation of scales on individual trees, and they always dealt with the end products of this adaptive process; insects were consistently chosen from heavily infested hosts. To better understand the mechanisms of host specificity, in the summer of 1978 we began field transferring experiments in which insects were taken from donor trees that represented a wide range of scale-infestation densities, in order to examine correlates of the adaptation process. Specifically, we asked the question, How does

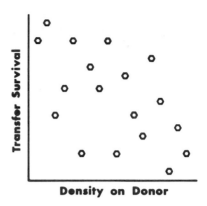

Fig. 2. Ranked average transfer success of individual scale demes plotted against the rank of their densities on the original donor–host. Density ranks increase from left to right on the abscissa, and average colonizing success rises from bottom to top on the ordinate.

the average colonizing ability into a variety of trees vary as adaptation to the original host individual increases?

Thus 18 donor trees were chosen and ranked according to the scale-insect-infestation densities that they carried. Three replicate transfers from every donor tree were moved into each of 10 receptor trees. In addition, within-tree control transfers from each donor were similarly transfered back into cleared branches of the original host. Initial establishment of first-instar larvae from each of the 612 transfers was quantified a week after larval settlement was complete. Insect survival was estimated in September and again in the following April. In each case, the census was made using an abundance scale that included 11 classes (0, 1–10, 10–25, 25–50, 50–75, 75–100, 100–150, 150–200, 200–250, 250–300, >300 insects per transfer twig). September and April survival ratios were calculated from the abundance data, dividing final class by initial class.

Average between-tree colonizing success for the 18 different donor populations is illustrated in Fig. 2, as a function of ranked infestation density on the donor trees. The negative relationship (Spearman rank correlation $r_s = 0.56$, $P = 0.01$) shows that populations occurring on their original donor–host at the lowest densities (those presumably least fitted to the host's defensive character) were most successful with respect to average colonizing success on a wide variety of receptor trees.

The use of insects from trees carrying different infestation densities involves assumptions that should be borne in mind as these experimental results are interpreted. We assume that insect density on a host is indicative of adaptation to that individual's defensive phenotype. In fact, there are many factors, including differences in predation, parasitism, maternal vigor, and nutritional quality of the host trees, that may produce variations in insect density among the pines without influencing host differentiation or colonizing success. Any of these mechanisms could support a density-dependent counterhypothesis, but we have demonstrated independently that density has little effect on survivorship (Fig. 1). Thus, although these data say little about mechanism or mode of inheritance, the ability to colonize new host individuals appears to be an intrinsic characteristic of the black pineleaf scale deme that declines through the ontogeny of increasing density on an single host pine. Adaptation to a single host reduces colonizing ability.

IV. SURVIVORSHIP PATTERNS AFFECT THE SCALE SEX RATIO

Sex is determined in black pineleaf scale by a haplodiploid mechanism involving obligate fertilization and elimination of paternal chromosomes early in the development of male progeny (Brown, 1958; Brown and McKenzie, 1962). Males carry the haploid chromosome number ($n = 4$) and females are diploid ($2n = 8$). Male eclosion, flight, and mating of scales occur in mid-May on ponderosa pines in the northwestern United States. A census of the insects just prior to male emergence showed wide variation in male/female ratios from one host tree to the next. We have not yet determined the sex ratios at hatching, but detailed observations of scale mortality show that reduced survivorship of males relative to females is an important component of this pattern. Table II shows data on the sex ratio of scale populations on 18 different host trees, taken during three successive years. The data show variations in the sex ratio between trees and between years. There are two patterns of great interest. First, male survivorship and the resulting sex ratio are correlated with the density of insects on the host tree (Spearman rank correlations for the three years are: 1979, $n = 11$, $r_s = 0.51$, $0.1 > P > 0.05$; 1980, $n = 18$, $r_s = 0.50$, $0.05 > P > 0.01$; 1981, $n = 18$, $r_s = 0.03$, NS; rank estimates of density used in the correlations were made in 1977). Trees are ranked in Table II from top to bottom, according to the abundance of insects and their presumed level of adaptation to the host defenses. High-density populations show improved male survivorship and a higher sex ratio. The second pattern in the data from Table II is a consistent increase in the male frequency from year to year. Ratios from each host tree remained correlated between sampling seasons, but the pattern of improved male survivorship between samples is highly significant statistically.

If annual increases in male survivorship reflect the process of selection that adapts insect populations to the defensive character of their host, then natural or artificial differences in gene flow between demes on

Table II
Sex Ratios of Scale-Insect Demes from 18 Different Host Trees

Rank	n (1979)	♂ / ♀	n (1980)	♂ / ♀	n (1981)	♂ / ♀
1	—	—	327	0.073	299	0.128
2	71	0.014	409	0.073	467	0.107
3	181	0.028	347	0.089	1037	0.101
4	126	0.000	403	0.032	192	0.091
5	—	—	327	0.052	519	0.126
6	188	0.005	412	0.068	381	0.085
7	203	0.005	337	0.113	580	0.064
8	108	0.009	368	0.098	335	0.196
9	122	0.025	382	0.055	912	0.068
10	141	0.052	208	0.087	86	0.323
11	—	—	399	0.043	382	0.117
12	147	0.007	356	0.076	468	0.093
13	76	0.101	260	0.162	344	0.147
14	—	—	358	0.101	462	0.079
15	580	0.034	246	0.166	398	0.223
16	—	—	366	0.109	509	0.077
17	—	—	384	0.081	489	0.153
18	—	—	389	0.090	414	0.092

[a]Sampled just before male eclosion in three successive years. Tree demes are ranked from low density (top) to high density (bottom).

different host trees should produce changes in male frequency. Gene flow counteracts selection and differentiation. It should increase genetic variance, increase the survivorship differential between the sexes, and decrease the resulting male/female ratio. To examine the effect of gene flow on the sex ratio, we chose 11 pairs of adjacent trees from a heavily scale-infested plot of ponderosa pines and censused insects on near and far sides of the tree crowns. Near-side samples were selected where foliage from the two different hosts either touched or was separated by a distance of less than 10 cm. The far-side samples were taken from each tree crown in a location separated by at least 5 m from the foliage of any other tree. We reasoned that near-side samples would receive more interdemic mating and gene flow than far-side samples and predicted that survivorship differences would reduce the near-side male/female ratios in comparison to far-side samples from the same tree. Of 22 pairwise comparisons from the data illustrated in Fig. 3, 19 support this prediction, and the overall pattern of lower near-side male/female ratios is highly significant (Wilcoxon matched-pairs signed-ranks test, $P < 0.001$).

Tree	A		B	C		D	Tree
183	0.225	>	0.054	0.091	<	0.112	184
185	0.040	>	0.030	0.035	<	0.108	186
187	0.171	>	0.117	0.129	<	0.190	188
189	0.073	<	0.116	0.092	<	0.113	190
199	0.123	>	0.054	0.097	<	0.118	200
26	0.135	>	0.048	0.086	>	0.074	27
29	0.161	>	0.076	0.113	<	0.146	38
30	0.169	>	0.076	0.077	<	0.126	31
32	0.106	<	0.127	0.056	<	0.112	33
35	0.094	>	0.058	0.058	<	0.069	34
37	0.196	>	0.153	0.052	<	0.068	36

Fig. 3. Sex ratios ($\male/\female$) from near and far sides of adjacent tree pairs. Samples were collected late in development, just prior to male eclosion and flight. Each row of data represents four samples from a single pair of pines. Columns A and D show far-side results, B and C near side. Samples from which the ratios were calculated range from 273 to 852.

V. A GENETIC MODEL OF ADAPTATION AND SPECIFICITY

Black pineleaf scale insects living on ponderosa pine show a characteristic ontogeny in the infestation of individual trees. A few scale insects become established and, if parasitoids are absent, population density increases very gradually over many annual generations, to levels that damage and kill the host. We have sampled contemporary trees showing a range of insect densities to demonstrate biological correlates of increasing abundance on a host individual. If we assume that this sample is a reasonable analog of the infestation ontogeny on a single host tree, then we have demonstrated four interesting features of that ontogenetic development.

1. There is continuing mortality among even those scale populations that we presume, because of their high density, are well adapted to the defenses of the host tree; but this mortality, at least through the third larval instar, is not strongly density dependent.

2. There is a density-dependent decline in fecundity as the quality of the damaged tree declines, but variance in fecundity changes inversely with the mean, suggesting that this decline is not a property of the scale genotype.

3. As insect density increases, colonizing potential and the ability to establish populations on different host individuals decline.

4. Changes in a survivorship differential between the sexes of the black pineleaf scale increase the male/female ratio on successive annual samples from a single tree. Male/female ratios are correlated with the density of insects on the host and appear to reflect a selective process, which is counteracted by gene flow between adjacent host trees.

We believe that the simplest model of adaptation and specificity in the black pineleaf scale that is consistent with these phenomena and with other circumstantial evidence (described in our earlier papers) is based on the selection of scale-insect demes with genetic adaptations that are appropriate for the defensive pattern of a particular host individual. Pines display great variability in their secondary chemistry (Smith, 1964; Hanover, 1975; Sturgeon, 1979), and each individual must carry some subset of the total spectrum of terpenoids, phenolics, quinones, etc. that is represented in the entire population. The high mortality that we observe among scale insects suggests that selection imposed by these plant defenses is intense. Because gene flow among the sedentary herbivores on different trees is probably small relative to this selective pressure, genetic differentiation of scale-insect demes on individual trees could result.

If selection and differentiation are the processes that underlie the ontogeny of increasing density on individual host trees, hypothetical mechanisms accounting for other biological features of this interaction may be suggested. If, for example, the colonization process requires the establishment of marginally preadapted insects on a new host, then the genetic variance of a scale deme will influence its ability to produce successful colonists. Demes with great genetic variance should be more successful in producing propagules that are sufficiently preadapted to survive on a diverse range of new hosts. Selection and differentiation on a single host individual should reduce genetic variance within the deme. This mechanism may explain the decline in average colonizing ability that we observe with increasing density on the host.

The selective process, which results in differentiation and reduced genetic variance, also suggests a mechanistic explanation of the sex-ratio phenomena that we have observed. In a highly polymorphic insect deme, females will carry more genetic information than the hemizygous males, and at intermediate frequencies their diploidy can mask deleterious genes. This information may facilitate their accomodation of complex chemical defenses in the host pine. As natural selection reduces the genetic variance in the scale-insect deme, however, the genetic character of males and females will become more nearly equivalent. If changes in male/female ratio reflect differences in the survivorship of the sexes, then this mechanism may account for the correlation of male frequency and insect density. Sex-ratio changes resulting from gene flow from an adjacent tree are also consistent with this hypothesis. Finally, the continuing mortality that we observe in scale demes at all points in the density ontogeny may reflect gene flow and the continued maintenance of genetic variability resulting from the interdemic mating activity of winged males.

We believe that genetic differentiation of scale demes on individual host trees is the simplest hypothesis compatible with all the facts and experimental results and that the accumulated evidence is very strong, but we are aware that alternative hypotheses remain.

VI. DISCUSSION: SOME IMPLICATIONS OF GENETIC VARIATION

The interaction of black pineleaf scale and ponderosa pines is complex and includes two distinct phenomena. Some characteristics of the host trees and the insects have similar effects on all of the opponents; they contribute main treatment variance to the survivorship data emerging from between-tree scale-insect-transfer experiments. Resin pressures reflecting the water balance of a pine might be one tree characteristic that would affect all black pineleaf scales in a similar way. Selection for these characteristics in a tree-breeding program would produce resistance against all types of black pineleaf scale. They are analogous to the *horizontal resistance* of Van der Plank (1968) and similar in some respects to the *quantitative defenses* of Feeny (1976; see also Rhoades and Cates, 1976).

The second class of interchange in the biology of black pineleaf scale and pines contributes interaction to the variance of our transfer experiments. Looking at one side of the exchange, there are features of individual trees that have variable effects on black pineleaf scale propagules and that depend on insect characteristics correlated with host origin. These are the interactions implying that scale-insect demes differentiate, specialize, and track individual trees. Such tree characteristics are analogous to the *vertical defenses* of Van der Plank (1968), and share many evolutionary features *qualitative defenses* of Feeny (1976).

Our data show that both phenomena are involved in the relationship of black pineleaf scale and ponderosa pines, but we are most excited by and have focused on the biological implications of the interactive, vertical, or qualitative mechanisms. These are the interactions that support an arms-race analogy or *red queen hypothesis*, in which both parties to a coevolutionary interaction must run at full speed simply to stay in the same place vis-à-vis each other. Inevitably, these ideas raise the observation that trees and insects have very different life spans. How can trees stay ahead or abreast of coevolving antagonists that have much shorter generation times?

Our work with the black pineleaf scale system on long-lived ponderosa pines suggests a much more static and equilibrial interaction than these analogies imply. The selective pressure of coevolving herbivores seems to produce diversity and intraspecific variation in the interactive or vertical defenses of pines. Hanover (1975) has suggested that their secondary chemistry is so variable that individual trees are essentially unique. Interaction in the analysis of variance from our transfer experiments suggests that these defenses are successfully countered by coevolved herbivores. Thus frequency-dependent selective pressures may account for their diversity. New defensive novelties will confer a large protective benefit. Old defenses that have been countered will decrease in frequency until herbivores forgo the expense of (for example) detoxification, preventing their loss from the plant's gene pool.

Data that we have presented in this chapter suggest that the intraspecific variability of ponderosa pines poses an evolutionary dilemma for insect herbivores. The difference in the length of life histories provides an opportunity for selection and differentiation among insect demes on individual trees, but, as black pineleaf scales become increasingly effective in the interaction with a single host individual, their reduced genetic variance interferes with the process of colonizing new host trees. Viewed in one context, gene flow results in an outbreeding depression. Alternatively, it sustains the variability that allows successful intertree mobility. There are several individual and interdemic selective arguments entwined here; we suggest that short-lived insect herbivores interacting with a host plant may find themselves on a continuum with two extremes. At one end, highly vagile insects might remain very generalized and ineffective against specific host genotypes. At the other, they become so channelized that their extinction must inevitably follow the demise of that host genotype.

The position of an insect population on this continuum must depend on the strength and duration of the selective pressure for differentiation on individual trees and on the amount of gene flow between them. As Hamrick *et al.* (1979) have noted, the amount of electrophoretically detectable variation in plant populations is correlated with the length of life history. Thus the duration and intensity of differentiating selection should be correlated, and short-lived plants are doubly unlikely to bear herbivores that differentiate on host individuals.

Variation in chemical defenses of hosts will have direct effects on physiological processes, but in some cases coloration and other characters used by taxonomists might be involved. Thus it seems reasonable that the genetic adaptation involved in shifting from one host to another will at times also involve an assortment of taxonomically perceivable characters. We suggest that there should be a correlation between the number of taxonomically difficult herbivorous groups and the relative longevity difference between host and pest. In essence, we believe that long-lived hosts are likely to have between-individual variations that correspondingly increase the variability of short-lived herbivores.

A genetic-variance model of adaptation and host specificity also has interesting implications related to the cyclical-outbreak dynamics of forest insect populations like those of the spruce budworm or the Douglas-fir tussock moth. Spruce budworms reach outbreak density on old, mature stands of balsam fir (Morris, 1963). If high densities of these insects follow a period of genic selection and adaptation to individual host defensive patterns, as they do with the black pineleaf scale, the genetic variance of insect demes on individual trees will change through the density cycle, falling as selection proceeds and numerical abundance increases. Because our experiments suggest that colonizing ability falls with genetic variance and adaptation to a single host tree, changes in genetic variance with the density cycle are extremely important. The process of new-tree colonization is a matching problem, requiring the arrival on the tree of a suitably preadapted genotype to survive on that host individual. Thus the dynamics of the outbreak involve a positive feedback. Higher insect abundance means that more genotypes are tried on more trees. On the other hand, if adaptation to host individuals involves intense selection and reduction of genetic variance in each host tree deme, then the feedback of abundance on outbreak dynamics could well be negative. High densities of insects may actually represent a very limited spectrum of genotypes. According to this model, the low-density intervals between outbreak situations may be the most contagious phase of the dynamic cycle.

ACKNOWLEDGMENTS

We are grateful to J. A. Endler, D. A. Polhemus, M. D. Rausher, and D. A. Tonkyn for their criticisms and comments, and to R. F. Denno and M. S. McClure for editorial help.

REFERENCES

Alstad, D. N., Edmunds, G. F., Jr., and Johnson, S. C. (1980). Host adaptation, sex ratio, and flight activity in male black pineleaf scale. *Ann. Entomol. Soc. Am.* **73**, 665–667.

Brown, S. W. (1958). Haplodiploidy in the Diaspididae—confirmation of an evolutionary hypothesis. *Evolution* **12**, 115–116.

Brown, S. W., and McKenzie, H. L. (1962). Evolutionary patterns in the armored scale insects and their allies. *Hilgardia* **33**, 141–170.

Edmunds, G. F., Jr. (1973). The ecology of black pineleaf scale. *Environ. Entomol.* **2**, 765–777.

Edmunds, G. F., Jr., and Alstad, D. N. (1978). Coevolution in insect herbivores and conifers. *Science* **199**, 941–945.

Edmunds, G. F., Jr., and Alstad, D. N. (1981). Responses of black pineleaf scales to host plant variability. *In* "Insect Life History Patterns" (R. F. Denno and H. Dingle, eds.), pp. 29–38. Springer-Verlag, New York and Berlin.

Feeny, P. P. (1976). Plant apparency and chemical defense. *Recent Adv. Phytochem.* **10**, 1–40.

Hamrick, J. L., Linhart, Y. B., and Mitton, J. B. (1979). Relationships between life history characteristics and electrophoretically detectable genetic variation. *Annu. Rev. Ecol. Syst.* **10**, 173–200.

Hanover, J. W. (1975). Physiology of tree resistance to insects. *Annu. Rev. Entomol.* **20**, 75–95.

Morris, R. F., ed. (1963). The dynamics of epidemic spruce budworm populations. *Mem. Entomol. Soc. Can.* **31**.

Rhoades, D. F., and Cates, R. G. (1976). Toward a general theory of plant antiherbivore chemistry. *Recent Adv. Phytochem.* **10**, 168–213.

Smith, R. H. (1964). Variation in the monoterpenes of *Pinus ponderosa* Laws. *Science* **143**, 1337–1338.

Sturgeon, K. B. (1979). Monoterpene variation in ponderosa pine xylem resin related to western pine beetle predation. *Evolution* **33**, 803–814.

Van der Plank, J. E. (1968). "Disease Resistance in Plants." Academic Press, New York.

D. N. Alstad
Department of Ecology and Behavioral Biology
University of Minnesota
Minneapolis, Minnesota

G. F. Edmunds, Jr.
Department of Biology
University of Utah
Salt Lake City, Utah

CHAPTER **13**

An Evolutionary–Genetic View of Host-Plant Utilization by Insects

CHARLES MITTER

DOUGLAS J. FUTUYMA

I. INTRODUCTION

In this chapter we shall consider the consequences for herbivorous insects of differences between their hosts, from the standpoint of evolutionary genetics. An important goal of this discipline, in particular that facet of it known as ecological genetics, is to explain the maintenence of genetic variation (or reasons for its absence) within populations. Thus one issue we shall examine in detail is the applicability to phytophages of recent theory on the promotion of such variability by environmental (in this case, among-host) heterogeneity. A chief task of evolutionary genetics is to provide an explanation in genetic terms of the patterns of evolutionary change, that is, the origin of new taxa or features. Thus we shall treat *host utilization* as an evolutionary character complex, asking what its temporal or spatial pattern of evolution is and whether it can be predicted from the genetic basis of variation. We shall also consider the possible influence of differences between hosts on the origin of new phytophagous species.

427

II. MAINTENANCE OF GENETIC VARIATION BY
ENVIRONMENTAL HETEROGENEITY: THEORY

Population geneticists have developed an extensive body of theory to describe the genetic consequences of variation in the environment. The seminal paper on this subject is that of Levene (1953). Felsenstein (1976) has reviewed the theoretical work of Levene and other authors, especially Dempster, Prout, Maynard Smith, Deakin, Strobeck, and Gillespie. The general conclusions are as follows.

Consider first the simplest case, two alleles at a single locus, and conceive of the environment as a patchwork of "islands" that differ in a key environmental feature, for example, host plant. For theoretical purposes it does not matter whether the islands are spatially separated or are intermingled as two plant species will often be. The first important distinction is whether the environmental variation is experienced by the insect as fine-grained or coarse-grained (Levins, 1968; Strobeck, 1975). If each individual is very mobile and does not choose one patch type over another, it experiences each kind of patch (i.e., each plant species) in proportion to the abundance of that patch type. The environment is then effectively the same for all individuals, and each genotype may be assigned a single value of average fitness. This is fine-grained environmental variation, and polymorphism will be stable only if there is heterozygote superiority in arithmetic mean fitness. Such apparent heterozygote advantage could result (here and in the models discussed later) from selection favoring a different homozygote in each habitat, a phenomenon known as *marginal overdominance* (Wallace, 1968).

At the other extreme, if each individual spends its whole developmental period in one patch or another, the environment is perceived as coarse-grained, and each genotype may be assigned a different fitness value for each environment. Assume, at first, that individuals emerge from all the patches, after developing in these, to form a single, randomly mating pool and that the offspring settle (or are deposited) at random into the two kinds of environment. Thus migration, or gene flow between patches, is maximal. In this situation the probability of stable polymorphism depends on the nature of population regulation. In the *constant zygote-number* model (Dempster, 1955), the number of individuals that survive and emerge from a patch to join the mating pool is proportional to the fraction of the zygotes settling into that patch that were of the genotype best adapted to it. There is *hard* selection (Wallace, 1968), so that the contribution of a patch to the total population of mating adults depends on gene frequency. Polymorphism in this case requries that the heterozygote have the highest arithmetic mean fitness.

In the *constant fertile-adult-number* model, however, ecological factors independently regulate the number of survivors in each patch, so that patch type 1 contributes a proportion C_1 to the adult population and patch type 2 a fraction C_2, whatever the genetic composition. Selection is *soft*, and population regulation is density dependent within each patch. Levene (1953) showed that, under these conditions, a polymorphism may be maintained if the harmonic mean fitness of each of the homozygotes is less than that of the heterozygote. Because a harmonic mean, the reciprocal of the mean of reciprocals, is less than an arithmetic mean, polymorphism may arise from a wider range of possible fitnesses than in the models described previously. Thus a coarse-grained environment with independent population regulation within patches creates favorable conditions for polymorphism, with each kind of patch or resource harboring a predominance of a particular well-adapted genotype.

Maynard Smith (1966; see also Maynard Smith and Hoekstra, 1980) has pointed out, however, that if the differences in fitness between the genotypes are small (less than about a 30% advantage of the superior genotype in each patch type), the polymorphism will persist only if the relative fitnesses and the abundances of the two kinds of patches bear a very precise relationship to each other. In a panmictic population, an allele favored only in one patch type will not persist if gene flow *(m)* of the alternate allele from outside that patch type is much greater than the selection against it within that patch. Thus, in a randomly mating population, a small, localized resource is unlikely to harbor a specially adapted genotype.

Two factors, however, may increase the likelihood of polymorphism. If individuals from the different patch types tend to mate *within* patches rather than at random, gene flow between patches is reduced, and polymorphism can persist even if selective differences are slighter. Clearly, such a situation will occur if patches are large relative to the dispersal distances of the animals when they seek mates, that is, if there is microgeographic variation in the environment. It is also possible for selection to favor alleles that confer reproductive isolation on the isolated genotypes, that is, for sympatric speciation to occur (Maynard Smith, 1966; see below), but the likelihood of this depends on several genetic factors, including the intensity of linkage between the genes that control mate choice and those that effect adaptation to different resources (Felsenstein, 1981).

The conditions for polymorphism are also relaxed considerably if the organisms practice habitat selection: if each genotype seeks out the resource or patch type to which it is specifically adapted or if females tend to lay eggs in the kind of patch in which they developed (Maynard

Smith, 1966). There would then be a corrrelation between host selection and the polymorphic trait that confers adaptation to one or the other host. This, like assortative mating, effectively lowers the flow of genes into the "wrong" patches, so that less intense selection is required to maintain a difference in gene frequency between patch types. A critical question is how such a correlation between habitat selection and substantive adaptation can be effected. In long-lived organisms such as birds or bees, an individual might learn by experience what kind of seeds or flowers, for example, it can exploit most effectively with its particular size of beak or tongue. In the case of holometabolous insects, in which the adult and larval food sources are different (e.g., lepidopterans), the only possibility for such matching would seem to be some form of imprinting or "conditioning" during the larval stage that carries through into adult oviposition behavior.

A correlation between host selection and morphological or physiological adaptation to the host plant can also be established if each trait is controlled by a polymorphic locus and if the loci are in linkage disequilibrium: if the alleles A_1 and A_2, controlling the physiological adaptation, and alleles B_1 and B_2, controlling host selection, are nonrandomly organized into the combinations A_1B_1 and A_2B_2. The strength of linkage disequilibrium depends on the tightness of linkage and on the degree of superiority of the "good" combinations A_1B_1 and A_2B_2 over the "bad" combinations A_1B_2 and A_2B_1. Clearly, a polymorphism for behavior that gets the individual onto the host to which it is adapted is more effective if the behavioral and physiological traits are controlled by single, closely linked loci than if each trait is polygenically determined by loci scattered throughout the chromosomes. It is important to point out that most traits in most organisms are polygenically inherited; if this is true also of behavioral and physiological adaptations of insects to host plants, the likelihood of stable, host-associated polymorphism may not be great.

Summarizing, the factors that will promote genetic polymorphism for host adaptation by a population of insects include pronounced differences in the ability of different genotypes to survive on different plants; independent regulation of population size on each host species; low mobility between hosts or extensive patches of one or the other host, which have the same effect of lowering gene flow between host-associated subdivisions of the population; assortative mating; and habitat selection, whereby individuals choose the host on which they or their offspring are more likely to survive. If habitat selection itself is based on genetic polymorphism, mono- or oligogenic inheritance of both behavior and adaptation and tight linkage of the two traits are more favorable to polymorphism than polygenic inheritance and loose linkage.

These models ascribe adaptation to a single locus. If adaptation is polygenically controlled, far more complex models are required. If adaptation entails only a single polygenic trait such as, perhaps, hatching time, different hosts may impose diversifying (or disruptive) selection by selecting for different means and maintain variation in the characteristic. The maintenance of variation again requires that the density of populations on the two hosts be independently regulated, otherwise there is directional selection for the genotypes that are adapted to the host on which survival is higher. It may sometimes happen, moreover, that adaptation to a host requires the possession of genes for several characteristics, for example, phenology as well as the ability to detoxify any of several plant compounds, but that no single characteristic confers an advantage unless coupled with the others. In this case a complex polymorphism of host-associated subpopulations differing in several characteristics may persist. The conditions for such a polymorphism are mathematically intricate, but they primarily require a balance between selection, which promotes the formation of coadapted gene complexes in linkage disequilibrium, and recombination, which breaks up the gene combinations. Thus tight linkage or other mechanisms such as close inbreeding or parthenogenesis, which reduce recombination, favor the maintenance of complex polymorphisms.

Although the theory just discussed tells us what to expect when disruptive selection occurs, it does not predict how often environmental discontinuity will actually impose such selection. Thus, for example, as noted by Gould (Chapter 17), the existence of disruptive selection imposed by differences between hosts, if widespread, would imply that adaptation to any particular host generally entails a correspondingly poor fitness on other hosts. However, there may often be single (homozygous) "compromise" genotypes with high fitness simultaneously on several hosts. This could come about, for example, if the physiological traits, such as detoxifying enzymes, that confer adaptation to the host were sufficiently broad in their action, or if they could be adjusted by short-term means to the characteristics of a particular host. In this case, different insect genotypes might differ only slightly in host-specific fitness profiles, and selection coefficients might be insufficient to maintain polymorphism. Moreover, many cases are known in which the evolutionary response to environmental variation is not genetic variability but some form of developmental "switch," yielding discretely different phenotypes adapted to different conditions. Thus the predictions about host-associated variation that might seem to follow from simple genetic theory may have to be modified by broader, organism-level considerations of adaption (see discussion in Levins, 1968; Slatkin, 1978; Mitter and Futuyma, 1979).

We have thus far centered attention on loci governing fitness in the particular environment (e.g., host) in which an individual finds itself. A somewhat different perspective emerges if we focus instead on genes responsible for the selection of different habitats or resources. For such characters there has begun to develop a partially independent body of theory derived from evolutionary ecology, specifically, the study of intraspecific competition and the evolution of *niche width*, reviewed by Roughgarden (1979). These models show that stable polymorphism for habitat preference is possible if the population is resource limited and if different genotypes use different resources; the likelihood of polymorphism is enhanced if there is some mechanism (such as, in the extreme, clonal reproduction; Roughgarden, 1972) for matching the proportion of each genotype produced each generation to the relative abundance of its particular resource. The important perspective added by the niche-width approach is that several genotypes might be equally well adapted to each of several hosts (perhaps for reasons like those discussed previously), but that stable polymorphism exist nevertheless, solely because each genotype selects a different host on which population size is independently regulated. (This is a version of the so-called Ludwig effect; Ludwig, 1950.) Suppose, for example, that a population of herbivores is limited by the number of hiding places from predators offered by its host and that a new mutant arises that selects a different host on which the herbivores are also able to feed and reproduce. The details of the outcome will depend on, among other things, the behavior of the heterozygote, but, in principle, such a mutant should increase to a frequency determined in part by the number of new hiding places supplied by the novel host. Of course, such a polymorphism may be replaced by a generalist genotype if one arises (see Matessi and Jayakar, 1975).

We have thus far treated different hosts or host genotypes as representing constant features of the herbivore's environment. It may sometimes be more realistic to suppose (especially in the case of variation within a single host species) that the host properties are themselves evolving in response to herbivore attack or are subject to significant environmental variation induced by the herbivores (see Rhoades, Chapter 6). The complications introduced by such temporal variation are discussed by Gould (Chapter 17). However, the majority of herbivores occupying two or more host taxa probably do so as a result of host shifts onto already differentiated plants, as opposed to parallel phylogenesis or *coevolution* (see Futuyma, 1983; Mitter and Brooks, 1983). In considering the genetic consequences of occupation of two or more species of hosts, then, it is probably realistic to suppose that the plants constitute a background for insect evolution that is heterogeneous but that is not changing in a consistent direction, at least in the short term.

III. EVIDENCE

A. Terminology

Before we can review the evidence on genetic variation in host utilization at different evolutionary levels, it will be necessary to clarify the relationships between the phenomena spoken of by evolutionary genetic theory and the terms that have been used in the literature to describe various kinds of genetic differences.

The literature that describes genetic differences in the responses of insects to host plants draws on the experience of classical taxonomy, agricultural entomology, and evolutionary genetics, and it has a correspondingly diverse vocabulary. A good deal of cryptic variation is discernible in the form of sibling species, which are morphologically so similar that they are often not recognized at first by taxonomists and are revealed by study of their ecology, behavior, chromosomes, or, more recently, allozymic differences. In some cases, subtle morphological differences in, for example, the genitalia, have been the clue to their existence. Geographic races, some of which are named as subspecies, are allopatric forms that differ in one or more traits, and they are taken to be conspecific. Within populations, the coexistence of discretely different genotypes is referred to as polymorphism; no clear distinction can be made between polymorphism, which usually refers to segregation at one or a few major gene loci, and continuous, quantitative, genetic variation that arises from segregation at a larger number of loci. The term *biotype* is used in agricultural entomology as a loose synonym for genotype. As Eastop (1973) has said, a biotype contains those individuals that perform whatever biological feat interests the observer. Biotypes are collections of individuals that differ in their response to a species or strain of plant, or in insecticide resistance, or in features such as coloration. They may be sympatric or allopatric, and as Claridge and den Hollander (1980) have pointed out in the case of the rice brown planthopper *(Nilaparvata lugens)*, each recognized biotype may be a genetically heterogeneous entity. A biotype is a phenotype that shows some degree of heritability.

The classical entomological literature bears many references to "host races," forms judged conspecific on morphological grounds but associated with different host plants and generally exhibiting other "biological" differences. Many of the so-called host races described in the early entomological literature have proved to be complexes of host-specific sibling species. This is true, for example, of the true fruit flies in the *Rhagoletis pomonella* complex that attack hawthorn, blueberry, and dogwood (Bush, 1969). The hawthorn- and apple-associated forms of the small ermine moth *Yponomeuta* differ in the form of the cocoon, the placing of eggs on the host, and (very subtly) in coloration (Thorpe, 1929), and they are now recognized as different species (Herrebout *et al.*, 1976). Two "host races" of the fall webworm *(Hyphantria cunea)* differ in larval coloration, site of egg laying, and form of the web, as well as host preference; given such a complex of differences, it is not surprising that allozyme analysis shows them to be reproductively isolated (Jaenike and Selander, 1980). Treehoppers in the *Enchenopa binotata* complex, referred to by Wood (1980) as host races on the basis of a variety of biological differences among collections taken from several woody plants, are also allozymically differentiated and are clearly sibling species (Guttman *et al.*, 1981). It seems probable that most of the sympatric "host races" of the older literature will turn out to be biological species.

B. Within-Population Variability in Host-Utilization Characters

1. Factors Promoting Match of Genotype to Host

We have described several phenomena that could serve to increase the likelihood of host-related variation by increasing the probability that a specifically adapted genotype will find itself on the appropriate host. To what extent are such effects prevalent in nature?

As noted previously, a correlation between host selection and adaptive characters could be established by learning. A model is provided by bumblebees, in which individual preferences for flowers of different corolla length are correlated with tongue length (Inouye, 1980). Presumably, such a correlation arises through learning, which may be more likely in long-lived insects. Cavener (1979) and Gelfand and McDonald (1980) have found that *Drosophila* genotypes differing at the alcohol dehydrogenase locus avoid ethanol to different extents. The avoidance reaction is more pronounced in late-instar larvae of genotypes with low alcohol dehydrogenase activity than in genotypes with high enzyme activity. There is no such correlation in the early instars, and Gelfand and McDonald (1980) have suggested that avoidance develops as a consequence of accumulation of aldehydes within the cells. Because of the limited mobility of *Drosophila* larvae, such alteration of behavior presumably does not affect host choice, but analogous systems might give rise to adaptive host choice in more mobile species. We are not aware of any similar cases in phytophagous insects (but see Gould, Chapter 17).

A somewhat different form of modification of food selection by prior experience has been demonstrated in a number of lepidopteran larvae, in which early feeding experience can influence, or "induce," feeding preferences in later larval life (Hanson, 1976; Barbosa *et al.*, 1979). Although an initially less preferred host can become more acceptable as a result of such "conditioning," an absolute preference for such a plant is seldom, if ever, developed. It is conceivable that this phenomenon could play a role in the maintenance of genetic variation, if "induction" tended to keep larvae on the same host to which they had been subjected to selection in the early instars.

A much stronger contribution to polymorphism would potentially result if such conditioning could affect adult oviposition preferences as well. Although early authors postulated that a female's larval experience could determine her oviposition preference (named by Craighead, 1921, the Hopkins' host-selection principle), no unequivocal examples of such an effect that cannot be explained by unconscious selection or inadequate technique have withstood critical scrutiny (Claridge and Wilson, 1978); see also Fox and Morrow, 1981; Tabashnik *et al.*, 1981). However, Jaenicke (1982) and Prokopy *et al.* (1982) have reported, for *Drosophila* and *Rhogoletis* flies, respectively, that previous exposure of adults to particular substrates can increase oviposition preference for these. These authors have argued that such adult conditioning may promote fidelity of oviposition to the host on which an adult has proven its fitness by successful development, if their larval hosts are the ones first encountered by emerging females.

There are few if any published cases in which variation in host adaptation in strictly sexual species is genetically correlated with variation in host preference (but compare with findings by S. Via, cited by Gould, Chapter 17), although it must be said that such evidence has almost never been sought. There are cases in which different biotypes of partially or obligately parthenogenetic forms differ in both preference and adaptation, but in these cases one cannot determine whether the correlation pre-dated and supplied a predisposition for the development of such forms or resulted from their clonal propagation.

Although the roles of learning and of genetic correlation between adaptation and host preference are ambiguous, many herbivores possess life history features that would seem to predispose them to maintenance of host-associated variation. In addition to the cyclical or obligate parthenogenesis and low vagility exhibited by many forms, there is the widespread habit of using the host as a rendezvous for mating. No general review of the prevalence of this phenomenon appears to exist, but it probably occurs in a great variety, perhaps even in the majority, of herbivorous groups (see, e.g., Bush, 1975b).

2. Documentation of Genetic Variation

Genetic variation in host-utilization characters within local populations of herbivores has been sought through artificial selection (e.g., Gould, 1979; Wasserman and Futuyma, 1981), responses of putative genotypes (families or individuals) to different hosts (e.g., Tabashnik *et al.*, 1981; Moran, 1981), and distributions of genetic variants across different hosts in the field (e.g., Menken, 1981; Mitter and Futuyma, 1979; Mitter *et al.*, 1979). Much of the evidence is summarized by Gould (Chapter 17, see especially Table IV).

The most general conclusion suggested by the findings to date is that within-population variability for host utilization may be very widespread. However, relatively few studies (on the order of a dozen) have addressed this question directly. Moreover, a considerable fraction of the information at hand concerns agricultural pests; for this literature especially it is difficult to be sure that the apparent prevalence of variation is free of unintentional bias against publication of "negative" results or against study of species for which there is not gross evidence of variation a priori.

a. Which Characteristics Vary?   From the standpoint of "multiple-niche polymorphism" models, it is useful to distinguish characters responsible for selection of the host from those determining fitness on particular hosts once these are chosen. For insects in which the feeding stage is mobile enough for choice to be exercised, this classification will generally correspond to a distinction between "behavioral" and "physiological" adaptations. In forms in which one stage or generation determines the host of its relatively immobile progeny, on the other hand, "fitness" may have both willingness-to-feed and physiological components, which are frequently very difficult to separate. Thus, if a young caterpillar or an aphid dies on a particular plant, it is usually hard to tell if it ate the plant and was poisoned or refused to eat it at all. Although this distinction is clearly important to the study of how insect host utilization evolves, in the present theoretical context it will be sufficient to regard host-related fitness as a single, albeit possibly complex, trait.

The conditions for stable "fitness" polymorphism may be severe in the absence of a mechanism guaranteeing fidelity of particular genotypes to particular hosts; in contrast, a purely "host-choice" polymorphism could arise in the absence of "fitness" variability, so long as there is genotype-independent, separate population regulation on different hosts. One might then predict that variability in host choice would be more common and more likely to occur alone than variability in host-related fitness.

In fact, no such pattern seems evident, although it must be stressed that the data are scanty. Variation has been discovered in both kinds of characters. In few studies has it been possible, however, to determine the relative amount of variability in each; in many cases, only one type of trait has been studied. Thus Tabashnik *et al.* (1981) found suggestive evidence of genetic differences in oviposition preference between two legume species in a population of the butterfly *Colias eurytheme;* corresponding variation in larval fitness within the same population was not sought. In contrast, Moran (1981) caged apterous *Uroleucon caligulatum* aphids of several clones on different clones of their goldenrod hosts and found a significant host-clone × herbivore-clone interaction with respect to first-instar size attained; the possibility of variation in host choice among alate aphids was not tested. In one of the few studies to consider both types of trait, Wasserman and Futuyma (1981) observed no response to selection for larval survival on two different hosts in the bean weevil *Callosobruchus maculatus,* but they were able to alter a complex adult trait that included oviposition preference. In contrast, in the Hessian fly, genetic variation in larval survival on different strains of wheat exists in the absence of comparable discrimination by ovipositing females (see review by Gould, Chapter 17). In summary, a reliable estimate of the frequency of intrapopulational variation in different kinds of characters will require further investigation.

b. What is the Genetic Basis of the Variation? Very few detailed studies of the inheritance of host-related variabiilty have been carried out, and most have examined only one generation. The only generalization that can be made thus far is that both mono- and polygenic variation have been discovered, in both host-choice and "fitness" traits. Thus, in the several selection experiments cited previously, the variation was found to be quantitative. In contrast, in one of the best studied cases, that of the Hessian fly, "virulence" to each different strain of wheat is effected by a single recessive allele at a different locus (Hatchett and Gallun, 1970). A similar mode of inheritance may govern the different strains of the raspberry aphid, *Amphorophora rubi* (Briggs, 1965). Various authors, (e.g., Bush, 1975a) have suggested that variation in host utilization may more frequently be monogenic than in most characters, but the number of thorough studies on which such a conclusion might be based is very small.

c. How is the Variation Maintained? The observed variation in host-related traits could represent "multiple-niche" polymorphism maintained by selection, but other factors also affect genetic variation, for example, recurrent mutation, which could be responsible for the existence of rare alleles. Mutation pressure, moreover, could be sufficient to maintain observed levels of genetic variance in polygenic characters

(Lande, 1975). Only a very few cases have been reported of host-related variability that an ecological geneticist could unhesitatingly regard as "polymorphic." These involve discrete markers, such as the larval coloration polymorphism of *Papilio demodocus* (Clarke *et al.*, 1963) or the clonal variation in *Alsophila pometaria* (Mitter *et al.*, 1979). On the other hand, some discrete within-population variation, such as that in the Hessian fly, appears to involve alleles rare enough to be plausibly ascribed to mutation pressure. On the basis of frequency distributions alone, one could not at present rule out recurrent mutation as the predominant cause of intrapopulational heritability in host utilization.

The most direct evidence for the importance of host difference as a selective factor maintaining genetic variation would come from observation or manipulation showing that the continued presence of some variants depended on the presence of different host(s). There is some evidence of this kind concerning the clonal polymorphism in *Alsophila pometaria* (Mitter *et al.*, 1979; see following discussion). Similarly, the possible progressive loss of variance in differentiated "demes" of *Nuculaspis californica* on individual pine trees (Alstad and Edmunds, Chapter 12) suggests that some scale genotypes might go extinct if pines were homogeneous. In contrast, Gould (Chapter 17) has observed that the several populations in which host-related characteristics have been successfully subjected to artificial selection had each been kept for long periods on single hosts. If we wish to invoke a "multiple-niche" explanation for the variation detected in these cultures, we must postulate either an important effect of unanalyzed heterogeneity *within* hosts, or small host-specific selection coefficients leading to very slow decay of polymorphism, even in homogeneous environments.

Suggestive but not conclusive evidence for polymorphism due to host difference would be fulfillment of one or more of the conditions (e.g., appropriate host-dependent reversals of genotype fitness) associated with such polymorphism under some model. Some of the only information of this kind pertains to a striking color polymorphism in larvae of the African swallowtail *Papilio demodocus*, in which the two forms appear maximally cryptic and suffer relatively less predation on different hosts; morph frequencies are the same on both hosts before selection (Clarke *et al.*, 1963). Another rarely sought expectation from "multiple-niche" theory, differentiation of subpopulations on different hosts, appears to be met in the black pineleaf scale (although the evidence for genetic variation is indirect; Alstad and Edmunds, Chapter 12) and the leafmining fly *Liriomyza brassicae*, larvae of which develop faster on the hosts from which their mothers have been collected than do progeny of females taken from other hosts; female flies also have more surviving progeny in their hosts of origin, given a choice at oviposition (Tavormina, 1982; for related studies, see Mitter and Futuyma, 1979; Mitter *et al.*, 1979; Menken, 1981).

In general, ecological genetics has provided few rigorous demonstrations of balanced polymorphism and even fewer conclusive demonstrations of selective mechanisms that maintain them. It is quite possible that a nonequilibrium view of the dynamics of allele frequencies and populations (see, e.g., Caswell, 1978) is more realistic than the supposition that polymorphism must be stable. Factors such as host differences might thus merely slow the rate of loss of genetic variation rather than maintain balanced polymorphisms.

d. Populations with Reduced Recombination, in Particular, the Fall Cankerworm. There is less information about the factors governing patterns of host-related variation in outbreeding species of insects than in populations subject to close inbreeding or parthenogenesis. Examples include the pine scale *Nuculaspis californica* (Alstad and Edmunds, Chapter 12) and the sympatric "biotypes" reported in several species of aphids (summarized by Futuyma, 1983, and Gould, Chapter 17). Fully inbred lines and those perpetuated by some forms of parthenogenesis share the property that complexes of traits persist without recombination, as long as the breeding system remains unchanged.

One instance of host-associated variation in a parthenogenetic form which we have investigated in some detail is that of the fall cankerworm, *Alsophila pometaria*. This species of geometrid moth is the only member of its genus and subfamily in North America, where it is very broadly distributed. The winged males and wingless females emerge after leaf drop in the late autumn, and there is a small spring emergence as well on Long Island, New York. Females climb the trunks of trees, apparently indiscriminately, mate, and lay a clutch of eggs that hatches at about the time of bud break in the spring. The hatchling larvae are capable of extensive dispersal by wind. They feed on the foliage of many families of deciduous trees and complete larval development within about 6 weeks (early June on Long Island), when they drop to the ground, burrow, and remain underground until autumn. The synchrony between hatching and bud break is critical in their success, for larvae whose development for any reason lags behind the maturation of the foliage enter pupation at small size or are incapable of pupating at all. In early June, on Long Island, we have found considerable numbers of stunted larvae that almost certainly did not survive. In many areas, on Long Island and elsewhere, populations are occasionally or chronically extremely dense.

In 1977, we reported (Mitter and Futuyma, 1977), on the basis of allozyme analysis, that although a small proportion (less than 10%, and usually less than 1%) of females reproduce sexually, the preponderance of reproduction in the population is parthenogenetic; the maternal, often highly heterozygous, genotype is transmitted intact to the progeny, which in these cases are all female. Mating, however, is required; unmated females lay few or no eggs, and the few eggs deposited do not hatch. Lawrence Harshman (unpublished observations) has found that a male genetic contribution is occasionally made to a few of a female's offspring, even if the majority of the brood has the maternal genotype. Thus sexually produced offspring can arise in low frequency from otherwise asexual genotypes. Harshman has also obtained evidence that asexual animals can arise from sexual parents, providing a likely mechanism for the generation of clonal diversity.

Most of the populations we have examined, from many localities in the eastern United States, are comprised largely (often more than 60%) of a few genotypes (identified by their elecrophoretic profile at three or four allozyme loci), the frequencies of which are far greater than if there were free recombination. Breeding tests have shown that many of the rarer genotypes are also parthenogenetically inherited. In several sites on Long Island, pronounced differences in the frequencies of common genotypes occur over narrow ecotones between woodlots dominated by red maple *(Acer rubrum)* and oaks *(Quercus* spp.) (Mitter *et al.*, 1979). Within mixed woodlots, however, we have not found associations between genotypes and tree species, a fact we attribute to dispersal (Futuyma *et al.*, 1981). Isolated trees, however, appear to build up differences in genotype frequencies within a single generation.

Most of our investigation of biological differences among the genotypes has focused on three of them: A, which is most prevalent in maple-dominated stands; B, which is the most abundant genotype in many stands of oak; and C, which we have found in greatest abundance in a mixed stand. These genotypes appear to differ in many respects, including average fecundity in nature, pupal weight attained when reared on the same host, and susceptibility to the irreversible melanization that occurs in the later larval instars when larvae are crowded (Futuyma *et al.*, 1981). When they were reared in mesh bags on natural hosts, their survival and pupal weight did not differ on oak, but the maple-associated genotype A showed far higher survival on red maple than did the others. Hatchling larvae of genotypes other than A disperse from red-maple foliage with dispatch, but not from oak foliage, whereas A larvae tend to remain on either oak or maple. Throughout larval life, larvae of genotype A appear to consume maple foliage more readily than does genotype B, although the genotypes' responses to oak foliage seem not to differ (D. Futuyma, R. Cort, I. van Noordwijk, unpublished observations). There is a corresponding difference in larval survival on maple foliage in the laboratory. We have not yet ascertained whether the differences in survival on maple observed in the laboratory and the field are attributable to differential ability to detoxify maple compounds, to differences in assimilation of nutrients, or entirely to differences in willingness to feed.

The most immediately apparent differences among the genotypes are phenological. Females of genotype A emerge in the autumn several weeks, on average, before B females, and there is a corresponding difference of almost a week in the average date of egg hatch. The hatching date appears to be influenced both by the date of oviposition and by other factors intrinsic to larval development or response to environmental cues (Mitter et al., 1979; Schneider, 1980). Because of the important effect of the schedule of foliage maturation on larval development, we have postulated that differences in hatching date are adaptations to the phenological difference between hosts. Red maple, with which the early hatching genotype A is associated, usually breaks bud before the oaks, on which genotype B is most abundant. This factor is the most likely cause we have found for A's rarity in oak-dominated stands, because this genotype suffers no evident disadvantage compared to B when reared on oak.

One of our chief reasons for studying the fall cankerworm is the belief that inbreeding or parthenogenetic forms are in some ways ideal for investigating ecological genetic problems. The discontinous nature of clonal inheritance can, through the use of markers such as allozymes, allow relatively direct estimation of the frequencies of the replicating units underlying variation, even in characters (e.g., phenology) ordinarily considered quantitative. Thus it is unnecessary to attempt the impossible task of estimating allele frequencies at each of the loci governing a quantitative trait in order to determine whether the observed variation represents underlying ecological genetic "polymorphism." Large numbers of individuals of identical genotype can be obtained for experiments on genotype × host interactions. Moreover, the fact that clones tend to represent genetic "packages" differing simultaneously at many loci increases the likelihood that biological differences between them will be strong enough to detect. Finally, reduced recombination should, for reasons discussed previously, be especially conducive to the maintenance of genetic variation by between-host differences. Parthenogenetic and inbreeding forms should thus be a kind of test case for the potential importance of this phenomenon.

Many of these putative advantages have proven to be real in the case of *Alsophila pometaria*. Thus we have determined that there is intrapopulational variation in host-utilization characters, that the clone frequencies are too high and too variable from place to place to be plausibly explained by recurrent mutation or *de novo* generation from the sexual population, and that neutral "drift" of clone frequencies can be ruled out by the observation of repeatable association of particular genotypes with particular types of forest. The evidence that host differences *maintain* clonal polymorphism, however, is not clear-cut.

Our earliest observations suggested that some genotypes were consistently reduced to frequencies plausibly explained by immigration alone in extensive stands of certain types of forest (Mitter *et al.*, 1979). Thus, for example, the maple-associated genotype A was all but absent from mature oak forests at two widely separated sites, suggesting that a universe composed only of such forest would not contain A. Maple stands do not appear to be the only habitat "protecting" type A from extinction, however. For example, this clone was a consistent, albeit not dominant, component of the fauna sampled in very extensive tracts of oak–pine scrub, from which red maple is entirely absent. If the continued existence of genotype A is dependent on some subset of the environments occupied by the fall cankerworm in our study sites, then that "niche" is defined by properties that do not coincide exactly with differences among host taxa.

Although there is some evidence that differences at the level of the composition of different stands of trees may contribute to the preservation of clonal diversity in a local region (e.g., the vicinity of Stony Brook, Long Island), we do not know what governs clonal diversity *within* habitats. The lack of host-specific differentiation in clone frequencies and the apparent high level of tree-to-tree dispersal make it implausible to suppose that any genotype is sufficiently restricted to any host to be "protected" by its presence. On average, all genotypes appear to face the same, fine-grained environment.

Assuming that "host-protected" polymorphism is a real, if not dominant, effect in this species, it is of interest to know if parthenogenesis contributes to its existence. In contrast to the differentiation in parthenogenetic *Alsophila*, we have found no evidence of linkage disequilibrium or of gene-frequency differences between adjacent populations in our allozyme survey of the males, which represent the sexual part of the population (Mitter *et al.*, 1979). Adjacent sexual populations may not be adapted to different hosts, or we may not be able to recognize such differentiation because recombination dissociates differentially adapted alleles from the allozyme loci we use as markers, but which presumably do not in themselves confer adaptations to different hosts. But the very same process that makes us incapable of recognizing differentially adapted sexual genotypes by recourse to allozyme markers may also frustrate the packaging of sets of alleles that confer adaptation to one host versus another. The parthenogenetic genotypes differ in a number of traits, of which several—behavioral and phenological, at least—seem to confer adaptation to different hosts, and of which each may be more effectively held in a polymorphic state when linked together than when disassociated. Thus, although we have no direct evidence on this point, it is possible that parthenogenesis holds "coadapted" blocks of genes in a polymorphic state. Finally, the absence of interhost gene flow resulting from dispersal by adult males should enhance the likelihood of polymorphism in the parthenogenetic population, even when host-related traits are considered individually.

Work in progress on the fall cankerworm may provide an especially useful test of the general hypothesis that parthenogenesis promotes host-related polymorphism. Thus, if the several characters adapting clones to their specific hosts are also highly variable in the sexual population and show a similar pattern of host-associated variation, the "complex-polymorphism" theory will be suspect, especially if it is established that there are no genetic correlations among these traits.

e. Electrophoretic Studies. Thus far we have considered variation in characters obviously related to host utilization. We and others, however, have also searched for associations with host differences in characters of a less obviously relevant sort, namely, allozyme markers. In addition to summarizing some of the results of this work, we shall offer some cautionary remarks on what we perceive as the limitations on its usefulness in the current context.

When we began this work, there was theoretical reason (Franklin and Lewontin, 1970; Maynard Smith and Haigh, 1974) to suppose that linkage disequilibrium might be more prevalent in natural populations than it now seems empirically to be, so we were perhaps naive in assuming that allozyme loci might mark blocks of genetic material that confer adaptation to one or another host. Contrasting four polyphagous with six mono- or oligophagous species of geometrid moths (Mitter and Futuyma, 1979), we found no evidence of greater genetic variation in the polyphagous forms; if anything, the more specialized feeders were more heterozygous. Without conviction, we suggested that specialized species might be less well buffered against slight variations in host quality than polyphagous species and thus be more polymorphic. However, examination of the difference in sensitivity to host-plant variation between a specialized lasiocampid (*Malacosoma americanum*, the eastern tent caterpillar) and its polyphagous congener (*M. disstria*, the forest tent caterpillar) revealed no difference (Futuyma and Saks, 1981). There is at present no strong reason to suppose that selection and, in particular, "multiple-niche" polymorphism, are responsible for the apparent difference we found in heterozygosity between specialized and generalized species.

In contrast to our findings, Lacy (1982) has reported a positive correlation between overall allozyme heterozygosity and the diversity of fungi on which a number of mycophagous *Drosophila* species feed. Heterozygosity is also correlated with abundance; the correlation with diet breadth appears to hold over and above the effect of abundance, although it is possible that effective population size, not perfectly reflected in observed abundance, might still be the dominant factor.

In view of the results of our cross-species comparison, it is perhaps not surprising that we found almost no evidence for host-specific differentiation in allozyme frequencies in several oligophagous and polyphagous geometrids, including the sexual form of the fall cankerworm. Similar results were reported for the polyphagous, mushroom-feeding *Drosophila falleni* (Jaenike and Selander, 1979) and the "red-headed" sibling species of the fall-webworm complex (Jaenike and Selander, 1980). On the other hand, Menken (1981) found consistent evidence, across loci, years, and localities, for differentiation between sympatric subpopulations on different hosts in the ermine moth *Yponomeuta padellus*.

Gene or genotype frequency differentiation between subpopulations on different hosts could have any of several causes. It could persist because of host-specific selection, at the marker locus or other linked characters, or because restricted migration between hosts perpetuates some historical effect such as a founder event, or because of some combination of these. The initial presumption of selection that might apply to host-associated differentiation in characters such as host-specific larval fitness is probably not warranted for allozyme differences in outbreeding forms. Conversely, allozymes are probably a relatively insensitive gauge of variation in host utilization, and it would not be proper to conclude from a failure to find host-related substructuring of electromorph frequencies that the population in question contained no variation for host-utilization characteristics. As has often been pointed out, for most of the enzymes commonly studied, which are parts of standard metabolic pathways, there is no strong a priori reason to expect a functional relationship to host differences. The likelihood of a correlation between genes effecting adaptation to host plants and a few randomly-scattered marker loci seems small given the probable rarity of linkage disequilibrium, for all but closely-linked loci, in outbreeding organisms (see, e.g., Clegg *et al.*, 1980). Sensitivity of the usual electrophoretic study, employing only a single set of conditions for each enzyme, is further hampered by the fact that "electromorphs" detected in this way may often be heterogeneous collections of alleles, responding in different ways, if at all, to ecological factors. Finally, allozyme characters will be of no use in detecting variability in host-utilization ability that is not partitioned among subpopulations on different hosts.

General surveys of genetic variation using allozymes have, in fact, revealed few convincing cases of correlation between genetic variation and environmental heterogeneity (Mitter and Futuyma, 1979; Futuyma, 1979). The heyday of optimism about the power of electrophoretic surveys to solve all the questions of population and ecological genetics has passed, and we are once again returned to the conclusion that genetic adaptation to particular features of the environment must be sought by examining the specific characteristics that are adaptively related to those particular features. Thus evidence of microgeographic differentiation in response to ethanol concentration can be found by examination of allozymes in natural populations of *Drosophila*, but it is found at the alcohol dehydrogenase locus (McKenzie and Parsons, 1974), not in enzymes chosen at random for their convenience of study (see also Cavener and Clegg, 1978). The electrophoretic approach has great value, however, in detecting extreme cases of discontinuous breeding structure, such as sibling species or parthenogenetic races, and in many cases it reveals the demic structure of populations that arises because of restricted dispersal. Moreover, at least a few cases have been described in which randomly chosen allozyme markers have shown response to ecological factors (see, e.g., Taylor and Powell, 1977; Eanes, 1978) in outbreeding species. Combined with the fact that electrophoresis generally provides unambiguously genetic characters with relatively little effort, these considerations suggest that allozyme studies will remain a useful complement to the direct study of host-associated adaptations, revealing likely candidates for host-related polymorphism. The question of whether host-related variation may occupy any point on a continuum from polymorphism under panmixia to full reproductive isolation or encompass only a more restricted range of population structures is an open one. Thus a case like that of *Yponomeuta padellus*, cited previously, should generously reward detailed biological investigation; perhaps it will prove to be one of the few known cases of host-associated subdivision within an interbreeding population. Finally, allozymes should be much more sensitive ecological markers and hence should find considerable use in demonstrating a genetic basis to host-associated variation in forms (such as the aphid and scale-insect species discussed previously) showing restricted recombination.

C. Evolutionary Change

1. Variation among Populations and Species

A chief reason for studying the nature of within-population variability is to account for patterns of evolutionary change. Such an attempt presupposes that the patterns to be explained have been well documented, but in the case of host utilization this is only beginning to be true.

There has been increasing interest in the question of "microevolutionary" change in host utilization, that is, variation among populations of the same species. Singer (1971), for example, investigated local variation within California in host selection by females of the butterfly *Euphydryas editha*. Marked differences were observed between some sets of populations in laboratory tests of oviposition behavior, the results of which may be taken as indicative of genetic differences. However, some populations that show very similar preferences under experimental conditions are found almost wholly on different plant species in the field. Although some of these differences appear attributable to other "intrinsic" factors (e.g., habitat preference) not expressed in the experiments, others seem to be simply a matter of local variation in relative host phenologies. That is, between-population variation in some host-utilization characters may have a large environmental component. Given the paucity of studies designed to separate environmental and genetic effects, it may be too early to interpret the frequent occurrence of geographic variation in host association that has been cataloged by Fox and Morrow (1981).

A few studies, however, have documented presumably genetic among-population variation in either host choice, host-specific "fitness," or both. For example, Hsaio (1978) observed differential adaptation by the Colorado potato beetle (*Leptinotarsa decemlineata*) to the locally abundant hosts used most prominently by each of several geographically separated populations. There does not appear to be corresponding variation in the behavior of ovipositing females, all of which appear to prefer the original wild host, *Solanum rostratum*. Scriber (Chapter 11) reports differential host-specific larval survival rates for geographically separated populations of the silkmoth *Callosamia promethea*; adult preferences were not tested. Rauscher (1982) found differential larval adaptation to the different hosts used by two of the *Euphydryas editha* populations previously studied by Singer (1971). Numerous additional examples can be found in the agricultural literature, involving "biotypes" able to attack previously resistant strains of crops (see review in Gould, Chapter 17).

It is not especially surprising to observe geographic variation in host-utilization characters; geographic variation has been found in most features in which it has been sought. Such variation, however, invites several questions that parallel to a degree those raised about intrapopulational variability.

First is the question of which kinds of characters, if any, show greater propensity for evolutionary change. In the case of the Colorado potato beetle, for example, larval adaptation to the use of different hosts follows upon a geographic pattern of host selection imposed directly by host abundance, there being no evolution of adult female preference. (One might expect differential female choice to evolve eventually in these populations, e.g., to increase host-finding efficiency.) In contrast, some of the differences in host association between populations of *Euphydryas editha* result from evolution of adult female behavior to favor one host over another, even though both may be available; in some such cases it is possible to relate these changes to environmental factors (e.g., predation intensity) that may cause differential larval fitness on the several hosts in question (Singer, 1971).

At present we cannot say which, if any, of the possible "modes" of origin of new feeding habits is the most common, or why. However, population genetic theory predicts that, other things being equal, the rate of evolution in a character should be proportional to the availability of genetic variation in that character. Thus we might expect local populations of the Colorado potato beetle to harbor less heritable variation for oviposition preference than for host-specific larval fitness. A related, though logically distinct prediction (Farris, 1969), is that intrapopulation variability for a character such as oviposition preference should be greater in taxa (e.g., *Euphydryas editha*) undergoing rapid evolution in that character than in taxa (such as *Leptinotarsa decemlineata*) in which the character is more conservative. Repeated failure of such predictions could imply that the evolution of feeding habits, at least within the range observed, is limited by factors other than the availability of genetic variation. The issue is clouded, however, by the fact that rapid evolution itself may deplete variability; proper investigation of this general question will necessitate distinction between populations exhibiting ancestral versus derived feeding habits (see following discussion).

Not only the level of host-related variability but also its mode of inheritance could have an important bearing on the propensity for evolutionary change. Suppose, for example, that an evolutionary shift from one to the other of two co-occurring hosts required simultaneous change in both preference and fitness characters. Then host utilization as a character complex could be said to exhibit multiple *adaptive peaks* (Wright, 1932) separated by *adaptive valleys* of unfit gene combinations. In this case, natural selection on single-gene variation alone will not effect change in feeding habits, and a host shift should be facilitated by the same genetic factors, that is, correlated and monogenic inheritance of preference and fitness traits, that promote host-associated polymorphism. Alternatively, the adaptive valley could be crossed by a *transilience* event (Templeton, 1981), such as assembly of favorable gene combinations by genetic drift in small founder populations. The need for such an event could add a considerable element of ecological indeterminism to the evolution of host utilization, which thus might not be closely associated with any inferred selection pressure favoring one habit over another. In this and any other case of genetic constraint on the evolution of feeding habits, species will not have "optimal" diets.

Despite its importance both to these issues and to theories of speciation, there is little information on the genetic basis of feeding-habit differences between populations or closely related species, although to be sure, the necessary experiments are often technically difficult. Anecdotal reports of crosses between forms differing in host are not uncommon, especially in the older literature (e.g., Brown, 1956; references in Scriber, Chapter 11). Unfortunately, these generally provide little information useful from a genetic point of view, beyond an occasional report that one habit showed dominance over another. There are almost no controlled experiments carried through at least two generations, with sample sizes adequate for statistical evaluation.

Knerer and Atwood (1972, 1973) reported dominance in both larval and adult preferences, in hybrids between "food races" of the sawfly *Neodiprion abietis*, and interpreted this (Knerer and Atwood, 1973) as evidence of monogenic inheritance of these traits. Although such results indicate that the genetic differences are not additive in effect, they do not distinguish single-locus from polygenic inheritance. Van Drongelen and van Loon (1980) found dominance or semidominance in larval hybrids of the small ermine moths *Yponomeuta cagnagellus* and *Y. malinellus*, for gustatory sensitivity to several compounds found in hosts of one or the other parent species. Huettel and Bush (1972) ascribed the complex results of crosses between two species of the tephritid fly *Procecidochares*, which are specific to different hosts, as reflecting oligogenic inheritance of oviposition preference, but other interpretations of the data are possible (see Futuyma and Mayer, 1980). In sum, although the limited data at hand are compatible with a hypothesis of predominantly oligogenic inheritance of at least the behavioral characters involved in host shifts, this notion cannot be considered well corroborated at present, and more experimentation is greatly desirable.

2. Predicting Evolutionary Sequences of Feeding Habits

Thus far, we have implicitly been treating between-population and between-species variation as if they were just additional levels in the great analysis of variance that is population genetics. Such a view, however, is not really appropriate for entities that are likely to be related by an evolutionary branching process. Thus a complete evolutionary genetic theory of host utilization will need to explain not only the patterns in such generalized population-genetic quantities as the rate of evolution, but also the ways in which genetic factors influence particular, historical sequences of feeding habits. A usual prerequisite for investigations of the latter kind will be a phylogenetic tree; at present such estimates are available for very few phytophagous groups for which there is also extensive life-history information (see Futuyma, 1983; Mitter and Brooks, 1983).

Once evolutionary sequences of host utilization have been established, generally on systematic grounds, a variety of questions about genetic constraints on them can be posed. For example, suppose that availability of genetic variation allowing shift to a particular host is an important limitation on the probability of that event. Then we might predict that populations most closely related to those in which such a shift has occurred, but which are restricted to the ancestral host, should show more variation for the ability to use the novel host than for acceptance of other hosts that on the basis of their ecological proximity might have seemed equally likely a priori candidates for colonization; such populations might also have more such variability than more distantly related ones belonging to lineages in which no host shift occurred.

There are also theoretical reasons to think that particular kinds of gene substitution affecting host utilization might be more frequent than others. For example, mutations that are advantageous when they first appear will spread faster if they are dominant rather than recessive, which implies that more recently evolved feeding habits might generally be dominant over older ones within any given lineage. A probable example of this effect, involving wing patterns of *Heliconius* butterflies, has been discussed by Turner (1975). On the other hand, if most evolution is a result of a changed environment acting on an existing pool of rare variants, we might expect derived habits to be generally recessive, because deleterious mutants (such as those causing selection of an unavailable host) can be perpetuated in heterozygous form.

The cases at hand in which genetic and phylogenetic information on feeding habits can be combined are too few to allow strong generalization, although neither supports the hypothesis of substitution by dominant genes. Thus the phylogenetic arrangement of *Neodiprion* depicted by Knerer and Atwood (1973; based largely on Ross, 1955) implies that this lineage shifted from pine to true firs, and thence to spruce. Female preference and larval survival in a balsam-fir form were dominant to the corresponding traits in a spruce-feeding population (Knerer and Atwood, 1973). The systematic evidence suggests that the host of *Ypono-*

meuta cagnagellus, Euonymus, was also the host of its common ancestor with the apple-feeding *Y. malinellus.* Larvae of *Y. malinellus* show no electrophysiological response to phloridzin, an apple compound that deters feeding by *Y. cagnagellus;* hybrid larvae show an intermediate response (van Drongelen and van Loon, 1980).

Further results of such conjunction between phylogenetic and genetic studies should say a great deal about how host utilization has evolved and, in particular, about the relative importance of genetic versus ecological factors.

3. The Role of Host Shifts in the Origin of Reproduction Isolation

It has frequently been postulated that the response to differences between hosts could be a primary factor in phytophagous-insect speciation. This is just a special case of the problem of the importance of ecological factors in the origin of reproductive isolation (see, e.g., Mayr, 1963). In broadest terms, the issue is whether the spatial or temporal restriction of interbreeding following directly from divergence in ecology is commonly an initiating factor in speciation. Habitat isolation seems to have been a primary isolating mechanism in a variety of groups (Anderson, 1948; Mayr, 1963). However, the evidence that host differences play an analogous role in the diversification of phytophagous insects is not extensive.

Controversy over the role of ecological factors has resulted from the proposal by many authors that the reproductive isolation and divergent selection imposed by ecological differences could operate over very small distances, so that speciation could occur on a very local scale. In principle, host-associated genotypes can be transformed into host-specific species sympatrically (Mather, 1955; Thorpe, 1930; Bush, 1975a). If mating does not occur on the host plant, strong selection, independent population regulation on the two hosts, and close linkage between the loci governing mating preference and the substantive adaptation to the hosts are necessary for speciation (Felsenstein, 1981). If mating does occur on the host plant, genetic differentiation between the incipient species requires either that there be strong selection against genes that find their way to the wrong host, therefore favoring reinforcement of reproductive isolation, or else that the attraction of different genotypes to different hosts impose a strong barrier to gene flow. This is most likely to occur if host attraction is governed by a single locus at which there is full dominance, that is, *AA* and *Aa* are attracted to one host, *aa* to the other, and full penetrance, that is, genotypes are not ambivalent or subject to frequent mistakes in host selection (see, e.g., Maynard Smith, 1966; Dickinson and Antonovics, 1973). The stringency of the conditions has led some authors to doubt that sympatric speciation by host-plant isolation is at all common (Mayr, 1947; Futuyma and Mayer, 1980; for a contrary view see Bush and Diehl, 1982).

Like so many questions involving speciation, the issue of host shifts as causative agents in the origin of reproductive isolation may be difficult to resolve. If such an effect is widespread, we should frequently find evidence that genetic adaptation or physiological response to host differences has reduced the potential for intermating between closely related herbivores on different hosts. For example, Smith (1953, 1954) reported that adult moths, including mating pairs, of the spruce budworm *(Choristoneura fumiferana)* and a sympatric sibling, the jackpine budworm *(C. pinus)*, are nearly always found on their respective hosts. Smith also suggested that the difference between species in time of emergence from larval diapause, with its consequent difference in reproductive flight period, might reflect adaptation to differing host phenology. Wood and Guttman (1982) found that adults of the six sympatric treehopper sibling species of the *Enchenopa binotata* complex tended strongly to remain on the individual hosts on which they were marked and released; here too, there are marked interspecies differences in immature emergence and breeding period that are correlated with differences in host phenology. Evidence of such host-related differences between species of true fruit flies has been reviewed by Bush (1975a).

In themselves, however, such differences are not conclusive evidence for a primary role of the host shift. Although few tabulations have been attempted, it seems evident that a large fraction of even host-specific, phytophagous insect species have originated in the absence of a host shift. Ross (1962), for example, calculated that in the evolution of three species flocks of the deciduous forest leafhopper *Erythroneura* (totaling about 500 species) there had been about 150 host transfers (probably an underestimate), implying that about 70% of the speciation events involved no host shift. In such cases, sympatric relatives must be isolated by "classical" mechanisms such as differences in courtship, behavior, diel periodicity, etc. To say that host-related differences in reproductive biology, when they occur, can significantly facilitate speciation, is to assert that they can partially or entirely take the place of isolating mechanisms known to operate in the absence of host shifts. The existence of complexes of species differing in host, but showing relatively weak development of non-host-related (e.g., ethological) isolating mechanisms, is thus potentially the most direct evidence for the role of host shifts (see Bush, 1975b, p. 352). In cases in which both ethological and host-associated differences appear sufficient, it is difficult to determine their relative historical importance.

Evidence on this point is scarce, in part no doubt because of the difficulty of carrying out definitive experiments. Thus Brown (1956) suggested that host differences might have been important in the origin of sibling species of *Chrysomela* beetles, because many species pairs will hybridize readily in the laboratory. A substantial (though imperfect) degree of artificial crossability has likewise been observed for at least one pair of sibling species of Tephritidae differing in host (McAlister and Anderson, 1935), although others exhibit nearly or entirely complete isolation under laboratory conditions (see, e.g., Hall, 1943). However, beetles confined in jars lose much, if not all, of their natural mating discrimination (Brown, 1956), and there is good evidence that laboratory studies in general underestimate the effectiveness in nature of premating isolation of all kinds (see, e.g., discussion in Dobzhansky, 1970). Considerable caution must therefore be exercised in interpreting hybridization under highly artificial conditions as evidence for the coexistence of ethologically compatible species. Laboratory studies could be of considerable value, however, for determining whether, under standardized conditions, species pairs differing in host show less mating discrimination than comparable pairs with similar feeding habits. Such an outcome for *Rhagoletis* fruit flies might be predicted from the fact that species groups with homogeneous feeding habits seem to show more differentiation in external coloration than groups characterized by host shifts (Bush, 1969).

In a study carried out under at least somewhat natural conditions, Wood (1980) found almost no hybridization among six *Enchenopa* species confined to the same enclosure; host preference and host-related phenological variation were not the only factors affecting intermating potential, because there was diurnal mating period separation at least and, probably, female discrimination. However, the relative contributions of these factors were not determined, and it is difficult to say whether differences not attributable to host specificity would themselves be sufficient to preserve the integrity of these species. Preliminary results of experiments designed to minimize host-related differences suggest, however, that ethological barriers are relatively weak (T. K. Wood, personal communication).

In observations made in the field, Smith (1954) found that in a year when the temporal and host-specificity barriers between the *Choristoneura* siblings cited previously were less than fully effective, because of unusual weather, there was nevertheless no evidence of hybridization. Earlier, smaller experiments under seminatural conditions had indicated complete ethological isolation (Smith, 1953), and subsequent work has revealed pheromone differences between these species (Sanders, 1971).

Pheromone differences have also been shown to separate several species of *Yponomeuta* moths that differ in host association (Hendrikse, 1978). Such differences may be the most important mechanism of isolation for many species of Lepidoptera (Roelofs and Cardé, 1974).

Although persuasive arguments have been advanced for a direct contribution of host shifts to speciation (e.g., Bush, 1969, 1975a,b), further detailed studies, for example, of isolating mechanisms, appear necessary to establish the generality of such a conclusion. Such investigations might, moreover, contribute to resolution of the debate over sympatric speciation. The widely accepted model (Bush, 1975a) for this process postulates a host shift as providing a sufficient initial isolating mechanism. If cases cannot be found in which host-related differences are demonstrably primary and necessary interbreeding barriers between species, the model might be judged unrealistic. Finding that a host shift *was* instrumental in speciation, however, like finding that host shifts involved only simple genetic changes, would not by itself rule out geographic in favor of sympatric speciation. Which observations would compel one to accept such a conclusion we leave for others to discuss.

Although we have focused on the potential role of host differences in the origin of isolating mechanisms, host shifts could also facilitate speciation by allowing otherwise similar forms to avoid competitive exclusion. It must be said, however, that the evidence for the operation of such a factor is at present weak (Lawton and Strong, 1981).

IV. SUMMARY AND CONCLUDING REMARKS

The current state of the evolutionary genetics of host-plant utilization by insects might be summarized as follows.

1. There is a modest but growing body of evidence to indicate that herbivore populations routinely harbor genetic variation for host-utilization traits.

2. The reasons for this variation and the degree to which it represents "polymorphism" in the ecological genetic sense are largely unknown; in a few cases, for example, *Papilio demodocus*, *Nuculaspis*, or parthenogenetic *Alsophila pometaria*, there is some evidence for diversifying selection and perhaps "multiple-niche" (i.e., host) polymorphism.

3. The degree to which populations occupying multiple hosts may be structured into host-associated subdemes is largely unknown.

4. Variation has been found in both host-choice and host-related fitness characters, with no indication that one or the other is more prone to vary.

5. The limited evidence on inheritance of host-related variation does not contradict but does not firmly establish the hypothesis that such variation, both within and between populations, is frequently discrete.

6. Genetically based geographic differences in host-utilization traits may be common; the relative contribution of environmental and genetic components to geographic variation in such features remains unknown.

7. The degree to which the rate and direction of evolution in host utilization are limited by the availability of genetic variation is not known.

8. There is suggestive but not conclusive evidence that host shifts are a significant predisposing factor to insect speciation.

At this stage, then, genetic studies of phytophagous insects have progressed only to the point to which it is possible to cite isolated probable examples of the phenomena that evolutionary genetics teaches us to looks for. Thus carefully documented cases of (or failures to find) host-maintained polymorphism, for example, or simple inheritance of host-utilization differences, will continue to be important contributions. As we have repeatedly stressed, moreover, there is even less support for any broader generalizations about the forces governing the prevalence of such observations. Although we have concentrated on genetic factors narrowly defined, the degree, nature, and spatial scale of variation in host utilization also undoubtedly varies in as yet unknown ways with the species' vagility, breadth of diet, mode of feeding, longevity, and other properties of ecological importance. One might, for example, expect an oligophagous insect to be genetically adapted to its particular local host(s), whereas more highly polyphagous species are likely to be "preadapted" to allopatric hosts and show consequently less geographic differentiation. The biochemical adaptations that enable an insect to use a wide range of hosts may provide adequate adaptation to novel hosts to which the population is exposed (see Tabashnik, 1983). Although these and many other predictions made in this chapter remain untested, we discuss them in the belief that the supply of clearly stated, general hypotheses may be a limiting resource in this field of inquiry.

ACKNOWLEDGMENTS

This chapter benefited in a major way from the advice and encouragement of Fred Gould. We also thank Scott Diehl for a number of helpful comments on the manuscript. The excellent secretarial assistance of S. Donkis, H. Lindsey, and J. Russo is much appreciated. We dedicate this work to the memory of Richard P. Seifert, 1946–1981.

Scientific Article no. A-3392, Contribution no. 6465 of the Maryland Agricultural Research Station, Department of Entomology.

REFERENCES

Anderson, E. (1948). Hybridization of the habitat. *Evolution* **2**, 1–9.

Barbosa, P., Greenblatt, J., Withers, W., Cranshaw, W., and Harrington, E. A., (1979). Host-plant preferences and their induction in larvae of the gypsy moth, *Lymantria dispar*. *Entomol. Exp. Appl.* **26**, 180–188.

Briggs, J. B. (1965). The distribution, abundance, and genetic relationships of four strains of the rubus aphid [*Amphorophora rubi* (Kalt.)] in relation to raspberry breeding. *J. Hortic. Sci.* **40**, 109–117.

Brown, W. J. (1956). The new world species of *Chrysomela* L. (Coleoptera: Chrysomelidae). *Can. Entomol.* **88**, Suppl. 3, 1–54.

Bush, G. L. (1969). Mating behavior, host specificity, and the ecological significance of sibling species in frugivorous flies of the genus *Rhagoletis* (Diptera—Tephritidae). *Am. Nat.* **103**, 669–672.

Bush, G. L. (1975a). Sympatric speciation in phytophagous parasitic insects. *In* "Evolutionary Strategies of Parasitic Insects and Mites" (P. W. Price, ed.), pp. 187–206. Plenum, New York.

Bush, G. L. (1975b). Modes of animal speciation. *Annu. Rev. Ecol. Syst.* **6**, 339–364.

Bush, G. L., and Diehl, S. R. (1982). Host shifts, genetic models of sympatric speciation, and the origin of parasitic insect species. *In* Insect and Host Plant—5th International Symposium on Insect–Plant Relationships (J. H. Visser and A. K. Minks, eds.). PUDOC, Wageningen.

Caswell, H. (1978). Predator-mediated coexistence: a nonequilibrium model. *Am. Nat.* **112**, 127–154.

Cavener, D. (1979). Preference for ethanol in *Drosophila melanogaster* associated with the alcohol dehydrogenase polymorphism. *Behav. Genet.* **9**, 359–365.

Cavener, D. R., and Clegg, M. T. (1978). Dynamics of correlated genetic systems. IV. Multilocus effects of ethanol stress environments. *Genetics* **90**, 629–644.

Claridge, M. F., and den Hollander, J. (1980). The "biotypes" of the rice brown planthopper, *Nilaparvata lugens*. *Entomol. Exp. Appl.* **27**, 23–30.

Claridge, M. F., and Wilson, M. R. (1978). Oviposition behavior is an ecological factor in woodland canopy leafhoppers. *Entomol. Exp. Appl.* **24**, 101–109.

Clarke, C. A., Dickson, C. G. C., and Sheppard, P. M. (1963). Larval color pattern in *Papilio demodocus*. *Evolution* **17**, 130–137.

Clegg, M. T., Kidwell, J. F., and Horch, C. R. (1980). Dynamics of correlated genetic systems. V. Rates of decay of linkage disequilibria in experimental populations of *Drosophila melanogaster*. *Genetics* **94**, 217–234.

Craighead, F. C. (1921). Hopkin's host-selection principle as related to certain cerambycid beetles. *J. Agric. Res.* **22**, 189–220.

Dempster, E. R. (1955). Maintenance of genetic heterogeneity. *Cold Spring Harbor Symp. Quant. Biol.* **20**, 25–32.

Dickinson, H., and Antonovics, J. (1973). Theoretical consideration of sympatric divergence. *Amer. Nat.* **107**, 256–274.

Dobzhansky, T. (1970). "Genetics of the Evolutionary Process." Columbia Univ. Press, New York.

Eanes, W. F. (1978). Morphological variance and enzyme heterogeneity in the monarch butterfly. *Nature (London)* **276**, 263–264.

Eastop, V. F. (1973). Biotypes of aphids. *Entomol. Soc. N. Z. Bull.* **2**, 40–51.

Farris, J. S. (1969). On the relationship between variation and conservatism. *Evolution* **24**, 825–827.

Felsenstein, J. (1976). The theoretical population genetics of variable selection and migration. *Annu. Rev. Genet.* **10**, 253–280.

Felsenstein, J. (1981). Skepticism towards Santa Rosalia, or why are there so few kinds of animals? *Evolution* **35**, 124–138.

Fox, L. R., and Morrow, P. A. (1981). Specialization: species property or local phenomenon? *Science* **211**, 887–893.

Franklin, I., and Lewontin, R. C. (1970). Is the gene the unit of selection? *Genetics* **65**, 707–734.

Futuyma, D. J. (1979). "Evolutionary Biology." Sinauer Assoc., Sunderland, Massachusetts.

Futuyma, D. J. (1983). Evolutionary interactions among herbivorous insects and plants. *In* "Coevolution" (Futuyma, D. J. and M. Slatkin, eds.) Sinauer Assoc., Sunderland, Massachusetts (in press).

Futuyma, D. J., and Mayer, G. C. (1980). Non-allopatric speciation in animals. *Syst. Zool.* **29**, 254–271.

Futuyma, D. J., and Saks, M. E. (1981). The effect of variation in host plant on the growth of an oligophagous insect, *Malacosoma americanum*, and its polyphagous relative, *Malocosoma disstria*. *Entomol. Exp. Appl.* **30**, 163–168.

Futuyma, D. J., Leipertz, S. L., and Mitter, C. (1981). Selective factors affecting clonal variation in the fall cankerworm, *Alsophila pometaria* (Lepidoptera: Geometridae). *Heredity* **47**, 161–172.

Gelfand, L. J., and McDonald, J. F. (1980). Relationship between ADH activity and behavioral response to environmental alcohol in *Drosophila*. *Behav. Genet.* **10**, 237–249.

Gould, F. (1979). Rapid host range evolution in a population of the phytophagous mite *Tetranychus urticae* Koch. *Evolution* **33**, 791–802.

Guttman, S., Wood, T. K., and Karlin, A. A. (1981). Genetic differentiation along host plant lines in the sympatric *Enchenopa binotata* complex (Homoptera: Membracidae). *Evolution* **35**, 205–217.

Hall, J. A. (1943). Notes on the dogwood fruit fly, a race of *Rhagoletis pomonella* (Walsh). *Can. Entomol.* **75**, 202.

Hanson, F. E. (1976). Comparative studies of induction of food choice preferences in lepidopterous larvae. *In* "The Host-plant in Relation to Insect Behavior and Reproduction" (J. Jermy, ed.), pp. 71–77. Plenum, New York.

Hatchett, J. H., and Gallun, R. L. (1970). Genetics of the ability of the Hessian fly, *Mayetiola destructor*, to survive on wheats having different genes for resistance. *Ann. Entomol. Soc. Am.* **63**, 1400–1407.

Hendrikse, A. (1979). Activity patterns and sex pheromone specificity as isolating mechanisms in eight species of *Yponomeuta*. *Entomol. Exp. Appl.* **25**, 172–180.

Herrebout, W. M., Kuyten, P. J., and Wiebes, J. T. (1976). Small ermine moths and their host relationships. *Symp. Biol. Hung.* **16**, 91–94.

Hsiao, T. H. (1978). Host plant adaptations among geographic populations of the Colorado potato beetle. *Entomol. Exp. Appl.* **24**, 437–447.

Huettel, M. D., and Bush, G. L. (1972). The genetics of host selection and its bearing on sympatric speciation in *Procecidochares* (Diptera: Tephritidae). *Entomol. Exp. Appl.* **15**, 464–480.

Inouye, D. (1980). The effect of proboscis and corolla tube lengths on patterns and rates of flower visitation by bumblebees. *Oecologia* **45**, 197–201.

Jaenike, J. (1982). Environmental modification of oviposition behavior in *Drosophila*. *Amer. Nat.* **119**, 784–802.

Jaenike, J., and Selander, R. K. (1979). Ecological generalism in *Drosophila falleni*: genetic evidence. *Evolution* **33**, 741–748.

Jaenike, J., and Selander, R. K. (1980). On the question of host races in the fall webworm, *Hyphantria cunea*. *Entomol. Exp. Appl.* **27**, 31–37.

Knerer, G., and Atwood, C. E. (1972). Evolutionary trends in the subsocial sawflies belonging to the *Neodiprion abietis* complex (Hymenoptera: Tenthredinoidea). *Am. Zool.* **12**, 407–418.

Knerer, G., and Atwood, C. E. (1973). Diprionid sawflies: polymorphism and speciation. *Science* **179**, 1090–1099.

Lacy, R. C. (1982). Niche breadth and abundance as determinants of genetic variation in populations of mycophagous drosophilid flies (Diptera: Drosophilidae). *Evolution* **36**, 1265–1275.

Lande, R. (1975). The maintenance of genetic variability by mutation in a polygenic character with linked loci. *Genet. Res.* **26**, 221–235.

Lawton, J. H., and Strong, D. R., Jr. (1981). Community patterns and competition in folivorous insects. *Am. Nat.* **118**, 317–338.

Levene, H. (1953). Genetic equilibrium when more than one ecological niche is available. *Am. Nat.* **87**, 331–373.

Levins, R. (1968). "Evolution in Changing Environments." Princeton Univ. Press, Princeton, New Jersey.

Ludwig, W. (1950). Zur Theorie der Konkurrenz. Die Annidation (Einnischung) als fünfter Evolutionsfaktor. *Neue Ergeb. Probl. Zool., Klatt-Festschr., 1950* pp. 516–537.

McAlister, L. C., and Anderson, W. H., (1935). Insectary studies on the longevity and preoviposition period of the blueberry maggot and on cross breeding with the apple maggot. *J. Econ. Entomol.* **28**, 675–678.

McKenzie, J. A., and Parsons, P. A., (1974). Microdifferentiation in a natural population of *Drosophila melanogaster* to alcohol in the environment. *Genetics* **77**, 385–394.

Matessi, C., and Jayakar, S. D. (1975). Models of density-frequency-dependent selection for the exploitation of resources. I. Intraspecific competition. *In* "Population Genetics and Ecology" (S. Karlin and E. Nevo, eds.), pp. 707–722. Academic Press, New York.

Mather, K. (1955). Polymorphism as an outcome of disruptive selection. *Evolution* **9**, 52–61.

Maynard Smith, J. (1966). Sympatric speciation. *Am. Nat.* **100**, 637–650.

Maynard Smith, J., and Haigh, J. (1974). The hitchhiking effect of a favorable gene. *Genet. Res.* **23**, 23–35.

Maynard Smith, J., and Hoekstra, R. (1980). Polymorphism in a varied environment: how robust are the models? *Genet. Res.* **35**, 45–57.

Mayr, E. (1947). Ecological factors in speciation. *Evolution* **1**, 263–288.

Mayr, E. (1963). "Animal Species and Evolution." Harvard Univ. Press, Cambridge, Massachusetts.

Menken, S. B. (1981). Host races and sympatric speciation in small ermine moths, Yponomeutidae. *Entomol. Exp. Appl.* **30**, 280–292.

Mitter, C., and Brooks, D. R. (1983). Phylogenetic aspects of coevolution. *In* "Coevolution" (D. J. Futuyma and M. Slatkin, eds.). Sinauer, Sunderland, Massachusetts (in press).

Mitter, C., and Futuyma, D. J. (1977). Parthenogenesis in the fall cankerworm, *Alsophila pometaria* (Lepidoptera, Geometridae). *Entomol. Exp. Appl.* **21**, 192–198.

Mitter, C., and Futuyma, D. J. (1979). Population genetic consequences of feeding habits in some forest Lepidoptera. *Genetics* **92**, 1005–1021.

Mitter, C., Futuyma, D. J., Schneider, J. C., and Hare, D. J. (1979). Genetic variation and host plant relations in a parthenogenetic moth. *Evolution* **33**, 777–790.

Moran, N. (1981). Intraspecific variability in herbivore performance and host quality: a field study of *Uroleucon caligatum* (Homoptera: Aphididae) and its *Solidago* hosts (Asteraceae). *Ecol. Entomol.* **6**, 301–306.

Prokopy, R., Averill, A. L., Cooley, S. S., and Roitberg, C. A. (1982). Associative learning in egglaying site by apple maggot flies. *Science* **218,** 76–77.

Rauscher, M. D. (1982). Population differentiation in *Euphydryas editha* butterflies: larval adaptation to different hosts. *Evolution* **36,** 581–590.

Roelofs, W., and Cardé, R. (1974). Sex pheromones in the reproductive isolation of lepidopterous species. *In* "Pheromones" (M. C. Birch, ed.), pp. 96–144., Elsevier, Amsterdam.

Ross, H. (1955). The taxonomy and evolution of the sawfly genus *Neodiprion. For. Sci.* **1,** 196–209.

Ross, H. (1962). "A Synthesis of Evolutionary Theory." Prentice-Hall, Englewood Cliffs, New Jersey.

Roughgarden, J. (1972). Evolution of niche width. *Am. Nat.* **106,** 683–718.

Roughgarden, J. (1979). "Theory of Population Genetics and Evolutionary Ecology: An Introduction." Macmillan, New York.

Sanders, C. J. (1971). Daily activity patterns and sex pheromone specificity as sexual isolating mechanisms in two species of *Choristoneura.* (Lepidoptera: Tortricidae). *Can. Entomol.* **103,** 498–502.

Schneider, J. C. (1980). The role of parthenogenesis and female aptery in microgeographic ecological adaptation in the fall cankerworm, *Alsophila pometaria* Harris (Lep., Geom.). *Ecology* **61,** 1082–1090.

Singer, M. C. (1971). Evolution of food-plant preference in the butterfly *Euphydryas editha. Evolution* **25,** 383–389.

Slatkin, M. (1978). On the equilibration of fitnesses by natural selection. *Am. Nat.* **112,** 845–859.

Smith, S. G. (1953). Reproductive isolation and the integrity of two sympatric species of *Choristoneura* (Lepidoptera: Tortricidae). *Can. Entomol.* **85,** 141–151.

Smith, S. G. (1954). A partial breakdown of temporal and ecological isolation between *Choristoneura* species (Lepidoptera: Tortricidae). *Evolution* **8,** 206–224.

Strobeck, C. (1975). Selection in a fine-grained environment. *Am. Nat.* **109,** 419–425.

Tabashnik, B. E. (1983). Host range evolution: the shift from native legumes to alfalfa by the butterfly *Colias philodice eriphyle. Evolution* (in press).

Tabashnik, B. E., Wheelock, H., Rainbolt, J. D., and Watt, W. B. (1981). Individual variation in oviposition preference in the butterfly *Colias eurytheme. Oecologia* **50,** 225–230.

Tavormina, S. J. (1982). Sympatric genetic divergence in the leaf-mining insect *Liriomyza brassicae* (Diptera: Agromyzidae). *Evolution* **36,** 523–535.

Taylor, C. E., and Powell, J. R. (1977). Microgeographic differentiation of chromosomal and enzyme polymorphisms in *Drosophila persimilis. Genetics* **85,** 681–695.

Templeton, A. (1981). Mechanisms of speciation—a population genetic approach. *Annu. Rev. Ecol. Syst.* **12,** 281–308.

Thorpe, W. H. (1929). Biological races in *Hyponomeuta padella* L. *J. Linn. Soc., London, Zool.* **36,** 621–634.

Thorpe, W. H. (1930). Biological races in insects and allied groups. *Biol. Rev. Cambridge Philos. Soc.* **5,** 177–212.

Turner, J. R. G. (1975). Müllerian mimicry: classical "beanbag" evolution and the role of ecological islands in adaptive race formation. *In* "Population Genetics and Ecology" (S. Karlin, and E. Nevo, eds.), pp. 185–218. Academic Press, New York.

van Drongelen, W., and van Loon, J. J. A. (1980). Inheritance of gustatory sensitivity in F_1 progeny of crosses between *Yponomeuta cagnagellus* and *Y. malinellus., Entomol. Exp. Appl.* **28** 199–203.

Wallace, B. (1968). Polymorphism, population size, and genetic load. *In* "Population Biology and Evolution" (R. C. Lewontin, ed.), pp. 87–108. Syracuse Univ. Press, Syracuse, New York.

Wasserman, S. S., and Futuyma, D. J. (1981). Evolution of host plant utilization in laboratory populations of the southern cowpea weevil, *Callosobruchus maculatus* Fabricius (Coleoptera: Bruchidae). *Evolution* **35,** 605–617.

Wood, T. K. (1980). Divergence in the *Enchenopa binotata* Say complex (Homoptera: Membracidae) effected by host plant adaptation. *Evolution* **34,** 147–160.

Wood, T. K., and Guttman, S. I. (1982). Ecological and behavioral basis for reproductive isolation in the sympatric *Enchenopa binotata* complex (Homoptera: Membracidae). *Evolution* **36,** 233–242.

Wright, S. (1932). The roles of mutation, inbreeding, crossbreeding, and selection in evolution. *Proc. Int. Congr. Genet., 6th, 1932* Vol. I, pp. 356–366.

Charles Mitter

Department of Entomology
University of Maryland
College Park, Maryland

Douglas J. Futuyma

Department of Ecology and Evolution
State University of New York at Stony Brook
Stony Brook, New York

PART IV

Host Variability and the Structure of Plant–Herbivore Communities

No other area of ecology is changing faster than community ecology. For decades our concept of what processes are important in organizing insect communities centered around interspecific competitive interactions. Now, well-designed field experiments are contributing to a rapidly growing data base that only infrequently finds competition to be a driving force in community organization. Consequently, alternative hypotheses that focus on host-plant heterogeneity and natural enemies are being erected to elucidate organizing forces. The current challenge to community ecologists is reflected by the flavor of the following three chapters, which underscore the importance of considering the variable nature of the host plant when unraveling the processes that structure herbivore communities.

Krischik and Denno (Chapter 14) begin this part by considering the role of herbivores as selective agents that affect the growth, age to first reproduction, fecundity, and mortality of plants. Having documented the cost of herbivory to the plant in terms of reduced fitness, the authors build a case for plant defense (e.g., allelochemistry and morphology of leaves) in which the magnitude and nature of the defense are related to the value of the plant tissue lost. They also consider shifts in allocation pattern of growth, reproduction, and defense in plants that might be partially influenced by herbivores. Individual, population, latitudinal, and altitudinal patterns in plant defense are described and discussed relative to herbivore pressure. The authors also suggest that some of the spatial and temporal variation in leaf chemistry found in nature is explained by the selective effects of herbivores and conclude by emphasizing the reciprocal impact of variation in leaf quality on herbivore–plant interactions.

Jones (Chapter 15) examines phytochemical variation as a contributing factor to host-plant heterogeneity, one that influences successful insect colonization and utilization of plants and ultimately the organization of the herbivore community. Because bracken fern (*Pteridium aquilinum*) is one of few plants in which both the phytochemistry and structure and population dynamics of the associated insect community are known, it provides an excellent model system. Jones discusses variation in eight distinct classes of allelochemicals as well as variation in the nutritional components of bracken fern relative to the constraints placed on insect feeding and provides evidence suggesting that chemical variation affects both nonadapted and bracken-adapted insects. Jones argues that an array of phytochemical features of bracken impede the frequency of successful colonization by nonadapted insects; for adapted insects phytochemical variation contributes to the fine division of resources, prevents monopolization by herbivores, and contributes to the regulation of herbivore abundance. Using this example, Jones discusses how phytochemistry influences species composition and herbivore community structure.

In Chapter 16, Price considers the extent to which herbivore communities consist of coexisting, interdependent populations and, in this inquiry, erects several major hypotheses to account for community organization. Price suggests that various characteristics of herbivore communities combine to make competition a weak influence in their organization and presents arguments suggesting that many ecological niches remain vacant in evolutionary time, reducing interactions between species. Similarly, in ecological time and space the patchy occupation of habitats with many uncolonized patches minimizes encounters between potential competitors. Price contends that low utilization of resources may reflect a combination of a herbivore's specialization to a particular resource state and the rapid changes in state, resulting in a narrow window when resources are suitable for attack. Consequently, herbivore communities may often be undersaturated and in a state of nonequilibrium. Price contends that under these conditions the individualistic colonization of resources by species is a more important structuring process in communities than competition.

CHAPTER **14**

Individual, Population, and Geographic Patterns in Plant Defense

VERA ABER KRISCHIK
ROBERT F. DENNO

I. INTRODUCTION

Of major concern to agriculture, silviculture, ecology, and evolutionary biology is the effect of variation in leaf allelochemistry and morphology on the distribution and abundance of herbivores. Plants are not homogeneous, but rather heterogeneous resources. Individual leaves differ on a shoot (Ikeda *et al.*, 1977a,b; Cranshaw and Langenheim, 1981; Raupp, 1982), leaves change over the growing season (Feeny, 1976; Rhoades and Cates, 1976; Lawton, 1976; Mooney *et al.*, 1980; Kraft and

VARIABLE PLANTS AND HERBIVORES
IN NATURAL AND MANAGED SYSTEMS

Denno, 1982), and individual plants vary within and between populations (Dolinger *et al.*, 1973; Cates, 1975; Gansel and Squillace, 1976; Smith, 1977; Edmunds and Alstad, 1978; Langenheim *et al.*, 1978). The objective of this chapter is to consider what has influenced the origin of such heterogeneity.

A number of authors have suggested that the evolution of differences in leaf morphology and plant chemistry has been at least partly influenced by herbivory (Frankel, 1959, 1969; Ehrlich and Raven, 1964; Janzen, 1966; Feeny, 1975; Gilbert, 1975; Rhoades and Cates, 1976; Williams and Gilbert, 1981). If insects, by feeding on leaves, reduce plant growth and reproduction, and if plant chemical and morphological characteristics confer resistance, then present patterns of leaf chemistry and morphology may be, in part, a result of past selection. However, constraints associated with growth and reproduction should prevent plants from exclusively maximizing commitments to defense or protecting all leaves equally. A reasonable extension of this thinking is that leaves having the greatest value to the plant are most strongly defended. Leaf value can be measured by determining the effect of the loss of that tissue on plant fitness. Consequently, spatial and temporal patterns of leaf defensive chemistry reflect nutrient availability, plant phenology, and the demands of growth and reproduction as well as the timing and intensity of parasite (e.g., insects, fungi, viruses) attack.

Plants may increase their investment in defensive compounds until a threshold is reached beyond which further allotment to chemistry must be balanced by the benefit gained (Chew and Rodman, 1979; McKey, 1979; Rhoades, 1979). The underlying assumption of this cost–benefit approach to chemical variation is that chemicals are costly to produce. Various ways to evaluate cost are the energetic cost of secondary compounds (e.g., number of ATPs involved in biosynthesis; Chew and Rodman, 1979), the physiological cost of different defensive compounds (e.g., production, translocation, and storage; McKey, 1979), and the ecological cost of investment in defense (McKey, 1979; Rhoades, 1979). Energetic and physiological costs are technically difficult to define and measure; however, ecological costs can be measured by comparing patterns of allocation of growth, reproduction, and defense within and between individual plants. Assuming that plants have an energy budget, allocation of resources to one category (e.g., growth) should affect investment in the others (Mooney and Chu, 1974; Rapport and Turner, 1977). Shifts in allocation between growth and reproduction have been shown in various organisms such as snails (Calow, 1978; Hamilton, 1979), aphids (Mackay and Wellington, 1975; Wratten, 1977), planthoppers (Kisimoto, 1965; Denno *et al.*, 1980), and annual and perennial plants

(Pitelka, 1977; Primack, 1979; Abrahamson, 1979; Monson and Szarek, 1981). Trade-offs between growth, reproduction, and defense have been found in plants (Cates, 1975) and snails (Hamilton, 1979). In addition to the variation in leaf defensive chemistry and morphology that occurs within and between individual plants in a population, geographic variation (e.g., latitudinal, altitudinal, and island–mainland) in phytochemistry and leaf morphology may be the result of differences in herbivore pressure as well.

In this chapter we use an empirical approach to evaluate the relationships between variation in leaf chemistry, leaf morphology, and herbivory. First, we ask whether herbivores contribute to host-plant heterogeneity by reducing plant fitness. Second, we test the hypothesis that not all leaves are of equal value to a plant. The loss of leaves to herbivores at certain positions on a shoot and during certain times of the year may not have equal impact on plant fitness. Third, we test the hypothesis that the most valuable leaves are best defended. Fourth, we consider the demands of growth and reproduction, the availability of nutrients, and plant phenology as factors that modify the allelochemical patterns of plants predicted solely from leaf value. Fifth, we review studies suggesting that individual, population, and geographic patterns in plant defense reflect selective pressures associated with the distribution and abundance of herbivores.

II. EFFECTS OF DEFOLIATION ON PLANT FITNESS

A. Trees and Shrubs

Here we review the effects of insect defoliation on the growth, survivorship, and fecundity of trees and shrubs. Trees and shrubs appear to withstand greater insect damage than annuals because the result of a bout of defoliation in trees is reduced root reserves rather than immediate death (Harris, 1972). However, if defoliation is severe or occurs repeatedly for several seasons, reserves may be exhausted, and trees may eventually die (Kozlowski, 1969; Kulman, 1971). Regrowth of a plant after defoliation is associated with a reduction in the plant's carbohydrate reserves, and the level of carbohydrates in roots is positively correlated with winter hardiness (Jameson, 1963). Defoliation of 65–70% of the current year's growth in shrubs has invigorating effects, but repeated defoliation is detrimental (Ellison, 1960). High levels of defoliation result in a reduced number and size of growth rings in stands of naturally growing trees (Varley and Gradwell, 1962; Morrow and La

Marche, 1978) as well as in cultivated trees (Williams, 1967; Kulman, 1971). Defoliation of larch *(Larix)* by spruce budworm *(Choristoneura fumiferana)* impairs annual shoot growth, and needle growth is diminished to 50% of normal (Baltensweiler *et al.*, 1977). Heavy defoliation of black cherry *(Prunus serotina)* by *Hydria prunivorata*, the cherry scallop moth, significantly reduces growth (Schultz and Allen, 1977). In field studies on natural infestations of various poplar *(Populus)* clones by *Chrysomela scripta*, the cottonwood leaf beetle, there is an 80% reduction of shoot growth in severely defoliated clones (Caldbeck *et al.*, 1978). Dixon (1971) has indicated that the main effect of aphid infestations on lime trees *(Tilia × vulgaris)* is reduced root growth, whereas the effect on sycamore maple *(Acer pseudoplatanus)* is reduced growth of all plant parts. Repeated artificial defoliation of the tropical shrub *Cordia macrostachya* results in the reduction of growth and reproduction (Simmonds, 1951).

Insects also reduce flowering and fruit or seed yields in trees and thereby reduce their fecundity. Defoliation reduces male-cone production in jack pine *(Pinus banksiana;* Heron, 1965; Kulman *et al.*, 1963). In apple trees, artificial removal of 10% of the leaf area results in significant loss in photosynthesis (Hall and Ferree, 1976). Yields of fruit are positively related to leaf area (Haller and Magness, 1925). In apples, complete or partial defoliation causes obvious reductions in growth, fruiting, or retention of fruits (Chester, 1950; Cutright, 1963; Powell *et al.*, 1970). The effects of defoliation were simulated by removing leaves from six species of tropical trees in Costa Rica. In defoliated trees 80% produced no fruit, whereas only 29.8% of controls failed to produce some fruit. The only damaged trees to produce fruit were trees that were only partially defoliated (Rockwood, 1973).

B. Agricultural Crops

An abundance of data from agricultural crops shows the negative effects of natural and artifical (leaf clipping) defoliation on plant growth and reproduction. Both the amount of leaf tissue removed and the seasonal time of defoliation have varying consequences on the plant. Insects reduce both the quantity and quality of vegetative and reproductive parts of plants. Damage can occur directly to the leaves, resulting in subsequent losses in yield of foliage and reproductive parts. Also, sap-feeding insects indirectly reduce growth and reproduction by removing nutrients from the leaves or stalks on which they feed. Furthermore, some insects transmit plant pathogens, so even small populations of vectors may be detrimental.

In a number of studies in which insects were released on or caged on plants during different times of the season, reductions in yield were found. Boll weevils (*Anthonomis grandis*) released at two intervals during the season severely reduced cotton yields (Walker *et al.*, 1976). Reduction in cotton yield was also found in caging studies with the pink bollworm, *Pectinophora gossypiella* (Brazzel and Gaines, 1956, 1957). In another study with pink bollworm, yield (lint) was reduced by 18–53% in cotton fields not sprayed with insecticide, and seed damage was correlated with larval density (Henneberry *et al.*, 1977). Sucking insects like the tarnished plant bug *(Lygus lineolaris)*, the clouded plant bug *(Neurocolpus nubilis;* Tugwell *et al.*, 1976), and the stink bugs *Euschistus conspersus* and *Chlorochroa uhleri* (Toscano and Stern, 1976) also reduce yield in cotton.

Field studies with *Graphognathus peregrinus* and *G. leucoloma* caged on soybeans resulted in a significant reduction in pod production (Ottens and Todd, 1980). The seed size and pod number of soybeans are reduced when caged plants are infested with the green stinkbug (*Acrosternum hilare;* Todd and Turnipseed, 1974; Yeargan, 1977).

Other studies report yield reductions from natural infestations of insects. For instance, yields of corn (*Zea mays*) decrease as levels of infestation by the European corn borer *(Ostrinia nubilalis)* increase (Lynch, 1980). Direct relationships between insect number and yield loss are found for Mexican bean beetle *(Epilachna varivestis)* on pinto beans (Michels and Burkhardt, 1981). *Leptinotarsa decemlineata*, the colorado potato beetle, causes substantial reduction in tomato yield, which is negatively correlated with plant damage (Schalk and Stoner, 1979). Data from small grains indicate a negative relationship between leaf area consumed (%) by cereal leaf beetles *(Oulema melanopus)* and oat yield (Wilson *et al.*, 1969). A positive relationship also exists between the density of lepidopterous larval pests and damage to celery plants (van Steenwyk and Toscano, 1981).

Some studies report little effect of insects on plant quality and yield, but these appear to be uncommon. For example, the carbohydrate content of grapes was not related to mite *(Tetranychus pacificus)* density (Laing *et al.*, 1972) and corn leaf aphid *(Rhopalosiphum maidas)* and greenbug *(Schizaphis graminum)* feeding did not influence sorghum yields (Wilde and Ohiagu, 1976).

Artificial defoliation studies allow for greater control over the degree and timing of defoliation. By artificially defoliating plants and preventing insects from colonizing the plant with insecticide treatments, the relationship between defoliation and plant response can be tested. Artificial defoliation studies on soybeans (Thomas *et al.*, 1974), corn (Baldridge, 1976), winter wheat (Naghad, 1979), wheat and oats (Womack and Thurman, 1962), and grain sorghum (Stickler and Pauli, 1961) all show that midseason defoliation, from early flowering through early fruiting, has the greatest effect on plant yield, compared to early- and late-season leaf loss.

C. Biological Control of Weeds

In programs on biocontrol of weeds, insects and other plant parasites have been used to regulate the density of pest plants by reducing their growth, fecundity, or survivorship. Often the plant is an alien species introduced into a new environment free of its parasites, predators, and competitors. An important feature in both aquatic and terrestrial weed control is for the insect to attack when the plant is least able to compensate for defoliation (Harris, 1973; Andres and Bennett, 1975). For instance, defoliation before winter or the dry season can be most effective, due to the weeds' inability to compensate. Also, repeated defoliations either by a multivoltine herbivore or by several herbivores are effective, because of severe depletion of root reserves (Harris, 1972). One of the suspected reasons behind the success of the beetle *Chrysolina quadrigemina* in controlling Klamath weed *(Hypericum perforatum)* in California is the feeding phenology of this herbivore. Beetles fed during the fall and winter months, when root reserves were depleted, and consequently the plants died (Huffaker, 1954). The cinnabar moth *(Tyria jacobaeae)* reduced ragwort *(Senecio jacobaea)* populations to 0.01% of their former size at Durham, Nova Scotia, whereas in Nanaimo, British Columbia populations of the weed remained stable. Both populations were defoliated during bloom, but in Nova Scotia the plant had only 2 months to compensate, whereas in British Columbia 4 months were available (Harris, 1973).

Regulation of alligator weed *(Alternanthera philoxeroides)* by the beetle *Agasicles hygrophila* in Jacksonville, Florida, resulted from intense herbivory during the times when the plants' carbohydrate reserves were low (Blackburn and Weldon, 1964; Gangstad *et al.*, 1973). Differences in the beetles' ability to control populations of alligator weed were attributable to the lack of synchrony between peak defoliation and the time when plants had the lowest levels of carbohydrates (Coulson, 1977). Thus poor synchrony between the timing of herbivory and plant susceptibility may explain the failure of some biological control programs on weeds (Andres and Goeden, 1971; Freeman, 1976).

D. Natural Systems

Studies of herbivory in natural systems show the same pattern of reduced plant growth, fecundity, and survivorship. The pipevine swallowtail *(Battus philenor)* consumes approximately 45% of the leaf area of its host, *Aristolochia reticulata.* Growth rates of plants subject to defoliation were less than for undefoliated controls. During the 2-yr study period, plants exposed to herbivory had a mortality rate of 9%, higher than the mean mortality for protected plants by a factor of 4.5 (Rausher and Feeny, 1980). Mortality from feeding was greater for small plants because they had fewer reserves to draw on after defoliation and larval feeding reduced root growth. Plants exposed to larval feeding grew slower and took longer to reach reproductive maturity. By extrapolating from data on protected plants, Rausher and Feeny (1980) predicted that the seed production potential of defoliated plants was lower. In another study, *Trirhabda virgata* and *T. borelis* frequently caused severe defoliation of tall goldenrod *(Solidago altissima).* Plants that escaped defoliation, due to the presence of ants, grew significantly taller and produced more achenes ("seeds") (Messina, 1981).

Herbivores also damage reproductive tissue and seeds directly. Primary umbel fruits of *Pastinaca sativa* are damaged by larvae of the parsnip webworm *(Depressaria pastinacella).* Plants with a basal stem diameter less than 8 mm suffer a reduction in seed set of 50% when the primary umbel is destroyed, but plants that are larger can compensate with increased fruit set of tertiary umbels, either by increasing the number of umbels that reach maturity or by increasing the number of fruits per umbel. Tertiary umbel fruits are smaller than those of the primary or secondary umbels, but this does not affect viability. Such compensation may be due to the long flowering period of *P. sativa* (Hendrix, 1979). There are large reductions in fruit set of *P. sativa* following attack by the parsnip webworm in other populations as well (Thompson, 1978).

In artificial defoliation studies on natural plants, results resemble those found in agricultural systems. Removal of the upper leaves from curled dock *(Rumex crispus)* during flowering reduced mean seed size by approximately one third. However, neither seed number nor viability was affected (Maun and Cavers, 1971). Similar trends in the reduction of seed size occurred when *Trifolium incarnatum* was defoliated (Knight and Hollowell, 1962). However, for many plants seedling survival is lower for plants grown from small seeds (Black, 1958; Kaufmann and McFadden, 1963). Artificial defoliation of native tropical trees caused reductions in numbers of fruits and seeds (Rockwood, 1973).

The distribution of native plants can be determined in part by herbivores. For example, the grasshopper *Hesperotettix viridis* apparently excludes the biennial herb *Machaeranthera canescens* from several habitats. *Machaeranthera canescens* transplanted to areas where the grasshopper was common were colonized within 3 days, and uncaged plants were completely defoliated after an average of 7.4 days. Of the protected control plants 77% grew and produced flowers. Seedlings of *M. canescens* were observed to occur in areas where *H. viridis* was present, but none survived to flower during 2 yr of observation (Parker and Root, 1981).

Data from natural and agricultural systems as well as biological control programs on weeds all show that insect feeding can drastically reduce the growth, reproduction, and survivorship of plants and affect their distribution. Furthermore, the timing of defoliation relative to plant phenology and its effect on plant fitness deserves detailed study, because it may provide insight into seasonal changes in commitments to defense.

III. VALUE OF LEAF TISSUE TO THE PLANT

In this section we test the hypothesis that leaves at different positions on a shoot (e.g., terminal versus basal) and leaves differing in phenological age (e.g., spring versus fall) have different value to a plant by virtue of their different photosynthetic and storage capabilities. The value of the various leaf classes will be assessed by measuring plant fitness after artificial defoliation. The second hypothesis we test is that leaves of high value are better defended than leaves of lesser value. We elucidate how well each leaf class is defended, with a knowledge of the concentration of allelochemicals in leaves and through feeding studies with herbivores. Ultimately, we relate leaf value, leaf defense, and herbivory.

For clear separation of the tests of hypotheses concerning leaf value and defense in regard to leaf position on a shoot or leaves of different phenological age, it is essential to interpret the existing data correctly. For instance, the meaning of "young" leaves has several connotations in the literature. Young leaves can be the terminal leaves on a shoot as opposed to "old" basal leaves, or they can be all the leaves present on a tree during spring compared to the "old" leaves present in fall. The hypothesis that leaf value varies with position on a shoot is tested by selective defoliations performed at *one* time, with subsequent measurements of plant fitness. The hypothesis that leaf value changes during the season is tested by comparing the relative fitness effects of *two or more* defoliations performed during different seasons.

A. Within-Shoot Differences in Leaf Value and Defense

1. Within-Shoot Differences in Leaf Value

Leaves on a shoot have a gradient of photosynthetic activity. A number of studies of temperate-zone conifers indicate that maximum photosynthetic efficiency and production of carbohydrates occur soon after a terminal leaf reaches full size (McKey, 1979). In red pine *(Pinus resinosa)* current-year terminal needles do not contribute carbohydrates until they are fully expanded, and 1-yr-old subterminal needles supply more photosynthate than 2- or 3-yr-old basal needles (Dickman and Kozlowski, 1958). Data from two other conifer species indicate that terminal needles, after they are fully expanded, photosynthesize more than basal needles (McKey, 1979). Also, terminal leaves contribute more plant hormones (Kozlowski, 1974), whereas basal leaves serve a storage function (Kramer and Wetmore, 1943; Kozlowski and Winget, 1964). In leaves of annuals and herbaceous perennials, peak photosynthetic rates are attained at or just before full leaf expansion and then immediately begin to decline (Fukai and Silsbury, 1976; Rawson and Woodward, 1976; Woledge, 1979; Mooney *et al.*, 1981a; Mooney and Gulmon, 1982). Leaves of woody perennials that remain on the plant for at least one growing season obtain peak photosynthetic rate when leaves are fully expanded, after which the rate declines (Freeland, 1952; Roads and Wedding, 1953; Nixon and Wedding, 1956; Syvertsen and Cunningham, 1977; Mooney and Gulmon, 1982).

Artificial defoliation of leaves at different positions along the shoot, with subsequent measurement of plant fitness, provides a test for the hypothesis that terminal leaves are of greater value to the plant than basal ones. Data from conifers indicates that removal of terminal and subterminal foliage has a greater effect on growth and survivorship than removal of older basal needles (McKey, 1979). For example, removal of the basal needles from jack pine *(Pinus banksiana)* has no significant effect on growth, whereas removal of terminal foliage induces high bud mortality and shoot elongation (reviewed in McKey, 1979).

A similar pattern emerges from the defoliation of agricultural crops. In sorghum, defoliation of either the upper half or the lower half of the plant at bud formation (late boot) and flowering (anthesis) resulted in greater yield loss at both times when the upper half of the plant was removed (Stickler and Pauli, 1961). Also, for potatoes there were greater yield reductions from the loss of terminal compared to basal leaves (Cranshaw and Radcliffe, 1980). Data on leaf removal in sunflower plants indicate that removal of the upper half of the plant reduces yield by 52%, whereas defoliation of the lower half reduces yield by only 14%

(Sackston, 1959). Based on the fitness ramifications of leaf loss, these data from agricultural and silvicultural systems strongly suggest that the terminal leaves of a shoot are of more value to a plant than basal ones. Now we may ask whether plants commit more allelochemistry to defense of terminal leaves.

2. Within-Shoot Differences in Leaf Defense

The terminal, juvenile needles of jack pine (*Pinus banksiana*) are not fed on by two species of spring-feeding diprionid sawflies that prefer basal foliage. A resin acid concentrated in the terminal leaves is responsible for this feeding pattern (Ikeda *et al.*, 1977a,b). As the season progresses, levels of the chemical drop in the terminal leaves, and the larvae move from the basal to the terminal leaves to feed. Such preferential feeding on basal needles occurs in other sawfly species as well (Ross, 1955; Smith, 1974). In the tropical tree *Hymenaea courbaril*, the highest yields of terpenes and total and condensed tannins and the greatest relative astringency were found in terminal buds and leaves (Crankshaw and Langenheim, 1981). Independent bioassays of resins confirmed that these terpenes deter feeding by generalist insects like *Spodoptera exigua* (Langenheim *et al.*, 1980). The terminal leaves of the desert shrubs *Larrea tridentata* and *L. cuneifolia* also contain the highest concentration of phenolic resins. Measured resin content of terminal leaves was 26% in *L. tridentata* and 44% in *L. cuneifolia*, decreasing to 11 and 15%, respectively, in the more basal leaves (Rhoades and Cates, 1976; Rhoades, 1977). Leaf-chewing insects preferred feeding on the less resinous basal leaves (Rhoades, 1977). Larvae of the specialist butterfly *Euphydryas chalcedona* feed primarily on the cohort of leaves third from the tips of the perennial shrub *Diplacus aurantiacus*. Leaves in this cohort have a slightly lower nitrogen content than terminal leaves, but they contain much less resin (Mooney *et al.*, 1981b), which inhibits larval growth in *E. chalcedona* (Lincoln *et al.*, 1982).

In the plants just mentioned, the terminal leaves contain higher concentrations of resinous defensive compounds than do the subterminal or basal leaves. Furthermore, Rhoades and Cates (1976) have suggested that the ephemeral tissues (e.g., terminal leaves) of many plant species are defended by greater concentrations of toxins. However, a tremendous number of herbivores feed on the terminal leaves of plants (e.g., Dixon, 1969; Phillips, 1976; Denno *et al.*, 1980; Raupp, 1982; Raupp and Denno, Chapter 4). Specialist herbivores, if they are able to cope with the toxins present in terminal leaves, may enjoy the benefits of feeding on a tender tissue that contains more water and nutrients (McNeill and Southwood, 1978; Mattson, 1980). Coping with toxins includes their detoxification (Brattsten, 1979) or avoidance, as can be the case in sap-feeding insects (Lawton, 1976). Thus, although terminal leaves are clearly valuable to the plant, several factors impinge on their defense and consequent herbivory. Covariance in concentration of nutrients, allelochemicals, and toughness of leaves along a shoot (Raupp, 1982), physiological constraints imposed on defending young, ephemeral tissue (McKey, 1979), shifts within a plant in the allocation of resources from defense to growth or reproduction (Mooney and Chu, 1974), and differences in the costs of synthesis, transport, and storage of allelochemicals (McKey, 1979) may predispose terminal leaves to attack, especially by specialists. Evidence supports the hypothesis that the most valuable, terminal leaves are the best-defended leaves on the shoot. However, the highly concentrated allelochemicals in terminal leaves primarily offer protection from generalist or nonadapted feeders.

B. Seasonal Change in Leaf Value and Defense

1. Seasonal Change in Leaf Value

The timing of defoliation during the season can have major consequences on a plant's ability to compensate for lost tissues. Such compensation will depend on the life history of the plant and the timing of resource allocation to growth, defense, and reproduction. The availability of nutrients in the soil also may affect a plant's ability to recover from defoliation. Compensation is probably easier for plants in agricultural systems, where nutrients, water, and root space are not as limiting. For instance, cotton grown in underfertilized clay soil did not compensate for early season, artificial defoliation, compared to plants similarly defoliated that were grown in better soil. Yield was 43% less for those plants, compared to controls (Tugwell *et al.*, 1976). Although defoliation studies in agricultural systems can serve as models for natural systems, their impact is likely an underestimate for natural systems.

Defoliation of young leaves can stimulate the plant to refoliate (Harris, 1972), and any remaining leaves may compensate for the loss by increasing their photosynthetic rate (Maggs, 1964; Hopkinson, 1966; Sweet and Wareing, 1966; Gifford and Marshall, 1973; Hodgkinson, 1974). Energy and nutrients are exported to produce young leaves, at the expense of root storage (Ryle and Powell, 1975). Consequently, early-season defoliation can increase the production of secondary shoots and stimulate plant growth (Harper, 1977).

In contrast, defoliation later in the season has greater effects on plant survivorship and fitness. Defoliation at the times of flowering or during seed production, when nutrients and energy are being translocated to reproductive tissue, can severely reduce plant fitness. Valuable tissue containing nutrients and carbohydrates to be exported for reproduction can be lost. Loss of the plant's ability to compensate and subsequently reproduce is due to a number of factors such as the loss of root reserves, direct loss of nutrients in leaves due to herbivory, and lack of time for regrowth of foliage. Tanskiy (1969) showed that the removal of cotton bolls during the first larval generation of bollworm (Heliothis obsoleta) significantly increased boll yield by 23.8%, but defoliation by second- and third-generation larvae reduced yield. Early-maturing cultivars of potatoes showed less ability to compensate for defoliation than later-maturing varieties, probably due to the shorter growing season (Cranshaw and Radcliffe, 1980). Maun and Cavers (1971) found that leaf removal in curled dock (Rumex crispus) during flowering reduced mean seed size by one-third. It has been established in other studies that small seeds usually have a higher mortality than larger seeds (Black, 1958; Kaufman and McFadden, 1963). Even if late-season defoliation does not adversely affect growth or reproduction, plants often show reduced survivorship and winter hardiness due to depleted root reserves (Jameson, 1963; Harris, 1972; Harper, 1977).

Studies conducted with agricultural crops on artificial defoliation (leaf removal), controlled field sprayings to establish differential insect infestations, and caging of herbivores in the field provide additional data suggesting that yield reduction is greatest when plants are defoliated at midseason, during flowering and early fruit formation (Chester, 1950).

There has been some criticism of artificial defoliation studies, concerning the magnitude of the plant response in relation to natural insect defoliation (Dyer and Bokhari, 1976). Comparison of defoliation by the grasshopper Melanoplus sanguinipes and by artificial defoliation revealed that insect defoliation has greater effect on seedling regrowth (Capinera and Roltsch, 1980). Also, insects feed in different manners. Piercing, sucking insects and leaf miners can secrete toxins and hormones that alter plant physiology (Englebrecht, 1971; Osborne, 1973; Tingey and Pillemer, 1977), and in some cases saliva from chewing insects stimulates plant growth (Dyer and Bokhari, 1976). Consequently, artificial defoliation may not always mimic herbivore damage. For our purposes, however, such studies provide a useful direction on the potential effects of herbivory.

In cotton, both artificial defoliation and field studies with clouded and tarnished plant bugs (Neurocolpus nubilus and Lygus lineolaris) indicate that midseason defoliation at the height of bud formation (4–6 weeks, square) reduces yield significantly compared to earlier or later defoliations (Tugwell et al., 1976). Similarly, field studies with the beet armyworm (Spodoptera exiqua) on cotton indicate that attacks early in bud formation (squaring) result in the greatest reduction in yield (Gutierrez *et al.*, 1975). Artificial infestations of the tobacco budworm *(Heliothis virescens)* on tobacco produced negative correlations between larval density and yield. The greatest loss due to defoliation occurred during periods of root formation (early season) and flower production (midseason), and the response was less during periods of rapid vegetative growth (Kolodny-Hirsh and Harrison, 1980).

Corn, artificially infested with European cornborer *(Ostrinia nubilalis)* at different stages of plant development, showed the greatest reduction in yield during the late whorl stage, intermediate reduction during male budding and male flowering (tasseling), and no reduction in yield compared to controls when plants were defoliated earlier or later in the season (Lynch, 1980). Yield of corn is most affected when leaves are removed during midseason, at the tasseling stage (Baldridge, 1976). Also, studies of sugar beets (Afanasiev, 1966), pinto beans (Woodbury and LeBaron, 1959) and field beans (Snyder and Mickelson, 1958) all report that maximum yield reduction occurred when plants were artificially defoliated at full bloom.

Soybeans can tolerate 33–55% defoliation before flowering with little yield loss (Kalton *et al.*, 1949; Carnery and Weber, 1953; Todd and Morgan, 1972). During pod formation defoliation has greater effect (Kalton *et al.*, 1949; McAlister and Krober, 1958; Turnipseed, 1972; Todd and Morgan, 1972), and damage is most severe when pods are filling and maturing (McAlister and Krober, 1958; Kincade *et al.*, 1971; Smith and Bass, 1972; Turnipseed, 1973). In another study of soybeans, 33% artificial defoliation during pod development and filling reduced yield, but the yields of plants defoliated by 33% earlier and later did not significantly differ from that of controls. Defoliation of at least 66% was necessary at early pod formation before there was a significant loss in yield (Thomas *et al.*, 1974). Artificial defoliation of lima beans at levels of 16, 66, and 100% caused yield reductions during pod filling, but only complete leaf loss caused reduction in yield at earlier and later dates (Coggin and Dively, 1980).

The pattern is much the same for potatoes. Artificial defoliation during midseason was most detrimental when vegetative growth slowed and nutrients were transported for tuber bulking. Plants recovered completely from 10 or 33% artificial defoliation inflicted early in the season, whereas midseason defoliation resulted in the greatest yield reduction (Cranshaw and Radcliffe, 1980). Defoliation by the Colorado potato beetle *(Leptinotarsa decemlineata)* during midseason resulted in a 64% yield reduction (Hare, 1980).

In guar *(Cyamopsis tetragonoloba)* bud removal during midseason (46–90 days after emergence) significantly reduced pod yields at all levels of defoliation when 30, 40, 50, or 100% of the buds were artificially removed. Production of pods increased by 10% in plants that had 100% of their buds removed before 45 days after emergence, whereas the removal of buds 90 days following emergence had no significant effects on pod production (Rogers, 1975).

Artificial defoliation of grain sorghum (Stickler and Pauli, 1961) during bud formation (late boot) had a greater effect on yield than during flowering (anthesis) one year, yet there was no significant difference in response the second year. Pauli and Laude (1959) found that winter wheat lost 32% of its grain yield when plants were completely defoliated artificially 5 days prior to midfruiting (heading), and smaller losses occurred if plants were defoliated at later stages. Yield losses due to defoliation were caused by the combined effects of depleted stored nitrogen, decreased subsequent nitrogen accumulation, and reduced quantities of synthesized and stored carbohydrate. Decreases in nitrogen accumulation after leaf removal were associated with reduced amounts of storage tissue. Removal of leaves at midfruiting (heading), when leaf nitrogen content was particularly high, reduced subsequent translocation of nitrogen to the grain. Apparently, much of the nitrogen used by wheat plants is taken up before heading and is stored in leaves and stems before being translocated to the developing kernels (Salmon, 1941). Kisselbach (1925) artificially removed leaves 3, 10, and 17 days after midfruiting (heading). Removing leaves 3 days after heading resulted in the greatest reduction in yield of grain and straw. Artificial defoliation studies by White (1946), Womack and Thurman (1962), and Naghad (1979) all confirm that yield of wheat is reduced most by damage incurred when plants begin to flower and fruit.

Although most of the available data on the effects of defoliation on plant fitness come from agricultural crops, one study provides information on a naturally growing woody shrub, *Baccharis halimifolia*. *Baccharis halimifolia* breaks bud in early spring and grows vegetatively until August, when reproductive shoots are produced. Plants flower from late August into December. Plants defoliated (75%) in April did not differ from controls in the number of flower heads per shoot (t test, $P > 0.05$; Fig. 1A). However, defoliation in late July caused a significant reduction in the number of flower heads per shoot, compared to controls and April defoliation (t test, $P < 0.05$; Fig. 1B). Plants cannot compensate for lost nutrients if defoliation occurs just prior to flowering.

Figure 2 illustrates the seasonal changes in potato yield reduction resulting from four levels of defoliation (70, 80, 90, and 100%), imposed throughout the growing season, and corroborates that midseason defoliation (near flowering) has the greatest effect on tuber yield (Hare, 1980). The parabolic shape of the relationship between the time of de-

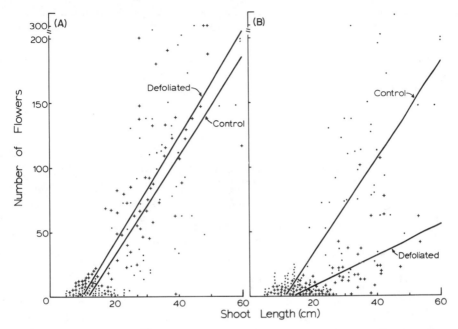

Fig. 1. Relationship between flower-head number and shoot length in control and defoliated (75%) shrubs of *Baccharis halimifolia*. (A) April defoiation, $y = 4.13x - 41.43$, $r = 0.826$, $P < 0.01$. (B) July defoliation, $y = 1.26x - 16.75$, $r = 0.678$, $P < 0.01$. (A and B) Control, $y = 3.89x - 44.58$, $r = 0.759$, $P < 0.01$. Shrubs defoliated in July differed from controls (t test, $P < 0.05$), whereas those defoliated in April did not (t test, $P > 0.05$). Shrubs defoliated in July differed from those defoliated in April (t test, $P < 0.05$).

foliation and yield reduction generated for potatoes is also supported by the tremendous volume of data from other crops that we have presented. Consequently, the hypothesis that leaf value changes during the season is substantiated.

2. Seasonal Change in Leaf Defense

Here we test the hypothesis that plants should defend themselves from herbivory during their most vulnerable phenological stage by increasing their defenses. Numerous studies indicate that phytophagous insects either grow faster, weigh more, survive better, and/or have higher fecundity when fed young, early-season leaves versus more mature, mid- to late-season foliage (Greenbank, 1956; Morris, 1967; De Wilde *et al.*, 1969; Feeny, 1970; Clarke *et al.*, 1975; Scriber, 1978; Mitter *et al.*, 1979; Smith *et al.*, 1979; Kraft and Denno, 1982; Raupp, 1982; see Fig. 3). Although these studies are consistent with the hypothesis that plants increase their defensive investment in valuable midseason leaves,

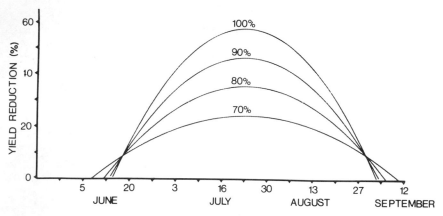

Fig. 2. Seasonal changes in potato yield reduction resulting from four levels of defoliation (70, 80, 90, and 100%) performed throughout the growing season. Note that midseason defoliation had the greatest effect on yield. From Hare (1980).

seasonal changes in defensive chemistry are often paralleled by changes in leaf nutrition, water content, and toughness, all of which can influence herbivore fitness (Tanton, 1962; Feeny, 1970; Lawton, 1976; Scriber, 1977; Mattson, 1980; Scriber and Feeny, 1979; Rausher, 1981; Kraft and Denno, 1982). Thus, to pursue more vigorously the relationship of leaf value, leaf chemistry, and patterns of herbivore feeding to each other, we must turn to specific studies that document seasonal changes in allelochemicals and their effects on herbivores.

The correlation between changes in defensive chemicals, insect response to these chemicals, and patterns of plant flowering is revealed in a study by Mooney *et al.* (1980) of the shrub *Diplacus aurantiacus* and the checkerspot butterfly *Euphydryas chalcedona*. Resin quantity in the shrub is lowest in March, increases through the season until October, and then begins to fall (Fig. 4A). The shrub flowers from mid-March to mid-July, and the postdiapausing larvae feed from mid-January until mid-May (Fig. 4B). When resin content is highest, larvae are diapausing. From mid-June until mid-July prediapause larvae occur, and the entire larval growth cycle falls closely within the winter and spring growth period of the shrub. This suggests that larvae feed when resin content of the leaves is lowest. Also, resin content increases when the shrub flowers. For *Diplacus*, it appears that defensive commitments are increased at flowering and that insects respond by entering diapause during this period. Prediapause larvae reared on an artificial diet containing leaf resin showed significantly depressed larval survivorship, growth rate, and body size with increased concentration of resin (Lincoln *et al.*, 1982).

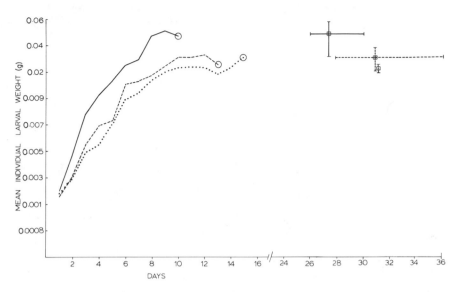

Fig. 3. Comparison of larval weight, development time, adult weight and emergence of *Trirhabda bacharidis* fed early-season (——), midseason (– – –), and late-season (·····) leaves of *Baccharis halimifolia*. Larvae reared on young leaves developed significantly faster than all others, but larvae fed midseason and late-season leaves developed at a similar rate. Adults emerging from larvae fed young leaves were significantly heavier than those fed midseason leaves, which were heavier than those fed late-season leaves. ○, Point at which 50% had pupated; □, adult emergence. All tests, SNK, $P < 0.05$. Ranges surround means. From Kraft and Denno (1982).

In the woody composite *Baccharis halimifolia* a similar pattern exists. There is a seasonal increase in a leaf resin that reduces feeding (Kraft and Denno, 1982), survivorship, and growth of generalist and non-adapted insects (Table I). Leaf resin is highest in August, at the time defoliation has the greatest consequence on plant fitness (Fig. 5). Peak herbivory from the specialist beetle *Trirhabda bacaridis* occurs during the early spring (April and May), when resin concentration is low (Kraft and Denno, 1982). However, levels of nitrogen, moisture, and toughness decline through the season as well, so high levels of secondary chemicals may not be the only factor restricting beetle feeding phenology (Kraft and Denno, 1982). However, the increase in resin is an effective defense against generalist herbivores (V. A. Krischik and R. F. Denno, unpublished data).

The size of the resin canals in the buds of Scots pine *(Pinus sylvestris)* increases through the season, as does the volume of bud resin (Harris, 1960). Larvae of the pine-shoot moth *(Rhyacionia buoliana)* are able to remove small amounts of resin from their bud mines in July, but mines

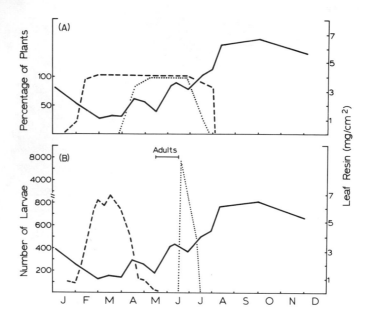

Fig. 4. (A) Seasonal patterns of growth (– – –), reproduction (·····), and defense (——) in the perennial shrub *Diplacus aurantiacus*. (B) Phenology of feeding by larvae of *Euphydryas chalcedona*. Note that postdiapausing larvae (– – –) feed when the concentration of leaf resin (——) is lowest. ·····, Prediapause larvae. From Mooney *et al.* (1980).

excavated in September are abandoned as they quickly become flooded with resin. As a consequence, larval mortality increases during the season (Harris, 1960).

Feeny (1968, 1970) has suggested that tannins have a defensive function against insects. Tannins increase through the season in *Quercus robur* leaves and further reduce nitrogen availability for herbivores. In *Heteromeles arbutifolia* cyanogenic glucoside levels are highest in young leaves and decrease through the season, whereas tannin levels increase to a maximum during fruiting and remain high (Fig. 6; Dement and Mooney, 1974; Mooney and Chu, 1974). A similar pattern is found in bracken fern *(Pteridium aquilinum),* in which two peaks of allelochemicals occur (Lawton, 1976; Cooper-Driver *et al.,* 1977). Cyanogenic compounds occur in the young fronds in June, and tannins increase throughout the season, peaking in late August in mature fronds. Tannin concentration declines at the end of the season in September (Cooper-Driver *et al.,* 1977). There is a negative relationship between the levels of tannin and cyanide in fronds and their palatability to the phytophagous locust *Schistocerca gregaria* (Cooper-Driver *et al.,* 1977).

Table I

Effects of Leaf Extracts of *Baccharis halimifolia* from Maryland and Florida on the Growth and Survivorship of the Generalist Feeder, *Spodoptera frugiperda*[a]

Extract origin	Leaf age	Extract in diet (%)	n	Survival to pupation (%)	Time to pupation[b] (days ± SE)	Pupal weight[b] (mg ± SE)
Maryland	May	0.25	60	90	15.36 ± 0.21(b)	236.29 ± 15.87(a)
Maryland	September	0.25	60	62	17.23 ± 0.25(c)	240.45 ± 33.60(a)
Florida	September	0.25	30	37	22.73 ± 0.35(d)	242.80 ± 772.40(a)
Extract-free diet	—	0.00	18	100	14.71 ± 0.01(a)	242.82 ± 16.57(a)

[a]Extracts were incorporated into synthetic diet and fed to larvae. Extracts were made by soaking 30 g of leaves in acetone. The residue was then gas evaporated and dissolved in a volumetric flask in chloroform. May leaves contain less residue than September leaves from Maryland plants, but HPLC data show no differences in the chemical composition of the residue. September leaves from Florida and Maryland plants have similar residue yields, but there are qualitative differences in the chemical composition of the residue (HPLC data).

[b]Means within columns followed by different letters are significantly different at the 0.05 level. (Data analysis by ANOVA and SNK.)

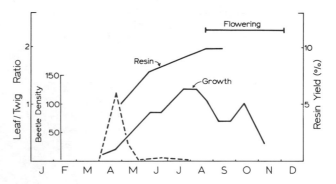

Fig. 5. Phenology of growth, reproduction, defense (resin), and herbivory (−−−) by the
beetle *Trirhabda bacharidis* in the woody shrub *Baccharis halimifolia*.

Generally, these data show that tannins and resins increase in concentration to a high in midseason and then level off or drop. The concentration of these allelochemicals increases rapidly prior to flowering
(*Quercus* excepted) or early fruit formation, when defoliation has the
greatest impact on plant fitness. However, patterns of toxin and tannin
deployment by plants are likely shaped by factors other than just herbivore pressure. The persistence of leaves and plants (Feeny, 1970;
Rhoades and Cates, 1976), nutrient availability (Mattson, 1980), shifts
in investment from defense to growth or reproduction (Mooney and
Chu, 1974; Mattson, 1980), differences in the growth and leaf-flushing
phenology of plants (Mattson, 1980; Mooney and Gulmon, 1982), additional functions of defensive chemicals (McKey, 1979), and the differential cost of synthesizing and storing allelochemicals (McKey, 1979)
may act to modify patterns of allelochemistry predicted by leaf value
alone.

For instance, nitrogen-based toxins such as alkaloids, cyanogenic compounds, and nonprotein amino acids are usually found in highest concentration in early-season foliage or in ephemeral plants (e.g., Dement
and Mooney, 1974; Cooper-Driver *et al.*, 1977; Mattson, 1980) and are
thus apparent exceptions to the predictions about the seasonal distribution of allelochemicals based on leaf value. This pattern may be related
to the availability of nitrogen early in the season and in early successional
habitats. Consequently, plants may translocate nitrogen from the soil
and store it in nitrogenous compounds that can be metabolized later,
when needed for growth. In young leaf tissue carbon is limiting, and
it is not until after expansion that leaves are partially self-sufficient and
can export carbon (Mattson, 1980). The use of nitrogen-based allelochemicals at this time may be a plant strategy for maximizing allocation

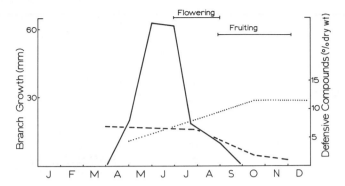

Fig. 6. Phenology of growth (——), reproduction, and defense (– – –, nitrogen-based cyanogenic glucosides; ·······, carbon-based tannins) in the woody shrub *Heteromeles arbutifolia*. Shifts in allelochemistry from nitrogen- to carbon-based compounds are influenced by nitrogen availability and physiological constraints. Adapted from Mooney and Chu (1974) and Dement and Mooney (1974).

demands and maintaining defensive chemistry. Later in the season carbon supply can exceed that demanded for growth, and a carbon surplus permits the production of carbon-based allelochemicals like tannins. Tannins are stable compounds; consequently, stored nitrogen could be released while the plant still maintained a defensive commitment. This availability hypothesis, provided by Mattson (1980), suggests that nitrogen-based defensive chemicals should occur when nitrogen supply is greater than the amount needed in growth. When nitrogen is limiting, plants should employ non-nitrogen-containing carbon-based defensive chemicals. Such correlations between nitrogen availability and patterns of defense can be expanded to the habitat level as well. Plants occurring in habitats with low available nitrogen could use carbon-based defensive chemicals like phenolics and terpenoids. There is some evidence for this. In nitrogen-poor communities like tropical sands, bogs, and climax forests, many of the allelochemicals are not nitrogen based (Mattson, 1980). Exceptions might be plants such as legumes, which can fix their own nitrogen. Nitrogen is less limiting for them and, as a consequence, they contain nitrogen-based allelochemicals (Mattson, 1980). The availability hypothesis (Mattson, 1980) implies that a plant optimizes its investment in growth, reproduction, and defense. It does not indicate that defensive commitments are merely a consequence of plant phenology and physiology, but that plants have evolved different allocations to defense due to constraints imposed by growth and reproduction.

Young leaves, which demand resources for growth, may contain nitrogen-based toxins due to their low cost of synthesis or translocation

(Rhoades and Cates, 1976; Rhoades, 1979; McKey, 1979). Investment in these toxins early in the season does not contradict our arguments concerning leaf value and defense. The majority of early-season leaves are terminal leaves of high value to the plant. Consequently, early-season investment in low-cost allelochemicals is consistent with the predictions of defense based on leaf value as well as constraints associated with growth.

IV. SEASONAL CHANGE IN ALLOCATION TO GROWTH, DEFENSE, AND REPRODUCTION

Plants have a limited season within which to grow and reproduce. Nutrients and space are often limited, so allocation of resources to growth early in the season would seem important. However, plants must also defend leaf tissue, otherwise valuable nutrients will be lost to herbivory. Plants have energy budgets in which allocation of nutrients and physiology to growth, reproduction, and defense are interrelated but competing categories. Investment in one category could reduce allocations to others. Investment in defense has a cost, so the quality and quantity of allelochemicals present represents a balance between the cost of their production and maintenance and the benefits accrued by the plant.

The shrub *Diplacus aurantiacus* shows shifts in allocation among growth, reproduction, and defense (Fig. 4A). Growth rate and twig elongation are high during January (early season), when defensive investments are low. Later on in the season, as the plant begins to reproduce, growth slows, and resin concentration increases but then eventually drops in the fall (Mooney et al., 1980).

Data for the woody composite *Baccharis halimifolia* also elucidate seasonally changing patterns of allocation (Fig. 5). *Baccharis* breaks bud in early spring (April in Maryland) and adds leaves until August when reproductive shoots are produced and flowering begins. The concentration of a defensive leaf resin increases from April to August (V. A. Krischik and R. F. Denno, unpublished data). Commitments to growth in spring have shifted to reproduction and defense by fall.

Mooney and Chu (1974) and Dement and Mooney (1974) investigated patterns of carbon gain and allocations to growth, reproduction, and defense in the evergreen shrub *Heteromeles arbutifolia* (Fig. 6). In the spring the major allocation is to growth, apparently for competitive purposes. Flowering occurs from July to mid-August, when allocation of resources must shift from growth to reproduction. Investment in reproductive tissue demands nitrogen that is apparently bound in storage tissue and nitrogen-based defensive chemicals like cyanogens. As

Fig. 7. Seasonal variation in the yield of volatile oil (——) and growth rate (– – –) of *Juniperus scopulorum*. From Powell and Adams (1973).

the plant accrues surplus photosynthate and carbon, investment in defense can switch to a carbon-based system (tannins). The reduction in the concentration of cyanogenic compounds through the season may represent reclamation of nutrients that are used for growth or reproduction (McKey, 1979; Mattson, 1980). Plants may also reclaim defensive compounds from leaves after they have lost their photosynthetic value. McKey (1979) has reported that cyanogenic glycosides and alkaloids can be withdrawn from senescing leaves.

As growth rate and nutrient demands change there can be concomitant shifts in defensive chemistry. For instance, there is a negative relationship between growth rate and the yield of volatile oils (carbon-based allelochemicals) throughout the season in *Juniperus scopulorum* (Powell and Adams, 1973). The decrease in yield of volatile oils during the winter months may reflect the breakdown of terpenoids for use elsewhere (Fig. 7). Powell and Adams (1973) reported a poor correlation between oil yield and environmental variables like temperature and moisture. Peppermint plants grown under controlled conditions showed a steady increase in monoterpenes until flower initiation, when their concentration decreased (Burbott and Loomis, 1969). Furthermore, late-season decreases in the concentration of leaf resin in *Diplacus* (Mooney *et al.*, 1980) and tannins in bracken fern are consistent with the hypothesis that plants can shift their investments in defense to other physiological processes.

Plants shift their patterns of resource allocation throughout the season. Changing patterns reflect different physiological demands during plant development that are associated with growth, defense, and reproduction. Consequently, "optimal" patterns of defensive chemistry predicted by leaf value and herbivore pressure may be altered by nutrient availability and allocation of resources to other physiological processes.

V. PATTERNS OF ALLOCATION IN PLANT MORPHS, CULTIVARS, AND SPECIES

In this section we present data showing that plant allelochemistry has a genetic basis with some environmental modification. Then we review data showing that some plant morphs, cultivars,and species contain more concentrated, diverse, and toxic chemicals than others and that these differences render plants more resistant to insect attack. Finally, we show that increased investment in defense can result in decreased growth and reproduction. These data are used to support the hypothesis that plants cannot maximize defensive commitments without incurring ecological costs that result in reduced reproduction and growth.

A. Genetic Determination of Leaf Allelochemistry

Quantitative and qualitative differences in secondary compounds are common among individuals in natural and cultivated plants. Quantitative variation involves varying amounts of defensive chemicals, whereas qualitative variation involves the addition or substitution of compounds. Both the quantity and quality of defensive compounds appear to be genetically controlled by a small number of loci (reviewed in Chew and Rodman, 1979), although there may be some modifying effects by the environment. Compositional differences in the leaf resins of the tropical leguminous tree *Hymenaea courbaril* are not due to the effects of photoperiod, temperature, or moisture. Little phenotypic plasticity for leaf resin composition is found, although the quantity (yield) of resin varies with light intensity (Langenheim *et al.*, 1981).

Resin composition in conifers appears to be under tight genetic control, although variation in resin quantity may be related to environmental factors (Squillace, 1976; Smith, 1977). Also, experiments under controlled environmental conditions and hybridization studies show that the monoterpenoid composition of yerba buena, *(Satureja douglasii)* is genetically controlled (Lincoln and Langenheim, 1978, 1981). However, the quantity of monoterpenoids has been correlated with light intensity (Lincoln and Langenheim, 1978, 1979), temperature (Lincoln and Langenheim, 1978) and moisture (Gershenzon *et al.*, 1978). Photoperiod does influence the composition of essential oils in *Mentha piperita* (Grahle and Holtzel, 1963); however, studies on other *Mentha* species and genotypes indicate that the quality and quantity of monoterpenes are under tight genetic control (Lincoln and Murray, 1978; Murray *et al.*, 1980). Populations of bracken fern growing in the open sun contain higher concentrations of cyanogenic compounds and tannins, compared to shaded populations (Cooper-Driver *et al.*, 1977). Furthermore, tannin concentration in bracken fern is influenced by moisture availability in the environment (Tempel, 1981). Although the environment certainly contributes to variation in plant allelochemistry, the data suggest that there is a strong genetic component as well.

B. Differences in Allelochemistry in Susceptible and Resistant Plants

Some of the insect-resistant properties of plants are attributable to the quality and quantity of secondary chemicals. For instance, a gene controls the production of bitter cucurbitacin in *Cucumis sativus*. The bitter chemical reduces feeding and increases mortality of the two-spotted mite by as much as 95%, compared to nonbitter cucumber plants (Da Costa and Jones, 1971). Total glycoalkaloid concentrations in the foliage varied greatly among 10 naturally growing, tuber-bearing species of *Solanum* (Raman *et al.*, 1979). Increasing the total concentration of glycoalkaloids in a diet reduced feeding and survival in the potato leafhopper, although some of the effects on leafhopper survival were not attributable to total concentration alone. The concentration and biological activity of specific glycoalkaloids proved to be important as well. Although glycoalkaloids confer resistance to potato plants, it is important to realize that levels of total glycoalkaloids in tubers and foliage are highly correlated, so breeding for resistant potato plants can result in tubers with glycoalkaloid concentrations in excess of the 0.02% health-hazard threshold (Raman *et al.*, 1979).

Cotton *(Gossypium hirsutum)* has a number of complex terpenoid phenolics like gossypol that are toxic to herbivores. Resistance of 130 lines from the USDA wild-cotton germplasm collection were examined in feeding tests with *Heliothis zea* and *H. virescens*. The concentration of gossypol was positively correlated with resistance, and the concentration of terpenoid phenolic compounds in resistant plants was approximately twice that found in susceptible plants (Seaman *et al.*, 1977). Wild tomato *(Lycopersicon hirsutum* f. *glabratum)* contains a nonalkaloid compound in a concentration that is 72× greater than that in the cultivated tomato *(L. esculentum)*. *Manduca sexta, Heliothis zea,* and *Aphis gossypii* died when exposed to filter paper treated with the chemical (Williams *et al.*, 1980).

In some plant species, the secondary chemicals common to a genus or family have been lost or additions and substitutions in secondary chemistry have occurred. Specialist herbivores may not be capable of utilizing these plants because the appropriate sensory cues are lacking, or the new chemicals may act as feeding deterrents. Some genera of the Cruciferae produce cardenolides or cucurbitacins in addition to the usual glucosinolates. Plants in these genera often escape attack from specialist insects that feed on the remainder of the family (Chew and Rodman, 1979). *Vernonia flaccidifolia* lacks sesquiterpene lactone fractions that are present in 16 of the 18 other species of *Vernonia* in eastern North America (Burnett *et al.*, 1977). In field tests with other species of *Vernonia, V. flaccidifolia* incurred less herbivory from insects. The sesquiterpene lactone glaucolide A, lacking in *V. flaccidifolia,* may be necessary for adapted insects to locate the plant, or the plant may divert energy to another as yet unknown feeding deterrent. Lab tests with artificial diets containing glaucolide A indicate that the chemical significantly reduces the growth rate of three generalist feeding Lepidoptera, whereas two others are unaffected (Jones *et al.*, 1979). *Vernonia flaccidifolia* flowers earlier than two other sympatric species, *V. gigantea* and *V. glauca,* and perhaps the lack of sesquiterpene lactones allows energy to be diverted to early seed production (Burnett *et al.*, 1977).

C. Allocation Patterns in Plant Cultivars and Polymorphic Species

Higher yielding varieties of crops are of central concern to agriculturists and plant breeders. Yet, higher yields may occur at the expense of plant defense. Here we examine trade-offs in allocation to growth, defense, and reproduction that might result in lower concentrations of defensive chemicals in cultivated crops and, subsequently, in increased susceptibility to insect attack. First, we provide data on cultivars, varieties, and species of agricultural plants, and then we use data from natural systems to support the occurrence of such trade-offs.

The hypothetical relationship between the survival of plant genotypes in a population and their investment in chemical defense is presented in Fig. 8. Individuals low in defensive commitment have reduced survivorship and/or fecundity as a consequence of herbivory. Genotypes with very high investments in defense allocate less to growth and reproduction and could lose the competitive battle to faster growing, more competitive individuals. Stabilizing selection should maintain investments in defense at a level that offers the best protection from generalized feeders and nonadapted herbivores, without drastically reducing growth and reproduction. Investments in defense are often below con-

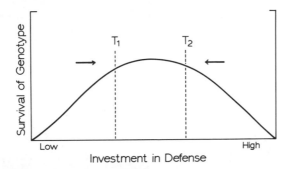

Fig. 8. Hypothetical relationship between the survival of plant genotypes in a population and their investment in chemical defense under conditions of constant herbivory. Fast-growing individuals with a small defensive investment are very susceptible to herbivory. Individuals with large defensive commitments, although they are well protected from herbivores, lose in competition with other plants due to slow growth. Stabilizing selection favors genotypes with moderate investments in defense. The investment in defensive chemistry necessary to protect a plant from generalist herbivores (T_1) is less than that required for protection from specialists (T_2).

centrations that are effective against adapted specialists. On the other hand, if herbivore pressure fluctuates, with palatable fast-growing morphs being favored in the absence of herbivores and unpalatable plants surviving in the presence of herbivores, allelochemical diversity should be maintained in a plant population.

The predictions of the model are confirmed by data from crop systems. For instance, genotypes selected for high yield are often more susceptible to attack by insects and pathogens (Pimentel, 1976). Cotton varieties bred for high yield, long-season fruiting, and responsiveness to fertilizers and irrigation are highly vulnerable to pest attack (Bottrell and Adkisson, 1977). Plants bred for palatability (reduced toxicity) often have higher yield (Rhoades, 1979). Scientists have had difficulty breeding high levels of gossypol (which conveys resistance to *Heliothis* sp.; Lukefahr and Houghtaling, 1969) into agronomically suitable cotton. Data from 400 wild and feral collections of cotton indicate that they have significantly higher levels of flower-bud gossypol than domestic varieties (Dilday and Shaver, 1976). About 100 high-gossypol derivatives of the high-gossypol Socorro Island Wild variety were crossed with agronomically acceptable lines. Among the offspring of this cross, flower-bud gossypol was negatively correlated with boll size in two tests ($r = -0.609, P < 0.05$; $r = -0.608, P < 0.05$), lint percentage in two of three tests ($r = -0.422, P < 0.05$; $r = -0.415, P < 0.05$), and total lint in two of three tests ($r = -0.419, P < 0.05$; $r = -0.521, P < 0.05$) (Dilday and Shaver, 1976).

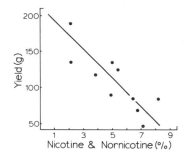

Fig. 9. Relationship ($r = 0.87$) between foliage yield and concentration of nicotine and nornicotine in 10 primitive, natural, and domesticated varieties of *Nicotinia tobacum* from Central and South America. Data from Vandenberg and Matzinger (1970).

Tobacco (*Nicotiana tabacum*) has many primitive and native strains in Central and South America. In a paper by Vandenberg and Matziner (1970), comparisons of tobacco foliage yield and nicotine and nornictone levels for 10 primitive and native strains showed an inverse relationship between yield and alkaloid concentration ($r = -0.87$, $P < 0.01$; Fig. 9). Nicotine incorporated into synthetic diets reduced survivorship, development rate, and pupal weight of the tobacco hornworm (*Manduca sexta*; Parr and Thurston, 1972). Varieties of soybeans resistant to the Mexican bean beetle had lower yields than susceptible varieties when grown under beetle-free conditions (Kenworthy and Elden, 1982). However, the mechanism of resistance, whether chemical, nutritional, or morphological, is not known for these soybean cultivars. Another study on different varieties of soybeans did not show such a trend (Elden and Paz, 1977). Some varieties of alfalfa that are resistant to alfalfa weevil have a lower yield than susceptible varieties (Barnes *et al.*, 1970). The mechanism of resistance was not indicated in the study, although the larval weight and survivorship of alfalfa weevils fed resistant cultivars were lower than those for larvae fed three nonresistant cultivars. Furthermore, weevils laid more eggs on the susceptible varieties (Barnes *et al.*, 1970). However, in another study on alfalfa, differences in yield of susceptible and resistant plants were not indicated (Kindler *et al.*, 1971). In corn, hybrids that are resistant to corn borer (*Ostrinia nubilalis*) have lower yields compared to more susceptible hybrids. In years when corn borer populations are low or moderate, the susceptible plant hybrid outyields the resistant hybrid (Lynch, 1980).

In natural systems, trade-offs between growth, reproduction, and defense are also found. For example, growth rates in pine trees are negatively correlated with total monoterpene resin content (Hanover, 1966). Mutants of *Nicotiana* and *Datura* high in alkaloid content have stunted

Table II
Comparisons of Dry Weight and Seed Production of the Palatable and Unpalatable
Morphs of Wild Ginger *(Asarum caudatum)*[a]

	Palatable plants (mean)	Unpalatable plants (mean)
Wet microhabitat[b]		
Dry weight production (mg)	3350	1960
Seed production per fruit	39.5	16.2
Dry microhabitat[c]		
Dry weight production (mg)	2730	2140
Seed production per fruit	29.0	28.5

[a]Each morph was grown in its natural microhabitat as well as transplanted to the reciprocal habitat of the other morph. From Cates (1975). Copyright 1975, the Ecological Society of America.
[b]Dominated by palatable individuals.
[c]Dominated by unpalatable individuals.

growth (Mothes, 1976). In fruits of *Xanthium strumarium* there is an inverse correlation between thickness of fruit and concentration of secondary compounds (Hare, 1978; Hare and Futuyma, 1978). Growth and reproduction are greater in the acyanogenic compared to the cyanogenic morphs of *Trifolium repens* (Foulds and Grime, 1972a,b). Jones (1966) showed in field and laboratory studies that acyanogenic and weakly cyanogenic plants of *Lotus corniculatus* are preferred by slugs and snails over strongly cyanogenic plants (see Jones *et al.*, 1978). However, when larvae of the southern armyworm *(Spodoptera eridania)* were fed acyanogenic and cyanogenic leaves of *Lotus corniculatus*, there were no differences in consumption rate, assimilation efficiency, or utilization of plant biomass (Scriber, 1978).

The most extensive study on allocations to growth, reproduction, and defense in plants is by Cates (1975) on wild ginger *(Asarum caudatum)*. Natural populations of wild ginger are polymorphic for growth rate, seed production, and palatability to the native slug *Ariolimax columbianus*. Wet habitats contain the palatable, fast growing, fecund morph of ginger. In dry habitats there is a less palatable, slower growing morph with fewer seeds. Although the mechanism for resistance was not determined, Cates (1975) postulated that, in the absence of grazing pressure, palatable, faster growing individuals would gain a competitive advantage over slower growing individuals, which commit more energy to defensive compounds. Reciprocal transplant studies with morphs seem to support a genetic basis for the polymorphism, although irreversible,

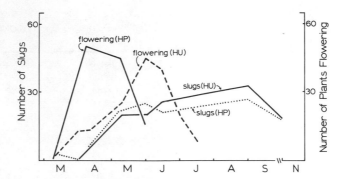

Fig. 10. Seasonal patterns of slug density and flowering of wild ginger (*Asarum caudatum*) in two habitats. Palatable morphs (HP) occur in the wet habitat and flower earlier than unpalatable morphs (HU) that dominate the dry habitat. From Cates (1975). Copyright 1975, the Ecological Society of America.

environmentally caused phenotypic change cannot be ruled out (Table II). The unpalatable morph flowers later than the palatable morph, suggesting that a trade-off occurs between defense and growth (days to first reproduction; Fig. 10).

Trade-offs between growth and reproduction also occur in plants. *Machaeranthera gracilis* has two genetically related but ecologically distinct chromosomal races that occur in the desert and foothills of Arizona. At 125 days after germination, the desert race has invested far more in reproductive (2154 mg dry wt per plant) than in vegetative growth (289 mg dry wt per plant), whereas the pattern is reversed in the foothill race, which invests more in vegetative growth (1342 mg dry wt per plant) than in reproduction (1158 mg dry wt per plant) (Monson and Szarek, 1981). Also, among annual species of *Lupinus*, those growing in costal habitats allocate a greater proportion of resources to reproductive structures, at the expense of vegetative growth and maintenance, than do the species in other habitats (Pitelka, 1977).

These data confirm that trade-offs between growth, reproduction, and defense do exist in plants. One ultimate consequence of this allocational pattern to plant breeding programs is that high-yielding cultivars may be more vulnerable to herbivore attack.

VI. DIFFERENCES IN LEAF DEFENSE BETWEEN PLANT POPULATIONS

There are many data documenting differences in leaf defense between conspecific populations of plants. In some cases differences in defense between plant populations can be correlated with the intensity of herbivore pressure in the habitat. In this section we build a case for herbivores as selective agents that shape patterns of allocation to defense in some plant populations.

Chemosystematic studies have documented population differences in plants based on secondary chemicals. Population differences in allelochemistry have been reported for numerous angiosperm taxa [monoterpenes in the *Hedeoma drummondii* complex (Labiatae), Irving and Adams, 1973; monoterpenes in *Satureja douglasii* (Labiatae), Lincoln and Langenheim, 1976; sesquiterpenes in *Hymenaea courbaril* (Leguminosae), Langenheim *et al.*, 1978; sesquiterpene lactones (Compositae) Mabry, 1970; Rodriguez, 1977; glucosinolates in *Cakile* (Cruciferae) Rodman, 1980; cardiac glycosides in *Asclepias* (Asclepiadaceae), Brower *et al.*, 1972; and flavonoids in *Phlox carolina* (Polemoniaceae), Levy and Fujii, 1978].

In a few of these studies, attempts were made to correlate populational differences in secondary chemicals to herbivory. Geographic patterns in the monoterpenoid composition of *Satureja douglasii* were investigated by Lincoln and Langenheim (1976). Five compositional types were determined, based on the relative proportions of carvone, pulegone, isomenthone, menthone, or bicyclic compounds in the leaves. Patterns of geographic variation were retained when individuals were transplanted to the greenhouse, although there was some modification in the amounts of principal constituents. Other studies indicate that the composition of monoterpenes is under genetic control (Lincoln and Langenheim, 1979, 1981). Types containing a high portion of bicyclic compounds (camphene and camphor) were more palatable to the native slug *Ariolimax dolichophallus* than were types containing high proportions of *p*-menthane compounds (isomenthone, pulegone, or carvone). Types containing camphor were the most palatable, pulegone was the most deterrent, and carvone and isomenthane were intermediate. The most palatable compositional types occurred in the least favorable habitats for slugs. Rice *et al.* (1978) suggested that slugs act as a selective force determining the composition of monoterpenes in *S. douglasii*.

Leaf resin composition of *Hymenaea courbaril*, a tropical leguminous tree, also varies among populations in Central and South America. Variation in leaf resin composition among populations was not explained by geographic differences in photoperiod, light intensity, temperature, or moisture (Langenheim *et al.*, 1978). There were differences in the growth rate and mortality of beet armyworm *(Spodoptera exigua)* larvae when they were fed on artificial diets containing extracts of *H. courbaril* leaves representing the different compositional types (Langenheim *et al.*, 1980). The authors suggested that feeding by generalist herbivores directs variation in the leaf resin composition in populations of trees.

Hemp *(Cannabis sativa)* achenes ("seeds") collected from four populations (Illinois, Panama, Nepal, and Jamaica) and grown under controlled conditions in growth chambers showed differences in net photosynthesis and total cannabinoid content. The lowest yield of cannabinoids was found in populations from Illinois and Panama, and the highest yields occurred in populations from Jamaica and Nepal. It was concluded that the four populations represent different ecotypes, genetically adapted to different areas (Bazzaz *et al.*, 1975).

Perennial lupine *(Lupinus)* plants, occurring in areas unsuitable for the specialist lycaenid butterfly *Glaucopsyche lygdamus*, contain low concentrations of specific bicyclic alkaloids in their inflorescences and lack alkaloid diversity (Dolinger *et al.*, 1973). In lupine populations where butterflies are abundant, plants contain higher alkaloid concentrations in inflorescences and have a greater diversity of alkaloids. Dolinger *et al.* (1973) have suggested that interplant variability in alkaloid composition provides an antiherbivore defense whereby specialist herbivores find it difficult to adapt to such diverse chemistry.

Although some studies show little leaf chemical variation among populations of conifers [leaf-oil terpene composition in western red cedar *(Thuja plicata)*; von Rudloff and Lapp, 1979], the majority of studies report populational differences in cortical oleoresins or leaf resins (*Cupressus* spp., Zavarin *et al.*, 1971; *Pinus strobus*, Bridgen *et al.*, 1979; *Pseudotsuga menziesii* and *P. macrocarpa*, von Rudloff, 1972, 1975; Snajberk and Zavarin, 1976; *Pinus elliottii*, Gansel and Squillace, 1976; *Pinus ponderosa*, Smith, 1977; *Pinus monticola*, Hunt and von Rudloff, 1977; *Abies procera* and *A. magnifica*, Zavarin *et al.*, 1978; *Juniperus ashei*, Adams, 1977). Chemical differences between populations have been related to herbivore abundance in only a few cases (Smith, 1977; Sturgeon, 1979). Environmental effects on terpene composition are minimal (Squillace, 1976). In pines, morphologically similar, adjacent individuals can differ greatly in plant chemistry, and well-defined geographic variability has been repeatedly documented. These chemical factors are under tight genetic control and seem most reasonably explained by the existence of selective pressures imposed directly on the chemicals (Zavarin, 1975).

Distinct geographic patterns occur in the monoterpene composition of cortical oleoresins of slash pine *(Pinus elliottii)* grown from seeds for 9 yr on plantations in Georgia and Florida (Gansel and Squillace, 1976). Variation in monoterpene composition and quantity was not affected by plantation site, but it was related to the original source of the populations. Gene inheritance has been reported for four of the five monoterpenes. Concentrations of individual monoterpenes show clinal variation latitudinally through Florida, with the steepest gradient in central Florida (Gansel and Squillace, 1976).

Eastern white pines *(Pinus strobus)* transplanted from 25 populations and grown for 19 yr on a pine plantation in Maine have been analyzed for oleoresin chemical composition and viscosity. Geographic patterns were found for three monoterpenes, α-pinene, 3-carene, and terpinolene (Bridgen *et al.*, 1979). Total monoterpene fractions showed no effects due to plantation site, a result consistent with other conifers (Hanover, 1974). Trees resistant to the white-pine weevil *(Pissodes strobi)* and susceptible trees showed no consistent differences in monoterpenes, although the F values for 3-carene and limonene were considerably higher than those of other monoterpenes (Bridgen *et al.*, 1979). However, high concentrations of limonene were correlated with weevil resistance in 1 of 3 yr (Bridgen *et al.*, 1979).

Ponderosa pine *(Pinus ponderosa)* in the western United States can be divided into five regional and four transitional types, based on the composition of monoterpenes. Resin composition is constant within a tree and is independent of tree morphology, growth, and climate. Regional and local variation in resin composition is explained by a large number of genetically inherited compositional types. Trees resistant to western pine beetle *(Dendroctonus brevicomis)* have high concentrations of limonene. However, the frequency of inherently resistant trees is low. High resin concentration makes a tree conditionally resistant to bark beetle attack, but resin quantity may be related to nongenetic environmental factors as well. The distribution of bark beetles can be associated with regional and transitional limits of average monoterpene composition (Smith, 1977). Smith (1969) has suggested that western pine beetle is most destructive in areas where the concentration of the major monoterpenes is equally balanced, compared to areas where one monoterpene is dominant. Pines in regions where the beetle has been destructive have the most balanced composition of monoterpenes, the greatest amount of β-pinene, which is the least toxic monoterpene, and the highest percentage of myrcene, a terpene that synergizes the attraction pheromone of western pine beetle. Geographical changes in the resin composition of ponderosa pine parallel shifts in the abundance of *Dendroctonus* (Smith, 1977). Whether these shifts are due to patterns of *Dendroctonus* abundance and feeding is yet to be determined.

VII. LATITUDINAL, ALTITUDINAL, AND ISLAND–MAINLAND PATTERNS IN PLANT DEFENSE

Leaf chemistry not only varies among populations in a region, it may also change along latitudinal and altitudinal gradients. Such variation in allelochemistry may result from the differential effects of environmental factors, but changes in herbivore pressure may play a role as well (Levin, 1976a). For instance, Janzen (1974, 1979) has argued that tropical forests with low productivity and diversity have high investments in defensive compounds because foliage loss there causes greater reduction in plant fitness there than in richer sites. The following studies on latitudinal patterns in plant allelochemistry support these arguments for increased commitments to defense in the tropics.

The proportion of alkaloid-bearing perennial plants increases toward the tropics and is correlated with the intensity of herbivore and pathogen pressure (Levin, 1976b). In addition, tropical plants contain alkaloids that are more toxic than those in subtropical and temperate plants (Levin and York, 1978). The quantity of sesquiterpene lactones in the genus *Parthenium* (Compositae) is higher in tropical thorn-forest species (1–2% dry wt) than in north temperate montane species (0.001% dry wt; Rodriguez, 1977). Also, the structural complexity of sesquiterpene lactones is far greater in tropical species (Rodriguez, 1977). Interspecific differences are also greater among tropical members, with only one or two lactones shared by one or two species, whereas in temperate taxa two lactones are shared by all species. Flavonoid and alkaloid constituents of the tropical and temperate taxa show a similar pattern, with the tropical members containing three flavonoid types, whereas the montane taxa contain insignificant amounts of only one flavonoid type (Rodriguez, 1977). However, in the study by Rodriguez (1977), latitudinal comparisons between tropical and temperate taxa were confounded by discrepancies in elevation among the sample sites.

The cardiac glycoside content of the umbels and seeds of *Asclepias curassavica* has been found to be higher in Costa Rica (Isman, 1979) than that in the umbels and seeds of five Californian milkweed species (Isman *et al.*, 1977). The gross cardenolide content of lygaeid bugs that feed on these milkweeds is also higher in Costa Rica. Cardiac glycoside concentrations in monarch butterflies *(Danaus plexippus)* sequestered from milkweeds (Asclepiadaceae) were found to decrease along a latitudinal gradient from Ontario to Florida by Brower *et al.* (1972), who suggested that the Florida milkweed may contain more-toxic cardiac glycosides.

The woody composite *Baccharis halimifolia* contains a defensive resin that shows dosage-dependent effects on larvae of the generalist lepidopteran *Spodoptera frugiperda* (Table I). Although the quantity of resin in the leaves increases during the season in both populations, plants from Florida have constituents in the resin that differ from those from Maryland. Furthermore, the leaf resin from Florida plants increases days to pupation and reduces survivorship of *S. frugiperda* compared to Maryland resin. The specialist chrysomelid beetle *Trirhabda bacharidis* is a major defoliator of the plant. However, populations of the insect are not as persistent in Maryland as in Florida, where they regularly defoliate *Baccharis* and prevent it from flowering.

There is a paucity of data concerning changes in the allelochemistry of plants along elevational gradients. However, Levin (1976b) reported that plants with the greatest yield of alkaloids occurred in the lowland rain forest, followed by the foothill rain forest and the montane rain forest in New Guinea.

Island floras seem to have fewer poisonous or highly aromatic plants than mainland floras. Levin (1976b) has pointed out that insular species of *Geranium* (Bate-Smith, 1973), *Senecio* (Glennie *et al.*, 1971), and *Empetrum* (Moore *et al.*, 1970) are depauperate in flavonoids compared to their mainland congeners. Levin went on to suggest that the reduced levels of allelochemicals in insular plants may be the result of reduced herbivore pressure. Mutualistic ants, like allelochemicals, perform a defensive function for plants by warding off herbivores and clipping away encroaching vines (Janzen, 1967; Bentley, 1977). Some studies indicate that mutualisms with ants have been lost in island and high-elevation populations of plants (Janzen, 1973). For example, *Cecropia peltata* does not have *Azteca* ants tending it on Puerto Rico and other Caribbean islands. The plant has lost the glycogen-rich food bodies (trichilia) that are a major part of the ants' diet in the mutualism with *Cecropia* on the neotropical mainland. Janzen (1973) suggested that this is due to reduced herbivore pressure and reduced interspecific competition for space with other plants. On the mainland, some high-elevation populations of *Cecropia* have also lost the mutualism with *Azteca*. Keeler (1979) reported that the frequency of plants with extra floral nectaries that attract ants is less (0.0%) at 1310-m elevation than at sea level (0.28%) on Jamaica.

From the few comparative data that exist on differences in allelochemistry between plant populations along latitudinal and altitudinal gradients, a pattern emerges. Plants growing at low latitudes and altitudes appear to contain higher concentrations and a greater diversity of defensive chemicals than their high-latitude and -altitude counterparts. Furthermore, the greater investment in defensive chemistry in plants at low latitudes and altitudes is suggested as a response to high parasite pressure.

VIII. SUMMARY AND CONCLUSION

Both natural and artificial defoliation of trees, shrubs, agricultural crops, and weeds reduce the fitness (growth, reproduction, and yield) of these plants. Consequently, the need for defensive chemistry and/or morphology seems apparent. More specifically, we have tested the hypothesis that not all leaves along a shoot (e.g., terminal versus basal) and not all leaves throughout the growing season (e.g., spring versus fall) are of equal value in terms of (photosynthetic or storage capability) to the plant. After examining the results of many studies, we conclude that the loss of terminal rather than basal leaves has the greatest effect on plant fitness. Also, defoliation at the time of flowering and early fruit formation (midseason) has the greatest impact on the fitness of perennials and annuals that flower from mid to late season.

We have then asked whether leaves of high value are better defended by the plant. With regard to terminal leaves the answer is a qualified yes. Rhoades and Cates (1976) have made the point that toxins are more concentrated in ephemeral (e.g., terminal) tissues. In addition, we have provided data from trees and perennial shrubs documenting that higher concentrations of leaf resins occur in terminal rather than basal leaves. However, the feeding patterns of herbivores do not necessarily reflect the distribution of allelochemicals in plants. For instance, many specialist herbivores feed on terminal leaves (Phillips, 1976; Rhoades and Cates, 1976; McNeill and Southwood, 1978; Cates, 1980; Denno et al., 1980; Raupp and Denno, Chapter 4), apparently because of their ability to cope with toxins and the nutritional advantages of feeding there (Rhoades and Cates, 1976; Rhoades, 1979). There are exceptions to this pattern. Diprionid sawflies (Neodiprion) and the checkerspot butterfly (Euphydryas chalcedona) are specialized feeders, yet both avoid the high concentration of resins in the terminal leaves of their hosts and feed on more basal tissues (Ikeda et al., 1977a,b; Mooney et al., 1981b). Many generalist herbivores either avoid feeding on terminal leaves when offered a choice or suffer decreased fitness when raised on them (Crankshaw and Langenheim, 1981; Raupp and Denno, Chapter 4). However, polyphagous herbivores like the winter moth (Operophtera brumata; Varley and Gradwell, 1968; Feeney, 1970) and the fall cankerworm (Alsophilia pometaria; Mitter et al., 1979) both feed on the young terminal leaves of their hosts. If defenses like resins are more concentrated in terminal tissues, they can be effective against both generalized and specialized feeders. Toxins alone may prove effective only against generalists and nonadapted insects (Rhoades and Cates, 1976).

Leaves present during flowering and early fruit formation (midseason leaves) appear to be of the most value to the plant. We have provided data showing that quantitative allelochemicals like resins and tannins increase in concentration throughout much of the growing season, level off, and then drop in some species. The concentration of these chemicals is either increasing rapidly or has peaked when the plant is in flower and when leaves are of high value to the plant. Defoliation at this time apparently reduces the translocation of nutrients from leaves to reproductive structures. The decline in the resin content of *Diplacus* (Mooney *et al.*, 1980) and *Juniperus* (Powell and Adams, 1973) at the end of the season is consistent with the hypothesis that investment in defense is commensurate with leaf value. It is important to realize that the data on the timing of defoliation and its effect on plant fitness and the subsequent value of leaves was generated largely from annual agricultural crops like corn and soybeans, which flower at the end of the season. Information on seasonal changes in defensive chemistry comes mainly from long-lived trees and perennial shrubs. Consequently, predictions concerning leaf value (from annuals) have been tested by examining allelochemical patterns in perennials. What little evidence exists concerning the effects of the timing of defoliation on the fitness of a perennial (*Baccharis halimifolia*, see Fig. 1) is consistent with that for annuals and points to the value of midseason leaves. However, it may well be that the seasonal patterns of leaf value for annuals may differ from those of other long-lived perennials that may compensate for losses over the course of several seasons. It is also likely that differences in plant development (e.g., evergreen versus deciduous) affect seasonal patterns of leaf value.

Apparent exceptions to our prediction that leaves present during flowering and early fruiting are the best defended come from qualitative allelochemicals (toxins; e.g., cyanogenic compounds and alkaloids) that often are most concentrated in early-season foliage (Rhoades and Cates, 1976; McKey, 1979). This pattern may be related to the availability of nitrogen in the environment and reclamation by the plant of bound nitrogen for other functions like growth and reproduction (McKey, 1979; Mattson, 1980). Also, even though plants are more likely to compensate for the loss of leaves early in the season, new leaves are very abundant at that time, offering a concentrated resource for herbivores. To lose them all repeatedly to herbivores may reduce plant fitness. Thus, to defend early-season leaves with cheap secondary compounds that can be translocated into the developing leaf (e.g., the nitrogen-based alkaloids or their precursors) rather than synthesizing allelochemicals *in situ* may be the only option for some plants (Rhoades, 1979; McKey, 1979). Tannins and other digestion-reducing polymers have not been reported to cross cell membranes, because of their high molecular weight, and they must be synthesized on site (Rhoades and Cates, 1976). Consequently, the frequencies of leaf-age and -position classes must be taken into account when forming predictions about allelochemical patterns.

Plants must respond to the demands placed on them not only by defense but also by growth and reproduction. Thus "optimal" patterns of defensive chemistry predicted by leaf value and herbivore pressure may be altered by the relative abundance of various leaf-age classes, nutrient availability, and allocation of resources to other physiological processes. However, at the level of the individual plant, temporal and spatial patterns of allelochemistry appear to be shaped, in part, by herbivore pressure, whereby the most valuable leaves are the best defended ones.

Just as herbivores have played a role in the fashioning of allelochemical patterns at the level of the individual plant, there is evidence that variation in allelochemistry among plant morphs, populations, and species results from differences in herbivore pressure. For instance, in habitats in which phytophagous slugs are abundant, wild ginger plants are less palatable than plants that occur where slugs are rare (Cates, 1975). Rice *et al.* (1978) have suggested that slugs also act as a selective force, determining the monoterpene composition in yerba buena. Geographical changes in the resin composition of ponderosa pines parallel shifts in the abundance of the western pine beetle (*Dendroctonus brevicomis;* Smith, 1977). Where herbivore pressure is greater in southern populations of the shrub *Baccharis halimifolia,* plants contain a leaf resin that is a greater deterrent to generalist herbivores. Although the environment certainly contributes to allelochemical variation among populations of plants, transplanted plants often maintain their defensive chemical integrity, suggesting a strong genetic basis for variation (Zavarin, 1975; Lincoln and Langenheim, 1978, 1981; Lincoln and Murray, 1978; Murray *et al.,* 1980; Langenheim *et al.,* 1981). What few data exist for populations and species of plants suggest that plants growing at low latitudes and altitudes contain higher concentrations and a greater diversity of allelochemicals than their high-latitude and -altitude counterparts. The greater investment in defensive chemistry in plants at low latitudes and altitudes appears to be associated with potentially high parasite pressure.

However, there is a cost associated with increasing investments in defense. Trade-offs appear to exist between defense, growth, and reproduction. For example, there is a negative relationship between the concentration of alkaloids and yield in strains of tobacco (Vandenberg and Matzinger, 1970). Similar negative relationships between defense (plant resistance) and growth or reproduction (yield) occur in cotton, soybeans, alfalfa, corn, and wild ginger (Barnes *et al.,* 1970; Cates, 1975; Dilday and Shaver, 1976; Lynch, 1980; Kenworthy and Elden, 1982).

In this chapter we have argued that variation in plant defensive chemistry originates from a multitude of sources, of which herbivore pressure is one. Nutrient availability and the demands of growth and reproduction are among other factors that interact to shape the allelochemical profiles of plants at the level of the individual and the population. The result at the level of the individual plant is a chemically diverse host that may be difficult for herbivores to exploit (Dolinger *et al.*, 1973; Smith, 1977; Edmunds and Alstad, 1978; Levin and York, 1978; Whitham, 1981; Jones, Chapter 15; Price, Chapter 16). Lastly, between-population differences in the concentration and diversity of allelochemicals may result from geographic differences in herbivore pressure. To better understand the origins of variation in plant defense, it is essential to know the contributions of genes and environment (e.g., moisture, light, nutrient availability). Then, detailed comparative studies of plants under high and low herbivore pressure will provide insight into the selective role of plant parasites in influencing patterns of allelochemistry in plants.

ACKNOWLEDGMENTS

This chapter benefited from discussions with Marvin K. Aycock, Jr., Pete Barbosa, Galen Dively, Tom C. Elden, William J. Kenworthy, Bill Mellors, and Roger Ratcliffe. Judd Nelson supported and directed the chemical work on *Baccharis*. Dan Hare, Suzanne Hamilton, Clive Jones, Mark McClure, Mark McKone, Graham Rotheray, and Doug Tallamy commented on various drafts. Shirley Donkis, Helen Lindsey, Mary Luetkemeyer, and Joan Russo typed the manuscript. We thank all of these people for their help and support.

Scientific Article no. A-3222, Contribution no. 6293 of the Maryland Agricultural Experiment Station, Department of Entomology.

REFERENCES

Abrahamson, W. G. (1979). Patterns of resource allocation in wildflower populations of field and woods. *Am. J. Bot.* **66**, 71–79.

Adams, R. P. (1977). Chemosystematics—analyses of populational differentiation and variability of ancestral and recent populations or *Juniperus ashei*. *Ann. M. Bot. Gard.* **64**, 184–209.

Afanasiev, M. M. (1966). The effect of simulated hail injuries on the growth, yield, and sugar content of beets. *Bull.—Mont., Agric. Exp. Stn.* **605**.

✳ Andres, L. A., and Bennett, F. D. (1975). Biological control of aquatic weeds. *Annu. Rev. Entomol.* **20**, 31–46.

✳ Andres, L. A., and Goeden, R. D. (1971). The biological control of weeds by introduced natural enemies. *In* "Biological Control" (C. B. Huffaker, ed.), pp. 143–164. Plenum, New York.

Baldridge, D. E. (1976). The effects of simulated hail injury on the yield of corn grown for silage. *Bull.—Mont., Agric. Exp. Stn.* **687**, 1–27.

Baltensweiler, W., Benz, G., Bovey, P., and Delucchi, V. (1977). Dynamics of larch bud moth populations. *Annu. Rev. Entomol.* **22**, 79–100.

Barnes, D. K., Hanson, C. H., Ratcliffe, R. H., Busbice, T.H., Schillinger, J. A., Buss, G. R., Campbell, W. V., Hemken, R. W., and Blickenstaff, C. C. (1970). The development and performance of Team alfalfa[:]a multiple pest resistant alfalfa with moderate resistance. *Crop Res. ARS* **34-115**, 1–41.

Bate-Smith, E. C. (1973). Chemotaxonomy of geranium. *Bot. J. Linn. Soc.* **67**, 347–359.

Bazzaz, R. A., Dusek, D., Seigler, D. S., and Haney, A. W. (1975). Photosynthesis and cannabinoid content of temperate and tropical populations of *Cannabis sativa*. *Biochem. Syst. Ecol.* **3**, 15–18.

Bentley, B. L. (1977). Extra floral nectaries and protection by pugnacious bodyguards. *Annu. Rev. Ecol. Syst.* **8**, 407–427.

Black, J. N. (1958). Competition between plants of different initial seed sizes in swards of subterranean clover (*Trifolium subterraneum* L.) with particular reference to leaf area and the light microclimate. *Aust. J. Agric. Res.* **9**, 299–318.

Blackburn, R. D., and Weldon, L. W. (1964). A Correlation of Carbohydrate Reserves in Alligatorweed to Time and Initial Treatment with Silvex, Annu. Rep. USDA, Agric. Res. Serv., Weed Investigations Aquatic and Non-crop Areas, Plantation Field Lab., Ft. Lauderdale, Florida.

Bottrell, D. G., and Adkisson, P. L. (1977). Cotton insect pest management. *Annu. Rev. Entomol.* **22**, 451–481.

Brattsten. L. B. (1979). Biochemical defense mechanisms in herbivores against plant allelochemicals. *In* "Herbivores: Their Interaction with Secondary Plant Metabolities" (G. A. Rosenthal and D. H. Janzen, eds.) pp. 200–270. Academic Press, New York.

Brazzel, J. R., and Gaines, J. C. (1956). The effect of pink bollworm infestations on yield and quality of cotton. *J. Econ. Entomol.* **49**, 852–854.

Brazzel. J. R., and Gaines, J. C. (1957). Cotton yield and quality losses caused by various levels of pink bollworm infestations. *J. Econ. Entomol.* **50**, 609–613.

Bridgen, M. R., Hanover, J. W., and Wilkinson, R. C. (1979). Oleoresin characteristics of eastern white pine seen sources and relationship to weevil resistance. *For. Sci.* **25**, 175–183.

Brower, L. P., McEvoy, P. B. Williamson, K. L., and Flannery, M. A. (1972). Variation in cardiac gylcoside content of monarch butterflies from natural populations in eastern North America. *Science* **177**, 426–428.

Burbott, A. J., and Loomis, W. D. (1969). Evidence for metabolic turnover of monoterpenes in peppermint. *Plant Physiol.* **44**, 173–179.

Burnett, W. C., Jones, S. B., and Mabry, T. J. (1977). Evolutionary implications of sesquiterpene lactones in *Vernonia* (Compositae) and mammalian herbivores. *Taxon* **26**, 203–207.

Caldbeck, E. S., McNabb, H. S., Jr., and Hart, E. R. (1978). Poplar clonal perferences of the cottonwood leaf beetle. *J. Econ. Entomol.* **71**, 518–520.

Calow, P. (1978). The evolution of life-cycle strategies in fresh-water gastropods. *Malacologia* **17**, 351–364.

Capinera, J. L., and Roltsch, W. J. (1980). Response of wheat seedlings to actual and simulated migratory grasshopper defoliation. *J. Econ. Entomol.* **73**, 258–261.

Carnery, M. P., and Weber, C. R. (1953). Effects of certain components of simulated hail injury on soybeans and corn. *Res. Bull.—Iowa, Agric. Exp. Stn.* **400**, 465–504.

Cates, R. G. (1975). The interface between slugs and wild ginger: some evolutionary aspects. *Ecology* **56**, 391–400.

Cates, R. G. (1980). Feeding patterns of monophagous, oligophagous, and polyphagous insect herbivores: the effect of resource abundance and plant chemistry. *Oecologia* **46**, 22–31.

Chester, K. S. (1950). Plant disease losses: their appraisal and interpretation. *Plant Dis. Rep., Suppl.* **193**, 190–362.

Chew, F. S., and Rodman, J. E. (1979). Plant resources for chemical defense. In "Herbivores: Their Interaction with Secondary Plant Metabolities" (G. A. Rosenthal and D. H. Janzen, eds.) pp. 271–307. Academic Press, New York.

Clarke, A. E., Knox, R. B., and Jermyn, M. A. (1975). Localization of lectins in legume cotyledons. J. Cell Sci. 19, 157–167.

Coggin, D. C., and Dively, G. P. (1980). Effects of depodding and defoliation on the yield and quality of lima beans. J. Econ. Entomol. 73, 609–614.

Cooper-Driver, G., Finch, S., Swain, T., and Bernays, E. (1977). Seasonal variation in secondary plant compounds in relation to the palatability of Pteridium aquilinum. Biochem. Syst. Ecol. 5, 177–183.

Coulson, J. (1977). Biological control of alligatorweed, 1959–1972. A review and evaluation. U.S., Agric. Res. Serv., Tech. Bull. 1547.

Crankshaw, D. R., and Langenheim, J. H. (1981). Variation in terpenes and phenolics through leaf development in Hymenaea and its possible significance to herbivory. Biochem. Syst. Ecol. 9, 115–124.

Cranshaw, W. S., and Radcliffe, E. B. (1980). Effect of defoliation on yield of potatoes. J. Econ. Entomol. 73, 131–134.

Cutright, C. R. (1963). Insect and mite problems of Ohio apples. Ohio, Agric. Exp. Stn., Res. Bull. 930.

Da Costa, C. P., and Jones, C. M. (1971). Cucumber beetle resistance and mite susceptibility controlled by the bitter gene in Cucumis sativus L. Science 172, 1145–1146.

Dement, W. A., and Mooney, H. A. (1974). Seasonal variation in the production of tannins and cyanogenic glucosides in the chaparral shrub, Heteromeles arbutifolia. Oecologia 15, 65–76.

Denno, R. F., Raupp, M. J., Tallamy, D. W., and Reichelderfer, C. F. (1980). Migration in heterogeneous environments: differences in habitat selection between the wing forms of the dimorphic planthopper, Prokelisia marginata (Homoptera: Delphacidae). Ecology 61, 859–867.

De Wilde, J., Bongers, W., and Schooneveld, H. (1969). Effects of host plant age on phytophagous insects. Entomol. Exp. Appl. 12, 714–720.

Dickmann, D. I., and Kozlowski, T. T. (1958). Mobilization by Pinus resinosa cones and shoots of C^{14}-photosynthate from needles of different ages. Am. J. Bot. 55, 900–906.

Dilday, R. H., and Shaver, T. N. (1976). Breeding for increased levels of flowerbud gossypol in cotton. Proc.—Beltwide Cotton Prod. Res. Conf. p. 87.

Dixon, A. F. G. (1969). Quality and availability of food for a sycamore aphid population. In "Animal Populations in Relation to their Food Resources" pp. 271–287. Blackwell, Oxford.

Dixon, A. F. G. (1971). The role of aphids in wood formation. I. The effect of the sycamore aphid, Drepanosiphum platanoides (Schr.) (L.). J. Appl. Ecol. 8, 165–179.

Dolinger, P. M., Ehrlich, P. R., Fitch, W. L., and Breedlove, D. E. (1973). Alkaloid and predation patterns in Colorado lupine populations. Oecologia 13, 191–204.

Dyer, M. I., and Bokhari, U. G. (1976). Plant–animal interactions: studies of the effects of grasshopper grazing on blue grama grass. Ecology 57, 762–772.

Edmunds, G. F., Jr., and Alstad, D. N. (1978). Coevolution in insect herbivores and conifers. Science 199, 941–945.

Ehrlich, P. R., and Raven, P. H. (1964). Butterflies and plants: a study in coevolution. Evolution 18, 586–608.

Elden, T. C., and Paz, P. E. (1977). Field cage studies to determine effects of Mexican bean beetle resistance in soybeans. J. Econ. Entomol. 70, 26–29.

Ellison, L. (1960). Influence of grazing on plant succession of rangelands. Bot. Rev. 26, 1–78.

✶ Englebrecht, L. (1971). Cytokinin activity in larval infected leaves. *Biochem. Physiol. Pflanz.* **162**, 9–27.

Feeny, P. (1970). Seasonal changes in oak leaf tannins and nutrients as a cause of spring feeding by winter moth caterpillars. *Ecology* **51**, 565–581.

Feeny, P. (1975). Biochemical coevolution between plants and their insect herbivores. *In* "Coevolution of Animals and Plants" (L. E. Gilbert and P. R. Raven, eds.), pp. 3–19. Univ. of Texas Press, Austin.

Feeny, P. (1976). Plant apparency and chemical defense. *Recent Adv. Phytochem.* **10**, 1–40.

Feeny, P. P. (1968). Effect of oak leaf tannins on larval growth of the winter moth *Operophtera brumata. J. Insect Physiol.* **14**, 805–817.

Foulds, W., and Grime, J. P. (1972a). The influence of soil moisture on the frequency of cyanogenic plants in populations of *Trifolium repens* and *Lotus corniculatus. Heredity* **28**, 143–146.

Foulds, W., and Grime, J. P. (1972b). The response of cyanogenic and acyanogenic phenotypes of *Trifolium repens* to soil moisture supply. *Heredity* **28**, 181–187.

Fraenkel, G. S. (1959). The raison d'être of secondary plant substances. *Science* **129**, 1466–1470.

Fraenkel, G. S. (1969). Evaluation of our thoughts on secondary plant substances. *Entomol. Exp. Appl.* **12**, 473–486.

Freeland, R. O. (1952). Effect of age of leaves upon the rate of photosynthesis in some conifers. *Plant Physiol.* **27**, 685–690.

✶ Freeman, T. E. (1976). "Proceedings of the IV International Symposium on Biological Control of Weeds." The Center for Environ. Programs, Inst. Food Agric. Sci., University of Florida.

Fukai, S., and Silsbury, J. H. (1976). Responses of subterranean clover communities to temperature. I. Dry matter production and plant morphogenesis. *Aust. J. Plant Physiol.* **3**, 527–543.

✶ Gangstad, E. O., Raynes, J. J., Mobley, G. S., Jr., and Zeiger, C. F. (1973). "Biological Control of Alligator Weed," Aquatic Plant Control Program, Tech. Rep. 3. U.S. Army Eng. Waterways Expt. Stn., CE, Vicksburg, Mississippi.

Gansel, C. R., and Squillace, A. E. (1976). Geographic variation of monoterpene in cortical oleoresin of slash pine. *Silvae Genet.* **25**, 149–232.

Gershenzon, J., Lincoln, D. E., and Langenheim, J. H. (1978). The effect of moisture stress on monoterpenoid yield and composition in *Satureja douglasii. Biochem. Syst. Ecol.* **6**, 33–43.

Gifford, R. M., and Marshall, C. (1973). Photosynthesis and assimilate distribution in *Lolium multiflorum* Lam. following differential tiller defoliation. *Aust. J. Biol. Sci.* **26**, 517–526.

Gilbert, L. E. (1975). Ecological consequences of a coevolved mutualism between butterflies and plants. *In* "Coevolution of Animals and Plants" (L. E. Gilbert and P. H. Raven, eds.) pp. 210–240. Univ. of Texas Press, Austin.

Glennie, C. W., Harborne, J. B., Rowley, G. D., and Marchant, C. J. (1971). Correlations between flavonoid chemistry and plant geography in the *Senecio radicans* complex. *Phytochemistry* **10**, 2413–2417.

Grahle, G., and Holtzel, C. (1963). Photoperiodische Abhängigkeit der Bildung des ätherischen Öls bei *Mentha piperita* L. *Naturwissenschaften* **50**, 552.

Greenbank, D. O. (1956). The role of climate and dispersal in the initiation of outbreaks of the spruce budworm in New Brunswick. *J. Zool.* **34**, 453–476.

Gutierrez, A. P., Flacon, L. A., Loew, W., Leipzig, P. A., and Van den Bosch, R. (1975). An analysis of cotton production in California: a model for acala cotton and the effects of defoliators on its yields. *Environ. Entomol.* **4**, 125–136.

Hall, F. R., and Ferree, D. C. (1976). Effects of insect injury simulation on photosynthesis of apple leaves. *J. Econ. Entomol.* **69**, 245–248.

Haller, M. H., and Magness, J. R. (1925). The relation of leaf area of the growth and composition of apples. *Proc. Am. Soc. Hortic. Sci.* **22**, 189–196.

Hamilton, S. (1979). Shell armor in freshwater gastropods: its protective advantages and potential liabilities. Ph.D. Dissertation, University of Maryland, College Park (unpublished).

Hanover, J. W. (1966). Genetics of terpenes. I. Gene control of monoterpene levels in *Pinus monticola* Dougl. *Heredity* **21**, 73–84.

Hanover, J. W. (1974). Biochemical analysis of tree speciation. *North For. Biol. Workshop, 3rd, 1974* pp. 106–131.

Hanover, J. W. (1975). Physiology of tree resistance to insects. *Annu. Rev. Entomol.* **20**, 75–95.

Hare, J. D. (1978). Variation and seed predation among local populations of *Xanthium strumarium* L. Ph.D. Thesis, State University of New York at Stony Brook.

Hare, J. D. (1980). Impact of defoliation by the Colorado potato beetle on potato yields. *J. Econ. Entomol.* **73**, 369–373.

Hare, J. D., and Futuyma, D. J. (1978). Different effects of variation in *Xanthium strumarium* L. (Compositae) on two insect seed predators. *Oecologia* **37**, 109–120.

Harper, J. L. (1977). "Population Biology of Plants." Academic Press, New York.

Harris, P. (1960). Production of pine resin and its effect on survival of *Rhyacionia buoliana* (Schiff) (Lepidoptera: Olethreutidae). *Can. J. Zool.* **38**, 121–130.

Harris, P. (1972). Insects in the population dynamics of plants. *Symp. R. Entomol. Soc. London* **6**, 201–209.

Harris, P. (1973). The selection of effective agents for the biocontrol of weeds. *Can. Entomol.* **105**, 1495–1503.

Hendrix, S. B. (1979). Compensatory reproduction in a biennial herb following insect defoliation. *Oecologia* **42**, 107–118.

Henneberry, T. J., Bariola, L. A., Fry, K. E., and Kittock, D. L. (1977). Pink bollworm infestations and relationships to cotton yield in Arizona. *U.S. Agric. Res. Serv., West. Reg.* [*Rep.*] *ARS-W* **ARS W-49**.

Heron, R. J. (1965). The role of chemotactic stimuli in the feeding behavior of spruce budworm larvae on white spruce. *Can. J. Zool.* **43**, 247–269.

Hodgkinson, K. C. (1974). Influence of partial defoliation on photosynthesis, Photorespiration, and transpiration by lucerne leaves of different ages. *Aust. J. Plant Physiol.* **1**, 651–578.

Hopkinson, J. M. (1966). Studies on the expansion of leaf surface. VI. Senescence and the usefulness of old leaves. *J. Exp. Bot.* **17**, 762–770.

Huffaker, C. B. (1954). Quantitative studies on the biological control of St. John's wort (Klamath weed) in California. *Proc. Pac. Sci. Congr. 7th, 1952* Vol. 4, pp. 303–313.

Hunt, R. S., and von Rudloff, E. (1977). Leaf-oil-terpene variation in western white pine populations of the pacific northwest. *For. Sci.* **23**, 507–516.

Ikeda, T., Matsumura, F., and Benjamin, D. M. (1977a). Mechanisms of feeding discriminating between matured and juvenile foliage by two species of pine sawflies. *J. Chem. Ecol.* **3**, 677–694.

Ikeda, T., Matsumura, F., and Benjamin, D. M. (1977b). Chemical basis for feeding adaptation of pine sawflies *Neodiprion rugifrons* and *Neodiprion swainei*. *Science* **197**, 497–499.

Irving, R. S., and Adams, R. P. (1973). Genetic and biosynthetic relationships of monoterpenes. *Recent Adv. Phytochem.* **6**, 187–214.

Isman, M. B. (1979). Cardenolide content of lygaeid bugs on *Asclepias curassavica* in Costa Rica. *Biotropica* **11**, 78–79.

Isman, M. B., Duffey, S. S., and Scudder, G. G. E. (1977). Variation in cardenolide content of the lygaeid bugs, *Oncopeltus fasciatus* and *Lygaeus kalmii* and of their milkweed hosts (*Asclepis* spp.) in central California. *J. Chem. Ecol.* **3**, 613–624.

✳ Jameson, D. A. (1963). Responses of individual plants to harvesting. *Bot. Rev.* **29**, 532–594.

Janzen, D. H. (1966). Coevolution of mutualism between ants and acacias in Central America. *Evolution* **20**, 249–75.

Janzen, D. H. (1967). Fire, vegetation structure, and the ant × acacia interaction in Central America. *Ecology* **48**, 26–35.

Janzen, D. H. (1973). Dissolution of mutualism between *Cecropia* and its *Azteca* ants. *Biotropica* **5**, 15–28.

Janzen, D. H. (1974). Tropical blackwater rivers, animals, and mast fruiting by Dipterocarpaceae. Biotropica **6**, 69–103.

Janzen, D. H. (1979). New horizons in the biology of plant defenses. *In* "Herbivores: Their Interaction with Secondary Plant Metabolites" (G. A. Rosenthal and D. H. Janzen, eds.) pp. 331–350. Academic Press, New York.

Jones, D. A. (1966). On the polymorphism of cyanogenesis in *Lotus corniculatus* L. I. Selection by animals. *Can. J. Genet. Cytol.* **8**, 556–567.

Jones, D. A., Keymers, R. J., and Ellis, W. M. (1978). Cyanogenesis in plants and animal feeding. *In* "Biochemical Aspects of Plant and Animal Coevolution" (J.B. Harborne, ed.) pp. 21–34. Academic Press, New York.

Jones, S. B., Jr., Burnett, W. C., Jr., Coile, N. C., Mabry, T. J., and Betkouski, M. F. (1979). Sesquiterpene lactones of *Vernonia*—influence of glaucolide-A on the growth rate and survival of lepidopterous larvae. *Oecologia* **39**, 71–77.

Kalton, R. R., Weber, C. R., and Eldredge, J. C. (1949). The effect of injury simulating hail damage to soybeans. *Res. Bull.—Iowa, Agric. Exp. Stn.* **359**, 739–796.

Kaufmann, M. L., and McFadden, A. D. (1963). The influence of seed size on the results of barley yield trails. *Can. J. Plant Sci.* **43**, 51–58.

Keeler, K. H. (1979). Distribution of plants with extrafloral nectories and ants at two elevations in Jamaica. *Biotropica* **11**, 152–154.

Kenworthy, W. J., and Elden, T. C. (1982). Performance of Mexican bean beetle resistant soybean lines in Maryland. University of Maryland, College Park (unpublished manuscript).

Kincade, R. T., Laster, M. L., and Hartwig, E. E. (1971). Simulated pod injury in soybeans. *J. Econ. Entomol.* **64**, 984–985.

Kindler, S. D., Kehr, W. R., and Ogden, R. L. (1971). Influence of pea aphids and spotted alfalfa aphids on the stand, yield of dry matter, and chemical composition of resistant and susceptible varieties of alfalfa. *J. Econ. Entomol.* **64**, 653–657.

Kisimoto, R. (1965). Studies on the polymorphism and its role playing in the population growth of the brown planthopper, *Nilaparvata lugens* Stal. *Bull. Shikoku Agric. Exp. Stn.* **13**, 1–106.

Kisselbach, T. A. (1925). Winter wheat investigations. *Res. Bull.—Nebr. Agric. Exp. Stn.* **31**.

Knight, W. E., and Hollowell, E. A. (1962). Response of crimson clover to different defoliation intensities. *Crop Sci.* **2**, 124–127.

Kolodny-Hirsch, D., and Harrison, F. P. (1980). Foliar loss assessments and economic decision-making for the tobacco budworm on Maryland tobacco. *J. Econ. Entomol.* **73**, 465–468.

Kozlowski, T. T. (1969). Tree physiology and tree pests. *J. For.* **67**, 118–122.

Kozlowski, T. T. (1974). Extent and significance of shedding of plant parts. *In* "Shedding of Plant Parts." (T. T. Kozlowski, ed.), pp. 1–44. Academic Press, New York.

Kozlowski, T. T., and Winget, C. H. (1964). The role of reserves in leaves, branches, stems, and roots on shoot growth of red pine. *Am. J. Bot.* **51**, 522–529.

Kraft, S. K., and Denno, R. F. (1982). Feeding responses of adapted and non-adapted insects to the defensive properties of *Baccharis halimifolia* L. (Compositae). *Oecologia* **52**, 156–163.

✕— Kramer, P. J., and Wetmore, T. H. (1943). Effects of defoliation on cold resistance and diameter growth of broad-leaved evergreens. *Am. J. Bot.* **30**, 428–431.

✕— Kulman, H. M. (1971). Effects of insect defoliation on growth and mortality of trees. *Annu. Rev. Entomol.* **16**, 289–324.

✕— Kulman, H. M., Hodson, A. C., and Duncan, D. P. (1963). Distribution and effects of jack-pine budworm defoliation. *For. Sci.* **9**, 146–157.

Laing, J. E., Calvert, D. L., and Huffaker, C. B. (1972). Preliminary studies of effects of *Tetranychus pacificus* on yield and quality of grapes in San Jonquin Valley, California. *Environ. Entomol.* **1**, 658–663.

Langenheim, J. H., Stubblebine, W. H., Lincoln, D. E., and Foster, C. E. (1978). Implications of variation in resin composition among organs, tissues, and populations in the tropical legume *Hymenaea. Biochem. Syst. Ecol.* **6**, 299–313

Langenheim, J. H., Stubblebine, W. H., and Foster, C. E. (1979). Effect of moisture stress on composition and yield in leaf resin of *Hymenaea courbaril. Biochem. Syst. Ecol.* **7**, 21–28.

Langenheim, J. H., Foster, C. E., and McGinley, R. B. (1980). Inhabitory effects of different quantitative compositions of *Hymenaea* leaf resins on a generalist herbivore *Spodoptera exigua. Biochem. Syst. Ecol.* **8**, 385–396.

Langenheim, J. H., Arrhenius, S. P., and Nascimento, J. C. (1981). Relationship of light intensity of leaf resin composition and yield in the tropical leguminous genera *Hymenaea* and *Copaifera. Biochem. Syst. Ecol.* **9**, 27–37.

Lawton, J. (1976). The structure of the arthropod community on bracken. *Bot. J. Linn. Soc.* **73**, 187–216.

✕— Levin, D. A. (1976a). The chemical defense of plants to pathogens and herbivores. *Annu. Rev. Ecol. Syst.* **7**, 121–160.

Levin, D. A. (1976b). Alkaloid-bearing plants: an ecogeographic perspective. *Am. Nat.* **110**, 261–284.

Levin, D. A., and York, B. M., Jr. (1978). The toxicity of plant alkaloids: an ecogeographic perspective. *Biochem. Syst. Ecol.* **6**, 61–76.

Levy, M., and Fujii, K. (1978). Geographic variation of flavonoids in *Phlox carolina. Biochem. Syst. Ecol.* **6**, 117–125.

Lincoln, D. E., and Langenheim, J. H. (1976). Geographic patterns of monoterpenoid composition in *Satureja douglasii. Biochem. Syst. Ecol.* **4**, 237–248.

Lincoln, D. E., and Langenheim, J. H. (1978). Effect of light and temperature on monoterpenoid yield and composition in *Satureja douglasii. Biochem. Syst. Ecol.* **6**, 21–32.

Lincoln, D. E., and Langenheim, J. H. (1979). Variation of *Satureja douglasii* monoterpenoids in relation to light intensity and herbivory. *Biochem. Syst. Ecol.* **7**, 289–298.

Lincoln, D. E., and Langenheim, J. H. (1981). A genetic approach to monoterpenoid compositional variation in *Satureja douglasii. Biochem. Syst. Ecol.* **9**, 153–160.

Lincoln, D. E., and Murray, M. J. (1978). Monogenic basis for reduction of ($+$) $-$ pulegone to ($-$) $-$ menthone in *Mentha* oil biogenesis. *Phytochemistry* **17**, 1727–1730.

Lincoln, D. E., Newton, T. S., Ehrlich, P. R., and Williams, K. S. (1982). Coevolution of the checkerspot butterfly *Euphydryas chalcedona* and its larval food plant *Diplacus aurantiacus*: larval response to protein and leaf resin. *Oecologia* **52**, 216–223.

Lukefahr, M. J., and Houghtailing, J. E. (1969). Resistance of cotton strains with high gossypol content to *Heliothis* sp. *J. Econ. Entomol.* **61**, 588–591.

Lynch, R. E. (1980). European corn borer: yield losses in relation to hybrid and stage of corn development. *J. Econ. Entomol.* **73**, 159–164.

Mabry, T. J. (1970). Infraspecific variation of sesquiterpene lactones in *Ambrosia* (compositae). Applications to evolutionary problems. *In* "Phytochemical Phylogeny" (J. B. Harborne, ed.), pp. 269–300. Academic Press, New York.

McAlister, D. F., and Krober, O. A. (1958). Response of soybeans to leaf and pod removal. *Agron. J.* **50**, 674–677.

Mackay, D. A., and Wellington, W. G. (1975). A comparison of the reproductive patterns of apterous and alate virginoparous *Acyrthosiphon pisum* (Homoptera: Aphididae). *Can. Entomol.* **107**, 1161–1166.

McKey, D. (1979). The distrubution of secondary compunds within plants. *In* "Herbivores: Their Interaction with Secondary Plant Metabolities" (G. A. Rosenthal and D. H. Janzen, eds.), pp. 56–133. Academic Press, New York.

McNeill, S., and Southwood, T. R. E. (1978). The role of nitrogen in the development of insect/plant relationships. *In* "Biochemical Aspects of Plant and Animal Coevolution" (J. B. Harbone, ed.), pp. 78–98. Academic Press, New York.

Maggs, D. H. (1964). Growth-rates in relation to assimilated supply and demand. I. Leaves and roots as limiting regions. *J. Exp. Bot.* **15**, 574–583.

Mattson, W. J., Jr. (1980). Herbivory in relation to plant nitrogen content. *Annu. Rev. Ecol. Syst.* **11**, 119–161.

Maun, M. A., and Cavers, P. B. (1971). Seed production and dormancy in *Rumex crispus*. I. The effects of removal of cauline leaves at anthesis. *Can. J. Bot.* **49**, 1123–1130.

Messina, F. J. (1981). Plant protection as a consequence of an ant–membracid mutualism: Interactions on goldenrod *(Solidago* sp.). *Ecology* **62**, 1433–1440.

Michels, G. J., Jr., and Burkhardt, C. C. (1981). Threshold levels of the Mexican bean beetle on pinto beans in Wyoming. *J. Econ. Entomol.* **74**, 5–6.

Mitter, C., Futuyma, D. J., Schneider, J. C., and Hare, J. D. (1979). Genetic variation and host plant relations in a parthenogenetic moth. *Evolution* **33**, 777–790.

Monson, R. K., and Szarek, S. R. (1981). Life cycle characteristics of *Machaeranthera gracilis* (Compositae) in desert habitats. *Oecologia* **49**, 50–55.

Mooney, H. A., and Chu, C. (1974). Seasonal carbon allocation in *Heteromeles arbutifolia*, a California evergreen shrub. *Oecologia* **14**, 295–306.

⚡Mooney, H. A., and Gulmon, S. L. (1982). Constraints on leaf structure and function in reference to herbivory. *BioScience* **32**, 198–206.

Mooney, H. A., Ehrlich, P. R., Lincoln, P. E. and Williams, K. S. (1980). Environmental controls on the seasonality of a drought deciduous shrub, *Diplacus aurantiacus* and its predator, the checkerspot butterfly, *Euphydras chalcedona*. *Oecologia* **45**, 143–146.

Mooney, H. A., Field, C., Gulmon, S. L., and Bazzaz, F. (1981a). Photosynthetic capacity in relation to leaf position in desert versus old-field annuals. *Oecologia* **50**, 109–112.

Mooney, H. A., Williams, K. S., Lincoln, D. E., and Ehrlich, P. R. (1981b). Temporal and spatial variability in the interaction between the checkerspot butterfly, *Euphydryas chalcedona* and its principal food source, the California shrub, *Diplacus aurantiacus*. *Oecologia* **50**, 195–198.

Moore, D. H., Harborne, J. B., and Williams, C. (1970). Chemotaxonomy, variation, and geographical distribution of the Empetraceae. *Bot. J. Linn. Soc.* **63**, 277–293.

Morris, R. F. (1967). Influence of parental food quality on the survival of *Hyphantria cunea*. *Can. Entomol.* **99**, 24–33.

⚡Morrow, P. A., and La Marche, V. C., Jr. (1978). Tree ring evidence for chronic insect suppression of productivity in subalpine *Eucalyptus*. *Science* **201**, 1244–1246.

Mothes, K. (1976). Secondary plant substance as materials for chemical high quality breeding in higher plants. *Recent Adv. Phytochem.* **10**, 385–405.

Murray, M. J., Lincoln, D. E., and Henfendehl, F. W. (1980). Chemogenetic evidence supporting multiple allele control of the biosynthesis of ($-$) $-$ menthone and ($+$) $-$ isomenthone stereoisomers in *Mentha* species. *Phytochemistry* 19, 2103–2110.

Naghad, K. (1979). Effects of natural and simulated cereal leaf beetle damage on the yield and quality of winter wheat. Ph.D. Dissertation, University of Maryland, College Park (unpublished).

Nixon, P. W., and Wedding, R. T. (1956). Age of date leaves in relation to efficiency of photosynthesis. *Proc. Am. Soc. Hortic. Sci.* 67, 265–269.

✳ Osborne, D. J. (1973). Mutual regulation of growth and development in plants and insects. *R. Entomol. Soc. London Symp.* 6, 33–42.

Ottens, R. J., and Todd, J. W. (1980). Leaf area consumption of cotton, peanuts and soybeans by adult *Graphognathus peregrinus* and *G. leucoloma*. *J. Econ. Entomol.* 73, 55–57.

✳ Parker, M. A., and Root, R. B. (1981). Insect herbivores limit habitat distribution of a native composite, *Machaeranthera canescens*. *Ecology* 62, 1390–1392.

Parr, J. C., and Thurston, R. (1972). Toxicity of nicotine in synthetic diets to larvae of the tobacco hornworm. *Ann. Entomol. Soc. Am.* 65, 1185–1188.

Pauli, A. W., and Laude, H. H. (1959). Protein and carbohydrate relationships in winter wheat as influenced by mechanical injury. *Argon. J.* 51, 55–57.

Phillips, W. M. (1976). Effects of leaf age on feeding 'preference' and egg laying in the chrysomelid beetle, *Haltica lythri*. *Physiol. Entomol.* 1, 223–226.

Pimentel, D. (1976). World food crisis: energy and pests. *Bull. Entomol. Soc. Am.* 22, 20–26.

Pitelka, L. F. (1977). Energy allocation in annual and perennial lupines (*Lupinus*: Leguminosae). *Ecology* 58, 1055–1065.

Powell, D., Janson, B., and Sharvelle, E. (1970). Diseases of apples and pears in the Midwest. *Circ.—Univ. Ill., Coop. Ext. Serv.* 909.

Powell, R. A., and Adams, R. P. (1973). Seasonal variation in the volatile terpenoids of *Juniperus scopulorum* (Cupressaceae). *Am. J. Bot.* 60, 1041–1050.

Primack, R. B. (1979). Reproductive effort in annual and perennial species of *Plantago* (Plantaginaceae). *Am. Nat.* 114, 51–62.

Raman, K. V., Tingey, W. M., and Gregory, P. (1979). Potato glycoalkaloids: effect on survival and feeding behavior of the potato leafhopper. *J. Econ. Entomol.* 72, 337–341.

Rapport, D. J., and Turner, J. E. (1977). Economic models in ecology. *Science* 195, 367–373.

Raupp, M. (1982). Spatial distribution and seasonal abundance of the imported willow leaf beetle, *Plagiodera versicolora* Laich: The effect of plant nutrition and defense, physical factors, and activities of competitors and predators. Ph.D. Dissertation, University of Maryland, College Park, (unpublished).

Rausher, M. D. (1981). The effect of native vegetation on the susceptibility of *Aristolochia reticulata* (Aristolochiaceae) to herbivore attack. *Ecology* 62, 1187–1195.

✳ Rausher, M. D., and Feeny, P. (1980). Herbivory, plant density, and plant reproductive success: the effect of *Battus philenor* on *Aristolochia reticulata*. *Ecology* 61, 905–917.

Rawson, H. M., and Woodward, R. G. (1976). Photosynthesis and transpiration in dicotyledonous plants. I. Expanding leaves of tobacco and sunflower. *Aust. J. Plant Physiol.* 3, 247–256.

Rhoades, D. F. (1977). Intergrated antiherbivore, anti-desiccant, and ultraviolet screening properties of creosote bush resin. *Biochem. Syst. Ecol.* 5, 281–290.

Rhoades, D. F. (1979). Evolution of plant chemical defense against herbivores. *In* "Herbivores: Their Interaction with Secondary Plant Metabolites" (G. A. Rosenthal and D. H. Janzen, eds.), pp. 4–54. Academic Press, New York.

Rhoades, D. F., and Cates, R. (1976). Toward a general theory of plant antiherbivore chemistry. *Recent Adv. Phytochem.* 10, 168–213.

Rice, R. L., Lincoln, D. E., and Langenheim, J. H. (1978). Palatability of monoterpeniod compositional types of *Satureja douglasii* to a generalist mollusean herbivore, *Ariolimax dolichophallus*. *Biochem. Syst. Ecol.* **6**, 45–53.

Roads, W. A., and Wedding, R.T. (1953). The photosynthetic and respiratory rates of citrus leaves of four different ages. *Citrus Leaves* **33**, 10–11.

⅄ Rockwood, L. L. (1973). The effect of defoliation on seed production of six Costa Rican tree species. *Ecology* **54**, 1361–1369.

Rodman, J. E. (1980). Population variation and hybridization in sea-rockets (Cakile: Cruciferae): seed glucosinolate characters. *Am. J. Bot.* **67**, 1145–1159.

Rodriguez, E. (1977). Ecogeographic distribution of secondary constituents in *Parthenium* (Compositae). *Biochem. Syst. Ecol.* **5**, 207–218.

Rogers, C. E. (1975). Effects of simulated damage by midges on seed production by guar. *J. Econ. Entomol.* **68**, 832–834.

Ross, H. H. (1955). The taxonomy and evolution of the sawfly genus *Neodiprion*. *For. Sci.* **1**, 196.

Ryle, G. J. A., and Powell, C. E. (1975). Defoliation and regrowth in the graminaceous plant: the role of current assimilate. *Ann. Bot. (London)* [N.S.] **39**, 297–310.

Sackston, W. E. (1959). Effects of artifical defoliation on sunflowers. *Can. J. Plant Sci.* **39**, 108–118.

Salmon, S. C. (1941). Climate and small grains. USDA Year. Agric. pp. 321–342.

Schalk, J. M., and Stoner, A. K. (1979). Tomato production in Maryland: effect of different densities of larvae and adults of the Colorado potato beetle. *J. Econ. Entomol.* **72**, 826–829.

Schultz, D. E., and Allen, D. C. (1977). Effects of defoliation by *Hydria prunivorata* on the growth of black cherry. *Environ. Entomol.* **6**, 276–283.

Scriber, J. M. (1977). Limiting effects of low leaf-water content on the nitrogen utilization, energy budget, and larval growth of *Hyalophora cecropia* (Lepidoptera: Saturniidae). *Oecologia* **8**, 269–287.

Scriber, J. M. (1978). Cyanogenic glycosides in *Lotus corniculatus*. *Oecologia* **34**, 143–155.

Scriber, J. M., and Feeny. P. (1979). Growth of herbivorous caterpillers in relation to feeding specialization and to growth form of their food plants. *Ecology* **60**, 829–850.

Seaman, F., Lukefahr, M. J., and Mabry, T. J. (1977). The chemical basis of the natural resistance of *Gossypium hirsutum* L. to *Heliothis*. *Proc.—Beltwide Cotton Prod. Res. Conf.* pp. 102–103.

Simmonds, F. J. (1951). Further effects of the defoliation of *Cordia macrostachys*. *Can. Entomol.* **83**, 24–28.

Smith, C. M., Wilson, R. F., and Brim, C. A. (1979). Feeding behavior of Mexican bean beetle on leaf extract of resistant and susceptible soybean genotypes. *J. Econ. Entomol.* **72**, 374–377.

Smith, D. R. (1974). Conifer sawflies, Diprionidae: key to North American genera, checklist of world species, and new species from Mexico (Hymenoptera). *Proc. Entomol. Soc. Wash.* **76**, 409.

Smith, R. (1969). Xylem resin as a factor in the resistance of pines to forced attacks by bark beetles. *Proc. World Consult. For. Tree Breed., 2nd, 1969*. FO-FTB-69-5/6, pp. 1–13.

Smith, R. H. (1977). Monoterpenes of ponderosa pine xylem resin in western United States. *USDA For. Serv. Tech. Bull.* **1532**, 1–48.

Smith, R. H., and Bass, M. H. (1972). Relationship of artificial pod removal to soybean yields. *J. Econ. Entomol.* **65**, 606–608.

Snajberk, K., and Zavarin, E. (1976). Mono- and sesqui-terpenoid differentiation of *Pseudotsuga* of the United States and Canada. *Biochem. Syst. Ecol.* **4**, 159–163.

Snyder, G. B., and Mickelson, L. (1958). The effect of simulated hail injury in beans. *Bull.—Idaho, Agric. Exp. Stn.* **322**.

Squillace, A. E. (1976). Biochemical genetics and selection composition of volatile terpenes. *IUFRO, Jt. Meet. Adv. Generation Breed.* p. 167–178.

Stickler, F. C., and Pauli, A. W. (1961). Leaf removal in grain sorghum. I. Effects of certain defoliation treatments on yield and components of yield. *Agron. J.* **53**, 99–102.

Sturgeon, K. B. (1979). Monoterpene variation in ponderosa pine xylem related to western pine beetle predation. *Evolution* **33**, 803–814.

Sweet, G. B., and Wareing, P. F. (1966). Role of plant growth in regulating photosynthesis. *Nature (London)* **210**, 77–79.

Syvertsen, J. P., and Cunningham, G. L. (1977). Rate of leaf production and senescence and effect of leaf age on net gas exchange in creosote bush. *Photosynthetica* **11**, 161–166.

Tanskiy, V. I. (1969). The harmfulness of the cotton bollworm, *Heliothis obsoleta* F. (Lepidoptera, Noctuidae), in southern Tadzhikistan. *Entomol. Rev. (Engl. Transl.)* **48**, 23–29.

Tanton, M. T. (1962). The effect of leaf toughness of the feeding of larvae of the mustard beetle *Phaedon cochleariae* Fab. *Entomol. Exp. Appl.* **5**, 74–78.

Tempel, A. S. (1981). Field studies of the relationship between herbivore damage and tannin concentration in brachen *(Pteridium aquilinum* Kuhn*)*. *Oecologia* **51**, 97–106.

Thomas, G. D., Ignoffo, C. M., Biever, K. D., and Smith, D. B. (1974). Influence of defoliation and depodding on yield of soybeans. *J. Econ. Entomol.* **67**, 683–685.

Thompson, J. N. (1978). Within-patch structure and dynamics in *Pastinaca sativa* and resource availability to a specialized herbivore. *Ecology* **59**, 443–448.

Tingey, W. M., and Pillemer, E. A. (1977). Lygus bugs: crop resistance and physiological nature of feeding injury. *Bull. Entomol. Soc. Am.* **23**, 277–287.

Todd, J. W., and Morgan, L. W. (1972). Effects of hand defoliation on yield and seed weight of soybeans. *J. Econ. Entomol.* **65**, 567–570.

Todd, J. W., and Turnipseed, S. G. (1974). Effects of southern green stink bug damage on yield and quality of soybeans. *J. Econ. Entomol.* **67**, 421–426.

Toscano, N. C., and Stern, V. M. (1976). Cotton yield and quality loss caused by various levels of stink bug infestations. *J. Econ. Entomol.* **69**, 53–56.

Tugwell, P., Young, S. C., Jr., Dumas, B. A., and Phillips, J. R. (1976). Plant bugs in cotton. Importance of infestation time, types of cotton injury, and significance of wild hosts near cotton. *Rep. Ser.—Arkansas, Agric. Exp. Stn.* **227**.

Turnipseed, S. G. (1972). Response of soybeans to foliage loss in South Carolina. *J. Econ. Entomol.* **65**, 224–229.

Turnipseed, S. G. (1973). Insects. *In* "Soybeans: Improvement, Production, and Uses" (B. E. Caldwell, ed.), pp. 545–572. Am. Soc. Agron., Madison, Wisconsin.

Vandenberg, P., and Matzinger, D. F. (1970). Genetic diversity and heterosis in *Nicotiana*. III. Crosses among Tobacco introductions and flue-cured varieties. *Crop Sci.* **10**, 437–440.

van Steenwyk, R. A., and Toscano, N. C. (1981). Relationship between lepidopterous larval density and damage in celery and celery plant growth analysis. *J. Econ. Entomol.* **74**, 287–290.

Varley, G. C., and Gradwell, G. R. (1962). The effect of partial defoliation by caterpillars on the timber production of oak trees in England. pp. 211–214. *Proc. Int. Congr. Entomol., 11th, 1960*.

Varley, G. C., and Gradwell, G. R. (1968). Population models for the winter moth. *Symp. R. Entomol. Soc. London* **4**, 132–142.

von Rudloff, E. (1972). Chemosystematic studies in the genus *Pseudotsuga*. I. Leaf oil analysis of the coastal and Rocky Mountain varieties of Douglas-fir. *Can. J. Bot.* **50**, 1025–1040.

von Rudloff, E. (1975). Volatile leaf oil analysis in chemosystematic studies of North America conifers. *Biochem. Syst. Ecol.* **2**, 131–167.

von Rudloff, E., and Lapp, M. S. (1979). Population variation in the leaf oil terpene composition of western red cedar, *Thuja plicata*. *Can. J. Bot.* **57**, 476–479.

Walker, J. K., Gannaway, J. R., and Niles, G. A. (1976). The age distribution of cotton bolls and damage from different generations of the boll weevil. *Tex. Agric. Exp. Stn. [Misc. Publ.], MP* **MP-1254C**, 1–15.

White, R. M. (1946). Preliminary observations on some effects of artificial defoliation of wheat plants. *Agric. Sci.* **26**, 225–229.

✗ Whitham, T. G. (1981). Individual trees as heterogeneous environments: Adaptation to herbivory or epigenetic noise? *In* "Species and Life History Patterns: Geographic and Habitat Variations" (R. F. Denno and H. Dingle, eds.), pp. 9–27. Springer-Verlag, New York/Berlin.

Wilde, G., and Ohiagu, C. (1976). Relation of corn leaf aphid to sorghum yield. *J. Econ. Entomol.* **69**, 195–197.

Williams, C. B. (1967). Spruce budworm damage symptoms related to radial growth of grand fir, Douglas fir, and Englemann spruce. *For. Sci.* **13**, 274–285.

✗ Williams, K. S., and Gilbert, L. E. (1981). Insects as selective agents on plant vegetative morphology: egg mimicry reduces egg laying by butterflies. *Science* **212**, 467–469.

Williams, W. G., Kennedy, G. G., Yamamoto, R. T., Thacker, J. D., and Bordner, J. (1980). 2-Tridecanone: a naturally ocurring insecticide from the wild tomato *Lycopersicon hirsutum* f. *glabratum*. *Science* **207**, 888–889.

Wilson, M. C., Treece, R. E., Shade, R. E., Day, K. M., and Stivers, R. K. (1969). Impact of cereal leaf beetle larvae on yields of oats. *J. Econ. Entomol.* **62**, 699–702.

Woledge, J. (1979). Effects of flowering on the photosynthetic capacity of ryegrass leaves grown with and without natural shading. *Ann. Bot. (London)* [N.S.] **44**, 197–207.

Womack, D., and Thurman, R. L. (1962). Effect of leaf removal on the grain yield of wheat and oats. *Crop Sci.* **2**, 423–426.

Woodbury, C. W., and LeBaron, M. (1959). A study of simulated hail injury in beans. *Bull.—Idaho, Agric. Exp. Stn.* **322**.

Wratten, S. D. (1977). Reproductive strategy of winged and wingless morphs of aphids *Sitobion avenae* and *Metopolophium dirhodum*. *Ann. Appl. Biol.* **85**, 319–331.

Yeargan, K. V. (1977). Effects of green stink bug damage on yield and quality of soybeans. *J. Econ. Entomol.* **70**, 619–622.

Zavarin, E. (1975). The nature, variability, and biological significance of volatile secondary metabolites from Pinaceae. *Phytochem. Bull.* **8**, 6–15.

Zarvarin, E., Lawrence, L., and Thomas, M. C. (1971). Compositional variations of leaf monoterpenes in *Cupressus macrocarpa*, *C. pygmaea*, *C. goveniana*, *C. abramisiana* and *C. sargentii*. *Phytochemistry* **10**, 379–393.

Zavarin, E., Critchfield, W. B., and Snajberk, K. (1978). Geographic differentiation of monoterpenes for *Abies procera* and *Abies magnifica*. *Biochem. Syst. Ecol.* **6**, 267–278.

Vera Aber Krischik
Robert F. Denno
Department of Entomology
University of Maryland
College Park, Maryland

CHAPTER **15**

Phytochemical Variation, Colonization, and Insect Communities: the Case of Bracken Fern (*Pteridium aquilinum*)

CLIVE G. JONES

I. INTRODUCTION

The host plants of phytophagous insects are spatially and temporally heterogeneous resources, varying in quality and quantity. Plant phenology and distribution are major sources of variation that could create resource patchiness and barriers against successful insect colonization and utilization (Preston, 1962a,b; MacArthur and Wilson, 1967). This chapter examines phytochemical variation as another factor contributing to resource heterogeneity. Phytochemical defense against herbivores has received considerable attention from ecologists and evolutionary biologists (see Wallace and Mansell, 1976; Rosenthal and Janzen, 1979). However, the extent to which chemical variation occurs in any plant and its impact on adapted and nonadapted phytophagous insects have not been extensively studied. There are few plants for which the variation of more than one biochemical class of compounds has been measured and for which the structure and population dynamics of the insect community are known. Bracken fern [*Pteridium aquilinum* (L.) Kuhn; Filicopsida: Dennstaedtiaceae] is one of these plants.

VARIABLE PLANTS AND HERBIVORES
IN NATURAL AND MANAGED SYSTEMS

Bracken is globally distributed (Page, 1976) and locally abundant. It occurs in over 90% of all 10-km squares in the British Isles (Perring and Walters, 1962), with over 400,000 acres covered in 1970 (M. Morrison, personal communication. *In* Rymer, 1976). Bracken is a spore-producing plant (i.e., there are no insects associated with pollination), but it frequently occurs as extensive, long-lived, clonal stands (Page, 1976). It is old in comparison to most angiosperms—fossil records for *Pteridium* date from the Oligocene, 38×10^6 yr ago (Page, 1976)—and it has an insect community that includes some "primitive" insects (Lawton, 1976). Bracken exhibits broad-spectrum antibiotic *(sensu stricto)* activity against competitors, consumers and decomposers (I. A. Evans, 1976; W. C. Evans, 1976; Gleissman, 1976; Cooper-Driver *et al.*, 1977; Jones and Firn, 1979a; J. Merryweather, personal communication on antimicrobial activity) and has at least eight distinct biochemical classes of putative allelochemicals. These characteristics make bracken a particularly suitable plant for examining the impact of chemical variation on plant–insect interactions.

II. CHEMICAL VARIATION: SOURCES, SCALES, AND IMPACTS

A plant is a dynamic system that is expected to show qualitative and quantitative chemical variation over space and time. This applies to production of exogenous (e.g., volatiles, exudates, and chemical components of seeds and litter) and endogenous materials. The sources of this variation are both intrinsic and extrinsic. Intrinsic variation arises from the genetic components of individuals (including somatic components, Whitham, 1981, Chapter 1; Whitham and Slobodchikoff, 1981), populations, varieties and species and changes associated with all aspects of growth, development, reproduction, and senescence. Extrinsic sources of variation are modifiers of these intrinsic events and are the abiotic and biotic interactions (e.g., climate, edaphy, consumers, decomposers, and pathogens).

The scales of chemical variation can be divided into spatial and temporal. Spatial scales are (1) structural variation within a biochemical class of compounds; (2) different biochemical classes; (3) intracellular distribution of these compounds; (4) intraplant variation, including cells, tissues and organs; (5) interplant variation, including variation in response to microhabitat; and (6) variation within and among populations, varieties, or subspecies, again including micro- and macrohabitat-induced variation. The spatial scale therefore encompasses the molecular to the biogeographic. Temporal scales of variation are (1) short-term biosynthetic turnover; (2) diurnal variation; (3) seasonal variation; (4) interyear variation, particularly that resulting from environmental changes; and (5) variation over evolutionary time scales that leads to speciation or to varietal differences. It will be seen that both spatial and temporal scales overlap at a number of levels and meet at the evolutionary, or speciation level. Extrinsic, biotic modification of intrinsic variation may also be manifested in a third source of variation—that of variation in biological activity or target specificity of nutritionally and allelochemically important components.

Table I summarizes the types of nutritional and putative allelochemical variation found in bracken and the biological activity or significance of these compounds to the various classes of organisms with which the plant interacts; this includes bracken itself (e.g., autoallelopathic inhibition of spore germination by phenolics; Gleissman and Muller, 1972). Although there are many gaps in our knowledge of this system, it is apparent that variation operates at all spatial and temporal scales and that biological activity involves all classes of competitors, consumers, and pathogens. Therefore, caution must be exercised in attributing variation to any one cause, and analysis of ecologically significant variation to insects, for example, must be applied to the spatial and temporal scales of the insect.

A. Nutritional Variation and Effects on Insects

In general, the nutritional requirements of most insects are not markedly different from other heterotrophs, with the possible exception of their inability to synthesize sterols (Dadd, 1973; Svoboda et al., 1975). The necessary qualitative requirements of amino acids, carbohydrates, steroids, lipids, vitamins, and cofactors, minerals, and water are present in most plants (Fraenkel, 1959, 1969), including bracken. Proteins (Moon and Pal, 1949), amino acids (Smith and Agiza, 1951), carbohydrates (Williams and Foley, 1976), lipids (Jarvis and Duncan, 1974, 1975), nucleotide sugars (Duncan and Jarvis, 1976), and steroids such as β-sitosterol, stigmast-4-en-3-one, and stigmasta-3,6-dione (Kuroyanagi et al., 1974a), do not appear to be atypical. The few studies on the nutritional quality of bracken and bracken silage for ruminants indicate that toxicity rather than qualitative absence of components is responsible for poor growth and survivorship of mammals (Ferguson and Armitage, 1944; Smith and Fenton, 1944; Moon and Pal, 1949; Hunter, 1953).

The qualitative argument that "all plants are green" does not explain insect host specificity or differential growth and utilization efficiencies on different host plants (e.g., Hodge, 1933; Soo-Hoo and Fraenkel, 1966;

Table I

Sources of Quantitative and/or Qualitative Variation in Phytochemicals of Bracken Fern and Their Biological Activity as *Direct* Impact on Physical, Physiological, Biochemical, or Behavioral Characteristics of Organisms[a]

Chemical class of compound	Molecules	Conjugated molecules	Organelles	Cells	Tissues	Organs	Biochemical class	Biochemical class	Cell	Tissue	Organ	Plant
			Between (Spatial)						Within			
Nutritional chemical												
Protein	√	√	(√)	(√)	(√)	?	?					√
Amino acids	√	√	(√)	(√)	(√)	?	?	(√)	(√)			√
Nucleic acids	√	(√)	(√)	(√)	(√)	(√)	(√)					√
Carbohydrates (mobile)	√	(√)	(√)	(√)	(√)	(√)	(√)					√
Carbohydrates (reserve)	√	(√)	(√)	(√)	(√)	(√)						√
Water	x	x	(√)	(√)	(√)	(√)						√
Inorganic ions	x	(√)	(√)	(√)	(√)							√
Lipids	√	(√)	(√)	?	?							√
Steroids	√	?	(√)	?	?	(√)						√
Ecdysteroids	√	√	?	?	?							√
Putative allelochemical												
Silica	x	(√)	(√)	(√)	?							√
Lignin	√	?	(√)	(√)	?							√
Condensed tannins	√	√	(√)	(√)	?							√
Cinnamic acids	√	√	?	?	?							√
Benzoic acids	√	√	?	?	?							√
Flavonols	√	√	?	?	?							√
Pterosins	√	√	?	?	?							√
Cyanogenic glycoside	x	x	(√)	(√)	(√)							√
β-Glucosidase	?	?	(x)	(√)	(√)							√
Oxynitrilase	?	?	?	(√)	?	(√)						√
Thiaminase	?	?	(x)	√	(√)	?	√	(√)				
Ant nectar	x	(√)	(√)	(√)	?	√	√					
Lactam	x	(√)	(√)	(√)	?	?	√					
Mutagen	?	?	?	?	?	√						

		Plants	Microhabitat (e.g., shade/open)
		Plants	Population
		Populations	Geographic region
		Geographic regions	Variety
		Varieties	Species

Temporal

		Day/night	24 hr
		Months	Season
		Seasons	—

Biological activity

		Bracken	
		Other plants	
		Microorganisms	
		Invertebrates	
		Vertebrates	

[a]See text for references. Key to symbols: √, Variation shown to occur; x, variation shown not to occur; (√), variation expected to occur, based on other systems; (x), variation expected not to occur, based on other systems; ?, variation unknown; −, biological activity determined to have negative effect; •, biological activity determined to have negative effect, based on other systems; (−), biological activity expected to have negative effect, based on other systems; 0, biological activity determined to have no effect; (0), biological activity expected to have no effect, based on other systems; •, biological activity determined to have positive effect; (•), biological activity expected to have positive effect, based on other systems; ?, biological activity effect unknown.

Bernays *et al.*, 1975; Scriber, 1978a, 1979). Although allelochemicals may explain many of these phenomena, there is growing evidence that plants are frequently nutritionally suboptimal (Gordon, 1961; van Emden, 1972; Southwood, 1973), particularly with respect to the quantity of nitrogen, vitamins, water, and amino acids (van Emden, 1972; Dadd, 1973; Scriber, 1978b; Scriber and Feeny, 1979). Although bracken may not be qualitatively nutritionally deficient, there are marked quantitative changes in crude protein and nitrogen (see Lawton, 1976, for summary of references; Watt, 1976), carbohydrates (Williams and Foley, 1976), water (Williams and Foley, 1976; Jones, 1977), certain ions (Ca^{2+}, K^+; Watt, 1976; Fig. 1), and amino acids over the growing season. Studies by J. Lawton (personal communication) indicate that several essential amino acids, notably methionine, lysine, histidine, and tryptophan, are very low or undetectable in late May. Lysine, histidine, and tryptophan levels rise in July and are present in reasonable quantities by the end of the summer. Proline, a potential methionine substitute, is present until June, whereupon it decreases to undetectable levels. Furthermore, a number of unidentified (potentially nonprotein amino acids; see Rosenthal and Bell, 1979) also occur. Thus, although nutritional quality may be adequate, nutritional quantity declines from early May onward. Such quantitative changes could markedly affect the spatial and temporal distribution of the adapted insect community. The aphid *Macrosiphum ptericolens* tends to move up the plant onto successively higher pinnae as the season progresses before becoming very abundant on lower, senescent pinnae later in the season (J. Lawton, personal communication). This insect may be chasing soluble nitrogen, as has been demonstrated for some aphids on Brassicaceae (van Emden, 1972). To elucidate the relative importance of variation in nutritional quality and quantity of bracken will require detailed studies of the growth and utilization efficiencies of the different bracken insects, at different times over the growing season, on different parts of the plant.

B. Allelochemical Variation and Effects on Insects

In contrast to the relative dearth of information on nutritional components, bracken allelochemistry has received more attention than that for most plants, probably as a consequence of its agricultural and medical importance (Braid, 1959; I. A. Evans, 1976; W. C. Evans, 1976). The diversity of biochemical classes and biological activities is considerable (see Table I). Most of the bracken compounds have been tentatively implicated in plant–insect interactions. These compounds are steroidal insect molting hormone mimics (the phytoecdysteroids); the structural components silica and lignin, the latter of phenolic origin; the phenolics,

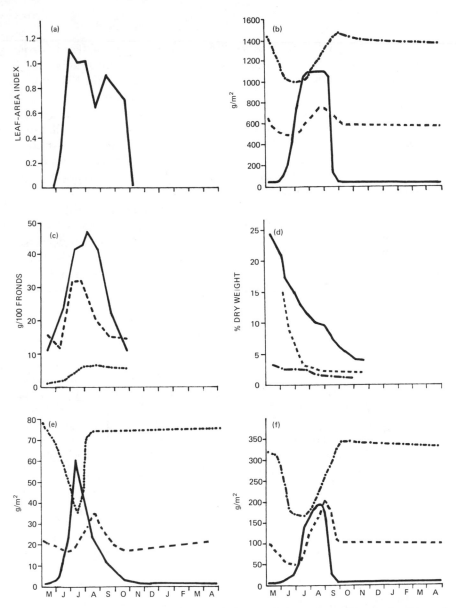

Fig. 1. Seasonal variation in architectural characteristics and nutritional chemistry of bracken fern. (a) Frond area as projected area of foliage per unit ground area. After Lawton (1976) and Roberts *et al.* (1980). (b) Dry weight. Fronds and buds (——), frond-bearing rhizome (– – –), storage rhizome (–·–·–). After Williams and Foley (1976). (c) Inorganic ions. Fronds: potassium (——), [phosphorus] × 10 (– – –), calcium (–·–··–). After Watt (1976). (d) Crude protein. Frond (——), rachis (– – –). After Lawton (1976). Nitrogen. Frond (–·–··–). After Watt (1976). (e) Mobile carbohydrates. Fronds and buds (——), frond-bearing rhizome (– – –), storage rhizome (–·–··–). After Williams and Foley (1976). (f) Reserve carbohydrates. Fronds and buds (——), frond-bearing rhizome (– – –), storage rhizome (–·–··–). After Williams and Foley (1976). (a) Copyright, in part, 1980, Blackwell Scientific Publications, Ltd.

including condensed tannins, flavonols, and their glycosides, benzoic and cinnamic acids and their derivatives; the sesquiterpene indan-1-ones or pterosins; the cyanogenic glycoside, prunasin; the enzyme thiaminase I; the sugar-producing axillary nectaries; and miscellaneous components such as a lactam (Takatori et al., 1972) and an unidentified mutagen (I. A. Evans, 1976). The variation and biological activity of all but the miscellaneous compounds will be examined in detail. Because most studies have been carried out on nonadapted insects, specific chemical effects on the adapted insect community are inferred in most cases and must remain speculative at present.

There are two distinct trends in the seasonal variation of these compounds in fronds—those that increase as the season progresses (phytoecdysteroids, silica, lignin, and some phenolics) and those that decrease (sesquiterpenes, cyanide, thiaminase, and ant nectaries; see Figs. 2 and 3). Although at first sight these patterns appear to be similar to the quantitative–apparent, qualitative–unapparent divisions made by Feeny (1976), it will be seen that the complexity of chemical variation and the interaction of environment and plant physiology with herbivores make such a division for bracken overly simplistic.

1. Phytoecdysteroids

There are five of these polyhydroxy sterols in bracken (Fig. 4). Ecdysone (α-ecdysone) and ecdysterone (β-ecdysone, crustecdysone) are insect molting hormone homologs and are the major components. Pterosterone, ponasterone A, and its glycoside, ponasteroside A, are structural analogs and are minor components (Kaplanis et al., 1967; Takemoto et al., 1968; Hikino et al., 1969). It is likely that they occur naturally in the glycosidic form, (e.g., ponasteroside A). Phytoecdysteroids were first isolated from fronds but are also known to occur in the rhizome (C. G. Jones, unpublished results) and in the thallus of the gametophyte generation (McMorris and Voeller, 1971). Bracken is not unique in containing phytoecdysteroids. Over 38 different structures have been found in 83 different families of angiosperms, gymnosperms, and pteridophytes (see Jones and Firn, 1978).

The initial discovery of ecdysteroids in plants (Nakanishi et al., 1966) led to the hypothesis that these insect molting hormone analogs and homologs evolved as defenses against insect attack (Galbraith and Horn, 1966; Staal, 1967). This hypothesis seems eminently reasonable, given their well known developmental role in insects (Hikino and Hikino, 1970). Reports that crude extracts of phytoecdysteroids had physiological activity in plants similar to that of the endogenous plant growth regulators, the gibberellins (Carlisle et al., 1963; Matsuoka et al., 1969), were not substantiated by work with pure ecdysteroids (Hendrix and Jones, 1972). These compounds were also reported not to have any effect on

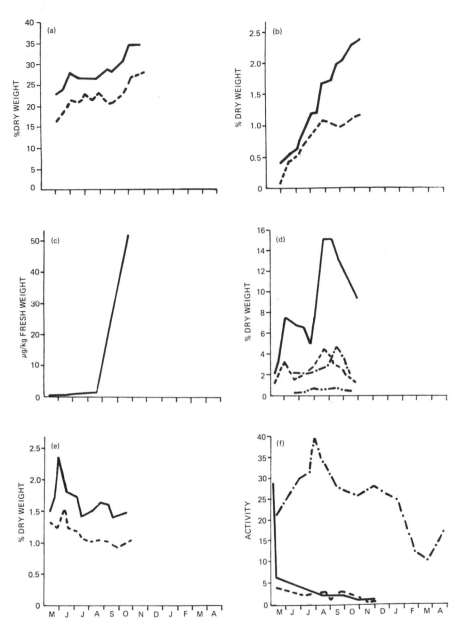

Fig. 2. Seasonal variation in allelochemicals of bracken fern. (a) Lignin. Frond (——), rachis (– – –). After Lawton (1976). (b) Silicate. Frond (——), rachis (– – –). After Lawton (1976). (c) Phytoecdysteroids. Fronds. After Jones and Firn (1978). (d) Condensed tannins. Frond (–··–··–), rachis (–···––···–). After Lawton (1976). Frond—open (——), frond—shade (– – –). After Cooper-Driver *et al.* (1977). (e) Flavonoids. Frond—open (——), frond—shade (– – –). After Cooper-Driver *et al.* (1977). (f) Thiaminase. As micrograms of thiamine destroyed per minute per gram dry weight. Frond (——), rachis (– – –), rhizome (–·–··–). After W. C. Evans (1976). (c) Copyright 1978, Plenum Publishing Corp. (d), (e) Copyright, in part, 1977, Pergamon Press, Ltd.

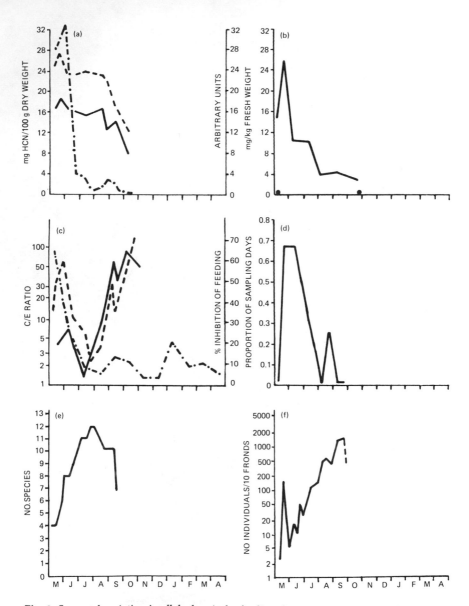

Fig. 3. Seasonal variation in allelochemicals, feeding-deterrent activity, ant activity, insect diversity, and insect abundance for bracken fern. (a) Cyanogenesis (populational). As micrograms of HCN per gram dry weight. Frond (–·—·–). After Lawton (1976). Cyanogenesis in an individual pinna. As arbitrary units. Pinna—open (——), pinna—shade (– – –). After Cooper-Driver *et al.* (1977). (b) Pterosin F. Frond (——), rhizome (●). After Jones and Firn (1979a). (c) Feeding-deterrent activity. As log of the C/E ratio divided by 2 times dry weight of frond-extracted equivalents (g) per milliliter methanol. Against *Pieris brassicae* (Lepidoptera) (–·—·–). After Jones and Firn (1979a). As percentage inhibition of feeding of *Schistocerca gregaria* (Orthoptera), compared to feeding on *Agropyron repens*: frond—open (——), frond—shade (– – –). After Cooper-Driver *et al.* (1977). (d) Ant activity at nectaries. As proportion of sampling days on which ants were recorded visiting axillary

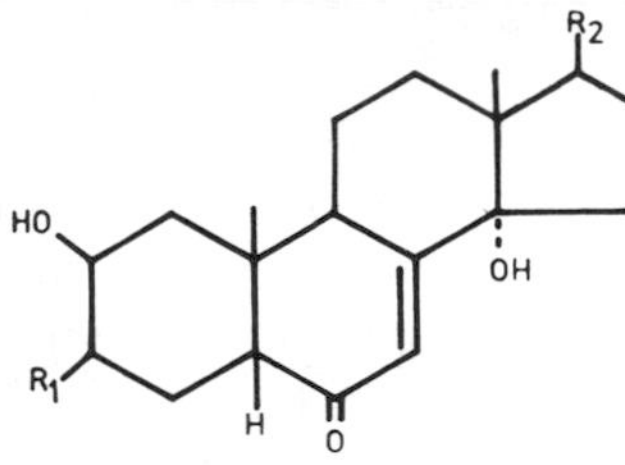

Phytoecdysteroids	R_1	R_2
Ecdysone	OH	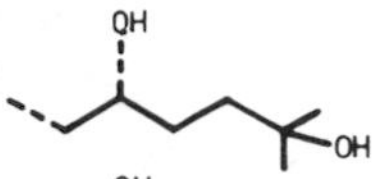
Ecdysterone	OH	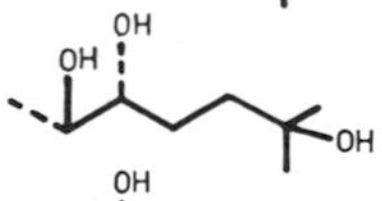
Ponasterone	OH	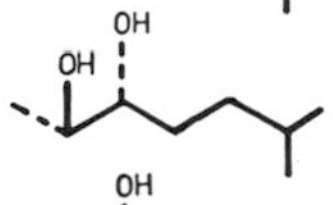
Ponasteroside	*O*-Glucose	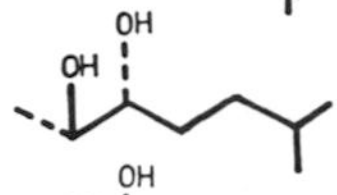
Pterosterone	OH	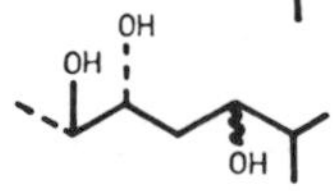

Fig. 4. Structural variation in bracken phytoecdysteroids.

flowering (Jacobs and Suthers, 1971), spore germination (McMorris and Voeller, 1971), vertebrate metabolism (Burdette, 1974; Ogawa *et al.*, 1974), or fungal growth (Jones, 1977). This evidence would substantiate a relatively target-specific mode of action against insects.

Bracken is the only plant for which the phytoecdysteroid insect defense hypothesis has been realistically assessed (Jones and Firn, 1978). Frond concentrations of ecdysone and ecdysterone are exceptionally low throughout the growing season (<0.3 μg/kg fresh wt, Fig. 2c) until October, when peak levels of 53 μg/kg fresh wt occurred. It should be noted that October is effectively the end of the season for bracken insects in Britain (Fig. 3e,f; Lawton, 1976). The highest frond concentrations were 10^{-3} and 10^{-6} that of the lowest levels known to have an adverse

nectaries. After Lawton (1978). (e) Insect diversity. As six seasons of data on a small patch of bracken. After Lawton (1978). (f) Insect abundance. For all herbivorous insects, one season of data (log). After Lawton (1976). (a)–(c) Copyright, in part, 1977, 1979, Pergamon Press, Ltd. (d), (e) Copyright 1978, Blackwell Scientific Publications, Ltd.

effect on phytophagous insect growth and development following ingestion of these materials.

The reasons why ingested phytoecdysteroids appear to have little or
no effect on phytophages is probably two-fold. First, insects have to
regulate endogenous ecdysteroid titres, and enzymes for converting these
hormones to more polar metabolites are present in the hemolymph at
certain times (King and Siddall, 1974; Nigg et al., 1974; Hikino et al.,
1975). These enzymes could rapidly metabolize exogenous ecdysteroids,
should they reach the hemolymph. The desert locust Schistocerca gregaria
can ingest large amounts of these compounds with little or no effect,
excreting polar metabolites (Carlisle and Ellis, 1968). Second, unlike most
steroids, ecdysteroids are polyhydroxy, polar compounds. Consequently, they have a reduced lipophilicity, compared to, say, cholesterol,
and may not be expected to be passively transported across the gut
membrane to the hemolymph.

Of course, it is possible that insects incapable of metabolizing large
quantities of these compounds and having membrane transport systems
that enable phytoecdysteroids to enter the hemolymph could be adversely affected. For these insects, the ability to recognize and avoid
phytoecdysteroid-containing materials might be selectively advantageous. Although a number of insects are deterred from feeding on their
host plants that have been treated with ecdysone and ecdysterone (Jones
and Firn, 1978) or from drinking ecdysteroid solutions (Schoonhoven
and Derksen-Koppers, 1973), the dose response curves show that deterrent concentrations are, at best, 10^{-1}–10^{-3} that of the highest levels
found in bracken frond. It would appear that phytoecdysteroids alone
are not an effective frond defense to nonadapted insects. This is not to
say that these compounds did not originally evolve as defenses or that
they may be effective against some insects, especially for plants that
contain much higher concentrations (see Jones and Firn, 1978, Table 4).

Interestingly, the predominant phytoecdysteroids in plants are the
insect molting homologs, ecdysone and ecdysterone, rather than the
inhibitory analogs. These analogs (e.g., cyasterone, inokosterone, and
ponasterone A) do occur, but they do not appear to be as widely distributed or quantitatively abundant as the homologs. If phytoecdysteroids were a highly effective defense, one would perhaps expect selection
to favor inhibitory analogs rather than homologs. Ecdysteroid within-
plant distribution may also be important. Bracken rhizome contains levels of ecdysteroids that are far higher than fronds (C. G. Jones, unpublished results), and these concentrations may be effective against insects
or nematodes that might attack the subterranean rhizome. It is notable
that many phytoecdysteroid-containing plants have the highest concentrations in bark, roots, or rhizomes. Perhaps, then, the peak of ecdy-

steroids in October fronds may be the consequence of a metabolic "spillover" from the rhizome system at the end of the frond growing season.

Although further studies of these compounds in other plant systems are sorely needed, two important points do emerge. First, apparent target specificity of any compound does not necessarily guarantee activity against that target, particularly because insects can adapt so rapidly. Second, spatial and temporal variation in components such as ecdysteroids do not necessarily guarantee ecological significance to a target. Thus structural variation, seasonal variation, interplant variation, and populational variation (bracken in Britain contains lower levels of frond ecdysteroids than bracken in Japan and North America; Kaplanis *et al.*, 1967; Hikino *et al.*, 1969; Jones and Firn, 1978; although these levels are still too low to have marked effects) all take place, and yet these variations may arise from intrinsic sources (i.e., genotypic or senescence-related ones) that are not necessarily of significance to the insect. Therefore, although chemical variation may provide a pool upon which natural selection may operate, the presence of variation is not an assurance that selection has operated or operates in that instance.

2. Silica and Lignin

These two components are structurally and biochemically distinct (lignins are phenolic, silica is inorganic), but they may be functionally similar. Lignin concentrations increase over the growing season in both stem and frond (Fig. 2a; Ferguson and Armitage, 1944). Silica also shows a similar pattern with season (Fig. 2b; Ferguson and Armitage, 1944; Moon and Pal, 1949). The role of these compounds as structural components of cell walls is well known, and the seasonal increase in concentrations is compatible with an increasing need for plant support. However, these materials do continue to increase in concentration after frond expansion and stem growth ceases in August. Because these compounds are important components of secondary, xylem, and phloem cell walls, inter- and intracellular variation in their distribution would be expected to occur.

Although little is known of the effect of these compounds on bracken insects, it is possible that silica and lignin increase plant toughness in a manner similar to that found in other systems (Sasamoto, 1961; Djamin and Pathak, 1967; Blum, 1968). This physical phenomenon would be expected to affect bracken insects in different ways, based on feeding locale, time, and mode. Because a number of bracken insects do feed in the late season (see Lawton, 1976), it must be assumed that these organisms are adapted to any increased toughness. These adaptations could include modified mandibles in chewers, mining and boring modes

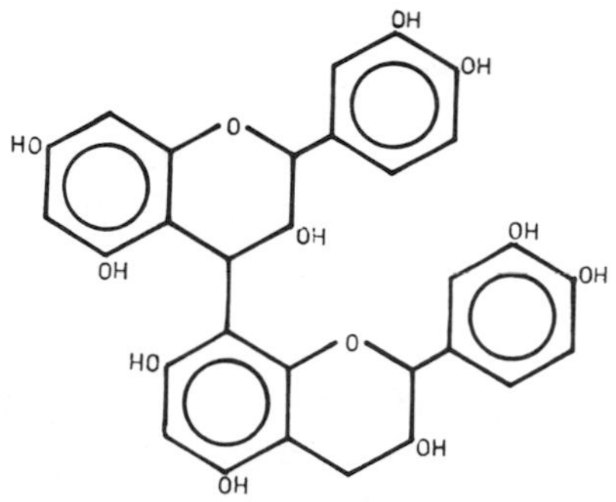

Fig. 5. Structure of proanthocyanidin dimer of bracken condensed tannin.

of feeding, modified stylets in sucking insects, and modification of plant tissues by gall formers. One interesting possibility is that soluble silicic acid could act as a feeding inhibitor, as has been suggested for delphacid plant hoppers on rice (Yoshihara *et al.*, 1979). In this example, silicic acid is invoked as a reason for the localized feeding behavior of the delphacids. Thus the suggestion that the changes in feeding site of the bracken aphid *Macrosiphum* are related to soluble nitrogen (see previous discussion) may be equally applicable to the occurrence of soluble feeding inhibitors such as silica. The study of Yoshihara *et al.* (1979) indicates that the assumption that sucking insects avoid many defensive compounds by virtue of their absence in phloem tissues (e.g., Lawton, 1976) is not necessarily true. There is evidence suggesting that aphids ingest a wide variety of compounds from phloem, including phenolic acids, plant growth regulators (Hussain *et al.*, 1974; Dixon, 1975), sterols, and pentacyclic triterpenes (B. Campbell, personal communication).

3. Condensed Tannins

Bracken contains condensed tannins, oligomers derived from the anthocyanins, procyanidin, and prodelphinidin (Fig. 5; Voirin, 1970). Concentrations in fronds increase over the season, but then decline in September–October (Fig. 2d; Moon and Pal, 1949; Cooper-Driver *et al.*, 1977; Tempel, 1981). Stem levels do not change markedly (Moon and Pal, 1949). Similar patterns have been shown to occur in other plants (Feeny and Bostock, 1968; Dement and Mooney, 1974). Concentrations also differ in shaded and bracken in the open (Cooper-Driver *et al.*, 1977), with higher levels in the open (Fig. 2d). This source of variation is also known for other plant systems (e.g., Hillis and Swain, 1959). Two further sources of variation may also take place. These are microdistributional variation in the vacuolar deposition of tannins, as is known to occur in other systems (e.g., Parham and Kaustinen, 1976, 1977; H.

Larew, personal communication on microdistribution of tannins in gall tissues), and changes in the molecular size and solubility of tannin oligomers, probably increasing in size in late season (Bate-Smith, 1975; Haslam et al., 1977). The increased oligomeric sizes may be responsible for reduced solubility, thus the reduced extraction efficiency and hence the apparent decline in tannin levels in September–October (Cooper-Driver et al., 1977). Because these different oligomers would be expected to have different chemical properties, their activity against herbivores may also vary.

Although early studies indicated that some insects are stimulated to feed by tannins (Grevillius, 1905), the widespread distribution of tannins in plants and their ability to complex with protein (Goldstein and Swain, 1965) led to the theory that tannins are a broad-spectrum antiinsect defense. These compounds are known to reduce available nitrogen for some insects (Feeny, 1968, 1970) and to be toxic to a number of insects (e.g., Bennett, 1965; Bernays and Chapman, 1977). However, there is now increasing evidence that these "quantitative" defenses (Feeny, 1976; Rhoades and Cates, 1976) are subject to insect adaptation, like any other defense system.

Insects differ widely in their response to dietary tannins. Polyphagous acridids do not appear to be adversely affected by hydrolyzable tannins at concentrations up to 20% dry-weight diet, whereas graminivorous species do show reduced growth rates and survivorship (Bernays et al., 1980). Condensed tannins had no adverse effect on growth or survivorship of a polyphagous or graminivorous acridid (Bernays, 1978), despite the fact that at low concentrations (0.1% dry wt) they depress feeding (E. A. Bernays, personal communication. In Cooper-Driver, 1976). Larvae of Pieris brassicae are also deterred by low concentrations of condensed tannins (Jones and Firn, 1979b). Similarly, the growth of certain Eucalyptus chrysomelids does not appear to be adversely affected by condensed tannins in the host plant (Fox and MacAuley, 1977; MacAuley and Fox, 1980). Growth of Lymantria dispar larvae (Lepidoptera) was inhibited at 0.1% dry-weight mixed tannins, but this growth inhibition did not increase with increasing tannins up to 10% dry-weight diet, and larval susceptibility to tannins decreased with increasing larval age (M. Montgomery, personal communication).

The adaptive mechanisms of insects to tannins are now beginning to be understood. Many leaf-feeding Lepidoptera and aquatic leaf-shredding insects have an alkaline gut pH (Berenbaum, 1979; Martin et al., 1980), and it is known that alkaline pH reduces or prevents tannin-protein complexes, especially in the presence of Ca^{2+} ions (Gadal and Boudet, 1965; Goldstein and Swain, 1965; Loomis and Battaile, 1966; Martin et al., 1980). Acridids must possess another mechanism, because their gut pH is neutral or acidic (Bernays, 1978). Studies by Bernays (1981) suggest that this mechanism involves the posterior portion of the alimentary canal, which is pocketed with caecae lined with peritrophic membranes. These regions rapidly take up water and accumulate macromolecules such as tannins. In this way the compounds are "packaged away from the midgut lumen" and can be "excreted in the peritrophic membrane enveloping the faecal pellets" (Bernays, 1981, p. 5).

The role of tannins in bracken is perhaps more enigmatic than the purely antiherbivore role suggested for these "quantitative" defenses (Feeny, 1976). Balick et al., (1978) could find no correlation between field measurements of herbivory and tannin content for ferns, including bracken. Lawton (1982) showed that more insects attack British bracken when it grows in the open than in the shade under trees, despite the fact that tannin content is lower in the shade. However, the reverse is true for bracken in Arizona and New Mexico (i.e., more insects in the shade, where tannins are lower). Tempel (1981) showed that, at best, only 25% of the variation ($r = 0.503$) in herbivore damage could be explained by variation in tannin concentration, and only for those fronds escaping damage until maturity. The data of Lawton (1982) and Tempel (1981) strongly suggest that environmental factors (e.g., water stress; Tempel, 1981) are of greater importance than herbivory in determining the variation in distribution and abundance of tannins.

It is clear that the mode of action of chemically distinct tannin types and oligomeric units, their distribution and plant physiological roles, and insect digestive physiology are all areas requiring further study before tannins can be implicated as broad-spectrum defenses against insects. However, is it still pertinent to ask why plants contain such high concentrations when insect growth inhibition is maximal at low concentrations. If, as suggested by Feeny (1976) and Rhoades and Cates (1976), these compounds are "costly" to make, production of high concentrations of tannins as purely antiinsect defenses would be counteradaptive. Perhaps these compounds are not costly to produce, and/or the cost is shared between environmentally related physiological roles, possibly antimicrobial (Cooper-Driver et al., 1977) or antimammalian roles, as well as antiinsect activity. If this turns out to be the case it will necessitate a reconsideration of the qualitative–quantitative apparency or predictability theories.

4. Flavonols

Bracken contains at least five flavonols, all of which probably occur naturally in the glycosidic form (Fig. 6; Nakabayashi, 1955; Voirin, 1970; Swain and Cooper-Driver, 1973; Wang et al., 1973). These compounds are the glycosides astragalin, rutin, isoquercetin, and tiliroside, and the aglycone quercetin. This structural variation within a biochemical class

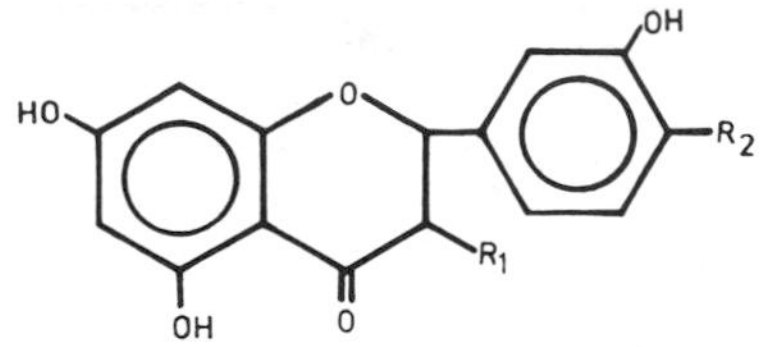

Compound	R_1	R_2
Quercetin	OH	OH
Isoquercetin	O-Glucose	OH
Rutin	O-Gluco-rhamnose	OH
Astragalin	O-Glucose	H
Tiliroside	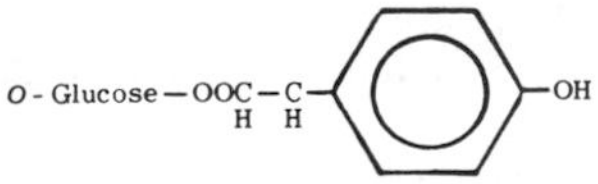 O - Glucose — OOC — C H₂ —〔ring〕— OH	H

Fig. 6. Structural variation in bracken flavonols and glycosides.

appears to be characteristic of the flavonoids (including phenolic acids), hence their use as chemosystematic indicators (Harborne, 1967; Swain and Cooper-Driver, 1973), but the ecological significance of this variation is unknown. Seasonal variation profiles for individual flavonols are not known, but total flavonoids increase slightly in early season before declining in July to a relatively constant level (Fig. 2e; Cooper-Driver *et al.*, 1977). As with condensed tannins, concentrations of flavonoids in bracken growing in the open are higher than in those in the shade. This microhabitat-related variation is almost certainly a reflection of increased plant productivity in the open. Bracken in the open has a greater stem density and plant height than shade bracken. It is important to note that if these microhabitat differences are of significance to bracken insects (cf. Klammath weed; Huffaker and Kennett, 1959), the phenomenon may be a recent one. Prior to man's forest-clearing activities in Neolithic Britain, bracken was predominantly a shade, woodland species (Watt, 1976).

Flavonols are known to show a diversity of biological activities against insects; these include feeding stimulation, feeding deterrence, and growth inhibition (Hedin *et al.*, 1974; Beck and Reese, 1976). This is true for the bracken flavonols. For example, quercetin and rutin both inhibit feeding of *Locusta migratoria* (Bernays and Chapman, 1977), whereas quercetin and related glycosides stimulate feeding in the boll weevil (Hedin *et al.*, 1968) and isoquercetin incites feeding in *Bombyx mori* (Hanamura *et al.*, 1962). This variation in effect also extends to responses of one species to the bracken flavonols. Jones and Firn (1979b) showed that although rutin and quercetin stimulate feeding in *Pieris brassicae*, astragalin has

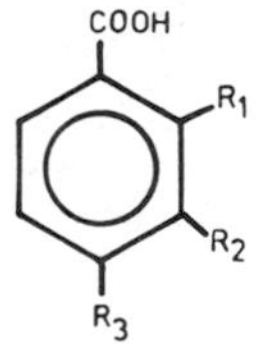

Acid	R_1	R_2	R_3
Benzoic	H	H	H
p-Hydroxybenzoic	H	H	OH
Protocatechuic	H	OH	OH
Vanillic	H	OCH$_3$	OH

Fig. 7. Structural variation in bracken benzoic acids.

no effect, and tiliroside is inhibitory. It is interesting to note that tiliroside has a cinnamic acid moiety attached to the flavonol nucleus and that this acid is, by itself, inhibitory to *P. brassicae*. The structure–activity relationships suggest that changes in the flavonol moiety are responsible for changes in activity, not the presence or absence of different sugars.

Because the responses of a single insect species may vary when exposed to these different compounds, it is difficult to assess their overall impact to adapted or nonadapted insects. It is worth noting that the quantitative activity of these compounds, based on dose–response curves, is less than that of other phenolics or other bracken chemicals (Jones and Firn, 1979a,b), and seasonal variation in flavonoids does not follow the seasonal variation in deterrent activity to insects as closely as some other compounds (cf. Fig. 3c and Cooper-Driver *et al.*, 1977; Jones and Firn, 1979a). Furthermore, the known antimicrobial and physiological activities of flavonoids (McClure, 1976) would suggest that a purely antiinsect defensive role for flavonoids is a potentially misleading generalization.

5. Benzoic and Cinnamic Acid Derivatives

Many of the considerations raised concerning the flavonoids are probably also true for these phenolics. Seasonal variation in the individual compounds is not known, but the seasonal flavonoid profiles (Fig. 2e; Cooper-Driver *et al.*, 1977) do include these compounds. Again, many of these compounds are demonstrably active against insects and other arthropods. These include feeling stimulation and inhibition, attraction, repulsion, and growth inhibition (Hedin *et al.*, 1974; Beck and Reese, 1976; Valiela *et al.*, 1979).

p-Hydroxybenzoic, protocatechuic, vanillic, benzoic, p-coumaric, caffeic, ferrulic, chlorogenic, and chicoric acids have all been reported from bracken (Figs. 7 and 8: Bohm and Tryon, 1967, 1968; Glass and Bohm,

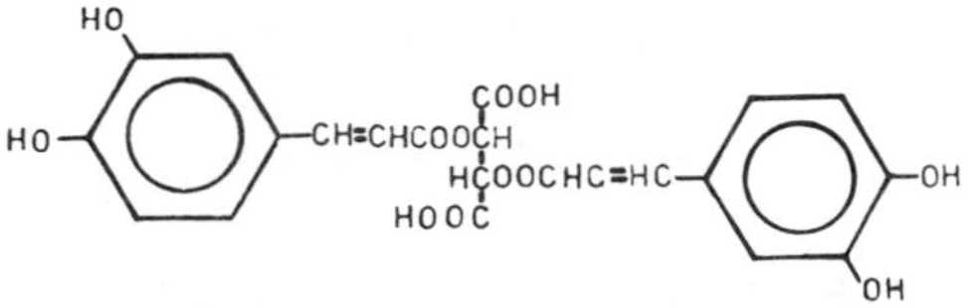

Fig. 8. Structural variation in (a) bracken cinnamic acids. Other bracken cinnamic acids: (b) chlorogenic acid, (c) dicaffeoyl-tartaric acid.

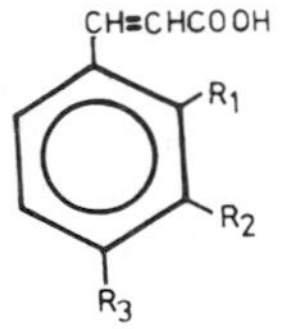

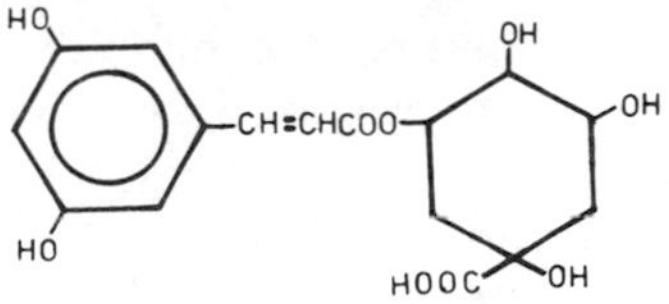

Acid	R_1	R_2	R_3
o-Coumaric	OH	H	H
p-Coumaric	H	H	OH
Caffeic	H	OH	OH
Ferulic	H	OCH_3	OH

1969a,b; Hasegawa and Taneyama, 1973; Kuroyanagi et al., 1974a; Cooper-Driver, 1976). Most have been recorded from fronds or unnamed parts of the plant, with the exception of chlorogenic acid, which is reported to occur in rhizomes (Kuroyanagi et al., 1974a) but not fronds (Bohm and Tryon, 1968). Cooper-Driver and Swain (1975) found a charged caffeic acid sulfate ester in fronds, a class of phytochemicals now being reported with increasing frequency (Harborne, 1977). Cinnamic acids appear to turn over rapidly in early frond development (May), but the benzoic acids do not show the same variation (Glass and Bohm, 1969b). Phenyl ammonia lyase activity—a key enzyme in cinnamic acid synthesis—is high at this time (Cooper-Driver, 1976). In addition to structural and seasonal variation, there are qualitative differences between bracken varieties. For example, o-coumaric and protocatechuic acids vary in their presence and absence between five varieties of bracken (Glass and Bohm, 1969a).

Feeding-deterrent activity of bracken benzoic and cinnamic acid derivatives show structurally related variation in activity in Pieris brassicae, as do the flavonols (Jones and Firn, 1979b). Generally speaking, the cinnamic acids appear to have a greater deterrent effect than the benzoic acids. However, it should be noted that synergistic effects of mixtures of these compounds may well be important. Adams and Bernays (1978) showed that although feeding of *Locusta migratoria* might not be reduced by single benzoic or cinnamic acids, additive mixtures were frequently inhibitory. This is an important aspect of chemical variation and structural diversity that is rarely considered in plant–insect interactions.

6. Sesquiterpene Pterosins

In the course of studies on the defenses of bracken against nonadapted insects, Jones and Firn (1979a) isolated a sesquiterpene indan-1-one, pterosin F (Fig. 9). Unlike the allelochemicals so far discussed, pterosin F concentrations show a marked decline with season (Fig. 3b). This seasonal pattern does closely correspond to part of the seasonal pattern in overall deterrent activity of bracken (Fig. 3c). Although pterosin F was a deterrent to five of seven insect species tested (representing four orders), the dose–response curves showed that bracken contains pterosin F at active concentrations for only two of the five species, and then only over the period May–June. This demonstrates the importance of establishing limits of variation if one wishes to indicate ecological significance.

There are other sources of variation in the pterosins. Pterosin F frond concentrations do vary from year to year, and rhizome concentrations are far lower than those in fronds (Fig. 3b; Jones and Firn, 1979a). Perhaps the greatest source of variation is that of structure. A total of 29 different pterosins have been isolated from various parts of the plant (Table II; Hikino *et al.*, 1970, 1971, 1972; Yoshihira *et al.*, 1971, 1972; Fukuoka *et al.*, 1972; Kuroyanagi *et al.*, 1974a,b). Although some of these compounds are variations on the glycone–aglycone theme, structural variation is considerable, and includes halogenated and fatty-acid-substituted compounds. Given that one of these bracken compounds is active against insects, it is not unreasonable to suppose that others may also be active. For example, fatty-acid substitution might increase membrane permeability, and halogenation—which is rare in terrestrial systems—may increase activity by virtue of reactivity.

The bracken pterosins were the first sesquiterpenes found in pteridophytes, but similar structural variation has also been found in angiosperms (e.g., sesquiterpene lactones in Compositae; Rodriguez *et al.*, 1976). To establish the ecological significance of these structural variations will necessitate detailed structure–activity studies.

7. Cyanide

Bracken contains the cyanogenic glycoside prunasin (Berti and Bottari, 1968) and a β-glucosidase enzyme, which are almost certainly compart-

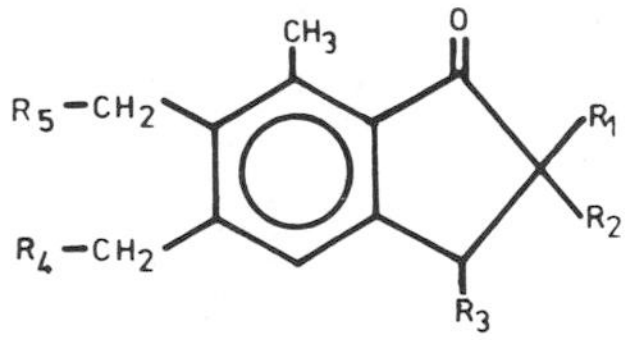

Fig. 9. Structure of sesquiterpene indan-1-one pterosin nucleus.

mentalized in cellular vacuoles, as has been found for dhurrin in *Sorghum* (Saunders *et al.*, 1977). Although the exact mechanism of cyanogenesis in bracken has not been fully established, it is probable that the process is similar to that found in other plants (Fig. 10; Conn, 1980, 1981). β-Glucosidase and glycoside mix on cellular disruption to produce the labile, alkali-unstable product mandelonitrile by hydrolysis. This product rapidly dissociates nonenzymatically at pH greater than 6 to produce benzaldehyde and gaseous HCN. However, at a pH of 5 or less, this dissociation is very slow, and an additional oxynitrilase enzyme is probably necessary (Conn, 1981). Because the pH optimum of the β-glucosidase is acidic (Conn, 1973), enzyme-free dissociation of the mandelonitrile would not take place rapidly at the same location and would require the oxynitrilase to produce gaseous HCN.

In bracken, frond cyanide levels are high in early May and decay rapidly with passage of the season (Fig. 3a; Moon and Raafat, 1951; Kofod and Eyjolfsson, 1966; Jones, 1977), in a manner similar to that known for other plants (Dement and Mooney, 1974). There is now some evidence that individual pinnae may remain cyanogenic over most of the growing season (Cooper-Driver *et al.*, 1977; Fig. 3a), declining at a much slower rate. Stem and rhizome appear to be relatively acyanogenic.

There are a number of other sources of variation in cyanogenesis that are of interest. First of all, structural variation does not occur. Bracken and most cyanogenic plants contain only one type of glycoside (Conn, 1980). This is in marked contrast to, say, sesquiterpenes, for which structural diversity is the norm. Why this should be is unknown, but I suspect that enzyme specificity and the inherent broad-spectrum activity of the active component, CN^-, as an electron-transport inhibitor may be contributory factors. Second, cyanide is microdistributed within cells; this includes the β-glucosidase enzyme, the glycoside, and, probably, the oxynitrilase. This vacuolar compartmentation is almost certainly necessary to prevent autotoxicity, especially because bracken—unlike many cyanogenic plants—does not appear to have evolved cyanide-resistant respiration (see Solomos, 1977). It may well be that this is the primary reason for the microdistribution of many plant phytochemicals.

Table II

Structural and Distributional Variation in Sesquiterpene Indan-l-One Pterosins of Bracken Fern[a]

Pterosin type	Plant part[b]	Substitution on pterosin nucleus				
		R_1	R_2	R_3	R_4	R_5
Pterosin A	F, R	CH_3	CH_2OH	H	H	CH_2OH
Pteroside A	F, R	CH_3	CH_2OH	H	H	CH_2-O-Glucose
Palmityl pterosin A	F	CH_3	CH_2OH	H	H	$CH_2OCOC_{15}H_{31}$
Acetyl pterosin A	N	CH_3	CH_2OH	H	H	CH_2OCOCH_3
Pterosin B	F, R	CH_3	H	H	H	CH_2OH
Pteroside B	F, R	CH_3	H	H	H	CH_2-O-Glucose
Benzoyl pterosin B	F	CH_3	H	H	H	$CH_2OCOC_6H_5$
Isocrotonyl pterosin B	F	CH_3	H	H	H	$CH_2OCOCH=CHCH_3$
Palmityl pterosin B	F	CH_3	H	H	H	$CH_2OCOC_{15}H_{31}$
Pterosin C	F, R	CH_3	H	OH	H	CH_2OH
Pteroside C	R	CH_3	H	OH	H	CH_2-O-Glucose
Phenyl acetyl pterosin C	F	CH_3	H	OH	H	$CH_2OCH_2C_6H_5$
Palmityl pterosin C	F	CH_3	H	OH	H	$CH_2OCOC_{15}H_{31}$
Acetyl pterosin C	F	CH_3	H	OH	H	CH_2OCOCH_3

Compound	Location[b]					
Pterosin D	F	CH_3	CH_3	OH	H	CH_2OH
Pteroside D	R	CH_3	CH_3	OH	H	CH_2-O-Glucose
Pterosin F	F, R	CH_3	H	H	H	CH_2Cl
Pterosin G	F	CH_2OH	H	H	H	CH_2OH
Pterosin J	F	CH_3	H	OH	H	CH_2Cl
Pterosin K	F	CH_3	OH	H	H	CH_2Cl
Pterosin L	F	CH_3	CH_2OH	OH	H	CH_2OH
Pterosin N	N	CH_2OH	CH_3	H	H	CH_2OH
Pterosin O	F	CH_3	CH_2OH	H	H	CH_2OH
Pterosin P	N	CH_3	H	H	OH	CH_2OH
Pteroside P	N	CH_3	H	H	OH	CH_2-O-Glucose
Pterosin Z	F	CH_3	CH_3	H	H	CH_2OH
Pteroside Z	N	CH_3	CH_3	H	H	CH_2-O-Glucose

[a] For structure of pterosin nucleus see Fig. 9. See text for references.
[b] F, Frond; R, rhizome; N, location in plant not reported.

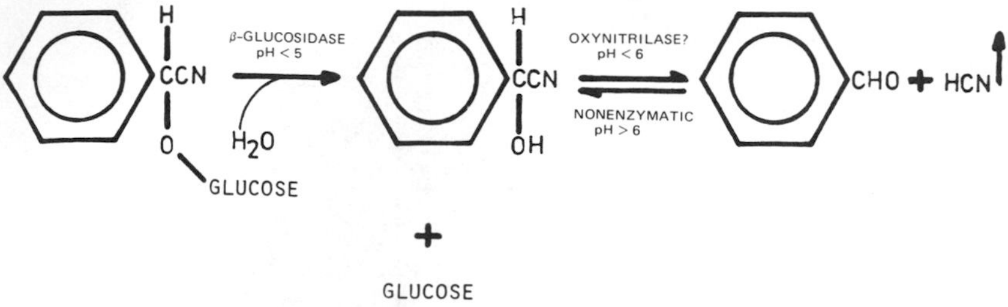

Fig. 10. Production of hydrogen cyanide from prunasin in bracken.

Third, bracken, like some other plants (notably *Lotus*; Jones, 1966) is polymorphic for cyanogenesis. Bracken may contain the glycoside, and/ or β-glucosidase enzyme, or neither (Cooper-Driver, 1976; Lawton, 1976). Populations at one site tend to have the same cyanogenic or acyanogenic character (Lawton, 1976), but there is some indication that cyanogenesis varies among plants in a population (Cooper-Driver *et al.*, 1977; Schreiner, 1980). It is not known whether the cyanogenesis in each individual plant is genetically fixed or environmentally plastic, nor whether the polymorphism also includes oxynitrilase production. Because bracken frequently grows in clonal stands, it is possible that the observed variation in cyanogenesis across a stand is genetically or environmentally plastic within a clone. Because cellular disruption and enzyme–glycoside mixing could arise from a number of circumstances (herbivores, pathogens, water stress, and frost damage), environmental plasticity in cyanogenesis could be of adaptive significance to the plant.

Bracken cyanogenesis is quantitatively higher in shade plants than in bracken in the open (Fig. 3a; Cooper-Driver *et al.*, 1977; Schreiner, 1980). This is the opposite from the flavonoids and tannins. It is conceivable that this difference is primarily related to microenvironmental conditions. Assuming for the moment that it is advantageous to the plant to maintain high cyanide concentrations as an antiherbivore defense but disadvantageous to do so where the risk of environmentally related autotoxicity is high (e.g., because of drought or frost), then one would expect cyanide levels to be higher in the shade (less water and temperature stress) than in the open. Studies by Schreiner (1980) show that the frequency of cyanogenic bracken in shaded stands is nearly twice that in sunny stands within a given geographic location. However, frequency did not differ at northern and southern geographic locations on a 600-mi transect in the northeastern United States. Obviously, further studies will be necessary before the environmental constraints influencing cyanogenesis can be clearly established.

The adaptive potential of bracken cyanide as a defense against generalist herbivores has been demonstrated (e.g., mammalian toxicity and selective grazing and deterrence to locusts; Cooper-Driver and Swain, 1976; Cooper-Driver et al., 1977; Jones, 1977). The situation for specialist insect herbivores appears more complex. Studies by Schreiner (1980) show that sawfly larvae are less numerous on cyanogenic than on acyanogenic fronds. This has been substantiated by field observations of reduced chewer damage (of which sawflies are one component) on cyanogenic fronds. Both *Strongylogaster impressata* and *S. multicinta* grew more slowly and had higher mortality when reared on cyanogenic fronds. However, aphid and lepidopteran abundance did not differ on cyanogenic and acyanogenic fronds.

This variation in activity to different adapted herbivores is to be expected. Because cyanide is compartmentalized, suckers (such as aphids), gall formers, and miners may well avoid this chemical (Lawton, 1976). In fact, observation of *Shizaphis graminum* feeding on *Sorghum* shows that the aphid avoids the cyanogen dhurrin, contained in the epidermal cells, by inserting the stylets between cells (B. Campbell, personal communication). Lepidopteran larvae provide some of the best examples of cyanide-enzyme detoxification systems in insects (e.g., rhodanase; Parsons and Rothschild, 1964; L.B. Brattsten, personal communication) and the bracken Lepidoptera may possess similar mechanisms. The situation is further complicated because bracken morphs that are β-glucosidase free and yet contain the glycoside (often termed "acyanogenic") may be capable of releasing HCN. J. Lawton and D. Howard (personal communication) have shown that ingested prunasin liberates HCN in the gut of *Pieris brassicae* by virtue of endogenous β-glucosidase activity. In this case prunasin entering the gut is converted to mandelonitrile by insect β-glucosidases active in alkaline pH, and the mandelonitrile, being alkali unstable, dissociates to HCN and benzaldehyde. Interestingly, *Pieris brassicae* larvae are not deterred by prunasin or mandelonitrile (Jones and Firn, 1979b), despite the release of HCN in the gut. It is conceivable that the mechanisms for processing toxic allylisothiocyanates in this insect preadapt the organism for detoxifying cyanide.

Thus for cyanide to function as a defense against bracken insects is a result of at least six factors.

1. The insect must encounter a cyanogenic frond which involves host-plant selection and plant environmental constraints such as shade versus open.
2. The insect must damage tissues that contain the cyanogen.
3. The frond must contain the glycoside and the β-glucosidase and oxynitrilase for gaseous HCN to be released at biting if the buccal cavity

pH is in the acidic or neutral range. If the buccal cavity pH is alkaline, then HCN may not be released.

4. If gaseous HCN in the vicinity of the mouthparts has no effect on behavior, it is unlikely that the doses received in this form would be toxic, because the HCN would rapidly dissipate.

5. Ingested glycoside will release HCN in an acidic or neutral gut only if the plant β-glucosidase and oxynitrilase are present or if the insect β-glucosidases are active at acidic or neutral pH and plant oxynitrilase is present. Ingested glycoside will release HCN in an alkaline gut pH irrespective of plant β-glucosidase and oxynitrilase, provided that the insect β-glucosidases hydrolyze the aglycone–sugar β-glucoside bond.

6. Liberated HCN will be potentially toxic to the insect only if no detoxification–binding system occurs, and a sufficient dose is received.

Given that variation in these plant and insect characteristics is known to occur in the bracken system, considerable caution must be exercised in drawing correlations between the presence–absence–quantity of cyanide and the amount of damage bracken receives.

8. Thiaminase

The enzyme thiaminase I (EC 2.5.12)—distinct from microbial thiaminases—appears to be restricted to certain pteridophytes, including bracken (W. C. Evans, 1976). This enzyme is responsible for antianeurin activity and avitaminosis syndromes in mammals that consume the plant (Evans et al., 1950). The enzyme causes catalytic decomposition of thiamine by nucleophilic displacement of the methylene on the pyrimidine moiety, producing pyrimidine and thiazole, at a pH optimum of 7–8 (W. C. Evans, 1976). Thiaminase activity is present in all parts of the plant, but each is quantitatively different over the growing season. Frond levels are highest in May and decline thereafter, stem levels remain low and relatively constant, and rhizome levels rise steadily over the season (Fig. 2f; W. C. Evans, 1976). The location of thiaminase synthesis and whether or not translocation of the enzyme occurs are not known. In addition to thiaminase I, other simple phenolics in bracken are capable of binding and degrading thiamine to thiols at the same pH. These compounds are isoquercetin, rutin, astragalin, and caffeic acid (see Figs. 6 and 8; Berüter and Somogyi, 1967; Somogyi, 1971; Murata et al., 1974; W. C. Evans, 1976).

Because insects require thiamine (vitamin B_1) for normal growth and development (Fraenkel, 1952), it is not unreasonable to suppose that thiaminase may be a defense against insects, especially because it is effective against vertebrates. Bracken does contain thiamine (Berti and Bottari, 1968). However, the evidence for thiaminase involvement in insects is scanty. Soo-Hoo and Fraenkel (1964) implicated thiaminase from the fern *Nephrolepis exaltata* in growth inhibition of *Prodenia* (= *Spodoptera*) larvae. Hendrix (1975) isolated a water-soluble, ether-insoluble, heat-labile fraction from bracken that was growth-inhibitory to *Trichoplusia ni* larvae. Unfortunately, Hendrix erroneously assumed that heat-stable, relatively ether-soluble and water-insoluble thiamine-binding phenolics were the only thiamine-degrading components present in bracken and concluded that thiamine degradation was not involved. In fact, the fraction that was isolated had properties very similar to those of the thiaminase I enzyme, so thiaminase could well have been involved. If thiaminase is an effective defense, there are potential insect adaptations. These could include feeding on the stem or when thiaminase levels are low, maintaining an acidic gut pH to inactivate the enzyme, utilizing symbionts to synthesize vitamin B_1 (see Koch, 1967), or obtaining the vitamin from other plants.

9. Ant Nectaries

Although this is not strictly a chemical defense, predator activity may be mediated via a chemical (carbohydrate) reward system. Bracken has axillary nectaries (Darwin, 1877), which are visited regularly by ants. Ant visitation declines from May onward (Fig. 3d; Lawton, 1978) and is correlated to nectar secretion. As seen with the phenolics, nectar production and ant visitation are higher in bracken growing in the open than in the shade (J.H. Lawton, personal communication). Lawton has also observed ants removing insects from the plant, as well as artificial baits and *Paltodora cytisella* (Lepidoptera) larvae removed from stem mines and placed on fronds.

Ant-mediated plant defenses are not unique to bracken (e.g., Janzen, 1966, 1967a,b; Bentley, 1977), but it is difficult to assess the overall impact of variation in nectar quality, quantity, and distribution on ant foraging and defensive efficacy, given the existing information. One interesting point is the high proportion of mining, boring, rolling, and gall-forming insects on bracken (Lawton, 1978). Although one cannot invoke ants as a sole reason for these feeding specializations, these feeding mechanisms do physically isolate herbivores from ant predation.

C. Genetic Variation in Bracken

Given the extensive variation in bracken nutritional components and allelochemicals, it is pertinent to ask how this variability can be maintained for a plant that may sexually reproduce infrequently and that often establishes extensive, long-lived clones. Studies by Chapman *et*

al. (1979) show that such a mechanism exists. The homosporous pteridophytes produce spores that form gametophytes, which in turn produce male and female gametes by mitotic cell division. Consequently,
all gametes produced from an individual gametophyte have identical
genotypes. Therefore, selfing produces zygotes with completely homozygous genotypes. However, there is a mechanism for storing and releasing genetic variation despite this homozygosity. Recombination
between duplicated, unlinked loci (homoeologous heterozygosity) results in genetic variation that is released through homoeologous pairing
of chromosomes at meiosis. Thus sporophytes produced through intragametophytic selfing are homozygous at the homologous-gene level but
carry homoeologous heterozygosity.

Therefore, when a single bracken spore develops into a gametophyte,
intragametophytic selfing occurs, producing a sporophyte of homologous homozygosity. Because of homoeologous pairing and crossing
over, the original colonizing spore can produce a genetically variable
population. Successful genotypes can then reproduce asexually by vegetative rhizomes, producing a series of clones arising from one individual
spore. So a stand of bracken arising from a single spore can have considerable genetic variability. The adaptive potential of such a mechanism
is obviously considerable and may explain why intrapopulational variation in, say, cyanogenesis, could take place. If, in addition, many of
the enzymes involved in allelochemical production are inducible (e.g.,
cyanogenesis), then even greater variation would be expected to occur.

III. BRACKEN DEFENSE AND THE INSECT COMMUNITY: AN OVERVIEW

The analysis of function, interaction, and influence on individual insect
adaptations will require more detailed studies of bracken chemical variation and insect response. However, the probable impact of phytochemistry can be assessed at this stage, from an overview of defensive
potential against nonadapted insects, adapted insect community structure and dynamics, phenology, and distribution of the plant.

A. The Myth of Fern Insect Resistance

It has often been assumed that the efficacy of a plant defense system
may be assessed from the number of insect species that feed on it, that
is, well-defended plants have few insects. This erroneous logic has been

applied to ferns since Victorian times (Schneider, 1892) and has, unfortunately, been perpetuated (Brues, 1920, 1946; Dethier, 1947; Soo-Hoo and Fraenkel, 1964; Kaplanis *et al.*, 1967; Carlisle and Ellis, 1968; Rees, 1971; Swain and Cooper-Driver, 1973; Huffaker, 1974; Hendrix, 1975, 1977, 1980; Balick *et al.*, 1978; Strong and Levin, 1979). Ferns "appear" to have few insects and are therefore resistant. This viewpoint is almost certainly an artifact of inadequate sampling of fern–insect communities. There are studies of a number of fern–insect associations that challenge the assumption of fern underutilization and indicate that it is based on biases of plant growth form and range and sampling effort (Lawton, 1976, 1978; Gerson, 1979; Auerbach and Hendrix, 1980). The extensive studies on bracken insects (Lawton, 1976; Kirk 1977) certainly show that this fern is not underutilized. British bracken has a total of 40 species of insects, from 8 orders, that have been recorded feeding on the plant, of which 18–20 are "key" species (Lawton, 1976). Bracken in New Guinea has at least 24 species (Kirk, 1977). In fact, bracken has about as many insect species as would be predicted for a plant of similar size, phenology, and distribution (Lawton, 1976).

Plants are subject to continuous visitation by adapted and nonadapted insects. Colonization of newly introduced plants can take place over very short evolutionary time scales (e.g., Evans, 1966; Strong, 1974; Bournier, 1977; Strong *et al.*, 1977), because of the dispersive, reproductive, and hence adaptive potential of insects. Therefore, there is no reason to suppose that the number of insect species (diversity) is directly related to the number or amount of a plant's defenses, except perhaps at the extreme ends of a resistant–susceptible gradient or in the case of an individual insect species and its host–nonhost plants. Because the natural insect community of a plant comprises adapted insects, the effects of chemistry on these insects are likely to be more subtle. Furthermore, absolute barriers against all nonadapted insects attempting to colonize are highly unlikely.

B. Defense against Nonadapted Insects

Insects do attempt to colonize bracken. J. H. Lawton (personal communication) has observed lepidopteran oviposition errors on the plant that led to larval emergence, consumption of foliage, and complete mortality. This was also true of a meloid, *Epicauta ruidosa* (Coleoptera). Jones (1977) observed starving larvae of the specialist hyponomeutid *Hyponomeuta evonymella* (Lepidoptera) attempting, unsuccessfully, to feed on bracken growing adjacent to their defoliated host plants *(Prunus padus).*

Adults of the weevils *Phyllobius pyri* and *P. argentatus* (Coleoptera) have also been observed falling off the host plant *(Betula)* onto bracken. If one accepts that colonization attempts will take place and that, sooner or later, some of these attempts will succeed, the best defense system is one that reduces the number of successful colonizations and hence the rate at which colonization occurs. This may be of considerable adaptive significance for a plant invading a new habitat, where biotic and abiotic stresses are likely to be great. Although phenology and distribution are of importance in this case, the broad-spectrum ability of a plant to repel, deter, and inhibit growth and reproduction of insects is also an important measure of this type of resistance.

Bracken does exhibit broad-spectrum insect deterrent, repellent, and toxic properties. Jones and Firn (1979a) showed that bracken extracts applied to host plants were deterrent or repellent to seven of nine species tested, representing insects from a range of host-plant specificities (specialist to generalist) and four different orders. Intact bracken deterred feeding by two remaining generalist species. Bracken was also toxic or deterrent to a number of other insects (Hendrix, 1975; Lawton, 1976; Cooper-Driver *et al.*, 1977; J. H. Lawton and D. Howard, personal communication). Deterrent activity was present at all times over the growing season but was maximal in the early year (May) and toward the end of the season (Fig. 3c; Cooper-Driver *et al.*, 1977; Jones and Firn, 1979a). This seasonal variation in activity against nonadapted insects is compatible with protection of vulnerable May croziers (damage to croziers, by cutting, frost, or insects, prior to net positive photosynthetic productivity can prevent regrowth and rhizome energy-reserve depletion; Watt, 1976; Williams and Foley, 1976) and with the seasonal changes in known allelochemicals (see Figs. 1–3). I suggest that the marked qualitative and quantitative changes in bracken allelochemistry are ultimately responsible for this broad-spectrum defensive capacity. However, one would not expect all chemical changes to correlate perfectly with defense capacity, given the intrinsic changes in the plant and the other abiotic, competitive, mammalian, and pathogen-related phenomena and variability in insect responses.

Insect colonists can come from closely related plant species or increasingly unrelated plants. Similarly, these insects may be generalists or specialists or exhibit intermediate forms of preference. Although the active components, threshold concentrations, synergistic effects, and local distribution of these compounds will affect each type of nonadapted insect in different ways, chemical variation probably influences overall colonization processes in the following ways.

1. Reduction of Identical Resources

Extensive chemical variation over space and time reduces the likelihood that an insect will find exactly the right mixture of feeding or oviposition cues at the spatial and temporal niche it attempts to occupy. This is especially true for insects coming from unrelated plants, but extensive intervarietal differences could function in the same manner. Obviously, any plant, irrespective of type or degree of chemical variation, accrues some of these benefits passively, by virtue of insect specialization.

2. Mismatch of Detoxification Capacities

Variation in chemical type and mode of action (i.e., structural and biosynthetic class) decreases the likelihood that an insect will encounter chemicals that it can detoxify at that place and time.

3. Maintenance of a Heterogeneous Resource over Time

An insect might succeed in finding a time or place on the plant that has the correct positive cues, lacks deterrents or repellents, and has chemicals that can be detoxified. However, the chances of that niche's remaining at constant suitability for a suffecient period of time for successful growth, development, and reproduction is markedly reduced if all nutritional and allelochemical characteristics are constantly changing.

4. Reduction of Detoxification Successes

Generalists, by definition, are capable of utilizing a variety of plants, and their detoxification capacity is correspondingly high (Brattsten, 1979a). In this case variation in the mode of action (i.e., structural variation within and differences between biochemical classes) reduces the likelihood of successful detoxification of all co-occurring compounds. Cases in point are the pH optima of cyanide for plant β-glucosidase (acidic), thiaminase (alkaline), and tannins (acidic) in bracken. If all three compounds were ingested simultaneously, it is unlikely that any insect system (located, say, in midgut) could inactivate all three toxins by manipulating pH or that the detoxification enzymes would be so pH insensitive that they could operate effectively over this wide pH range.

On the basis of resistance to attempted colonization, it can be seen that the adaptive benefit to a plant such as bracken of maintaining a high degree of chemical variation is to decrease the likelihood of a "good fit" between prospective colonist and plant. This argument also extends to diversity in defense against pathogens and vertebrates. Perhaps for this reason, there is no a priori rationale for assuming that this type of defense should necessarily involve selection for specific antiinsect defenses rather than broad-spectrum antibiotics. In fact, the allelochemicals of bracken and many other plants are of broad-spectrum activity (e.g., CN^-, thiaminase, silica, phenolics). Therefore, to invoke a defense as having evolved against a particular group of organisms such as insects, it is necessary to demonstrate that these organisms are most frequently responsible for selection pressures or are sufficiently distinct for natural selection to operate in a target-specific manner.

C. The Adapted Insect Community

Both abundance and species diversity of bracken insects are low early in the season, reach a maximum in August, and decline in September (Fig. 3e,f; Lawton, 1976, 1978). Thus the adapted insect community utilizes the plant at a time when the nutritional quantity is not maximal. Lawton (1976) originally suggested that this was a consequence of the diversity of allelochemicals in fronds early in the year (cyanide, pterosins, ant nectary exudates, thiaminase). A similar argument could be applied to the decline in insect abundance and diversity later in the year and the increase in other allelochemicals (phenolics, silica, lignin) and reduced levels of nutritional components. At first sight, it appears that there may be only a short exploitation window between June and August, during which insects could utilize the plant.

However, the abundance and diversity relationships are almost certainly based on more than considerations of the presence of abundant allelochemicals or low nutrient content. Because the insects are adapted to the plant there must be a certain degree of flexibility in their ability to deal with allelochemicals and nutrient availability, because these problems are always present to a greater or lesser extent. There are also temporal constraints arising from insect intrinsic growth rates and abiotic factors (e.g., temperature) that limit the time during which the plant can be utilized. Perhaps of considerable importance is size of the physical resource.

Lawton (1978) showed that there is a good correlation between the area of plant available and the number of species utilizing the plant at that time. This species–area relationship appears to hold true at the biogeographic scale, for bracken islands or stands and for the area and architectural complexity of individual plants and fronds (Lawton, 1978; Lawton and Schroeder, 1976, 1978; Rigby and Lawton, 1981). The highest coefficient of determination (r^2) between species number and area characteristics of bracken islands was 0.708 (Rigby and Lawton, 1981), when a stepwise maximum r^2 determination included area, frond density, litter dry weight, and resource availability (frond weight with time). Thus

70% of the variation in species diversity was associated with variation in these parameters. This suggests that spatial and architectural considerations of habitat heterogeneity are primary determinants of species diversity on bracken. This may also be true of insect abundance, because this follows a seasonal pattern similar to that of species diversity. The relationships of resource availability in the physical sense (i.e., area) to insect diversity for bracken appear similar to those described for other plant systems, whether the island size is a part of the plant, whole plant, or stand of plants (see MacArthur and Wilson, 1967; Janzen, 1968, 1973; Johnson and Simberloff, 1974; Simberloff, 1974; Strong, 1979; Strong and Levin, 1979; Connor and McCoy, 1979; Kuris *et al.*, 1980; Lawton *et al.*, 1981).

More recent studies (Lawton, 1983) have also shown that there is little or no convergence in the structure of the community along the area gradient from that of the biogeographic to the bracken stand. Niches that can be occupied by a particular feeding specialization (e.g., miner, roller, chewer, sucker, gall former) are often vacant or only partially filled. Lawton has envisaged that this lack of convergence reflects an absence of competition for niches on bracken as a result of natural enemies. However, this phenomenon may well also be related to chemical variation.

Because both architecture (area) and chemistry vary simultaneously, it is not possible to say whether or not chemistry is a component of phenological heterogeneity or an independent contributory factor in the 30% unexplained variation mentioned earlier. This distinction cannot be established unless it can be shown that an insect utilizes a physical niche (e.g., a piece of frond), provided the niche remains constant in availability, irrespective of any chemical changes that take place within the piece of frond. In such a case chemical variation would not be important. Alternatively, if the insect utilizes the physical niche for a period of time shorter than it remains physically constant, then other factors such as chemical variation, competition, or predation would be important.

Taking into account the species–area relationship and the lack of competition on the plant, it is now possible to visualize how chemical variation may affect the adapted insect community and keep successful colonists rare (Lawton and McNeill, 1979).

1. Type of Insect

The adapted insect community is comprised of successful representatives of attempted colonizations. A logical extension of the arguments applied to nonadapted insects can be applied to the type of successful colonist and, hence, the guild composition. Chemical variation may not have a major effect on the overall number of species, because the time scale has been sufficient for many colonists to succeed. However, chemical variation may well have a marked effect on the type of insect that succeeds and the time and place that it occupies (Lawton, 1978). Because chemical variation occurs at all spatial and temporal levels, it may well exclude insects with certain types of feeding specialization and that lack certain detoxification abilities. For example, cyanide-susceptible chewers may not be able to occupy early-season frond niches. Borers with unmodified mandibles may not be able to occupy mid- to late-season silica- and lignin-rich stem niches. Therefore, marked qualitative and quantitative variation in nutritional and allelochemical character produces a resource that requires multiple adaptations or preadaptations by insects.

If this is the case, one would not necessarily expect any strong taxonomic relatedness among insects, other than that arising from similarities in feeding mechanisms, chemical cues, and detoxification capacity. In fact, the structures of bracken communities in Britain and New Guinea show little or no taxonomic similarity (familial, generic, or ordinal), but they do show a remarkable similarity in feeding-specialization types (i.e., proportions of chewers, suckers, miners, rollers, and gall formers; Lawton, 1978). Because not all types of feeding specialization cause the same amount of fitness-related damage, the type of insect may well be one clue to the evolution of plant defenses against insects. Thus, if plants protect their vulnerable (fitness-related) parts successfully, then the adapted guild should feed more on less vulnerable parts and at less vulnerable times (cf. Feeny, 1976; Rhoades and Cates, 1976; Krischik and Denno, Chapter 14).

2. Local Specialization

Studies on other plant systems (Cates, 1980; Fox and Morrow, 1981) indicate that insects frequently exhibit a narrower range of host specificity at any particular locale than that across their range. I suggest that a major factor contributing to this local specialization is chemical variation. Within-plant, between-plant, and within-population variation over time could reduce the likelihood of a successful transfer between plants within a population, and even within a plant. Adjacent plants may well be out of chemical synchrony. Insects that may feed on, say, frond and stem across their range may be restricted to either fronds or stems at one locale, because they are chemically very different. Local specialization for chemical characteristics is compatible with insect-induced preference (Jermy et al., 1968; Ali, 1976; Hanson, 1976; Saxena and Schoonhoven, 1977; Cassidy, 1978; Barbosa et al., 1979) and induction of detoxification systems (Brattsten and Wilkinson, 1973; Brattsten et al.,

1977; Brattsten, 1979a,b). These may permit insects to adjust to a chemically variable resource, but their plasticity is almost certainly less than all chemical variation in the plant at all spatial and temporal levels.

3. Division of Niches

Lawton (1983) has suggested that the lack of convergence in bracken insect-community structure reflects a lack of competition. If this is true, then resource limitation and resource concentration do not occur. Why is there no resource concentration, and what is the significance to plant and insect? One explanation is, of course, that natural enemies (predators, parasitoids, and diseases) keep most species rare (Lawton and McNeill, 1979). This may well be the case, but phenological and chemical variation almost certainly play a role. It is certainly true that area and architectural complexity are important because they can divide up the plant, reduce niche breadth and, hence, resources available for growth and reproduction, and make location of niches more difficult. However, phenology has its limits of scale (smallest physical unit of plant used), whereas the limits of scale of chemical variation extend to the molecular level. Applying the same logic to chemical variation would result in an even greater division of niches, further reductions in niche breadth, and reduced likelihood of locating the same niche twice (either within or between plants). As a consequence, each niche may be too finely grained for resource concentration to occur and for the insect populations to build up. Because division of niches would affect location by any species, some niches may well be unoccupied. In those situations in which resource concentration did occur, competition would be expected to occur rapidly, because of the reduced size of the niche. This competition could be an additional benefit accruing to the plant.

4. Cost of Living

Homeostasis, growth and reproduction are all energy-requiring processes. Finely divided niches are more difficult to find and require a corresponding diversion of energy from growth and reproduction to what is required for locating the niche. Furthermore, niches containing one or more chemicals requiring detoxification or specialized utilization will have a higher energetic cost associated with them than a homogeneous source of nutritional compounds. It is almost certain that adapted insects do have a cost-of-living component, because their growth can be better on artificial diets than on the host-plant (see Singh, 1977) and utilization efficiencies vary between different host-plants (e.g., Beck and Reese, 1976; Scriber, 1978b). Although some of these differences almost certainly reflect nutritional components, there is no reason to suppose that adaptation to a plant automatically liberates an insect from detoxification costs. In fact, the data on tannins (see previous discussion) suggest that a cost to the insect may always be present (e.g., *Lymantria* larval growth is reduced at 0.1% dry wt of tannins, well below plant concentrations, compared to the same diet without tannins, even though the insect can feed on diets with up to 10% tannins with no further reduction in growth; M. Montgomery, personal communication). Additional allelochemicals would be expected to further divert energy from reproduction. Even if these costs are minimal in comparison to nutritional costs (Scriber, 1978b), the combinatory effect of all energy-diverting processes (location, utilization, and detoxification) is of potential adaptive significance to the plant.

IV. SUMMARY AND CONCLUSION

I have shown that there is extensive chemical variation in bracken fern and that many of the nutritional components and allelochemicals are involved in plant–insect interactions. This chemical variation affects both nonadapted insects attempting to colonize the plant and the adapted insect community. The probable major effect of chemical variation on nonadapted insects is to reduce the frequency of successful colonization, by decreasing the chances of a good chemical fit between plant and insect. Such an effect may involve chemical cues, nutritional quality and quantity, allelochemical detoxification, and reduced allelochemical constancy of niches over time. Effects of the adapted insect community probably involve determination of the type of successful colonist, the location and timing of its success (an extension of defenses against nonadapted insects), and its abundance. This probably involves regulation of insect abundance by fine division of resources, which prevents resource concentration, reducing successful transfer within and between plants by division of resources, and imparting a higher cost of living by diversifying defense type, number, and location (also see Price, Chapter 16).

One fundamental principle is seen as the major factor influencing the ecological significance of phytochemical variation. This is the phenomenon of resource heterogeneity. In this respect chemical variation may be visualized as either a subset of phenological variation or as an additional component together with phenology and distribution.

Confirmation of the role of chemical variation in increasing resource heterogeneity for insects will come only from quantitative studies of chemical changes in plants, at the ecologically relevent spatial and temporal niche of the insect. This will necessitate quantifying and qualifying the natural products chemistry of a large number of samples of small amounts of plant material. Investigators should also be aware of the importance of other biotic and abiotic interactions, the multiple role of many allelochemicals, the consequences of synergism, the necessity for detailed structure–activity studies, the consequences of chemical movement through trophic levels, and the importance of interactions between chemistry, phenology, distribution, competition, predation, parasitism, and microorganisms.

ACKNOWLEDGMENTS

I thank Lena Brattsten, Bruce Campbell, and Mike Montgomery for use of unpublished data, and John Lawton for unpublished data and critical comment.

REFERENCES

Adams, C. M., and Bernays, E. A. (1978). The effect of combinations of deterrents on the feeding behaviour of *Locusta migratoria*. *Entomol. Exp. Appl.* **23**, 101–109.

Ali, M. (1976). Studies on the induction of food preference in alfalfa ladybird, *Subcoccinella punctata* L. (Coleoptera: Coccinellidae). *Symp. Biol. Hung.* **16**, 23–28.

Auerbach, M. J., and Hendrix, S. D. (1980). Insect–fern interactions: macrolepidopteran utilization and species–area association. *Ecol. Entomol.* **5**, 99–104.

Balick, M. J., Furth, D. G., and Cooper-Driver, G. A. (1978). Biochemical and evolutionary aspects of arthropod predation on ferns. *Oecologia* **35**, 55–89.

Barbosa, P., Greenblatt, J., Withers, W., Cranshaw, W., and Harrington, E. A. (1979). Host plant preferences and their induction in larvae of the gypsy moth, *Lymantria dispar*. *Entomol. Exp. Appl.* **26**, 180–188.

Bate-Smith, E. C. (1975). Phytochemistry of proanthocyanidins. *Phytochemistry* **14**, 1107–1113.

Beck, S. D., and Reese, J. C. (1976). Insect–plant interactions, nutrition and metabolism. *Recent Adv. Phytochem.* **10**, 41–92.

Bennett, S. E. (1965). Tannic acid as a repellent and toxicant to alfalfa weevil larvae. *J. Econ. Entomol.* **58**, 372.

Bentley, B. L. (1977). The protective function of ants visiting the extrafloral nectaries of *Bixa orellana* (Bixaceae). *J. Ecol.* **65**, 27–38.

Berenbaum, M. (1979). Adaptive significance of midgut pH in larval Lepidoptera. *Am. Nat.* **115**, 138–146.

Bernays, E. A. (1978). Tannins: an alternative viewpoint. *Entomol. Exp. Appl.* **24**, 44–53.

Bernays, E. A. (1981). A specialized region of the gastric caeca in the locust, *Schistocerca gregaria*. *Physiol. Entomol.* **6**, 1–6.

Bernays, E. A., and Chapman, R. F. (1977). Deterrent chemicals as a basis of oligophagy in *Locusta migratoria* L. *Ecol. Entomol.* **2**, 1–18.

Bernays, E. A., Chapman, R. F., Cook, A. G., McVeigh, L. J., and Page W. W. (1975). Food plants in the survival and development of *Zonocerus variegatus* (L.). *Acrida* **4**, 33–46.

Bernays, E. A., Chamberlain, D., and McCarthy, P. (1980). The differential effects of ingested tannic acid on different species of Acridoidea. *Entomol. Exp. Appl.* **28**, 158–166.

Berti, G., and Bottari, F. (1968). Constituents of ferns. *Prog. Phytochem.* **1**, 589–685.

Berüter, J., and Somogyi, J. C. (1967). 3,4-Dihydroxycinnamic acid, an antithiamine factor of fern. *Experientia* **23**, 996–997.

Blum, A. (1968). Anatomical phenomena in seedlings of sorghum varieties resistant to the sorghum shootfly *(Atherigona varia soccata)*. *Crop Sci.* **8**, 388–391.

Bohm, B. A., and Tryon, R. M. (1967). Phenolic compounds in ferns. I. A survey of some ferns for cinnamic acid and benzoic acid derivatives. *Can. J. Bot.* **45**, 585–593.

Bohm, B. A., and Tryon, R. M. (1968). Phenolic compounds in ferns. III. An examination of some ferns for caffeic acid derivatives. *Phytochemistry* **7**, 1825–1830.

Bournier, A. (1977). Grape insects. *Annu. Rev. Entomol.* **22**, 355–376.

Braid, K. W. (1959). "Bracken, a Review of the Literature." Commonwealth Agricultural Bureau, Hurley, Berkshire, England.

Brattsten, L. B. (1979a). Ecological significance of mixed-function oxidations. *Drug. Metab. Rev.* **10**, 35–58.

Brattsten, L. B. (1979b). Biochemical defense mechanisms in herbivores against plant allelochemicals. *In* "Herbivores: Their Interaction with Secondary Plant Metabolites" (G. A. Rosenthal and D. A. Janzen, eds.), pp. 199–270. Academic Press, New York.

Brattsten, L. B., and Wilkinson, C. F. (1973). Induction of microsomal enzymes in the southern armyworm *(Prodenia eridania)*. *Pestic. Biochem. Physiol.* **3**, 393–407.

Brattsten, L. B., Wilkinson, C. F., and Eisner, T. (1977). Herbivore–plant interactions: mixed-function oxidases and secondary plant substances. *Science* **196**, 1349–1352.

Brues, C. T. (1920). The selection of food plants by insects, with special reference to lepidopterous larvae. *Am. Nat.* **54**, 313–332.

Brues, C. T. (1946). "Insect Dietary." Harvard Univ. Press, Cambridge, Massachusetts.

Burdette, W. J. (1974). The concept of hormonal heterophylly. *In* "Invertebrate Endocrinology and Hormonal Heterophylly" (W. J. Burdette, ed.), pp. 331–337. Springer-Verlag, New York and Berlin.

Carlisle, D. B., and Ellis, P. E. (1968). Bracken and locust ecdysones. Their effects on moulting in the desert locust, *Schistocerca gregaria*. *Science* **159**, 1472–1474.

Carlisle, D. B., Osborne, D. J., Ellis, P. E., and Moorhouse, J. E. (1963). Reciprocal effects of insect and plant growth substances. *Nature (London)* **200**, 1230.

Cassidy, M. D. (1978). Development of an induced food plant preference in the Indian stick insect, *Carausius morosus*. *Entomol. Exp. Appl.* **24**, 87–93.

Cates, R. G. (1980). Feeding patterns of monophagous, oligophagous, and polyphagous insect herbivores: the effect of resource abundance and plant chemistry. *Oecologia* **46**, 22–31.

Chapman, R. H., Klekowski, E. J., Jr., and Selander, R. K. (1979). Homoeologous heterozygosity and recombination in the fern *Pteridium aquilinum*. *Science* **204**, 1207–1209.

Conn. E. E. (1973). Cyanogenic glycosides: Their occurrence, biosynthesis and function. *Int. Dev. Res. Cent. [Monogr.] IDRC*. **IDRC–010e**, 55–63.

Conn, E. E. (1980). Cyanogenic glycosides. *Encyl. Plant Physiol., New Ser.* **8**, 461–492.

Conn, E. E. (1981). Cyanogenic glycosides. *In* "The Biochemistry of Plants" (E. E. Conn, ed.)., Vol. 7, pp. 479–500. Academic Press, New York.

Connor, E. F., and McCoy, E. D. (1979). The statistics and biology of the species–area relationship. *Am. Nat.* **113**, 791–832.

Cooper-Driver, G. A. (1976). Chemotaxonomy and phytochemical ecology of bracken. *Bot. J. Linn. Soc.* **73**, 35–46.

Cooper-Driver, G. A., and Swain, T. (1975). Sulphate esters of caffyl-*p*-coumaric-glucose in ferns. *Phytochemistry* **14**, 2506–2507.

Cooper-Driver, G. A., and Swain, T. (1976). Cyanogenic polymorphism in bracken in relation to herbivore predation. *Nature (London)* **260**, 604.

Cooper-Driver, G. A., Finch, S., Swain, T., and Bernays, E. A. (1977). Seasonal variation in secondary plant compounds in relation to the palatability of *Pteridium aquilinum*. *Biochem. Syst. Ecol.* **5**, 177–183.

Dadd, R. H. (1973). Insect nutrition: current developments and metabolic implications. *Annu. Rev. Entomol.* **18**, 382–419.

Darwin, F. (1877). The nectaries of the common brake fern. *Bot. J. Linn. Soc.* **15**, 398–409.

Dement, W. A., and Mooney, H. A. (1974). Seasonal variation in the production of tannins and cyanogenic glucosides in the chaparral shrub, *Heteromeles arbutifolia*. *Oecologia* **15**, 65–76.

Dethier, V. G. (1947). "Chemical Insect Attractants and Repellents." H. K. Lewis & Co. Ltd., London.

Dixon, A. F. G. (1975). Aphids and translocation. *Encyl. Plant Physiol., New Ser.* **1**, 154–170.

Djamin, A., and Pathak, M. D. (1967). Role of silica in resistance to Asiatic borer, *Chilo suppressalis* (Walker), in rice varieties. *J. Econ. Entomol.* **60**, 347–351.

Duncan, H. J., and Jarvis, M. C. (1976). Nucleotides and related compounds in bracken. *Bot. J. Linn. Soc.* **73**, 79–85.

Evans, I. A. (1976). Relationship between bracken and cancer. *Bot. J. Linn. Soc.* **73**, 105–112.

Evans, J. W. (1966). The leafhoppers and froghoppers of Australia and New Zealand. *Mem. Aust. Mus.* **64**, 70–75.

Evans, W. C. (1976). Bracken thiaminase-mediated neurotoxic syndromes. *Bot. J. Linn. Soc.* **73**, 113–131.

Evans, W. C., Jones, N. R., and Evans, R. A. (1950). The mechanism of the antineurin activity of bracken *(Pteris aquilina)*. *Biochem. J.* **46**, 38.

Feeny, P. P. (1968). Effect of oak leaf tannins on larval growth of the winter moth *Operophtera brumata*. *J. Insect Physiol.* **14**, 805–817.

Feeny, P. P. (1970). Seasonal changes in oak leaf tannins and nutrients as a cause of spring feeding by winter-moth caterpillars. *Ecology* **51**, 656–681.

Feeny, P. P. (1976). Plant apparency and chemical defense. *Recent. Adv. Phytochem.* **10**, 1–40.

Feeny, P. P., and Bostock, H. (1968). Seasonal variation in the tannin content of oak leaves. *Phytochemistry* **7**, 871–880.

Ferguson, W. S., and Armitage, E. R. (1944). The chemical composition of bracken. *J. Agric. Sci.* **34**, 165–171.

Fox, L. R., and MacAuley, B. J. (1977). Insect grazing on *Eucalyptus* in response to variation in leaf tannins and nitrogen. *Oecologia* **29**, 145–162.

Fox, L. R., and Morrow, P. A. (1981). Specialization: species property or local phenomenon? *Science* **211**, 887–893.

Fraenkel, G. S. (1952). The nutritional requirements of insects for known and unknown vitamins. *Trans. Int. Congr. Entomol., 9th, 1951* Vol. 1, pp. 277–279.

Fraenkel, G. S. (1959). The *raison d'être* of secondary plant substances. *Science* **129**, 1466–1470.

Fraenkel, G. S. (1969). Evaluation of our thoughts on secondary plant substances. *Entomol. Exp. Appl.* **12**, 473–486.

Fukuoka, M., Kuroyanagi, M., Toyama, M., Yoshihira, K., and Natori, S. (1972). Pterosins J, K, and L and six acylated pterosins from bracken, *Pteridium aqulinum* var. *latiusculum*. *Chem. Pharm. Bull.* **20**, 2282–2285.

Gadal, P., and Boudet, A. (1965). Inhibition of enzymes by tannins of *Quercus sessilis* leaves: inhibition of β-amylase. *C.R. Hebd. Seances Acad. Sci.* **260**, 4252–4255.

Galbraith, M. N., and Horn, D. H. S. (1966). An insect moulting hormone from a plant, *J. Chem. Soc., Chem. Commun.* No. 24, pp. 905–906.

Gerson, U. (1979). The associations between pteridophytes and insects. *Fern Gaz.* **12**, 29–45.

Glass, A. D. M., and Bohm, B. A. (1969a). The accumulation of cinnamic and benzoic acid derivatives in *Pteridium aquilinum* and *Athyrium felix-femina*. *Phytochemistry* **8**, 371–377.

Glass, A. D. M., and Bohm, B. A. (1969b). A further survey of ferns for cinnamic and benzoic acids. *Phytochemistry* **8**, 629–632.

Gleissman, S. R. (1976). Allelopathy in a broad spectrum of environments as illustrated by bracken. *Bot. J. Linn. Soc.* **73**, 95–104.

Gleissman, S. R., and Muller, C. H. (1972). The phytotoxic potential of bracken [*Pteridium aquilinum* (L.) Kühn]. *Madroño* **21**, 299–304.

Goldstein, J. L., and Swain, T. (1965). The inhibition of enzymes by tannins. *Phytochemistry* **4**, 185–192.

Gordon, H. T. (1961). Nutritional factors in insect resistance to chemicals. *Annu. Rev. Entomol.* **6**, 27–54.

Grevillius, A. Y. (1905). Zur Kenntniss der Biologie des Goldafters (*Euproctis chrysorrhoea* Hbn.) *Bot. Centralbl. Bl. Beih.* **18**, 22.

Hanamura, Y., Hayashiya, K., Naito, K., Matsuura, K., and Nishida, J. (1962). Food selection by silkworm larvae. *Nature (London)* **194**, 754–755.

Hanson, F. E. (1976). Comparative studies on induction of food choice preferences in lepidopterous larvae. *Symp. Biol. Hung.* **16**, 71–78.

Harborne, J. B. (1967). "Comparative Biochemistry of the Flavonoids." Academic Press, New York and London.

Harborne, J. B. (1977). Flavonoid sulfates: a new class of natural product of ecological significance in plants. *Prog. Phytochem.* **4**, 189–208.

Hasegawa, M., and Taneyama, M. (1973). Chicoric acid from *Onychium japonicum* and its distribution in the ferns. *Bot. Mag.* **86**, 315–317.

Haslam, E., Opie, C. T., and Porter, T. J. (1977). Procyanidin metabolism: a hypothesis. *Phytochemistry* **16**, 99–101.

Hedin, P. A., Miles, L. R., Thompson, A. C., and Minyard, J. P. (1968). Constituents of a cottonbud. X. Formulation of a bollweevil feeding stimulant mixture. *J. Agric. Food Chem.* **16**, 505–513.

Hedin, P. A., Maxwell, F. G., and Jenkins, J. N. (1974). Insect plant attractants, feeding stimulants, repellents, deterrents, and other related factors affecting insect behavior. *In* "Proceedings of the Summer Institute for the Biological Control of Plant Insects and Diseases" (F. G. Maxwell and F. A. Harris, eds.), pp. 494–527. Univ. of Mississippi Press, Jackson.

Hendrix, S. D. (1975). The resistance of *Pteridium aquilinum* (L.) Kuhn (bracken fern) to insect attack. Ph.D. Thesis, University of California, Berkeley.

Hendrix, S. D. (1977). The resistance of *Pteridium aquilinum* (L.) Kuhn to insect attack by *Trichoplusia ni* (Hübn.). *Oecologia* **26**, 347–361.

Hendrix, S. D. (1980). An evolutionary and ecological perspective of the insect fauna of ferns. *Am. Nat.* **115**, 171–196.

Hendrix, S. D., and Jones, R. L. (1972). The activity of β-ecdysone in four gibberellin bioassays. *Plant Physiol.* **50**, 199–200.

Hikino, H., and Hikino, Y. (1970). Arthropod moulting hormones. *Prog. Chem. Org. Nat. Prod.* **28**, 256–312.

Hikino, H., Arihara, S., and Takemoto, T. (1969). Ponasteroside A. a glycoside of insect metamorphosing substance from *Pteridium aquilinum* var. *latiusculum*. *Tetrahedron* **25**, 3909–3917.

Hikino, H., Takahashi, T., Arihara, S., and Takemoto, T. (1970). Structure of pteroside B, glycoside of *Pteridium aquilinum* var. *latiusculum*. *Chem. Pharm. Bull.* **18**, 1488–1489.

Hikino, H., Takahashi, T., and Takemoto, T. (1971). Structure of pteroside Z and D, glycosides of *Pteridium aquilinum* var. *latiusculum*. *Chem. Pharm. Bull.* **19**, 2424–2425.

Hikino, H., Takahashi, T., and Takemoto, T. (1972). Structure of pteroside A and C, glycosides of *Pteridium aquilinum* var. *latiusculum*. *Chem. Pharm. Bull.* **20**, 210–212.

Hikino, H., Ohizumi, Y., and Takemoto, T. (1975). Detoxification mechanism of *Bombyx mori* against exogenous phytoecdysone ecdysterone. *J. Insect Physiol.* **21**, 1953–1963.

Hillis, W. E., and Swain, T. (1959). The phenolic constituents of *Prunus domestica*. II. The analysis of tissues of the Victoria plum tree. *J. Sci. Food Agric.* **10**, 135–144.

Hodge, C. (1933). Growth and nutrition of *Melanoplus differentialis* Thomas (Orthoptera, Acrididae), I. Growth on a satisfactory mixed diet and on diets of single food plants. *Physiol. Zool.* **6**, 306–328.

Huffaker, C. B. (1974). Some implications of plant–arthropod and higher level arthropod–arthropod food links. *Environ. Entomol.* **3**, 1–9.

Huffaker, C. B., and Kennett, C. E. (1959). A ten-year study of vegetational changes associated with biological control of Klamath weed. *J. Range Manage.* **12**, 69–82.

Hunter, J. G. (1953). The composition of bracken: some major and trace-element constituents. *J. Sci. Food Agric.* **4**, 10–20.

Hussain, A., Forrest, J. M. S., and Dixon, A. F. G. (1974). Sugar, organic acid, phenolic acid and plant growth regulator content of extracts of honeydew of the aphid *Myzus persicae* and of its host plant, *Raphanus sativus*. *Ann. Appl. Biol.* **78**, 65–73.

Jacobs, W. P., and Suthers, H. B. (1971). The culture of apical buds of *Xanthium* and their use as a bioassay for flowering activity of ecdysterone. *Am. J. Bot.* **58**, 836–843.

Janzen, D. H. (1966). Co-evolution of mutualism between ants and acacias in Central America. *Evolution* **20**, 249–275.

Janzen, D. H. (1967a). Interaction of the bulls'-horn Acacia (*Acacia cornigera* L.) with an ant inhabitant (*Pseudomyrmex furruginea* F. Smith) in eastern Mexico. *Univ. Kan. Sci. Bull.* **47**, 315–358.

Janzen, D. H. (1967b). Fire, vegetation structure, and the ant × acacia interaction in Central America. *Ecology* **48**, 26–35.

Janzen, D. H. (1968). Host-plants as islands in evolutionary and contemporary time. *Am. Nat.* **102**, 592–595.

Janzen, D. H. (1973). Host-plants as islands. II. Competition in evolutionary and contemporary time. *Am. Nat.* **107**, 786–790.

Jarvis, M. C., and Duncan, H. J. (1974). Distribution of glycolipids and phospholipids in *Pteridium aquilinum*. *Phytochemistry* **13**, 979–981.

Jarvis, M. C., and Duncan, H. J. (1975). Diurnal variation in lipids of bracken fronds. *Phytochemistry* **14**, 77–78.

Jermy, T., Hanson, F. E., and Dethier, V. G. (1968). Induction of specific food preference in lepidopterous larvae. *Entomol. Exp. Appl.* **11**, 211–230.

Johnson, M. P., and Simberloff, D. S. (1974). Environmental determinants of island species numbers in the British Isles. *J. Biogeogr.* **1**, 149–154.

Jones, C. G. (1977). Chemical content and insect resistance of bracken fern [*Pteridium aquilinum* (L.) Kuhn]. D.Phil. Thesis, University of York, England.

Jones C. G., and Firn, R. D. (1978). The role of phytoecdysteroids in bracken fern, *Pteridium aquilinum* (L.) Kuhn, as a defense against phytophagous insect attack. *J. Chem. Ecol.* **4**, 117–138.

Jones C. G., and Firn, R. D. (1979a). Resistance of *Pteridium aquilinum* to attack by non-adapted phytophagous insects. *Biochem. Syst. Ecol.* **7**, 95–101.

Jones, C. G., and Firn, R. D. (1979b). Some allelochemicals of *Pteridium aquilinum* and their involvement in resistance to *Pieris brassicae*. *Biochem. Syst. Ecol.* **7**, 187–192.

Jones, D. A. (1966). On the polymorphism of cyanogenesis in *Lotus corniculatus:* selection by animals. *Can. J. Genet. Cytol.* **8**, 556–567.

Kaplanis, J. N., Thompson, M. J., Robbins, W. E., and Bryce, C. H. (1967). Insect hormones: alpha ecdysone and 20-hydroxyecdysone in bracken fern. *Science* **157**, 1436–1438.

King, D. S., and Siddall, J. B. (1974). Biosynthesis and inactivation of ecdysone. *In* "Invertebrate Endocrinology and Hormonal Heterophylly" (W. J. Burdette, ed.), pp. 147–152. Springer-Verlag, Berlin and New York.

Kirk, A. A. (1977). The insect fauna of the weed *Pteridium aquilinum* (L.) Kuhn (Polypodiaceae) in Papua New Guinea: a potential source of biological control agents. *J. Aust. Entomol. Soc.* **16**, 403–409.

Koch, A. (1967). Insects and their endosymbionts. *In* "Symbiosis" (S. M. Henry, ed.), Vol. 2, pp. 1–106. Academic Press, New York.

Kofod, H., and Eyjolfsson, R. (1966). The isolation of the cyanogenic glycoside prunasin from *Pteridium aquilinum*. *Tetrahedron Lett.* No. 12, pp. 1289–1291.

Kuris, A. M., Blaustein, A. R., and Alió, J. J. (1980). Hosts as islands. *Am. Nat.* **116**, 570–586.

Kuroyanagi, M., Fukuoka, M., Yoshihira, K., and Natori, S. (1974a). The absolute configurations of pterosins, 1-indanone derivatives from bracken, *Pteridium aquilinum* var. *latiusculum*. *Chem. Pharm. Bull.* **22**, 723–726.

Kuroyanagi, M., Fukuoka, M., Yoshihira, K., and Natori, S. (1974b). Pterosin N and O, phenylacetyl pterosin C, and pteroside P from bracken, *Pteridium aquilinum* var. *latiusculum*. *Chem. Pharm. Bull.* **22**, 2762–2764.

Lawton, J. H. (1976). The structure of the arthropod community on bracken. *Bot. J. Linn. Soc.* **73**, 187–216.

Lawton, J. H. (1978). Host-plant influences on insect diversity: the effects of space and time. *Symp. R. Entomol. Soc.* **9**, 105–125.

Lawton, J. H. (1983). Non-competitive populations, non-convergent communities and vacant niches: the herbivores on bracken. *In* "Ecological Communities: Conceptual Issues and the Evidence" (D. R. Strong, Jr., D. Simberloff, and L. G. Abele, eds.). Princeton Univ. Press, Princeton, New Jersey (in press).

Lawton, J. H., and McNeill, S. (1979). Between the devil and the deep blue sea: on the problem of being a herbivore. *In* "Population Dynamics" (R. M. Anderson, B. D. Turner, and L. R. Taylor, eds.), pp. 223–244. Blackwell, Oxford.

Lawton, J. H., and Schroeder, D. (1976). Effects of plant type, size of geographical range and taxonomic isolation on number of insect species associated with British plants. *Nature (London)* **265**, 137–140.

Lawton, J. H., and Schroeder, D. (1978). Some observations on the structure of phytophagous insect communities: the implications for biological control. *In* "Proceedings of the IVth International Symposium on the Biological Control of Weeds" (T. E. Freeman, ed.), pp. 57–73. Center for Environment Programs, Institute of Food and Agricultural Sciences, University of Florida, Gainesville.

Lawton, J. H., Cornell, H., Dritschilo, W., and Hendrix, S. D. (1981). Species as islands: comments on a paper by Kuris *et al. Am. Nat.* **117**, 623–627.

Loomis, W. D., and Battaile, J. (1966). Plant phenolic compounds and the isolation of plant enzymes. *Phytochemistry* **5**, 423–438.

MacArthur, R. H., and Wilson, E. O. (1967). "The Theory of Island Biogeography." Princeton Univ. Press, Princeton, New Jersey.

MacAuley, B. J., and Fox, L. R. (1980). Variation in total phenols and condensed tannins in *Eucalyptus:* leaf phenology and insect grazing. *Aust. J. Ecol.* **5**, 31–35.

McClure, J. W. (1976). Progress toward a biological rationale for the flavonoids. *Nova Acta Leopold.* **7**, 463–496.

McMorris, T. C., and Voeller, B. (1971). Ecdysones from gametophytic tissues of a fern. *Phytochemistry* **10**, 3253–3254.

Martin, M. M., Martin, J. S., and Kukor, J. J. (1980). The digestion of protein and carbohydrate by the stream detritivore *Tipula abdominalis* (Diptera: Tipulidae). *Oecologia* **46**, 360–364.

Matsuoka, T., Imai, S., Sakai, M., and Kamada, M. (1969). Studies on phytoecdysones—a review of our works. *Annu. Rep. Takeda Res. Lab.* **28**, 221–271.

Moon, F. E., and Pal, A. K. (1949). The composition and nutritive value of bracken. *J. Agric. Sci.* **39**, 296–301.

Moon, F. E., and Raafat, M. A. (1951). Some biochemical aspects of bracken poisoning in the ruminant animal. II. The significance of the cyanogenetic principle of bracken. *J. Sci. Food Agric.* **2**, 327–336.

Murata, K., Tanaka, R., and Yamaoka, M. (1974). Reaction mechanisms of thiamine with thermostable factors. *J. Nutr. Sci. Vitaminol.* **20**, 351–362.

Nakabayashi, T. (1955). The isolation of astragalin and isoquercitrin from bracken *(Pteridium aquilinum). Bull. Agric. Chem. Soc. Jpn.* **19**, 104–109.

Nakanishi, K., Koreeda, M., Sasaki, S., Chang, M. L., and Hsu, H. Y. (1966). Insect hormones. The structure of ponasterone A, an insect-moulting hormone, from the leaves of *Podocarpus nakaii* Hay. *J. Chem. Soc., Chem. Commun.* No. 24, pp. 915–917.

Nigg, H. N., Svoboda, J. A., Thompson, M. J., Kaplanis, J. N., Dutky, S. R., and Robbins, W. E. (1974). Ecdysone metabolism: ecdysone dehydrogenase–isomerase. *Lipids* **9**, 971–974.

Ogawa, S., Nishimoto, N., and Matsuda, H. (1974). Pharmacology of ecdysones in vertebrates. *In* "Invertebrate Endocrinology and Hormonal Heterophylly" (W. J. Burdette, ed.), pp. 341–344. Springer-Verlag, New York and Berlin.

Page, C. N. (1976). The taxonomy and phytogeography of bracken—a review. *Bot. J. Linn. Soc.* **73**, 1–34.

Parham, R. A., and Kaustinen, H. M. (1976). Differential staining of tannin in sections of epoxy-embedded plant cells. *Stain Technol.* **51**, 237–240.

Parham, R. A., and Kaustinen, H. M. (1977). On the site of tannin synthesis in plant cells. *Bot. Gaz. (Chicago)* **138**, 465–467.

Parsons, J., and Rothschild, M. (1964). Rhodanase in the larva and pupa of the common blue butterfly *(Polyommatus icarus* [Rott.]) (Lepidoptera). *Entomol. Gaz.* **15**, 589.

Perring, F. H., and Walters, S. M. (1962). "Atlas of the British Flora." Bot. Soc. Br. Is. and Nelson, London.

Preston, F. W. (1962a). The canonical distribution of commonness and rarity. I. *Ecology* **43**, 185–215.

Preston, F. W. (1962b). The canonical distribution of commonness and rarity. II. *Ecology* **43**, 410–432.

Rees, H. H. (1971). Ecdysones. In "Aspects of Terpenoid Chemistry and Biochemistry" (T. W. Goodwin, ed.), pp. 181–222. Academic Press, New York and London.

Rhoades, D. F., and Cates, R. G. (1976). Toward a general theory of plant anti-herbivore chemistry. Recent Adv. Phytochem. 10, 168–213.

Rigby, C., and Lawton, J. H. (1981). Species–area relationships of arthropods on host plants: herbivores on bracken. J. Biogeogr. 8, 125–133.

Roberts, J., Paymar, C. F., Wallace, J. S., and Pitman, R. M. (1980). Seasonal changes in leaf area, stomatal and canopy conductances and transpiration from bracken below a forest canopy. J. Appl. Ecol. 17, 409–422.

Rodriguez, E., Towers, G. H. N., and Mitchell, D. (1976). Review: biological activities of sesquiterpene lactones. Phytochemistry 15, 1573–1580.

Rosenthal, G. A., and Bell, E. A. (1979). Naturally occurring, toxic nonprotein amino acids. In "Herbivores: Their Interaction with Secondary Plant Metabolites" (G. A. Rosenthal and D. H. Janzen, eds.), pp. 353–386. Academic Press, New York.

Rosenthal, G. A., and Janzen, D. H., eds. (1979). "Herbivores: Their Interaction with Secondary Plant Metabolites." Academic Press, New York.

Rymer, L. (1976). The history and ethnobotany of bracken. Bot. J. Linn. Soc. 73, 151–176.

Sasamoto, K. (1961). "Resistance of Rice Plant Applied with Silicate and Nitrogenous Fertilizers to the Rice Stem Borer, Chilo suppressalis Walker," No. 3. Proc. Fac. Lib. Arts Educ., Yamanashi Univ. Japan.

Saunders, J. A., Conn, E. E., Lin, C. H., and Shimada, M. (1977). Localization of cinnamic acid 4-monooxygenase and the membrane-bound enzyme system for dhurrin biosynthesis in Sorghum bicolor seedlings. Plant Physiol. 60, 629–634.

Saxena, K. N., and Schoonhoven, L. M. (1977). Induction of orientational and feeding preferences in Manduca sexta larvae for an artificial diet containing citral. Entomol. Exp. Appl. 23, 72–78.

Schneider, G. (1892). "The Book of Choice Ferns," Vol. I. L. Upcott Gill, London.

Schoonhoven, L. M., and Derksen-Koppers, I. (1973). Effects of secondary plant substances on drinking behaviour in some Heteroptera. Entomol. Exp. Appl. 16, 141–145.

Schreiner, I. H. (1980). Cyanogenesis and the herbivorous insects of bracken fern (Pteridium aquilinum). Ph.D. Thesis, Cornell University, New York.

Scriber, J. M. (1978a). Cyanogenic glycosides in Lotus corniculatus. Oecologia 34, 143–155.

Scriber, J. M. (1978b). The effects of larval feeding specialization and plant growth form upon the consumption and utilization of plant biomass and nitrogen: an ecological consideration. Entomol. Exp. Appl. 24, 694–710.

Scriber, J. M. (1979). The effects of sequentially switching food plants upon biomass and nitrogen utilization by polyphagous and stenophagous Papilio larvae. Entomol. Exp. Appl. 25, 203–215.

Scriber, J. M., and Feeny, P. P. (1979). Growth of herbivorous caterpillars in relation to feeding specialization and to the growth form of their food plants. Ecology 60, 829–850.

Simberloff, D. S. (1974). Equilibrium theory of island biogeography and ecology. Annu. Rev. Ecol. Syst. 5, 161–182.

Singh, P. (1977). "Artificial Diets for Insects, Mites and Spiders." IFI/Plenum, New York.

Smith, A. M., and Agiza, A. H. (1951). The amino-acids of several grassland species, cereals and bracken. J. Sci. Food Agric. 2, 503–519.

Smith, A. M., and Fenton, E. W. (1944). The composition of bracken fronds and rhizomes at different times during the growing season. J. Soc. Chem. Ind., London 63, 218–219.

Solomos, T. (1977). Cyanide-resistant respiration in higher plants. Annu. Rev. Plant Physiol. 28, 279–297.

Somogyi, J. C. (1971). On antithiamine factors of fern. J. Vitaminol. 17, 165–174.

Soo-Hoo, C. F., and Fraenkel, G. S. (1964). Resistance of ferns to the feeding of *Prodenia eridania* larvae. *Ann. Entomol. Soc. Am.* **57**, 790–791.

Soo-Hoo, C. F., and Fraenkel, G. S. (1966). The consumption, digestion and utilization of food plants by a polyphagous insect, *Prodenia eridania* (Craner). *J. Insect Physiol.* **12**, 711–730.

Southwood, T. R. E. (1973). The insect/plant relationship—an evolutionary perspective. *Symp. Ry. Entomol. Soc.* **6**, 3–30.

Staal, G. B. (1967). Insect hormones in plants. *Meded. Rijsfac. Landbouwwet., Gent* **32**, 393–400.

Strong, D. R., Jr. (1974). Rapid asymptotic species accumulation in phytophagous insect communities: the pests of cacao. *Science* **185**, 1064–1066.

Strong, D. R., Jr. (1979). Biogeographical dynamics of insect–host plant communities. *Annu. Rev. Entomol.* **24**, 89–119.

Strong, D. R., Jr., and Levin, D. A. (1979). Species richness of plant parasites and growth form of their hosts. *Am. Nat.* **114**, 1–22.

Strong, D. R., Jr., McCoy, E. D., and Rey, J. R. (1977). Time and the number of herbivore species: the pests of sugar cane. *Ecology* **58**, 167–175.

Svoboda, J. A., Kaplanis, J. N., Robbins, W. E., and Thompson, M. J. (1975). Recent developments in insect steroid metabolism. *Annu. Rev. Entomol.* **20**, 205–220.

Swain, T., and Cooper-Driver, G. A. (1973). Biochemical systematics in the Filicopsida. *Bot. J. Linn. Soc., Suppl.* **1**, 111–134.

Takatori, K., Nakano, S., Nagata, S., Okumura, K., Hirono, I., and Shimuzu, H. (1972). Pterolactam, a new compound isolated from bracken. *Chem. Pharm. Bull.* **20**, 1087.

Takemoto, T., Arihara, S., Hikino, Y., and Hikino, H. (1968). Isolation of insect moulting hormone from *Pteridium aquilinum* var. *latiusculum. Chem. Pharm. Bull.* **16**, 762.

Tempel, A. S. (1981). Field studies on the relationship between herbivore damage and tannin concentration in bracken (*Pteridium aquilinum* Kuhn). *Oecologia* **51**, 97–106.

Valiela, I., Koumjian, L., and Swain, T. (1979). Cinnamic acid inhibition of detritus feeding. *Nature (London)* **280**, 55–57.

van Emden, H. F. (1972). Aphids as phytochemists. *In* "Phytochemical Ecology" (J. B. Harborne, ed.), pp. 25–43. Academic Press, New York and London.

Voirin, B. (1970). Recherches chimiques, taxonomiques et physiologiques sur les flavonoides des pteridophyte. Thèse Doct. l'Université de Lyon.

Wallace, J. W., and Mansell, R. L., eds. (1976). "Biochemical Interaction Between Plants and Insects," Recent Adv. Phytochem., Vol. 10. Plenum, New York.

Wang, C. Y., Pamukcu, A. M., and Bryan, G. T. (1973). Isolation of fumaric acid, succinic acid, astragalin, isoquercetin and tiliroside from *Pteridium aquilinum. Phytochemistry* **12**, 2298–2299.

Watt, A. S. (1976). The ecological status of bracken. *Bot. J. Linn. Soc.* **73**, 217–239.

Whitham, T. G. (1981). Individual trees as heterogeneous environments: adaptation to herbivory or epigenetic noise. *In* "Insect Life History Patterns" (R. F. Denno and H. Dingle, eds.), pp. 9–27. Springer-Verlag, New York and Berlin.

Whitham, T. G., and Slobodchikoff, C. N. (1981). Evolution by individuals, plant–herbivore interactions, and mosaics of genetic variability: the adaptive significance of somatic mutations in plants. *Oecologia* **49**, 287–292.

Williams, G. H., and Foley, A. (1976). Seasonal variations in the carbohydrate content of bracken. *Bot. J. Linn. Soc.* **73**, 87–93.

Yoshihara, T., Sogawa, K., Pathak, M. D., Juliano, B. O., and Sakamura, S. (1979). Soluble silicic acid as a sucking inhibitory substance in rice against the brown plant hopper (Delphacidae, Homoptera). *Entomol. Exp. Appl.* **26**, 314–322.

Yoshihira, K., Fukuoka, M., Kuroyanagi, M., and Natori, S. (1971). 1-Indanone derivatives from bracken. *Pteridium aquilinum* var. *latiusculum. Chem. Pharm. Bull.* **19,** 1491–1495.

Yoshihira, K., Fuhuoka, M., Kuroyanagi, M., and Natori, S. (1972). Further characterisation of 1-indanone derivatives from bracken, *Pteridium aquilinum* var. *latiusculum. Chem. Pharm. Bull.* **20,** 426–428.

Clive G. Jones
New York Botanical Garden Cary Arboretum
Millbrook, New York

CHAPTER 16

Hypotheses on Organization and Evolution in Herbivorous Insect Communities

PETER W. PRICE

I. INTRODUCTION

Progress in understanding herbivore communities has been greater in the 1970s and 1980s than in any previous decade. Whereas indirect synoptic evidence such as dominance–diversity curves and ratios of species per genus dominated the earlier study of communities, a new emphasis on specific mechanisms and trophic relations, working "from the bottom up," has since prevailed. An emphasis on resources and how individual species respond to these resources and in concert form a community makes a powerful analytical approach to understanding community organization. The individualistic approach to plant communities (e.g., Gleason, 1926; Whittaker, 1967) has been applied to animal communities.

These are exciting times for an insect ecologist because these new approaches have led to new insights, and general patterns have started to emerge. The study of insect communities has indicted that major paradigms in community ecology may not hold all the time. Such communities should play a major role in testing paradigms fundamental to all of ecology and in the development of alternatives. With the basis of a strong experimental approach to community organization, we are

VARIABLE PLANTS AND HERBIVORES
IN NATURAL AND MANAGED SYSTEMS

poised for major developments in understanding. The seminal paper by Lawton and Strong (1981) illustrates the powerful impact that the study of herbivorous insect communities can have on conceptual ecology.

This book will pave the way for an even closer look at resources as a basis for understanding communities. With its emphasis on variable host quality, it forces a detailed examination of variation in community structure within species of plants, requiring an understanding of host-plant population structure and demography that has yet to become a major emphasis for understanding assemblages of insect herbivores.

Community organization involves processes resulting in the kinds and numbers of species in communities and their relative abundance. A community is simply an assemblage of species in a particular area, if we accept the null hypothesis that species presence or absence is an individualistic, idiosyncratic phenomenon. To what extent communities consist of "coexisting *interdependent* populations" (Price, 1975, p. 3) will be examined in this chapter. Root (1973) has recognized subunits of communities as component communities, assemblages of species associated with some microenvironment or resource such as tree holes, rotting logs, or a particular plant taxon. The study of component communities has become a major analytical approach among students of insect communities on crucifer plants (e.g., Root, 1973), bracken (Lawton, 1976), *Heliconia* (e.g., Seifert and Seifert, 1976, 1979; Strong, 1977), mangroves (Simberloff, 1978; Simberloff and Wilson, 1970), *Spartina* in salt marshes (e.g., Denno *et al.*, 1981; Rey, 1981), and umbellifers (e.g., Thompson, 1978; Berenbaum, 1981a). Root (1973) defined the compound community as a complex mixture of component communities that interact to varying degrees, as in a meadow, wood lot, or pond. Even component communities may contain many species, but they are sufficiently simple locally to allow detailed analysis of organizational processes, thus much attention in this chapter will be devoted to communities reflecting this important bias in the literature. Compound communities can be so complex that we have very little idea of how the components are linked and how they interact. Discussion of compound communities will be delayed until component communities have been treated, and a clear distinction will be maintained in this chapter between the two.

Before considering the major hypotheses erected to account for community organization, it is necessary to examine the players in this ecological theater. Are we studying an evolutionary play in this ecological theater, as Hutchinson (1965) has proposed, or is it rather an ecological play, as the individualistic concept of organismal association would suggest (Gleason, 1926; Whittaker, 1967)? Are evolutionary processes involved in community organization, and does membership in a community necessitate an evolutionary change in a species?

II. THE EVOLUTION OF SPECIALISTS

The study of component communities has usually involved specialist herbivores, specialized at least in exploiting the family of plants to which the host belongs. Indeed, component communities on plants have usually been selected for this reason, because the fauna and its resources can be readily identified. Members of these faunas occur together regularly, and organizing influences are more likely among species that habitually occur together. Resources for specialist herbivores are narrowly defined by what is available on a single plant species or population.

Overall, it can be argued that the generalized strategy is more adaptive, providing an organism with many alternative sources of food and shelter. Many authors, such as Hering (1951), have regarded the generalist strategy as the primitive one from which specialized species have been derived. Specialization seems to be an environmentally induced necessity. We must therefore ask the question, Where and why does specialization occur?

Taxonomic specialization is relatively easy to describe. As the intimacy between host plant and insect increases, the tendency toward specialization increases. At the most intimate extreme, gall formers that must modify plant growth and live within plant tissues most of their lives are among the most specialized herbivores, usually being found on only one plant species (Eastop, 1973). It is clear that gall formation is an evolutionary step, with a genetic commitment to adapting for exploitation of a plant species. When such genetic constraints occur, host range extensions can be made only by deviations from the parental stock, which are probably sufficient to produce significant reproductive isolation and almost instantaneous speciation, as in the model by Bush (1975). A significant observation is that herbivorous insects with intimate relationships with the host plant (e.g., gall formers, borers, and miners) are not only specific but have undergone very extensive adaptive radiations. The largest family of herbivores in the British Isles is the Cecidomyiidae, or gall-forming midges (Price, 1977, 1980), and the next largest is the Curculionidae, the larvae of which bore into stems, roots, or fruits. External feeders on plants are also well represented by specialists. Specialists therefore contribute very significantly to the species richness of component communities on plant species.

To narrow down the question of when specialization evolves, it helps to focus on a relatively specialized group of herbivores and examine where more or less specialization occurs. Plant-mining flies in the family Agromyzidae are mostly specialized to exploiting only one species of host plant (Lawton and Price, 1979), with 57% of species in Britain in this category (Price, 1980). The agromyzid fauna in Britain is largely known (Spencer, 1972) and the flora almost completely described (Clapham *et al.*, 1957), so we can test the hypothesis that colonization of plant families has been random and observe the extent to which the evolution of specialized species influences the species distribution of agromyzids among plant families.

With 291 agromyzid species of known host-plant relationships (from Spencer, 1972) and 2177 nonaquatic plants available for colonization (from Clapham *et al.*, 1957), we can calculate an expected number of agromyzids on each family of plants and compare this with the number observed. The hypothesis that colonization is random among families must be rejected. Using only families of plants with an expected number of agromyzid species over 5, the χ^2 statistic for goodness to fit gives a probability of much less than 0.005 that the distribution is random ($n = 16$, $\chi^2 = 153.90$). Some families of plants have many more agromyzid species than expected, and others have fewer (Table I). One reason for this is that certain plant families have more specialized species (i.e., utilizing only one or two host species) than others, and where increased specialization occurs we usually see more than the expected number of agromyzids (Table I). When reduced specialization occurs, in most cases fewer agromyzid species than expected are found. This pattern conforms to the theory of competition that predicts the coexistence of many specialists on a resource but few generalists. Whether these patterns result from competitive interaction will be examined in Section V.

The description of where most specialization occurs helps us with an answer to the more difficult question of why it occurs. Hering (1951) noted that for leaf-mining taxa in general the most specialized species occur on families like the Umbelliferae and Compositae, or small families with monospecific genera like the Cannabinaceae (see Table I). A conspicuous common characteristic in these families is the high diversity of aromatic chemicals resulting in significant differences in chemical constituents between plant species (e.g., Hegnauer, 1971; Berenbaum, 1981a,b; on Umbelliferae), which presumably select for genetic specialization for enzyme systems that can detoxify or utilize such chemicals. The detailed study of herbivore communities on umbellifers in relation to plant chemistry made by Berenbaum (1981a) supports this argument. As plant defense, in the form of furanocoumarins, is escalated, so the tendency is for communities to become dominated by specialists, both in terms of the number of species associated with plant species and the number of specialist individuals present (Table II). Umbellifer species with no furanocoumarins have on average only two specialized herbivore species, and 67% of individuals in communities are generalists,

Table I

Numbers of Observed and Expected Agromyzid Species (with Many More or Less than the Expected Number) and the Specificity of Agromyzids on Each Family[a]

Family	Plant species in family (no.)	Observed agromyzid species (no.)	Expected agromyzid species (no.)	Agromyzid species on one host species (%)	Agromyzid species on two host species (%)
Families of plants with more attacks than expected					
Ranunculaceae*	49	20	6.55	60	95
Papilionaceae*	95	24	12.70	54	75
Umbelliferae*	74	22	9.89	68	73
Urticaceae	5	5	0.67	100	100
Cannabinaceae	2	2	0.27	100	100
Salicaceae	29	8	3.88	50	88
Boraginaceae	31	8	4.14	63	75
Labiatae*	65	13	8.69	38	46[b]
Campanulaceae	14	5	1.87	20	40[b]
Rubiaceae	21	6	2.81	83	100
Caprifoliaceae	13	6	1.74	33	100
Dipsacaceae	6	5	0.80	60	80
Compositae*	235	64	31.41	45	69
Gramineae*	164	34	21.92	44	59[b]
Mean		15.86	7.67	58.43	78.57
Families of plants with fewer attacks than expected					
Polypodiaceae*	39	2	5.21	0	50
Cruciferae*	138	4	18.44	50	50
Caryophyllaceae*	93	3	12.43	33	33
Chenopodiaceae*	43	2	5.75	50	50
Rosaceae*	167	5	22.32	40	60
Scrophulari-aceae*	98	7	13.10	29	43
Liliaceae*	44	2	5.88	50	50
Cyperaceae*	111	8	14.84	75	88[b]
Mean		4.13	12.25	40.88	53.00
Families of plants with no attacks when three or more were expected					
Onagraceae	24	0	3.21		
Polygonaceae*	48	0	6.42		
Ericaceae	25	0	3.34		
Orchidaceae	56	0	7.49		
Mean		0	5.12		

[a]Based on the percentage attacking one or two species of host in Britain. Plant families are listed as in Clapham et al. (1957). Families with an asterisk are those with an expected number of agromyzid species over five, used in the analysis of goodness of fit to a random distribution of species.
[b]Data on specificity that do not fit the general pattern are discussed in the text.

Table II
Relative Abundance of Specialist and Generalist Insect Species and Individuals on
13 Species of Umbelliferae[a]

Furanocoumarins present	Host species (no.)	Species per host species (mean no.)		Individuals (mean %)	
		Specialists	Generalists	Specialists	Generalists
None	5	2.0	2.6	33	67
Linear only	3	2.7	1.7	62	38
Linear and angular	5	5.0	3.8	75	25

[a]In relation to type of chemical defense of the host-plant species. Data from Berenbaum (1981a).

whereas host species with both linear and angular furanocoumarins average five species of specialists per component community, and 75% of individuals are specialists. The pattern generally seen in a fauna when more specialists coexist than generalists is reflected in this detailed study on the local scale.

The degree to which a plant species is biologically different from other species therefore seems to be important in defining whether it can be attacked by generalists or specialists. Quite what the differences are needs more investigation, but they are reflected in a taxonomist's view of biological distinctness. As Hering (1951) noted, monospecific genera of plants frequently have monospecific leaf miners. When species within a genus are subdivided into subgenera or sections, herbivores tend to be monospecific when such taxa are monospecific. This is seen in *Yucca* moths, in which highly specific moths in the genera *Tegeticula* and *Prodoxus* occur on the most distinct species of *Yucca* (each isolated in a separate taxonomic section), *Y. brevifolia* and *Y. whipplei* (Davis, 1967). Interestingly, whereas taxonomic isolation has been regarded as a possible negative influence on species richness of herbivores on a plant species (Lawton and Schröder, 1977; Lawton and Price, 1979), the isolated *Y. whipplei* has a richer moth fauna than any other species.

Clearly, much more study is needed of the evolution of specialization and its impact on species richness. Although patterns are emerging, important exceptions exist. Some families have more agromyzid species than expected, and yet the species are no more specialized than those on depauperate families (e.g., Labiatae, Campanulaceae, and Gramineae, in Table I). One family has highly specialized agromyzids but fewer species than expected (Cyperaceae). The Gramineae, with a rich agromyzid fauna, is not conspicuously diverse in chemicals regarded as inhibitory to generalist herbivores. Clearly, other mechanisms are involved in specialization and radiation of herbivore species.

Another mechanism resulting in specialization, or more likely another dimension of the same mechanism, has been extensively studied by plant breeders. Genetic analysis of plant defense and herbivore attack has demonstrated repeatedly that there is a gene-for-gene relationship between genes conferring defense in the plant and genes conferring the capacity to attack in herbivores (Flor, 1971; Day, 1974). Although most studies relate to pathogenic fungi, such relationships do exist in insect herbivores, as demonstrated in the hessian fly (*Myetiola destructor*; Hatchett and Gallun, 1970). With this matching of genes in the plant by genes in the herbivore, not only is specificity limited to plant species, it is also limited to plant genotypes. It is even conceivable that within-plant specialization is selected for by genotypic variation in plants resulting from somatic mutations (Whitham and Slobodchikoff, 1981). Such specificity has not been commonly considered by community ecologists (Fox and Morrow, 1981), and yet it may explain much of the species richness in communities. A hypothesis is developed in Section III on the genetic diversity of host plants, which is in need of extensive testing. This book documents the large amount of heterogeneity in plant populations important to insect herbivores, much of it no doubt of genetic origin. The need for incorporating this information into the community ecology of herbivores is obviously apparent and should lead to major advances in understanding them.

Understanding of the evolution of specialist herbivores is important to an understanding of community organization, because plants selecting for specialists will have community structures qualitatively different from those that enable many generalists to enter, as Berenbaum (1981a) has emphasized. Also, specialists contribute very significantly to the richness of insect herbivore communities and represent one of the most important evolutionary processes in such communities. Where specialists are concerned we must understand the evolutionary play involved, whereas with generalists a simpler ecological play is probably more common.

III. HYPOTHESES ON COMMUNITY ORGANIZATION

A. The General Case

Many hypotheses on the mechanisms involved with community organization invoke the importance of heterogeneity of the environment in some form or another (see references under Sections III,B,3, C,1 and

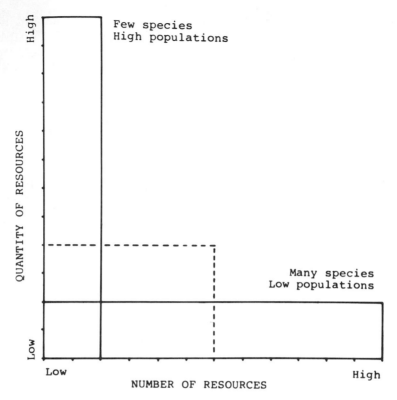

Fig. 1. The resource base in a community, and population responses of species to varying numbers of resources and quantity of resources. Although the total amount of resources remains constant in the three cases illustrated, species richness and number of individuals per species change significantly. The dashed lines illustrate an intermediate case. After Price (1975).

4). As environmental heterogeneity increases, more species are likely to coexist in a community because more ecological niches exist and because no resources are abundant enough to enable a few species to become dominant and exclude others through interspecific competition. This heterogeneity may involve habitats, resources within habitats, or genetic heterogeneity in the host-plant population.

The general case describes the simple relationship between high heterogeneity and high species richness with relatively low numbers of individuals per species, and the other extreme is low heterogeneity, low species richness, but high numbers of individuals per species, given an equal amount of resource in each community (Fig. 1). The general case incorporates the major qualities of communities, species number and relative abundance, but it says nothing about the types of species present or the role of higher trophic levels in community organization.

The specific hypotheses are discussed in the following subsections and relate to component communities of insects on plants. The hypotheses are not mutually exclusive, and several may be applicable to one component community, with some species being influenced by one mechanism and others by another. The first set of hypotheses (Sections III,B,1–5) relate to differences in communities on the same host-plant species, and the second set (Sections III,C,1–5) to differences between host-plant species.

When this distinction is made it becomes necessary to deal with very similar processes in different sections. For example, the hypothesis in Section III,B,2 involves mechanisms very similar to those in Section III,C,3 and 4; those in Sections III,B,5 and C,5 both relate to enemy impact on herbivores. However, this dichotomy helps to clarify the necessary difference between within-species variation in community structure and between-species variation and the studies that relate to these areas.

B. Within-Host Species Hypotheses

1. The Genotypic-Heterogeneity Hypothesis

This hypothesis has not been proposed before in relation to the organization of insect communities. It was stimulated by the subject matter of this book and the need for understanding basic mechanisms in community organization. The hypothesis states that as the genetic diversity in a plant population increases the diversity of insect herbivores increases. The mechanism involved is that each herbivore species in a locality is likely to be adapted to one or a few plant genotypes, so herbivore species are accumulated in a community as the number of plant genotypes increases.

Tests of this hypothesis should help in the fusion of two independently developed literatures, neither of which has entered into the consideration of insect herbivore communities. A remarkable dichotomy exists in the literature concerning the understanding of the population dynamics of small herbivores. On the one hand, a population of host plants has been regarded as homogeneous, so a large sample of randomly selected plants has been used to estimate the mean herbivore population size and the standard error of the mean (e.g., see references in Morris, 1955, 1963; Klomp, 1968; Baltensweiler, 1970). Even when a few host plants were sampled the data were pooled (Varley and Gradwell, 1968). This was in spite of the early recognition that the major source of variance in herbivore number was between plants (Morris, 1955), with several sets of data showing the same pattern: spruce budworm (Morris, 1955), European spruce sawfly (Prebble, 1943), winter moth (Morris and Reeks, 1954), large aspen tortrix (Prentice, 1954), and lodgepole needle miner (Stark, 1952). Morris (1955) was moved to assert, "The fact that the variability in insect population between trees is so much greater than the variability within trees . . . may well prove to be a principle common to all forest insects [p. 244]." And yet few researchers in the following 20 yr investigated in detail the mechanisms resulting in this pattern. The debate centered around population regulation by means of density-dependent or density-independent factors, with very little concern for plant quality.

In contrast to the *plant-homogeneity* viewpoint, wherever important variation in a plant population in relation to small herbivores was sought it was usually discovered (Strong, 1982, provides an exception). Resistance factors to insect herbivores were repeatedly found in plant populations, with an extensive literature going back to the 1880s. For example, Painter (1951) was able to discuss resistance in wheat to 15 species of herbivores, and the genetic basis for host resistance and susceptibility and herbivore virulence and avirulence are now well understood. Day (1974) considered that the gene-for-gene relationship between host plant and herbivore discovered in the very simple genetic structure of agricultural crops must exist, but in a more complex form, in natural populations. Unfortunately, the *plant-heterogeneity* viewpoint has not been prominent in the ecological literature.

Fortunately, plant heterogeneity has received much more attention from ecologists in the recent past, as this book illustrates. But concentration has been on the influence of host-plant variation on herbivore populations, and not on herbivore communities. And yet, if we are to understand the evolution of herbivore communities, the subject of this chapter, we must have knowledge of how the genetic basis of plant heterogeneity to herbivores influences groups of populations that form communities. This level of understanding is primitive. The role of plant heterogeneity within populations has not been applied before to the understanding of insect herbivore communities. Major emphasis has been on why different plant species and different plant populations have different numbers and relative abundances of herbivore species (Lawton and Price, 1979; Strong, 1979; and references in Price, 1980), without examining within-species or plant population heterogeneity. The hypothesis that the genotypic diversity of a host-plant population influences the diversity of insect hervibores on the population has not been tested.

The evidence to support this hypothesis is scanty, to say the least, but there are indications that genetic heterogeneity plays a role in defining the species richness and relative abundance of herbivores. Work on the willow *Salix lasiolepsis* and its tenthredinid sawflies in the genera *Euura, Pontania,* and *Phyllocolpa* (P. W. Price and K. M. Clancy, unpublished) has indicated that a population of willows is composed of many clones. Each clone differs from others in many characters, including phenology of flowering and vegetative growth, stem and bud color, stem diameter and growth characteristics, phenol glycoside content, and susceptibility to herbivore attack. We have yet to prove that these differences are genetically based, but evidence is mounting. There are no obvious environmental differences between clones that show very different characters, and many clones occur within one or a few meters of others, some with interlocking shoots. In a newly established willow garden, cuttings from many clones planted in identical soil preserve parental traits. A detailed analysis of characters of plants in the willow garden can begin only in 1982. The abundance of tenthredinid sawflies on these clones can be accurately estimated, because each species studied alters plant growth to form a gall or a leaf fold. Thus we sample the actual choices made by ovipositing female sawflies, not the adult populations, which may sample many clonal genotypes but select only a few for oviposition.

In two plots near Flagstaff, Arizona, 16 clones were sampled, each plot about 50 m along a creek and 0–10 m away from the creek. The number of sawflies on each clone, expressed as the number on stems developed from 15 shoots from the previous growing season, differed dramatically from clone to clone and from plot to plot (Table III), with clone size not contributing to these differences. The notable observation relevant to the genetic-heterogeneity hypothesis is that most clones (14 of 16) did not support all four herbivore species. Clone 1 supported only one species, and many clones had only two species. Clone 2 had a large population of the stem galler and, being very favorable for herbivore development, may well have acted as a reproductive source, whereas the other clones acted as reproductive sinks for this species. Clone 6 had a large population of the leaf-folding sawfly, which was rare or absent on most other clones. But in each plot all herbivores were present. We cannot exclude the possibility that habitat effects influenced the large differences in abundance of leaf gallers between plots I and II and between clones 8–14 and 15–16 in plot II.

There is no doubt that clonal quality affects species presence or absence and the relative abundance of species. By including more clones of dif-

Table III
Number of Sawflies (Four Species) on Willow Clones in 1981[a]

| | | Galls (no.) | | | Phyllocolpa |
| | | Euura Stem | Euura Petiole | Pontania Leaf | Leaf folds (no.) |
Plot	Clone				
I	1	0	0	4	0
	2	60	1	2	0
	3	15	2	0	3
	4	0	1	1	0
	5	1	0	3	0
	6	8	1	4	41
	7	3	0	1	0
II	8	5	3	235	9
	9	0	0	119	0
	10	9	0	114	0
	11	3	0	125	0
	12	3	0	50	0
	13	3	0	262	0
	14	15	1	100	0
	15	13	0	0	0
	16	36	0	2	0

[a]Numbers are sawflies on shoots developed from 15 stems which grew in 1980.

ferent quality in the community, we obtained more herbivore species. This is not a simple species–area effect, because the species–area curve would assume very different shapes, depending on the order in which clones were sampled. The genetic-heterogeneity hypothesis remains a viable explanation in this case.

Another case concerns cecidomyiid gall flies on birches in Holland, studied by Roskam and van Uffelen (1981). The birches *Betula pendula* and *B. pubescens* hybridize freely, forming a gradient of genotypes from the most *B. pendula*-like to the most *B. pubescens*-like plants. *Semudobia betulae* is more abundant on *B. pendula*, and *S. tarda* more abundant on *B. pubescens*. It is quite likely that pure stands of each birch species would support only one *Semudobia* species, and only trees of hybrid origin support the two species. Genetic heterogeneity is important in determining the presence and abundance of these highly specialized insects.

The chapters in this book by Whitham (Chapter 1) and Alstad and Edmunds (Chapter 12) and the chapters in Part II on interplant variation in host quality relate to the population biology of herbivores. However, it is clear that such variation must have community effects, because species presence and abundance are influenced. It is very likely that genetic differences dictate host-plant quality differences in many cases.

Clearly, the genetic-heterogeneity hypothesis needs vigorous testing, but the evidence presented in this book suggests that we have the baseline data to make this a relatively simple task in the systems represented. Studies like those of Burdon (1980) and Burdon and Marshall (1981), which tested resistance to pathogenic fungi in natural populations of plants, would be very valuable when applied to insect herbivores (see also Burdon, 1978). A strong experimental approach should be developed also, using varieties of agricultural plants in which gene-for-gene relationships are understood and simple. A comparison of species diversity in stands of one genotype with stands of increasing genetic diversity would provide a direct test of this hypothesis. Both insects and pathogenic fungi could be studied on varieties of wheat, oats, barley, or flax, well studied by plant pathologists (see Day, 1974). It is also desirable to extend the gene-for-gene concept to the study of component communities of plants in natural environments.

2. The Phenotypic-Heterogeneity Hypothesis

This hypothesis states that phenotypic differences, uninfluenced by genetic traits, influence the herbivores in the component community. The influence could take many forms, involving environmentally induced chemical differences such as allelochemicals or basic nitrogen metabolism, architectural change resulting from plant age, or differences in plant phenology.

Evidence in support of this hypothesis is not abundant, because it is only relatively recently that studies have been sufficiently detailed to provide an understanding of how variable phenotypic quality influences insect herbivore communities. This book supports the contention that this hypothesis is an important one, and it is in need of more direct testing. Many studies illustrate phenotypic effects on insect populations, but not community-wide effects (e.g., White, 1976, 1978; McNeill and Southwood, 1978; Cates, 1980; Haukioja, 1980).

Plant architecture is a labile character that affects herbivores. Where wild parsnip (*Pastinaca sativa*) grows in isolation, the plants are large and provide resources over a prolonged period of time and accumulate a large number of the specialized herbivores, *Depressaria pastinacella* (Thompson and Price, 1977). Where the plant grows in clumps, plants are small, resource availability synchronized and brief, and populations of the herbivore small. Such dramatic differences in resource availability have been observed within populations of wild parsnip. An almost converse effect of patch size has been seen in bracken fern, in which large patches had fern fronds larger than in small patches, and large fronds supported more herbivores than small fronds (Rigby and Lawton, 1981).

The expression of plant traits may also vary according to the habitat in which a plant is growing. Berenbaum (1978, 1981a) has noted that the defensive furanocoumarins in some umbellifers are activated by sunlight. Therefore, plants growing in the sun will define a rather specialized community, whereas shaded plants may permit more generalists to enter the herbivore community. Bracken fern also supports partially different assemblages of species and numbers of species, depending on whether it grows shaded and unshaded (Lawton, 1982, 1983).

Clearly, it is desirable in distinguishing between the genotypic- and phenotypic-heterogeneity hypotheses to adopt the now classic approach used by Clausen et al. (1948) to study ecotypic variation in Achillea. Plants expressing different phenotypes can be grown in uniform conditions to observe the plasticity in characters. The colonization of herbivores in such gardens could also be studied if they were located close to sources of colonists. If potted plants were utilized, these could be moved into natural populations to observe how herbivores respond. Reciprocal transplants between localities will test for plant effects on a community with the same array of potential colonizers. The experimental approach to insect herbivore communities can be developed readily, and it provides the opportunity for gaining leadership in the conceptual development of community ecology.

3. The Resource-Concentration Hypothesis

Root (1973) proposed this hypothesis, based on studies of arthropod communities on crucifers. The hypothesis states that simple, pure stands of a plant species represent a concentrated resource for specialized herbivores, which increases the attraction and accumulation of these species, the time they spend in the stand, and their reproductive success. As a result, a few species whose requirements are entirely met by the pure stand will become very abundant and contribute heavily to the herbivore load on the plant population (see Kareiva, Chapter 8). Conversely, plants of a species in a mixed stand represent a diluted resource and will be less easily detected by specialized herbivores; the herbivores are less likely to remain, and reproduction will be less successful because finding food is a greater problem. The herbivores will therefore contribute less to the total biomass of insects in the component community, with a probable increase in species richness and evenness. Part of the mechanism resulting in lower herbivore abundance on diluted resources appears to involve the *associational resistance* of the plant community in which the component community is situated (Tahvanainen and Root, 1972). Nonhost plants appear to interfere with finding host plants and the feeding on them, thus affecting colonization, survival, and reproductive success in mixed-species stands.

Evidence supporting this hypothesis has been provided by Root (1973). In pure stands of collards one species of flea beetle, *Phyllotreta cruciferae*, became very abundant and depressed the general species diversity (e.g., H') in the component community, probably as a result of interspecific competition. When collards were grown in a matrix of wild plants, providing diluted resources, this species was less dominant and species diversity was higher. These results were apparent in the absence of evidence that natural enemies had differential impact on populations in concentrated and diluted resources. Root (1973) provided other references with data supporting the resource concentration hypothesis, and Ralph (1977a,b), Bach (1980), and Risch (1981) added weight to its validity. In addition, the island-size hypothesis (discussed next), when applied on the local scale, is consistent with the resource-concentration hypothesis, although it concentrates on patch size without accounting for other aspects of patch quality emphasized by Root (see Lawton, 1978, for references).

The resource-concentration hypothesis involves many mechanisms, and they do not operate in all communities on all species. It is now important to identify the most important mechanisms, differences in mechanisms between communities, and any patterns in the kind of species that show the resource-concentration effect and which do not. For example, whereas flea beetles on collards support the hypothesis (Root, 1973), *Pieris rapae* butterflies do not, causing Cromartie (1975) to assert that "the diversity of the crucifer fauna is maintained by each species having a different pattern of colonization behaviour [p. 531]." This conclusion is also supported by McLain's (1981) study of hemipteran herbivores on *Senecio smallii*. Studying the gelechiid moth *Frumenta nundinella*, which is a specialist on leaves and fruits of *Solanum carolinense*, Solomon (1981) found no significant resource-concentration effect. Distance between concentrated resources and the source of colonists also plays a role, as illustrated by the moth *Cactoblastis cactorum* on populations of *Opuntia* cactus in Australia (Myers *et al.*, 1981), and the elm leaf beetle, *Pyrrhalta luteola*, on *Ulmus* seedlings (Lemen, 1981).

4. The Island or Patch-Size Hypothesis

This hypothesis was proposed by MacArthur and Wilson (1963, 1967) in their theory of island biogeography. The hypothesis states that area alone has a direct and positive effect on the number of species on an island, because a larger area has a higher probability of receiving colonists, and colonists will persist longer because the larger populations on larger islands or patches are less readily pushed to extinction by competitors, natural enemies, or simple stochastic population change. Thus the number of species on an island or patch is defined by a dynamic equilibrium between the colonization by new species and the extinction of resident species. Janzen (1968, 1973) made the now widely accepted claim that host plants represent islands available to insect herbivores for colonization (although discussion between critics and proponents is current: Kuris and Blaustein, 1977; Kuris et al., 1980; O'Connor et al., 1977; Rey et al., 1981; Lawton et al., 1981).

The most detailed experimental tests of the theory, by Wilson and Simberloff on mangrove islands (Simberloff, 1978) and Rey (1981) on *Spartina* islands, provide strong support. Defaunated islands were colonized rapidly, and the predefaunation number of species was largely reestablished, although the species differed. The equilibrium number of species present on islands was certainly dynamic, with high species colonization and extinction rates. When islands were reduced in size, without changing habitat diversity, the equilibrium number of species declined.

Many studies now support the prediction that as islands or patches of a plant species increase in area, the number of herbivore species increases (references in Lawton, 1978; Strong, 1979; Price, 1980). However, the mechanisms resulting in this pattern have not been adequately studied, and the pattern itself is not sufficient evidence that the MacArthur and Wilson immigration–extinction hypothesis is valid (Strong, 1979; Connor and McCoy, 1979; Lawton and Strong, 1981). Much more detailed work is needed.

In addition, where a species–area correlation holds, alternative hypotheses to the MacArthur and Wilson model have been seldom tested. When such alternatives have been investigated, as in the study by Rigby and Lawton (1981) on insect herbivores on bracken, other explanations are more viable. In the bracken component community the species–area relationship is best explained by differences in plant quality in patches of different size. Larger patches have plants with larger fronds, and larger fronds support more species than small fronds. Again, the detailed mechanisms resulting in this pattern need further study.

5. The Enemy-Impact Hypothesis

This hypothesis states that members of the third trophic level in a community based on plants influence the species richness and relative abundance of herbivores. Brower (1958) suggested that predators will limit similarity between prey species, and diet breadth will be restricted to plants on which protection from enemies is most effective. Ricklefs and O'Rourke (1975) and Otte and Joern (1977) followed with support for this argument. Askew (1961) argued that cynipid gall-wasp communities on oaks are organized by competition for avoidance of enemies. Root (1973) provided a concise review of the "enemies" hypothesis, as he called it, and more recent reviews have argued that enemy impact may well be more important than competition in organizing herbivore communities (Price *et al.*, 1980; Lawton and Strong, 1981). Parasitoids may cause extinction of some species in the community (Washburn and Cornell, 1981) and may keep populations below levels at which competition becomes important (Faeth and Simberloff, 1981a,b). Lawton (1978) introduced the term "enemy-free space," arguing that competition for such space was a viable alternative to competition for food.

Within plant species effects of enemy impact have been recorded repeatedly. Plants growing in monocultures usually support herbivores that are less attacked by enemies than those growing in diverse stands of plants. Associated plants provide important resources for enemies (Pimentel, 1961a,b; van Emden, 1963, 1965; Leius, 1967; Atsatt and O'Dowd, 1976; Price *et al.*, 1980).

The hypothesis that predators and parasites play an important organizing role in communities has not been adequately tested. We have little evidence yet of "keystone species" in the third trophic level regulating herbivore diversity as in intertidal communities (Paine, 1966, 1969), although Risch and Carroll (1982) have shown that the predaceous ant *Solenopsis geminata* can act in this way, greatly reducing diversity and abundance of species. Perhaps the most convincing evidence on the importance of enemy-free space is the great diversity seen in gall morphology within component communities. Askew (1961) noted this and made the cogent argument that divergence in gall morphology is most likely selected for by the action of enemies. Divergence in gall morphology could have no effect on competition for food between species, and there is no evidence that gall morphology influences quality of food for the herbivore. We know that gall formers are heavily attacked by parasitoids and inquilines and that communities of gall formers on plants are very rich [e.g., 19 species of cynipids in the genus *Andricus* in British oaks (Darlington, 1975), 16 species of cecidomyiid gall midges on creosote bush in the Tucson region of Arizona, most in the genus *Asphondylia* (G. Waring, personal communication)]. The link between high impact of enemies and high species richness in communities of gall formers is suggestive but has not been adequately established. It forms the most likely mechanistic explanation for the remarkable variety of gall shapes seen on one plant species.

C. Between-Host Species Hypotheses

Several of the hypotheses used to investigate changes in herbivore communities within plant species have been applied to the study of between-host-plant species differences. The resource-concentration, island-size, and enemy-impact hypotheses have their counterparts in between-host species studies. One assumption has been that communities are restricted to relatively small areas so that geographical effects do not play a role. Within-habitat differences have been discussed already. When comparisons are made between plant species, the concept of the community changes to a geographical scale rather than a within-habitat scale. It would be useful to distinguish between comparison of herbivore communities on different plants in the same habitat and on a geographical scale, but seldom have the two aspects of community analysis been combined. We know practically nothing about how within-habitat effects contribute to the variation seen in major trends such as species–area relationships.

1. The Island or Patch-Size Hypothesis

The same hypothesis has been applied to within-plant species and between-plant species comparisons (see Section III,B,4). In the latter case a positive relationship between area of plant species and species richness of herbivores has been demonstrated repeatedly (Connor and McCoy, 1979; Strong, 1979; Price, 1980), but the mechanisms resulting in this pattern have not been adequately studied. As Connor and McCoy (1979) have pointed out, three hypotheses are equally viable at present: (a) the *area per se hypothesis* defined in Section III,B,4; (b) the *habitat-diversity hypothesis* proposed by Williams (1964), in which the increase in island or patch size increases the number of habitats sampled and the number of species living in each habitat (see Section III,C,3, the habitat-heterogeneity hypothesis); and (c) the *passive-sampling hypothesis* defined by Connor and McCoy (1979)—larger areas sample passively larger numbers of colonists and thus contain more species, independent of any population phenomena or interaction between species. Passive sampling is the null hypothesis for the mechanism explaining the species–area relationship. This hypothesis is akin to the *species-exhaustion hypothesis* proposed by Lawton and Strong (1981), in which a plant species receives samples of insects until none is left that is readily capable of colonizing that plant. Because colonization is a probabilistic phenomenon, plants occupying larger areas receive more colonists, all else being equal. Southwood (1960) recognized this possibility and showed that the most common trees in Hawaii have the largest number of herbivores on them, the trend being the same for both specialist and generalist herbivores. The importance in distinguishing between these hypotheses is great, for they are central to the understanding of herbivore communities on plants. The resolution is fundamental to the debate on the importance of competition and predation in natural communities (Lawton and Strong, 1981; see Section V on competition). Opler (1974) showed that hosts with the largest geographic range also have the highest local number of species, supporting hypothesis (a). Fowler and Lawton (1982) showed that area of plant species has no effect on agromyzid species richness, once the effect of habitat number occupied by a plant was removed, adding support to hypothesis (b).

Hypothesis (b) necessitates a more detailed understanding of the kinds of species present in a community than has been achieved until now. Questions that need to be answered are, When and from where do generalists and specialists arrive in a community? How many habitat specialists exist in a community, and how do they contribute to the area effect? What are the relative colonizing abilities of the species? Opler (1974) demonstrated clearly that species differ in their colonizing abilities and that these qualitative effects create patterns in leaf-miner communities on oaks. Oak species with small areal range support only the best colonizers, those in the genera *Cameraria* and *Lithocolletis*. An increasing array of species are able to adapt to oak as the oak species become more abundant, with some insect species, in the genera *Careospina* and *Neurobathra*, restricted to the most common oak species. The number of species per genus among good colonizers also increases with increasing geographic range of host. Identification of such patterns reveals important insights into the mechanisms involved in the development of insect communities on plants.

2. The Time Hypothesis

This hypothesis states that older communities have more species than younger ones, because evolutionary time is necessary for the increase in species richness. Southwood (1961) presented data in support of this hypothesis, showing that species of trees in Britain with a more extensive fossil record had more species of insects than those less well represented. However, Strong (1974a,b) has shown that present area of these trees is a better correlate of herbivore species number than evolutionary time. But in many cases herbivore communities seem to be so depauperate relative to the resources available that evolutionary time may well be important in the enrichment of communities (Lawton and Price, 1979).

Using new estimates of residence times of trees in Britain, Birks (1980) reconfirmed the likelihood of a time effect on the number of insect species per tree species.

Wilson (1969) proposed that communties develop in four phases: noninteractive, interactive, assortative, and evolutionary. The noninteractive phase occurs early in community development, when species number and population density are low and enemies poorly established. Biotic interaction is absent, except for the important relationship between plants themselves and the herbivore colonists. The interactive phase results when populations become large enough for competition to play a role and enemies are established, resulting in a likely decline in species number and the establishment of a dynamic equilibrium of species number, imposed by equalized colonization and extinction rates. The assortative phase results in an increased equilibrium number of species as species are sorted in favor of those species that can most efficiently utilize resources and coexist with others. Finally, an evolutionary phase is reached in which the equilibrium number of species increases by the coevolution of species, which adapts them for more efficient coexistence. The assumption here is that communities are usually saturated with species from the interactive phase onward and that the experimental addition of species would not change the equilibrium number of species in the long run.

The stage in community development in which herbivore communities on plants exist is a debatable point. Although the role of competition in organizing communities has become a part of conventional wisdom in ecology (e.g., Ricklefs, 1973; Pianka, 1974), there is increasing realization that interaction between members of the same trophic level is minimal in insect communities on plants (Lawton, 1978; Strong, 1979; Lawton and Strong, 1981). The keys in this debate lie in understanding the nature of equilibrium in herbivore communities and the role of competition, discussed in Sections IV and V.

3. The Habitat-Heterogeneity Hypothesis

Plant species may occur in several habitats, or they may provide habitats for herbivores. In the first case, Williams' (1964) hypothesis (described in Section III,C,1) holds that the more habitats in which a plant species occurs, the more insect herbivores are likely to occur in the component community based on that plant [hypothesis (a)]. The difficulties in isolating the habitat effect from the pure effect have been discussed in Section III,B,4 and C,1. Several authors have acknowledged the likelihood that the mechanism resulting in the island-size hypothesis actually involves habitat heterogeneity (Strong, 1979; Connor and

McCoy, 1979; Lawton and Strong, 1981), and this has been supported by evidence concerning agromyzid flies on British Umbelliferae (Fowler and Lawton, 1982).

The hypothesis that plants provide habitats for herbivores and that as plant architecture increases in complexity the number of herbivores on that plant increases [hypothesis (b)] has been tested several times. As plant size increases, the number of associated herbivores increases, when gross comparisons are made between structural groupings such as herbs, shrubs, and trees (Lawton and Schröder, 1977, 1978; Price, 1977; Strong and Levin, 1979). A more detailed study on architecture in *Opuntia* species by Moran (1980) showed that as plant complexity increased, the number of specialized herbivore species it supported increased. Using an "architectural rating," based on height of plant, number and area of cladodes, cladode texture and spininess, and extent of woody stem development, 69% of the variance in herbivore species richness was accounted for. A similar pattern was seen in specialized herbivores on milkweeds in Illinois (Price and Willson, 1979). Plant height accounted for a small amount of variance in species richness of leaf miners on plants, in addition to the area effect (Lawton and Price, 1979). In all of these studies, plant size was a significant component, meaning that the island-size hypothesis can be involved in all of its three forms: the area per se hypothesis [see Sections III,B,4 and C,1, hypothesis (a) above], the habitat-diversity hypothesis [Sections III,C,1, hypothesis (b), and III,C,3], and the passive-sampling hypothesis [Section III,C,1, hypothesis (c)] (Strong, 1979; Connor and McCoy, 1979).

4. The Resource-Diversity Hypothesis

This hypothesis states that the number of species in a community "is proportional to the number of kinds of packages of resources available in that community [Karr, 1975, p. 162]" (see also Orians, 1969). Karr noted that the number of birds in tropical communities is greater than in temperate regions, largely because more resources are present. Additional guilds of birds are present in the tropics, because of resources like large insects and fruits that are not abundant enough to be specialized on in temperate regions. The relationship of this hypothesis to the general case (Fig. 1) is clear.

Therefore, for insect herbivores, for which the habitat-heterogeneity hypothesis has been applied to plant architecture, the resource-diversity hypothesis is likely to be pertinent. As a plant increases in size, it adds resources available to herbivores: first a root, stem, and cotyledons, then petioles, midribs, and leaf laminae, followed by stems of inflorescences, pedicels, flowers, nectar, and pollen, and, finally, enlarged ovaries and seeds, senescent leaves and stems, and decaying leaves. All of these resources may be present at once in the later stages of plant development. The number of herbivores in the component community should change as resources develop, a pattern seen in bracken (Lawton, 1978), nettle (Davis, 1973), and soybean (Price, 1976; Kogan, 1981). In addition, plants of large stature, like trees, provide more resources than the more diminutive herbs (Strong, 1979). A stem has heart and sap wood, an active cambium, cortex, and bark. Bark may be thick at the base and thin on the branches, a gradient along which species such as bark beetles may specialize (Price, 1975); furrows and bark scales add to the diversity of bark, a diversity not present in herbs (Morris, 1974). Bark also allows the development of an epiphytic flora, adding enormously to the richness of resources for herbivores (e.g., Rose, 1974).

Another perspective on resource diversity was provided by Berenbaum (1981a), who showed that the defensive chemistry of plant hosts influences community structure. As the chemical defenses become more diverse in the form of linear and then angular furanocoumarins, so the bias shifts from communities of generalists to communities of specialists (Table II; see also Futuyma, 1976).

The habitat-heterogeneity and the resource-diversity hypotheses have been used interchangeably in the literature. It is desirable to segregate effects on community structure into the two mechanisms involved, by detailed studies of the idiosynchratic responses to plants as habitats sought by herbivores and to plants as providers of resources utilized by herbivores.

5. The Enemy-Impact Hypothesis

This hypothesis relates to differences between component communities on different plant species, and it has been stated in Section III,B,5. Presence and absence of herbivores is dictated by the efficacy of enemies in preventing colonization. *Heliconius melpomene* is specific to *Passiflora oerstedii* in nature, although it feeds and grows on four other *Passiflora* species when placed on them. Smiley (1978) has suggested that enemy impact imposed by predators and parasitoids on the latter species causes "ecological monophagy" to *P. oerstedii*, in the absence of "coevolved monophagy" (Gilbert, 1979). Atsatt (1981a) has made a convincing case that in the speciose subfamilies of lycaenid butterflies, Theclinae and Polyommatine, butterflies have adapted to associating with ants that protect eggs and larvae and that "larval diet has been significantly altered to achieve ant-associated enemy-free space [p. 639]" (see also Atsatt, 1981b; Pierce and Mead, 1981). The dramatic dietary differences between closely related lycaenids suggests that speciation results when ants are located on new, unrelated host plants and that such shifts have provided the mechanism resulting in the great species richness in these subfamilies. Thus the acquisition of enemy-free space, by associating with ants, affects species richness of herbivores directly, the plant species on which they occur, and their abundance (Atsatt, 1981a).

A counterexample, using a much cruder approach, indicates that the number of herbivores on plants is not related to the number of parasitoids associated with those plants (Lawton and Price, 1979).

Now that the hypothesis is widely regarded as viable and important (e.g., Lawton, 1978; Holloway and Herbert, 1979; Lawton and McNeill, 1979; Price *et al.*, 1980; Lawton and Strong, 1981; and references in Section III,B,5), it is desirable to develop direct tests of its validity. Following Askew's (1961) lead on cynipid gall wasps on oaks, this and similar communities of gall formers would be ideal subjects, because the diversity of gall form seems to relate more to interaction with enemies than to the host plant. The lycaenid butterflies studied by Atsatt (1981a,b) and *Heliconius* butterflies studied by Gilbert and Smiley (1978; Smiley, 1978; Gilbert, 1979) also provide excellent opportunities. Any plant that develops extrafloral nectaries suggests that its component community of herbivores will be influenced significantly by the enemies attracted to this rich carbohydrate source (e.g., Bentley, 1977). Any component community that includes herbivores that produce honeydew will again be influenced by ants, which are likely to act as enemies to the other herbivores (e.g., Messina, 1981). The effect of herbivore enemies on community structure is probably ubiquitous, but it needs much more study.

IV. COMMUNITIES AT EQUILIBRIUM OR NONEQUILIBRIUM?

Community equilibrium is defined as the state in which the rate of immigration of new species is equal to the rate of extinction of resident species (MacArthur and Wilson, 1967). Therefore, patches of equal size should have the same number of species at equilibrium. This definition may be applied to communities in both ecological and evolutionary time.

An obvious condition for community equilibrium is that resources persist and remain stable. If resources change in number and abundance, the species number and relative abundance will be altered (see Fig. 1). This clearly happens in many communities, more commonly than not in temperate component herbivore communities based on living plants (Davis, 1973; Price, 1976; Lawton, 1978). For herbivores utilizing leaves, resources expand at such a rate that much remains unexploited. Resources change so rapidly in quality that only a brief period is available for colonization (Thompson and Price, 1977). A shortage of time dominates the process of community development, even though resources are apparently superabundant. Resources are displayed in rapid succession, and conditions provided by the plant change, contributing substantially to change in species number (Price, 1976). Then senescence of the plant or plant parts initiates a general decline in species number. Local component communities in temperate regions are always in a state of flux and are unlikely to exist in an equilibrium state. Any component community of insects on plants in markedly seasonal habitats, which is the vast majority, will exist largely in a nonequilibrium condition in ecological time (see also Price, 1980, 1983).

Even in tropical environments, where resources persist throughout the year, individual units of resource may be ephemeral, with similar impact on utilization by herbivores. The rolled leaves of *Heliconia* used by hispine chrysomdid beetles are always present in a patch of plants, but each leaf may remain rolled and available for only a few days (Strong, 1981, 1982), with the result that usually less than 0.5% of the leaf is eaten by the chrysomelids and all other herbivores combined.

In evolutionary time a similar picture emerges. For example, in a well-studied flora and fauna, only 291 species of leaf-mining flies (Agromyzidae) exploit 2177 nonaquatic plants in the British Isles. This is an expected 0.13 species of herbivore per plant; yet some plant species support up to 9 species of agromyzid, others none (Spencer, 1972). When species of plant with similar geographic ranges are compared, enormous differences in species number of agromyzids are observed (Lawton and Price, 1979; Price, 1980). An equilibrium number of species is not apparent in these studies. Attempts to explain this on the basis of preemption of resources by other taxa in the leaf-mining guild have failed. Leaf-mining moths are positively, not negatively correlated with agromyzid species number (Lawton and Price, 1979). The only conclusion available is that with more evolutionary time the herbivore fauna on a plant species will become richer, so ultimately community equilibrium will be reached. At present, communities are undersaturated and, from an evolutionary perspective, in a nonequilibrium condition. Several other studies have shown that plant species with similar geographic range have numbers of herbivore species that are significantly different, leading to a species–area regression that acccounts for less than 50% of the variance (Strong and Levin, 1975; Claridge and Wilson, 1976, 1978; Cornell and Washburn, 1979). This suggests that many plant species could be enriched with herbivore species in evolutionary time, without causing extinction of resident species. In addition, there is no evidence to suggest that even the plant species with the richest herbivore communities are saturated with herbivore species (Lawton and Price, 1979; Price, 1980, 1983; Lawton, 1982, 1983).

V. THE ROLE OF COMPETITION

Four factors appear to dominate the organization of component communities on plants (Price, 1980, 1983).

1. Species colonize in an idiosyncratic manner, showing an individualistic response to available resources (see Section III,B,3). The probability of frequent contact between species is therefore low (see following discussion).

2. There is a shortage of time when resources are available for colonization, and once colonized resources are not available long enough to permit complete utilization (see Section IV).

3. Many herbivorous insects are highly specialized (see Section II), not only to plant species, but to plant parts, simply because a small organism cannot adapt to exploiting a wide range of resources.

4. Contact and interaction with the host plant affect 100% of the individuals in these component communities. Selective pressures imposed by the plant will be strong. The probability of interaction between herbivore species on a plant is usually much less than 100%. For example, the study by Roskam and van Uffelen (1981) indicates that the probabilities of encounter between two species ranges around 0.003 and 0.007, or less than 1% of resources. Therefore, evolutionary responses of herbivores to hosts will always be stronger than such responses to other members of the herbivore community.

These characteristics of herbivore communities combine to make competition a weak influence in their organization. The most persuasive statements to this effect have been made by Connell (1980) for the general case and Lawton and Strong (1981) for herbivorous insect communities in particular. When communities are undersaturated both in ecological and evolutionary time, selection from competitors will be weak or absent (Price, 1980, 1983). Considering the concept of community development proposed by Wilson (1969; Section III,C,2), it appears that many communities exist at the noninteractive phase. Even those that show an apparent equilibrium number of species may result from the passive sampling of available species [Section III,C,1, hypothesis (c)] or the species-exhaustion hypothesis proposed by Lawton and Strong (1981), which states that the plant population's or species' accumulation of herbivore species "is rapidly asymptotic by quickly exhausting the pool of species that have high probabilities of colonization [p. 326]."

Those communities that enter the interactive phase may well be organized by enemies rather than by competition. But, as Lawton and Strong (1981) have said, the effect of enemies is poorly understood and needs much more study. Whether insect herbivore communities have ever reached equilibrium under assortative and evolutionary influences remains in doubt.

VI. VACANT NICHES IN ECOLOGICAL AND EVOLUTIONARY TIME

Hutchinson (1957) viewed the niche as an n-dimensional hypervolume in the environment, the perimeter of which circumscribes the space in which a species can reproduce indefinitely. The niche, from this perspective, is a property of the environment. Therefore, the question can be asked, Do vacant niches exist in the environment? Are there hypervolumes in nature that seem to be suitable for supporting a species, even though no such species exists?

Specialist insect herbivores are particularly valuable in attempts to answer this question, because of the following properties (see also Price, 1983).

1. Insect herbivores usually live on the food plant for a prolonged period, enabling an accurate assessment of resources on the plant that an insect needs to complete development.

2. Once the resources are known, these can easily be quantified on per-plant and per-plant-patch bases.

3. Hosts provide homologous habitats. Each herbaceous plant species provides the same set of resources in terms of stems, leaves, roots, flowers, seeds, etc. available for colonization by herbivores. Trees provide all of these plus additional resources, as discussed in Section III,C,4. Therefore, if one herbaceous plant species supports ten herbivore species, we can assume that ten such ecological niches exist on other herbaceous plants for a similar array of herbivore species. A strong comparative and predictive approach can be applied to these herbivore assemblages, and unoccupied niches can be identified.

4. Specialist species provide a clear picture of the organisms' needs, an organismal perspective of the ecological niche, and the scale at which we should be studying niche occupation.

When this approach is taken, it can be demonstrated repeatedly that many plant species could support many more herbivore species. Only

291 agromyzid species occur on 2177 species of plants in Britain (see Section II), but some host plants support 9 species. In Canada, an average of 5 agromyzid species are found per 100 plant species (Price, 1977). Attempts to explain absence of species in one taxon by preemption of resources by members of another taxon have failed (Lawton and Price, 1979). In fact, positive relationships have been found between numbers of species of leaf-mining flies and leaf-mining moth larvae, suggesting that insect species in different taxa colonize plant species independently—a recurring theme in this chapter. Other examples in which the slope of regression of number of species in a taxon versus the number of hosts available is very low are given by Price (1980).

This perspective indicates a world that is very depauperate compared to the number of species that could be supported. Many ecological niches remain vacant in evolutionary time. This poses a paradox of major proportions. Specialized herbivorous insects exist under conditions conducive to rapid evolution and speciation (Price, 1977, 1980), yet adaptive radiation is nowhere nearly as extensive as resources seem to permit. Resolution of this paradox is central to the understanding of insect herbivore communities.

If many ecological niches on plants remain vacant in evolutionary time these will dilute the interactions between species, because many gaps on resource gradients will exist. In contrast to the tight species packing invoked by theoreticians dealing with competition (e.g., MacArthur, 1972), species will not be packed at all, being more like sardines in an ocean than sardines in a tin, with much ecological space between species.

In ecological space and time the conclusion is similar—local occupation of habitats is very patchy, many patches remain uncolonized, and the probability of encounter between potential competitors is low. Rathcke (1967a,b), studying the stem-boring insect guild in tall-grass prairie plants, with 13 common insect species present, estimated that usually less than 10% of resources in a stem is utilized by a boring insect, usually less than 20% of stems attacked, and that the cooccurrence of species fits the pattern generated assuming random distribution of species. Rathcke concluded that competition has not been a major organizing force within the guild of stem borers, because resources of food and space were generally not limiting. In addition, predation on stem boring larvae was virtually absent (Rathcke, 1976a). Rathcke (1976b) noted that insects seldom exist in equilibrium populations "a condition necessary for most predictions of competition theory [p. 85]."

Low occupancy of resources is typical of insects on plants. In a survey of 12 relatively common insect herbivore species on 6 milkweed species (*Asclepias* spp.) over 2 yr, 21 plot–yr of data were collected (Price and Willson, 1979). In 95% of the cases in the matrix of the 12 herbivore species and 21 plot–yr, the herbivores occurred at densities of less than 10% of stems occupied by a species, and 46% of entries in the matrix were zero. When all species were combined, 43% of the 21 plot–yr showed less than 10 individuals per 100 stems, and 76% showed less than 30 individuals per 100 stems, whereas each stem has the biomass to support many insect herbivores. The distribution of the common herbivores was very patchy, and compared to food resource availability they were rare. It seems that patches of these herbaceous plants are hard to find, as predicted by Feeny (1976) and Rhoades and Cates (1976).

The distribution of eight *Erythroneura* leafhopper species on sycamore *(Platanus)* becomes increasingly patchy as distance from the center of distribution increases (McClure and Price, 1976). Many habitats were found to be totally unoccupied: an average of 3% sampled in the center of the species range, 52% at the edge of the range, and 34% midway between these extremes (from McClure's original data). Within these habitats distributions were very uneven, also, even for species close to the center of their range. These data show that throughout much of the range of these species resources were superabundant. Competition has been shown to occur between these species in experimental enclosures (McClure and Price, 1976), but any real effects in natural communities have yet to be demonstrated.

Low utilization of resources may result from a combination of specialization to a particular resource state and rapid change in state, resulting in shortage of time when resources are suitable for attack and exploitation (Price, 1972; Jones, Chapter 15). One example concerns the parsnip webworm *(Depressaria pastinacella)*, which lays eggs on unopened umbels of the wild parsnip *(Pastinaca sativa)*. This time of attack coincides with a period of very rapid development, from rosette to flowering (Thompson and Price, 1977), during which any one unopened umbel may remain suitable for oviposition for only 48 hr, or only two nights when moths are flying. Therefore, a small plant with two or three umbels may provide resources for the moth for only a few days. Plants in patches develop in synchrony, so a patch could easily be missed while resources are suitable for attack. In a high-density stand of parsnip, resources were available for about 13 days, and less than 50% of umbels were attacked on only 52% of the plants, leaving about 75% of resources unutilized. Larger plants in uncrowded conditions displayed more umbels over a larger period of time. Unopened umbels were attacked for a period of 29 days, and 90% of plants and 68% of umbels were utilized, leaving little less than 40% of resources unutilized. The majority of umbels in this old field were produced in dense stands, so resources in general were superabundant, even at epidemic population levels of the webworm. This study was done in one of two years when the population was greatest, between 1970 and 1979.

When specialist herbivores are considered, the conclusion seems to be justified that many vacant niches remain in evolutionary time and that many resources or resource patches remain uncolonized in ecological time. Under these conditions communities are likely to result from the individualistic colonization of resources by species, in the absence of competition as an organizing force.

VII. COMPOUND COMMUNITIES

Root (1973) noted that "the organization of component communities should be more obvious than that of compound communities, in which the critical interactions are observed by combining relatively distinct systems [p. 96]." His observation that "little is known about how components influence one another [p. 96]" is as valid today as it was when written.

One important link between component communities, especially those with many specialized herbivores, is likely to be at the third trophic level, in which enemies of herbivores cross component-community boundaries. Evidence discussed in Section III,B,5 suggests that enemy impact is greater in assemblages of component communities than in monocultures. Such linkage is seen in the component communities on wild blackberries and wild grape growing in riparian habitats in California (Doutt and Nakata, 1973), where the species in common is the egg parasite *Anagrus epos*, which attacks the specialist cicadellid herbivores *Dikrella cruentata* on blackberry and *Erythroneura elegantula* on grape (Fig. 2). The important point, made by Atsatt and O'Dowd (1976), is that such cross linkage at the third trophic level may influence evolutionary patterns, even between the plants in the compound community. The study of interaction between component communities is therefore very important, but it is still on a very elementary level.

Another interaction between component communities concerns other aspects of "associational resistance" (Tahvanainen and Root, 1972) beyond the impact of enemies. Plants grown in association with other species usually have lower herbivore loads than those in monocultures (Tahvanainen and Root, 1972; Root, 1973; Bach, 1980; Risch, 1981). This may result from a pure plant-density effect or interference by associated plants with host discovery and feeding.

Compound communities have been investigated by studying the effects of plant species diversity on insect species diversity (e.g., Hurd *et*

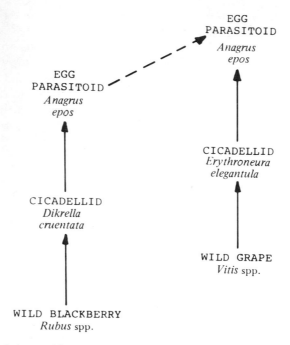

Fig. 2. Food chains on blackberries and grape, illustrating linkage at the third trophic level. The displacement of the grape food chain upward illustrates the later phenology of grape and its herbivore, so that parasitoids reared on blackberry emerge and attack eggs of the herbivore on grape. Movement of the parasitoid between component communities is illustrated by the dashed line.

al., 1971; Murdoch *et al.*, 1972; Hurd and Wolf, 1974; Sharp *et al.*, 1974; Gibson, 1976). In general, the relationship accounts for little of the variance in insect species richness, reinforcing the view that synoptic approaches to community organization of insect herbivores cannot cope with the individualistic nature of these herbivores to available resources.

Even though Root's (1973) assertion is correct that interactions are more easily observed in component communities than in compound communities, the many viable hypotheses depicting major organizational influences in component communities indicate that major research effort is needed in order to reach some general conclusions on their relative importance. More research programs should be designed specifically to distinguish between alternative hypotheses, and, as Connell (1980) has emphasized, only well-designed field experiments are adequate for the task. There is also a need for more explicit hypotheses defining the mechanisms that result in the major aspects of community structure: the number of species present, the type of species present, the relative abundance of species, the stage in community development, and the equilibrium status of the community.

ACKNOWLEDGMENTS

I am grateful to John H. Lawton, Richard B. Root, Donald R. Strong, and John N. Thompson for their very helpful reviews of the manuscript. Financial support was provided by National Science Foundation grant DEB 80-21754.

REFERENCES

Askew, R. R. (1961). On the biology of the inhabitants of oak galls of Cynipidae (Hymenoptera) in Britain. *Trans. Soc. Br. Entomol.* **14**, 237–268.

Atsatt, P. R. (1981a). Lycaenid butterflies and ants; selection for enemy-free space. *Am. Nat.* **118**, 638–654.

Atsatt, P. R. (1981b). Ant dependent oviposition by the mistletoe butterfly *Ogyris amaryllis*. *Oecologia* **48**, 60–63.

Atstatt, P. R., and O'Dowd, D. J. (1976). Plant defense guilds. *Science* **193**, 24–29.

Bach, C. E. (1980). Effects of plant density and diversity on the population dynamics of a specialist herbivore, the striped cucumber beetle, *Acalymma vittata* (Fab.). *Ecology* **61**, 1515–1530.

Baltensweiler, W. (1970). The relevance of changes in the composition of larch and moth populations for the dynamics of its numbers. *Proc. Adv. Study Inst. Dyn. Numbers Popul., 1970* pp. 208–219.

Bentley, B. L. (1977). Extrafloral nectaries and protection by pugnacious bodyguards. *Annu. Rev. Ecol. Syst* **8**, 407–427.

Berenbaum, M. (1978). Toxicity of a furanocoumarin to armyworms: a case of biosynthetic escape from insect herbivores. *Science* **201**, 532–534.

Berenbaum, M. (1981a). Patterns of furanocoumarin distribution and insect herbivory in the Umbelliferae: plant chemistry and community structure. *Ecology* **62**, 1254–1266.

Berenbaum, M. (1981b). Effects of linear furanocoumarins on an adapted specialist insect *(Papilio polyxenes)*. *Ecol. Entomol.* **6**, 345–351.

Birks, H. J. B. (1980). British trees and insects: a test of the time hypothesis over the last 13,000 years. *Am. Nat.* **115**, 600–605.

Brower, L. P. (1958). Bird predation and foodplant specificity in closely related procryptic insects. *Am. Nat.* **92**, 183–187.

Burdon, J. J. (1978). Mechanisms of disease control in heterogeneous plant populations— an ecologist's view. *In* "Plant Disease Epidemiology" (P. R. Scott and A. Bainbridge, eds.), pp. 193–200. Blackwell, Oxford.

Burdon, J. J. (1980). Variation in disease-resistance within a population of *Trifolium repens*. *J. Ecol.* **68**, 737–744.

Burdon, J. J., and Marshall, D. R. (1981). Inter- and intra-specific diversity in the disease-response of *Glycine* species to the leaf-rust fungus *Phakopsora pachyrhizi*. *J. Ecol.* **69**, 381–390.

Bush, G. L. (1975). Sympatric speciation in phytophagous parasitic insects. *In* "Evolutionary Strategies of Parasitic Insects and Mites" (P. W. Price, ed.), pp. 187–206. Plenum, New York.

Cates, R. G. (1980). Feeding patterns of monophagous, oligophagous, and polyphagous insect herbivores: the effect of resource abundance and plant chemistry. *Oecologia* **46**, 22–31.

Clapham, A. R., Tutin, T. G., and Warburg, E. F. (1957). "Flora of the British Isles." Cambridge Univ. Press, London and New York.

Claridge, M. F., and Wilson, M. R. (1976). Diversity and distribution patterns of some mesophyll-feeding leafhoppers of temperate woodland canopy. *Ecol. Entomol.* **1**, 231–250.

Claridge, M. F., and Wilson, M. R. (1978). British insects and trees: a study in island biogeography or insect/plant coevolution? *Am. Nat.* **112**, 451–456.

Clausen, J., Keck, D. D., and Hiesey, W. M. (1948). Experimental studies on the nature of species. III. Environmental responses of climatic races of *Achillea. Carnegie Inst., Washington Pub.* **581**, 1–129.

Connell, J. H. (1980). Diversity and the coevolution of competitors, or the ghost of competition past. *Oikos* **35**, 131–138.

Connor, E. F. and McCoy, E. D. (1979). The statistics and biology of the species–area relationship. *Am. Nat.* **113**, 791–833.

Cornell, H. V., and Washburn, J. O. (1979). Evolution of the richness–area correlation for cynipid gall wasps on oak trees: a comparison of two geographic areas. *Evolution* **33**, 257–274.

Cromartie, W. J. (1975). The effect of stand size and vegetational background on the colonization of cruciferous plants by herbivorous insects. *J. Appl. Ecol.* **12**, 517–533.

Darlington, A. (1975). "A Pocket Encyclopaedia of Plant Galls in Colour," Rev. ed. Blandford Press, Poole, Dorset.

Davis, B. N. K. (1973). The Hemiptera and Coleoptera of stinging nettle *(Urtica dioica* L.*)* in East Anglia. *J. Appl. Ecol.* **10**, 213–237.

Davis, D. R. (1967). A revision of the moths of the subfamily Prodoxinae (Lepidoptera: Incurvariidae). *Bull.—U.S. Nat. Mus.* **255**, 1–170.

Day, P. R. (1974). "Genetics of Host–Parasite Interaction." Freeman, San Francisco.

Denno, R. F., Raupp, M. J., and Tallamy, D. W. (1981). Organization of a guild of sap-feeding insects: equilibrium vs. nonequilibrium coexistence. *In* "Insect Life History Patterns" (R. F. Denno and H. Dingle, eds.), pp. 151–181. Springer-Verlag, New York and Berlin.

Doutt, R. L., and Nakata, J. (1973). The *Rubus* leafhopper and its egg parasitoid: an endemic biotic system useful in grape-pest management. *Environ. Entomol.* **2**, 381–386.

Eastop, V. F. (1973). Deductions from the present day host plants of aphids and related insects. *Symp. R. Entomol. Soc. London* **6**, 157–178.

Faeth, S. H., and Simberloff, D. (1981a). Population regulation of a leaf-mining insect, *Cameraria* sp. nov., at increased field densities. *Ecology* **62**, 620–624.

Faeth, S. H., and Simberloff, D. (1981b). Experimental isolation of oak host plants: effects on mortality, survivorship, and abundances of leaf-mining insects. *Ecology* **62**, 625–635.

Feeny, P. (1976). Plant apparency and chemical defense. *In* "Biochemical Interaction Between Plants and Insects" (J. W. Wallace and R. L. Mansell, eds.), pp. 1–40. Plenum, New York.

Flor, H. H. (1971). Current status of the gene-for-gene concept. *Annu. Rev. Phytopathol.* **9**, 272–296.

Fowler, S. V., and Lawton, J. H. (1982). The effects of host-plant distribution and local abundance on the species richness of agromyzid flies attacking British umbellifers. *Ecol. Entomol.* **7**, 257–265.

Fox, L. R. and Morrow, P. A. (1981). Specialization: species property of local phenomenon? *Science* **211**, 887–893.

Futuyma, D. J. (1976). Food plant specialization and environmental predictability in Lepidoptera. *Am. Nat.* **110**, 285–292.

Gibson, C. W. D. (1976). The importance of foodplants for the distribution and abundance of some Stenodemini (Heteroptera: Miridae) of limestone grassland. *Oecologia* **25**, 55–76.

Gilbert, L. E. (1979). Development of theory in the analysis of insect–plant interactions. *In* "Analysis of Ecological Systems" (D. J. Horn, G. S. Stairs, and R. D. Mitchell, eds.), pp. 117–154. Ohio State Univ. Press, Columbus.

Gilbert, L. E., and Smiley, J. T. (1978). Determinants of local diversity in phytophogous insects: host specialists in tropical environments. *Symp. R. Entomol. Soc. London* **9**, 89–104.

Gleason, H. A. (1926). The individualistic concept of the plant association. *Bull. Torrey Bot. Club* **53**, 7–26.

Hatchett, J. H. and Gallun, R. L. (1970). Genetics of the ability of the Hessian fly, *Mayetiola destructor*, to survive on wheats having different genes for resistance. *Ann. Entomol. Soc. Am.* **63**, 1400–1407.

Haukioja, E. (1980). On the role of plant defenses in the fluctuation of herbivore populations. *Oikos* **35**, 202–213.

Hegnauer, R. (1971). Chemical patterns and relationships of Umbelliferae. *In* "The Biology and Chemisty of the Umbelliferae" (V. H. Heywood, ed.), pp. 267–277. Academic Press, New York and London.

Hering, E. M. (1951). "Biology of the Leaf Miners." Junk, The Hague.

Holloway, J. D., and Herbert, P. D. N. (1979). Ecological and taxonomic trends in macrolepidopteran host plant selection. *Biol. J. Linn. Soc.* **11**, 229–251.

Hurd, L. E., and Wolf, L. L. (1974). Stability in relation to nutrient enrichment in arthropod consumers of old-field successional vegetation. *Ecol. Monogr.* **44**, 465–482.

Hurd, L. E., Mellinger, M. V., Wolf, L. L., and McNaughton, S. J. (1971). Stability and diversity at three trophic levels in terrestrial successional ecosystems. *Science* **173**, 1134–1136.

Hutchinson, G. E. (1957). Concluding remarks. *Cold Spring Harbor Symp. Quant. Biol.* **22**, 415–427.

Hutchinson, G. E. (1965). "The Ecological Theater and the Evolutionary Play." Yale Univ. Press, New Haven, Connecticut.

Janzen, D. H. (1968). Host plants as islands in evolutionary and contemporary time. *Am. Nat.* **102**, 592–595.

Janzen, D. H. (1973). Host plants as islands. II. Competition in evolutionary and contemporary time. *Am. Nat.* **107**, 786–790.

Karr, J. R. (1975). Production, energy pathways, and community diversity in forest birds. *In* "Tropical Ecological Systems: Trends in Terrestrial and Aquatic Research" (F. B. Golley and E. Medina, eds.), pp. 161–176. Springer-Verlag, New York and Berlin.

Klomp, H. (1968). A seventeen-year study of the abundance of the pine looper, *Bupalus piniarius* L. (Lepidoptera: Geometridae). *Symp. R. Entomol. Soc. London* **4**, 98–108.

Kogan, M. (1981). Dynamics of insect adaptations to soybean: impact of integrated pest management. *Environ. Entomol.* **10**, 363–371.

Kuris, A. M. and Blaustein, A. R. (1977). Ectoparasitic mites on rodents: application of the island biogeographic theory? *Science* **195**, 596–598.

Kuris, A. M., Blaustein, A. R., and Alió, J. J. (1980). Hosts as islands. *Am. Nat.* **116**, 570–586.

Lawton, J. H. (1976). The structure of the anthropod community on bracken. *Bot. J. Linn. Soc.* **73**, 187–216.

Lawton, J. H. (1978). Host-plant influences on insect diversity: the effects of space and time. *Symp. R. Entomol. Soc. London* **9**, 105–125.

Lawton, J. H. (1982). Vacant niches and unsaturated communities: a comparison of bracken herbivores at sites on two continents. *J. Anim. Ecol.* **51**, 573–595.

Lawton, J. H. (1983). Non-competitive populations, non-convergent communities, and vacant niches: the herbivores on bracken. *In* "Ecological Communities: Conceptual Issues and the Evidence" (D. R. Strong, D. Simberloff, and L. G. Abele, eds), Princeton Univ. Press, Princeton, New Jersey (in press).

Lawton, J. H., and McNeill, S. (1979). Between the devil and the deep blue sea: on the problem of being a herbivore. *Symp. Br. Ecol. Soc.* **20**, 223–244.

Lawton, J. H., and Price, P. W. (1979). Species richness of parasites on hosts: agromyzid flies on the British Umbelliferae. *J. Anim. Ecol.* **48**, 619–637.

Lawton, J. H., and Schröder, D. (1977). Effects of plant type, size of geographical range and taxonomic isolation on number of insect species associated with British plants. *Nature (London)* **265**, 137–140.

Lawton, J. H., and Schröder, D. (1978). Some observations on the structure of phytophagous insect communities: the implications for biological control. *In* "Proceedings of the IVth International Symposium on the Biological Control of Weeds" (T. E. Freeman, ed.), pp. 57–73. Center for Environmental Programs, Institute of Food and Agricultural Sciences, University of Florida, Gainesville.

Lawton, J. H., and Strong, D. R., Jr. (1981). Community patterns and competition in folivorous insects. *Am. Nat.* **118**, 317–338.

Lawton, J. H., Cornell, H., Dritschilo, W., and Hendrix, S. D. (1981). Species as islands: comments on a paper by Kuris *et al. Am. Nat.* **117**, 623–627.

Leius, K. (1967). Influence of wild flowers on parasitism of tent caterpillar and codling moth. *Can. Entomol.* **99**, 444–446.

Lemen, C. (1981). Elm trees and elm leaf beetles: patterns of herbivory. *Oikos* **36**, 65–67.

MacArthur, R. H. (1972). "Geographical Ecology: Patterns in the Distribution of Species." Harper & Row, New York.

MacArthur, R. H., and Wilson, E. O. (1963). An equilibrium theory of insular zoogeography. *Evolution* **17**, 373–387.

MacArthur, R. H., and Wilson, E. O. (1967). "The Theory of Island Biogeography." Princeton Univ. Press, Princeton, New Jersey.

McClure, M. S., and Price, P. W. (1976). Ecotope characteristics of coexisting *Erythroneura* leafhoppers (Homoptera: Cicadellidae) on sycamore. *Ecology* **57**, 928–940.

McLain, D. K. (1981). Resource partitioning by three species of hemipteran herbivores on the basis of host plant density. *Oecologia* **48**, 414–417.

McNeill, S., and Southwood, T. R. E. (1978). The role of nitrogen in the development of insect/plant relationships. *In* "Biochemical Aspects of Plant and Animal Coevolution" (J. B. Harborne, ed.), pp. 77–98. Academic Press, New York.

Messina, F. J. (1981). Plant protection as a consequence of an ant–membracid mutualism: Interactions on goldenrod (*Solidago* sp.). *Ecology* **62**, 1433–1440.

Moran, V. C. (1980). Interactions betwen phytophagous insects and their *Opuntia* hosts. *Ecol. Entomol.* **5**, 153–164.

Morris, M. G. (1974). Oak as a habitat for insect life. In "The British Oak" (M. G. Morris and F. H. Perring eds.), pp. 274–297. Classey, Faringdon, Berks.

Morris, R. F. (1955). The development of sampling techniques for forest insect defoliators, with particular reference to the spruce budworm. Can. J. Zool. 33, 225–294.

Morris, R. F., ed. (1963). The dynamics of epidemic spruce budworm populations. Mem. Entomol. Soc. Can. 31, 1–332.

Morris, R. F., and Reeks, W. A. (1954). A larval population technique for the winter moth [Operophtera brumata (Linn.) (Lepidoptera: Geometridae)]. Can. Entomol. 86, 433–438.

Murdoch, W. W., Evans, F. C., and Peterson, C. H. (1972). Diversity and pattern in plants and insects. Ecology 53, 819–829.

Myers, J. H., Monro, J., and Murray, N. (1981). Egg clumping, host plant selection and population regulation in Cactoblastis cactorum (Lepidoptera). Oecologia 51, 7–13.

O'Connor, B., Dritschilo, W., Nafus, D., and Cornell, H. (1977). Ectoparasitic mites on rodents: application of the island biogeographic theory? Science 195, 598.

Opler, P. A. (1974). Oaks as evolutionary islands for leaf-mining insects. Am. Sci. 62, 67–73.

Orians, G. H. (1969). The number of bird species in some tropical forests. Ecology 50, 783–801.

Otte, D., and Joern, A. (1977). On feeding patterns in desert grasshoppers and the evolution of specialized diets. Proc. Acad. Nat. Sci. Philadelphia 128, 89–126.

Paine, R. T. (1966). Food web complexity and species diversity. Am. Nat. 100, 66–75.

Paine, R. T. (1969). The Pisaster–Tegula interaction: prey patches, predator food preference, and intertidal community structure. Ecology 50, 950–961.

Painter, R. H. (1951). "Insect Resistance in Crop Plants." Univ. of Kansas Press, Lawrence.

Pianka, E. R. (1974). "Evolutionary Ecology." Harper & Row, New York.

Pierce, N. E., and Mead, P. S. (1981). Parasitoids as selective agents in the symbiosis between lycaenids and ants. Science 211, 1185–1186.

Pimentel, D. (1961a). The influence of plant spatial patterns on insect populations. Ann. Entomol. Soc. Am. 54, 61–69.

Pimentel, D. (1961b). Species diversity and insect population outbreaks. Ann. Entomol. Soc. Am. 54, 76–86.

Prebble, M. L. (1943). Sampling methods in population studies of the European spruce sawfly, Gilpinia hercyniae (Hartig), in eastern Canada. Trans. R. Soc. Can., Sect. V 37, 93–126.

Prentice, R. M. (1954). "The Life History and Some Aspects of the Ecology of the Large Aspen Tortrix, Archips conflictana (Wlk.)," Interim Tech. Rep. Laboratory of Forest Zoology, Canadian Department of Agriculture, Winnipeg, Manitoba.

Price, P. W. (1975). "Insect Ecology." Wiley, New York.

Price, P. W. (1976). Colonization of crops by arthropods: non-equilibrium communities in soybeam fields. Environ. Entomol. 5, 605–611.

Price, P. W. (1977). General concepts on the evolutionary biology of parasites. Evolution 31, 405–420.

Price, P. W. (1980). "Evolutionary Biology of Parasites." Princeton Univ. Press, Princeton, New Jersey.

Price, P. W. (1983). Communities of specialists: vacant niches in ecological and evolutionary time. In "Ecological Communities: Conceptual Issues and the Evidence" (D. Simberloff, D. Strong, and L. Abele, eds.). Princeton Univ. Press, Princeton, New Jersey.

Price, P. W., and Willson, M. F. (1979). Abundance of herbivores on six milkweed species in Illinois. Am. Midl. Nat. 101, 76–86.

Price. P. W., Bouton, C. E., Gross, P., McPheron, B. A., Thompson, J. N., and Weis, A. E. (1980). Interactions among three trophic levels: influence of plants on interactions between insect herbivores and natural enemies. *Annu. Rev. Ecol. Syst.* **11**, 41–65.

Ralph, C. P. (1977a). Effect of host plant density on populations of a specialized, seed-sucking bug *Oncopeltus fasciatus. Ecology* **58**, 799–809.

Ralph, C. P. (1977b). Search behavior of the milkweed bug, *Oncopeltus fasciatus* (Hemiptera: Lygaeidae). *Ann. Entomol. Soc. Am.* **70**, 337–342.

Rathcke, B. J. (1976a). Insect–plant patterns and relationships in the stem-boring guild. *Am. Midl. Nat.* **99**, 98–117.

Rathcke, B. J. (1976b). Competition and coexistence within a guild of herbivorous insects. *Ecology* **57**, 76–87.

Rey, J. R. (1981). Ecological biogeography of arhtropods on *Spartina* islands in northwest Florida. *Ecol. Monogr.* **51**, 237–265.

Rey, J. R., McCoy, E. D., and Strong, D. R., Jr. (1981). Herbivore pests, habitat islands, and the species–area relation. *Am. nat.* **117**, 611–622.

Rhoades, D. F., and Cates, R. G. (1976). Toward a general theory of plant antiherbivore chemistry. *In* "Biochemical Interaction Between Plants and Insects." (J. W. Wallace and R. L. Mansell, eds.), pp. 168–213. Plenum, New York.

Ricklefs, R. E. (1973). "Ecology." Chiron Press, Newton, Massachusetts.

Ricklefs, R. E., and O'Rourke, K. (1975). Aspect diversity in moths: a temperate–tropical comparison. *Evolution* **29**, 313–324.

Rigby, C. and Lawton, J. H. (1981). Species–area relationships of arthropods on host plants: herbivores on bracken. *J. Biogeog.* **8**, 125–133.

Risch, S. J. (1981). Insect herbivore abundance in tropical monocultures and polycultures: an experimental test of two hypotheses. *Ecology* **62**, 1325–1340.

Risch, S. J., and Carroll, C. R. (1982). Effect of a keystone predaceous ant, *Solenopsis geminata*, on arthropods in a tropical agroecosystem. *Ecology* **63**, 1979–1983.

Root, R. B. (1973). Organization of a plant–arthropod association in simple and diverse habitats: the fauna of collards *(Brassica oleracea). Ecol. Monogr.* **43**, 95–124.

Rose, F. (1974). The epiphytes of oak. *In* "The British Oak" (M. G. Morris and F. H. Perring, eds.), pp. 250–273. E. W. Classey, Faringdon, Berkshire.

Roskam, J. C., and van Uffelen, G. A. (1981). Biosystematics of insects living in female birch catkins. III. Plant–insect relation between white birches, *Betula* L., Section Ex-celsae (Koch) and gall midges of the genus *Semudobia* Kieffer (Diptera, Cecidomyiidae). *Neth. J. Zool.* **31**, 533–553.

Seifert, R. P., and Siefert, F. H. (1976). A community matrix analysis of *Heliconia* insect communities. *Am. Nat.* **110**, 461–483.

Seifert, R. P., and Siefert, F. H. (1979). A *Heliconia* insect community in Venezuelan cloud forest. *Ecology* **60**, 462–467.

Sharp, M. A., Parks, D. R., and Ehrlich, P. R. (1974). Plant resources and butterfly habitat selection. *Ecology* **55**, 870–875.

Simberloff, D. S. (1978). Colonization of islands by insects: immigration, extinction, and diversity. *Symp. R. Entomol. Soc. London* **9**, pp. 139–153.

Simberloff, D. S., and Wilson, E. O. (1970). Experimental zoogeography of islands: a two-year record of colonization. *Ecology* **51**, 934–937.

Smiley, J. (1978). Plant chemistry and the evolution of host specificity: new evidence for *Heliconius* and *Passiflora. Science* **201**, 745–747.

Solomon, B. P. (1981). Response of a host-specific herbivore to resource density, relative abundance, and phenology. *Ecology* **62**, 1205–1214.

Southwood, T. R. E. (1960). The abundance of the Hawaiian trees and the number of their associated insect species. *Proc. Hawaii. Entomol. Soc.* **17**, 299–303.

Southwood, T. R. E. (1961). The number of species of insect associated with various trees. *J. Anim. Ecol.* **30**, 1–8.

Spencer, K. A. (1972) "Handbooks for the Identification of British Insects," Vol. 10, Part 5(g), Diptera, Agromyzidae. Royal Entomological Society of London, London.

Stark, R. W. (1952). Analysis of a population sampling method for the lodgepole needle miner in Canadian Rocky Mountain parks. *Can. Entomol.* **84**, 316–321.

Strong, D. R., Jr. (1974a). Nonasymptotic species richness models and the insects of British trees. *Proc. Nat. Acad. Sci. U.S.A.* **71**, 2766–2769.

Strong, D. R., Jr. (1974b). The insects of British trees: community equilibrium in ecological time. *Ann. Mo. Bot. Gard.* **61**, 692–701.

Strong, D. R., Jr. (1977). Insect species richness: hispine beetles of *Heliconia latispatha*. *Ecology* **58**, 573–583.

Strong, D. R., Jr. (1979). Biogeographic dynamics of insect–host plant communities. *Annu. Rev. Entomol.* **24**, 89–119.

Strong, D. R., Jr. (1981). The possibility of insect communities without competition: hispine beetles on *Heliconia*. In "Insect Life History Patterns" (R. F. Denno and H. Dingle, eds.), pp. 183–194. Springer-Verlag, New York and Berlin.

Strong, D. R., Jr. (1982). Harmonious coexistence among hispine beetles on *Heliconia* in experimental and natural communities. *Ecology* **63**, 1039–1049.

Strong, D. R., Jr., and Levin, D. A. (1975). Species richness of the parasitic fungi of British trees. *Proc. Nat. Acad. Sci. U.S.A.* **72**, 2116–2119.

Strong, D. R., Jr., and Levin, D. A. (1979). Species richness of plant parasites and growth form of their hosts. *Am. Nat.* **114**, 1–22.

Tahvanainen, J. O., and Root, R. B. (1972). The influence of vegetational diversity on the population ecology of a specialized herbivore, *Phyllotreta cruciferae* (Coleoptera: Chrysomelidae). *Oecologia* **10**, 321–346.

Thompson, J. N. (1978). Within-patch structure and dynamics in *Pastinaca sativa* and resource availability to a specialized herbivore. *Ecology* **59**, 443–448.

Thompson, J. N., and Price, P. W. (1977). Plant plasticity, phenology and herbivore dispersion: wild parsnip and the parsnip webworm. *Ecology* **58**, 1112–1119.

van Emden, H. F. (1963). Observations on the effect of flowers on activity of parasitic Hymenoptera. *Entomol. Mon. Mag.* **98**, 265–270.

van Emden, H. F. (1965). The effect of uncultivated land on the distribution of cabbage aphid *(Brevicoryne brassicae)* on an adjacent crop. *J. Appl. Ecol.* **2**, 171–196.

Varley, G. C., and Gradwell, G. R. (1968). Population models for the winter moth. *Symp. R. Entomol. Soc. London* **4**, 132–142.

Washburn, J. O., and Cornell, H. V. (1981). Parasitoids, patches, and phenology: their possible role in the local extinction of a cynipid gall wasp population. *Ecology* **62**, 1597–1607.

White, T. C. R. (1976). Weather, food and plagues of locusts. *Oecologia* **22**, 119–134.

White, T. C. R. (1978). The importance of a relative shortage of food in animal ecology. *Oecologia* **33**, 71–86.

Whitham, T. G., and Slobodchikoff, C. N. (1981). Evolution by individuals, plant–herbivore interactions, and mosaics of genetic variability: the adaptive significance of somatic mutations in plants. *Oecologia* **49**, 287–292.

Whittaker, R. H. (1967). Gradient analysis of vegetation. *Biol. Rev. Cambridge Philos. Soc.* **42**, 207–264.

Williams, C. B. (1964). "Patterns in the Balance of Nature." Academic Press, New York and London.
Wilson, E. O. (1969). The species equilibrium. *Brookhaven Symp. Biol.* **22**, 38–47.

Peter W. Price
Department of Biological Sciences
Northern Arizona University
Flagstaff, Arizona

PART V

Host Variability and Herbivore Pest Management

Previous chapters of this book have discussed the various factors that contribute to variation in host plants, the importance of resource variability as a defense mechanism of plants, and the ecological and evolutionary consequences of host variability for herbivores. In view of our growing appreciation and understanding of the causes and effects of host-plant variability, evident from the preceding chapters, it seems prudent to integrate this knowledge in our tactics to manage populations of herbivorous pests. As the mechanisms by which host plants maintain variability become better known, it should become increasingly feasible to manipulate the quantity and quality of resources available to herbivores and to employ such manipulations in pest control strategies.

The application of basic research to the constant battle against agricultural and silvicultural pests should be a common objective of all scientists studying plant–herbivore interactions. Unfortunately, there remains a gap between theoretical and applied studies that impedes progress toward this goal. The chapters in this concluding part of the book discuss the potential value of manipulating host-plant variability for herbivore population management and the benefits of more intensive interaction between applied and basic studies of plant–herbivore relationships.

In Chapter 17, Gould discusses patterns of variation and the genetic basis for variation in plants and herbivores and explains how basic studies of genetic interactions between plants and their herbivores may strengthen the ability of applied biologists to develop and manage resistant crops, concurrently providing important information for the basic disciplines of plant–herbivore biology and evolutionary ecology. Gould discusses current procedures and concepts used by entomologists and plant breeders in the development and deployment of resistant plant varieties and reviews theoretical genetic arguments on plant–herbivore interaction and empirical information available on the genetics of economically important plants and their herbivores. In Chapter 18, Hare explains how host-plant variability can be manipulated in time and space in agroecosystems and discusses how a more complete understanding of the effects of host variation on herbivorous insects will lead to new, effective approaches for managing populations of herbivore pests. Hare draws upon his own work on the utilization of alternate hosts, seasonal variation in phytochemicals, and feeding-deterrent fungicides on the Colorado potato beetle, as well as numerous other examples from the literature to illustrate the wide range of methods available to manipulate host variability within the limits of current agricultural and silvicultural practice.

CHAPTER 17

Genetics of Plant–Herbivore Systems: Interactions between Applied and Basic Study

FRED GOULD

I. INTRODUCTION

In their classic paper on the coevolution of butterflies and plants, Ehrlich and Raven (1964) suggested that the patterns of plant–herbivore associations we see today are the outcome of evolutionary events that occurred over a time scale spanning geological ages. They envisioned herbivore-resistant plant genotypes arising that could succeed in lowering their herbivore load long enough to undergo other genetic changes necessary, not only for speciation but also for radiation into new adaptive zones. Conversely, herbivore genotypes that finally overcame a resistance factor gained long term benefits. Evolutionary biologists wish they had a way of testing the generality of Ehrlich and Raven's hypothesis, but economic entomologists just wish that they knew how to make crop systems obey Ehrlich and Raven's hypothesis, at least the part of it dealing with the rate at which herbivores evolve to overcome the resistance of plant genotypes. As it is, economic entomologists have a difficult

    599

time finding resistant plant genotypes that will remain resistant for the span of a resistance breeder's career. Although such rapid herbivore adaptation in crop systems in no way refutes the possibility of stepwise coevolution between plants and herbivores over a geological time span, it certainly suggests that some evolutionary interactions between plants and herbivores occur at a much quicker pace.

The goal of this chapter is to demonstrate that basic studies of genetic interactions between economically important plant species and their herbivorous enemies may strengthen the applied entomologists' ability to develop and manage crop varieties to maximize the stability of the crop's resistance to herbivores, concurrently providing important information for the basic disciplines of plant–herbivore biology and evolutionary ecology. To achieve this goal, I shall first discuss current procedures and concepts used by entomologists and plant breeders in the development and deployment of resistant plant varieties. I shall follow this by a review of theoretical genetic arguments relevant to applied and basic study of plant–herbivore interactions and empirical information available on the genetics of economically important plant and herbivore species. Finally, I shall discuss how some of the goals of applied entomologists and evolutionary ecologists could be met by cooperative studies.

II. CURRENT PROCEDURES AND CONCEPTS IN THE DEVELOPMENT AND DEPLOYMENT OF RESISTANT VARIETIES

On average, entomologists and plant breeders devote 12 yr to developing a new pest-resistant crop variety (F. Gould, unpublished survey). This time span may, in exceptional cases, be as short as 5 yr or as long as 25 yr. In all cases, a large expenditure of time and money is involved, and it is therefore disappointing to find that pests may genetically overcome the resistance in less time than it took to develop it. Entomologists and plant breeders yearn for a method of judging a priori the longevity of a resistance factor in the field.

The present procedures for development of resistant varieties, reviewed by Russell (1978), can be divided into two steps: screening crop varieties and related species for resistant genotypes and breeding this resistance into agronomically acceptable varieties. In the screening process over 1000 plant genotypes may be tested for resistance. The effort involved in screening is often reduced by the development of greenhouse or laboratory assays, which are quicker than true field screening.

Assuming that these assays do reflect qualities that confer resistance in the field (see Kennedy, 1978; Smith, 1978), the problem remains of choosing genotypes that will maintain their resistance in the field over time. Insects used in bioassays rarely come from more than one laboratory population, so genetic diversity is low. Moreover, resistance is usually assayed based on the performance of one stage of the pest's life cycle (often one instar). This tends to favor the selection of plant genotypes causing acute negative effects on the pest, when those that cause low-level chronic effects may offer more stable resistance, as discussed in the following sections. Although somewhat less problematic, field screening procedures are also limited because they often involve one or a few local insect populations that have never encountered the resistant varieties before. The genetic potential of these insect populations is, therefore, never assessed.

Another problem that a resistance breeder faces in screening the hundreds of available plant genotypes is where to begin. The usual order of screening is as follows. The first screening is of current agronomic varieties. Second, land races (i.e., varieties grown in areas of the world where each farmer or village maintains his or its own seed from one season to the next), are examined. Having failed to find resistance at this point, the search may expand to include related species that can be crossed to the crop species and, finally, to more distantly related species for which the plant breeders have "bridge species" that enable transfer of genetic material to the crop species. Plants in the last two groups are ignored by some entomologists and breeders, because moving resistance from them into agronomic varieties is thought of as "a young man's game" (R. Fery, personal communication), because it may take the entire span of a resistance breeder's career to accomplish. Of course, if a breeder were confident that resistance from such a source would last much longer in the field than resistance found within the crop species, he or she would be less reluctant to pursue such an effort. The search for resistant land races and wild species is subject to an ordering by some breeders who believe that resistance is more likely to occur in plant samples from areas of sympatry with the pest. Some empirical support for this approach exists (Dinoor, 1977), but Harris (1975) has argued that, theoretically, allopatric sources of resistance would be more stable in the field.

process, deciding which of the resistant genotypes should be chosen for further development, assuming that more than one source has been found, which is usually the case. From my survey of the literature, the characteristics of resistance regarded favorably in selecting a breeding line are are (1) genotypes with the highest level of resistance according to the bioassay, (2) genotypes most similar to modern varieties in characteristics other than resistance, (3) genotypes whose resistance is easily transferred to modern varieties, and, at least by some, (4) genotypes whose resistance is polygenic in nature. Only characteristic (4) may be related to increased stability of resistance. Polygenic sources of resistance are considered by many to be less vulnerable to pests evolving mechanisms to counteract the resistance (Gallun and Khush, 1980). The strength of this logic will be addressed in Section II. The important factor here is that characteristic (4) is usually not compatible with characteristic (3) and is often not compatible with characteristic (1), which are deemed more important for practical reasons.

Once a resistant source is selected, one of a number of breeding systems is chosen to raise the agronomic quality of the resistance-bearing plants (Russell, 1978). For monogenic sources of resistance, backcrossing to one or a few currently popular agronomic varieties is usually undertaken. The progeny of each cross are assayed for resistance; the most resistant progeny are used in the next backcross. This procedure is continued until all undesirable characteristics in the parental source of resistance are discarded. For polygenic sources of resistance, many generations of mass selection are commonly used.

The assays used for resistance during these selection procedures are often the same as those used for screening. In cases in which the morphological or chemical basis for resistance is known, these characters are sometimes measured directly without the use of any insects. When insects are used to assay resistance, rarely is the plant tested against more than one or two genetically distinct insect populations (for an exception, see Gallun, 1980). Therefore, in the entire period of resistance development, from screening through breeding, genetic variation in the pest species is almost completely ignored.

Once resistance has been incorporated into a modern variety, it is sometimes grown for one or two seasons in a number of locations where the pest is a problem. These small-plot tests may show geographic variation in the pest's ability to deal with the resistance factor (Dunn and Kempton, 1972), but they offer no information on the capacity of the pest populations to adapt to the resistant varieties. The question that must be addressed is, Can a better theoretical and empirical understanding of the genetics of plant–herbivore interactions offer any practical help to the resistance breeder's decision-making and testing, or is the present blend of pragmatism and science the best solution for the future?

III. THEORETICAL CONSIDERATIONS

A. Effects of Spatial and Temporal Environmental Variation on Herbivore and Plant Adaptation

Two questions of interest to resistance breeders and individuals studying basic plant–herbivore interactions that deserve consideration are, (1) What influences the manner in which herbivore populations respond genetically to spatial variation in host-plant qualities? (2) What influences the manner in which these same herbivore populations respond genetically to temporal genetic change in their host plants' qualities?

The population genetic theory related to question (1) is generally discussed as the theory of *multiple-niche polymorphism* (Levene, 1953; Felsenstein, 1976; Lewontin *et al.*, 1978; Maynard-Smith and Hoekstra, 1980). Mitter and Futuyma (Chapter 13) include an excellent review of this theory as it is related to plant–herbivore systems. Their concern is mainly with what combinations of geographic host-quality variation and herbivore population biology would lead to genetic polymorphism or monomorphism in the herbivore population. In summary, they conclude that the following characteristics will theoretically favor polymorphism for host utilization by an herbivore population.

1. Pronounced negatively correlated differences in the ability of different genotypes to survive on different host types
2. Independent regulation of population sizes on each host type
3. Low mobility between hosts, or extensive patches of one or the other host, which have the same effect of lowering gene flow between host-associated subdivisions of the population
4. Assortative mating and habitat selection whereby individuals choose the host on which they or their offspring are more likely to survive

Additionally, they point out that if this habitat selection is based on genetic polymorphism, mono- or oligogenic inheritance of both behavior and adaptation and tight linkage of the two traits should be more favorable to polymorphism than polygenic inheritance and loose linkage. Their theoretical insights could prove important to agriculturalists if a relationship between genetic polymorphism (genetic substructuring) of a pest population and its ability to damage crops exists. Because agriculturalists sometimes have the power to vary the geographic arrangement of varieties of a single crop (Browning, 1980) and the species of a multiple crop system, they may be able to select arrangements that would minimize pest adaptedness to the crop(s), with a concomitant lowering of the related economic losses. For example, crop arrangements could be set up which would maintain a pest population that was only partially adapted to each of two crops (or varieties), or an arrangement of crops could be set up that caused monomorphism in the pest population, such that the pest was best adapted to the crop that could tolerate the most damage without economic loss. Of course, the utility of this type of management would depend on a negative correlation between pest-genotype fitnesses on the crop varieties or crop species, and we must assume that a less "fit" pest causes less damage (see Price *et al.*, 1980).

The second question, the one on which I shall concentrate, involves genetic changes educed in an herbivore if the quality of its host plant(s) varies over time. Temporal change in host quality may either be responsive to or independent of the herbivore population, and these changes in quality may be cyclical or directional. Cyclic change would be exemplified by a plant population that initially contains 10% tannin-producing individuals and 90% nonproducers, changing to 50% of each, then back to the original frequency; directional change would proceed only in one direction. Therefore, four classes of temporal change in host quality, cyclic–independent, cyclic–responsive, directional–responsive, and directional–independent may be realized.

1. Cyclic–Independent Change in Host Quality

In cases in which host quality cycles because of selection factors unrelated to the herbivore in question, effects on the herbivore's population polymorphism for host adaptation are similar but somewhat more restrictive than those of spatial variation in host quality (Hedrick *et al.*, 1976). Such cyclic changes may be related to seasonal host-plant phenology or resistance induced by other herbivores or pathogens (see Hare, Chapter 18). If genetic polymorphism in the herbivore is maintained, the interaction of the host-quality cycling period and rate of genetic tracking on the part of the herbivore population may lead to less herbivore damage, due to a lag time in adaptation of the herbivore.

2. Cyclic-Responsive and Directional–Responsive Changes in Host Quality

The same lag-time effect may exist in the case of herbivore-responsive cycling in host-plant quality. Conditions that will maintain herbivore-responsive cycling were outlined theoretically by Haldane (1949) and

Pimentel (1961) as a special case of frequency-dependent selection, and they have been addressed in detail and modeled by plant pathologists and parasitologists (e.g., Clarke, 1976; Leonard and Czochor, 1980). Most of the current models deal with a single-locus, two-allele system with one allele (S) causing susceptibility to the pathogen (or herbivore) and the other allele (R) conferring resistance. Haploid systems are usually used for convenience and because they offer a conservative estimate of the conditions necessary for cycling. The most essential condition for host-quality cycling is that S cause lower host fitness than R in the presence of the pathogen and that, due to pleiotropy or tight gene linkage, R cause lower fitness than S in the absence of the pathogen. The interaction of the polymorphic host population with an herbivore population that is either genetically monomorphic or polymorphic with regard to utilization of S and R genotypes can maintain the stable cycle in the host. In the case of a monomorphic herbivore and a plant population with an initially low R frequency, the selective damage done by the herbivore to S genotypes will raise the frequency of R. However, as R increases and S decreases there is a negative effect on the herbivore's fitness, due to the scarcity of S-bearing individuals. The decrease in efficiency will be most pronounced if the herbivore cannot discriminate between S- and R-bearing individuals or has limited mobility. This will cause a decline in the herbivore population. Because in the absence of the herbivore S-bearing individuals are more fit, their frequency in the population increases and, following it, there is an increase in the herbivore population. And so the cycle proceeds. Models of this system assume that populations of plants and herbivores are closed to migration from other areas. If the herbivore population has higher mobility than the plant population or can utilize an alternate plant species as a host, the cycle may be destabilized, because the frequency of R- and S-bearing host individuals will have less effect on the herbivore population dynamics. With the breakdown in the cycle we wind up with directional change in the plant and, ultimately, fixation of R alleles.

If the herbivore population is polymorphic with regard to utilization of S- and R-bearing plants, we have a more complex situation. In this case the R plant is not as resistant to herbivores of genotype V (virulent) as they are to herbivores of genotype N (nonvirulent). Unless models of this situation assume that there is a cost to virulence (i.e., N is more fit on hosts of genotype S), the herbivore population undergoes directional selection and becomes fixed for allele V, bringing us back to the original situation involving the monomorphic herbivore. Leonard (1977) tested a model for a plant–pathogen system that incorporated population dynamics and resembled conditions found in agricultural multiline varieties. The crop's gene (R and S) frequencies changed once a year, while the pathogen gene (V and N) frequencies changed 1 or 10 times per year. Selection coefficients leading to stable cycles of crop- and pathogen-genotype frequencies were quite broad as long as S-bearing plants were most fit in the absence of the pathogen, and N-bearing pathogens were most fit on S-bearing plants. It is very interesting that in contrast to Leonard's results Sedcole (1978) found that, when he examined a case in which the crop gene frequency changed during a season, stable cycles became less likely. In all models, when conditions do not maintain a stable limit cycle, the pathogen population undergoes directional selection and reaches fixation for V very quickly. Once fixation for V is achieved, the plant population, if yet polymorphic, increases in S frequency if C (the cost of resistance) is greater than 0, and the V pathogen causes equal damage to R and S-bearing plants. Over many generations R may be lost unless C is small or the V-bearing pathogen causes less damage to R-bearing plants. Thus the concept of an arms race in which the plant and pathogen carry "obsolete" armaments from past interactions would hold only in specific cases.

3. Directional–Independent Change in Host Quality

In directional–independent change of host-plant quality, something other than the herbivore in question causes the change in plant quality, but this change affects the herbivores. If the herbivore responds genetically to this host quality change, an evolutionary process sometimes labeled *genetic host tracking* occurs. Although this is obviously not coevolution, there is no way to use present-day patterns of plant–herbivore associations to clearly distinguish the results of this process from coevolution, because in both cases the herbivore genetically tracks changes in the host. Only detailed studies can indicate whether the change in the host was a response to the herbivore in question or some other herbivore, pathogen, or plant competitor or was a neutral change in terms of plant fitness (see Mitter and Brooks, 1983).

In all models already discussed, each plant had only one "enemy," and each enemy only one host-plant species. The real world is more complex. If we give each host three enemies and each enemy three hosts, the interactions become quite intricate. Questions regarding the general effectiveness of one resistance factor, considering all the enemy species, and one virulence factor, considering all hosts, are of primary importance. An additional simplification used in this discussion, which may not be justified, is the reliance on one-locus models. The addition of a polygenic system of inheritance complicates models for temporal change in host quality, as it did the models dealing with spatial change in host quality, which is addressed by Mitter and Futuyma (Chapter 13).

The theory of genetic interactions of plants and herbivores involving temporal changes in host quality may be complex. However, it is important from a basic and an applied perspective, because it helps us narrow down the conditions that lead to a variety of evolutionary interactions between host and herbivore. This theory certainly develops a framework that points to specific characteristics of plant–herbivore systems requiring measurement, and it leads to the next question, which is, What types of R are most likely to impede evolution of V genotypes of the pest population?

B. Are Some Types of Resistance Inherently More Stable than Others?

1. Polygenic versus Monogenic Resistance

Van der Plank (1968), a plant pathologist, concluded that the number of genes involved in conferring resistance to a crop variety should influence the rate at which V genotypes of pathogens evolve. Van der Plank felt that monogenic sources of resistance would, in general, be more rapidly overcome than polygenic sources of resistance (i.e., would be less stable). This would be true because polygenic resistance would involve many plant characteristics unsuitable for the pest. Therefore, more complex adaptations by the pathogen would be required to deal with polygenic resistance than the more simple monogenic resistance. In this scheme, cost of virulence was not considered as much as the probability of a virulent genotype ever arising. Some entomologists have adopted this generalization too readily (see Maxwell and Jennings, 1980). "Permanent" and "temporary" have become synonyms for polygenic and monogenic sources of insect resistance, respectively. Indeed, there is now a school of resistance breeders (Robinson, 1980) that feels that resistance-breeding programs should discard resistance sources controlled by single genes conferring strong resistance, on the assumption that they will confer only temporary resistance. Although such a scheme may in some cases be profitable for those breeding for disease resistance, for those concerned with insect pests such a generalization may prove damaging. Even if, on average, monogenic sources of resistance are somewhat more often overcome by genetic changes in the insect pest than is the case with polygenic sources of resistance, is that enough to go on? The assumption that polygenic resistance should involve production of an array of plant characteristics that combine to make the plant unsuitable for insects is unfounded. For example, resistance due to a high level of a single secondary plant compound may be controlled by many loci (e.g., cucurbitacin in cucumbers; dePonti and Garretsen, 1980). Conversely, a single gene change that causes production of one different metabolic enzyme may result in production of an array of new secondary compounds (e.g., sesquiterpenes in cotton species; Bell *et al.*, 1978).

2. The Relationship between Stability of a Resistance Factor and Its Effect on the Herbivore's Fitness

Instead of emphasizing examination of the genetic nature or physical and physiological complexity of a resistance factor, I feel that emphasis should be placed on studying the direct biological effect that resistance has on the pest insect. With this information we could attempt to predict whether the genetic change required on the part of the pest to circumvent the biological effect of a plant defense would be simple or complex. We could also compute what the selection coefficients would be on genotypes that circumvent the resistance.

Indeed, not all forms of host resistance cause a biological effect on the pest that impairs the fitness of the pest, for resistance has in some cases been found that is entirely due to tolerance of a pest (Painter, 1951). The only biological effect of this type of resistance would be lessening of the effect of the pest on fitness of plants bearing it, for the pest would survive equally well on tolerant and intolerant host genotypes. Whether such resistance were controlled by one or many genes, it would theoretically cause no genetic change in the pest. Because resistance based on herbivore tolerance would be very stable to herbivore evolution, it is interesting to question how common such evolved tolerance is in natural plant populations. Such tolerance would always be selected for at the individual plant level (assuming no strong pleiotropic effects), but it would not necessarily be selected for at the population level, because it could lead to larger herbivore populations than those in areas where plants had other forms of resistance, such as antibiosis.

Although it is rarely stated in the literature (Gallun, 1972; Carter and Dixon, 1981), some insect-resistance breeders apparently feel that sources of plant resistance that cause either a repulsive or nonattractive effect on the insect while it is choosing a host (i.e., nonpreference resistance) will be more stable than resistance that operates by debilitating or killing the insect after it has chosen the host (i.e., antibiosis, defined broadly). Although this is not acceptable as a generalization, under certain circumstances the effect of a naturally evolved or man-introduced source of nonpreference may indeed have little or no effect on the fitness of pest individuals, and, in those cases, resistance should remain stable.

For an example, consider individuals of a generalist insect population that develop equally well on a number of host-plant species and whose population size is not regulated by density-dependent factors (Andrewartha and Birch, 1954; Lawton and Strong, 1981). Evolution of a characteristic in one host-plant species that causes avoidance by the insect will decrease the insect's fitness only if the energetic cost or risk involved in foraging or ovipositing increases a significant amount, due to increased search time. In contrast, a characteristic that decreases survival of progeny once eggs are laid (i.e., antibiosis) would necessarily decrease the insect's fitness in relation to the severity of the antibiotic effect and the proportion of progeny placed on or that chose that host, compared to the other host plants. In this case, an insect genotype unaffected by the antibiotic factor could increase in frequency more rapidly than one unaffected by the nonpreference factor. If instead of a generalist we considered a very specialized insect, there would be no reason a priori to expect more stability of a nonpreference factor (compared to an antibiotic factor) in terms of selection pressure on the insect, for not feeding on its one host would ultimately cause death of the specialist herbivore.

3. Stability of Resistance Causing Antibiotic Effects

For the purposes of this discussion it is important to differentiate "antibiotic effects" into three categories: (1) slower development and reproductive rates, (2) lower survival, and (3) lower total reproduction. A single resistance factor may cause any or all of these effects in the herbivore. Theoretically, each effect may lead to differing resistance stability.

In most insect species, it is reasonable to assume that lowered survival or fewer total progeny produced would cause lowered fitness. Therefore, we might assume that herbivore genotypes unaffected by such resistance would increase in frequency if the resistant host were common. In contrast, resistance causing slower developmental rates or reproductive rates may in some cases lower herbivore fitness, but in other cases it may be expected not to do so. For example, consider a univoltine foliage-feeding species that survived equally well whether it reached its diapause state in August or September. A plant characteristic lengthening development time would have little effect on such an insect's fitness. This plant characteristic would, nonetheless, provide resistance to the plant if the longer development time caused the last instar's feeding period to occur after the plant set seed or ripened fruit in late July.

An interesting although, perhaps, uncommon condition is a resistance factor causing slower development in a specialist insect, which lowers the insect's future fitness, but that is stable in face of newly arisen insect genotypes that circumvent it. This may occur if there is *predator satiation*, in which the probability of predation or parasitism is inversely related to herbivore density. In the presence of often important insect egg predators, eggs that are laid far to either side of a pest generation's peak oviposition period may be most likely to be eaten. If a common host resistance factor lengthened the average developmental rate of a multivoltine insect population, any rare individuals of a newly evolved genotype, unaffected by this resistance, would develop more rapidly than other individuals in the population and would lay their eggs long before the peak oviposition period of the population. The low density of eggs at this time would lead to high predation rates and low fitness, compared to that of individuals affected by the resistance. Of course, this system depends on the resistance factor becoming very common before the unaffected genotype became frequent, and therefore, it may apply more to agricultural systems, in which humans may dictate such an occurrence.

4. Increased Effectiveness of Resistance due to Herbivore Evolution

The next question that arises is whether we can ever expect plant resistance factors that directly lower herbivore survival to remain resistant, when they are common. Not only would we sometimes expect such plants to remain resistant, we would, in special cases, actually predict an increase in effectiveness of such plant resistance, due to evolution of the insect population. Although our biases may cause initially negative reaction to this suggestion, such evolution may be expected in the case of a generalist herbivore, if before or after establishment of the antibiotic resistance factor in host species A, a genotype arose in the herbivore population that preferred an alternate host-plant species. If, after establishment of the resistance factor, the herbivore had higher fitness on the alternate host-plant species, the new herbivore genotype would be favored and increase in frequency, and what was originally only antibiotic resistance would yield nonpreference resistance as well. How common such a situation is and whether it can be manipulated by resistance breeders is yet to be investigated. Of course, if the alternate host is a crop to which the herbivore also causes damage, such an evolutionary event would not necessarily be helpful.

5. Stability of Resistance Causing both Antibiotic and Nonpreference Effects

Instead of relying upon natural selection to produce a common insect genotype that does not prefer the host that has antibiotic resistance, the resistance breeder may have the option of combining a nonpreference and antibiotic resistance factor in a single crop variety. If the resistance is to a generalist herbivore, the herbivore will instantly be more fit on its other hosts than on the resistant crop. This resistance should be stable unless an insect genotype arises that is affected by neither the antibiosis nor the nonpreference factor. As discussed later, even in the event that an individual with such a genotype did arise, its increase in frequency would still be questionable.

It is useful to discuss this double-barreled resistance in detail from an agricultural as well as a naturalistic perspective, because any pest adaptation to the resistant crop variety just described would be very similar to Bush's (1974) conception of host-plant switching in natural situations. Let us examine some factors that will favor or disrupt the evolution of a genotype that "breaks" the resistance of or that is "adapted" to the former nonhost. One important characteristic, pointed out by Rausher (1982) and Tabashnik (1982), is the strength of each resistance factor. If nonpreference is qualitative in effect (i.e., no individuals of the original insect population feed on it), there will be no selective advantage at all to a mutant genotype that is unharmed by the antibiosis. However, if nonpreference is quantitative in its effect on the insect population (i.e., some individuals feed on it), selection will favor a mutant genotype that is unaffected by the antibiosis in relation to the proportion of the insect population that winds up on the nonpreferred host. Whether we consider individuals circumventing the effects of the nonpreference and antibiotic factors as due to mutations in the insect population or initially low-frequency alleles, the probability of the two types ever being combined in one individual would be enhanced if the nonpreference resistance were quantitative. In such a case the rare alleles for circumventing antibiosis could rise in frequency independent of the co-occurrence in individuals of an allele for circumventing the nonpreference factor. Once the alleles for circumventing antibiosis became common, the probability of individuals sharing these alleles and the rare alleles for circumventing nonpreference would be much greater. Given that individuals occurred that had alleles for circumventing both the antibiosis and nonpreference factors, an increase in frequency of alleles for circumventing the nonpreference factor would not occur unless the individuals with this combination of alleles were, on average, more fit in the population's total habitat than individuals of other genotypes. Such heightened fitness of this combination would not be likely unless there was density-dependent population regulation or a high risk associated with host finding, so plant resistance could still remain stable.

I have been discussing this situation as if there were one allele for totally circumventing antibiosis and one for totally circumventing non-preference factors in the plant. If many loci were involved in each of these two herbivore traits, the probability of proper combinations would be more complex to predict, as would be the fitness profiles for each possible combination, especially if epistasis were involved. A meaningful attack on this problem is beyond the scope of this discussion and would require computer simulation of specific cases and that would include parameters related to the population's mating structure and mutation rates.

On the other hand, analysis of adaptation to a nonpreferred, antibiotic plant could be simpler than the scenario presented here. This would be the case if genes for overcoming the antibiosis were the same genes that caused circumvention of nonpreference. Such a pleiotropic relationship would decrease the stability of the plant resistance, because it would lead to optimal host selection, that is, herbivore genotypes would select a host in relation to their fitness on the host. As an example, consider an insect whose behavioral program causes it to leave a plant if it becomes "sick" or not satiated while feeding on the plant. If single alleles in the insect caused less "sickness" (i.e., less antibiosis), they would also cause less nonpreference response, and the insect would remain on the plant and bear young. If the same alleles were active in adults and immatures, the young would wind up on plants to which they were adapted. This could not occur in insects such as butterflies, in which the adult is not herbivorous, but it is plausible in many totally herbivorous insects because, in general, alleles coding for physiological characteristics in the adult stage of an insect are expressed to some extent in the immature stages as well (Georghiou et al., 1966; O'Brien and MacIntyre, 1978).

6. Common Sense and Quantitative Genetics

It is important to examine as many theoretically plausible genetic interactions as we can, for, although they may turn out to be uncommon, we shall never know this if we do not open our minds to their possible existence. While exploring these theoretical possibilities as we have so far, there is also a need to keep ourselves firmly rooted in biological common sense. One needs only to look at the specific effects of certain resistance factors on an insect to predict their stability. If a plant breeder finds an aphid-resistance gene that produces a single, very sticky substance over the entire plant, completely entangling alighting females, the breeder might rest assured of stability of the resistance to the aphid. In doing this, the breeder is making a judgement about the genetic variation in the aphid population, concluding that the variation necessary to be unaffected by this substance is absent. When biological common sense is of no help in making such an assessment, the next best indicators of genetic potential appear to be quantitative genetics and "pest breeding."

By using quantitative genetic techniques (Falconer, 1981), one may be able to assess whether a specific herbivore population contains the genetic variation that would be necessary to overcome a specific resistance factor in the plant. Quantitative genetic techniques could also be used to determine if there are genetic "costs" involved in the adaptation to a resistance factor. As an alternative to careful quantitative genetic studies, it may in some cases be possible to set up a simple "pest-breeding" program (Gould, 1978), in which one could determine the genetic potential of a pest species for circumventing a resistance factor by imposing a selection regime on a number of lab populations for adaptation to the resistant host. Although quantitative genetics and "pest breeding" may be of little help in detecting very rare monogenic characteristics in a population of herbivores (Frankham and Nurthen, 1981), they certainly could be of use in identifying specific plant resistance factors that would have a high probability of being rapidly overcome by genetic changes in the pest, as would be true if a pest population showed easily detected, highly heritable genetic variation for adaptation to the resistance factor.

C. Conclusions from Theory

Perhaps the most general conclusion that can be drawn from the theoretical arguments just discussed is that, for both natural and agricultural systems, the rate and direction of change in herbivore adaptation to plant genotypes depends on interactions between the ecology and the genetics of the specific herbivore and plant populations. Broad generalizations about stability of resistance based on single factors such as the number of genes involved in a plant's resistance to an herbivore cannot, by themselves, offer accurate predictions of a variety's future resistance when grown commercially. In making predictions about future resistance of crop varieties or plants in a natural community, we need data on a number of important genetic and ecological parameters.

The genetic parameters include

1. How much variation there is in the plants regarding resistance to the insect and how it is distributed geographically
2. How much genetic variation exists within the herbivore populations in regard to adaptation to the resistant plants
3. What pleiotropic costs to the herbivore's fitness are associated with adaptation to the plant defenses

4. Whether host preference and fitness on a host are genetically (or phenotypically) linked
5. Whether there is mating and, if so, whether there is assortative mating based on larval host

The ecological parameters include

1. Significance of density-dependent effects in the population regulation of the herbivore
2. Suitability of alternate hosts as food sources
3. Energetic costs associated with avoiding resistant plants as oviposition sites (e.g., increased distance flown and increased time needed to deposit full compliment of eggs)
4. Mortality factors associated with avoiding resistant plants as oviposition sites (e.g., increased predation)

As can be seen from examining some of the scenarios depicted in this section, changes in the values of each of the parameters listed here can lead to important differences in the rates and, in some cases, directions of herbivore adaptation to plant genotypes. Where the interactions between parameters are also important, it may be impossible to use intuition to predict future resistance. In these cases there is a need for analytic and simulation modeling of specific plant–herbivore systems if our predictions are to be accurate. There is a need to at least develop a general body of data on the parameters discussed so that we can narrow our future research to those that will most likely influence future resistance in specific systems. Such knowledge may help resistance breeders in choosing resistance characteristics to breed for in a given system and may also aid agronomists in choosing deployment patterns of resistant varieties that will minimize adaptation by herbivore populations.

IV. AVAILABLE DATA ON THE GENETICS OF PLANT–HERBIVORE INTERACTIONS

The theoretical discussion in the previous sections points us to many basic types of empirical information that are needed both to further our understanding of basic plant–herbivore biology and to strengthen our predictions of future resistance of crop varieties. I shall attempt here to review the available genetic data. Some of the ecologically relevant data are discussed elsewhere in this book (e.g., Schultz, Chapter 3; Rausher, Chapter 7).

I shall review the genetic parameters listed in Section III within the following format: (A) information on how genetically variable plants and their herbivores are in space and over limited periods of time, (B) the nature of genetic factors underlying this variation, and (C) the frequency and magnitude of negative pleiotropic effects (i.e., costs) related to host resistance factors and herbivore adaptations for overcoming this resistance.

A. Intraspecific Variation in Plants and Herbivores

1. Patterns of Genetic Variation in Plant Resistance to Herbivores

In order to put all of our theory in perspective, it is first of all important to know how common it is for a plant species or population to vary genetically in its resistance to herbivores. Although some information is available from the basic literature, most of our knowledge comes from economically important plant species.

In terms of genetic variation found within a species, a wealth of information is available from the resistance breeders. Table I outlines some of the numerous cases in which variability in resistance has been found in crop species (or closely related species), indicating that such variation is not rare. What is not represented in this table, however, is the distribution of this variation *within* and *among* the populations that provided the original material for screening. Such information would help us understand how plant species respond genetically to herbivores in natural situations (see Section III,A). To acquire this information, we must go back to the sometimes obscure literature on initial screening tests. Often, even this literature indicates only which samples were most resistant. However, in cases in which the range of resistance has been reported, we can get a feeling for the among-population variation existing in wild populations of the crop or related species. For example, I found that good information is available on the range of resistance of wild potato species to the green peach aphid *(Myzus persicae)* and the potato aphid *(Macrosiphum euphorbiae)* (Radcliffe *et al.,* 1981). For 14 of the potato species with betweeen 14 and 67 genotypes tested, I calculated a variety of statistics related to variation in resistance within these species (Table II). These figures offer a conservative estimate of the variation among populations, because some crossing between samples may have occurred in experimental gardens used to propagate the germ-plasm collection, and a few samples may have been collected from nondistinct populations. However, on a gross level, such data are very informative. Because the material was not collected based on resistance properties, each plant sample tested can be assumed to be a random sample, and the values may be considered representative of the species.

Table I

Some Economically Important Plant Species in which Genetic Variation for Herbivore Resistance Exists[a]

Plant	Herbivore	Genetic control of variation	General type of resistance	Reference
Zea mays (corn)	European corn borer	Polygenic	Antibiosis (DIMBOA)	Scott and Guthrie (1967), Russell et al. (1975)
	Corn earworm	Polygenic	Antibiosis, nonpreference, tolerance	Widstrom and McMillian (1973)
	Corn-leaf aphid	Conflicting reports	Antibiosis, nonpreference (DIMBOA?)	Long et al. (1976), Pathak and Saxena (1976), Chang and Brewbaker (1975)
	Maize stem borers	?	Antibiosis	Kalode and Pant (1967), Mathur and Jain (1972)
	Fall armyworm	Polygenic	?	Widstrom et al. (1972)
Oryza sativa (rice)	Brown planthopper	2 dominant and 2 recessive genes with independent effects	Antibiosis, nonpreference	Lakshimnarayana and Khush (1977), Song et al. (1972)
	Green leafhopper	4 dominant genes and 1 recessive gene with independent effects	Antibiosis + ?	Krishnaiah (1975)
	Rice stem borer	Monogenic in some crosses, polygenic in others	Antibiosis, nonpreference (mechanical)	Oliver and Gifford (1975), Lee et al. (1974)
	Rice gall midge	Conflicting reports	Antibiosis	Heinrichs and Pathak (1981)
Triticum spp. (wheat)	Hessian fly	7 dominant genes, 1 recessive gene, with independent effects	Antibiosis	Gallun et al. (1975)
	Greenbug	1 + recessive genes	?	Abdel-Malik et al. (1966)
	Cereal-leaf beetle	Polygenic	Nonpreference, antibiosis (pubescence)	Ringlund and Everson (1968), Gallun et al. (1975)

616

Plant	Insect	Genetic basis	Mechanism	References
Hordeum vulgare (barley)	Wheat stem sawfly	1 major gene and modifiers	Antibiosis (solid stem)	McKenzie (1965), McNeal et al. (1971)
	Hessian fly	1 dominant gene at low temperature, 2 epistatically interacting genes at high temperature	Antibiosis?	Olembo et al. (1966)
Sorghum bicolor (sorghum)	Cereal-leaf beetle	1 recessive gene	Nonpreference	Hahn (1968)
	Corn-leaf aphid	1 dominant gene	Antibiosis	Cartier and Painter (1956), Gallun and Khush (1980)
	Greenbug	1 dominant gene	Antibiosis	Weibel et al. (1972)
	Shoot fly	?	?	Starks and Doggett (1970)
Medicago sativa (alfalfa)	Spotted alfalfa aphid	Polygenic	Nonpreference, antibiosis, tolerance	McMurtry and Stanford (1960) Harvey et al. (1960)
	Pea aphid	1+ dominant genes (?)	Antibiosis + ?	Jones et al. (1950), Ortman et al. (1960)
Gossypium spp. (cotton)	Boll weevil	1 gene for some traits	Nonpreference (red leaves, frego bract)	Isely (1928), Stephens and Lee (1961)
	Jassids	1 dominant gene, modifiers, and 2 epistatically interacting genes	Antibiosis, nonpreference (pubescene, thickness of cells)	Knight (1952), Muttuthamby et al. (1969), and Batra and Gupta (1970)
	Corn earworm, tobacco budworm	1–few genes, depending on trait	Nonpreference, antibiosis (gossypol, tannin, other secondary compounds, glabrous leaves)	Lukefahr and Martin (1966), Wilson and Lee (1971), Waiss et al. (1981)
Cucurbits	Cucumber beetles	1 recessive gene	Nonpreference	DaCosta and Jones (1971)
	Two-spotted spider mite	1 dominant gene, modifiers	Antibiosis or nonpreference	Gould, (1978), dePonti (1978)
	Melon aphid	1 dominant gene in some tests	Tolerance, antibiosis	Bohn et al. (1973)
	Squash bug	Polygenic	Nonpreference	Benepol and Hall (1967), Novero et al. (1962)

(Continued)

Table I (Continued)

Plant	Herbivore	Genetic control of variation	General type of resistance	Reference
Rubus idaeus (raspberry)	European raspberry aphid	9 dominant genes with independent effects	Nonpreference, antibiosis	Keep and Knight (1967), Keep et al. (1970)
	American raspberry aphid	1 dominant gene	Nonpreference, antibiosis	Kennedy et al. (1973), Daubeny (1966), Kennedy and Schaefers (1974)
Beta vulgaris (sugar beets)	Green peach aphid	Polygenic	Nonpreference, antibiosis	Russell (1978)
Lactuca sativa (lettuce)	Root aphid	?	Antibiosis	Dunn and Kempton (1974)
Malus robusta (apple)	Rosy apple aphid	1 dominant gene	Nonpreference (hypersensitivity)	Alston and Briggs (1970)
	Wooly apple aphid	1 dominant gene		Painter (1951)
	Rosy leaf-curling aphid	1 dominant gene	?	Alston and Briggs (1968)
Picea sp. (spruce)	Black-marked tussock moth	?	Avoidance	von Schonborn (1966)
	Spruce sawfly	?	Tolerance + ?	von Schonborn (1966)
	Spruce gall aphid	1 gene(?)	?	Thielges and Campbell (1972); Hanover (1980)
Pinus silvestris (Scots pine)	Shoot borer	?	?	Steiner (1974)
	Pine-root collar weevil	?	?	Wright and Wilson (1972)
	European pine sawfly	?	Antibiosis	Wright et al. (1976)

[a]The information presented represents probabilistic inferences that I, or the various authors referred to, have drawn concerning genetic control and mechanisms responsible for resistance. It is impossible in most of the cases presented to make absolute statements based on available data.

Table II
Distribution of Resistance to the Green Peach Aphid and Potato Aphid in 14 Species of Wild Potato[a]

Series and species of Solanum	Sample size	Origin	Green peach aphid resistance					Potato aphid resistance					Correlation[b]
			Mean	Range	CV	g₁	g₂	Mean	Range	CV	g₁	g₂	
Bulbocastana / S. bulbocastanum	33	Guatemala, Mexico	1.1	0.1–3.0***[c,d]	68.5	0.55 NS	2.72***	0.9	0.1–2.7***	68.5	1.04*	3.68***	0.403*
Pinnatisecta / S. cardiophyllum	19	Mexico	1.8	0.7–4.1 NS	57.3	0.90 NS	2.65**	2.2	0.7–5.2*	58.3	0.86 NS	2.86**	0.020 NS
Commersoniana / S. chacoense	44	Argentina	7.1	2.0–26.8**	73.3	1.73***	6.30***	5.0	1.3–24.0***	73.4	3.24***	17.35***	0.255 NS
Commersoniana / S. tarijense	14	Argentina	2.9	0.6–7.7****	102.7	1.34*	−3.20*	4.8	3.6–8.4 NS	49.1	−0.98 NS	3.38*	0.017 NS
Acaulia / S. acaula	67	Argentina	6.8	1.8–52.1***	118.6	3.87***	19.39***	1.8	0.5–5.0**	66.3	0.98**	3.97***	0.169 NS
Demissa / S. demissum	46	Mexico, Guatemala	5.6	2.0–12.5*	54.4	0.58 NS	2.27*	1.6	0.4–2.9 NS	66.7	0.92**	3.76***	−0.031 NS
Longipecicellata / S. stoloniferum	47	Mexico	2.1	0.8–10.0	71.5	3.31***	16.52***	1.1	0.3–2.6****	59.8	0.77*	2.67****	0.436**
Longipecicellata / S. polytrichon	19	Mexico	3.5	0.1–7.8****	62.0	0.25 NS	1.89 NS	1.5	0.4–3.0****	53.8	0.59 NS	2.35*	0.155 NS
Cuneoalata / S. infundibuliforme	19	Argentina, Bolivia	1.6	0.7–3.5 NS	45.2	1.30**	0.43 NS	1.6	0.2–3.3 NS	56.7	0.33 NS	2.53**	−0.026 NS
Megistacroloba / S. raphanifolium	25	Peru	4.8	1.7–11.6*	52.3	1.01*	3.35***	3.1	1.0–14.2*	87.6	2.79**	11.64***	0.018 NS
Tuberosa / S. canasense	36	Peru, Bolivia	2.2	0.1–16.7****	140.6	3.49***	14.88***	1.8	0.6–11.3***	121.7	3.60***	15.39***	0.908**
Tuberosa / S. multidissectum	19	Peru	1.6	0.6–2.8***	37.0	−1.08*	2.59*	1.1	0.2–2.6**	63.9	0.86 NS	2.74**	−0.182 NS
Tuberosa / S. sparsipilum	21	Bolivia, Peru	6.7	2.4–14.6 NS	41.6	0.91 NS	4.18***	3.9	1.1–6.4 NS	51.5	0.62 NS	3.19**	0.312 NS
Tuberosa / S. phureja	57	Colombia	3.9	1.3–9.5*	56.2	1.29***	3.64***	2.7	0.9–5.6 NS	51.5	0.97*	3.53***	0.201 NS

[a]The ratio of the number of aphids on a test sample and on a control genotype was used as the resistance value. All of the statistics are based on these values. CV, Coefficient of variation; g₁, skewness; g₂, kurtosis. Correlation between mean resistance of species of potato to the two aphids was 0.55 ($r < 0.05$).
[b]Correlation between potato aphid and green peach aphid performance.
[c]Significance level: *, <0.05; **, <0.01; ***, <0.001; ****, <0.0001.
[d]Only samples tested more than once were used in ANOVA for within-species variation.

In Table II the mean values presented represent the mean ratio of the number of aphids on a test plant compared to the number on a consistantly used, partially resistant control plant. Therefore, any value below 1.0 would indicate a test plant more resistant than the control, and any value above 1.0 a test plant of less resistance. We can see from the table that the means for the potato species vary considerably for both aphids but that the coefficients of variation (CVs) within potato species are usually between 50 and 100, with no correlation between the CV and the mean. A conservative analysis of variance indicates that 11 of the 14 potato species were genetically variable in their resistance to the green peach aphid and that 9 were genetically variable regarding resistance to the potato aphid. If this result is exemplary of most plant–herbivore systems, genetic variation is indeed common. But what about the potato species not exhibiting genetic variation? Their mean resistance levels and CVs among genotypes are not significantly different from the others. What stands out is that fewer replicates were used per test in these cases than the average. I ran a simple linear regression to determine whether the statistical value of P from the analysis of variance (ANOVA) for each potato species and aphid combination was related to the average number of replicate tests conducted per potato genotype. The results indicate that 27% of the variation in P is accounted for by the number of replicates per genotype ($P < 0.005$). According to the regression equation [$P = 0.656 - 0.068 \times$ (number of replicates)], running 8.9 replicates per genotype would, on average, yield significant variation within a potato species for resistance to these aphids. (Number of genotypes tested per potato species was not significant for the range of values in the data set.)

Analysis of skewness and kurtosis (g_1 and g_2 in Table II) of the distribution of resistance among genotypes within these wild potato species tells us two things. First, resistance is not normally distributed, as might be expected with a polygenic, additively inherited characteristic under no selection pressure and, second, it is not bimodally distributed, as would be expected if populations were fixed for one of two alleles coding for resistance or susceptibility. Why all potato species show a leptokurtic distribution of resistance that is almost always skewed toward susceptibility is impossible to determine from this data set, but some tenable answers are worth considering, especially if this pattern proves more general. For example, selection pressure for resistance may have been very strong in only a few areas, or only a few populations may have had the genetic variation necessary to respond dramatically to selection. Because the data set does not allow separation of within- and among-population variation, we, unfortunately, cannot rule out the possibility that the genetic variation we have demonstrated is due totally to within-population variation. To gain a real grasp of the dynamics of genetic interactions between plants and herbivores, it is important to have information on both within- and among-population variation, for the within-population variation can often help us determine why we see specific patterns of among-population variation. Unfortunately, this has not been of much concern to resistance breeders, who are under pressure to find as many sources of resistance as possible and assume that there is much more among- than within-population variation.

Another bit of useful information unavailable from this potato data set and most other published data on economically important plants is the geographic distribution of resistance. Knowing whether the variation in resistance to an insect is distributed over a long cline or forms a checkered pattern could help in studying causal factors of variation and could also aid resistance breeders in focusing more sharply their future searches for resistant plant material (see Krischik and Denno, Chapter 14).

In exceptional cases, in which geographic distributions have been published, results can be intriguing. For example, Gibson (1979) collected samples of two *Solanum* species *(S. berthaultii* and *S. tarijense)* along a latitudinal gradient from Bolivia through Argentina. Although the sample sizes were small, it can be seen (Fig. 1) that both potato species varied in a resistance character (sticky tipped hairs) along the gradient. Moreover, in one general area where they were sympatric, both showed variation for the character. The genetic analysis indicated that the same locus governed expression of resistance in both species and that they probably were of common ancestry. What maintains this single-locus variation in both species is yet to be studied.

Extensive studies of *among*-population genetic variation in resistance to herbivores in economically unimportant species are unavailable. However, three studies stand out in which geographic surveys of the genetic variation in resistance in economically important plants has been studied with the primary goal of gaining insight into the basic ecology and evolution of plant—herbivore systems. Jones (1966, 1968, 1972, 1973, 1977) conducted long-term studies of wide-area and microgeographic patterns of resistance through cyanogenesis in *Lotus corniculatus.* Jones found very long geographic clines in resistance to mollusks and vertebrates across Europe and much microgeographic differentiation within small areas. Jones later distrusted many of the patterns, for *Lotus* is an agricultural species that has become more and more commonly sown from pedigreed seed stocks, and this could have produced unnatural patterns (Jones, 1977). Similar studies of *Trifolium repens*, which also exhibits cya-

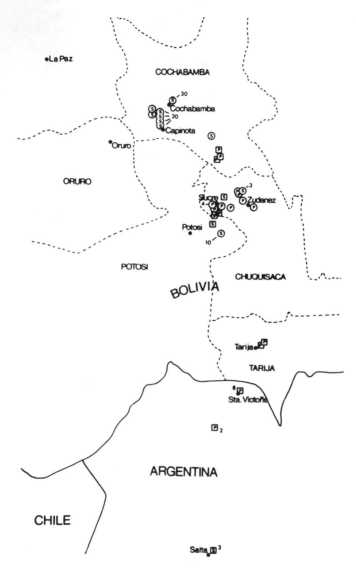

Fig. 1. Geographic variation in the resistance of two wild potato species: ○, *Solanum berthaultii*; □, *S. tarijense*. S, Samples with sticky hairs conferring resistance; P, samples with pointed hairs not bearing any sticky exudate. From Gibson (1979).

nogenesis, have been conducted and reveal patterns of *among*- and *within*-population variation grossly similar to that of *Lotus* (Daday, 1954a,b, 1965; Jones, 1968). These, too, are suspect, according to Jones (1977).

From a similar perspective, Hare (1980) and Hare and Futuyma (1978) have studied the weedy cocklebur *(Xanthium strumarium)* and its resistance to attack by two seed feeders. Their results demonstrate *among*-population variation over a transect of about 16 km of beachfront that was certainly not distributed in a cline-like fashion.

Although more such studies of *among*-population variation would be helpful, what we really lack and need are studies of *within*-population variation in resistance. Whereas knowledge of among-population variation gives us a feeling for the importance of genetic variation in the interactions of plants and herbivores, it is knowledge of within-population variation that helps us to understand the evolutionary processes producing this variation.

Agricultural examples of within-population variation that do exist are either of the type exemplified by Gibson (1979) or are from studies of modern crop varieties. The studies of genetic variation for resistance within modern crop varieties are actually very revealing, for, although crops are often considered to be more genetically homogeneous than wild plants, resistance breeders have often had good luck in searching for resistance within nonhybrid agronomic cultivars of alfalfa (Harvey *et al.*, 1960), sugar beet (Russell, 1966), maize (Widström *et al.*, 1972), carrots (dePonti and Freriks, 1980), and Brussels sprouts (Dunn and Kempton, 1971).

Harvey *et al.* (1960) were able to select alfalfa plants from one variety for resistance to damage by the spotted alfalfa aphid in one generation. In testing after the first generation of selection, 35% of the plants in the control population died from aphid attack compared to 18% in the selected population. A reanalysis of Dunn and Kempton's (1972) work on Brussels sprouts (Table III, Fig. 2b) indicates that within single cultivars of Brussels sprouts there may exist three or more genotypes yielding distinct interactions with the cabbage aphid.

Three studies on economically unimportant flowering plants illustrate existence of within-population variation in resistance. Another on bracken fern is reported by Jones (Chapter 15) and will therefore not be discussed. Moran (1981) found that within one field of goldenrod *(Solidago)* there was genetic variation among clones in resistance to the aphid *Uroleucon caligatum*. One could argue about the genetic inference drawn in the study, but the evidence is generally strong. Service (1982) demonstrated that two clones of *Rudbeckia luciniata* from one site differed

Table III

Variation among Seven Aphid Populations Regarding Their Reproductive Capacities on Eight Brussels Sprouts Clones

| All clones[a] | | | | Clones within varieties[b] | | | | G Tests for each clone[c] | | | |
| | | | | Heterogeneity test | | | | | | | |
Tests	df	G	P	Tests	df	G	P	Tests	df	G	P
Pooled	6	13.991	<0.05	BG-10 + BG-9	6	15.54	<0.025	BG-10	6	17.183	<0.01
Heterogeneity	42	132.108	<0.001	VI-2 + VI-4	6	20.51	<0.005	BG-9	6	11.900	NS
Total	48	146.099	<0.001	G-2 + G-19	6	2.774	NS	BG-11	6	2.208	NS
								VI-2	6	6.184	NS
								VI-4	6	12.717	<0.05
								D-2	6	3.581	NS
								G-2	6	11.9108	NS
								G-19	6	12.755	<0.05

[a]Results of replicated G test including all clones. The significant heterogeneity G value indicates presence of clone × aphid-population interaction.

[b]Results of a priori test for clone × aphid-population interaction for clones derived from the same Brussels sprouts variety (letters represent variety; numbers represent clones).

[c]G Test to detect significance of variation in reproduction of the seven aphid populations on each clone.

All of these results represent conservative estimates of statistical significance. A two-way ANOVA would have been more appropriate, but original data were not available from Dunn and Kempton's (1972) paper. Their analysis indicates that each aphid population was genetically distinct ($P < 0.05$).

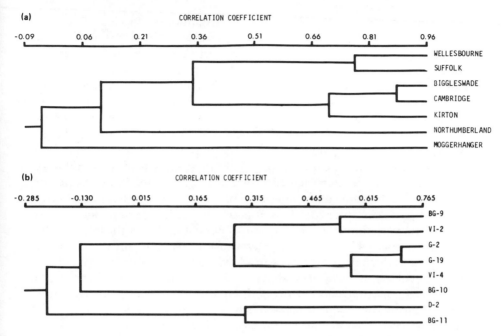

Fig. 2. (a) Similarity of aphid populations based on correlations between them in reproductive rate on seven resistant Brussels sprouts clones. (b) Similarity of eight Brussels sprouts clones [seven aphid resistant, one susceptible (BG-11)], based on correlations between them regarding reproductive rates of the seven aphid populations. Cophenetic correlation coefficients: (a), 0.840; (b), 0.814. Analysis of Dunn and Kempton's (1972) data.

significantly in their suitability to the aphid *U. rudbeckiae*. Service also found genetic variation in suitability on a larger geographic scale. A detailed field-plot study of *Oenothera biennis* by Kinsman (1982) yielded a complex pattern of genetic variation within and among populations in resistance to a number of herbivore species.

In all three of these studies the plant species were or "acted," at least partially, as parthenogenetic reproducers. The term *within population* refers more to the essential fact that the plants were all taken from areas easily within the range of a single herbivore population that could exert the selective pressure to maintain the genetic variation (rather than referring to an interbreeding set of plants). Even based on the few available studies, we can conclude that genetic variation *within* and *among* plant populations for resistance to herbivores is probably quite common. However, the selective forces (if they exist) that maintain this variation are still elusive.

2. Patterns of Variation in Herbivore Adaptations to Host Plants

As discussed in the theoretical sections of this chapter, one factor that may contribute to genetic variation in host-plant resistance is genetic variation in herbivore adaptation to the host plants. Conversely, it is the variation in the plants that may foster genetic variation in the herbivore.

As is true of our data on genetic variation in host plants, most of our data on genetic variation in herbivores come from economically important species. Table IV lists herbivore species for which I could find convincing evidence of genetic variation in adaptation to host plants. One potential problem with a number of these studies is lack of certainty with regard to whether each recorded species is indeed one species or a number of discrete sibling species. This problem is discussed by Mitter and Futuyma (Chapter 13). As is apparent in Table IV, many of the cases of genetic variation involve parthenogenetic aphids. In these cases the biological species concept is not very useful. Because in many of the areas from which the differences in adaptation of the aphids are recorded there never is a sexual phase, distinguishing a "clone" or "biotype" from a "species" is impossible. In this discussion we shall accept currently prevailing phenetic species classifications, with the understanding that for some purposes it may be more useful to equate clones of asexual organisms with sibling species of sexual organisms than to distinguish the two categories.

Although there is less evidence for genetic variability in host-plant adaptation of herbivore species (Table IV) than there is evidence for genetic variation for resistance in host plants (Table I), this probably reflects the amount of effort invested in finding genetic variation, rather than a true difference in the frequency of genetic variation. Additionally, whereas the data on genetic variation in resistance within host-plant species can often be assumed to be an unbiased estimate of the genetic variation within the species, this is rarely the case with the agricultural data on herbivores. With few exceptions, genetic variation in herbivore pests is not searched for by researchers. Instead, this variation in the herbivore finds the researcher when pest outbreaks occur on "resistant" crops. For this reason, only large genetic differences in pest adaptability are usually reported, and the true picture of the pattern of variation among populations is obscured.

As I said, there are exceptions, most of which result from attempts to develop a resistant crop variety when geographic variation in the pest is anticipated. In some of these cases researchers may conduct a general survey of pest populations in search of genetic variation. Dunn and Kempton's (1972) investigation of aphid resistance in Brussels sprouts (a study referred to previously as evidence that there may be genetic

Table IV
Genetic Variation within Herbivore Species for Response to Host-Plant Resistance[a]

Order and species of herbivore	Host plant(s) involved in expression of variation	Mode of reproduction and genetic control of variation	Type of plant resistance involved	Scale of reported variation	Reference
Hemiptera					
Amphorophora rubi (European raspberry aphid)	Raspberry	Seasonally parthenogenic, series of single dominant genes	NP + AB, series of single dominant genes	Within districts in England	Briggs (1965)
Schizaphis graminum (greenbug)	Wheat, barley	Parthenogenic, 4 biotypes	Single gene +	Within Texas	Wood (1971), Daniels (1981)
Rhopalosiphum maidis (corn-leaf aphid)	Sorghum, maize, wheat, barley, oats	Parthenogenic, 5 biotypes	NP + AB, monogenic + polygenic	Within Kansas	Wilde and Feese (1973), Cartier and Painter (1956), Pathak and Painter (1959)
Therioaphis maculata (spotted alfalfa aphid)	Alfalfa	Parthenogenic in some areas, 6 biotypes	NP, AB, T, polygenic	Within Canada, United States, and California	Stanford (1977), Nielson and Don (1974a,b)
Aphis gossypii (melon aphid)	Muskmelon	?	T + AB, single gene?	Populations from California, se United States	Ivanoff (1957), Kishaba et al. (1971)
Acyrthosiphon pisum (pea aphid)	Alfalfa, pea	Parthenogenic in some areas (crosses performed, intricate results)	NP + AB, single gene+	Within United States, Canada, and local area of Germany	Cartier et al. (1965), Muller (1971), Muller and Hubert-Dahl (1973), Bournoville (1981)

(Continued)

Table IV (Continued)

Order and species of herbivore	Host plant(s) involved in expression of variation	Mode of reproduction and genetic control of variation	Type of plant resistance involved	Scale of reported variation	Reference
Aulacorthum solani (foxglove aphid)	Lungwort, foxglove, potato	Seasonally parthenogenic, additive on potato, dominance on foxglove and lungwort (in opposite directions)	AB + NP	Within local area of Germany	Muller (1976)
Uroleucon caligatum	Goldenrod	Seasonally parthenogenic?	AB + ?	Within a field	Moran (1981)
Uroleucon rudbeckiae	Rudbeckia luciniata	Seasonally parthenogenetic	AB + NP	Within local area in North Carolina	Service (1982)
Eriosoma lanigerum (wooly apple aphid)	Apple	Seasonally parthenogenic	Single gene	Within Australia	Sen Gupta and Miles (1975)
Nilaparvata lugens (brown planthopper)	Rice	Sexual polygenic? 3 biotypes?	AB + NP, series of 4 single genes	Philippines and se Asia	Claridge and denHollander (1980), Lakshminarayana and Khush (1977), Sogawa, (1981a,b)
Nephotetix cincticeps (green rice leafhopper)	Rice	Sexual, 2 biotypes	NP + AB, series of 5 single genes	800 km	Sato and Sogawa (1981)
Nuculaspis californica (black pine leaf scale)	Ponderosa pine	Haplodiploid, additive?	AB	Local area	Alstad and Edmunds (Chapter 12)

Diptera					
Mayetiola destructor (Hessian fly)	Wheat	Sexual, series of single genes	AB, series of 8 single genes	A field, within United States	Painter *et al.* (1931), Gallun *et al.* (1975)
Pachydiplosis oryzae (rice gall midge)	Rice	Sexual, 4 biotypes	AB	India	Heinrichs and Pathak (1981)
Liriomyza sativae	Tomato, pea	Sexual	AB + NP	Within 1 county of North Carolina	S. Via (unpublished data)
Liriomyza brassicae	*Barbarea vulgaris, Thlaspi arvense, Brassica nigra*	Sexual	AB + NP	Within a field	Tavormina (1982; personal communication)
Coleoptera					
Cassidinae spp. (tortoise beetles)	Morning glory	Sexual	?	Within 1 county	M.D. Rausher (unpublished data)
Callosobruchus maculatus	Pigeon pea, adzuki bean	Sexual, additive	?	Lab population	Wasserman and Futuyma (1981)
Sitophilus oryzae	Split pea	Sexual, single recessive gene	AB	Worldwide	Coombs *et al.* (1977), Thind and Muggleton (1981)
Lepidoptera					
Colias philodice (clouded sulfur)	Alfalfa, vetch	Sexual	AB + ?	1 area of Colorado	Tabashnik (1982)
Laspeyresia pomonella (codling moth)	Apple, walnut, plum	Sexual	Avoidance in time	1 area of California	Phillips and Barnes (1975)
Alsophila pometaria (fall cankerworm)	Oaks, maple	Parthenogenetic	AB + NP	1 woodlot, New York, New Jersey	Mitter and Futuyma (Chapter 13)
Papilio polytenes (tiger swallowtail)	Carrot	Sexual	AB	United States, Costa Rica	Blau (1978)

(Continued)

Table IV (*Continued*)

Order and species of herbivore	Host plant(s) involved in expression of variation	Type of plant resistance involved	Mode of reproduction and genetic control of variation	Scale of reported variation	Reference
Papilio glaucus (tiger swallowtail)	Birch, aspen, tulip tree, cherry	AB	Sexual, dominance	United States, Canada	Scriber (Chapter 11)
Euphydryas editha (checkerspot)	*Pedicularis, Plantago, Collinsia*	NP + AB	Sexual	California	Singer (1970), Rausher (1982)
Acarina					
Tetranychus urticae (two-spotted spider mite)	Cucumber, potato, *Plantago,* tobacco	AB, single gene + modifiers	Haplodiploid, additive	Within 1 orchard and within United States	Gould (1978, 1979)

[a]Information on genetic control of variation in herbivore responses is even less precise than that for genetics of host resistance, so care must be taken in drawing absolute conclusions from this table. Biotypes of parthenogenic species may be equivalent to sibling species. AB, Antibiosis; NP, nonpreference; T, tolerance.

variation for herbivore resistance within single crop varieties) provides such an example. Once Dunn and Kempton found resistance within their Brussels sprouts varieties, they wanted to determine if populations of *Brevicoryne brassicae*, the cabbage aphid, existed that were not affected by the resistance factors. In pursuit of this, they tested the response to the resistance factors by seven cabbage-aphid populations from various geographic areas in England. Figure 2a and Table III provide a reanalysis of their data in which the similarities of the seven aphid populations, based on the correlations in their reproductive rates on eight Brussels sprouts clones (seven resistant and one susceptible), are depicted. Each population is apparently unique, genetically, in terms of response to the Brussels sprouts clones. Even the Biggleswade and Cambridge populations, which have a correlation coefficient of 0.89 are statistically distinguishable ($P < 0.05$) on two of the Brussels sprouts clones. An analysis of clone similarity and geographic location shows no apparent correlation of biological similarity of aphid populations and geographical proximity. Indeed, the Moggerhanger and Biggleswade populations, which are quite dissimilar biologically, come from the same district, whereas the distinctly clustered Wellesbourne and Suffolk populations come from the center and east coast of England, respectively. The Suffolk population is actually closer to Cambridge and Moggerhanger than to Wellesbourne. Temporal stability of this geographic pattern is supported by the fact that the Wellesbourne population was tested over a number of years and maintained its host-utilization profile.

A similar lack of correspondence between geographic distance and biological response to a host-plant resistance factor was found by Gould (1978). Results of testing 13 field populations of the two-spotted spider mite on a resistant variety of cucumber indicated that there was as much genetic difference between populations found 3.0 mi apart as there was between populations from New York and California. Temporal stability in this case appeared to be low.

The most intensive geographic analysis of "biotype" distribution that I could find involved a study of the corn-leaf aphid. Pathak and Painter (1959) collected samples of this aphid from the short- and long-grass areas of Kansas in 1956 and 1957 and classified them as either one of two "biotypes" (1956) or one of four "biotypes" (1957). (This difference in classification was due to differential sensitivity of the testing procedure used in the two years.) A total of 286 samples were collected. The results are summarized in Table V and Fig. 3. A localized pattern of variation is apparent. All of the 1956 and 1957 samples from the short-grass area were collected almost exclusively from sorghum, whereas one-third of the long-grass-area samples were collected from corn (*Zea*).

Table V
Occurrence of Corn-Leaf Aphid Biotypes in the Short-Grass (West) and Long-Grass (East) Areas of Kansas[a]

	Samples					
	Short-grass region		Tall-grass region		Total	
Biotypes	(no.)	(%)	(no.)	(%)	(no.)	(%)
1956 Survey						
KS-1	44	65.7	38	67.9	82	66.7
KS-2	23	34.3	18	32.1	41	33.3
	67		56		123	
1957 Survey						
KS-1	26	61.9	68	56.7	94	58.0
KS-2	9	21.4	38	31.7	48	29.0
K-3	1	2.4	2	1.7	3	1.9
KS-4	6	14.3	10	8.3	16	9.9
Mixed KS-2 and						
KS-3	0	0	2	1.7	2	1.2
	42		120		163	

[a]After Pathak and Painter (1959).

The frequencies of the four biotypes were nonetheless similar in both areas in 1957. If the four biotypes of 1957 are condensed to become the two biotypes of 1956 (KS-4 = KS-1; KS-3 = KS-2), we see a strong similarity of total biotype frequencies in the two years. That the corn-leaf aphid may be highly migratory should be considered in the interpretation of these patterns.

Not all herbivorous pests show such patterns of local genetic differentiation. In some cases it appears as if the scale of differentiation is much larger. For example, Hsiao (1978) found genetic variation in the utilization of the host plant *Solanum elaeagnifolium* by Colorado potato beetle populations from Arizona to Texas. The Utah population, which was geographically intermediate, was also intermediate in terms of the mean number of offspring a female could produce when reared on *S. elaeagnifolium*. Information on such broad geographic variation in other pest species is also available, but, as in the case of the potato beetle, data regarding the local scale of variation have never been presented, so comparison is impossible. The differences in host utilization are sometimes so great, however, that had there been comparable local variation it surely would have been noticed. One early case of such broadscale variation was reported by Painter (1930), who found that Hessian flies in eastern Kansas could survive on all varieties of hard and soft wheat

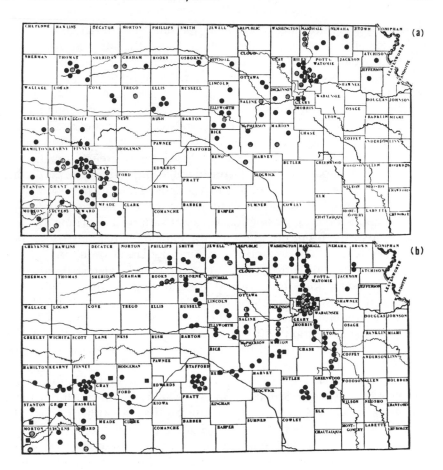

Fig. 3. Geographic distribution of corn-leaf aphid biotype in Kansas for the years 1956 (a; ●, KS-1; ⊖, KS-2; ◗, KS-1 and KS-2 mixed) and 1957 (b;●, KS-1; ⊖, KS-2; ⊗, KS-3; ■, KS-4, ⊙, KS-2 and KS-3 mixed). From Pathak and Painter (1959).

that were being grown at the time, whereas Hessian flies from western Kansas and California could only develop on hard-wheat and some soft-wheat varieties. Other agricultural examples may be extracted from Table IV. In terms of nonpest species, Scriber (Chapter 11), Blau (1978), and Straatman (1962) have described broad geographic patterns of genetic variation in host utilization by populations or "subspecies" of Papilionidae and Saturniidae.

In order to relate these patterns of geographic variation to the theory in the Section III of this chapter, one must ask not only whether these "subspecies" of butterflies or locally differentiated populations of aphids and mites are genetically different from each other in host utilization, but, also, whether a subset of the genetic variability responsible for the differentiation among the populations is to be found within populations. For example, if the differences among herbivore populations are due to genetic response to a cline in host-plant quality, does the genetic variation within herbivore populations also reflect this clinal variation in the host plants, or do we find genetic homogeneity within populations? From the applied perspective, knowledge of the degree of genetic variation within populations is of considerable importance in predicting how rapidly a pest may adapt to a man-imposed change in host quality. Although among-population variation may contribute to a single herbivore population's adaptation to a resistant variety, due to long distance immigrants from other populations, the immediate response of an herbivore population will depend on within-population variation.

As is the case with studies of genetic variation in plants, there are at this point, few studies that address the question of within-population variation in herbivores. The few that do exist demonstrate a great deal of within-population variation. One of the first demonstrations of variation in host utilization within an interbreeding herbivore population was published in a technical bulletin of the Kansas Agricultural Experiment Station (Painter et al., 1931). This bulletin reported two types of evidence that indicated within-population variation in the ability of Hessian flies from western Kansas to infest a variety of wheat (Illini Chief), which had never been grown there. In the first experiment, single females were caged in pots containing Illini Chief and another variety of wheat (Kanred). Females showed no significant preference for either wheat variety as an oviposition site, but in most cases the immatures only survived on Kanred wheat. An "occasional" fly's progeny would survive equally well on both varieties. Flies of these two types were isolated and maintained for three generations, during which time they retained their respective survival characteristics. In a second experiment, which amounted to mass selection of a central Kansas population of flies, it proved possible to develop a subpopulation that could infest Illini Chief. These results were confirmed by experiments of Cartwright and Noble (1947) and by Gallun et al. (1961), who demonstrated that, within a small sample (64 females) from an Indiana population, there existed at least four fly genotypes that were distinct in their ability to infest an array of wheat varieties. Adding to the remarkable nature of this finding is the fact that, prior to the testing by Gallun et al. (1961), this "sample" had been reared in the greenhouse for 12 generations on one wheat variety. (The size of the sample during these 12 generations was, unfortunately, not recorded.) As if this were not amazing enough, we must also note that the Hessian fly is not native to North America. It was introduced to the United States by Hessian soldiers around 1774, and perhaps again by Russian immigrants around 1870, so its genetic base was probably not as broad as that of endemic species.

These results with the Hessian fly stood alone and unnoticed by evolutionary biologists and most entomologists for many years. If this were the only case of such striking within-population variation in host utilization, it may not have deserved too much attention; however, more recent studies of other herbivores have demonstrated similarly striking variation. Response to a selection regime for adaptation to a resistant cucumber variety by a small sample of two-spotted spider mites demonstrated that there was significant genetic variation within the sample (Gould, 1979). After approximately 15 generations of selection, cucumber leaves causing 70% mortality of the control line caused only 20% mortality of the selected line. This sample originated from approximately 200 individuals collected from one area, and they had been maintained in the laboratory on one host (beans) for 16 generations before the selection experiment began. The notable factor in this case was that the genetic variation for adaptation to cucumber found in this one sample was equal to that found in a hybrid sample composed of individuals from 12 populations (Gould, 1978).

Similarly, Pathak and Heinrichs (1982), working with the brown planthopper, succeeded in increasing a laboratory colony's ability to survive on two resistant rice varieties by mass selection of a portion of the colony on each rice variety for seven generations. The resultant planthopper lines developed as well as resistance-breaking "biotypes" collected in areas where the resistant varieties had been grown. This laboratory colony had been maintained on a susceptible rice variety for 12 yr prior to the selection experiment. In light of our earlier theoretical analysis of factors that favor maintenance of genetic polymorphism within populations, we must postulate either that there were rather low pleiotropic "costs" associated with genes for adaptation to the resistant host plants or that some type of balancing selection existed in the apparently homogeneous environment used to maintain the herbivore prior to the selection experiments, in each of the three cases described.

These findings of genetic variation in laboratory populations lead us to ask, How much variation can be found in a naturally occurring population? Along these lines, Bournoville (1981) conducted a rough (but revealing) analysis of the variation in reproductive capacity of aphid clones growing on lucerne. Bournoville measured the variance in net reproduction among clones derived from (1) one parthenogenetic female, (2) one population, and (3) three geographically separated populations (Normandy, central west, and central east France). Variance in reproduction of clones ($n = 19$) derived from one female was less than one-tenth that of clones developed from 27 females collected in the same lucerne field ($F = 10.71$), indicating within-population genetic variation. Variance in the reproduction of clones from the three regions of France was surprisingly similar to that of the clones from the single field ($F = 1.17$). Bournoville's experimental design could have been better constructed, but the results at least strongly suggest that genetic variance within a population for host-plant adaptation may equal the genetic variance among a number of populations. When trying to generalize from this result to other species, it must be recognized that alate pea aphids are highly mobile. For less mobile insects, the among-population component of variation may be more important.

With the possible exception of the planthopper case the previous studies only found genetic variation in ability to adapt to antibiotic resistance. Wasserman and Futuyma (1981) have demonstrated similar genetic variation within a small population for a host-preference characteristic of the seed-feeding weevil *Callosobruchus maculatus*. This population had been reared in the laboratory for about 300 generations, and, although it showed no genetic variation in terms of development and survival on various hosts, a selection experiment did alter its host-selection behavior. Tavormina (1982), in a study of a single population of the leaf miner *Liriomyza brassicae*, found genotypic variation for both oviposition preference and development time on three host species. In a quantitative genetic experiment, S. Via (unpublished data) found significant variation for oviposition preference among subpopulations and a genotype × environment interaction for pupal weight on tomato and peas, indicating specialization of local subpopulations of another leaf miner, *L. sativae*. Additionally, within some subpopulations there was significant genetic specialization among individuals for larval utilization of different crops.

High levels of genetic variation for host-plant adaptation seem to be frequent, but there are cases in which investigators have searched for genetic variation within and among herbivore populations with no success. Guthrie *et al.* (1982) selected a laboratory colony of European corn borers for adaptation to resistant corn plants (containing DIMBOA) for 16 generations and found no response to selection. E. B. Radcliffe (unpublished data) found no population × plant interaction when New York and Minnesota populations of *Myzus persicae* were tested on 61 genotypes of wild potato. Whalon and Smilowitz (1979) measured a number of fitness-related characters of three colonies of this polyphagous aphid grown on cultivated potato. Although the colonies originated from widely separated areas (i.e., Pennsylvania, Maine, and Washington state), no biologically significant differences were found. This result was supported by electrophoretic data on 12 structural proteins that were obtained for two of these colonies (Mack and Smilowitz, 1980). Not only were there no differences in the proteins between the colonies, each colony appeared to be entirely homozygous. This result may be considered artifactual, because the colonies had been held in the lab for a number of generations, but an independent study of field-collected samples of nine aphid populations on potato, tobacco, and tomato yielded a similar result (May and Holbrook, 1978). This study revealed no heterozygosity in any of the nine populations at any of the 19 structural proteins studied. Moreover, there were no differences between populations. (Although lack of electrophoretic variability does not preclude the existence of biotypes, it does support the biological findings.) May and Holbrook (1978) concluded that some of the biotypes of M. persicae that have been reported may have been due to contamination of colonies with other species of Myzus. They felt that M. persicae's lack of electrophoretic variability may be due to a population bottleneck that occurred when the species was introduced from the eastern hemisphere, where some genetic variation has been found. (A. H. Eenink, personal communication, has found two biotypes in the Netherlands. One does best on lettuce, and the other does best on pepper.) Considering that M. persicae populations are at least cyclically parthenogenic, it would appear, based on genetic theory, a likely candidate for within- and among-population polymorphism. Certainly, Mitter and Futuyma (Chapter 13) show convincing evidence for this. It will be very interesting to see whether biotypes of M. persicae do evolve in North and South America, and, if so, whether they evolve in areas where M. persicae is completely or partially parthenogenetic.

B. Underlying Genetic Basis for Variation in Plants and Herbivores

Genetic theory suggests that polymorphism within herbivore populations may be more likely when there is strong substructuring of a population and that this is enhanced by assortative mating (or no mating) and adaptive habitat selection. The number of genes involved in producing variation in habitat selections and fitness on particular hosts may also be important, for the fewer genes involved, the more likely the proper biologically potent linkage between habitat-selection "genes" and fitness "genes." On the other hand, the more loci involved in an herbivore's host adaptation or in a plant resistance mechanism, the more likely a mutation that generates rare variants upon which selection may act.

In general, morphological characteristics appear to be inherited polygenically (Wright, 1978). However, it is useful to examine the mode of inheritance of resistance characteristics of plants and, more so, the inheritance of "resistance-breaking" characteristics in herbivores, because characteristics that adapt these herbivores to synthetic plant defenses (i.e., pesticides) are often inherited in a monogenic fashion (Brown and Pal, 1971). Tables I and IV present some of the data available on inheritance of these plant and herbivore characteristics. It is apparent from these tables that monogenic or polygenic control may be involved in specific cases. What is notable is the frequency of monogenically controlled variation in these characteristics.

Because almost all of the data in Table I come from the agricultural literature, it is fair to question whether there may be any bias involved in the information published on genetics of plant resistance characteristics. Because, as mentioned earlier, it is so much easier to use monogenically controlled resistance traits in breeding programs, it is possible that findings of monogenetically controlled variation are more often published. It is difficult to obtain a good answer to this question, but, considering the number of cases in which monogenically controlled variation in resistance has been found within crop species and wild relatives, we certainly cannot dismiss this mode of inheritance as unimportant. When we consider what would bias the reporting of resistance in wild relatives of crop plants, it is probably more the magnitude of resistance than the mode of inheritance, so a bias would arise primarily from monogenically controlled resistance characteristics being more potent, an important factor in itself.

One distinction that is very important to make in this discussion is that between the number of genes responsible for *variation* in plant species' resistance and the number of genes necessary for the production of a resistance characteristic. For example, although a single locus in cucumber has been found that determines absence or presence of cucurbitacin C (DaCosta and Jones, 1971), it is certainly not the only locus involved in the enzymatic steps necessary for producing cucurbitacin C (Rehm *et al.*, 1957; dePonti and Garretsen, 1980). A mutation at any locus coding for enzymes in the cucurbitacin synthetic pathway could presumably cause variation in the presence or absence or concentration of cucurbitacin C. So, although the presence–absence variation we see in cucumber is due to alleles at one locus, production of variation in this characteristic by mutation depends on the sum of mutation rates at all loci involved in cucurbitacin synthesis and degradation. As pointed out earlier, phenotypic variation in plant resistance may be enhanced further by the fact that an enzyme in the secondary metabolic pathway could cause variation in more than one secondary plant compound.

A distinction must also be made regarding the number of genes involved in genetic variation in an herbivore's ability to overcome resistance and the number of genes involved in producing the trait. Although, as seen in Table IV, there is some evidence of monogenically controlled variation in characteristics for overcoming plant resistance, this does not mean that alleles at one locus are the only ones that can produce this variation. Although the monogenic control of variation in adaptation to hosts may, theoretically, increase the chance that a polymorphism will be maintained, the polygenic nature of the system involved in producing a characteristic for adaptation will, theoretically, increase the probability of producing new genetic variation in adaptative characteristics. Taken together, they may act synergistically and help explain why we see so much genetic variation within herbivore populations.

In the theoretical section of this paper, it was suggested that an association between a genotype's habitat selection and its fitness in the chosen habitat would favor maintenance of polymorphism and allow more rapid adaptation to previously resistant host plants. If habitat selection and fitness in a habitat were controlled by separate genes, the probability of such an association's being maintained, once established, would be higher if there were assortative mating or parthenogenesis. As explained in Section III,B,5, this type of association could also be maintained if genes that were biologically active in the adult stage of a completely herbivorous insect were also active in the immature stage. If alleles in an adult insect that allowed it to overcome the toxic or repulsive characteristics of a resistant plant also enabled its immature stage to overcome the resistance in the plant, and the adult oviposits as it feeds (as if often the case), there would be a high probability that eggs would be laid on those plants upon which they could survive best. Adults of genotypes that were negatively affected by a plant's toxins or that were repelled by the plant would choose another, more suitable plant for feeding and ovipositing.

This scenario seems to apply quite well to the raspberry aphid (*Amphorophora rubi*). Briggs (1965) found four strains of this aphid in England that differed in their response to a number of varieties of raspberry. Based on hybrid crosses of the strains, Briggs found support for the hypothesis that differences in host-plant adaptation are controlled by single dominant alleles. When an aphid adult of strain 1, 2, or 3 was placed on a variety that was resistant to it, the aphid would usually leave the plant within 24 hr (Knight et al., 1958). When placed on a plant that was not resistant to it, the aphid would almost always feed on the plant and bear young. By repeatedly putting new adults on plants which were repellent to them, Keep and Knight (1967) were able to induce

enough reproduction to get five young aphids on plants that were repulsive to their parents. In none of these cases did the young survive
to maturity. In contrast, when young were produced on plants preferred
by an adult, survival was quite high. (Although a maternal effect could
have theoretically been involved in this result, its importance is limited
by the fact that females were placed on the host plants for only a short
period of time.)

In an insectary test (Keep *et al.*, 1970), 5 adult females of *Amphorophora
rubi*, strain 4, were placed on each of 10 raspberry plants resistant to the
strain and 4 plants susceptible to the strain; 7 days later the resistant
plants had an average of 4.6 nymphs in poor condition and 0 adults.
On the susceptible plants, there was an average of 67.3 nymphs in good
health and an average of 3.8 adults remaining from the 5 original aphids
placed on the plants. (Development time in this aphid genus is about
10 days.)

A more quantitative study of adaptive habitat selection, which may
have been due to a mechanism similar to that in the raspberry aphid
(or to linkage), was conducted by S. Via (unpublished data). Via found
that female leaf miners whose young grew larger on pea than tomato
preferred to oviposit on pea. The reverse held true for females whose
young grew to a larger size on tomato. A quantitative relationship was
found between the intensity of a female's preference and the degree of
difference in her offspring's pupal size on the two hosts.

Adaptive habitat selection based on genetically controlled phenotypic
resemblance of parent and offspring, described here, may turn out to
be quite common in insects in which both life stages are herbivorous or
in which each life stage is very mobile (e.g., grasshoppers). In insects
such as the Lepidoptera, this mechanism for habitat selection is not
feasible, because the adult is generally a nectar feeder. We may, therefore, ask whether there are differences between Lepidoptera and totally
herbivorous insects in the rates at which they adapt to new host plants
in natural and agricultural settings. This difference in life cycle may also
influence levels of within-population polymorphism and the probability
of "sympatric" speciation.

C. Pleiotropic Effects and Genetic Correlations

As discussed earlier, maintenance of polymorphism for resistance to
herbivores within plant populations may be strongly favored by existence
of negative pleiotropic (or linkage) effects of resistance, in terms of adaptiveness to other aspects of the plant's environment. The same would

hold true on a geographic scale larger than that occupied by one population if gene flow between populations occurred. Unfortunately, few hard data useful in determining pleiotropic effects in natural populations exist. Although we may infer from the literature that production of high concentrations of tannins in leaves and fruits would require energy that could otherwise be used for growth and reproduction, this is only inference and cannot easily be used to generalize about the cost of plant defenses such as low quantities of alkaloids or leaf pubescence.

The best evidence might come from a genetic analysis of covariance between expression of herbivore resistance in a plant genotype and a number of other fitness-related characteristics such as reproductive output, vegetative growth, intra- and interspecific competition, and resistance to other stress (e.g., drought, other herbivores, pathogens). The closest approximation to such data is in work on the reproductive output of isolines of seed- and fruit-producing crop plants that differ from each other solely in genes for herbivore resistance and genes linked tightly to them. Data from these isolines indicate that the cost of strong resistance to a single herbivore is often negligible in terms of reproductive output, for existence of a significant cost would make it difficult for a resistance breeder to convince agronomists and seed companies to market a resistant variety. Unfortunately, published reports of a breeder's failure to bring a resistant variety up to proper yield standards are rare, so we do not know the frequency of "low-cost" herbivore resistance.

Although the experiments have not to my knowledge been performed, the experimental material for rigorous testing of the pleiotropic costs of resistance to herbivores is available. Plant introduction centers teem with genetically variable seed from crop varieties and their wild relatives. The simplest experiments could be carried out on systems such as the wild potato variants collected by Gibson (1979), in which pleiotropic effects of single-locus differences in herbivore resistance could be tested in the area of origin. Because plant breeders in some cases know what the physiological or morphological causes of resistance in plant introductions are, it might be possible to contrast the cost of a number of types of resistance mechanisms.

Another useful approach for determining the cost of resistance has been taken by plant pathologists working with inducible fungal resistance, and this may be useful in evaluation of certain inducible herbivore-resistance mechanisms. Smedgaard-Petersen and Stølen (1981) measured the grain yield and protein content of barley exposed to an avirulent (i.e., symptomless) powdery mildew strain that nonetheless induced a defensive reaction in the host. They compared these results with yield and protein content of grain from unexposed control plants.

They found a 7% reduction in yield and an 11% reduction in protein content. This reduction appeared to be related to increased respiration rates in the exposed plants.

One fact that we know for certain from the agricultural literature is that genes for resistance to one herbivore may have positive or negative pleiotropic effects on resistance to other herbivores. For example, genes resulting in pubescent stems and leaves in cotton yield resistance to jassids and susceptibility to a number of lepidopterous pests (Batra and Gupta, 1970). Genetic stocks of spruce trees that avoid damage by the black-marked tussock moth, due to their late flushing of foliage, are most susceptible to the spruce sawfly (von Schonborn, 1966). If we look at the analysis of potato resistance to aphids (Table II), we can see that in 3 of the 14 potato species there is a significant positive correlation between the resistance of a genotype to the green peach aphid and its resistance to the potato aphid. In contrast to these 3 species, there are other species that exhibit high variation in resistance to both aphids but that have correlation coefficients incredibly close to zero, indicating independent inheritance of the two types of resistance. On a larger scale there is a positive correlation between the mean resistance of a potato species to the green peach aphid and potato aphid ($r^2 = 0.55$, $P < 0.05$).

In terms of pleiotropic effects of characteristics that adapt herbivores to plants, we might expect to find that in adapting to one host plant an herbivore becomes less adapted to a second host plant (Dethier, 1954). However, few experimental data are available that bear on this problem. In a selection experiment referred to earlier, in which I selected a single mite population for adaptation to a resistant cucumber variety, I found a negative relationship between adaptation to cucumber and adaptation to lima beans (Gould, 1979). Of equal interest, however, was the fact that I found a positive relationship between adaptation to the cucumber and adaptation to two other resistant plant species (potato and tobacco), which are members of a plant family only distantly related to cucumber. Additionally, no relationship at all was found between adaptation to cucumber and adaptation to yet another distantly related plant species (Plantago).

The question of positively and negatively correlated genetic effects is certainly of general interest to evolutionary ecologists (see Arnold, 1981). It may also be of great importance to resistance breeders. For instance, a low acreage of tobacco by itself may be insufficient to select for mite adaptation to tobacco. However, introduction of a large acreage of cucumber in the same area could cause adaptation of the mites to the cucumber and concurrent cross-adaptation to the tobacco.

We have, in the past few decades, seen the devastating effects of the positive genetic correlations involved in adaptation of herbivores to a

Table VI
Adaptation and Cross-Adaptation to Plant Defenses by *Heliothis virescens* Larvae[a]

Strain	Quercetin (13 days)	Nicotine (11 days)	Tomatine (11 days)
C	0.079 ± 0.008	0.027 ± 0.004	0.059 ± 0.010
S	0.112 ± 0.010	0.049 ± 0.007	0.125 ± 0.019
	$P < 0.02$	$P < 0.02$	$P < 0.005$

[a] Weights in grams of larvae reared on artificial diets containing secondary plant compounds. Strain S had been selected for adaptation to quercetin; strain C was maintained on an unadulterated artificial diet. Weight plus or minus standard error.

wide array of pesticides. We are at the point now at which it is difficult to find a new pesticide to which some insect pests are not already pre-adapted by selection with other pesticides (e.g., Colorado potato beetle in New York, tobacco budworm in Mexico). If positive genetic correlations in the adaptation of herbivores to resistant crop varieties are also common, we may someday face a similar problem in the field of resistance breeding. Although the search for negative correlations in adaptedness of insects to pesticides has been for the most part unsuccessful (Brown and Pal, 1971), this may not be the case in terms of adaptation to host-plant defenses, but the necessary supporting evidence is yet to be collected for herbivore species (see Leonard and Czochor, 1980, for data on plant pathogens).

A resistance breeder, armed with information about the types of resistance that would be overcome by positively correlated genetic changes in a pest species, could guard against utilizing combinations of crops with these types of resistance in the same area. Conversely, knowledge that adaptation by an insect to one type of resistance would cause a negative effect on the insect's fitness when exposed to a second plant defense would give the breeder the option of alternating these two resistance factors in time and space, to maintain a genetically inefficient pest population.

Absolute knowledge of the resistance factors that would cause positive and negative correlations in a specific pest population's pattern of adaptation would be impossible to achieve, but even probabilistic knowledge, based on analysis of genetic covariation of a few insect species in their response to a variety of plant defenses, would be helpful. In this context, F. Gould (unpublished data) selected two populations of the polyphagous lepidopteran, *Heliothis virescens*, for adaptation to quercetin, an antibiotic flavonoid found in some of its hosts. Once adaptation to quercetin was established, testing for cross-adaptation by one of the selected lines to other antibiotic compounds also found in crops hosts of *H. virescens* (Table VI) revealed positive but no negative relationship, even though the other compounds were chemically unrelated to quercetin. The positive correlations between adaptation to quercetin and adaptation to other compounds dictate caution in breeding for high concentrations of these compounds in crops grown in the same area, because adaptation of an insect population to one compound could yield adaptation to the others as well.

V. THE NEED FOR FUTURE INTERACTION BETWEEN RESISTANCE BREEDERS AND EVOLUTIONARY BIOLOGISTS

I hope that by this point it has become apparent that the empirical data provided by resistance breeders are of utility to individuals studying the evolutionary biology of plant–herbivore interactions and that the basic findings of these evolutionary biologists may be of use to resistance breeders.

Although researchers in both areas have occasionally quoted each other (e.g., Hayes, 1935; Smith, 1941), there is a need for more active interaction between the two fields. Because the primary goals of resistance breeders are different from those of basic evolutionary biologists, there has been a tendency for resistance breeders to discard or overlook information that is available to them and that could be of importance to evolutionary biologists. On the other hand, many evolutionary biologists still cling to the notion that for their research to be meaningful it must involve "natural" systems, when, in reality, studies of some "unnatural" systems could offer just as much basic information while being of use to resistance breeders. Additionally, the base-line information available on some agriculturally related species may make them more amenable to rigorous genetic investigations than other species.

In this chapter I have quoted a few studies in which basic investigations of the evolutionary biology of agricultural systems have been fruitful, but much more interaction is possible and desirable. I am certain that if one evolutionary ecologist worked with each resistance-breeding program in the United States, much previously unavailable information would be gathered.

For example, the data on potato resistance collected by Radcliffe et al. (1981), which are discussed in this chapter, offer much more extensive information on within-species variation in resistance than any nonagricultural study yet conducted. However, as pointed out in Section IV,A,1, it is impossible to separate the genetic variation into within- and among-population components. These components of variation could be identified if future collections of potato germ plasm emphasized accurate coding of locality data on each potato sample collected and efforts were divided between within- and among-population sampling. Accurate coding of locality data could also aid in mapping geographic patterns of resistance. These types of data could be used in determining if and how a resistance factor maintained its effectiveness in its natural habitat. Armed with this information, an evolutionary ecologist could conduct detailed field experiments in search of the actual selective factors maintaining this variation. If within-population variation stood out as an essential component maintaining resistance effectiveness (as found in some plant–pathogen systems; Dinoor, 1977; Browning, 1980), the breeder and agronomist would be well advised to try to mimic nature when deploying such resistance in a crop variety.

Evolutionary ecologists could also help a breeding team determine how much variation existed in their target pest, regarding its ability to adapt to the resistance being bred. Quantitative genetic and pest-selection experiments could be conducted to determine the existence of such variation and to aid in predicting field stability of the resistance.

Data on ecological factors (see Section III,C), such as cost involved in host selection, could also be determined, and, finally, the genetic and ecological information could be used in developing population-simulation models of the host plants and pests in a number of areas into which the resistant variety was to be introduced. Predictions of resistance stability in these areas could be made, based on differences in the biology of the pest and the plants in these areas. These predictions could be tested by monitoring the pest population once the variety was introduced.

Of course, resistance breeders could do all of this on their own, but, in general, their goals set priorities that preclude such detailed investigations. Evolutionary ecologists, though interested in developing testable evolutionary theory, lack the resources and well-controlled natural systems for such grandiose experiments. Although I do not suggest development of detailed models for all resistance programs, there are some in which the stakes are high enough to merit such cooperative ventures, and the results of these studies could be valuable in developing more accurate generalizations regarding factors involved in determining stability of herbivore resistance.

In conclusion, I should like to emphasize that there is much valuable information that must be gathered and many experiments that must be performed if the fields of resistance breeding and plant–herbivore biology are to progress. The gap between applied and basic studies of plant–herbivore interactions impedes such progress. This gap must, therefore, be removed.

ACKNOWLEDGMENTS

I thank R. Giroux and W. Olson for help with data analysis and A. Massey for editorial assistance. O. M. B. dePonti, S. Diehl, J. D. Hare, M. K. Harris, G. G. Kennedy, A. Massey, C. Mitter, E. B. Radcliffe, M. Rausher, R. Roush, J. Schneider, and S. Via made valuable comments on earlier versions of the manuscript. G. Satterwhite kindly typed the manuscript.

REFERENCES

Abdel-Malik, S. H., Heyne, E. G., and Painter, R. H. (1966). Resistance of F_1 wheat plants to green bugs and Hessian fly. *J. Econ. Entomol.* **59,** 707–710.

Alston, F. H., and Briggs, J. B. (1968). Resistance to *Sappaphis devecta* (Wld.) in apple. *Euphytica* **17,** 468–472.

Alston, F. H., and Briggs, J. B. (1970). Inheritance of hypersensitivity to rosy apple aphid *Dysaphis plantaginea* in apple. *Can. J. Genet. Cytol.* **12,** 257–258.

Andrewartha, H. G., and Birch, L.C. (1954). "The Distribution and Abundance of Animals." Univ. of Chicago Press, Chicago.

Arnold, S. J. (1981). Behavioral variation in natural populations. I. Phenotypic, genetic and environmental correlations between chemoreceptive responses to prey in the garter snake, *Thamnophis elegans. Evolution* **35,** 489–509.

Batra, G. R., and Gupta, D. S. (1970). Screening of varieties of cotton for resistance to jassid. *Cotton Grow. Rev.* **47,** 285–291.

Bell, A. A., Stipanovic, R. D., O'Brien, D. H., and Fryxell, P. A. (1978). Sesquiterpenoid aldehyde quinones and derivatives in pigment glands of *Gossypium. Phytochemistry* **17,** 1297–1305.

Benepol, P. S., and Hall, C. V. (1967). The genetic basis of varietal resistance of *Cucurbita pepo* L. to squash bug *Anasa tristis* (DeGeer). *Proc. Am. Soc. Hortic. Sci.* **90,** 301–303.

Blau, W. S. (1978). A comparative study of the ecology, life histories, and resource utilization of temperate and tropical populations of the black swallowtail butterfly, *Papilio polyxenes* Fabr. Ph.D. Thesis, Cornell University, Ithaca, New York.

Bohn, G. W., Kishaba, A. N., Principe, J. A., and Toba, H. H. (1973). Tolerance to melon aphid in *Cucumis melo. J. Am. Soc. Hortic. Sci.* **98,** 37–40.

Bournoville, R. (1981). Variability of the net reproductive rate of clones of the pea aphid on lucerne. *Breed. Resistance Insects Mites, Bull. SROP WPRS Bull., Rep. 2nd Meet., 1980* pp. 129–132.

Briggs, J. B. (1965). The distribution, abundance, and genetic relationships of four strains of the *Rubus* aphid (*Amphorophora rubi* Kalt.) in relation to raspberry breeding. *J. Hortic. Sci.* **40,** 109–117.

Brown, A. W. A., and Pal, R. (1971). "Insecticide Resistance in Arthropods." World Health Organ., Geneva.

Browning, J. A. (1980). Genetic protective mechanisms of plant–pathogen populations: their coevolution and use in breeding for resistance. *In* "Biology and Breeding for Resistance to Arthropods and Pathogens in Agricultural Plants" (M. K. Harris, ed.), pp. 52–75. Tex. Agric. Exp. Stn., Texas A&M University, College Station.

Bush, G. L. (1974). The mechanism of sympatric host race formation in the true fruit flies (Tephritidae). *In* "Genetic Mechanisms of Speciation in Insects (M. J. D. White, ed.), pp. 3–23. Australia & New Zealand Book Co., Brookvale, New South Wales.

Carter, N., and Dixon, A. F. G. (1981). The use of insect population simulation models in breeding for resistance. *Breed. Resistance Insects Mites, Bull. SROP WPRS Bull., Rep. 2nd Meet., 1980* pp. 21–24.

Cartier, J. J., and Painter, R. H. (1956). Differential reactions of two biotypes of the corn leaf aphid to resistant and susceptible varieties, hybrids and selections of sorghums. *J. Econ. Entomol.* **49,** 498–508.

Cartier, J. J., Isaak, A., Painter, R. H., and Sorenson, E. L. (1965). Biotypes of pea aphid *Acyrthosiphon pisum* (Harris) in relation to alfalfa clones. *Can. Entomol.* **97,** 754–760.

Cartwright, W. B., and Noble, W. B. (1947). Studies on biological races of the Hessian fly. *J. Agric. Res.* **75,** 147–153.

Chang, S. H., and Brewbaker, J. L. (1975). Genetic resistance in corn to the corn leaf aphid. *Misc. Publ.—Hawaii Agric. Exp. Stn.* no. 122, 16.

Claridge, M. F., and den Hollander, J. (1980). The "biotypes" of the rice brown planthopper, *Nilaparvata lugens. Entomol. Exp. Appl.* **27,** 23–30.

Clarke, B. (1976). The ecological genetics of host–parasite relationships. *In* "Genetic Aspects of Host–Parasite Relationships" (H. E. R. Taylor and R. Muller, eds.), pp. 87–103. Blackwell, Oxford.

Coombs, C. W., Billings, C. J., and Porter, J. E. (1977). The effect of yellow splitpeas (*Pisum sativum* L.) and other pulses on the productivity of certain strains of *Sitophilus oryzae* (L.) (Col. Curculionidae) and the ability of other strains to breed thereon. *J. Stored Prod. Res.* **13,** 53–58.

DaCosta, C. P., and Jones, C. M. (1971). Cucumber beetle resistance and mite susceptibility controlled by the bitter gene in *Cucumis salivus* L. *Science* **172,** 1145–1146.

Daday, H. (1954a). Gene frequencies in wild populations of *Trifolium repens.* I. Distribution by latitude. *Heredity* **8,** 61–78.

Daday, H. (1954b). Gene frequencies in wild populations of *Trifolium repens.* II. Distribution by latitude. *Heredity* **8,** 377–384.

Daday, H. (1965). Gene frequencies in wild populations of *Trifolium repens* L. IV. Mechanism of natural selection. *Heredity* **20,** 355–365.

Daniels, N. E. (1981). Migration of greenbugs in the Texas panhandle in relation to their biotypes. *Tex. Agric. Exp. Stn. [Misc. Publ.] MP* **MP–1487** (1–4).

Daubeny, H. A. (1966). Inheritance of immunity in the red raspberry to the North American strain of the aphid, *Amphorophora rubi* Kitb. [sic]. *Proc. Am. Soc. Hortic. Sci.* **88,** 346–351.

dePonti, O. M. B. (1978). Resistance in *Cucumis sativus* L. to *Tetranychus urticae* Koch. 3. Search for sources of resistance. *Euphytica* **27,** 167–176.

dePonti, O. M. B., and Freriks, J. C. (1980). Breeding of carrot *(Daucus carota)* for resistance to carrot fly *(Psila rosae). Res. Rep.—Inst. Hortic. Plant Breed.* **707,** 169–172.

dePonti, O. M. B., and Garretsen, F. (1980). Resistance in *Cucumis sativus* L. to *Tetranychus urticae* Koch. 7. The inheritance of resistance and bitterness and the relation between these characters. *Euphytica* **29,** 513–523.

Dethier, V. G. (1954). Evolution of feeding preferences in phytophagous insets. *Evolution* **8,** 33–54.

Dinoor, A. (1977). Oat crown rust resistance in Israel. *Ann. N.Y. Acad. Sci.* **287,** 357–366.

Dunn, J. A., and Kempton, D. P. H. (1971). Differences in susceptibility to attack by *Brevicoryne brassicae* (L.) on Brussels sprouts. *Ann. Appl. Biol.* **68,** 121–134.

Dunn, J. A., and Kempton, D. P. H. (1972). Resistance to attack by *Brevicoryne brassicae* among plants of Brussels sprouts. *Ann. Appl. Biol.* **72,** 1–11.

Dunn, J. A., and Kempton, D. P. H. (1974). Lettuce root aphid control by means of plant resistance. *Plant Pathol.* **23,** 76–80.

Ehrlich, P. R., and Raven, P. H. (1964). Butterflies and plants: a study in coevolution. *Evolution* **18,** 586–603.

Falconer, D. S. (1981). "Introduction to Quantitative Genetics," Longmans Green, New York.

Felsenstein, J. (1976). The theoretical population genetics of variable selection and migration. *Annu. Rev. Genet.* **10**, 253–280.

Frankham, R., and Nurthen, R. K. (1981). Forging links between population and quantitative genetics. *Theor. Appl. Genet.* **59**, 251–263.

Gallun, R. L. (1972). Genetic interrelationships between host plants and insects. *J. Environ. Qual.* **1**, 259–265.

Gallun, R. L. (1980). Breeding for resistance to insects in wheat. *In* "Biology and Breeding for Resistance to Arthropods and Pathogens in Agricultural Plants" (M. K. Harris, ed.), pp. 245–262. Texas A&M University, College Station.

Gallun, R. L., and Khush, G. S. (1980). Genetic factors affecting expression and stability of resistance. *In* "Breeding Plants Resistant to Insects" (F. G. Maxwell and P. R. Jennings, eds.), pp. 64–85. Wiley, New York.

Gallun, R. L., Deay, H. O., and Cartwright, W. B. (1961). Four races of Hessian fly selected and developed from an Indiana population. *Purdue Univ. Res. Bull.* **732**, 1–5.

Gallun, R. L., Starks, K. J., and Guthrie, W. D. (1975). Plant resistance to insects attacking cereals. *Annu. Rev. Entomol.* **20**, 337–357.

Georghiou, G. P., Metcalf, R. L., and Gidden, F. E. (1966). Carbamate-resistance in mosquitoes. *Bull. W. H. O.* **35**, 691–708.

Gibson, R. W. (1979). The geographica distribution, inheritance and pest-resisting properties of sticky-tipped foliar hairs on potato species. *Potato Res.* **22**, 223–236.

Gould, F. (1978). Predicting the future resistance of crop varieties to pest populations: a case study of mites and cucumbers. *Environ. Entomol.* **7**, 622–626.

Gould, F. (1979). Rapid host range evolution in a population of the phytophagous mite *Tetranychus urticae* Koch. *Evolution* **33**, 791–802.

Guthrie, W. D., Jarvis, J. L., Reed, G. L., and Lodholz, M. L. (1982). Plant damage and survival of European corn borer cultures reared for sixteen generations on resistant and susceptible genotypes of corn. *J. Econ. Entomol.* **75**, 134–136.

Hahn, S. K. (1968). Resistance of barley (*Hordeum vulgare* L. emend. Lam.) to cereal leaf beetle (*Oulema melanopus* L.). *Crop Sci.* **8**, 461–464.

Haldane, J. B. S. (1949). Disease and evolution. *Ric. Sci., Suppl.* **19**, 68–76.

Hanover, J. W. (1980). Breeding forest trees resistant to insects. *In* "Breeding Plants Resistant to Insects" (F. G. Maxwell and P. R. Jennings, eds.), pp. 487–512. Wiley, New York.

Hare, J. D. (1980). Variation in fruit size and susceptibility to seed predation among and within populations of the cocklebur, *Xanthium strumarium* L. *Oecologia* **46**, 217–222.

Hare, J. D., and Futuyma, D. J. (1978). Different effects of variation in *Xanthium strumarium* L. (Compositae) on two insect seed predators. *Oecologia* **37**, 109–120.

Harris, M. K. (1975). Allopatric resistance: searching for sources of insect resistance for use in agriculture. *Environ. Entomol.* **4**, 661–669.

Harvey, T. L., Hackerott, H. L., Sorensen, F. L., Painter, R. H., Ortman, E. E., and Peters, D. C. (1960). The development and performance of Cody alfalfa, a spotted alfalfa aphid resistant variety. *Kans., Agric. Exp. Stn., Tech. Bull.* **114**, 1–26.

Hayes, W. P. (1935). Biological races of insects and their bearing on host plant resistance. *Entomol. News* **46**, 20–23.

Hedrick, P. W., Ginevan, M. E., and Ewing, E. P. (1976). Genetic polymorphism in heterogeneous environments. *Annu. Rev. Ecol. Syst.* **7**, 1–32.

Heinrichs, E. A., and Pathak, P. K. (1981). Resistance to the rice gall midge, *Orseolia oryzae* in rice. *Insect Sci. Appl.* **1**, 123–132.

Hsiao, T. H. (1978). Host plant adaptations among geographic populations of the Colorado potato beetle. *Entomol. Exp. Appl.* **24**, 437–447.

Isely, D. (1928). The relation of leaf color and leaf size to boll weevil infestation. *J. Econ. Entomol.* **21**, 553–559.

Ivanoff, S. S. (1957). The homegarden cantaloupe, a variety with combined resistance to downy mildew, powdery mildew, and aphids. *Phytopathology* **47**, 552–556.

Jones, D. A. (1966). On the polymorphism of cyanogenesis in *Lotus corniculatus*. Selection by animals. *Can. J. Genet. Cytol.* **8**, 556–567.

Jones, D. A. (1968). On the polymorphism of cyanogenesis in *Lotus corniculatus* L. II. The interaction with *Trifolium repens* L. *Heredity* **23**, 453–455.

Jones, D. A. (1972). On the polymorphism of cyanogenesis in *Lotus corniculatus* L. IV. The Netherlands. *Genetica* **43**, 394–406.

Jones, D. A. (1973). On the polymorphism of cyanogenesis in *Lotus corniculatus* L. V. Denmark. *Heredity* **30**, 381–386.

Jones, D. A. (1977). On the polymorphism of cyanogenesis in *Lotus corniculatus* L. VII. The distribution of the cyanogenic form in western Europe. *Heredity* **39**, 27–44.

Jones, L. S., Briggs, F. N., and Blanchard, R. A. (1950). Inheritance of resistance to the pea aphid in alfalfa hybrids. *Hilgardia* **20**, 9–17.

Kalode, M. B., and Pant, N. C. (1967). Studies on the amino acids, nitrogen, sugar and moisture content of maize and sorghum varieties and their relation to *Chilo zonellus* (Swin.) resistance. *Indian J. Entomol.* **29**, 139–144.

Keep, E., and Knight, R. L. (1967). A new gene from *Rubus occidentalis* L. for resistance to strains 1, 2 and 3 of the *Rubus* aphid *Amphorophora rubi* Kalt. *Euphytica* **16**, 209–214.

Keep, E., Knight, R. L., and Parker, J. H. (1970). Further data on resistance to the *Rubus* aphid, *Amphorophora rubi* (Kalt.). *Annu. Rep., East Malling Res. Stn., Kent* **57**, 129–131.

Kennedy, G. G. (1978). Biological and environmental considerations in experimental design and measurement of resistance: entomological aspects. *Proc. Bienn. Plant Resist. Workshop, 3rd, 1978*, pp. 65–73.

Kennedy, G. G., and Schaefers, G. A. (1974). Evidence for non-preference and antibiosis inn aphid-resistant red raspberry cultivars. *Environ. Entomol.* **3**, 773–777.

Kennedy, G. G., Schaefers, G. A., and Ourecky, D. K. (1973). Resistance in red raspberry to *Amphorophora agathonica* Hottes and *Aphis rubicola* Oestlund. *Hort Science* **8**, 311–313.

Kinsman, S. (1982). Herbivore responses to *Oenothera biennis* (Onagraceae): effects of host plant genotype and population genetic diversity. Ph.D. Dissertation, Cornell University, Ithaca, New York.

Kishaba, A. N., Bohn, G. W., and Toba, E. H. (1971). Resistance to *Aphis gossypii* in muskmelon. *J. Econ. Entomol.* **64**, 935–937.

Knight, R. L. (1952). The genetics of jassid resistance in cotton. I. The genes H_1 and H_2. *J. Genet.* **51**, 47.

Knight, R. L., Keep, E., and Briggs, J. B. (1958). Genetics of resistance to *Amphorophora rubi* (Kalt.) in the raspberry. *J. Genet.* **56**, 261–277.

Krishnaiah, K. (1975). Resistance to green leafhoppers in rice. *Entomol. Newsl.* **5**, 30.

Lakshminarayana, A., and Khush, G. S. (1977). New genes for resistance to the brown planthopper in rice. *Crop Sci.* **17**, 96–100.

Lawton, J. H., and Strong, D. R., Jr. (1981). Community patterns and competition in folivorous insects. *Am. Nat.* **118**, 317–338.

Lee, J. O., Park, J. S., and Kim, H.-S. (1974). Studies on varietal resistance of rice to striped rice borer, *Chilo suppressalis* Walker. *Korean J. Plant Prot.* **13**, 83.

Leonard, K. J. (1977). Selection pressures and plant pathogens. *Ann. N.Y. Acad. Sci.* **286**, 207–222.

Leonard, K. J., and Czochor, R. J. (1980). Theory of genetic interactions among populations of plants and their pathogens. *Annu. Rev. Phytopathol.* **18**, 237–258.

Levene, H. (1953). Genetic equilibrium when more than one ecological niche is available. *Am. Nat.* **87**, 331–333.

Lewontin, R. C., Ginzburg, L. R., and Tuljapurkar, S. D. (1978). Heterosis as an explanation for large amounts of genic polymorphism. *Genetics* **88**, 149–170.

Long, B. J., Dunn, G. M., Bowman, J. S. and Routley, D. G. (1976). Relation of hydroxamic acid concentration (DIMBOA) to resistance to the corn leaf aphid. *Maize Genet. Co-op. Newsl.* **50**, 91.

Lukefahr, M. J., and Martin, D. F. (1966). Cotton plant pigments as a source of resistance to the boolworm and tobacco budworm. *J. Econ. Entomol.* **59**, 176–179.

Mack, T. P., and Smilowitz, Z. (1980). Soluble protein electrophoretic patterns from two biotypes of *Myzus persicae* (Sulzer). *Am. Potato J.* **57**, 365–369.

McKenzie, H. (1965). Inheritance of sawfly reaction and stem solidness in spring wheat crosses. *Can. J. Plant Sci.* **45**, 583–589.

McMurtry, J. A., and Stanford, E. H. (1960). Observations of feeding habits of the spotted alfalfa aphid on resistant and susceptible alfalfa plants. *J. Econ. Entomol.* **53**, 714–717.

McNeal, F. H., Wallace, L. E., Berg, M. A., and McGuire, C. F. (1971). Wheat stem sawfly resistance with agronomic and quality information on hybrid wheats. *J. Econ. Entomol.* **64**, 939–941.

Mathur, L. M. L., and Jain, P. C. (1972). Effect of maize germ plasm on the survival and development of *Chilo zonellus* S. under laboratory conditions. *Madras Agric. J.* **59**, 54–56.

Maxwell, F. G., and Jennings, P. R., eds. (1980). "Breeding Plants Resistant to Insects." Wiley, New York.

May, B., and Holbrook, F. R. (1978). Absence of genetic variability in the green peach aphid *Myzus persicae* (Hemiptera: Aphididae). *Ann. Entomol. Soc. Am.* **71**, 809–812.

Maynard-Smith, J., and Hoekstra, R. (1980). Polymorphism in a varied environment; how robust are the models? *Genet. Res.* **35**, 45–57.

Mitter, C., and Brooks, D. R. (1983). Phylogenetic aspects of coevolution. *In* "Coevolution" (D. J. Futuyma and M. Slatkin, eds.). Sinauer Associates, Sunderland, Massachusetts (in press).

Moran, N. (1981). Intraspecific variability in herbivore performance and host quality: a field study of *Uroleucon caligatum* (Homoptera: Aphididae) and its *Solidago* hosts (Asteraceae). *Ecol. Entomol.* **6**, 301–306.

Muller, F. P. (1971). Isolationsmechanismen zwischen sympatrischen bionomischen Rassen and Beispiel der Erbsenblattlaus *Acyrthosiphon pisum* (Harris) (Homoptera: Aphididae). *Zool. Jahrb., Abt. Syst. (Oekol.),* Geogr. Biol. **98**, 131–152.

Muller, F. P. (1976). Hosts and non-hosts in subspecies of *Aulacorthum solani* (Kaltenbach) and intraspecific hybridizations (Homoptera: Aphididae). *Symp. Biol. Hung.* **16**, 187–190.

Muller, F. P., and Hubert-Dahl, M. L. (1973). Wirtspflanzen und Überwinterung eines an Erbse lebenden Biotyps von *Acyrthosiphon pisum* (Harris). *Dtsch. Entomol. Z.* **20**, 321–328.

Muttuthamby, S., Aslam, M., and Khan, M. A. (1969). Inheritance of leaf hairiness in *Gossypium hirsutum* L. cotton and its relationship with jassid resistance. *Euphytica* **18**, 435–439.

Nielson, M. W., and Don, H. (1947a). A new virulent biotype of the spotted alfalfa aphid in Arizona. *J. Econ. Entomol.* **67**, 64–66.

Nielson, M. W., and Don, H. (1947b). Probing behavior of biotypes of the spotted alfalfa aphid on resistant and susceptible alfalfa clones. *Entomol. Exp. Appl.* **17**, 477–486.

Novero, E. S., Painter, R. H., and Hall, C. V. (1962). Interrelations of squash bug, *Anasa tristis* and six varieties of squash. *J. Econ. Entomol.* **55,** 912.

O'Brien, S. J., and MacIntyre, R. J. (1978). Genetics and biochemistry of enzymes and specific proteins for *Drosophila*. *In* "The Genetics and Biology of *Drosophila*" (M. Ashburner and T. R. F. Wright, eds.), Vol. 2, pp. 396–526. Academic Press, New York.

Olembo, J. R., Patterson, F. L., and Gallun, R. L. (1966). Genetic analysis of the resistance to *Mayetiola destructor* (Say) in *Hordeum vulgare* L., *Crop Sci.* **6,** 653–656.

Oliver, B. F., and Gifford, J. R. (1975). Weight differences among stalk borer larvae collected from rice lines showing resistance in field studies. *J. Econ. Entomol.* **68,** 134–135.

Ortman, E. E., Sorensen, E. L., Painter, R. H., Harvey, T. L., Hackerott, H. L. (1960). Selection and evaluation of pea aphid-resistant alfalfa plants. *J. Econ. Entomol.* **53,** 881–887.

Painter, R. H. (1930). The biological strains of Hessian fly. *J. Econ. Entomol.* **23,** 322–329.

Painter, R. H. (1951). "Insect Resistance in Crop Plants." Macmillan, New York.

Painter, R. H., Salmon, S. C., and Parker, J. H. (1931). Resistance of varieties of winter wheat to Hessian fly *Phytophaga destructor* (Say). *Kans., Agric. Exp. Stn., Bull.* **27,** 1–58.

Pathak, P. K., and Heinrichs, E. A. (1982). Selection of populations of *Nilaparvata lugens* by exposure to resistant rice varieties. *Environ. Entomol.* **11,** 85–90.

Pathak, M. D., and Painter, R. H. (1959). Geographical distribution of the four biotypes of corn leaf aphid, *Rhopalosiphum maidis* (Fitch) in Kansas. *Trans. Kans. Acad. Sci.* **62,** 1–8.

Pathak, M. D., and Saxena, R. C. (1976). Insect resistance in crop plants. *Curr. Adv. Plant Sci.* **27,** 1233–1252.

Phillips, P. A., and Barnes, M. M. (1975). Host race formation among sympatric apple, walnut, and plum populations of the codling moth, *Laspeyresia pomonella*. *Ann. Entomol. Soc. Am.* **68,** 1053–1060.

Pimentel, D. (1961). Animal population regulation by the genetic feedback mechanism *Am. Nat.* **95,** 65–79.

Price, P. W., Bouton, C. E., Gross, P., McPheron, B. A., Thompson, J. N., and Weis, A. E. (1980). Interactions among three trophic levels: influence of plants on interactions between insect herbivores and natural enemies. *Annu. Rev. Ecol. Syst.* **11,** 41–65.

Radcliffe, E. B., Lauer, F. I., Lee, M.-H., and Robinson, D. P. (1981). Evaluation of the United States potato collection for resistance to green peach aphid and potato aphid. *Minn., Agric. Exp. Stn., Tech. Bull.* **331.**

Rausher, M. D. (1982). Population differentiation in *Euphydryas editha* butterflies: larval adaptation to different hosts. *Evolution* **36,** 581–590.

Rehm, S., Enslin, P. R., Meeuse, A. D. J., and Wessels, J. H. (1957). Bitter principles of the Cucurbitaceae. VII. The distribution of bitter principles in this plant family. *J. Sci. Food Agric.* **8,** 679–686.

Ringlund, K., and Everson, E. H. (1968). Leaf pubescence in common wheat *Triticum aestivum* L. and resistance to the cereal leaf beetle, *Oulema melanopus* (L.). *Crop Sci.* **8,** 705–710.

Robinson, R. A. (1980). The pathosystem concept. *In* "Breeding Plants Resistant to Insects" (F. G. Maxwell and P. R. Jennings, eds.), pp. 157–170. Wiley, New York.

Russell, G. E. (1966). Preliminary studies in breeding for aphid-resistance in beet. *J. Int. Sugar Beet Res. Inst. (IIRB)* **1,** 117.

Russell, G. E. (1978). "Plant Breeding for Pest and Disease Resistance." Butterworth, London.

Russell, W. A., Guthrie, W. D., Klun, J. A., and Grindeland, R. (1975). Selection for resistance in maize to first-brood European corn borer by using leaf-feeding damage of the insect and chemical analysis for DIMBOA in the plant. *J. Econ. Entomol.* **68,** 31.

Sato, A., and Sogawa, K. (1981). Biotypic variations in the green rice leafhopper, *Nephotettix cincticeps* Uhler (Homoptera: Deltocephalidae) in relation to rice varieties. *Appl. Entomol. Zool.* **16**, 55–57.

von Schonborn, A. (1966). The breeding of insect-resistant forest trees in central and northwestern Europe. *In* "Breeding Pest Resistant Trees" (H. D. Gerhold *et al.*, eds.) pp. 25–27. Pergamon, Oxford.

Scott, G. E., and Guthrie, W. D. (1967). Reaction of permutations of maize double crosses to leaf feeding of European corn borers. *Crop. Sci.*, **7**, 233–235.

Sedcole, J. R. (1978). Selection pressures and plant pathogens: stability of equilibria. *Phytopathology* **68**, 967–970.

Sen Gupta, G. C., and Miles, P. W. (1975). Studies on the susceptibility of varieties of apple to the feeding of two strains of woolly aphid (Homoptera) in relation to the chemical content of the tissues of the host. *Aust. J. Agric. Res.* **26**, 157.

Service, P. M. (1983). Genotypic interactions in an aphid–host plant relationship: *Uroleucon rudbeckiae* and *Rudbeckia laciniata*. (in review).

Singer, M. C. (1970). Evolution of food-plant preference in the butterfly *Euphydryas editha*. *Evolution* **25**, 383–389.

Smedegaard-Petersen, V., and Stølen, O. (1981). Effect of energy-requiring defense reactions on yield and grain quality in a powdery mildew-resistant barley cultivar. *Phytopathology* **71**, 396–399.

Smith, C. M. (1978). Factors for consideration in designing short-term insect–host plant bioassays. *Bull. Entomol. Soc. Am.* **24**, 393–395.

Smith, H. S. (1941). Racial segregation in insect populations and its significance in applied entomology. *J. Econ. Entomol.* **34**, 1–13.

Sogawa, K. (1981a). Biotypic variations in the brown planthopper, *Nilaparvata lugens* (Homoptera: Delphacidae) at the IRRI, the Philippines. *Appl. Entomol. Zool.* **16**, 129–137.

Sogawa, K. (1981b). Hybridization experiments on three biotypes of the brown planthopper, *Nilaparvata lugens* (Homoptera: Delphacidae) at the IRRI, the Philippines. *Appl. Entomol. Zool.* **16**, 193–199.

Song, Y. H., Choi, S. Y., and Bak, J. (1972). Studies on the resistance of Tong-il rice variety, IR667, to *Nilaparvata lugens*. *Korean J. Plant Prot.* **11**, 61.

Stanford, E. H. (1977). Genetic resources in alfalfa and their preservation. *Calif. Agric.* **31**, 22–23.

Starks, K. J., and Doggett, H. (1970). Resistance to a spotted stem borer in sorghum and maize. *J. Econ. Entomol.* **63**, 1790–1795.

Steiner, K. (1974). Genetic differences in resistance of Scotch pine to eastern pineshoot borer. *Great Lakes Entomol.* **7**, 103–107.

Stephens, S. G., and Lee, H. S. (1961). Further studies on the feeding and oviposition preferences of the boll weevil (*Anthonomus grandis*). *J. Econ. Entomol.* **54**, 1085–1090.

Straatman, R. (1962). Notes on certain Lepidoptera ovipositing on plants which are toxic to their larvae. *J. Lepid. Soc.* **16**, 99–103.

Tabashnik, B. E. (1983). Host range evolution: The shift from native legume hosts to alfalfa by the butterfly, *Colias philodice eriphyle*. *Evolution* (in press).

Tavormina, S. J. (1982). Sympatric genetic divergence in the leaf-mining insect *Liriomyza brassicae* (Diptera: Agromyzidae). *Evolution* **36**, 523–534.

Thielges, B. A., and Campbell, R. L. (1972). Selection and breeding to avoid the eastern spruce gall aphid. *Am. Christmas Tree J.* **16**, 3–6.

Thind, B. B., and Muggleton, J. (1981). Inheritance of the ability of strains of *Stiophilus oryzae* (L.) (Coleoptera: Curculionidae) to breed on split-pea (*Pisum sativum*). *Bull. Entomol. Res.* **71**, 419–424.

van der Plank, J. E. (1968). "Disease Resistance in Plants." Academic Press, New York.

Waiss, A. C., Jr., Chan, B. G., Elliger, C. A., Dreyer, D. L., Binder, R. G., and Gueldner, R. C. (1981). Insect growth inhibitors in crop plants. *Bull. Entomol. Soc. Am.* **27,** 217–221.

Wasserman, S. S., and Futuyma, D. J. (1981). Evolution of host plant utilization in laboratory populations of the southern cowpea weevil, *Callosobruchus maculatus* Fabricius (Coleoptera: Bruchidae). *Evolution* **35,** 605–617.

Weibel, D. E., Starks, K. J., Wood, E. A., and Morrison, R. D., (1972). Sorghum cultivars and progenies rated for resistance to greenbugs. *Crop Sci.* **12,** 334–336.

Whalon, M. E., and Smilowitz, Z. (1979). The interaction of temperature and biotype on development of the green peach aphid, *Myzus persicae* (Sulz.). *Am. Potato J.* **56,** 591–596.

Widström, N. W., and McMillian, W. W. (1973). Genetic effects conditioning resistance to earworm in maize. *Crop Sci.* **13,** 459–461.

Widström, N. W., Wiseman, B. R., and McMillian, W. W. (1972). Resistance among some maize inbreds and single crosses to fall army worm injury. *Crop Sci.* **12,** 290–292.

Wilde, G., and Feese, H. (1973). A new corn leaf aphid biotype and its effect on some cereal and small grains. *J. Econ. Entomol.* **66,** 570–571.

Wilson, F. D., and Lee, J. A. (1971). Genetic relationship between tobacco budworm feeding response and gland number in cotton seedlings. *Crop Sci.* **11,** 419–421.

Wood, E. A., Jr. (1971). Designation and reaction of three biotypes of the greenbug cultured on resistant and susceptible species of sorghum. *J. Econ. Entomol.* **64,** 183–185.

Wright, J. W., and Wilson, L. F. (1972). Genetic differences in Scotch pine resistance to pine root collar weevil. *Mich., Agric. Exp. Stn., Res. Rep.* **159.**

Wright, J. W., Lemmian, W. A., Bright, J. N., Day, M. W., and Sajdak, R. L. (1976). Scotch pine varieties for Christmas tree and forest planting in Michigan. *Mich., Agric. Exp. Stn., Res. Rep.* **293.**

Wright, S. (1978). "Evolution and the Genetics of Populations," Vol. 4. Univ. of Chicago Press, Chicago.

Fred Gould
Department of Entomology
North Carolina State University
Raleigh, North Carolina

CHAPTER 18

Manipulation of Host Suitability for Herbivore Pest Management

J. DANIEL HARE

I. INTRODUCTION

Previous chapters in this volume show the many ways in which host-plant variation can influence the ecological relationships between plants and their insect herbivores, and they show how those relationships themselves vary in ecological and evolutionary time. The suitability of individual hosts may vary temporally as a result of intrinsic factors of plant growth and development (Schultz, Chapter 3; Raupp and Denno, Chapter 4; Denno, Chapter 9) or as the result of certain extrinsic factors such as abiotic stress (Rhoades, Chapter 6) or prior attack (Ryan, chapter 2; McClure, Chapter 5). Moreover, genetic differences among individuals of host species may also influence their suitability for herbivorous insects (Whitham, Chapter 1; Alstad and Edmunds, Chapter 12).

Intra- and interspecific variation in host suitability may influence the genetic structure of insect populations (Scriber, Chapter 11; Mitter and Futuyma, Chapter 13) and may also influence how herbivores locate, assimilate, and track their suitable hosts in space and time (Rausher, Chapter 7; Mitchell, Chapter 10). Spatial and temporal variation in host suitability therefore has been a critical component in the evolution of contemporary plant and insect communities (Kareiva, Chapter 8; Jones, Chapter 15; Price, Chapter 16).

Most of the scientific evidence showing the importance of variable hosts on phytophagous insects has been obtained only in the last few years, yet growers have been exploiting herbivore sensitivity to host-plant variation since the beginning of agriculture (Smith, 1978). Successful techniques to manipulate host suitability, however, have been largely empirically and often serendipitously derived; cultural techniques and management practices that alleviate pest pressure in one cropping system may confer no benefit or may even be harmful in other systems. As insect ecologists learn more about the mechanisms in which spatial and temporal variation among host plants affect herbivores, it may become increasingly possible to predictably and systematically manipulate host suitability for enhanced insect pest control.

My objectives in this chapter are to show how host-plant suitability can be manipulated in time and space within agroecosystems and to suggest that a more complete understanding of how genetic and phenotypic variation in host suitability affects phytophagous insects will lead to new, effective approaches to insect pest management. Entomologists engaged in both applied and basic research may find this information useful in their efforts not only to develop economically and ecologically sound pest-management programs, but also to design and perform more advanced experiments for evaluating the impact of variable hosts on the ecology and evolution of phytophagous insects.

Plants are complex, dynamic chemical entities that vary in both time and space. Although entomologists know and appreciate how variation in particular "nutritional" or "defensive" plant chemicals affect particular species of phytophagous insects, we know and understand comparatively little about how simultaneous variation in the concentrations of several such chemicals within host plants ultimately affect insect behavior, growth, and reproduction (Reese, 1979). The importance of quantitative variation in phytochemicals that deter insect feeding may be more than offset by simultaneous, parallel variation in other phytochemicals required for insect growth. The deleterious effects of saponins on insect growth, for example, can be ameliorated by adding sterols to insect diets (Applebaum and Birk, 1979), and the deleterious effects of quantitative increases in steroidal glycoalkaloids can be offset by a simultaneous quantitative increase in foliage protein content (Hare, 1983). Alternatively, other plant compounds are known to act as synergists for synthetic insecticides, and these same compounds may also interact synergistically with natural plant toxins as well (Brattsten, 1979). Fundamental growth in our understanding of the role of variation in host-plant phytochemistry in the dynamics, ecology, and evolution of herbivore populations in natural and applied systems will require broader and more quantitative studies that explore these interactions in detail (see also Jones, Chapter 15).

II. MANIPULATION OF THE SUITABILITY OF INDIVIDUAL HOST PLANTS

A. Cultural Manipulations

Manipulating the habitat and growing conditions of agricultural crops for insect pest management is not a new idea (Smith, 1978), and such manipulations are still useful components of several modern, successful, integrated pest management (IPM) programs (Stern et al., 1976; Knipling, 1979). My objective is not to catalog the numerous cases in which insect pest populations have been reduced by cultural manipulations, but to consider in detail a few cases in which such manipulations have caused specific physiological changes that reduce the suitability of host plants for phytophagous insects (see also Rhoades, Chapter 6).

1. Phenological Manipulation

The availability of young, succulent foliage is critical to the survival of many insect species, and asynchrony between the production of new foliage by plants and insect egg hatch can be an important factor in the dynamics of insect populations (Schultz, Chapter 3) and the evolution of insect life histories (Mitter and Futuyma, Chapter 13). Growers of annual crops can manipulate planting and harvesting dates to some extent to increase asynchrony between host and herbivore. In conjunction with other cultural practices to hasten crop maturity, early planting of short-season varieties serves as the basis for a contemporary program of cotton insect pest management (Adkisson et al., 1982). Similarly, in conjunction with the use of sprout inhibitors, timely destruction of tobacco stalks reduces the quantity of young, succulent foliage available to the tobacco hornworm (Manduca sexta) and the subsequent size of the overwintering population (Tappan, 1965; Rabb, 1969). There are, however, definite limits over which plant phenology can be shifted before crop production is affected, and reliance on manipulation of planting and harvesting dates as a primary means of insect control would require extensive knowledge of the relationships between plant growth and insect development and daily and seasonal temperatures.

2. Water and Nutrient Manipulations

The quantity of foliar nitrogen can greatly alter the suitability of plants to their herbivores (reviewed by McNeil and Southwood, 1978; Mattson, 1980). Plant water stress can also alter host-plant suitability, but the precise changes may vary with the duration and frequency of water shortage and the herbivore species in question (Wearing, 1972; Scriber, 1977; Lewis, 1979).

Changes in plant water or nutrient supply affect plants at a basic developmental level. Therefore, such changes can cause rather general and complex changes in plant physiology. An example has been provided by Leigh *et al.* (1970), who found that cotton susceptibility to lygus bugs is determined more by the interaction between irrigation and fertilizer treatments than by their direct effects. Similarly, Wolfson (1980) showed that reducing soil nitrogen available to *Brassica nigra* reduced foliage water content in an experiment in which water was not limiting. Apparently, leaves are thicker and more dense when grown under low-nitrogen regimes. Oviposition preference of the imported cabbage butterfly *(Pieris rapae)*, was more strongly correlated with high foliage water content than with nitrogen availability or leaf mustard oil content.

Differences in herbivore responses to the same plant stress is well illustrated by consolidating several studies of the effect of water stress on different varieties of cucumber (*Cucumis sativus*) and of the changes in host suitability perceived by cucumber beetles and spider mites. The presence or absence of cucurbitacins, a group of triterpenoid phytochemicals, is determined by a single locus in cucurbit species (Barham, 1953; see also Gould, Chapter 17). Some cucurbitacins stimulate feeding by several species of cucumber beetle (Chambliss and Jones, 1966). The same compounds are toxic to the two-spotted spider mite *(Tetranychus urticae)*. Therefore, cucumber varieties that produce cucurbitacins are simultaneously more attractive to cucumber beetles and more resistant to spider mites than are the cucurbitacin-free varieties (DaCosta and Jones, 1971). The dry-weight concentration of cucurbitacins increases after a short period of wilting in cucurbitacin-producing varieties. Therefore, previously wilted plants are simultaneously more attractive to cucumber beetles (Haynes and Jones, 1975) and more resistant to spider mites (Gould, 1978). Wilting had no significant effect on the suitability of cucurbitacin-free varieties as perceived by either herbivore species. In short, the effect of water stress on the suitability of cucumber for its arthropod herbivores may be positive, neutral, or negative, depending on which combination of plant genotype and herbivore species is examined.

The complexity of these relationships between water and nutrient stresses and the subsequent effects on herbivores does not mean that such manipulations are too complex ever to be used in insect pest management, however. The necessary conditions under which host suitability could be manipulated for insect control by irrigation management include (1) little or no rainfall, (2) one or a few pest species known to be adversely affected by host-plant water stress, and (3) a predictable pattern of insect seasonal abundance, so that only a short, properly timed period of water stress need be imposed. The association between *Heliothis zea*, the cotton bollworm, and cotton on the high plains of Texas meets most of these conditions. The peak period of adult oviposition can be predicted within about 3 days, using data from light-trap collections. Cotton irrigated shortly before peak oviposition is more succulent and attractive to adults and/or more suitable for larval survival than unirrigated cotton. Thus growers who time their irrigation treatments so that plants are left unirrigated during the peak oviposition period can effectively reduce the size of bollworm populations that ultimately develop (Slosser, 1980).

B. Induced Resistance

To the extent that there is a reproductive cost for plants to produce defensive chemicals (Chew and Rodman, 1979; Krischik and Denno, Chapter 14), there should be a selective advantage for plants that direct photosynthate from reproduction to defense only when threatened. The production of secondary metabolites in plants following either mechanical damage or plant disease infection is widely known (Horsfall and Cowling, 1980; Ryan, Chapter 2). Although far less numerous, a few studies have demonstrated plant resistance induced against insects. The time period over which resistance can be observed varies from a few days (Haukioja and Niemelä, 1977) to several seasons (Wallner and Walton, 1979; Werner, 1979; Rhoades, Chapter 6).

The reduction in host quality in some cases is known to be caused by specific changes in host-plant phytochemistry. The relationship between the density of scale insects in one season and the quantity of foliar nitrogen in the following season, for example, is the basis for self-regulation of the elongate hemlock scale *(Fiorinia externa)* on eastern hemlock (McClure, Chapter 5). Other examples demonstrate that the decreased suitability of previously attacked plants at both the local level (reduced suitability of a previously attacked leaf) and at the systemic level (reduced suitability of unattacked leaves on a previously attacked plant) is caused by increased synthesis and/or transport of allelochemicals (Haukioja and Niemelä, 1979; Carroll and Hoffman, 1980).

Of more practical interest to applied biologists is the phenomenon of general or cross-protection, whereby attack by one pest or pathogen induces resistance not only to the inducer, but to other unrelated pests as well (Matta, 1980). Some tobacco varieties, for example, are "hypersensitive" to tobacco mosaic virus (TMV), meaning that the virus is confined to a local lesion a few millimeters around the point of infection. The virus is not translocated throughout hypersensitive tobacco varieties and therefore does not cause systemic infection. Nevertheless, local virus infections induce not only local, but also systemic, simultaneous protection against the fungi *(Phytophthora parasitica* var. *nicotianae* and *Peronospora tabicina)*, the bacterium *(Pseudomonas tabaci)*, and also TMV (McIntyre *et al.*, 1981). In the same study, the daily reproductive rate of the green peach aphid *(Myzus persicae)*, was reduced an average of 11.1% when parthenogenetic females were allowed to feed and reproduce on developing leaves at plant apexes at least six nodes above the site of virus infection.

Except for the virus lesions on inoculated leaves, there were no discernable differences between infected and uninfected plants. Extensive phytochemical analysis of hypersensitive tobacco varieties has failed to show any gross changes in host physiology following the initial TMV infection. For example, there were no detectable changes in amino acid composition (Bozarth and Ross, 1964), chlorogenic acid or total phenolic concentration (Simons and Ross, 1971b), or total metabolic activity (Simons and Ross, 1971a) in systemically protected tobacco leaves. Thus the major difference between protected and unprotected leaves was the greater speed with which the former responded with specific defense mechanisms to subsequent challenge (Simons and Ross, 1971a); McIntyre *et al.*, 1981; see also Kuc, 1977).

Using a standard gravimetric technique (Waldbauer, 1968), we (J. D. Hare, J. L. McIntyre, and J. A. Dodds, unpublished data) found that the growth rates of fourth-instar tobacco hornworms *(Manduca sexta)* were reduced 27 and 16% when reared on locally and systemically protected tobacco leaves, respectively (Table I). In this analysis, the growth rate (GR) is defined as the product of the consumption index (CI) and the gross growth efficiency (ECI). The reduced GR of larvae reared on locally protected leaves was accompanied by a significant reduction in CI, whereas the reduction in GR of larvae reared on systemically protected leaves was accompanied by a significant reduction in ECI. This indicates that the reduced larval growth on locally protected leaves was due to TMV-induced changes that reduced the rate at which foliage was in-

Table I
Growth Rate, Consumption, and Growth Efficiency of Fourth-Instar Tobacco Hornworms Reared on Unprotected, Systemically Protected, or Locally Protected Tobacco Leaves[a]

	Leaf type		
	Unprotected	Systemically protected	Locally protected
Larval duration (Days)	3.5 ± 0.12[b]	3.36 ± 0.14	3.96 ± 0.10*
Relative growth rate (GR)[c]	0.464 ± 0.015	0.390 ± 0.022*	0.337 ± 0.034**
Consumption index (CI)	4.003 ± 0.291	4.265 ± 0.462	2.804 ± 0.248*
Gross efficiency (ECI)	11.93 ± 0.79	9.53 ± 0.61*	12.27 ± 1.48
Sample size	8	8	5[d]

[a] *, $P \leq 0.05$; **, $P \leq 0.01$.
[b] Means ± SE.
[c] Notation follows Waldbauer (1968).
[d] Three larvae died during the experiment.

gested, whereas that of systemically protected leaves was due to reduced efficiency at which ingested tissue was assimilated. Further research is in progress to better understand how localized infection by plant pathogens induces sytemic resistance against other pathogens and reduces the suitability of host plants for phytophagous insects.

The existence of general, inducible mechanisms of plant defense would be of little value to applied biologists if they could be activated only by such deleterious procedures as mechanical injury or attack by plant pathogens. Ryan (Chapter 2), however, has reviewed research to identify the specific biochemical compounds responsible for the induction of specific defense mechanisms in several plant species. Soon, it may be possible to routinely, artificially induce plant defense mechanisms (Cartwright et al., 1977, 1980; Moesta and Grisebach, 1980). More recent reports of inducible plant defense mechanisms against insects (Benedict and Bird, 1981; Hart, 1982) lend support to the hypothesis that growers may manipulate plant defenses in agroecosystems for routine pathogen and herbivore control.

C. Manipulation of Host Suitability with Plant Growth Regulators

Synthetic plant growth regulators are assuming an expanding role in contemporary crop production. Among their uses are the initiation of flowering, control of vegetative growth, thinning of fruit crops, promotion of synchronous fruit ripening, and inhibition of sprout formation. In general, growth regulators are being used to lessen the amount of manual labor in agricultural production, and present economic conditions favor wider applications and more intensive use of synthetic growth regulators in commercial agriculture.

Natural and synthetic plant growth regulators can directly influence the growth and development of insects (Carlisle *et al.*, 1969; Scheurer, 1976). For example, the dependence of sexual maturation of desert locusts on the gibberellic acid concentration of its host's foliage may be a means to maintain synchrony between plant and insect development (Ellis *et al.*, 1965). Synthetic growth retardants may also affect phytophagous insects indirectly by reducing the nutritional quality of plant tissues (van Emden, 1969; Honeyborne, 1969) or by shortening the time period that susceptible tissues are available to insects (Kittock *et al.*, 1973).

Because plant growth regulators affect all aspects of plant growth, the particular entomological consequences of applying such compounds may be unpredictable (Smith, 1969). Hall (1972), for example, found that daminozide, a compound widely used in apple production, reduced densities of the apple aphid *(Aphis pomi)* but not the European red mite *(Panonychus ulmi)*. Singer and Smith (1976) showed that daminozide and chlormetquat chloride had similar effects on the growth of black currant, *(Ribes niger)*, but they differed in their effects on the aphid *Hyperomyzus lactucae*; chlormetquat chloride reduced *H. lactucae* populations, but daminozide did not. Furthermore, although chlormetquat chloride reduced *H. lactucae* populations on black currant, the growth regulator did not affect *H. lactucae* populations on sow thistle *(Sonchus asper)*. Clearly, particular plant growth regulators affect plant–herbivore associations in specific and poorly understood ways.

Where insect pests are difficult to control by conventional means and where chemical control of plant growth is desirable and practical, growth regulators can contribute substantially to insect pest management, despite an imperfect understanding of all mechanisms involved. The pear psylla *(Psylla pyricola)*, for example, is a serious pest of pears in Oregon and is difficult and expensive to control conventionally. The nymphs feed primarily on the new, succulent shoots produced during the current growing season. Two carefully timed applications of daminozide reduced shoot growth 33%, psylla nymph density 35%, and fruit damage 57%, but commercial yields were not affected over a 3-year study (Westigard *et al.*, 1980). Although observed levels of psylla control were less than could have been obtained with multiple insecticide applications, the use of chemical growth regulators in conjunction with other cultural techniques could reduce the number of insecticide applications required.

Plant growth regulators can be used not only to control the nutritional quality but also the seasonal availability of susceptible plant tissue. Sprout inhibitors used in tobacco fields to inhibit sucker growth also reduce the quantity of young, succulent tobacco leaves most suitable for the tobacco hornworm (*Manduca sexta*; Rabb *et al.*, 1964). This, coupled with timely postharvest stalk destruction (previously described), has resulted in the tobacco hornworm becoming a minor pest of tobacco (Rabb, 1969).

An important component in the management of the pink bollworm (*Pectinophora gossypiella*) is to reduce the number that successfully diapause (Noble, 1969). Diapause is induced by photoperiod, and bollworms induced to diapause in late August to mid-September attack and overwinter in cotton bolls less than about 30 days old. If these bolls were destroyed or if their formation were prevented, then the size of the overwintering population could be greatly reduced.

One way to reduce the number of bolls suitable for bollworm diapause is to kill or completely defoliate plants before insect diapause occurs (Adkisson, 1962). Because some cotton varieties will continue to flower and produce cotton bolls until killing frost, artificially ending the growing season early to prevent bollworm overwintering may also reduce yield. The economic benefit of increased bollworm control must at least offset this potential yield reduction if early application of defoliants or dessicants is to be economically viable.

In theory, an equally effective but economically more favorable approach would be to selectively inhibit the formation of bolls suitable for insect diapause late in the season, while allowing older bolls to continue to mature. Such a procedure would allow plants to attain their maximum yield potential while reducing the number of sites available for diapausing bollworms (Kittock *et al.*, 1973). A number of plant growth regulators have been found that terminate the initiation of young cotton bolls, thereby reducing the overwintering population of pink bollworms, while allowing older but still immature bolls to reach full maturity at harvest (Bariola *et al.*, 1976, 1981; Thomas *et al.*, 1979; Kittock *et al.*, 1980).

In summary, several commercially available chemicals that regulate plant growth also alter the suitability of plants to their phytophagous insect pests. Although these effects may be neither sufficiently effective nor predictable at this time to warrant their use as a primary means of insect pest management, the choice among two or more growth regulators having the same desired horticultural effect might be based on their incidental value in insect control. Probably the first use of plant growth regulators as a primary means of insect pest management would be to promote asynchrony between plant growth and insect development.

D. Manipulation of Host Acceptability with Feeding Deterrents

Insect feeding can be deterred by many chemicals; thus feeding deterrents offer an alternative means of insect pest management (Chapman, 1974; Munakata, 1977). The advantages and disadvantages of feeding deterrents relative to chemical insecticides for insect control have been presented in detail by others (Jermy, 1971; Chapman, 1974). In brief, the main advantage of feeding deterrents is that they need not be toxic to be effective. Therefore, they may be safer to use and more compatible with biological control. The main disadvantage of exogenous feeding deterrents are that (1) plants must be thoroughly covered, and the feeding deterrent must persist on plants for a reasonable length of time; (2) leaf miners, aphids, and other nonchewing insects may be little affected by feeding deterrents applied only to leaf surfaces; and (3) feeding deterrents, whether exogenous or endogenous, may protect plants locally without providing any regional control of insect populations. When encountering plants treated with feeding deterrents, mobile and polyphagous herbivores may simply leave the treated plants and finish their development on other, untreated host plants. In general, the disadvantages continue to outweigh the advantages, and feeding deterrents per se have, as yet, no significant role in insect pest management.

Some chemicals that deter insect feeding, however, also have important additional agricultural uses, and these additional uses may mitigate the potential problems in exploiting their value as insect feeding deterrents. Several plant fungicides, for example, also deter insect feeding (Backman *et al.*, 1977; Chalfant *et al.*, 1977; Livingston *et al.*, 1978; Higgins and Pedigo, 1979). The potential use of plant fungicides to alter the suitability of plants for phytophagous insects while also protecting plants from disease is illustrated by the following example.

Potato *(Solanum tuberosum)* is susceptible to the fungal diseases early blight, *(Alternaria solani)* and late blight *(Phytophthora infestans)*. Growers usually apply fungicides regularly throughout the growing season at intervals ranging from 5 to 14 days, depending upon weather conditions. One of the earliest fungicides, Bordeaux mixture, was also recommended to control aphids, flea beetles, and leafhoppers as well as potato diseases (Dunlap and Turner, 1934). Adult females of the Colorado potato beetle *(Leptinotarsa decemlineata)* ceased feeding and ovipositing within 24 hr after transfer to potato leaves treated with 1% Bordeaux mixture in the laboratory (Jermy, 1961). In related field tests, Bordeaux mixture protected plants almost completely against *L. decemlineata* populations. Bordeaux mixture has long been abandoned for potato disease control because it is slightly phytotoxic and reduces potato yield in its own right (Horsfall and Turner, 1943).

In the laboratory, two currently registered but little-used fungicides formulated from cupric hydroxide or triphenyltin hydroxide inhibited potato beetle feeding up to 60 and 95% when applied to potato leaves at concentrations equivalent to those used for potato disease control in the field. Moreover, total egg production was reduced up to 99% by cupric hydroxide and 100% by triphenyltin hydroxide. Larval survival on leaves treated with cupric hydroxide was reduced 98%, and the developmental period of survivors was extended nearly 60%. All larvae starved when offered leaves treated with triphenyltin hydroxide (J. D. Hare, unpublished data).

Newly emerged *Leptinotarsa decemlineata* adults do not have fully developed wing muscles and cannot fly until at least 9 days after emergence, even when fed nutritious host plant foliage (de Kort, 1969). When fed on host plants of poor suitability, newly emerged adults enter diapause within 1–3 weeks (Larczenko, 1957; de Wilde *et al.*, 1969; Hsiao 1978; Hare, 1983). The lack of flight capacity in young *L. decemlineata* adults may make this insect especially susceptible to management with antifeedant fungicides. In some commercial-scale field tests, growers who incorporated these antifeedant fungicides into their regular potato-disease-control program were able to reduce the number of needed insecticide applications by up to 50%. Further research is in progress to incorporate antifeedant fungicides into an efficient, coordinated program of potato insect and pathogen management.

III. MANIPULATION OF THE SPATIAL VARIATION IN HOST SUITABILITY

A. Crop Diversity and Pattern

Previous chapters have shown how spatial variation within and among host plants affects the behavior, growth, and survival of phytophagous insects. One might reasonably conclude, therefore, that increasing the spatial heterogeneity within agroecosystems would reduce the risk to crops of discovery and attack by some of their adapted herbivores.

Although the potential dangers inherent in simplifying the genetic and phenotypic structure of agroecosystems are widely recognized and accepted within the scientific community (Horsfall, 1972; Day, 1977), insect pest management practices have not, in general, changed to alleviate these dangers. The major barriers against utilizing vegetational diversity as a means of insect pest management are based, in large part, on the absence of definite answers to several economic and ecological questions.

The major economic barriers are (1) potential difficulties in harvesting crops from diverse stands without incurring additional expenses and (2) the potential income loss directly associated with the dilution of valuable plant species per unit area of crop land. Obviously, the net economic benefit of the reduced cost of insect control resulting from increasing agroecosystem diversity must at least offset such potential losses before such changes can be fully integrated into economically viable pest-management programs. The ecological problems stem from our present inability to predict, in general, how insect populations will change in response to changes in agroecosystem structure (Southwood and Way, 1970; Murdoch, 1975; Risch, 1981).

One of the major areas of uncertainty is the scale of spatial variation necessary to affect host selection by herbivores. As Alstad and Edmunds (Chapter 12) have shown, variation among adjacent conspecific trees within a forest is sufficient to promote the differentiation of demes of scale insects on individual trees. On the other hand, Whitham (Chapter 1) and Rausher (Chapter 7) have demonstrated that at least some insect species can discriminate within and among individuals of host-plant species for oviposition.

Kareiva (Chapter 8) has reviewed the theoretical framework and empirical evidence for the resource-concentration hypothesis, that is, that herbivores are more likely to find and remain on host individuals when grown in pure, large, and/or dense patches. Kareiva has pointed out a number of exceptions and complications to the resource-concentration hypothesis, depending on the herbivore species, the various hosts and nonhosts studied, and the spatial and temporal scale over which vegetation texture is experimentally manipulated. Although the resource-concentration hypothesis may be a valid qualitative generalization, the empirical evidence at hand offers applied entomologists little in the way of quantitative predictability for designing an optimally diverse agroecosystem to exploit fully the benefits of resource concentration (or dilution) within the limitations of commercial crop production.

There are at present only a few cases in which manipulations of ecosystem structure have been used as a primary means of insect pest control, and the specific manipulations have been derived largely from empirical rather than theoretical bases. The examples presented here were selected because the two agricultural systems in question are at the extreme ends of agriculture's size and labor–capital spectra. That vegetational heterogeneity is an effective insect-management technique in both the small-scale, labor-intensive agriculture of Central America and the large-scale, captital-intensive agriculture of California's Central Valley should encourage further research in other, less extreme agroecosystems, to learn how vegetational diversity can be most economically and effectively manipulated for insect pest management.

When grown in triculture, maize, beans, and squash had lower abundances of six galerucine beetle species than when each was grown in monoculture (Risch, 1981). The benefits of this ancient polyculture derive from the fact that the three crops are not all equally suitable for all insect species. The poorer hosts promoted a greater level of adult insect activity; thus emigration rates from polycultures were higher than from monocultures. Additionally, maize, in particular, lowered adult insect abundances because of its growth habit. Adult insects avoided the shade that maize provided the other two crops, and erect stalks interfered with insect flight. Within-plot diversity had no effect on mortality from natural enemies in any of the mono-, di-, or tricultures. The reduced insect abundances were primarily the result of associational resistance that each crop provided the others and the particular ways in which one of them, maize, adversely affected the insects' physical environment (Risch, 1981).

In contrast, where poorer hosts repel pests or hide more suitable hosts, is the following example, based on the observation that a more tolerant crop is more attractive to insect pests than a less tolerant crop. Alfalfa is more attractive to pest species of *Lygus* than is cotton (Sevacherian and Stern, 1975). This differential preference has been exploited in lygus control in cotton, by using alfalfa as a trap crop (Stern, 1969). Alfalfa strips 20 ft wide as far as 540 ft apart within cotton fields are sufficient to keep nearly all lygus bugs out of cotton. There were at least $25 \times$, and occasionally $200–300 \times$ as many lygus bugs in alfalfa as in neighboring cotton (Sevacherian and Stern, 1974). That there were no significant differences in the density of lygus in cotton adjacent to the alfalfa compared to the middle of the cotton field 270 ft distant suggests that the strips could be spaced at even greater intervals before lygus bugs react to an interplanted field as they do to a conventionally planted field. Short-term benefits of insect control via trap crops must be balanced against the loss of at least 5% of land from cotton production. The alfalfa, of course, may have some economic value, but less than if the strips were combined in a continuous field. The requirement to maintain a continuous supply of attractive, succulent foliage within strips necessitates that only half of each strip be harvested at a time, further complicating the harvesting plan and potential value of alfalfa within strips.

Strip-harvesting has been effectively applied to full-sized alfalfa fields as well. Like many forage crops, alfalfa is mowed several times during the growing season. If only half of the field is mowed at a time, then phytophagous insects (and their natural enemies) migrate only to the unmowed half, rather than to neighboring alfalfa fields or fields of more susceptible crops (e.g., cotton) (van den Bosche and Stern, 1969). Thus selective harvesting minimizes the environmental disruption of prey–predator relationships within alfalfa agroecosystems and the need for chemical pest control. There is little more expense in harvesting half as much alfalfa twice as often, though this is practicable only if access to machinery and labor are not limiting.

Contemporary studies of insect responses to hosts and nonhosts in the field are leading to a better understanding of the specific mechanisms by which plant community stucture affects the dynamics of phytophagous insect populations. The more entomologists understand the specific mechanisms, the more predictable agroecosystem manipulations may become. In many cases the biological background information already exists, but currently there is no effective way to apply it. There are many examples of an imperfect correlation between host attractiveness for adult oviposition and host suitability for larval growth and survival (Chew, 1977), thus such host species may eventually be used as trap plants for insect pest control. It would be necessary, however, to complete a number of large-scale field experiments to learn how such trap species could be best deployed within the agroecosystem to obtain the maximum insect control with a minimum loss of land for crop production.

B. Genetic Structure of Host-Plant Populations

Differences in insect resistance among several crop varieties may be utilized to increase the spatial and temporal heterogeneity within crop species, perhaps reducing the rate at which phytophagous insects become adapted to any one variety. Although planting resistant varieties in large, uniform blocks may be most effective in suppressing pest populations quickly (Knipling, 1979), such uniform and widespread plantings may also constitute the most effective selection regime favoring insect biotypes tolerant to those resistant varieties.

The technique of physically combining several varieties differing in resistance within the same crop stand is known as multilining, and it has been used successfully to minimize the rate at which plant pathogens develop virulence to resistant crop varieties (Browning and Frey, 1969). The value of multilining to preserve the usefulness of resistant varieties against insect pests, however, is virtually unexplored (Gallun and Khush, 1980). Multilining may be most effective in preserving the lifetime of resistant varieties when it is used against pathogens and insect pests that disperse passively, rather than against insects that can discriminate between resistant and nonresistant hosts (Trenblath, 1977).

If multilining were used against insect pests that discriminate between conspecifics, host-plant resistance should probably be based on antibiosis rather than nonpreference. Otherwise, herbivores may simply select the least resistant varieties in a stand and develop as though the whole field were a low-density stand of a susceptible variety. Gould (Chapter 17) has discussed in detail the genetic consequences to the pest population of host-plant resistance based on antibiosis, nonpreference, and their combination.

In order to determine the optimal scale and pattern of intraspecific genetic variation necessary to minimize the rate that insect pests adapt to new resistant varieties, once again it would be necessary to perform several large-scale field studies. The optimal scale and pattern for one insect species would most likely differ from that for other pest species, due to differences in dispersal capacity, host range, and host-finding behavior.

In general, entomologists currently can better predict the consequences of manipulating individual host plants on their associated herbivore assemblages than they can the consequences of manipulating plant communities. In order to better understand how changes in plant community structure affect insect population dynamics, extensive field experimentation is essential. The task of applying the results of this research to crop protection will be simplified if the experimental designs are based not only on prior knowledge of plant–herbivore–enemy interactions in the laboratory, but also on a practical understanding of contemporary agricultural practices.

IV. EFFECTS OF HOST-PLANT VARIATION ON THE PARASITOIDS OF PHYTOPHAGOUS INSECTS

A. Host-Plant Influences on Parasitoid Success

Price et al. (1980) have suggested that natural enemies of herbivores should be considered to be mutualistic with plants and components of plant defense. Because properties of individual plants and plant communities strongly influence the herbivore–parasitoid interaction, neither plant–herbivore nor herbivore–parasitoid interactions can be fully understood without considering all trophic levels.

Among the ways in which host plants can affect herbivore–parasitoid interactions is to change the suitability of hosts for parasitoid development (Vinson and Iwantsch, 1980). Although it has long been known that variation within and among host-plant species can indeed affect parasitoid survival (Morgan, 1910; Flanders, 1942), the ecological significance of three-level interactions is only now beginning to be appreciated. The following examples illustrate how variation among host plants can affect not only parasitoid survival, but also parasitoid growth rate, longevity, and sex ratio. To the extent that these parameters determine parasitoid reproductive potential, host-plant variation may affect the capacity of parasitoids to regulate populations of an insect pest on different crop species.

Smith (1957) confirmed the observation of Flander (1942) that California red scale (Aonidiella aurantii) reared on Sago palm (Cycas revoluta) is the least suitable for the two encyrtid parasitoids Habrolepis rouxi and Comperiella bifasciata. Scale reared on Yucca filipendula and Agave decipiens were most suitable, whereas scale reared on grapefruit, lemon, and orange were of intermediate suitability. Although yucca was also the best host for red scale, there was not a perfect correspondence for the rest of the plant species between scale growth and parasitoid performance. Smith (1957) suggested the greater growth and higher fecundity of red scale on lemon, coupled with greater parasitoid mortality on lemon-reared scale, may be responsible for the observation that California red scale is a more serious pest on lemon than on orange or grapefruit (DeBach et al., 1949). More recently, survival and emergence of H. rouxi was shown to vary also with the host species of the oleander scale (Aspidiotus nerii; Blumberg and DeBach, 1979). The mechanisms by which scale-host plant species confer differential suitability to the scales' parasitoids are not yet known.

Mueller (1980) studied the oviposition behavior and host utilization of the braconid parasitoid Microplitis croceipes in the laboratory by offering it two Heliothis species reared on each of three different host-plant species. When reared on the same plant species, M. croceipes did not discriminate between H. zea and H. virescens. The parasitoid, did, however discriminate among Heliothis larvae reared on cotton, bean, and tomato. Host larvae reared on cotton were most preferred for parasitoid oviposition, and larvae reared on tomato were least preferred. Cotton-reared H. zea were also most suitable for M. croceipes development, as measured by differences in parasitoid larval survival and pupal weight. In this study, the differences in the ability of M. croceipes to utilize H. zea larvae reared on different host-plant species paralleled the differences in H. zea's ability to utilize the three host-plant species. Again, the specific plant factors responsible for differential selection and utilization of herbivore larvae reared on different host species were not identified, but the differences in the attractiveness of *Heliothis* larvae reared on different host plants may be due to an interaction between host-plant chemical constituents and a chemical (13-methylhentriacontane) produced by *Heliothis* spp. and utilized by *M. croceipes* in host location (Mueller, 1980).

Cheng (1970) reported greater parasitoid success of the tachinid parasitoid *Lypha dubia* on winter moth *(Operophtera brumata)* reared on hawthorn, witch hazel, or blackthorn compared to winter moth larvae reared on oak. Prey development was faster on oak, and oak-reared prey were larger when parasitoids were active in the field. Larger moth larvae encapsulated a greater proportion of developing parasitoids. Thus, because *O. brumata* grew faster on oak than on the other host plants, the moth population reared on oak was less synchronized with the parasitoid population.

A similar asynchrony exists between the gypsy moth *(Lymantria dispar)* and its braconid parasitoid, *Apanteles melanoscelus* (Weseloh, 1976), although this asynchrony is not necessarily host-plant related. Adult parasitoids successfully attack first- through third-instar gypsy moth larvae, but they have difficulty ovipositing in fourth and larger instars. The first generation of *A. melanoscelus* successfully utilizes early-instar gypsy moth larvae, but the second-generation parasitoids emerge after most gypsy moth larvae have molted to the fourth or later instars. It would appear that any factor that delayed gypsy moth development in the field would increase the ability of *A. melanoscelus* to control gypsy moth populations.

R. M. Weseloh, T. G. Andreadis, and co-workers and R. A. Fusco (unpublished data) found that sublethal doses of commercial formulations of the bacterial insecticide *Bacillus thuringiensis* (Bt) retard gypsy moth larval development and, therefore, promote increased parasitization by *Apanteles melanoscelus* in both the laboratory (Weseloh and Andreadis, 1982) and field (Weseloh *et al.*, in press). Apparently, the endotoxin associated with Bt paralyses the gut of gypsy moth larvae and prevents feeding and growth sufficiently to delay the third molt until after *A. melanoscelus* adults emerge. Sublethal doses of Bt had no discernable effect on *A. melanoscelus* oviposition behavior or larval survival. Thus Bt acts synergistically to increase *A. melanoscelus* success. Presumably, other compounds that retard gypsy moth larval growth would also improve *A. melanoscelus* control of gypsy moth populations.

Although reducing the growth rate of gypsy moth larvae by reducing consumption may benefit *Apanteles melanoscelus*, such a manipulation may harm the pupal gypsy moth parasitoids, the chalcid *Brachymeria intermedia* and the ichneumonid *Coccygomimus turionellae*. Gypsy moth pupae reared on different host species differed significantly in size and internal carbohydrate and free amino acid composition (Greenblatt and Barbosa, 1981). Pupae also differed in their suitability for survival and assimilation by *B. intermedia* and *C. turionellae*. Growth and survival of the polyphagous *C. turionellae* was strongly associated with the suitability of the herbivore's host species, in that gypsy moth pupae reared on their most suitable host, gray birch, were most digestible and produced the largest *C. turionellae* adults. Variation in host quality affected the more specialized *B. intermedia* differently, in that gypsy moth pupae reared not on their most suitable but their most common host, red oak, were most digestible and produced the largest *B. intermedia* adults.

The two parasitoids also differentially utilized pupae from different phases of the gypsy moth's population cycle (Greenblatt and Barbosa, 1980). *Brachymeria intermedia* survived better and grew larger when reared on pupae from high-density populations. *Coccygomimus turionellae*, however, better utilized pupae from low- and moderate-density gypsy moth populations, and this effect was more pronounced when *C. turionellae* was reared on the smaller male pupae.

Thus the capacity of *Brachymeria intermedia* and *Coccygomimus turionellae* to utilize gypsy moth pupae varies both with the gypsy moth's host species and with the phases of the gypsy moth's population cycle. The two parasitoids, in general, were differentially affected by these two sources of host variation. These results, when coupled with the reciprocal interaction between host-plant suitability and gypsy moth population density (Wallner and Walton, 1979), suggest a series of dynamic, interdependent relationships between spatial and temporal host-plant variation, herbivore population dynamics, and the suitability of herbivores for parasitoid utilization.

B. Compatibility of Host-Plant Resistance with Biological Control

The ways in which the host's diet can influence host suitability for parasitoid development are not fully understood. In some cases, hosts may sequester plant products for their own defense (Duffey, 1980). Morgan (1910) and Gilmore (1938) suggested that the variation in the emergence of *Apanteles congregatus*, a parasitoid of *Manduca sexta*, resulted from differences in the nicotine content of the tobacco varieties from which parasitized *M. sexta* were collected. Thurston and Fox (1972) confirmed that nicotine doses sublethal to *M. sexta* inhibited *A. congregatus* emergence, but there was no consistent effect on parasitoid development before emergence.

Campbell and Duffey (1979) showed that *Heliothis zea* acquired tomatine, an allelochemical from tomato. The ichneumonid parasitoid

Hyposerter exugae was adversely affected by sequestered tomatine. *Hyposerter exugae* had a longer development time, lower survival, and reduced adult size and longevity when reared on *H. zea* that were themselves reared on synthetic diets containing tomatine. The deleterious effects of tomatine on *H. exugae*, however, could be ameliorated, if not eliminated, by including equimolar quantities of cholesterol in *H. zea*'s diet. Thus the two important conclusions from this investigation were, first, that differential susceptibility of parasitoids and prey to plant allelochemicals implies that plant resistance based on antibiosis may not always be compatible with biological control and, second, that the particular consequences of variation in defensive phytochemical concentration on either host or parasitoid depend on the concentration of other phytochemicals.

Applied entomologists often assume that host-plant resistance is compatible with biological control (Kogan, 1975; Adkisson and Dyck, 1980), and, in a short-term, qualitative sense this is probably true (Starks *et al.*, 1972; Pimentel and Wheeler, 1973). The particular circumstances in which the deployment of resistant varieties would disrupt biological control so that insect-pest problems would become greater are probably rare. On the other hand, differential susceptibility to plant allelochemicals may only reduce herbivore populations while driving local populations of parasitoids to extinction. If so, then the deployment of resistant varieties would predispose pest populations for outbreaks whenever growers returned to nonresistant varieties or when pest populations overcame host-plant resistance. In order to accurately predict both the short- and long-term compatibility of host-plant resistance and biological control for integrated pest management, the diverse effects of intra- and interspecific variation in host-plant suitability must be included in the study of herbivore–parasitoid population dynamics. The results of such studies would promote the development of pest management programs tailored specifically to particular crop species and varieties.

V. CONCLUSIONS AND DIRECTIONS FOR FURTHER RESEARCH

The many ways in which spatial and temporal variation within and among host-plant species affect phytophagous insects are still poorly and incompletely understood. Not surprisingly, most current methods to manipulate host suitability are primitive and nonspecific. Growers may believe, therefore, that such manipulations are inferior to chemical methods as a means of insect pest management. The various manipulations presented here, primitive as they may be, however, demonstrate how variable host-plant manipulations can be exploited as one of several tactics in the integrated management of agricultural and forest insect pests.

These examples should not be construed to be a complete list of all possible ways in which host plants may be manipulated for insect pest management. Rather, I have limited the examples in this chapter to those illustrating the range of methods available within the limits, more or less, of current agricultural practices. I have also limited the examples to those bearing most directly on the economic issues of insect pest management, because such issues must be resolved before growers will incorporate new techniques into their pest-mangement programs. Therefore, I have omitted a number of potentially important manipulations that may not yet be economically favorable. The general use of trap plants and the manipulation of a crop's spatial and temporal genetic structure are two such examples.

Progress toward fully integrating variation in host suitability into pest-management programs will require extensive quantitative research on plant–herbivore–enemy interactions under both laboratory and field conditions. Laboratory research should emphasize insect behavioral and physiological responses to variation in particular aspects of host physiology. Field studies should test predictions drawn from the laboratory and determine the scale at which phytophagous insects respond to spatial variation in host suitability. Long-term studies are also necessary to obtain accurate data for predicting the specific results of various host-plant manipulations on herbivore population dynamics. Natural enemies must also be studied in order to learn how variation among host plants affects the capacity of natural enemies to provide and maintain biological control of pest populations. Plant physiologists and plant pathologists must be consultants, if not participants, during all phases of research, in order to formulate mutually compatible and synergistic recommendations for crop production.

In summary, research programs to take fullest advantage of variation in host-plant quality for insect pest management will encompass a broad range of basic and applied ecological research. The quantitative, experimental approach illustrated by this book should inspire the development of precise and creative methods to utilize and enhance natural variation within and among host-plant species for ecologically sound and economically viable pest-management programs.

ACKNOWLEDGMENTS

I thank D. J. Futuyma, F. L. Gould, M. Kogan, R. L. Rabb, and R. M. Weseloh for their thoughtful criticisms and suggestions on an earlier draft.

REFERENCES

Adkisson, P. L. (1962). Timing of defoliants and dessicants to reduce populations of the pink bollworm in diapause. *J. Econ. Entomol.* **55,** 949–951.

Adkisson, P. L., and Dyck, V. A. (1980). Resistant varieties in pest management systems. *In* "Breeding Plants Resistant to Insects" (F. G. Maxwell and P. R. Jennings, eds.), pp. 233–251. Wiley, New York.

Adkisson, P. L., Niles, G. A., Walker, J. K., Bird, L. S., and Scott, H. B. (1982). Controlling cotton's insect pests: a new system. *Science* **216,** 19–22.

Applebaum, S. W., and Birk, Y. (1979). Saponins. *In* "Herbivores, Their Interactions with Secondary Plant Metabolites" (G. A. Rosenthal and D. H. Janzen, eds.), pp. 539–566. Academic Press, New York.

Backman, P. A., Harper, J. D., Hammond, J. M., and Clark, F. M. (1977). Antifeeding effects of the fungicide guazatine triacetate on insect defoliators of soybean and peanuts. *J. Econ. Entomol.* **70,** 374–376.

Barham, W. S. (1953). The inheritance of a bitter principle in cucumbers. *Proc. Am. Soc. Hortic. Sci.* **62,** 441–442.

Bariola, L. A., Kittock, D. L., Arle, H. F., Vail, P. V., and Henneberry, T. J. (1976). Controlling pink bollworms: effects of chemical termination of cotton fruiting on populations of diapausing larvae. *J. Econ. Entomol.* **69,** 633–636.

Bariola, L. A., Henneberry, T. J., and Kittock, D. L. (1981). Chemical termination and irrigation cut-off to reduce overwintering populations of pink bollworms. *J. Econ. Entomol.* **74,** 106–109.

Benedict, J. H., and Bird, L. S. (1981). Relationship of microorganisms within the plant and resistance to insects and diseases. *Proc. Beltwide Cotton Prod. Res. Conf. 1981* pp. 149–150.

Blumberg, D., and DeBach, P., (1979). Development of *Habrolepis rouxi* Compere (Hymenoptera: Encyrtidae) in two armoured scale hosts (Homoptera: Diaspididae) and parasite egg encapsulation by California red scale. *Ecol. Entomol.* **4,** 299–306.

Bozarth, R. F., and Ross, A. F. (1964). Systemic resistance induced by localized virus infection: extent of change in uninfected parts. *Virology* **24,** 446–455.

Brattsten, L. B. (1979). Biochemical defense mechanisms in herbivores against plant allelochemicals. *In* "Herbivores, Their Interaction with Secondary Plant Metabolites" (G. A. Rosenthal and D. H. Janzen, eds.), pp. 200–270. Academic Press, New York.

Browning, J. A., and Frey, K. J. (1969). Multiline cultivars as a means of disease control. *Annu. Rev. Phytophathol.* **7,** 355–382.

Campbell, B. C., and Duffey, S. S. (1979). Tomatine and parasitic wasps: potential incompatibility of plant antibiosis with biological control. *Science* **205,** 700–702.

Carlisle, D. B., Ellis, P. E., and Osborne, D. J. (1969). Effects of plant growth regulators on locusts and cotton stainer bugs. *J. Sci. Food Agric.* **20,** 391–393.

Carroll, C. R., and Hoffman, C. A. (1980). Chemical feeding deterrent mobilized in response to insect herbivory and counteradaptation by *Eplilachna tredecimotata. Science* **209,** 414–416.

Cartwright, D. W., Langcake, P., Pryce, R. J., and Leworthy, D. P. (1977). Chemical activation of host defense mechanisms as a basis for crop protection. *Nature (London)* **269,** 511–513.

Cartwright, D. W., Langcake, P., and Ride, P. J. (1980). Phytoalexin production in rice and its enhancement by a dichlorocyclopropane fungicide. *Physiol. Plant Pathol.* **17,** 259–267.

Chalfant, R. B., Todd, J. W., Taylor, W. K., and Mullinix, B. (1977). Laboratory studies on the antifeeding effect of a fungicide, guazatine triacetate on eleven species of phytophagous insects. *J. Econ. Entomol.* **70,** 513–517.

Chambliss, O. L., and Jones, C. M. (1966). Chemical and genetic basis for insect resistance in cucurbits. *Proc. Am. Soc. Hortic. Sci.* **89,** 394–405.

Chapman, R. F. (1974). The chemical inhibition of feeding by phytophagous insects. *Bull. Entomol. Res.* **64,** 339–363.

Cheng, L. (1970). Timing of attack by *Lypha dubia* Fall (Diptera: Tachinidae) on the winter moth, *Operophtera Brumata* (L.) (Lepidoptera: Geometridae) as a factor affecting parasite success. *J. Anim. Ecol.* **39,** 313–320.

Chew, F. S. (1977). Coevolution of pierid butterflies and their cruciferous food plants. *Evolution* **31,** 568–579.

Chew, F. S., and Rodman, J. E. (1979). Plant resources for chemical defense. *In* "Herbivores, Their Interaction with Secondary Plant Metabolites" (G. A. Rosenthal and D. H. Janzen, eds.), pp. 271–307. Academic Press, New York.

DaCosta, C. P., and Jones, C. M. (1971). Cucumber beetle resistance and mite susceptibility controlled by the bitter gene in *Cucumis sativus*. *Science* **172,** 1145–1146.

Day, P. R., ed. (1977). "The Genetic Basis of Epidemics in Agriculture," Ann. N.Y. Acad. Sci. No. 287. N.Y. Acad. Sci., New York.

DeBach, P., Fleschner, C. A., and Dietrick, E. J. (1949). California red scale—studies in possible control by natural enemies. *Calif. Agric.* **3**(3), 12, 15.

de Kort, C. A. D. (1969). Hormones and the structural and biochemical properties of the flight muscle of the Colorado beetle. *Meded. Landbouwhoges. Wagingen* **69**(2), 1–63.

de Wilde, J., Bongers, W., and Schooneveld, H. (1969). Effects of hostplant age on phytophagous insects. *Entomol. Exp. Appl.* **12,** 714–720.

Duffey, S. S. (1980). Sequestration of plant natural products by insects. *Annu. Rev. Entomol.* **25,** 447–477.

Dunlap, A. A., and Turner, N. (1934). Potato spraying. *Conn., Agric. Exp. Stn., New Haven, Circ.* **102,** 1–8.

Ellis, P. E., Carlisle, D. B., and Osborne, D. J. (1965). Desert locusts: sexual maturation delayed by feeding on senescent vegetation. *Science* **149,** 546–547.

Flanders, S. F. (1942). Abortive development in parasitic hymenoptera induced by food-plant of the insect host. *J. Econ. Entomol.* **35,** 834–835.

Gallun, R. L., and Khush, G. S. (1980). Genetic factors affecting expression and stability of resistance. *In* "Breeding Plants Resistant to Insects" (F. G. Maxwell and P. R. Jennings, eds.), pp. 63–85. Wiley, New York.

Gilmore, J. U. (1938). Notes on *Apanteles congregatus* (Say) as a parasite of tobacco hornworms. *J. Econ. Entomol.* **31,** 712–715.

Gould, F. (1978). Resistance of cucumber varieties to *Tetranychus urticae*: genetic and environmental determinants. *J. Econ. Entomol.* **71,** 680–683.

Greenblatt, J. A., and Barbosa, P. (1980). Interpopulation quality in gypsy moths with implications for success of two pupal parasitoids: *Brachymeria intermedia* (Nees) and *Coccygomimus turionellae* (L.). *Ecol. Entomol.* **5,** 31–38.

Greenblatt, J. A., and Barbosa, P. (1981). Effects of host's diet on two pupal parasitoids of the gypsy moth: *Brachymeria intermedia* (Nees) and *Coccygomimus turionellae* (L.). *J. Appl. Ecol.* **18,** 1–10.

Hall, E. R. (1972). Influence of Alar on populations of European red mite and apple aphid on apple. *J. Econ. Entomol.* **65,** 1751–1753.

Hare, J. D. (1983). Seasonal variation in plant–insect associations: utilization of *Solanum dulcamara* (L.) by *Leptinotarsa decemlineata* (Say). *Ecology*. (in press).

Hart, S. V. (1982). Effects of soybean phytoalexins on food choice and nutrition of the soybean looper, *Pseudoplusia includens* (Walker), and Mexican bean beetle, *Epilachna varivestis* Mulsant. M.Sc. Thesis, University of Illinois at Urbana-Champaign.

Haukioja, E., and Niemelä, P. (1977). Retarded growth of a geometrid larva after mechanical damage to leaves of its host tree. *Ann. Zool. Fenn.* **14**, 48–52.

Haukioja, E., and Niemelä, P. (1979). Birch leaves as resource for herbivores: seasonal occurrence of increased resistance in foliage after mechanical damage of adjacent leaves. *Oecologia* **39**, 151–159.

Haynes, R. L., and Jones, C. M. (1975). Wilting and damage of cucumbers by spotted and striped cucumber beetles. *HortScience* **10**, 265–266.

Higgins, R. A., and Pedigo, L. P. (1979). Evaluation of guazatine triacetate as an antifeedant/feeding deterrent of the green cloverworm on soybeans. *J. Econ. Entomol.* **72**, 680–686.

Honeyborne, C. H. B. (1969). Performance of *Aphis fabae* and *Brevicoryne brassicae* on plants treated with growth regulators. *J. Sci. Food Agric.* **20**, 388–390.

Horsfall, J. G. (1972). "Genetic Vulnerability of Major Crops." Natl. Acad. Sci., Washington, D.C.

Horsfall, J. G., and Cowling, E. B., eds. (1980). "Plant Disease: An Advanced Treatise," Vol. 5. Academic Press, New York.

Horsfall, J. G., and Turner, N. (1943). Injuriousness of Bordeaux mixture. *Am. Potato J.* **20**, 308–320.

Hsiao, T. H. (1978). Host plant adaptations among geographic populations of the Colorado potato beetle. *Entomol. Exp. Appl.* **24**, 237–247.

Jermy, T. (1961). The rejective effect of some inorganic salts on Colorado beetle (*Leptinotarsa decemlineata* Say) adults and larvae. *Novenyved. Kut. Intez. Evk.* **8**, 121–130.

Jermy, T. (1971). Biological background and outlook of the antifeedant approach to insect control. *Acta Phytopathol. Acad Sci. Hung.* **6**, 253–260.

Kittock, D. L., Mauny, J. R., Arle, H. F., and Bariola, L. A. (1973). Termination of late-season cotton fruiting with growth regulators as an insect control technique. *J. Environ. Qual.* **2**, 405–408.

Kittock, D. L., Arle, H. F., Henneberry, T. J., Bariola, L. A., and Walwood, V. T. (1980). Timing late-season fruiting of cotton with potassium 3,4-dichloroisothiazole-5-carboxylate. *Crop Sci.* **20**, 330–333.

Knipling, E. F. (1979). The basic principles of insect population suppression and management. *U.S. Dep. Agric., Agric. Handb.* **512**.

Kogan, M. (1975). Plant resistance in pest management. *In* "Introduction to Insect Pest Management" (R. L. Metcalf and W. H. Luckman, eds.), pp. 103–146. Wiley, New York.

Kuc, J. (1977). Plant protection by the activation of latent mechanisms for resistance. *Neth. J. Plant Pathol.* **83**, Suppl. 1, 463–467.

Larczenko, K. (1957). Feeding and diapause in the Colorado potato beetle. *Rocz. Nauk Roln., Ser. A* **74**, 287–314.

Leigh, T. F., Grimes, D. W., Yamada, H., Bassett, D., and Stockman, J. R. (1970). Insects in cotton as affected by irrigation and fertilization practices. *Calif. Agric.* **24**(3), 12–14.

Lewis, A. C. (1979). Feeding preference for diseased and wilted sunflower in the grasshopper, *Melanoplus differentialis*. *Entomol. Exp. Appl.* **26**, 202–207.

Livingston, J. M., Yearian, W. C., and Young, S. Y. (1978). Insecticical activity of selected fungicides: effects on three lepidopterous pests of soybeans. *J. Econ. Entomol.* **71**, 111–112.

McIntyre, J. L., Dodds, J. A., and Hare, J. D. (1981). Effects of localized infection of *Nicotiana tabacum* by tobacco mosaic virus on systemic resistance against diverse pathogens and an insect. *Phytopathology.* **71**, 297–301.

McNeil, S., and Southwood, T. R. E. (1978). The role of nitrogen in the development of insect–plant relationships. *In* "Biochemical Aspects of Plant and Animal Coevolution" (J. B. Harborne, ed.), pp. 77–98. Academic Press, New York and London.

Matta, A. (1980). Defenses triggered by previous disease invaders. *In* "Plant Disease: An Advanced Treatise" (J. G. Horsfall and E. B. Cowling, eds.), Vol. 5, pp. 345–361. Academic Press, New York.

Mattson, W. J. (1980). Herbivory in relation to plant nitrogen content. *Annu. Rev. Ecol. Syst.* **11**, 119–161.

Moesta, P., and Grisebach, H. (1980). Effects of biotic and abiotic elicitors on phytoalexin metabolisms in soybeans. *Nature (London)* **286**, 710–711.

Morgan, A. C. (1910). An observation upon the toxic effect of the food of the host upon its parasites. *Proc. Entomol. Soc. Wash.* **12**, 72.

Mueller, T. F. (1980). Comparative studies on the host relations of three *Heliothis* species and a braconid parasitoid. Ph.D. Thesis, State University of New York at Stony Brook.

Munakata, K. (1977). Insect feeding deterrents in plants. *In* "Chemical Control of Insect Behavior: Theory and Applications" (H. H. Shorey and J. J. McKelvey, eds.), pp. 93–102. Wiley, New York.

Murdoch, W. W. (1975). Diversity, complexity, stability, and pest control. *J. Appl. Ecol.* **12**, 795–807.

Noble, L. W. (1969). Fifty years of research on the pink bollworm in the United States. *U.S. Dep. Agric., Agric. Handb.* **357.**

Pimentel, D., and Wheeler, A. G. (1973). Influence of alfalfa resistance on a pea aphid population and its associated parasites, predators, and competitors. *Environ. Entomol.* **2**, 1–11.

Price, P. W., Bouton, C. E., Gross, P., McPheron, B. A., Thompson, J. N., and Weis, A. E. (1980). Interaction among three tophic levels: influence of plants on interaction between herbivores and natural enemies. *Annu. Rev. Ecol. Syst.* **11**, 41–65.

Rabb, R. L. (1969). Environmental manipulation as influencing populations of tobacco hornworms. *Proc. Tall Timbers Conf. Anim. Control Habitat Manage., 1968* Vol. 1, pp. 175–191.

Rabb, R. L., Neunzig, H. H., and Marshall, H. V. (1964). Effect of certain cultural practices on the abundance of tobacco hornworms, tobacco budworms, and corn earworms after harvest. *J. Econ. Entomol.* **57**, 791–792.

Reese, J. C. (1979). Interaction of allelochemicals with nutrients in herbivore food. *In* "Herbivores, Their Interaction with Secondary Plant Metabolites" (G. A. Rosenthal and D. H. Janzen, eds.), pp. 309–330. Academic Press, New York.

Risch, S. J. (1981). Insect herbivore abundance in tropical monocultures and polycultures: an experimental test of two hypotheses. *Ecology* **62**, 1325–1340.

Scheurer, S. (1976). Influence of phytohormones and growth regulating substances on insect development processes. *In* "The Host-Plant in Relation to Insect Behavior and Reproduction" (T. Jermy, ed.), pp. 255–259. Plenum, New York.

Scriber, J. M. (1977). Limiting effects of low leaf water content on the nitrogen utilization, energy budget, and larval growth of *Hyalophora cecropia* (Lepidoptera: Saturniidae). *Oecologia* **28**, 269–287.

Sevacherian, V., and Stern, V. M. (1974). Host plant preferences of lygus bugs in alfalfa-interplanted cotton fields. *Environ. Entomol.* **3**, 761–766.

Sevacherian, V., and Stern, V. M. (1975). Movements of lygus bugs between alfalfa and cotton. *Environ. Entomol.* **4**, 163–165.

Simons, T. J., and Ross, A. F. (1971a). Metabolic changes associated with systemic induced resistance to tobacco mosaic virus in Samsun NN tobacco. *Phytopathology* **61**, 293–300.

Simons, T. J., and Ross, A. F. (1971b). Changes in phenol metabolism associated with induced systemic resistance to tobacco mosaic virus in Samsun NN tobacco. *Phytopathology* **61,** 1261–1265.

Singer, M. C., and Smith, B. D. (1976). Use of the plant growth regulator, chlormetquat chloride, to control the aphid, *Hyperomyzus lactucae* on black currants. *Ann. Appl. Biol.* **82,** 407–414.

Slosser, J. E. (1980). Irrigation timing for bollworm management in cotton. *J. Econ. Entomol.* **73,** 346–349.

Smith, B. D. (1969). Spectra of activity of plant growth retardants against various parasites of one host species. *J. Sci. Food. Agric.* **20,** 398–400.

Smith, J. M. (1957). Effects of the food plant of the California red scale, *Aonidiella aurantii* (Mask), on reproduction of its hymenopterous parasites. *Can. Entomol.* **89,** 219–230.

Smith, R. F. (1978). History and complexity of integrated pest management. *In* "Pest Control Strategies" (E. H. Smith and D. Pimentel, eds.), pp. 41–53. Academic Press, New York.

Southwood, T. R. E., and Way, M. J. (1970). Ecological background to pest management. *In* "Concepts of Pest Management" (R. L. Rabb and F. E. Guthrie, eds.), pp. 6–29. North Carolina State University, Raleigh.

Starks, K. J., Muniappan, R., and Eikenbary, R. D. (1972). Interaction between plant resistance and parasitism against greenbug on barley and sorghum. *Ann. Entomol. Soc. Am.* **65,** 650–655.

Stern, V. M. (1969). Interplanting alfalfa in cotton to control lygus bugs and other pests. *Proc. Tall Timbers Conf. Ecol. Anim. Control Habitat Manage., 1968* Vol. 1, pp. 55–69.

Stern, V. M., Adkisson, P. L., Beingola, O. C., and Victorov, G. A. (1976). Cultural controls. *In* "Theory and Practice of Biological Control" (C. B. Huffaker and P. S. Messenger, eds.), pp. 593–613. Academic Press, New York.

Tappan, W. B. (1965). The decline of tobacco hornworm populations on cigar-wrapper tobacco. *J. Econ. Entomol.* **58,** 771–772.

Thomas, R. O., Cleveland, T. C., and Cathey, G. W. (1979). Chemical plant growth suppressants for reducing late-season cotton bollworm feeding sites. *Crop Sci.* **19,** 861–863.

Thurston, R., and Fox, P. M. (1972). Inhibition by nicotine of emergence of *Apanteles congregatus* from its host, the tobacco hornworm. *Ann. Entomol. Soc. Am.* **65,** 547–550.

Trenblath, B. R. (1977). Interactions among diverse hosts and diverse parasites. *Ann. N.Y. Acad. Sci.* **287,** 124–150.

van den Bosche, R., and Stern, V. M. (1969). The effects of harvesting practices on insect populations of alfalfa. *Proc. Tall Timbers Conf. Ecol. Anim. Control Habitat Manage., 1968* Vol. 1, pp. 47–54.

van Emden, H. F. (1969). Plant resistance to aphids induced by chemicals. *J. Sci. Food Agric.* **20,** 385–387.

Vinson, S. B., and Iwantsch, G. F. (1980). Host suitability for insect parasitoids. *Annu. Rev. Entomol.* **25,** 397–419.

Waldbauer, G. P. (1968). The consumption and utlization of food by insects. *Adv. Insect Physiol.* **5,** 229–288.

Wallner, W. E., and Walton, G. S. (1979). Host defoliation: A possible determinant of gypsy moth population quality. *Ann. Entomol. Soc. Am.* **72,** 62–67.

Wearing, C. H. (1972). Responses of *Myzus persicae* and *Brevicoryne brassicae* to leaf age and water stress in Brussels sprouts grown in pots. *Entomol. Exp. Appl.* **15,** 61–80.

Werner, R. A. (1979). Influence of host foliage on development, survival, fecundity, and oviposition of the spear-marked black moth, *Rheumaptera hastata* (Lepidoptera: Geometridae). *Can. Entomol.* **111,** 317–322.

Weseloh, R. M. (1976). Reduced effectiveness of the gypsy moth parasite, *Apanteles melanoscelus* in Connecticut due to poor seasonal synchrony with its host. *Environ. Entomol.* **5**, 743–746.

Weseloh, R. M., and Andreadis, T. G. (1982). A possible mechanism for synergism between *Bacillus thuringiensis* and the gypsy moth (Lepidoptera: Lymantriidae) parasitoid, *Apanteles melanoscelus* (Hymenoptera: Braconidae). *Ann. Entomol. Soc. Am.* **75**, 435–438.

Weseloh, R. M., Andreadis, T. G., Dubois, N. R., Moore, R. E. B., Anderson, J. F., and Lewis, F. B. (1983). Field confirmation of a mechanism causing synergism between *Bacillus thuringiensis* and the gypsy moth parasitoid, *Apanteles melanoscelus. J. Inverteb. Pathol.* (in press).

Westigard, P. H., Lombard, P. B., Allen, R. B., and Strang, J. G. (1980). Population suppression through host modification using daminozide. *Environ. Entomol.* **9**, 275–277.

Wolfson, J. L. (1980). Oviposition response of *Pieris rapae* to environmentally induced variation in *Brassica nigra. Entomol. Exp. Appl.* **27**, 223–232.

J. Daniel Hare
Department of Entomology
The Connecticut Agricultural Experiment Station
New Haven, Connecticut

Index

A

Abies, host for *Fiorinia externa*, 133
Abies amabilis, systemic defense, 199
Abies balsamea
  cyclic outbreak of herbivores, 425
  effect of leaf age on herbivore fitness, 96
  host for spruce budworm, 197–200
  preference for reproductive trees by herbivore, 244
Abies concolor, effect of leaf age on herbivore fitness, 96
Abies grandis, systemic defense, 199
Abies magnifica, population variation in leaf resin and oleoresin, 494
Abies procera, population variation in leaf resin and oleoresin, 494
Abiotic factors, effect on leaf suitability, 114–115
Acalymma thiemei, response to interplanted hosts, 269
Acalymma vittata
  response to cucurbitacin, 175
  response to host density, 626
  response to host diversity, 269–270
Acer pensylvanicum, host for Geometridae, 80
Acer pseudoplatanus
  effects of defoliation on growth, 466
  effect of leaf nitrogen on herbivore fitness, 4
Acer rubrum
  effect of leaf age on fitness, 96, 97, 98, 100
  host for *Alsophila pometaria*, 440–442
  interaction with herbivore genotype, 233
Acer saccharum
  effect of leaf age on herbivore fitness, 96
  interleaf variation in digestibility, 65
Acer spicatum, host for Geometridae, 80
Achillea, ecotypic variation, 572

Acrosterum hilare, effect on soybean yield, 467
Acyrthosiphon pisum
  alfalfa resistance, 617
  interaction of genotype and host, 233, 627
  response to saponin, 172
Adalia bipunctata, searching behavior, 112
Adaptive radiation
  herbivore, 561, 564, 585
  host plants, 599
Adelges piceae, response to host-plant phenolics, 199
Adzuki bean, *see Vigna angularis*
African armyworm
  migration, 194
  phase change, 196
Agasicles hygrophilia, biocontrol of alligator weed, 468
Aggregation, response to predation, 282–283
Agrilus, effect of twig girdling, 174
Agromyzidae, host-plant utilization, 561–563
Agropyron intermedium, response to herbivore attack, 168–169
Agrotis orthogonia, effect of feeding time on growth, 80
Alder sawfly, *see Eriocampa ovata*
Alfalfa, *see Medicago sativa*
Alfalfa weevil
  effect of resistant alfalfa varieties, 490
  response to saponin, 172
Alkaloid
  in advanced plants, 160
  correlation with plant growth, 490
  diurnal fluctuation in plants, 93
  effect on insect fitness, 160, 490
  effect on thrips, 172
  elevational patterns, 496
  feeding deterrent, 227
  interaction with nitrogen, 163–164
  latitudinal variation, 496–497
  population variation in *Lupinus*, 494